W9-BXE-583

Illinois Central College
Learning Resources Center

CROWELL CASEBOOKS

AVANT GARDE DRAMA

A Casebook

Edited by

Bernard F. Dukore
University of Hawaii

and

Daniel C. Gerould
City University of
New York   Graduate Center

Thomas Y. Crowell Company
New York, New York

Thomas Y. Crowell Company
666 Fifth Avenue
New York, New York 10019

Manufactured in the United States of America

Contents

Plays

Avant-Garde Drama

Documents

Introduction

Toward the end of the nineteenth century, small, experimental theatres began to spring up in leading European cities, and modern drama began to experience what became a series of avant-garde movements, three in all, almost continuous, and all based in some degree upon reactions against the established theatre and the principles of realism. From the vantage of 1976 we can distinguish the major generations of avant-garde dramatists: first, the turn-of-the-century symbolists, such as Maeterlinck and Hauptmann; then, the revolutionary playwrights of the interwar years, such as Brecht and Pirandello; finally, the Absurdists of the 1950s, represented by Beckett, Ionesco, and Pinter.

Perhaps the most remarkable and far-reaching of these assaults on conventional theatre is the second wave, which is framed by the two World Wars. Today one may perceive the interwar period as the peak of various tendencies and movements away from nineteenth-century realism. This period sustained one of the most widespread, innovative outbursts in the history of theatre. Four years of catastrophic war, plus revolution in Russia, had made a striking and irreversible rupture with the past and helped to fashion the experience and outlook of dramatists who became contemptuous not only of the old dramaturgy but also of the audiences to whom it catered. They were determined to break with the past, to create something entirely new.

The avant-garde drama of the period 1918–1939 has a distinctive character and special urgency. The plays of this time not only look backward toward one world catastrophe but seem to anticipate an even greater cataclysm. This brief, blazing, twenty-one year dramatic era—acutely conscious of a "now" so different from the past and of a future which could crush that "now"—can rank with other glorious moments in world drama. These years saw the flourishing of modern American drama and the one and only great period in Soviet theatre. Brecht, Pirandello, and Witkiewicz became their countries' greatest dramatists and the fervent experimentalism of the movement crossed national boundaries to create new cosmopolitan modes, such as surrealism and epic theatre.

No other theatrical avant-garde has been as colorful and flamboyant, none has made so violent an attack on existing society and prevailing conventions of the stage, none has been so rich in new ideas and theories about drama and theatre. To be sure, the playwrights of the 1920s owed much to their pre-Armistice precursors and, indeed, brought to fruition many of the turn-of-the-century notions of total theatre. But whereas the symbolists and their contemporaries were murky and cosmic, the between-wars avant-garde playwrights were social as well as metaphysical, and more often than not, irreverent and mocking, tough-minded and flippant, ironic and dynamic. Significantly, this second avant-garde was the first movement in theatre to be affected directly by new scientific techniques and advanced technology of the machine age. The plays have an essentially new tempo and rhythm that mirror the pace of industrial life, the speed of the automobile, the airplane, and the intercut and edited film. This drama overwhelms the spectator with fast, broken images and movements more in keeping with the sports arena and movie screen than with the solemnity of the bourgeois theatre or the symbolist temple of art.

For these dramatists neither worldly nor otherworldly

absolutes exist, reality is hopelessly fragmented, values are relative. With the loss of belief in objective truth came as well the demise of illusionistic and atmospheric playwriting and staging. Instead, the interwar avant-garde created drama that calls attention to itself as drama, that frankly utilizes popular arts and popular culture—circus, cabaret, jazz, and sports—and that delights in artifice, tricks, razzle-dazzle, spectacle, and theatrical process. Further, these avant-garde playwrights regarded former notions of the self as sadly or laughably obsolete. They saw the autonomous individual as a moribund species. Their plays no longer focus on private life but rather reflect the instability and dissolution of an old society. Toller, Brecht, Witkiewicz, even Ghelderode (who set many plays in the decadent splendor of bygone days) created images of decay, and Olyesha perceived remnants of a dying but not quite dead world in the midst of the new. Toller solemnly, and Cummings joyously, broke with realism; Brecht rejected illusionism; and Pirandello dismantled conventional partitions between stage and auditorium. Witkiewicz, Artaud, and Brecht advocated an end to traditional drama, though each proposed something different to replace it. Proclaiming the end of the old, they also proclaimed—sometimes explicitly, at other times implicitly—the beginning of the new.

Paradoxically, the avant-garde drama of the second wave seems very close to us and at the same time rooted in a particular historical period. Brecht called for a drama based on science and Witkiewicz for one derived from pictorial art. Breton demanded a literature made from dreams, Artaud an end to literature. Cummings dramatized fascist Italy, Olyesha postrevolutionary Russia, and Brecht, Toller, and Witkiewicz capitalism in embattled turmoil. Ghelderode conjured up a grotesque universe in the process of disintegration, Pirandello a theatrical world in disarray, Cummings a vaudevillian circus in a whirl, and Brecht an explosively Marxist demonstration in multimedia. The seven plays in this collection and the critical documents that follow—major texts of or on the avant-garde drama of the interwar period—bring alive its excitement and pertinence, and facilitate its study.

ABOUT THE EDITORS

Bernard F. Dukore

is Professor, Department of Drama and Theatre, the University of Hawaii. He is the author of *Bernard Shaw, Director*, and *Bernard Shaw, Playwright*, as well as studies of Pinter, Brecht, and others, and coeditor with the late John Gassner of *A Treasury of the Theatre*. He is the editor of *Dramatic Theory and Criticism: Greeks to Grotowski* and of *17 Plays, Sophocles to Baraka* (Crowell, 1976).

Daniel C. Gerould

is Professor, Ph.D. Program in Theatre, Graduate Center, City University of New York. He spent 1968–1970 in Poland as a Fulbright lecturer in American Drama. With C.S. Durer he has translated and edited the first collected edition of Witkiewicz's plays to appear in English. A volume of *Twentieth-Century Polish Avant-Garde Drama* which he has prepared is soon to appear, as well as a critical study of Witkiewicz.

Explosions and Implosions: Avant-Garde Drama Between World Wars

The assassination of the Austrian Archduke Franz Ferdinand at Sarajevo on June 28, 1914 started a four-year period of slaughter and mutilation. Among the victims was the realistic play of the well-made school. Although the nineteenth-century theatre was not killed outright in the first of the great world wars, it did receive a series of blows from which it would never fully recover. The stable world of the pre-war era, reflected in a theatre that had catered to a bourgeois audience and held the mirror up to their lives and morals, began to disintegrate.

With a million killed at the battle of Verdun and another million during the Russian offensive of 1916, with countries appearing, disappearing, and reappearing on the map of Europe, what did it matter if Madame X committed adultery with her husband's best friend, or if Monsieur Dupont succeeded in marrying off his daughters? After the holocaust, the theatre's depiction of the marital and financial problems of the bourgeoisie became irrelevant and even obscene. Two parts Scribe and one part Ibsen (who was himself one part Scribe), the realistic tradition and well-made play were of course not killed in battle but only maimed and shell-shocked. They continue to drag out a senile existence in the rest homes of our commercial theatre.

The war exploded old conventions and preconceptions. The Russian Revolution of 1917 showed that the most sacred structures were subject to violent change. The theatrical avant-garde of the post-World War I era was revolutionary socially, politically, and psychologically as well as artistically.

The patron saints of the theatrical revolutionists of the between-wars period were an unlikely pair, Sigmund Freud and V. I. Lenin. Implosions and explosions, dreams and revolutions, the conquest of the irrational and the triumph of the proletariat—these extremes lent form and substance to the avant-garde theatre of the twenties. Expressionism and surrealism, the two major movements of the period in painting and in drama, unite subjective and social, dream and revolution, in the aim of transcending and transforming reality by releasing the subconscious and leveling all social barriers. Coincidentally, in the year before the revolution, Lenin lived directly across the street from the Cabaret Voltaire, the famous cafe in Zurich where Dada was born. In their rejection of the old society, the surrealists, heirs of Dada, looked eastward, toward Moscow, for fraternity and inspiration and maintained a prolonged, if stormy and vacillating, attachment to the French Communist Party and the Third International. The expressionists, almost to a man, were socialists and pacifists. In their plays and poems they blended oneiric hallucinations with pictures of violent social change. Revolution grows out of a dream of spiritual rebirth, and the grimly realistic moves with shocking rapidity into the fantastic and visionary.

In words appropriate to our own day as well as to the 1920s, the surrealist writer and painter André Masson recently described the origin of the artistic revolt of the twenties as disgust with "the colossal slaughter" of the war, the "obscene 'brain-washing' that had been inflicted on the civilians," the "militant stupidity" and "sick society of the 'between the wars' years." Angrily rejecting the past, the avant-garde dramatists also rejected traditional ways of regarding and portraying reality. Seeing reality in new ways, they created a daringly experimental drama which reflected these new views. The Bolshevik Revolution and Freudian psychoanalysis tore down old walls and conventions in society and in the self. No wonder the walls and conventions of the realistic theatre were also demolished—walls between stage and auditorium, actors and audience, author and play; and conventions about illusion, character, and plot.

The seven plays in this volume offer different versions of revolution, social and artistic, played out on different levels and shifting planes. An uprising of the masses occurs in the plays by Toller, Witkiewicz, Brecht, Cummings, and Ghelderode; Olyesha's play concerns the aftermath and consequences of the revolution. In *Each in His Own Way*, the revolution is transferred from the street to the theatre. Instead of bloodshed at the barricades, there is fighting in the lobby. Rebellion takes place on a theatrical level as members of the audience invade the backstage area and disrupt the performance.

Freud and Lenin demonstrated that reality, the basis for "realism," was neither objective nor unchanging. Inner and outer walls were crumbling. Man's psyche, the psychoanalysts showed, was a heap of fragments; an entire society, the Bolsheviks proved, could be blown up. The avant-garde dramatists of the twenties explored dramatic form in order to express this shattered reality. Dramatizing human society and human nature in constant flux and disintegration, the new playwrights used the fluidity of dreams and the chaos of revolutions to expose subterranean forces in society and in the self. Avant-garde drama between world wars reflects the instability of that period: its shifting planes of reality, changing perspectives on society, multiple images of personality, and drastic transpositions through space and time. Shattered mirrors, images within images, and apocalyptic visions create a series of vivid pictures of a violently changing world.

In Russia, the revolution became the starting point for the

new, theatrically as well as politically and economically, and made the Soviet stage pre-eminent for experimentation during the dozen years after the fall of St. Petersburg. Pilgrimages to Moscow to see the work of Vakhtangov, Tairov, Meyerhold, Akimov, and Mikhoels became mandatory for anyone interested in the future of the theatre. Westerners were unaware, however, that in Poland during the twenties and thirties a lonely and misunderstood figure, the painter-playwright-novelist-philosopher Stanisław Ignacy Witkiewicz, who had recently returned from the Tsarist army and direct observation of the revolution, was creating a proto-Absurdist theatre and a theory of abstract drama based on an analogy with modern painting. In the West, the German expressionists, such as Toller and Kaiser, radically transformed dramatic structure and staging, with an impact felt across the Atlantic. For the first time American drama and theatre joined the international mainstream of experimentation, and produced the avant-garde drama of Eugene O'Neill, E. E. Cummings, and Thornton Wilder. Using expressionistic techniques, Brecht created an anti-expressionistic drama that evolved into epic theatre, whose influence seems only to have begun. Immediately after the war, France, which had enjoyed commercial rather than artistic leadership in the drama during the century from Scribe to Bernhardt and Sardou, regained its traditional role of importance in the avant-garde through the theatrical renovations of Jacques Copeau and his pupils (Louis Jouvet, Charles Dullin, Gaston Baty, and Georges Pitoëff) and the experiments of the surrealists. Antonin Artaud, whose radical insights bore fruit a generation later, began his work as playwright-actor-director-theorist-prophet during this period of renaissance in the French theatre. In Italy, Pirandello shattered traditional conceptions of theatrical illusion and dramatic character, though it was the French productions by Dullin and Georges and Ludmilla Pitoëff which made the Sicilian's new dramatic vision known throughout Europe and America, launching Pirandelloism as a joint Franco-Italian enterprise. Theatrically, the between-wars period was an international era, important both in itself and for its influence on the drama after the Second World War.

Although the recent avant-garde, such as the Theatre of the Absurd and the Theatre of Cruelty, grows directly from the innovations of the between-wars period, major differences exist between these two periods and styles of experimentation and between their attitudes toward the past. The impress of history on the avant-garde of the between-wars period is overwhelming: the sense of rupture with the past is fresh, exhilarating, and immediate. Revolutionary zeal and flamboyance characterize the new drama following World War I. Contempt for the past and a feeling of the power to build a new world embolden playwrights to push language and staging to new extremes. The complex staging and huge casts of the seven plays in this collection typify this flamboyance. *Each in His Own Way* contains a dozen characters in the inner play and at least three times that many in the outer play. *Him* calls for 105 characters in twenty-two scenes. Both *Man and the Masses* and *Saint Joan of the Stockyards* demand huge choruses of workers, bankers, and stockbrokers. Mobs and crowds figure in each of the plays. The masses burst onto the stage; we see them in factories, at strike meetings, and at football matches. Unruly playwrights in boots and bandoleers, challenging the limitations of the stage and of the audience's expectations, explode the boundaries of the real into fantastic visions of worlds beyond. Such exuberance is unlike much of the avant-garde drama of the 1950s and '60s, which often contains only three or four characters, trapped in a single room, conversing laconically and cryptically in clichés and thereby revealing an irreducible human condition.

To represent the revolutionary and explosive spirit of the avant-garde theatre between world wars, we have chosen seven plays that illustrate the major movements of the period. *Man and the Masses* is one of the clearest and most coherent examples of expressionism. Surrealism is represented by *Him* and *The Water Hen* and epic theatre by *Saint Joan of the Stockyards*. Pirandelloism reveals its quintessence in *Each in His Own Way* and Ghelderode's *Chronicles of Hell* embodies Artaud's vision of a theatre of cruelty. In *The Conspiracy of Feelings*, we have a text expressive of the spirit of the new Russian theatricalism.

Avant Garde Drama

The avant-garde credentials which these plays offer include the fact that all but two of them (the Toller and Pirandello) were not fully accepted in their own day but were so subversive of the social, political, or artistic establishment which then prevailed that they were ignored or suppressed until our own time, when they could be re-evaluated in the perspective of today's experimental theatre. *The Water Hen* received one production in the between-wars period, running for only two nights; it had to wait until 1962 to be published and until 1964 to be successfully performed by a professional company. *Saint Joan of the Stockyards*, forbidden by the Nazis, was not performed on a German stage until 1959. Although *The Conspiracy of Feelings* received two major productions in 1929, it was condemned as negative in ideology and expressionistic in form; not until 1968 was it published in Russia. *Him*, performed in 1928 to the incomprehension and annoyance of most drama critics, has rarely been revived since. *Chronicles of Hell* was not performed until 1949, when it created a scandal because of its alleged blasphemy. The playwrights in this collection are innovators in the most comprehensive sense of the word: revolutionaries demanding fundamental changes in society, in the mind, in the theatre.

The first four plays in this collection—*The Water Hen, Man and the Masses, Saint Joan of the Stockyards*, and *The Conspiracy of Feelings*—represent four successive stages in social upheaval and change. Following these are plays demonstrating a changed theatrical reality, *Each in His Own Way* and *Him*. Next, *Chronicles of Hell* represents a universe whose very foundations appear to have cracked. Following these plays are documents concerning the nature of the avant-garde in this period as well as comments on and by the particular playwrights and their plays.

A SPHERICAL TRAGEDY IN THREE ACTS

by Stanisław Ignacy Witkiewicz

the
water
hen

Translated by

Daniel C. Gerould
and C. S. Durer

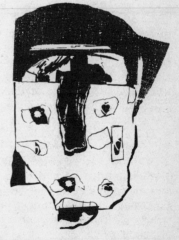

Kurka Wodna, written in 1921, was first performed at the
Słowacki Theatre, Cracow, on July 20, 1922,
and first published in 1962. This translation
was first published in *First Stage,* VI (Summer, 1967).

In the chronology of revolution, *The Water Hen* presents the first picture of the old society's dissolution. Until the end of the last act, *The Water Hen* is pre-revolutionary. Using 1917 as the crucial date, we can reconstruct the time-table of events. Evidently the first two acts take place around 1907 since Tadzio is then ten; in Act III, when the revolution occurs ten years later, he is twenty. Although the basic unit of this play is the family, as in the bourgeois drama and world, the family in *The Water Hen* is breaking down, and with it all of society. Two sets of fathers and sons are in opposition, with Edgar playing the role of father in one pair and son in the other—thereby doubly alienated and isolated. "My friend's wife—my mistress's son," Edgar exclaims. "At last I've created a family for myself!" Like everything else in the lives of these characters breathing their last gasps under the *ancien régime*, Edgar's "family" is synthetic and constantly disintegrating.

Therefore, at the end of *The Water Hen*, when without any explicit preparation the revolution suddenly breaks out, it is totally unexpected but nevertheless seems inevitable. The dissolution of a whole society, inherent in the relationship of individuals, may be inferred from these personal relationships. Finally the war of son against father takes to the streets, and the characters themselves greet the violent destruction of the old with a sense of relief. But even revolution may produce repetition, rather than rebirth. Edgar realizes that he is doomed simply to lead another life, not a new life. Nothing can break the "vicious circle" of "boredom and suffering" or bring about a spiritual transformation. The Captain will become a revolutionary admiral; new scoundrels will replace the old ones.

The accelerating breakdown of the social order leads to the collapse of "character" as it has traditionally been conceived and to the disintegration of individual psychology.

Edgar, a conglomeration of scraps of different periods of civilization and a receptacle for others' ideas and suggestions, has no identity. He is a prism reflecting light from outside, like the eight concentric beams from the Lamplighter's lantern. Faced with an unreal, chaotic, and absurd universe, Edgar tries desperately, by various poses and pretenses, to create inner meaning for his life through external forms. Although he is confronted with multiple possibilities and has a choice of identities, he lacks the conviction to commit himself even to an illusion. Directed like a marionette by others, he has no personality not imposed upon him from outside. None of the roles thrust on him stick, and no force of life within him can either make him feel the reality of life or enable him to turn his anguish into art. In Nevermore Palace, a spectral mansion inspired by the raven of his namesake Edgar Allan Poe (beloved of the surrealists and emulated by Ghelderode), Edgar is the recipient of second-hand roles, hand-me-down costumes, fake gestures, and artificial penance.

Edgar tries repeatedly to break through to reality, to become someone and feel something deeply. He resorts to the most extreme acts and postures in order to produce, from the outside in, powerful emotional responses: pain, violence, murder. But nothing works. Even killing the Water Hen, an act forced upon him, must be repeated. The play abounds in doubles and images within images. As husband to the Duchess, Edgar is a repetition of Edgar Nevermore. The past, to which Edgar looks for some kind of fixity and identity, offers only masquerade and ham acting. The future holds nothing for him, since he cannot accept the role of artist planned for him by his father. The present, in which he must recreate himself at every moment, is too painful for him to face.

With the breakdown of character and of a stable, moral universe, the quest for greatness and nobility becomes meaningless. How can man achieve heroic stature and experience grand emotions in a world where the absolute is no longer possible? A modern Everyman, Edgar searches for greatness and the heroic gesture, but has neither talent nor character. According to the Water Hen's acute analysis, greatness comes only from what is irreversible and can occur only once, like first love, loss of virginity, and death. But in Edgar's preposterous world, death itself is reversible. After killing the Water Hen twice, Edgar attempts yet another theatrical gesture: he blows his own brains out. As his father observes, he continues to be a ham even in his style of dying.

A painter by profession, Witkiewicz brings the experimental daring of modern painting to the theatre, making drama part of the same universe created by Picasso. His conception of a radically new theatre analogous to painting was a prophetic insight that anticipates the direction of much avant-garde drama toward extensive use of visual images. Tadzio paints his dreams in watercolors, and the entire play explores the pictorial dimensions of the unconscious. The opening of *The Water Hen* presents a landscape that suggests the paintings of Giorgio de Chirico, the Italian forerunner of surrealism, whose work, like Witkiewicz's, raises obsessive questions about man's relation to the universe and expresses his sense of insignificance and awe in the face of infinity. As dusk falls, Edgar feels intensely alone. Objects have a mysterious and indefinable significance—the mound, the crimson-colored lamp pole, the green octagonal lantern. The horizon meets the sea, creating a strange, empty perspective in which man is little and lost. "People are like insects," Tadzio observes, "and Infinity surrounds them and summons them in a mysterious voice." The moon appears from behind fleeting clouds. Edgar feels the terror hidden in one of Chirico's streets or seacapes: "Nothing happens, nothing. I thought that something would happen, but there's no change —the same silence everywhere, and the earth silently revolves on its axis. The world is a desert without meaning."

As the comparison with Chirico suggests, *The Water Hen* may profitably be discussed in terms of surrealism and is, in fact (along with *Him*), one of the greatest surrealist plays. A basic aim of the surrealists was to reveal a new reality by exploring hitherto unexplored dimensions of human experience and art. In opening doors onto the mysterious world of the subconscious, they changed our way of seeing. Through distortion, strange juxtapositions, and shifting planes of reality, the surrealists penetrated to life's essence. They believed, with Charles Baudelaire, precursor of surrealism, that "true reality is to be found in dreams alone." They reveled in the incongruities and obsessions that produce laughter and in the multiplicity of phenomena that provoke feelings of wonder and amazement. Freud, analyzing the logic of dreams, showed them to be the basis of man's actions. The surrealists tried to liberate the forces hidden in dreams, and saw life itself as a dream. On his first appearance in *The Water Hen*, Tadzio has the feeling that he has just waked up. Throughout the play, he continues to wake up from his dream, or rather to try to wake up from it. When he wakes up for the third time in the last act, it is his final awakening: revolution breaks out and reality now seems a dream. There are "heaps of corpses out there in the street," Typowicz exclaims. "It's all a dream!"

Surrealism opens perspectives on both infinity and dreams —outer and inner space. To accomplish this in the theatre, the logical bonds of cause and effect must be broken and the categories of time and space extended and inverted. In *The Water Hen*, time and space are stretched like the elastic band that ties Edgar to the Water Hen. A drastic distortion of normal dimensions occurs the first time the Water Hen dies. As we watch, the setting shifts mysteriously: *"the field becomes the courtyard of a barracks. Two walls are slid in from the sides; a dim light appears in the center windows and at the gate below."* Not only has the scene changed, but time itself has altered radically. Although the Water Hen's body is still on the ground, months or even years may have elapsed: the barracks, Edgar tells the Water Hen in Act II, were built after he shot her. Time and space have become interchangeable. "Time," as Henri Bergson wrote, "understood in the sense of a milieu where one distinguishes and counts, is nothing else but space." The causal chain is wrenched when Edgar first shoots the Water Hen: "One miss. The other straight through the heart," she observes, but shows no effects until five minutes later. The chain is broken completely when the Hen later returns, not only none the worse for having been shot through the heart, but in the third act looking even younger and more seductive than before.

Having destroyed the logical concatenation of events, Witkiewicz is free to work by suggestion and juxtaposition. After shooting the Water Hen, for example, Edgar says, "There's one thing I've forgotten—what am I going to tell my father?" His question "causes" Tadzio to appear. When the Water Hen tells the boy to go to his father, Tadzio calls Edgar "papa." The word *father* starts a process of transference that operates in lieu of causality. By another process of transference, the lights in the barracks window begin to blink after Edgar notices the barracks and remarks that he feels as though he is in prison: the setting comes to life only after Edgar observes it. In the last act, there is a second change of time and space when the scene shifts back to the past and to the setting of the beginning of the play. As the cherry-colored curtain is opened, the landscape from the first scene, with the pole and lighted lantern, appears between the columns. The Lamplighter reappears, pointing out the landscape from many years before. This locale then becomes, through trans-ference, the "cause" of Edgar's repeating his previous action, the shooting of the Water Hen. In Witkiewicz, perspectives appear within perspectives—as much of time as of space.

Surrealist elements in *The Water Hen* include explora-tion of the unconscious and the dream, acknowledgment of the essential ambiguity of human experience (we never know whose son Tadzio really is), use of chance as a compositional technique, and investigation of the problem of identity and of life lived like an automaton. Most im-portant, Witkiewicz's presentation of man's insecure posi-tion in an absurd world and of his futile questioning is or-ganized and integrated by the comedy and irony essential to the surrealist vision. In surrealism, the contradictions, in-congruities, and terrors of life find expression in laughter. And so in *The Water Hen* startling coincidences, wild meta-phors, nonsensicality, and extreme distortion reveal man's potentially tragic metaphysical condition to be ludicrous and laughable.

characters

FATHER (*Albert Valpor, an old man, former skipper of a merchant ship. Short, broad-shouldered, but not obese. Nautical garb. Beret with a light blue pompom. White Vandyke beard. White moustache*)

HE (*Edgar Valpor, his son. About 30 years old. Clean-shaven. Good-looking*)

SMALL SON (*Tadzio, a boy 10 years old, with long blond hair*)

LADY (*Duchess Alice of Nevermore, a tall blonde, rather majestic and very beautiful, about 25 years old*)

WATER HEN (*Elizabeth Gutzie-Virgeling, a person of unknown origin, about 26 years old. Flaxen-haired. Light eyes. Average height. Very pretty, but not at all seductive. Nose turned up just a little bit. Lips very wide, thick, and liver red*)

SCOUNDREL (*Richard de Korbowa-Korbowski*, recte* *Tom Hoozy, good-looking, dark-haired, very scoundrelly, about 20 years old. Looks like Edgar Valpor*)

THREE OLD MEN:

    EPHEMER TYPOWICZ (*a businessman, clean-shaven, short grey hair, grown corpulent with power*)

    ISAAK SPECTER (*tall, thin, grizzled Semite, with a black moustache and a Vandyke beard. Refined gestures, an Assyrian type*)

    ALFRED EVADER (*nervous, red-haired Semite, with gold pince-nez. Skinny and tall. A moustache, no trace of a beard, a typical Hittite*)

---

* Witkiewicz uses the Latin *recte* and *false* throughout the play to indicate this character's true and assumed names.

FOOTMAN (*Jan Parblichenko, an ordinary flunkey. Reddish-brown hair, pimply. Completely clean-shaven*)

FOUR MORE FOOTMEN (*with long hair, two dark, two albino. All of them [including Jan] dressed in blue frock coats, shirts with ruffled fronts, and white stockings. They wear a great many military medals on their frock coats. Middle-aged. Jan is distinguished from the others by red aiguillettes*)

THREE DETECTIVES (*head detective, Adolph Orsin, blond hair and a big moustache. One of the other two has a moustache and wears glasses. The other has a long black beard. They appear artificial and banal*)

NANNY (*Afrosia Ivanovna Yupupova, an old woman with a heart of gold. A fat blonde 40 years old*)

THE LAMPLIGHTER (*a bearded individual in a workman's blue coat*)

Supplementary instructions from the central authority: speak without affectation and not from the guts, even at the worst moments.

act I   (*An open field, sparsely overgrown with juniper bushes. Some of the juniper bushes are shaped like cypress [two to the left and three to the right]. Here and there bunches of yellow flowers [something in the poppy line]. The horizon meets the edge of the sea. In the center of the stage a mound a little over three feet high. A crimson-colored pole [five feet high] rises from the mound. Hanging from the pole there is a very large octagonal lantern with green glass [the lantern may be silver and ornate]. The* WATER HEN, *wearing a chemise, stands under the pole. Her hands are bare. She has rather short hair, tied with a blue ribbon, forming a large top-knot; the rest of her hair falls loosely around her head. A sheer black crinoline petticoat shows beneath her short skirt, and her legs are bare.* HE *stands to the left, dressed in the style of the three bound men in the illustrated edition of* Robinson Crusoe. *Three-cornered hat, boots with very wide tops turned down [eighteenth-century style]. He's holding a double barreled shotgun of the worst make. At this very moment he is loading it, with his back and side almost turned to the audience. To the left, a red sunset. The sky is covered with fantastic clouds.*)

WATER HEN (*gently reproachful*): Couldn't you be a little quicker about it?

EDGAR (*finishing loading*): All right—I'm ready, I'm ready. (*Shoulders the gun and aims at her—a pause.*) I can't. Damn it. (*He lowers the gun.*)

WATER HEN (*as before*): You're wearing us both out quite unnecessarily. We've already decided everything. I thought that after so much anguish we'd finally understood each other. And now you're hesitating again. Be a man. Hurry up and aim.

EDGAR (*raising his shotgun*): There's one thing I hadn't thought of. But what does it matter? (*Shoulders the gun and aims: a pause.*) I can't. No, I can't pull the trigger. (*Lowers the gun.*) The difficulty is that I won't have anyone to talk to any more. Who will I talk to if you're gone, Lizzie?

WATER HEN (*sighing*): Oh! You'll spend more time in your own company then. It will be very good for you. Be brave. Only for a moment. Afterwards you'll be able to figure it out.

EDGAR (*sits on the ground in Turkish fashion*): But I don't want to be by myself.

WATER HEN (*sits resignedly on the mound*): You liked solitude in the old days. Do you remember how you used to run away from me? What's happened to you now?

EDGAR (*angrily*): I've grown accustomed to you. It's awful. I feel that there's a special kind of elastic band between us. I haven't been alone for the past two years. Even when you were far away, the elastic stretched, but never broke.

WATER HEN: Well, try something different for once. I have nothing new to offer you. Your chances will be better without me. I'm not talking about women, but about things in general.

EDGAR: You're trying to work on my baser instincts. Just like a woman. (*He jumps up.*) You must have a suicide mania. You're afraid yourself, and you use me like a piece of machinery. As if I were an extension of this shotgun. It's humiliating.

WATER HEN: What a ridiculous idea! Death means nothing to me. That's the absolute truth. But I really don't want to die. Yet life means nothing to me either. What tires me most is standing here under this pole. (*The sun is setting, dusk is falling, and then it slowly turns dark.*)

EDGAR (*clutching the gun in his hands*): I can't stand this. You know what—let's stop all this and get away from here. This is a hateful place. Nothing can ever happen here.

WATER HEN (*gently*): No, Edgar, you have to make up your mind. It has to be decided today. We've already made up our minds. And that's all there is to it. I can't live the way I used to any more. Something's snapped inside me, and it will never come back again.

EDGAR (*groaning with indecision*): Hm. I hate to think what'll happen to me during the night. Boredom and suffering—a vicious circle, endless and self-contained and closed in upon itself forever. And there'll be no one to tell it to. After all, that's my only joy in life.

WATER HEN (*reproachfully*): Even at a time like this you're being small. But, honestly, you used to mean much more to me than I ever thought you could. You were my child and my father—something indefinable, something without form and without contour, filling my world with its indeterminateness. (*Changing her tone.*) You're not a child, but you're so little, so hopelessly little.

EDGAR (*angrily*): Yes. I know. I'm not an undersecretary of state, a factory manager, a revolutionary, or a general. I'm a man without a profession and without a future. I'm not even an artist. At least artists know how to die in style.

WATER HEN: Life for life's sake! Do you remember the theory of your friend the Duke of Nevermore? The so-called "creative life." Ha, ha!

EDGAR: The insignificance of that concept is the cause of all my misfortunes. I waged a futile battle against myself for ten years, and after all that, you wonder why I can't make up my mind about such a trivial matter as killing you. Ha, ha! (*He knocks the shotgun against the ground.*)

WATER HEN: How stupid he is! Greatness is always irrevocable.

EDGAR: There are limits to my endurance. Let's not have any contrived scenes. Even in the most idiotic plays it's definitely against the rules.

WATER HEN: All right, but even you'll agree it's a vicious circle. Everything irrevocable is great, and that explains the greatness of death, first love, the loss of virginity, and so forth. What everyone can do several times is by its very nature trivial. (*A pale gleam of moonlight shows through the clouds.*) You want to be great, and yet you don't want to do anything that can't be undone.

EDGAR (*ironically*): What about courage, self-sacrifice, suffering for someone else's sake, acts of renunciation? Aren't these forms of greatness too? But they're really not; as soon as you deny yourself something, you become so smug about your own greatness that it makes you petty. Every work of art is great because it's unique. Let's sacrifice ourselves for each other right now, or else join the circus.

WATER HEN (*ironically*): Anything that lives is unique too, and hence great. You are great, Edgar, and so am I. If you don't shoot me this very minute, I'll despise you as a perfect walking zombie.

EDGAR: All this bores me. I'll shoot you like a dog. I hate you. You're my guilty conscience. It's I who despise you.

WATER HEN: Let's not quarrel. I don't want to say goodbye to you in the middle of a scene. Come, kiss me on the forehead for the last time, and then shoot. We've thought it all out. Well, come on. (*After putting down the gun,* EDGAR *approaches her hesitantly and kisses her on the forehead.*) And now go back to your place, my dear. Don't hesitate anymore.

EDGAR (*goes to his former place stage left, and picks up his shotgun*): Well, all right. It's all settled. I accept the inevitable. (*Examining the gun.*)

WATER HEN (*clapping her hands*): O, how splendid!

EDGAR: Stand still. (*The* HEN *stands still—*EDGAR *shoulders the gun, aims for a long time, and fires from both barrels at short intervals. A pause.*)

WATER HEN (*still standing, her voice completely unchanged*): One miss. The other straight through the heart.

EDGAR (*silently ejects the cartridges from the shotgun and then slowly lays the gun on the ground and lights a cigarette*): There's one thing I've forgotten—what am I going to tell my father? Perhaps . . . (*While he is speaking,* TADZIO *crawls out from behind the mound, dressed in a boy's navy blue suit with a lace collar; he hides in* HEN's *petticoats.*)

WATER HEN (*standing*): Go to your papa, Tadzio.

EDGAR (*turns around, notices* TADZIO, *and speaks with reluctance*): O, more surprises!

TADZIO: Papa, papa, don't be angry.

EDGAR: I'm not angry, my child, I only want a little rest after all this. Where did you come from?

TADZIO: I don't know. I woke up when I heard the shots. And you're my papa.

EDGAR: Who knows? Maybe I'm a father too. You see, my young man, it's all the same to me. For all I know, I might even be your father, although I can't stand children.

TADZIO: But you won't beat me, papa?

EDGAR (*somewhat dementedly*): I don't know, I don't know. (*Controlling himself.*) You see, something's happened here. I can't tell you now. This woman (*Pointing to the* HEN.) in some way or other . . . Why am I telling you this?

TADZIO (*picking up the shotgun*): Please tell me, what were you shooting at?

EDGAR (*menacingly*): Put that down right now. (TADZIO *puts down the gun; more gently.*) I was shooting because . . . How can I tell you? Well, you see I was . . .

WATER HEN (*in a weak voice*): Don't say anything . . . in just a moment . . .

EDGAR: Yes, my boy, it's not as simple as you think. Assume I'm your father, if you will. But whoever your father may be, who is he really? What kind of a man will he turn out to be? These are still unanswered questions.

TADZIO: But you're a grown-up, papa, you know everything.

EDGAR: Not as much as you think. (*To the* HEN.) Something fatal's happened. I have so much to tell you that a whole lifetime wouldn't be long enough; then suddenly this little brat appears, and our last moments are hopelessly spoiled.

WATER HEN (*in a dying voice*): I'm dying. Remember what I told you. You must be great in one way or another.

EDGAR (*advances a few steps towards her*): Great, great, but how? At fishing or blowing soap bubbles?

WATER HEN (*weakly*): Don't come near me. This is the end. (*She slowly crumples on the mound. The moon behind the fleeting clouds occasionally lights up the stage. Now it shines rather brightly.*)

TADZIO: Papa, what's the matter with that lady?

EDGAR (*signaling him to be quiet; not turning away from the* HEN): Quiet, wait. (*He gazes in silence at the* HEN *who is expiring half-crumpled on the mound with her hands pressed to her breast. She breathes heavily and gives a death rattle. A cloud completely covers the moon. It is dark.*)

TADZIO: Papa, I'm afraid. It's scary here.

WATER HEN (*scarcely able to speak*): Go to him . . . I don't want . . . (*She dies. At this point the setting changes so that the field becomes the courtyard of a barracks. Two walls are slid in from the sides; a dim light appears in the center windows and at the gate below. At the same time* EDGAR *comes up to* TADZIO *and silently puts his arms around him.*)

EDGAR: Well, I am alone now. I can take care of you.

TADZIO: I'm afraid. What happened to the lady?

EDGAR (*letting go of* TADZIO): I'll tell you the truth. She's dead.

TADZIO: Dead? I don't know what dead means.

EDGAR (*surprised*): You don't know! (*Somewhat impatiently.*) It's exactly as though she went to sleep, but she'll never wake up.

TADZIO: Never! (*In a different tone of voice.*) Never. I said I'd never steal apples, but that was different. Never—I understand now, it's the same forever and ever.

EDGAR (*impatiently*): Well, yes, that's the infinite, the eternal.

TADZIO: I know God is infinite. I never could understand that. Papa, I know so much now. I understand everything. Only it's too bad about the lady. I'd like to tell her so.

EDGAR (*partly to himself, grimly*): There's a great deal I'd like to tell her too. Much more than you.

TADZIO: Papa, tell me the whole truth. Why won't you tell me? It's very important.

EDGAR (*waking up, after having been lost in his thoughts*): You're right. I have to tell you. There's no one else I can tell it to. (*Emphatically.*) I killed her.

TADZIO: You killed her? So you were the one who shot her. How funny! Ha, ha . . . As though you were out hunting.

EDGAR: Tadzio, Tadzio, don't laugh like that. It's dreadful.

TADZIO (*becoming serious*): It's not dreadful at all, if it really happened the way you say it did. I was shooting too, but at crows with a bird gun. You look so big, papa. But it all seems as if some insects had eaten one another. People are like insects and Infinity surrounds them and summons them in a mysterious voice.

EDGAR: Where did you get that? Did you read it somewhere?

TADZIO: Perhaps I dreamed it. I have such strange dreams. Please go on talking, papa. I'll explain everything to you.

EDGAR (*sitting on the ground*): You see, it was like this. I should have been somebody, but I never knew what, or rather who. I don't even know whether I actually exist, although the fact that I suffer terribly is certainly real. That woman (*Pointing backwards with the index finger of his left hand.*) wanted to help me; she was the one who asked me to kill her. Eventually all of us will die. Desperately un-happy people find consolation in that thought. (*Enter from stage right the* LAMPLIGHTER; *he lights the lantern. Eight concentric rays of intense green light fill the stage.* TADZIO *sits down next to* EDGAR—*they talk to each other without paying any attention to the* LAMPLIGHTER, *who is listening to them.*) Why, why? If a man doesn't live like everybody else, if he doesn't work towards a goal, like a horse with blinders over his eyes walking around in a treadmill, then let me tell you Tadzio, quite truthfully, that he's completely in the dark. The goal is in the goal itself, as my friend Edgar, Duke of Nevermore, used to say. But I never could fathom that deep truth.

TADZIO (*nodding seriously*): Oh, I understand. I'm not satisfied with just anything either, but right now I don't want anything at all, nothing at all—do you understand?

EDGAR (*putting his arms around him*): Oh yes, I under-stand. You're starting pretty early, my young friend. What'll you be like when you're my age? (*The* LAMPLIGHTER, *who has listened for a while, silently leaves through stage right.*)

TADZIO: I'll be a robber.

EDGAR (*moving away from him in disgust*): Shut up. Don't talk that way. Sometimes I'd like to do something terrible too.

TADZIO: Ha, ha. How funny you are, papa! There's really nothing terrible at all. Only there are certain times when it's best not to be afraid. And terrible things, really terrible things I paint in watercolors only—do you know what I mean? I have pastel colors like that, so I'm only really afraid when I'm asleep.

EDGAR (*jumping up*): Nothing happens, nothing. I thought that something would happen, but there's no change—the same silence everywhere, and the earth silently revolves on its axis. The world is a desert without meaning. (*He looks around him and notices the barracks.*) Look, Tadzio, I have the impression we're in prison. Yellow walls. (*Lights blink in the center windows of the barracks.* TADZIO *stands up and looks around him.*)

TADZIO: I know this house. Soldiers are stationed here. The seashore is over there. (*He points to the gate of the bar-racks.*)

EDGAR (*disillusioned*): Oh, yes, I thought it was a prison. I feel like a dog on a chain who's been set free, but doesn't know how to run. For the rest of my life I'll walk around the kennel, and I won't have the courage to run away. Because—who knows?—I'll probably feel that perhaps it isn't true, I'm still on the chain. (*To* TADZIO.) But tell me, once and for all, what were you doing here in the first place?

TADZIO (*after a moment's reflection*): I don't know and I don't even want to remember. I was very ill in a kind of institution for boys. I didn't have a mother. And then I woke up as you were shooting, but I know this house, perhaps from my dreams.

EDGAR (*waves his hand contemptuously*): That's hardly very important. Tomorrow I'll begin your upbringing. (*At this moment* EDGAR's FATHER, *wearing nautical garb, enters from stage right; he stops and listens to* EDGAR *and* TADZIO *without being noticed by them.*)

TADZIO: You'll never be able to bring me up, papa. You couldn't.

EDGAR: Why?

TADZIO: You've had no upbringing yourself. I know that much about you at least.

FATHER (*coming up to them*): You talk very well, sonny boy. (*To* EDGAR.) Where did you unearth such a precocious little imp?

EDGAR (*getting up*): I don't know. He crept out from behind that mound. (*The* FATHER *turns around and notices the* WATER HEN's *dead body.*)

FATHER: What's this? (*With a wave of his hand.*) After all, it hardly matters. I don't meddle in your personal affairs. The Water Hen is dead. Since there'll be no supper at home, I trust you'll approve of our having something to eat here. I'll give orders to have the body carried out. I can't stand corpses flopping about where they have no business to be. (*He blows his whistle which he wears on a yellow string.* EDGAR *and* TADZIO *remain standing silently.*)

TADZIO: This is funny. I can see myself painting it in pastels and even then . . . (*Four* FOOTMEN *rush in and fall in a row.*)

FATHER (*pointing to the* HEN's *corpse*): Carry the lady out. There ought to be a cold cellar somewhere in this barracks. (*He uses his finger to point to one of the* FOOTMEN.)

Tell the orderly that I'll send for the corpse tomorrow. Don't ask any questions, and don't go blabbing about it. And then bring a table here and serve supper.

FOOTMEN: Yes, we understand. At your service. (*They immediately pounce on the* HEN's *corpse and carry her out stage left.*)

FATHER (*to* TADZIO): Well, young man, how do you like all this? Huh?

TADZIO: It's really hilarious. Still there's something missing. I don't know what.

EDGAR: Father, won't you leave him in peace? I've adopted him. I'll take care of the formalities tomorrow. I'm beginning another life. Not a new life, but another one— do you understand, father?

FATHER: You can even start at the end and go backwards. You can't escape. Gauguin didn't begin to paint until he was 27, Bernard Shaw didn't begin to write plays until after he was 30. But what's the point of giving examples? I tell you you'll be an artist, just as sure as I'm Albert Valpor, former skipper of the *Oronteso*, a vessel of 10,000 tons. Our story today is only the beginning—but a promising one. Own up to it, Ed, you killed the Water Hen.

EDGAR: Yes, I did. But she asked me to.

FATHER: Naturally. She preferred death to living with you. And yet she couldn't live without you. Poor silly Hen. I'm sorry about it. But what'll you do now? Who'll listen to your long, pedantic lectures justifying your downfall? Eh? Perhaps this young ward of yours. Huh?

TADZIO: How wise you are, Captain! Papa has gone over everything with me. (*The* FOOTMEN *bring in a table from stage left, place it before the mound, and set it for five people. A simple table, simple wicker chairs.*)

FATHER: Didn't I tell you so? You've had a rendezvous with destiny, my adopted grandson. Edgar Valpor, the great artist of the future, has taken you into his confidence. Never forget that.

EDGAR: Must you joke, father? This is hardly an appropriate time. (*He notices the table.*) Why so many place settings?

FATHER: I'm expecting guests. I want to provide you with enemies disguised as friends and vice versa, friends disguised as the bitterest enemies. You don't know how to live simply and normally, so you'll have to live your life in reverse and walk backwards along wayward paths. My patience is at an end. I've had enough.

EDGAR: And so, father, you . . . (TADZIO *plays with the double barreled shotgun.*)

FATHER: Yes, yes, I knew what would happen. I foresaw a great deal. Not everything, of course. I didn't know you'd shoot her. Now I don't want to spoil you. Still, I must admit that I'm somewhat impressed. Somewhat, I repeat, despite the fact that you've behaved like a thoroughly cheap stinker.

EDGAR: You're not a man, you're a devil. So you knew all along, father?

FATHER: There's nothing remarkable about that. Don't you remember when the three of us lived in the little house on the other side of the bay at Stockfish Beach? Remember her mania for feeding lemons to my ginger cat? I was able to observe the two of you very closely then. You both thought I was only searching for buried treasure. Remember, when she gave you that purple flower and said: "A great man does not ask how to become great, he is great." I even wrote it down.

EDGAR: Don't say anything more, father. Poor Elizabeth, poor Water Hen. (*He covers his face with his hands.*)

TADZIO (*comes up to him with the shotgun in his hand*): Don't cry, papa. These are only little pictures God paints with his magic pastels.

EDGAR (*opens his eyes and notices the gun*): Take it away! I cannot bear to look at that thing. (*He grabs the gun out of* TADZIO'*s hands and throws it to the right. All this time the* FOOTMEN *pay no attention and set the table.*)

FATHER: Easy. Easy. Ham—bleeding heart—sentimental ass. (EDGAR *stands still staring at the ground.*) Remember you're leading another life. Another life—as you've so aptly put it. Go live on Mars or on the star Antares if you can't get along here. My guests are about to arrive, do you understand? Don't you dare let me down with that hang-dog look! Don't you forget it! (*Nonsensical sounds from an accordion are heard from the right.*) They're coming. (*To* EDGAR.) Chin up. Not a whimper!

TADZIO: Captain, you're wonderful! Like an evil sorcerer.

FATHER (*Moved*): Call me grandfather. At last there's someone who appreciates my style. (*He strokes* TADZIO'*s head. The accordion playing gets closer.*)

EDGAR (*explaining*): I appreciate your style too. I just don't want you to jump to conclusions about . . .

FATHER: Then don't let me jump over you as if I were a horse and you were a hurdle. Silence. The guests are coming. (DUCHESS ALICE *enters from stage right. She is dressed in a ball gown the color of the sea. She wears a scarf, but no hat. She is followed by* TOM HOOZY [false RICHARD DE KORBOWA-KORBOWSKI], *dressed in a frock coat without a hat; he enters playing the accordion. Three* OLD MEN *come in after them.*)

LADY: How do you do, Captain? (FATHER *kisses her hand, playing the young man.* HOOZY *has stopped playing the accordion and observes the situation.*)

FATHER: My dear lady—so delighted to see you. The situation here is rather snarled, but we can unsnarl it. It was hardly necessary for the Duchess to bring these gentlemen. (*Points to the* OLD MEN.) However, we'll have to do the best we can.

LADY: But these gentlemen are quite charming. Let me introduce them to you.

FATHER: O, we already know one another. (*He greets the* OLD MEN *in a perfunctory manner.*) And now, if your Grace will allow me, I'll present to you my son, who was a great friend of your late husband. Ed, greet her Grace. My son—Duchess Alice of Nevermore.

EDGAR: Good heavens, is Edgar dead?

FATHER: We'll talk about it later—behave yourself.

EDGAR (*kisses the* DUCHESS's *hand*): Please tell me what happened to Edgar.

LADY: A tiger devoured him in a Janjapara-Jungle. He was always putting his courage to the test until finally the Supreme Being lost his patience. He died two days after the accident and I assure you he died beautifully. His belly was torn to pieces and he suffered terribly. But up to the last moment he was reading Russell and Whitehead's "Principia Mathematica." You know—all those symbols.

EDGAR: Yes, I know. What strength! Poor Edgar. (*To his* FATHER.) Why didn't you tell me about it before, father? I'm buffeted by so many blows all at once. My God, did Elizabeth know about it?

LADY: Has anything else happened? Tell me. I've heard so much about you from Edgar. He considered you the most interesting character on the face of our small globe.

EDGAR: Yes—something strange has happened. I'm on the threshold of another life. Beyond the grave almost . . .

FATHER: That's enough. As a matter of fact, today he shot the Water Hen like a dog. At her own request. Wouldn't you agree, Duchess, that's a lousy thing to do?

LADY: Oh, that Elizabeth Virgeling! I've heard so much about you two from Edgar! My poor husband often received letters from her. She wrote such strange things. Afterwards he was never quite himself.

FATHER: I'd still like to know whether or not you think it's a lousy thing to do.

LADY: But Mr. Albert—women love to sacrifice themselves: what good luck to have the chance to die for someone else. Isn't that so, Mr. . . . Edgar? It's strange to say that name again.

EDGAR: Well, yes . . . I suppose so . . . I don't know. I killed her half an hour ago.

LADY: What a pity. I so much wanted to meet her.

EDGAR: Edgar was in love with her and worshipped her from a distance. He wrote me that she was the only woman he could really . . .

LADY (*dissatisfied, she interrupts him*): Edgar loved only me, my dear sir. (TADZIO *stands to the left and looks at everyone delightedly.*)

EDGAR: But my dear lady, I'll show you Edgar's letters.

LADY: That doesn't mean anything at all. He was lying. Let's go for a stroll and I'll explain everything to you. (*All this time the* FOOTMEN *have been standing stiffly between the mound and the table. The* LADY *and* EDGAR *pass to the left. The* FATHER *stands looking now at the* OLD MEN *and* HOOZY, *now at them. As she passes by.*) Who's this charming little boy?

EDGAR: That's my adopted son. I adopted him exactly twenty minutes ago.

LADY (*smiling*): Half an hour ago you killed her. Twenty minutes ago you adopt some boy or other. It seems to me you've really been through enough for one day. Edgar told me you were strong as Hercules. What's your name, little boy?

TADZIO: My name is Tadeusz Gutzie-Virgeling. (*To the*

DUCHESS.) You're a very beautiful woman. Like the fortune teller in the picture I drew.

EDGAR: What? That too? I'll go out of my mind.

FATHER (*bursts out laughing*): Ha, ha, ha. That's a good one. (*He beats his hands rapidly up and down on his knees.*)

EDGAR: Did you know about that too, father? You knew Elizabeth had a son and you didn't tell me anything about it?

FATHER (*laughing*): As sure as I am the skipper of the *Oronteso,* I knew nothing about it. It's a surprise to me. Come here, Tadzio, let me give you a hug. (TADZIO *goes to him.*)

EDGAR: What was it you wanted to tell me?

LADY: I want to prove to you that it's all a mistake. (*They pass to the left and whisper.* HOOZY *plays the accordion impatiently.*)

EVADER: Mr. Specter, this is an extraordinary affair. I think we'd better go have supper at the Astoria. Or else we'll have to face the consequences.

SPECTER: Take my word for it, Mr. Evader. Nothing bad's going to happen.

FATHER (*lets go of* TADZIO): But gentlemen, please stay to supper, they'll set the tables for you right away. (*To a* FOOTMAN.) Get a move on! Three more place settings and more wine; hurry up! (*The* FOOTMEN *dash to the left.*) Tonight we'll drink till we all fall overboard. Isn't that right, Mr. Korbowski? You were in the Navy.

KORBOWSKI (*produces a wild sob from the accordion*): All right, Mr. Valpor. But I don't like that flirtation between Alice and your only son. (*Points to the left.*) She's no morsel for degenerates, my Alice isn't! Alice is mine! (*He throws down his accordion, which gives a wail. The others turn around.*)

EVADER: Mr. Specter, let's go.

SPECTER: I quite agree. I smell trouble.

TYPOWICZ: Wait! We're invited to supper. It's an amusing situation.

EDGAR (*to the* LADY): Who's that swine? Oh, excuse me —he came with you, but after all . . .

LADY (*passing to the right*): He's my only consolation in life, Mr. Korbowski—Mr. Edgar Valpor. (*The* MEN *greet*

each other; the FOOTMEN *set three new places at the table.*)
He's utterly primitive. If it weren't for him, I wouldn't have
survived Edgar's death. We met in India. Now we go everywhere together and see the most revolting things in the
world. You have no idea how beautifully he conducts himself in every situation.

KORBOWSKI: Alice, darling, please don't joke. You're twisting the lion's tail. I want to be treated with respect whether
we're in company or alone.

EDGAR: Why is he so familiar with you? What's going
on?

KORBOWSKI: I'm this lady's lover. Understand? I was invited here by your father and no uncouth only son is going
to get in my way. (*The* DUCHESS *looks at both of them
through her lorgnette.*)

EDGAR: Don't go too far . . . or I won't be responsible for
my actions. I've had enough for today. Please. (*The* FOOT-
MEN *have set the table and stand in a row behind it.*)

KORBOWSKI: I'm not going to let Alice carry on with the
first amoeba who happens to come along. I'm her lover and
I draw a yearly salary of 40,000 francs—with the approval
of the late Duke Edgar.

EDGAR: So you're just a kept man, an ordinary Alphonse . . .

KORBOWSKI (*coldly with passion*): I'm not Alphonse, I'm
Richard and a quite extraordinary one at that. Take a good
look at that. (*He shoves his fist under his nose.*)

EDGAR: What? Shoving your filthy paw in my face! (*He
strikes him between the eyes with his fist. A short fight.*)

KORBOWSKI: You only son . . .

EDGAR: Take that and that! I'll show you! (*He throws*
HOOZY *out stage right and runs out after him.*)

LADY (*to* FATHER): Why, your son is an athlete! He
overpowered Korbowski! And besides he's so good-looking.
The photograph doesn't do him justice. It lacks expression.
And what intelligence! I've read his letters to Edgar.

FATHER (*bowing*): It's only nervous energy. I never could
persuade him to do his morning exercises. Nerves. Nervous
energy. The way madmen in an asylum break their cell bars.
Yes, nerves. We're descended from old nobility.

LADY: Why, with nerves like that, who needs an athlete's
muscles? What a magnificent specimen of masculinity!

FATHER: I was sure your Grace would be pleased.

LADY: Call me daughter, Mr. Valpor. It's all settled. (*The* FATHER *bows.* EDGAR *comes back.*)

EDGAR (*the ruffles of his shirt are crumpled—without his hat*): Do you know what he was shouting as he ran away? That you (*Pointing to the* DUCHESS.) couldn't live without him and his evil ways, his rotten tricks, to be more precise, as he himself put it. He claims that you're an utterly depraved woman. So did Edgar.

LADY (*coquettishly*): Find out for yourself. Starting tomorrow, I'm going to be your wife. Your father's already given his consent.

EDGAR: So soon? I don't really know who I am yet. Perhaps in a day or two.

FATHER: Idiot, when you can get something for nothing, take it, and don't ask questions. Such a high-class woman, and yet he hesitates.

LADY (*to* FATHER): It's only bashfulness. (*To* EDGAR.) I'm sure you'll be happy with me. We've already become acquainted through all those letters and also because of what Edgar himself told me. He actually brought us together a long time ago, although he loved only me. Please believe me.

EDGAR: But I do believe you, I have to. (*Takes her by the hand.*) Is it really true? Can I start another life?

LADY: Yes, with me. With me everything is possible.

EDGAR: But that Korbowski. I'm afraid of what he's got in mind . . .

LADY: Don't be afraid. With you I'm not afraid of anything. (*She takes his head in her hands and kisses him.*)

TADZIO: Grandfather, will I really get such a beautiful mother?

FATHER: Yes, my boy, You've won first prize. She's a genuine English Duchess. (*To* EVERYBODY.) And now, gentlemen, we can sit down to supper. Please. (*He points to the table.* TADZIO *comes up to the* LADY, *who hugs him.*)

LADY: My child, from now on you may call me mama.

EDGAR (*deep in thought, near the front of the stage, partly to himself*): My friend's wife—my mistress's son. At last I've created a family for myself! But won't it be too much for me? (*To his* FATHER.) Listen to me, father. Should I humor myself this way? Shouldn't I undergo some kind of penance first?

FATHER: Sit down at the table and don't bother me.

EDGAR (*to* EVERYBODY, *as though justifying himself*): It's people and circumstances that have always made me what I am. I'm a mannikin, a marionette. Before I can create anything, everything happens all by itself exactly the way it always has, and not because of anything I've done. What is this? Some sort of a curse?

LADY: You can tell me all about it later. Now let's go eat. I'm desperately hungry. (*They sit down.*)

(A salon in Nevermore palace. To the left by the wall a round table. Armchairs. There are no windows.

act II

Door to the left and to the right. Pictures on the walls. Everything in strawberry hues which gradually become suffused with a warm blue. In the center a wide niche and three steps which end in four thin columns made of rosy-orange marble. Behind the columns a dark cherry curtain. To the left, in the armchair, three-fourths turned towards the auditorium, the LADY *sits doing embroidery. Her small* SON *is playing on the carpet, constructing some fairly large mechanical device. His hair is cut short and looks velvety, and he's wearing a dark carmine suit. The* LADY *is wearing a light cold grey dress. Dusk is slowly falling. A moment of silence.)*

TADZIO (*without stopping his tinkering*): Mama, I forgot why he's my papa.

LADY: It doesn't make any difference if you have. No one knows why things are the way they are and not some other way. You can ask such questions endlessly and never find any answers.

TADZIO: I know—Infinity. I'll never forget how I first came to understand what it means. Ever since then everything's really been all right. I think everything's infinite and has to be the way it is. But there's just one thing: why exactly is he my papa and not someone else?

LADY: Perhaps you'd prefer to have Mr. Korbowski as your papa, my little philosopher?

TADZIO: Don't talk to me like that, mama. I'll tell you something else: as soon as you appeared, I forgot everything that had happened before. It's like one of those dreams you can never recall. I remember only my name. Nothing else.

LADY: That's a great deal. Apparently you had to forget everything else.

TADZIO: I want to find out how I came to be: where I came from and where everything's going. Things keep on going all by themselves and seem to be heading somewhere. What's it all about? Where's it all rushing so fast?

LADY (*slightly disconcerted*): Ask your father. Even I don't know that.

TADZIO: Mother, you're keeping something from me. But I know more than I'm letting on. Your eyes are double, like those little boxes with a secret drawer.

LADY: Now it's my turn to say: don't talk to me like that. I'm very fond of you and I don't want to have to hurt you.

TADZIO: Haven't I been good? Nothing seems right. Everything's happening as if I were dreaming. (*With sudden animation.*) You know, I've never been afraid of anything except in my dreams. And now that everything seems like a dream, I'm really afraid that at any moment something dreadful will happen and I'll be much more terrified than I ever was in any dream. I feel so frightened sometimes. I'm afraid of fear. (JAN PARBLICHENKO *enters and lights the electric candelabra hanging from the ceiling.*)

LADY: Jan, has the master returned?

JAN: Not yet, your Grace.

LADY: Don't forget the special liqueurs. There'll be guests for dinner.

JAN: Yes, your Grace.

TADZIO (*standing up*): So there'll be more of those repulsive characters who torment papa. (JAN *leaves stage left.*)

LADY (*somewhat venomously*): And Mr. Korbowski will be here.

TADZIO: He's a man out of a bad dream. But I like him. I like to look at him. He's like a snake who eats small birds.

LADY (*ironically*): And you're a small bird, aren't you?

TADZIO: Mama, why do you talk to me the way you would to a grown-up? I asked you not to talk that way.

LADY: I never had any children and I don't know how to talk to them. If you want to, go to Afrosia.

TADZIO: She doesn't have double eyes. Still she bores me. I don't like good people, but bad people make me suffer.

LADY (*smiling*): Am I bad?

TADZIO: I don't know. But you make me suffer, mama, and I like to be with you because you make me suffer.

LADY (*with a smile*): What perversity!

TADZIO: That's a word for a grown-up. I know. Why can't

I wake up? Everything seems wrong somehow. (JAN *enters from the right.*)

JAN: Mr. Korbowski, your Grace.

LADY: Ask him to come in. (*Exit* JAN. TADZIO *becomes silent, his gaze fixed on the door to the right.* KORBOWSKI *enters wearing a frock coat.*)

KORBOWSKI: Good evening. Am I late?

LADY: No, dinner is late. Edgar hasn't come back yet.

KORBOWSKI (*kisses her hand and sits down next to her facing forward*): Alice, how can you call that soggy wet noodle by the same name as your husband, the late Duke? I may not be very refined, but it gives me a kind of psychological ache. (TADZIO *makes a gesture as though he wanted to throw himself on* KORBOWSKI, *but he restrains himself.*)

LADY (*with a smile*): Well—as long as it's not physical, you can stand it.

KORBOWSKI: Don't laugh. I wear my soul in a sling like a broken arm, like fruit stolen out of my own garden which my enemy has leased. I feel a morganatic attraction for you, strong as an American tornado. I am consumed with passion for a misalliance, transformed by a clever writer into a self-libel, with which I flog my own impotent destiny.

LADY: But there's no sense at all to anything you're saying.

KORBOWSKI: I know, that's why I say it. I read night and day and my head is spinning. (*He stretches his legs out, leaning his head back behind the armchair.*)

LADY: Sit up properly.

KORBOWSKI: I don't have the strength. I'm like a shirt that's been embraced by a wringer. I'm afraid of time whirling past me like the wind on the pampas around the rushing antelope. I'm exhausted.

TADZIO (*seriously*): You put that very nicely. When I wake up from this dream, I'll paint it.

KORBOWSKI: Listen, young aesthete, suppose you go to sleep? Really and truly, to bed, huh?

TADZIO (*leaning against the* LADY's *armchair*): I won't go. You're just a handsome tramp, and this is my home.

KORBOWSKI: You're as much of a tramp as I am. Go to sleep, that's my advice.

LADY: Mr. Korbowski is right. Both of you have an equal right to be here with me.

TADZIO: That's not true. If I knew why he's my papa, I'd answer you differently. It's a mystery.

KORBOWSKI: There's no mystery at all. Your so-called father is a common murderer. He may be hanged at any moment. He lives by the grace of the Duchess, like a dog on a chain. Understand?

TADZIO: That's not true. If he wanted to, papa could be great, but he doesn't want to. I heard that somewhere.

KORBOWSKI (*gets up and pushes* TADZIO *away brutally*): You little moron, I'll give you greatness! Clear out! (TADZIO *falls down on the carpet, crawls up to the machine, and starts to operate it again, stooping over—not saying anything.* KOR-BOWSKI *stands bending over the* LADY.) Alice! I can't take it any longer. You don't belong here. Throw that Valpor out once and for a tired wet noodle. I can't go on living like this. I can feel something new and strange, something colossally rotten growing inside me, and it'll be nasty for anyone who gets in my way. Understand? Everything I read (and I don't do anything else) I eagerly pervert into evil—odious, hairy, cruel, redhot evil. Don't push me over the brink. Will you leave all this and come with me now! I don't want to go back to being what I was without you. I know I'm nothing. What are you paying me for? Why do I go on living? (*He clutches his head in his hands.*)

TADZIO (*turns around and looks at him ecstatically*): Blow up, Mr. Korbowski, go ahead and blow up. (*The* LADY *bursts out laughing.*)

KORBOWSKI (*shaking his fist at him*): Shut up! (*To the* LADY.) Alice, I'm nothing at all—that's just it! That's why I used to be the happiest man in the world. Now that I have everything I've always dreamed about, it all seems worthless without you. I might as well put a bullet through my head. I'll go stark raving mad!

LADY (*coldly*): Have you been unfaithful to me?

KORBOWSKI: No, no, no! Don't question me about it so casually. I can't stand it.

LADY: He's suffering too.

KORBOWSKI: What's that to me? Let him go on suffering in peace and quiet. You've turned this house into a colossal torturetorium. I don't want any part of it.

LADY (*with a smile*): Then go away!

KORBOWSKI (*bending over her*): I can't. Will you leave all this and come with me now! (JAN *enters.*)

JAN: Messieurs Specter, Evader, and Typowicz, your Grace.

LADY: Show them in. (*Exit* JAN. *Enter the three* OLD MEN *wearing frock coats.*)

KORBOWSKI (*bending over her embroidery, aloud*): What lovely needlework! The blues and yellows complement each other so exquisitely. (*Softly, through his teeth.*) Will you leave all this and come with me now!

LADY (*gets up, passes by him, and goes to greet the* OLD MEN): Gentlemen, you'll forgive us, Edgar is late. (*The* OLD MEN *kiss the* LADY'S *hand.*)

TYPOWICZ: Oh, that's all right. But how are we doing with our new venture, the Theosophical Jam Company?

LADY: We're putting up all our capital. We'll secure the balance with real estate as collateral. Even the name is marvelous. Edgar has gone to the Union Bank. He should be back any minute.

KORBOWSKI: Alice!

LADY (*turning away, in a cold voice*): Mr. Korbowski, must I ask you to leave our house? (KORBOWSKI *rolls up in a ball and falls into an armchair, covering his face with his hands.*)

TYPOWICZ: Dear lady, this is a great day for the corporation.

EVADER: You're the only member of the aristocracy who . . .

SPECTER (*interrupts him*): Yes—you alone had the courage. Your example ought to . . .

LADY: I can't talk about all this before dinner. Gentlemen, please sit down. (*Goes to the left; the* OLD MEN *follow her; they sit down without greeting* KORBOWSKI.) I'm in favor of a total Semitico-Aryan coalition. The Semites are the race of the future.

EVADER: Yes. The spiritual rebirth of the Jews is the key to the future happiness of mankind.

SPECTER: We'll show what we can do as a race. Up until now we've produced only individual geniuses. (*The curtain in the back is drawn and* EDGAR *quickly runs down the stairs, dressed in a black frock coat.* TADZIO *flings himself towards him.*)

TADZIO: Papa, I can't stand it any more! I don't know when she's telling the truth. (*He points to the* LADY.)

EDGAR (*shoving him away*): Go away. (*To everybody.*) Dinner is served.

TADZIO: Papa, I'm so all alone. (EDGAR *talks with the* OLD

MEN, *paying no attention to* TADZIO. KORBOWSKI *sits like a mummy.*)

LADY (*rings;* AFROSIA, *dressed entirely in green, runs in from the left side of the stage; a green scarf on her head*): Afrosia Ivanovna, take this child away. See that he drinks his herb tea and put him to bed! (AFROSIA *takes* TADZIO *by the hand and they go off to the left. From the right hand side of the stage the* WATER HEN *enters, dressed as in Act I, but she's wearing silk stockings, patent leather pumps, and a cape thrown over her shoulders.*)

LADY: And who is this?

EDGAR (*turning around*): It's she! You're alive?

WATER HEN: That should hardly be any concern of yours.

TADZIO (*stopping at the door to the left—shouts*): Mama! (*He runs to the* HEN.)

EDGAR (*to the* HEN): Is he your son? You lied about everything.

WATER HEN (*astounded*): I have never lied. I don't know this boy at all. (*She pushes* TADZIO *away, and he clings to her.*)

TADZIO: Mama! You don't know me?

WATER HEN: Calm down, child. I never was your mother.

TADZIO: So I have no one at all! (*He cries.*) And I can't wake up.

EDGAR: Afrosia Ivanovna, take Tadzio out of here this very minute; see that he goes to bed immediately. (AFROSIA *takes* TADZIO *away to the left; as he goes, he is convulsed with tears.*)

LADY (*nudging* EDGAR): Tell me, who is that woman?

EDGAR: It's the Water Hen—Elizabeth Virgeling.

LADY: But what does this mean? You killed her.

EDGAR: Apparently not, since she just walked in and is standing right there. That would appear to be fairly conclusive evidence.

KORBOWSKI (*getting up*): So she's really alive! I'm ruined. There goes my last chance of getting rid of that bad dream! (*To* EDGAR.) Rest assured, Mr. Valpor, the attempted blackmail didn't work.

EDGAR: You and your blackmail mean nothing to me. I tolerate your presence here in this house of my own free will. I'm devoting my entire life now to penance. (*To the* HEN.) Penance for what I've failed to accomplish. I failed and I've got to suffer for it and do penance. You should be delighted—it's all your fault. Can you imagine anything worse?

WATER HEN: You're still not suffering enough. Not nearly enough. And that's why everything seems so awful to you. (FATHER *enters from the right hand side of the stage, in a frock coat, his beard shaved.*)

EDGAR: Oh, father, please look after the guests. I want to talk privately with this woman. It's the Water Hen—she's alive! Judging by your complete lack of surprise, I suppose you knew exactly what was going to happen.

FATHER (*cheerfully*): Well, of course.

EDGAR: You monster!

FATHER: Your late mother spoiled you. I've got to make up for it, so I'm bringing you up in my own way. And now, ladies and gentlemen, will you please come to the dining room. (*To the* LADY.) Alice—has Mr. de Korbowa-Korbowski been invited too?

LADY: Of course. (*To the* HEN.) After you've talked with my husband, please join us at the table. And after dinner you and I will have a little chat.

WATER HEN: And who are you, may I ask?

LADY: I am Edgar Valpor's wife and Edgar Nevermore's widow. Apparently you're the one woman my first husband was in love with—from a distance of a thousand miles. Ha, ha! (*To the* GUESTS.) Please come, gentlemen. (KORBOWSKI *offers her his arm. She motions him away and offers her arm to* TYPOWICZ. *They go up the stairs.* JAN *draws the curtain. The two* OLD MEN *follow them, the* FATHER *comes next, and in the rear* KORBOWSKI *drags along, completely shattered. All this while* EDGAR *and the* HEN *stand still, looking at each other. All the others disappear behind the curtain, which is then drawn.*)

WATER HEN: Do you love her?

EDGAR: Don't even say that word in my presence. I hate the very sound of it.

WATER HEN: Once and for all, answer my question.

EDGAR: No, no, that's an entirely different matter. I'm just a marionette. I'm outside of whatever happens to me. And I watch myself like a Chinese shadow moving on a screen. I can only observe the movements, but have no control over them.

WATER HEN: So nothing has happened as a result of my death?

EDGAR: What's happened is that I suffer a thousand times more than I ever did. I've started another life—not a new one. I gave that up a long time ago. ANOTHER LIFE! I'm creating a new skeleton inside of what already exists. Or rather they are—my father and the Duchess.

WATER HEN: And the utter void? I mean as far as feelings are concerned.

EDGAR: It goes on and on.

WATER HEN: What does your father expect of you? The same as always?

EDGAR: Yes, he says I'll certainly become an artist.

WATER HEN: But you have no talent—not for anything whatever.

EDGAR: That's precisely the point. I don't have any and never will. It's as impossible as changing one's complexion. Black hair can be bleached but can a black character?

WATER HEN: Will you be angry if I ask you something: How's the greatness problem coming?

EDGAR: Greatness? Monstrosity perhaps? I've already told you: I'm a buffoon, a plaything of unknown forces. I'm great—like a marionette. Ha, ha!

WATER HEN: Don't laugh. What about real life?

EDGAR: I manage my wife's estate, I've invested all of it in the Theosophical Jam Company. Those three men are making all the arrangements. I'm only a mannikin. (A pause.)

WATER HEN: Don't get angry if I tell you something. You're not suffering enough.

EDGAR: You dare say that to me? Don't you understand how absolutely ghastly my life is?

WATER HEN: I understand, but it's really nothing, nothing at all. The only way to get anything out of you is to torture you. I know what I'm talking about.

EDGAR: Haven't I suffered enough already? My wife keeps that Korbowski in constant tow. The slimy maggot! I hate him, I loathe him, I despise him, and yet I have to put up with him all the time. Now he'll be on the board of the new company. I don't know whether he's her lover or not; I don't ask, I don't want to find out. Isn't that enough for you? All my evenings are pinnacles of utter degradation.

WATER HEN: But you don't love her.

EDGAR: You're a woman, my dear. You'll never understand. For you women it's only: he loves me, he loves me not, he loves me, he loves me not. You never understand suffering any more complicated than the wrong answer to that question.

WATER HEN: Go on. What else makes you suffer?

EDGAR: You know how I hate reality. From early morning on I'm up to my ears in business: board meetings at banks, the stock exchange, negotiations with wholesalers and big accounts. Now it's really starting. Imagine me, Edgar, a businessman! It's the height of agony.

WATER HEN: It's not enough. A propos, what about Tadzio?

EDGAR: Your deathbed bequest . . .

WATER HEN: I swear I never saw that boy before.

EDGAR: The facts are against you. But I don't want to go over that old story again. Besides, facts don't interest me. So you're not his mother?

WATER HEN: But you know I can't be a mother!

EDGAR: Miracles happen. Did you know they've built a huge barracks where I once tried to kill you without much success? But no matter.

WATER HEN: Tell me, what's the relationship between you?

EDGAR: Between Tadzio and me? Frankly, I'm insanely attached to him, but I have a deep suspicion that he'll grow up to be a scoundrel so monstrous that Korbowski will seem a saint by comparison. Along with my insane attachment to him, I feel an unbearable physical disgust. He doesn't love me at all and doesn't want to regard me as his father. He admires Korbowski—he's his artistic ideal. Now I've listed my principal sufferings. Isn't that enough?

WATER HEN: That's nothing.

JAN (*appears from behind the curtain*): Her Grace requests that you come to the table.

EDGAR: Right away. (JAN *disappears.*) That's nothing? What more do you want?

WATER HEN: I don't know . . . Perhaps a prison sentence or maybe physical pain will cure you. There have been cases of conversion . . .

EDGAR: To what? Theosophy?

WATER HEN: No—to a belief in the positive values of life.

EDGAR: Wait! Physical pain. That's a new idea! (*He runs over to the table and rings. The* HEN *watches him curiously. Four* FOOTMEN *run in from the left.*) Listen to me: go to the Duchess's museum immediately and bring me the Spanish instrument of torture; you know, the one with the green and yellow stripes. Hurry. (*The* FOOTMEN *leave quickly stage left.* EDGAR *paces up and down nervously. The* HEN *goes to the left, sits down in an armchair, and follows him with her eyes.*)

EDGAR: Well, now I'll show you . . .

WATER HEN: Just don't lie to yourself.

EDGAR: Quiet! Now I'm master of my own fate. I know what I'm doing and I'll do it myself without anyone else's help. (*Stamping his foot on the floor.*) Quiet! I tell you . . . (*The* FOOTMEN *come in carrying a box eight feet long, the sides of which are latticed with yellow and green strips of board; at the corners there are yellow wheels which are connected to cranks; inside there's a small bench, and thick ropes hang from the cranks; the box looks very old.*) Set it down in the middle of the room! (*The* FOOTMEN *put the box down and stand very stiffly by its four corners.*) And now listen to me: you'll torture me with this machine. No matter how much I cry out and beg for mercy, you're to stretch me till I stop screaming. Do you understand? Tie my hands and legs and then turn the cranks.

FOOTMEN: Yes sir, all right, we understand.

EDGAR: Well—hurry up! (*He takes off his frock coat and throws it on the ground; he's wearing a bluish shirt; then he quickly climbs into the box and lies down on the bench, his head to the left.*) Hurry! (*The* FOOTMEN *tie the ropes with frantic speed and begin to turn the cranks, at first rapidly, then slowly, with effort.* EDGAR *starts to groan horribly at regular intervals. The* HEN *laughs demonically in her armchair. When* EDGAR *isn't groaning, her laughter can clearly be heard.*) Stop—aaa! I can't stand it. Aaa! Aaa! Mercy! Enough! Aaa! (*He croaks the last "Aaa" horribly and is suddenly silent. The curtain is drawn and the* LADY *can be seen looking in. The* MEN *crowd behind her. The* FOOTMEN *stop and look into the box, without letting go of the cranks, which remain in the same position.*)

WATER HEN: What are you gaping at? Keep on turning it. (*The* COMPANY *from the dining room comes slowly down into the drawing room, with the* LADY *leading the way.* JAN *follows them. The* HEN *stops laughing and sits quietly, staring madly straight ahead.*)

FOOTMAN I: He's fainted.

FOOTMAN II: He's had enough, poor fellow.

FATHER (*runs over to the box and looks into it*): Has he gone mad or what? (*To the* FOOTMEN.) Get him out of there! (*The* FOOTMEN *untie* EDGAR *with frantic speed and pull him out, absolutely limp.*) Put him on the couch. (*To the* HEN.) Elizabeth, was this hideous business your idea? (*At this moment from the left side of the stage,* TADZIO, *in a night shirt and stockings, runs in with a cry.* AFROSIA *follows him. The* LADY *and her staff stay where they are, a little to the right. The* FOOTMEN *carry* EDGAR *to a small red couch, to the right, and stand erect to the right of it.* JAN *goes over to them. They whisper.*)

TADZIO: Papa, papa! Don't cry like that ever again! (*He falls on his knees by the couch, on the far side to the rear of the stage;* EDGAR *opens his eyes and his face brightens.*) Papa, I love you, I woke up from my dream. (EDGAR *strokes his head.*) Papa, she's the one who's torturing you, that strange lady who didn't want to be my mother. I don't want her here. Take her away. (*He buries his head in* EDGAR'S *chest;* EDGAR *hugs him.*)

KORBOWSKI (*speaks at the top of his voice in the midst of the silence*): This is barren metaphysical suffering in the fourth dimension.

FATHER: Silence. (*To the* FOOTMEN.) Take that damned box out of here. Hurry up. (*The* FOOTMEN *fling themselves at the box and carry it off to the left.* AFROSIA *stands silently to the left.* EDGAR'S *black frock coat remains in the middle of the stage on the ground until the end of the act.*)

WATER HEN (*gets up and speaks to the* LADY *in a fiery voice*): Do you think that Edgar Nevermore loved you? He loved only me. I have his letters right here. I want you to know everything. I've always kept them with me, but now they're useless. (*She throws down a packet of letters at the* LADY'S *feet. The packet becomes untied and the letters scatter about.* KORBOWSKI *picks them up eagerly.*)

LADY: I know all that and I've already proved to my second husband that your theory's wrong. You were only a kind of make-believe mother that certain men feel they need. Such an experiment works best at a great distance. Edgar loved only me. Korbowski knows something about it.

WATER HEN: Mr. Korbowski may know a great deal, but in matters of feelings of the sort which united me with Duke Edgar, he simply isn't competent to judge.

LADY: You're just a phantom. An imagined value. I'm not

at all jealous of you. I prefer reality to your spiritual seductions in the fourth dimension. Edgar told me that he wrote you nonsensical letters which you took seriously. It's all ridiculous and petty.

WATER HEN: That's not true.

KORBOWSKI: The Duke told me so just before he died; he was reading that big fat book full of symbols and expiring at the same time.

LADY: Yes, he was reading Russell and Whitehead's "Principia Mathematica" after his entrails had been torn out by a tiger. He was a hero. He was fully conscious when he said he'd duped you into a metaphysical flirtation. He called it the psychopaths' metaphysical flirtation. Yet he wasn't a madman himself.

WATER HEN: (*bursts out laughing suddenly*): Ha, ha, ha! I was the one who was pulling his leg. I lie about everything. I don't exist at all. I live only by lying. Is there anything more sublime than lying for its own sake? Read those letters. That man believed in me, but he had moments of horrible despair and tried to convince himself that he was the one who was lying. In that lay the drama of his life. That's why he was so brave. I was the one who didn't want to meet him.

LADY: Yes, because he would have been disillusioned. He didn't even have a photo of you; you wanted to be something in the nature of a myth. That's why you never have your picture taken. Everybody knows all about that. (*The* HEN *wants to say something in answer.*)

TADZIO (jumps up): Take that woman away. I don't want her here. She tells lies. (*He stamps his foot.*)

EDGAR (*in a weak voice*): Tadzio, don't—behave yourself!

LADY: Jan, show that woman out this instant. (JAN, *who up until now has stood erect near* EDGAR's *head, moves towards the* HEN.)

FATHER: I'll escort her to the door myself. Elizabeth, give me your hand. In your own way you are great. (*They go towards the door hand in hand.* TADZIO *sits down at* EDGAR's *feet.*)

EDGAR (*still lying down*): So you're against me too, father?

FATHER (*turning around at the door*): Not against you, but with you against life. I'm waiting for you to finally become an artist.

EDGAR (*still lying down*): Alice, save me from him; save me from myself. (*He notices* KORBOWSKI *standing irresolutely with the letters in his hand.*) Out, scum! Out!

LADY: You may take them with you, Mr. Korbowski. Reading that correspondence will be good for your psyche; you'll be more mixed up than ever. Please go right ahead. (*She points to the door on the right.* AFROSIA *sits down in the armchair to the left.* KORBOWSKI *hesitates.*) Jan! (JAN *shoves* KORBOWSKI *gently towards the door.* KORBOWSKI *scarcely resists.*)

JAN: All right, Tom, none of your tricks. (*They go off to the right.*)

TYPOWICZ (*pulls some papers out of his side pocket and goes over to* EDGAR): Mr. Valpor, as guardian of your wife's estate, will you please sign here. We've drawn up the final version of the charter of the Theosophical Jam Company. (*He gives him a fountain pen.* EDGAR *signs lying down.*)

EDGAR: And now, gentlemen, forgive me, but I can't go on. (*The three* OLD MEN *bow, kiss* ALICE's *hand, and leave.*) Alice, I beg you. Let's start a new life.

LADY (*with a smile*): Not another one, but a new one?

EDGAR: That was impossible. (*He looks at* TADZIO *as if he hadn't noticed him before.*) Tadzio, go to bed this minute!

TADZIO (*getting up*): But won't you believe me now? I believe in you, my dear, dear papa. I woke up when that woman said she didn't want to be my mother. I want to be good.

LADY: I want to be good too.

EDGAR (*paying no attention to what she has said. To* TADZIO): How will wanting to be good help, if there's evil in the very depths of your soul? Besides, I must admit I've gone beyond such categories today. Ethics is only the consequence of a large number of individuals thinking the same way. A man on a desert island wouldn't have any notion of what it means. Tadzio, go to bed.

TADZIO: But won't you believe me, papa? I'm not talking about you, mama; you have double eyes. Now I know why you're my father.

EDGAR: I want to believe you, just as you want to be good. (*He kisses him on the forehead. Without saying good-bye to the* LADY, TADZIO *goes slowly to the left, his head lowered.* AFROSIA *gets up and follows him.*)

LADY (*sitting down beside* EDGAR *on the small couch*): Do you really feel as though you were on a desert island?

EDGAR: Save me, Alice. I'm tired of being a superman. The temptation of penance was too much for me. Father's against me, and so is Elizabeth. Together the two of them tempt me. (*He speaks feverishly.*) There's an even worse temptation waiting for me—he inoculated me with it: the temptation to become an artist. I'm defending myself with what little strength I have left. I have no talent, I'm great in my utter nothingness. Today life has lost all meaning.

LADY: Just because that liar walked out on you?

EDGAR (*still more feverishly*): No, no. This suffering . . . I don't even want to talk about it. I can't describe it. Rescue me from art; I hate art and I'm afraid of it. Now that life has lost its meaning, that other temptation's becoming stronger and stronger. I won't be able to resist it unless you protect me. Alice, I hardly dare ask you; all my bones ache after those tortures. For once, kiss me as if you really loved me.

LADY (*bending over him*): I feel that I really do love you now. (*She kisses him on the lips. A long kiss.*)

EDGAR (*pushing her away*): But it's all petty, petty, petty.

LADY (*getting up and stretching*): Only in lying is there greatness.

EDGAR (*raising himself up a little*): Oh, so you're against me too? Life awaits us in all its horror.

LADY (*slowly, emphatically*): I won't leave you. Neither you nor Tadzio.

EDGAR: Like condemned prisoners we'll drag on and on until death.

act III   (*The same room as in Act II. Evening. The chandelier is
lighted. Ten years have elapsed. A suite of furniture
stands on the right hand side of the stage. A small
couch covered in something green on
the left. On the right, by the door, a small
folded card-table.* TADZIO, *as a young man
twenty years old, sits lost in thought in an armchair on the
left. He's dressed in a grey suit. Suddenly he begins nervously
to tap his right foot against the floor.*)

TADZIO: When will this ghastly nightmare ever end? It's
just like a life sentence. God knows what father expects of
me; he's a failure himself. What a fine example! (*Gets up.*)
For the time being I'll listen dutifully. But as soon as it all
blows up, I won't have to look up to anybody. Korbowski—
there was a man. What a pity he wasn't my father! (*Walking up and down.*) You forget everything—even that women
exist! Mathematics, mathematics! It's a hell of a life! (*Knocking at the door to the right.* JAN *enters.*)
JAN: Sir, the lady who was here ten years ago wishes to
speak to you.
TADZIO: What? (*Remembers.*) Oh! Show her in. Hurry up.
I behaved so badly then. (*He goes to the door. The* WATER
HEN *enters, dressed as in Act II, but she wears a black cape
and a black hat, something in the style of Napoleon's "en
bataille," and an orange sweater. She hasn't aged at all. On
the contrary, she is very seductive. Her eyes seem more
slanted and her lips redder. Her whole face is lighted up
with sensuality, of which there was no trace in Acts I and
II. Her hair is cut short and is curled.*)
WATER HEN: Are you Mr. Tadeusz Valpor?
TADEUSZ (*flustered*): Yes, I am. In the old days we both
had the same name.

WATER HEN: I know that. A pure coincidence. That's why people suspected I was your mother. You were the one who desperately wanted me to be your mother, and you got offended when I refused. Ha, ha. What a ridiculous rumor! Don't you agree? (JAN *leaves smiling.*)

TADEUSZ (*still more flustered*): I was a child then. But please—do sit down. (*The* HEN *sits down in the armchair to the left where he had been sitting;* TADEUSZ *near her, his left profile to the audience.*) But you look even younger now, as far as I can remember from the old days.

WATER HEN (*greatly flustered*): Yes . . . It's Indian yoga, plus American massage. Ludicrous, isn't it? Ha, ha! (*She conceals her embarrassment by laughing. She laughs "till her sides split," loudly.* TADEUSZ *is grimly flustered. It is evident that the* HEN *is making one hell of an erotic impression on him.*)

TADEUSZ (*sullenly*): Properly speaking, why are you laughing?

WATER HEN (*pulling herself together*): Properly speaking, I'm laughing quite improperly. And what are you doing these days? (*With an ironic stress on* "you.")

TADEUSZ: Me? I'm not doing anything. I study. Mathematics. They torture me with mathematics, even though I don't have any talent for it.

WATER HEN: That runs in your family. Your grandfather was dead set on making an artist out of your father. So far as I know, it was a complete failure.

TADEUSZ: That's true, as of now. Although it's still a subject of endless controversy. (*Returning to the original topic.*) You know, what I'm going to say may sound absurd: I'm so busy that I sometimes forget women exist. Yesterday as I was going to class, I caught sight of a good-looking woman and I swear for a minute I didn't know what sort of a creature I was looking at. Then I realized that there are such things as women, and I was deliriously happy. (*He breaks off and becomes embarrassed; the* WATER HEN *has become gloomy.*) What I'm saying is all nonsense. Maybe it seems very childish to you, but . . .

WATER HEN (*takes off her hat and puts it on the table; she tosses her cape back on the arm of the chair; her face brightens*): Well, and what else?

TADEUSZ: Nothing. You said there was something that runs in our family. But you know that I'm only my father's adopted son.

WATER HEN (*flustered*): Yes, I know.

TADEUSZ: But sometimes I could swear that it was you who first called him my father. I was very ill then—that's for certain.

WATER HEN (*suddenly moves a little closer to him and asks with sudden shamelessness*): Do I appeal to you?

TADEUSZ (*momentarily, as they say, "thunderstruck"; suddenly takes a deep breath and speaks in a choked voice*): I like you tremendously. I love you. (*He throws himself at her. She pushes him away, laughing.*)

WATER HEN: Just like that, "I love you." And what about that woman in the street? When all of a sudden you remembered that women exist.

TADEUSZ: That was nothing. I love only you. Let me kiss you . . . (*He kisses her on the lips violently. The* HEN *yields.*)

WATER HEN (*pushing him away*): That's enough . . . Someone's coming.

TADEUSZ (*out of his mind*): Tell me you love me. I've just kissed you for the first time. It's tremendous. Tell me you love me.

WATER HEN (*kisses him violently*): I love you—you innocent little thing. You'll be my . . . (*Enter* FATHER *and* EDGAR. *They stand on the threshold astounded.* TADEUSZ *jumps away from the* HEN. *The* FATHER, *clean-shaven but much older.* EDGAR, *who has aged a great deal, looks over fifty; both are dressed in the same way, like* TADEUSZ.)

FATHER: Here's a new development! (*He recognizes the* HEN; EDGAR *stands by the door absorbed;* TADEUSZ, *flustered, to the left.*) Good evening, Elizabeth. (*The* HEN *gets up.*) I haven't seen you for ages! You're quite the coquette now, aren't you! (*To* TADEUSZ.) Well, you rascal, playing footsie with her already, eh?

TADEUSZ: I love this woman and I intend to marry her. I've awakened from my dream again. Now I know what it all means and what all of you wanted from me. Nothing doing. I don't want to be that kind of person. I don't accept any of these new theories!

WATER HEN (*taking his arm*): He's mine. He's suffocating here with all of you. He's handsome. He has a beautiful soul. He'll become great through me.

EDGAR (*coming up to her, angry*): All of a sudden he's got a beautiful soul and greatness too just because you find him attractive. You don't know him. And you'll probably make him great the way you wanted to make me great. It's all petty, disgustingly petty.

FATHER: Greatness has gone to your heads. In my time at least it was possible to become a great artist. But now even that doesn't work . . .

WATER HEN (*not paying attention to him*): You two want to warp his life the way I warped yours. (*She points to herself and to* EDGAR *in a certain crude way.*)

FATHER: You warped my cat's life too, Elizabeth, by feeding him lemons. But the cat died, and in this case we've got to go on living, or else we'd better blow our brains out right away.

EDGAR: That's just it. I won't let you use Tadeusz for your suicidal experiments or for your artificial crimes. He'll be a scholar. The only profession in the world that hasn't already gone to the dogs or to some still worse creatures.

TADEUSZ: I don't want to be a scholar at all. I love Miss Elizabeth.

EDGAR: You think that'll satisfy you? You're not a woman, that won't fill your life. Look at him; he's invented a new career: being in love! A third-rate Don Juan—what am I saying—a common Juan without the Don.

WATER HEN: He knows intuitively who he is. You two can distort anything. If you won't let a criminal be a criminal, he'll become something still worse—a fake, a fraud. Father, you're the one who's contaminating everyone with your programs.

EDGAR: Since when have you repudiated lying? A long time ago? Or is this a new lie especially created for the present situation?

WATER HEN: There's no truth in words or in any actions or professions men devise. Truth is what is actually happening.

EDGAR: Look here, what sort of real-life dadaism is that? Do as the apes do, live in trees! But I'm going to remind you once more of that other time. (*To his* FATHER.) Father, talk with them. I'll be right back. (*He leaves, almost running, to the left.*)

FATHER: Well, what do you say about that, youngsters?

TADEUSZ: Nothing. Either father lets me marry this woman, or I'll run away from home. That's final.

FATHER: I have nothing more to say to you. I'll watch what happens as a spectator. (*The* LADY *enters from the left side of the stage, dressed in an azure dressing gown trimmed in lace. She is very well-preserved, but slightly made up.*)

LADY: Oh, it's you. New revelations about my first husband perhaps?

WATER HEN: That topic doesn't concern me any more. I've destroyed the past completely.

LADY (*coming up to her and speaking with venom*): But you haven't destroyed yourself in the process, have you? You look very pretty. I realized at once that something was going on when Edgar rushed in like a lunatic racing against time and changed into his eighteenth-century outfit. Apparently he wants to entice you with the past.

WATER HEN: It won't work. I love Tadeusz. He's going to marry me.

LADY: So soon? (*To* TADEUSZ.) Tadzio, is that true?

TADEUSZ (*in a hard tone of voice*): Yes. I've finally awakened from my dream and seen through all your lies. Manufacturing artificial people, artificial crimes, artificial penance, artificial everything.

LADY: This one is always waking up from some dream or other and beginning to understand everything. How many times now have you come to understand everything? What's the grand total?

TADEUSZ: I've understood twice. But everything is infinite, there's no point in talking about actual quantities of anything. When I understand for the third time, it may very well be the end. (*The* HEN *nestles close to him in silence.*)

LADY: A regular little Solomon. Watch out you don't tempt fate by talking about that third time. Watch out! (*She shakes her finger at him.* JAN *enters from the right.*)

JAN: Tom Hoozy, your Grace.

LADY: Hoozy?

JAN: *False* de Korbowa-Korbowski, your Grace.

LADY (*amazed*): I didn't know that was his real name. Ask Mr. Hoozy to come in. (*Exit* JAN.)

FATHER: Here's a new complication. Undoubtedly he knew all about it. Life holds no interest for me any more. (KOR-BOWSKI *enters, dressed in a threadbare sports coat, sports cap, a thick walking stick in his hand. His face is ravaged and aged, but handsome. He looks more noble than before.*)

LADY: Mr. Korbowski, *recte* Hoozy, sit down and be a silent witness to events. (KORBOWSKI *bows and sits in the armchair to the right. At this moment* EDGAR *runs in, dressed in the costume he wore in Act I, with a hat.*)

WATER HEN: What kind of a masquerade is this? Ham. He's changed into his old costume to create an atmosphere. Too bad you didn't dress up as a Mexican general or Julius Caesar.

TADEUSZ: Really, papa, that's too much, you're making a farce of a very serious situation.

EDGAR: Silence. I forbid you to marry that person.

KORBOWSKI (*gets up*): Mr. Valpor, please wait a minute. I apologize for being here, but I've been authorized by the Duchess. I still love her. For the last five years I've been observing your life together. I spent five years in the Argentine.

EDGAR: What's that to me? Get to the point.

KORBOWSKI: As soon as that witch appeared, I knew that today would be the crucial day. (*Points to the* HEN.) The police are on my track, but since I was a former witness, I took the chance and came to help you. Besides, there's a revolution going on and I mean to come out on top. If everything comes crashing down today, I'll have nothing to fear.

EDGAR (*who has been listening impatiently*): That will do, you can finish later. Tadzio, today you're at the turning point of your life. If you insist on staying with that woman, you're lost.

TADEUSZ: That's because you're sweet on her yourself, father. The proof is that you've changed your clothes. You overdo everything.

EDGAR: Tadzio, I'm telling you for the last time. I love you, but my patience . . .

TADEUSZ (*interrupts him brutally*): Father, you're an old ham and besides you're not my father at all. Don't forget that while I'm talking to you, father, I'm wide awake, not dreaming.

EDGAR (*petrified, he roars*): You scoundrel!

TADEUSZ: Yes, I'm a scoundrel . . .

EDGAR: Shut up! Shut up! (*Throws himself at* TADZIO *and tears him away from the* HEN.) You won't marry her. I won't let you.

TADEUSZ: If that's the case, I'm leaving the house right now and you'll never see me again. Understand, father? Not another word.

KORBOWSKI (*to* EDGAR): Mr. Valpor, come to your senses.

First of all, we've got to kill this slut. (*Mysteriously, to the* LADY.) Follow my game, Alice? (*To* EDGAR.) It's the only way out, Mr. Valpor.

EDGAR: Yes, you're right, Mr. Korbowski. I'm glad you've come. Thank you. (*Shouts.*) Jan! Jan! (JAN *appears in the door to the right.*) My double barreled shotgun, a bullet in each barrel! (JAN *disppears.*)

WATER HEN: That's enough play-acting. Tadeusz, we're leaving right now. I can't stand petty lying.

EDGAR: This is no lie, I'm not joking. (*The* LAMPLIGHTER *enters.*)

LAMPLIGHTER: The lantern has been lit.

EDGAR: What lantern? Who are you? (*The cherry-colored curtain is drawn and between the columns appears the landscape from Act 1 with the pole and lighted lantern. The mound is not visible behind the stairs.*)

LAMPLIGHTER: Playing dumb! As though you'd just dropped in out of the blue! Look over there! (*He points out the landscape. Everybody looks in that direction.*)

EDGAR: Oh, that! I'd forgotten. Thank you, my good man, you may go now. (*He gives him a tip. The* LAMPLIGHTER *goes away muttering something unintelligible. At the door he meets* JAN *carrying the gun.*)

JAN: It's loaded, sir. (*Everybody turns around.* EDGAR *takes the gun.*)

WATER HEN (*to* TADEUSZ): Are you coming or not?

TADEUSZ (*gives a start, as if awakened from a dream, and speaks in a daze*): I'm coming.

EDGAR: Not one step! (*To the* HEN.) Stand over there. (*He points to the stairs.*)

WATER HEN: I wouldn't dream of it. I'm sick of your idiotic jokes.

EDGAR: Jan, get that woman and hold her. I'm going to shoot her.

JAN: I'm afraid; you just might shoot me too.

EDGAR: Hold that woman, I said. (*The* HEN *makes a movement towards the door.*)

JAN: Please stop joking, sir.

EDGAR: You blockhead, you know I'm an excellent shot. *Tir aux pigeons*—first prize. Take her and put her on target, or I'll shoot you dead as a dog without a moment's hesitation. (*He says the last words in a threatening tone.* JAN *grabs her and drags her to the left towards the stairs.*)

WATER HEN: I've had enough of these idiotic jokes. Let

go of me, you boor. Edgar, have you really gone mad? (JAN *drags her onto the stairs. They stand against the background of the landscape.* TADEUSZ *has raised his hands to his head in incredulous horror. He stands petrified. The* LADY *and* FATHER, *craning their necks this way and that, look first at* EDGAR *and then at the group on the stairs, with horrified curiosity.*)

EDGAR (*to* JAN): Hold her still. (*He aims.*)

WATER HEN (*shouts*): Edgar, I love you, only you. I was only trying to make you jealous.

EDGAR (*coldly*): Too late!

WATER HEN: He's a madman, he already shot me once. Save me! (EDGAR *aims, moving the barrel to follow the* HEN's *movements as she struggles to tear herself away. Two shots are fired.* JAN *lets go of the* HEN *and she falls down on the threshold between the columns.*)

JAN (*bending over her*): Her head's split wide open! (*Coming down.*) You sure are a whale of a madman! Damned if you're not! (*He scratches his head admiringly.*)

EDGAR (*calmly*): It all happened once before, only a little differently. (*To* JAN.) Take this. (JAN *takes the shotgun and exits. At the door he passes the three* DETECTIVES *whom no one sees.*)

TADEUSZ: Now I've finally awakened from my third dream. I know everything now. I'm an unmitigated scoundrel.

EDGAR: Serves you right. I hate you. I haven't even got an adopted son. I'm all alone. (*Remembering.*) What about you, Alice?

LADY (*pointing to the door*): Look over there, look over there. (*Two* DETECTIVES *throw themselves on* KORBOWSKI *and pin his arms back. The curtain is drawn shut.*)

ORSIN: My apologies, ladies and gentlemen. But we've been tipped off that Tom Hoozy, one of the most dangerous criminals in the world, just came in here.

LADY: Richard, I've been the cause of your undoing. I left you for that idiot. (*She points to* EDGAR.)

KORBOWSKI (*held by the* DETECTIVES): It doesn't matter. There's a revolution going on. We'll meet again. This won't last long. Perhaps today we'll all be free. Alice, I loved you and you only even in the thick of crimes so monstrous as to be four-dimensional and non-Euclidean in their swinishness. (*The* LADY *wants to go over to him.*)

ORSIN (*noticing the* HEN's *body*): Stay where you are. Who's that lying over there? (*He points to the stairs.* EDGAR *makes a gesture, as though he wanted to say something.*)

LADY (*quickly*): I killed that woman, because she was in love with him. (*She points to* KORBOWSKI, *who smiles blissfully.* TADEUSZ, *taking advantage of the confusion, sneaks away to the left towards the door.* EDGAR *stands still.* FATHER, *completely bewildered, is silent.*)

ORSIN: Quite a cosy little nest! Madam—I mean, Duchess Nevermore—ho, ho—*secundo voto** Valpor—so this is how you operate? (TADEUSZ *flees impetuously through the door on the right.* ORSIN *flings himself after him.* TADEUSZ *escapes.*)

KORBOWSKI (*shouting after him*): Don't worry, we'll meet again. (*To the* LADY.) Don't you understand, Alice, now he's really turned into a hopeless scoundrel. And in times like these he may be destined to play a great role. (JAN *pulls the* HEN's *body to the other side of the curtain.*)

ORSIN: That's enough talk. Take them both to prison. (*Sounds like the pounding of feet, confused singing, and shouting can be heard in the street.*)

FIRST DETECTIVE: I don't know if we'll make it; things are starting to get hot out there.

ORSIN: We'd better hurry. (*Two shots are heard, followed by a burst of machine-gun fire.*)

KORBOWSKI: It's going nicely. Let's go out into the streets. I like the atmosphere of a revolution. There's nothing more agreeable than to swim in the black sea of a mob gone mad. (*The din offstage continues.*)

LADY: Richard, I love and admire you. Can there be any greater happiness than not to despise the man one loves? (*The two* DETECTIVES *lead* KORBOWSKI *out.* ALICE *follows him.* ORSIN *follows them. Passing across the stage.*) Good-bye, father. I'm leaving the house and the money to you. (*She leaves without looking at* EDGAR.)

FATHER: Well, sonny, now what? We've gone bankrupt. All we need now is for Tadzio to turn out to be Korbowski's son. But we'll never know about that. Perhaps now you'll become an artist. You could even become an actor; after all, actors are now creative artists too, ever since Pure Form became all the rage. (EDGAR *stands silently; the noise offstage becomes louder and louder; bursts of machine-gun fire.*)

---

* Latin, "according to vow," i.e., by marriage.

Well, make up your mind! Surely nothing ties you to life any more? Now you've got to become an artist.

EDGAR: Death still ties me to life. That's the last thing to be disposed of.

FATHER: How?

EDGAR (*pulls a revolver out of his pocket*): Like this. (*He shows it to his* FATHER.)

FATHER: You'd be an excellent actor, especially in those preposterous plays they write nowadays. But why did you use a shotgun when you had a revolver? So it would be more difficult to figure out? Huh?

EDGAR: Because I wanted it to be the same as before.

FATHER: I've always said you were an artist. Everything's neatly worked out in prepared speeches. You could write plays. Come here, let me give you a hug.

EDGAR: Later, I don't have time now. Good-bye, father. (*He shoots himself in the right temple and falls to the ground.* FATHER *stands goggle-eyed for a moment.*)

FATHER (*affectedly*): "Oh, thus the artist dies"—without any self-knowledge. Not like that other ham. (*He shouts.*) Jan! Jan! (JAN *runs in.*) The young master has killed himself. Call the albinos, have them carry him out.

JAN: I always thought it would turn out this way. (*He bends down over the corpse.*) It was a perfect shot. A tiny little hole like a nail makes. (*The noise in the street reaches its peak.*) What a shot that guy was! But he sure gave me a good scare today!

FATHER: Jan, open the door, they're beating on it. The mob must be tearing everything down. (JAN *goes out.*) It's strange how old age and sea duty blunt everything in a man. I honestly don't feel anything at all—either for good or evil. Damn it all, a man isn't a ship! (*Enter* TYPOWICZ, EVADER, *and* SPECTER.) At last! (*To the* OLD MEN.) My son killed himself. His nerves got the better of him. Too bad. Well, what's going on out there?

TYPOWICZ (*pale, the others frightfully dejected*): Mr. Valpor, cheer up. Everything's going to the devil. The Semites will always find a way. There are heaps of corpses out there in the street. We came on foot. Our chauffeur ran away. They took our car. We saw a strange sight. The Duchess was walking along the street in her dressing gown with Korbowski; some thugs were holding them prisoner. We couldn't get near them. (*The* ALBINOS *come in.*) Kor-

bowski kept shouting something. Then the mob beat the
thugs to a pulp, and Korbowski and the Duchess went off
with the crowd to the barricade near Roughneck Road. But
what am I saying? It's all a dream! Our company no longer
exists. The new government has abolished all private enterprise. All we have left is what we've got abroad in foreign
banks. (*During this speech, the* ALBINOS *carry out* EDGAR'S
body to the left.) And what about our homes?

EVADER: They're community property too. We've lost
everything.

FATHER: I wonder if my adopted grandson will fight his
way to the top. (*Suddenly.*) Well, gentlemen, it's our last
night; the gangsters will probably butcher us tomorrow, so
let's amuse ourselves for the last time. (*Shouts.*) Jan! (JAN
in the doorway.) Set up the card table. (JAN *throws himself
forward and with incredible speed sets up the card table in
the middle of the room.*)

EVADER: Have you gone out of your mind? To play cards
at such a critical time?

FATHER: At our age it's the only way of whiling away the
time during a social upheaval. What else could we do?
Whist or auction bridge? "That is the question."*

TYPOWICZ: Why not whist? (*Burst of machine-gun fire.*)

FATHER: Oh, did you hear that? How could we do anything else except play cards? Everything's falling to pieces
anyway.

SPECTER: It would seem that you're right.

FATHER: Of course. Jan, cold supper *extra fin* and plenty
of wine for all. We'll drink like dragons. We've got to drink
away three abortive generations. Maybe I'll still become a
revolutionary admiral, but those others—ugh—what a come-
down! (TYPOWICZ, SPECTER, *and* EVADER *sit down at the
table, leaving a place facing the audience for* FATHER. TY-
POWICZ *with his back to the audience,* EVADER *on the left,*
SPECTER *to the right. Faint bursts of machine-gun fire and a
distant roar of heavy artillery shells exploding.*)

FATHER (*to* JAN, *who stands in the doorway*): Jan, one
thing more. Go get those girls to keep us company at dinner,
you know—the ones the young master and I used to visit.

JAN: But will they want to come when all hell's breaking
loose?

---

* In English in the original.

FATHER: Certainly they'll want to; promise them any-thing. (*Exit* JAN; FATHER *goes over to the table and inspects the cards.*) There's no need to worry, gentlemen, perhaps we can still get jobs in the new government.

TYPOWICZ: One club.

EVADER: Two clubs.

FATHER (*sitting down*): Two diamonds. (*A red glare floods the stage and the monstrous boom of a grenade exploding nearby can be heard.*) Banging away in fine style. Your bid, Mr. Specter.

SPECTER (*in a quivering, somewhat plaintive voice*): Two hearts. The world is collapsing. (*Fainter red flashes of lighting and immediately afterwards two shells exploding a little further off.*)

TYPOWICZ: Pass.

A PLAY OF THE SOCIAL REVOLUTION IN
SEVEN PICTURES

by Ernst Toller

Translated by

Louis Untermeyer

man and the masses

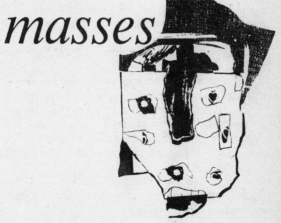

Masse-Mensch was first produced at the Volksbühne, Berlin,
on September 29, 1921, and published the same year.

Toller's famous play dramatizes the relationship between man, the state, and the masses—a major theme in much of the avant-garde drama of the period—in the abstract style of expressionism. *Man and the Masses* presents a stage of social upheaval following that depicted in *The Water Hen*. Whereas Witkiewicz's "spherical tragedy" deals primarily with the crumbling of the old regime, showing the eruption of revolution only at the last moment from the viewpoint of dreamers stumbling through a nightmare-like life, *Man and the Masses* takes as its entire subject the process of revolutionary uprising caused by war and capitalist oppression. Curiously, however, the revolution is still dramatized in the form of a dream. But Toller's expressionist dream offers hope as well as terror, aspiration as well as destruction, and conveys powerful emotions and messianic fervor.

Despite many overlapping techniques and areas of concern, the expressionist and the surrealist visions differ. Although the term *expressionism* is sometimes used loosely and imprecisely to refer to virtually all modern, non-realistic drama, the expressionist movement produced a type of play, definable by theme and form, which flourished in Germany from 1912 to 1925 and which influenced English, Irish, and American drama of the twenties and thirties. The confusion between expressionism and surrealism usually results from the attempt to analyze them solely on a formal basis. Since each is concerned with dream and revolution as both subject and technique, they often use similar methods in their departures from realism. Unlike the later movement, surrealism, expressionism was ideological and conceptual, with a strongly moral, essentially Christian belief in the possibility of man's regeneration and rebirth through love. Expressionism's typical dramatic structure, a series of scenes or stages in man's life, comes from the stations of the cross; its tendency toward allegory from the morality play; its denunciation of capitalism as much from a hatred of Mammon as the root of all evil as from Marx; its love of the underdog, the downtrodden, and the proletariat from such Biblical aphorisms as "Blessed are the poor" and "Many that are first shall be last, and the last shall be first"; its use of the martyr as a scapegoat dying to save others from the story of Christ's crucifixion and resurrection. Surrealism is fundamentally a comic vision, unbelieving and nihilistic in its stress on life's irreducible incongruities. Expressionism is a tragic or transcendent vision, religious even in its scathing denunciation of official Christianity and its "whited sepulchers." Surrealism remains cool and playfully ironic; expressionism is hot and intensely passionate.

In a typical expressionist play like *Man and the Masses,* the alienated hero is in quest of salvation. Searching for brotherhood and an end to spiritual isolation, he wants a new life, not simply another life. But the mechanized, industrialized society in which he lives reduces men to robots enslaved by machines. A key image for the expressionist is man's imprisonment in the cage of a dehumanized world. For the expressionist hero, the only hope for salvation lies in a radical change, not only in society, but, perhaps more important, in man himself. *Man and the Masses* is the journey of the heroine's soul through real and dream experiences of social upheaval during a revolutionary strike called to end an imperialist war. But this revolt is at the same time a subjective rebellion for the heroine, since she leaves her place in society and breaks with her husband, an authoritarian figure who represents both the state and the masculine principle of dominance to which she has been bound physically and psychologically. Her personal redemption blends with the transformation of society. In the experience of revolution, in which all former habits, conventions, and certainties are destroyed, the real seems dream-like and the dream-like real. The audience participates in the spiritual history of the heroine's soul, freed from the normal bonds of time and space, as she strives toward a salvation that can be accomplished only through the affirmation of love over the institutions of the industrial state and the triumph of man over the concept of the masses.

Sonia Irene L., the central figure of *Man and the Masses,* is the only character who has a name—and it is Russian. The characters of expressionist drama are almost always generic figures. Representatives of classes, defined and identified by their social functions and outer appearances, the other characters in *Man and the Masses* are not individuals but abstract, universal types. The masses themselves become a generalized chorus, oppressed and enslaved by capitalistic, militaristic, and bureaucratic institutions which have depersonalized them and drained them of individuality. Man's inner life is denied by the external reality in which he lives, and Death-in-Life (an abstraction from Toller's first play, *Transfiguration*) proves more deadly than actual death on the battlefield or before the firing squad. From the rupture between man and his social environment come the non-realistic techniques of expressionism, polarized toward dream consciousness on the one hand and the mechanical gestures and movements of masses on the other.

Telescoping and exaggeration, the shorthand of psychic reality, portray the distorted world of expressionism, in which the entire drama is seen through the subjective consciousness of the hero. All the principal voices and figures may be fragments of his own mind and extensions of his own inner conflicts. The hero's identity is subject to change; objects and characters undergo multiple transformations and incarnations. As Strindberg wrote in his influential prefatory note to *A Dream Play* (1902), "Characters split, double, and multiply; they evaporate, crystallize, dissolve, and reconverge." The heroine's husband in the first scene of *Man and the Masses* becomes the clerk in the dream sequence at the stock exchange in the Second Picture; he is the Man, symbol of allegiance to the system. In the dream vision in the Fourth Picture, the face of the prisoner changes into the face of the guard, for victim and victimizer are interchangeable as long as force rules. The Nameless One appears in many different guises: demagogue, revolutionist, vengeance, fate. If *Man and the Masses* is viewed as the inner struggle of the heroine, then the Man (her husband) and the Nameless One are projections of her own psyche and conflicting viewpoints within her own nature, her ties to her own past versus her passionate feeling of the need for social change at all costs.

The text of *Man and the Masses* conveys only a small part of its theatrical impact. Derived, like surrealism, from a movement in painting, expressionism relies heavily on visual and sensory effects. New lighting techniques in the 1920's permitted a theatrical chiaroscuro capable of creating a dreamlike atmosphere, an abstract sense of timelessness and spacelessness, and the feeling of vast groupings of faceless masses. In Jürgen Fehling's celebrated production of *Man and the*

Masses at the Berlin Volksbühne in 1921, the stage was empty except for a great staircase and dark curtains which, when drawn, seemed to open onto an infinity of space. Light and shadows molded the masses and their shifting shapes into subjective visions. In expressionism not only does the visual dominate the narrative, as three-dimensional stage pictures, painted by electric lighting, replace thousands of words, but, paradoxically, the lyric dominates the dramatic in the form of choral declamation and ritualistic chant. The dialogue itself often becomes elliptical, fragmentary, and dissociative.

The only play in this collection that was a great success in its own time and whose initial production was influential, *Man and the Masses* fell from prominence with the demise of expressionism and what seemed to be the end of revolutionary politics. Until recently Toller's play appeared to have only historical interest. However, once again *Man and the Masses* has immediate impact for a world in which major cities are racked by riots and revolutionary strikes. Taking as his subject the contemporary ethical problem of the use of violence in bringing about social justice and urgent changes in society, Toller dramatizes the dilemma of the intellectual: are revolutionary means justified by revolutionary ends? This drama is enacted in the mind of the Woman as her emotions drive her toward and against revolution. Can violence, abhorred as a weapon of the warfare state, be used against the state to destroy violence and create pressing social changes? In *Man and the Masses,* Toller analyzes the crisis of the bourgeois liberal who recognizes the need for change but draws back before the consequences when conscience is translated into action.

World Revolution.
Bearer of New Forces.
Bearer of New Folk-Unity.
The Century is a red glare.
Pyres are bloody with guilt.
Earth crucifies itself.

characters

WORKMEN
WORKWOMEN
THE NAMELESS ONE
OFFICER
PRIEST
MAN (*an official*)
SONIA IRENE L. (*the Woman*)

FIGURES IN THE VISION

SONIA IRENE L. (*the Woman*)
THE COMPANION
BANKERS
THE OFFICIAL
SENTINELS
PRISONERS
SHADOWS

The Second, Fourth, and Sixth Pictures are visionary, projections of a dream.

first picture

(Back room of a workmen's tavern. On the whitewashed wall are pictures of soldiers' councils and heroes of the masses. In the centre of the room, a crude table around which a WOMAN *and several* WORKMEN *are sitting.)*

FIRST WORKMAN: Hand-bills have been distributed
In the great convention hall.
To-morrow the factories will close early.
The masses seethe.
To-morrow—the decision.
Are you ready, comrade?
    THE WOMAN: I am.
Strength grows with every breath—
How I have longed for this hour,
Where the heart's blood finds words,
And words grow into deeds!
Impotence shook me often—and I clenched
My hands in shame and agony and fury.
When filthy papers trumpet "Victory,"
A million hands take hold of me
And cry:
"You are guilty of our death!"
Yes, every horse with shivering, foaming flanks,
Accuses me in silence . . . accuses me.—
Yet, since I sound the final call to-morrow,
There, where my conscience flames up in the hall,
Shall I not be the one to proclaim the strike?
Mankind cries, Strike! Nature cries, Strike!
The river hisses, Strike!
Even the dog, it seems, barks for it as he leaps
When I come home. . . .
I feel it in each vein. The masses rise,
Free of red tape, of webs spun out

By well-fed gentlemen around green tables.
Armies of mankind, with overpowering purpose,
Will build a structure of peace to unknown heights.
The red flag ... flag of bright beginnings ...
Banner of daybreak ...
Who will lead with it?

SECOND WORKMAN: You! They follow you!
(*Silence flickers.*)

THE WOMAN: Can we be sure no one has talked?
You think the police have had no information?
Suppose the soldiers form a chain around the hall?

FIRST WORKMAN: The police know nothing. And if they do,
They never know our real intentions.
When once the masses can possess the hall
They'll make a raging flood that no police
Can tame into a plashing, park-like fountain.
Besides, the police won't dare to interfere,
Broken ranks have eaten up their sense of power.
The regiments, moreover, are on our side—
Councils of soldiers everywhere!
To-morrow—comrade—the decision!
(*A knock.*)
Betrayed!

SECOND WORKMAN: They must not find you.

FIRST WORKMAN: Only one door.

SECOND WORKMAN: Through the window!

FIRST WORKMAN: The window opens on an air-shaft.

THE WOMAN: And the struggle so near ...
(*A louder knocking. The door is opened. The* MAN, *his coat-collar pulled up, comes in, looks about him quickly, and raises his derby.*)
A—friend ... And there's no danger ...
You come to me;
You find me.

THE MAN: Good evening.
(*Softly.*) Please don't introduce me.
May I speak with you?

THE WOMAN (*to the* OTHERS): Comrades ...

THE WORKMEN: Good-night.
Until to-morrow.   (*Exeunt.*)

THE WOMAN: Good-night; until to-morrow.

THE MAN: I must make it clear,
I did not come to help you.

THE WOMAN: Forgive the dream that blossomed for a
moment.

THE MAN: My honour's threatened—that is why I'm here.

THE WOMAN: And I'm the cause? How strange . . .

Honour, you say. Honour of the bourgeois class?

And were there tongues of disapproval?

Did the outraged majority

Threaten to bar you from its sacred ranks?

THE MAN: Please don't be flippant.

Consideration for others—an emotion to which you are a
stranger—

Is law for me.

For me the strictest code of honour still survives.

THE WOMAN: To stamp its pattern on you.

THE MAN: Self-control implies subordination.

We must submit . . .

Your thoughts are not upon my words.

THE WOMAN: I see your eyes.

THE MAN: Don't disconcert me.

THE WOMAN: You . . . You . . .

THE MAN: To come to the point,

You must give up your work.

THE WOMAN: You . . .

THE MAN: The desire for social service—

Laudable, I'll grant—

Can be fulfilled in our own circle.

Let's say, a home for illegitimate children.

Ideas are the foundation of all work,

Proof of the very culture you deride.

Even your new-found friends, your so-called comrades,

Despise the unmarried mother.

THE WOMAN: Go on . . . go on . . .

THE MAN: You are not free to act as you may choose.

THE WOMAN: I am free . . .

THE MAN: I think I may assume some personal consideration,

A certain measure of respect—

If not from conviction, then for appearances.

THE WOMAN: I have respect for nothing but my work.

That work commands me; that is all I serve.

THE MAN: Let's analyze you:

A wish for a new sort of service prompts your actions—

A wish born of a conflict of emotions.
I am, you understand, far from implying
That this wish springs from any base desires.
   THE WOMAN: How you can wound me with your words . . .
Tell me, have you ever seen the pictures of Madonnas
In peasants' houses?
Swords pierce the breast, the heart bleeds great dark tears.
Those gaudy, hideous, terribly moving prints . . .
So common—and so great . . .
You . . . you . . .
You speak of desires?
I know—a chasm yawns between us . . .
But it was not a whim that made me turn,
No *wish* to change my way of living.
It was a *need* . . . Need of my very self,
Need of the darkest depths of my existence.
Need alters us, I tell you, need changes us.
Not moods or spells or fits of boredom,
But need—the need to be a human being.
   THE MAN: Need? Have you the right
To speak of need?
   THE WOMAN: You . . . my husband . . . do not torture
                                    me . . .
Now I hold your head . . .
Now I kiss your eyes . . .
You . . .
Say no more . . .
   THE MAN: To hurt you was the last thing I intended . . .
But this place . . .
Can any one overhear us?
   THE WOMAN: Suppose a comrade does hear us?
They have understanding even though they lack your "code of
                                   honour."
Oh, if you only understood them,
If you could only get a breath of their great need.
Need . . . which is—which must be . . . ours!
You—you have lowered them . . .
And, in lowering them, you have debased yourself;
You have become your own executioner . . .
I do not want the pity in your eyes!
I'm not neurotic,
Not the least bit sentimental.
And since I'm not, I belong to them.

Oh, those miserable little hours you put aside
For social betterment—
A soothing syrup for your pity and weakness.
Many a comrade feels ashamed for you,
When they don't . . . laugh at you . . .
As I am laughing.
    THE MAN: So—you may as well know everything.
They know about you—the authorities.
I took an oath of loyalty to the State.
The chief detective has been informed . . .
Otherwise, progress in my career would be impossible.
    THE WOMAN: And . . .?
    THE MAN: I tell you this,
Regardless of the consequences,
Which, you may be sure,
Affect me, too,
Especially since you would harm both the career
Of your husband and the welfare of the State . . .
You help the enemy within our gates.
This gives me grounds for a divorce.
    THE WOMAN: Of course . . . if I have harmed you,
If I have stood in your way . . .
    THE MAN: There still is time.
    THE WOMAN: Then, of course,
Then . . . I am prepared . . .
I accept the blame . . .
You need not fear, the trial will not harm you.
You . . .
You . . . my arms stretch out to you
With hungry need.
You . . . my blood swells to you . . .
See—I am a withered leaf without you.
You are the dew that makes me blossom.
You are the storm whose April strength
Flings flaming torches in my thirsty veins. . . .
There were warm nights . . . calls of young boys in spring
Exulting in the vigour of their blood. . . .
Take me away to meadows, fields, or woodlands;
Meekly will I bow down and kiss your eyes. . . .
I know I will be very weak
Without you . . . unbelievably. . . .
    (*Short pause.*)
Forgive me—I was weak just now.

I see the situation clearly; I understand your action.
Nevertheless—to-morrow I appear before the masses—
To-morrow I speak to them.
To-morrow I attack the State, to which you swore allegiance,
Tearing the old mask from its murderous face.
   THE MAN: Your act is treason to the State.
   THE WOMAN: Your State makes war;
Your State betrays the people!
Your State exploits, grinds down
And robs the people of their rights!
   THE MAN: The State is holy. . . . War insures its life.
Peace is a phantom of weak minds.
War is nothing but an interrupted armistice,
In which the State continually lives,
Constantly threatened by its foes without
And enemies within.
   THE WOMAN: How can a body live that's eaten up by plague
And burned by fire?
Have you seen the naked body of the State?
Have you seen the worms that feed upon it?
Have you seen the stock exchanges, the financiers
That gorge themselves with human flesh?
You have not seen it. . . . You have sworn allegiance to the
                                   State;
You do your duty and your conscience is quieted.
   THE MAN: And this decision is your last word?
   THE WOMAN: My last word.
   THE MAN: Good-night!
   THE WOMAN: Good-night!
     (*As the* MAN *starts to go.*)
May I go with you?
To-night for the last time . . .
Or am I shameless?
Or am I shameless . . .
Shameless in my desire? . . .
     (*The* WOMAN *follows the* MAN. *The stage darkens.*)

second picture

(DREAM-PICTURE)

(*A room of the stock exchange. At the desk, a* CLERK; *about him* BANKERS *and* BROKERS. *The* CLERK *has the face of the* MAN *of the first scene.*)

CLERK: Recorded.

FIRST BANKER: Munition works,
Three-fifty.

SECOND BANKER: I offer
Four hundred.

THIRD BANKER: Four hundred
Offered.

(*The* FOURTH BANKER *draws the* THIRD BANKER *toward the front. In the background there is the murmur of bidders and sellers.*)

FOURTH BANKER (*to the* THIRD BANKER): Did you hear?
Retreat necessary.
Great offensive
Can't succeed.

THIRD BANKER: Reserves?

FOURTH BANKER: Human material
Running poor.

THIRD BANKER: Food inadequate?

FOURTH BANKER: That also.
Although
Professor Ude
Thinks
That rye
Ground down
With ninety-five percent of chaff
Will make
A food for epicures.

THIRD BANKER: The leaders?

FOURTH BANKER: Splendid.

THIRD BANKER: Not enough alcohol?

FOURTH BANKER: Distilleries
Working
Overtime.

THIRD BANKER: What's wrong?

FOURTH BANKER: The General
Has called ninety-three professors
To headquarters.
Also our expert,
Councillor Glubor.
There'll be results.

THIRD BANKER: They are?

FOURTH BANKER: Not to be discussed
In bourgeois circles.

THIRD BANKER: Are the soldiers weakened
By love of man?

FOURTH BANKER: Strangely enough, no.
Man hates man.
Something's missing.

THIRD BANKER: What's missing?

FOURTH BANKER: The mechanics
Of life
Have been laid bare.

THIRD BANKER: What's missing?

FOURTH BANKER: Masses need joy.

THIRD BANKER: What's missing? . . .

FOURTH BANKER: Love.

THIRD BANKER: That's enough!
Then war,
As our chief instrument,
The mighty powerful instrument,
That takes the State,
Kings, ministers,
Parliaments,
Newspapers, churches,
And makes them dance,
Dance on this ball of earth,
Dance over the sea—
This war is lost?

Answer me: Lost?
Is that the net result?
   FOURTH BANKER: Your calculation's poor.
The root of the trouble's been found—
Will be adjusted.
   THIRD BANKER: Through what?
   FOURTH BANKER: Through international arrangements.
   THIRD BANKER: Is this known?
   FOURTH BANKER: On the contrary.
We'll dress it up in national colours
And independent
Of the exchange.
   THIRD BANKER: And well financed?
   FOURTH BANKER: Syndicate of the largest banks
Will underwrite it.
   THIRD BANKER: The profit?
Dividends?
   FOURTH BANKER: Will be divided regularly.
   THIRD BANKER: The form of the enterprise sounds good.
But what's the scheme?
   FOURTH BANKER: We'll camouflage and call it
Recreation Home:
A Place to Strengthen the Desire to Win!
The real thing:
National brothels.
   THIRD BANKER: Magnificent!
I subscribe one hundred thousand.
Just one more question,
Who regulates the amount of time,
Energy to be spent, et cetera?
   FOURTH BANKER: Experienced generals.
They know
The standard regulations.
   THIRD BANKER: The plan
Drawn up yet?
   FOURTH BANKER: To be regulated,
As I just said.
Three prices.
Three divisions.
Brothel for officers:
Stay there all night.

Brothel for corporals:
One hour.
Brothel for privates:
Fifteen minutes.

THIRD BANKER: Thanks.
When does the market open?

FOURTH BANKER: Any minute.
(*Noise in the background.* THIRD *and* FOURTH BANKER *go to the rear.*)

THE CLERK: New issue ready:
National bonds,
War Recreation Home
Ltd.

FIRST BANKER: I have no order to buy.

SECOND BANKER: The dividend does not tempt me.

THIRD BANKER: I subscribe to one hundred thousand
At par.

THE CLERK: Recorded.

FOURTH BANKER: Same here.

FIRST BANKER (*to the* SECOND BANKER): The cool one's
buying. . . .

What do you think?

SECOND BANKER: Just got a telegram:
The drive on the West front
Has been lost. . . .

FIRST BANKER: Gentlemen,
The drive on the West front has been lost.
(*Cries, screams, shrieks.*)

VOICES: Lost!

A VOICE: I offer
Munition works
At one-fifty.

A VOICE: I offer
Liquid Flame Trust.

A VOICE: I offer
War Prayer-Book, Ltd.

A VOICE: Offer
Poison-Gas Works.

A VOICE: Offer
War loans.

THIRD BANKER: I'll take another
One hundred thousand.

A VOICE: What?
When prices are tumbling?
A VOICE: Who said we had lost the drive?
A VOICE: Is the rumour true?
Or just a trick to get control of the market?
The cool one
Has bought his second hundred thousand.
SECOND BANKER: Something's wrong!
Switch my order!
I buy—
One-fifty.
A VOICE: I bid
Two hundred.
A VOICE: I buy
Three hundred.
A VOICE: Who bids?
Four hundred?
I buy.
THE CLERK: Recorded.
FOURTH BANKER (*to the* THIRD BANKER): The old fox has
guessed . . .
THIRD BANKER: Excuse the question.
Has our most important method
Been saved?
FOURTH BANKER: How can you even ask that?
Mechanics of life
Are so simple—
There was a leak . . .
It is discovered
And stopped at once.
A rise
Or a fall to-day
Means nothing.
The important thing
Is to keep our machinery going.
And so it follows
The system is safe.
THE CLERK: Recorded.
(*The* COMPANION *enters. His face is a composite of the
features of death and the most radiant life. He leads the*
WOMAN.)
THE COMPANION: Gentlemen,

You're ordering too quickly.
"Blood—and the System!"
"Man—and the System!"
You cannot unite them.
One stamp of the foot
And your whole mechanism
Is broken
Like a child's toy.
Look out!
    (*To the* WOMAN.)
Speak to them!
    THE WOMAN (*quietly*): Gentlemen:
Human beings . . .
I say it again:
Human beings!
    (*The* COMPANION *and the* WOMAN *fade. Sudden silence.*)
    THIRD BANKER: You hear?
A disaster in the mines.
Seems
People are in distress.
    FOURTH BANKER: I have an idea:
A Charity Festival.
Dance
On the floor of the stock exchange.
Dance
To aid the suffering.
Help
The unfortunates.
If it's convenient,
A little dance.
Gentlemen,
I contribute
One bond
War Recreation Home
Ltd.
    A VOICE: How about women?
    FOURTH BANKER: As many as you want.
Someone tell the doorman:
Five hundred
Gay
Young girls

Wanted here!
Meanwhile . . .
   THE BANKERS: We donate!
We dance!
Help
The unfortunates!
    (*Music of clinking gold-pieces. The* BANKERS *in their high silk hats dance a fox-trot around the exchange. The stage darkens.*)

third picture

CHORUS OF THE MASSES (*as from a vast distance*): We who
are huddled for ever
In cañons of steel, cramped under cliffs of houses,
We who are delivered up
To the mockery of the machine,
We whose features are lost in a night of tears,
We, torn for ever from our mothers,
Out of the depths of factories, we cry to you:
When shall we, living, know the love of life?
When shall we, working, feel the joy of labour?
When shall deliverance come?
> (*The stage becomes light. A great hall. On the platform a
> long narrow table. At the left, the* WOMAN *is sitting. In
> the room,* WORKING MEN *and* WORKING WOMEN *are
> packed closely together.*)

GROUP OF YOUNG WORKING GIRLS: And struggle breeds new
struggles!
No compromising with these masters,
No loose agreements, feeble compacts.
Give orders to a group of comrades:
Dynamite in the machines!
To-morrow factories will explode into the air.
Machinery herds us all like beasts in stockyards,
Machinery clamps us in its metal vise,
Machinery pounds our bodies day by day
And turns us into rivets ... screws ...

Screws ... three millimeters ... screws ... five millimeters,
Withers our eyes, eats up our fingers,
While bodies go on living ...
Down with the factories! Down with machinery!

SCATTERED CRIES IN THE HALL: Down with the factories!
Down with machinery!

THE WOMAN: Once when I was blind, and felt the rods
Of engines pierce me and machines suck up my blood,
I, too, cried your despairing cry. . . .
It is a dream that limits your own vision,
A dream of children, frightened by the night.
For, see—this is the twentieth century.
We must realize
The factory cannot be wiped out.
Take all the dynamite on earth,
And, in one night, blast all the factories,
By next spring, they will rise again
To live more terribly than ever.
Factories must no longer be the master,
And man the raw material.
Factories must be our servants,
Helping to make a richer life.
The soul of man must master factories.

GROUP OF YOUNG WORKMEN: Let them and us be de-
stroyed together!
See how our words rush to revenge and fury.
The masters live in palaces;
Our brothers rot in filthy trenches.
Somewhere there's lively pleasure, dances, songs—
At night we read of them and grind our teeth!
And longing burns in us for light and knowledge. . . .
They took this holy thing
And it turned horrible.
Sometimes, but rarely, it shines out at us
In the theatre,
And it is sweet ... and clean ... and always mocking!
In school their hatred cheated us of youth,
In schoolrooms they destroyed our souls.
Nothing but need makes us cry out. . . .
What are we to-day?
We will not wait!

GROUP OF AGRICULTURAL LABOURERS: They turned us away
from our mother earth.

These rich men buy up land as they buy street girls,
Amuse themselves with her, the holy mother,
And toss our raw flesh into munition plants.
But we grow sick, uprooted from our soil,
The unhappy cities sour us, break our strength.
We want the land!
The land for everybody!
   CROWD IN THE HALL: The land for everybody!
   THE WOMAN: I went through the slums.
Gray rain dripped from dirty roofs;
Fungus sprouted from mouldy walls.
And in one room there sat an invalid
Who stuttered, "We were better off out there. . . .
Here we live in a pig pen . . .
Isn't it true . . . in a pig pen?"
A shamefaced smile slipped from his eyes.
And his shame shamed me. . . .
Brothers, do you want to know the way out?
There's one way left us weaklings,
For us who hate all war.
Strike! No more contracts, compromises.
Let our answer be, Strike!
We weak ones will become as strong as granite,
No weapon made can hope to conquer us.
Call to our mute battalions!
Summon our silent armies!
I cry, Strike!
Hear me:
I cry, Strike!
Moloch has fattened on our bodies
For six long years.
Pregnant women collapse upon the streets,
So starved they cannot even carry
The burden of the unborn.
Want stares at you in your homes;
Pestilence and madness glare at you,
And hunger, festering hunger. . . .
But there—look over there!
The bankers spend themselves in bacchanalia;
Champagne drowns every hard-fought victory;
Lust leaps and license stirs the dance
Around the golden altars.
And at the front?

Can you see the withered faces of your brothers?
Feel their bodies
Clammy in the fog and frost
Of twilight?
Smell the breath of that decay?
Hear their cries? I ask you.
Hear them calling?
"Brothers, we turn to you!
We, chained to the flanks of cannon,
We helpless ones,
We cry to you:
Help! Be our saviours!
You—be our rescue!"
Hear me. I cry, Strike!
Whoever again eats munition wages
Betrays his brother.
What did I say—betrays?
He *kills* his brother.
And you, you women!
Do you know the story of those wives
Who remain barren
Because they helped forge deadly weapons?
Think of your men out there!
I cry, Strike!
    CROWD IN THE HALL: We cry, Strike!
We cry
STRIKE!
        (*Out of the crowd in the hall, the* NAMELESS ONE *emerges.
        He hurries to the platform, placing himself to the right of
        the table.*)
    THE NAMELESS ONE: The man who wants to build a bridge
Must pay attention to the pillars.
A strike to-day is a hasty bridge without supports.
We must have more than just a strike. . . .
Let's grant the thing's successful.
Suppose your strike forces them to a peace,
It is not Peace you've won—you've made *a* peace.
Instead of peace, you have a pause. That's all.
War must be stopped entirely,
Once and for all time.
But first, one final, desperate battle!
What will you gain if you halt this one struggle?
The peace that you create

Will leave your situation as it is.
On one hand, a false peace and old conditions.
On the other, a swift war and new conditions!
You fools, break down foundations;
Break the foundations, I tell you!
Then let the flood of your power wash away
The mouldering structure
Which only gold chains
Keep from falling apart.
Let us build a system under which we can live.
The factories belong to all the workers
And not to old man Capital.
The time has passed when, on our burdened backs,
He looked around with greedy eyes
For foreign treasures,
And planned fresh wars, enslaved an alien people,
Compelled the lying tongues of newspapers to scream:
"The Fatherland! All for the Fatherland!"
While underneath it rang the real refrain:
"For me! For me!"
That time has passed!
The masses of all nations have one cry:
The factories belong to all the workers!
All power to the workers!
All for us all!
I cry for more than Strike!
I cry, War!
I cry, Revolution!
Our enemy up there won't pay attention
To any pretty speeches.
Force against force!
Violence! . . . Violence!
   A VOICE: Arms!
   THE NAMELESS ONE: Yes, arms are all we need!
Go out and get them!
Storm the city hall!
The battle cry: Victory!
   THE WOMAN: Hear me!
I must . . .
   THE NAMELESS ONE: Quiet yourself, comrade.
Frantic appeals, clasped hands, and tearful prayers
Produce no children.

Consumptives can't get well on watered soup.
You have to use an axe to chop down trees.
   THE WOMAN: Hear me . . .
I do not want fresh murders.
   THE NAMELESS ONE: Silence, comrade.
What can you know?
You suffer our distress, I grant you that.
But have you worked ten hours in the mines,
A homeless child in blind, enormous rooms;
Ten hours in the mines—and the dark hut at evening? . . .
That is how day comes daily to the workers.
You are not one of them.
I am the Mass!
The Mass knows its own future.
The Mass is destiny!
   A VOICE: Is destiny . . .
   THE WOMAN: But think a moment,
Mass is powerless.
Mass is weak.
   THE NAMELESS ONE: How little do you realize the truth!
Mass is leader!
Mass is strength!
   CROWD IN THE HALL: Is strength!
   THE WOMAN: Emotion pulls me toward the darkness
But all my conscience cries out, No!
   THE NAMELESS ONE: Keep silent, comrade!
The cause demands it.
What does one person matter?
His feelings? or his conscience?
Only the Mass must count!
Just think of it: a single bloody battle
And then, eternal peace.
No empty peace, a mask of mockery,
Hiding the face of war,
War of the strong against the weak,
War of exploiters, war of greed.
Think of it: the end of misery!
Think of it: crime a half-remembered fable!
It is the dawn of freedom for all people! . . .
You think I reckon lightly?
It is no longer a matter of choice.
War's a necessity for us.

Your advice means discord.
For the sake of the cause,
Keep silent.

> THE WOMAN: You . . . are . . . Mass.

You . . . are . . . right.

> THE NAMELESS ONE: Beat in the pillars of the bridge, O
> comrades!

Drive over everyone who stands in our way.
Mass is action!

> CROWD IN THE HALL (*as they storm out*): Action!
> (*The stage darkens.*)

fourth picture

(*A court with a high wall is suggested. On the ground in the middle of the court, a lantern which gives a miserable light.* WORKER GUARDS *suddenly emerge from the corners of the court.*)

(DREAM-PICTURE)

FIRST GUARD (*sings*): My mother
Bore me
In the mud of a trench.
Lalala la,
Hm, Hm.

SECOND GUARD: My father
Lost me
In a brawl with a wench.

ALL THE GUARDS: Lalala la,
Hm, Hm.

THIRD GUARD: Three years
I breathed
In the prison stench.

ALL THE GUARDS: Lalala la,
Hm, Hm.

(*With silent, ghostly steps, the* NAMELESS ONE *appears from somewhere. He stands near the lantern.*)

FIRST GUARD: Dear father
Forgot
To pay mother's fee.

ALL THE GUARDS: Lalala la,
Hm, Hm.

SECOND GUARD: Poor mother
Never
Gave anything free.

ALL THE GUARDS: Lalala la,
Hm, Hm.

THIRD GUARD: I troubled
The goddam
Bourgeoisie!
ALL THE GUARDS: Lalala la,
Hm, Hm.
THE NAMELESS ONE: Come, dance!
I'll play for you.
THE GUARDS: Halt!
Who are you?
THE NAMELESS ONE: Did I ask your names,
Nameless ones?
THE GUARDS: The password?
THE NAMELESS ONE: Mass is nameless!
ONE OF THE GUARDS: Is nameless.
He's one of us.
THE NAMELESS ONE: I'll play for you,
I, who announce
The great decision.

> (*The* NAMELESS ONE *begins to play a harmonica. The
> rhythms of his tune are alternately rousing, swaying, and
> lascivious, then ponderous and stormy. A* CONDEMNED
> MAN, *a rope around his neck, steps out of the dark.*)

THE CONDEMNED MAN: In the name
Of those condemned to die,
We beg a final
Favour:
Let us join the dance.
The dance is the very centre
Of things.
Life, born of the dance,
Urges and runs
To the dance;
To the dance of desire,
To whirling Time
And its dance of death.
THE GUARDS: One should always
Grant the condemned
Their last request:
Invited.
THE NAMELESS ONE: Come, then!
One is as good as another.

THE CONDEMNED MAN (*calls in the darkness*): All those
Condemned to death,
Step up!
The last dance!
Let the waiting coffins
Wait.
> (*All the* CONDEMNED, *with ropes around their necks, step
> out of the darkness.* GUARDS *and the* CONDEMNED *dance
> about the* NAMELESS ONE.)

THE GUARDS (*singing*): In the mud of a trench . . .
> (*They dance on. After a short pause.*)

In a brawl with a wench . . .
> (*They dance on. After a short pause.*)

In the prison stench . . .
> (*They dance on. The* NAMELESS ONE *breaks off suddenly.*
> PROSTITUTES *and* THOSE CONDEMNED TO DIE *run off to the
> dark corners of the court. Night swallows them up. The*
> GUARDS *strike a posture. Silence surrounds the* NAMELESS
> ONE. *The* COMPANION, *in the guise of a guard, glides
> through the wall. He holds a* WOMAN, *who has the face
> of the* WOMAN *of the preceding scenes, close to him.*)

THE COMPANION: The journey
Is difficult.
The result
Repays your trouble.
Look there—
The drama
Is about to begin.
If the impulse tempts you,
Act with it.
> (*A* GUARD *brings in a* PRISONER *who has the features of
> the* MAN *and leads him to the* NAMELESS ONE.)

THE NAMELESS ONE: Condemned
By the tribunal?
A GUARD: He brought death
Upon himself.
He shot at us.
THE PRISONER: Death?
THE NAMELESS ONE: It frightens you?
Listen:
Guard! Answer me.
Who taught us

Capital punishment?
Who gave us weapons?
Who said "Hero" and "noble deed"?
Who glorified violence?
   THE GUARDS: Schools.
Barracks.
War.
Always.
   THE NAMELESS ONE: Force . . . violence and force.
Why did you shoot?
   THE PRISONER: I swore
To protect the State.
   THE NAMELESS ONE: You die
For your convictions.
   THE GUARDS: To the wall with him!
   THE NAMELESS ONE: Guns loaded?
   THE GUARDS: Loaded.
   THE PRISONER (*against the wall*): Life!
Life!
     (*The* WOMAN *tears herself from the* COMPANION.)
   THE WOMAN: Don't shoot!
There stands my husband.
Forgive him
As I, too, humbly, forgive him.
Forgiveness is so strong
And far beyond all struggles.
   THE NAMELESS ONE: Do they forgive
Us?
   THE WOMAN: Do they struggle
For the people?
Do they fight
For humanity?
   THE NAMELESS ONE: The Mass counts.
   THE GUARDS: To the wall!
   A GUARD: Forgiveness is cowardice.
Yesterday I escaped
From the enemy over there.
They stood me up against the wall,
My body covered with bruises.
Next to me the man
Who was to murder me.
I had to dig

My grave
With my own hands.
In front of us
The photographer,
Eager to etch
Murder
On his plates.
I say, to hell with the Revolution
If it lets
Those grinning murderers over there
Make monkeys of us.
I say,
To hell with the Revolution!
    THE GUARDS: To the wall!
        (*The face of the* PRISONER *changes to that of one of the*
        GUARDS. *The* WOMAN *speaks to the* GUARD *who has just*
        finished.)
    THE WOMAN: Yesterday they stood you
Against the wall.
Now you are standing
Against the wall again.
That is you
Who are standing there
Against the wall to-day.
Man—
You are he.
Recognize yourself—
You are man.
    A GUARD: The Mass counts.
    THE WOMAN: The Man counts.
    ALL THE GUARDS: The Mass counts!
    THE WOMAN (*despairingly*): I give
Myself . . .
All of myself . . . to you . . .
        (*The* GUARDS *laugh lewdly. Placing herself next to the*
        MAN.)
Shoot then!
I give up. . . .
I am so tired . . .
        (*The stage darkens.*)

fifth
picture

(*The hall. Gray dawn crawls through the windows.
The platform is illuminated with a gloomy light.
The* WOMAN *sits at the left of the long
table, the* NAMELESS ONE *at the right.*
WORKER GUARDS *at the doors of the hall.
In the hall, isolated* WORKMEN *and*
WORKWOMEN *huddle about tables.*)

THE WOMAN: Has any news come within the last hour?
Forgive me, comrade, I slept.
THE NAMELESS ONE: Report crowds upon report.
War is war;
A bloody game and one to be played coolly.
Before midnight we occupied the station.
At one o'clock we lost it.
Detachments are moving up now
For a fresh assault.
The post-office is in our hands.
At this very moment
Telegrams are being sent to the nations,
Telling them of our work.
THE WOMAN: Work! What a holy word!
THE NAMELESS ONE: A holy word, comrade!
It calls for more than speeches and a warm heart,
It calls for implements of steel,
It calls for ruthless war.
(*A second's flickering silence in the hall.*)
THE WOMAN: Comrade, for all you say, I cannot be con-
vinced.
To fight with weapons is to win through force.
THE NAMELESS ONE: Mental weapons are also a force in
battle.
Words can be murderers.—

Don't be so startled, comrade.
I deal in naked truths.
Why, if I thought as you, I'd be a monk
Walking some cloister in eternal silence.
> (*Silence seems to sink heavily upon the hall.* FIRST
> WORKMAN *enters.*)

FIRST WORKMAN: I bring news.
We advanced three times against the station.
The place is thick with dead.
Damn them, they're well fortified,
Supplied with every kind of weapon,
Flame-throwers, hand-grenades, poison gas.

THE NAMELESS ONE: You advanced three times.
And the fourth time?

FIRST WORKMAN: We did not advance four times.
The others charged on us.

THE NAMELESS ONE: You held them.
Do you need support?

FIRST WORKMAN: We have been scattered.

THE NAMELESS ONE: Reverses were to be expected.
Attention! Go to the thirteenth district;
The reserves are there.
Go—hurry!   (*The* WORKMAN *goes.*)

THE WOMAN: He spoke of dead.
Many hundreds.
Yesterday I cried out against all war—
And to-day . . . I let them kill;
I let brothers be flung to death.

THE NAMELESS ONE: Your vision is not clear.
In yesterday's war we fought as slaves.

THE WOMAN: And to-day?

THE NAMELESS ONE: To-day in battle we are free.
> (*Fevered silence.*)

THE WOMAN: In both wars . . . human beings . . .
In both wars . . . human beings . . .
> (*Silence reels.* SECOND WORKMAN *stumbles in.*)

SECOND WORKMAN: The post-office is lost!
Our men are retreating!
The enemy gives no quarter.
Any one captured is shot!
> (FIRST WORKMAN *rushes in.*)

FIRST WORKMAN: I come from the thirteenth district.
Struggle is useless.

The streets are closed.
The district has surrendered.
They're giving up their weapons.
THIRD WORKMAN: The city's lost!
The work has failed.
  THE WOMAN: It had to fail . . .
  THE NAMELESS ONE: Once more, keep silent, comrade!
Our work is not a failure.
If we were not strong enough to-day,
To-morrow there'll be fresh battalions.
  FOURTH WORKMAN (*crying in the hall*): They're coming out
                                                 against us!
O terrible slaughter!
They shot my wife;
My father's murdered.
  THE NAMELESS ONE: They died for the masses.
Erect barricades!
We're the defenders!
Our blood is ripe for battle!
Let them come!
      (WORKMEN *storm into the hall*.)
  FIFTH WORKMAN: They're butchering everyone.
Men, women, children.
We won't surrender to be killed
Like captured cattle!
They're butchering everyone; we must resist them to the end.
International law protects the enemy's soldiers,
But they can murder us like jungle beasts,
And set a premium on our flesh. . . .
Weapons are in our hands.
We're bringing bourgeoisie that we've captured;
I gave an order to shoot half of them.
We'll shoot the other half if their shock-troops get us.
  THE NAMELESS ONE: You avenge your brothers.
Mass is revenge for the wrongs of centuries.
Mass is revenge.
  THE WORKMEN: Is revenge!
  THE WOMAN: Madmen, drunk with battle!
I stay your arms!
Mass should be a band of loving brothers.
Mass should be one firm community.
Community is not revenge.
Community tears up the roots of all injustice.

Community plants the flowers of righteousness.
The man who revenges himself creates nothing;
He only destroys.—
You shot half of your prisoners!
That was not self-defense?
Blind rage, not service to the cause.
You kill men.
Do you kill, with them, the spirit of the State
Which you are fighting? . . .
I'm going to help those men out there.
I was prepared
To cripple my own conscience
For the sake of the Mass.
I cry:
Break up the system!
But you—you want to break up men.
I can't keep silence, not to-day.
Out there are men,
Born in the blood of suffering mothers . . .
Men for ever brothers. . . .

    THE NAMELESS ONE: For the last time, keep quiet, comrade.
Force . . . we need force. . . .
The enemy thinks nothing of our lives,
They will not spare us.
War is a grim affair; it can't be won
With pious looks.
Don't listen to this woman.
Prattle of petticoats!

    THE WOMAN: I cry, Stop!
And you . . . who . . . are . . . you?
Are you driven by an unchained lust for power—
A lust that has been caged for centuries?
Who . . . are . . . you?
Murderer . . . or . . . Messiah . . . ?
Murderer . . . or . . . Messiah . . . ?
Nameless one—your face?
You are . . . ?

    THE NAMELESS ONE: Mass!

    THE WOMAN: You! . . . Mass!
I cannot bear you!
I must protect those men out there.
For many years I've walked along with you.
I know—you've suffered more than I. . . .

I have grown up in light and happy rooms,
Never knew hunger,
Never heard crazy laughter
Reeling from filthy hangings.
Still—I could feel for you
And know you.
See, I come to you now, a pleading child,
Quietly, humbly.
Listen to me:
Break down the pillars of injustice.
Break the old chains of hidden slavery.
But also break the weapons of a rotting age.
Shatter hate! Shatter revenge!
Revenge is not the purpose to reorganize.
Revenge is not Revolution.
Revenge is nothing but an axe that splits
The clean and glowing metal,
The power of Revolution.

THE NAMELESS ONE: How dare you, woman from another
class,

Poison us in the hour of our decision?
I hear another accent in your talk.
You hope to shield those with whom you have grown up.
That's your real purpose.
You are betrayal.

CROWD IN THE HALL (*pressing threateningly about the*
WOMAN): Betrayal!

A CRY: An intellectual!

A CRY: To the wall with her!

THE NAMELESS ONE: Your shielding them is treason.
The hour calls for conflict,
Pitiless conflict.
Who is not with us is against us.
The Mass must triumph.

CROWD IN THE HALL: Must triumph!

THE NAMELESS ONE: You are arrested.

THE WOMAN: I . . . shield those . . . with whom I have
grown up?

No—I shield you!
It is you who are standing there against the wall!
I shield your souls!
I shield humanity, divine humanity.
Insane accusers . . .

Is there fear in my words? . . .
Never as low as that . . .
I have chosen . . .
You lie . . . you lie . . .

> (*A* WORKMAN *enters the hall.*)

WORKMAN: One of our prisoners barks,
Barks the same tune, barks all the time.
Wants to be taken to the woman who leads us.

> THE NAMELESS ONE: Proof.

> THE WOMAN: Again . . . you lie . . .

Who wants to speak to me—who?
Perhaps the man.
I never would betray my word for him.
But you betray yourselves . . .
I know nothing more. . . .

> (*The* NAMELESS ONE *leaves the platform, diving into the crowd below him in the hall.* WORKERS *throng in from outside.*)

> WORKERS: Lost!

> CRIES: Fly! Slaughter!

> (*Scattered shots outside. The* WORKERS *crowd to the door.*)

The door is blocked . . .
Caught like rats in a trap!

> (*Silent waiting for death.*)

> A CRY: We die!

> (SOMEONE *begins to sing the "Internationale."* OTHERS *join in. Powerfully.*)

Awake, ye slaves of every nation,
Enchained to hunger, want, and shame.
The depths are loud with liberation;
The dawn grows bright—the torches flame.
The way is clear, old bonds are breaking;
Rise up, ye masses, seize command!
A new world's ours for the taking,
We slaves bring power where we stand.

Comrades of every nation,
March on, our flag's unfurled.
Arise to your salvation!
Arm, arm—and free the world!

> (*Suddenly a short rattle of machine guns. The song is snapped off. The door at the principal entrance and the*

side doors are burst in with a single blow. SOLDIERS *with
guns in firing position stand at every door.*)

OFFICER: No use to resist!

Hands up!

Hands up, I command!

Where is the woman that leads you?

Why don't you stick up your hands?

Here—put on the handcuffs.

(SOLDIERS *handcuff the* WOMAN. *The stage darkens.*)

sixth picture

(DREAM-PICTURE)

(*Boundless space. In the heart of it, a cage surrounded by a cone of light. Crouching within the cage is a handcuffed person who has the face of the* WOMAN. *Close to the cage is the* COMPANION *in the form of a* KEEPER.)

THE HANDCUFFED ONE: Where am I?

THE KEEPER: In the place
Where man reviews himself.

THE HANDCUFFED ONE: Drive away the shadows.

THE KEEPER: Drive them away yourself.

(*A gray* SHADOW *without a head appears from somewhere.*)

FIRST SHADOW: You know me, one they shot to death?
Murderess!

THE HANDCUFFED ONE: I am not
Guilty.

(*A second gray* SHADOW *without a head appears from somewhere.*)

SECOND SHADOW: You murdered me,
Also.

THE HANDCUFFED ONE: You lie!

(*Other gray* SHADOWS *without heads emerge from somewhere.*)

THIRD SHADOW: You murdered me.

FOURTH SHADOW: And me.

FIFTH SHADOW: And me.

SIXTH SHADOW: And me.

THE HANDCUFFED ONE: Help me, keeper!
Good keeper!

THE KEEPER: Ha ha! Hahaha!

THE HANDCUFFED ONE: I did not want
Bloodshed.

FIRST SHADOW: You kept silent.

SECOND SHADOW: Silent when they attacked
The city hall.

THIRD SHADOW: Silent when they stole
The weapons.

FOURTH SHADOW: Silent when they fought.

FIFTH SHADOW: Silent when they went
For the reserves.

SIXTH SHADOW: You are guilty.

ALL THE SHADOWS: You are guilty.

THE HANDCUFFED ONE: I wanted
To save
The others
From shooting.

FIRST SHADOW: Don't deceive yourself.
Before that,
They shot us.

ALL THE SHADOWS: You murdered
All of us.

THE HANDCUFFED ONE: Then I am ...

THE SHADOWS: Guilty!
Thrice guilty!

THE HANDCUFFED ONE: I ... am ... guilty ...
        (*The* SHADOWS *fade.* BANKERS *in high silk hats emerge
        from somewhere.*)

FIRST BANKER: I offer
Guilty Bonds
At par.

SECOND BANKER: Guilty Bonds
Are not listed
Any more.

THIRD BANKER: Bad investment!
Guilty Bonds,
Worthless scraps of paper.

THE THREE BANKERS: Guilty Bonds
Are a total loss.
        (*The* HANDCUFFED ONE *raises herself up.*)

THE HANDCUFFED ONE: I ... am ... guilty.
        (*The* BANKERS *fade.*)

THE KEEPER: Foolish one,
With your sentimental

Attitude to life—
If they were alive,
They would be dancing
About the golden altar
Where thousands have sacrificed.
And you, also.

THE HANDCUFFED ONE: I, Man, am guilty.

THE KEEPER: Mass is to blame.

THE HANDCUFFED ONE: Then I am doubly guilty.

THE KEEPER: Life is to blame.

THE HANDCUFFED ONE: And therefore must I
Assume the burden of its guilt?

THE KEEPER: Everyone lives in himself.
Everyone dies his own death.
Man,
Like every tree and flower,
Bound by destiny,
Moulded by patterns;
Ripening each in separate ways,
Withering by themselves . . .
Discover the answer for yourself!
Life is everything.

(*From somewhere,* PRISONERS *in their convicts' clothes
enter, walking five paces apart. They have pointed caps
on their heads, from which hang tattered rags concealing
their faces and allowing room only for eye-holes. They
walk, in a monotonous rhythm, silently around the cage.*)

THE HANDCUFFED ONE: Who are you,
Forms without faces?
Figures!
Who are you?
Mass
Of featureless forms?

DULL ECHO FROM A DISTANCE: Mass . . .

THE HANDCUFFED ONE: O God!

THE ECHO (*dying*): Mass . . .
(*Silence drips.*)

THE HANDCUFFED ONE (*crying out*): Mass is necessity!
Mass cannot be guilty!

THE KEEPER: Man cannot be guilty.

THE HANDCUFFED ONE: God is guilty!

DISTANT ECHOES: Guilty . . .
Guilty . . .
Guilty . . .

THE KEEPER: God is within you.

THE HANDCUFFED ONE: Then I will triumph over God.

THE KEEPER: Worm!

Blasphemer!

THE HANDCUFFED ONE: Did I dishonour

God?

Or did God

Dishonour Man?

O frightful

Decrees of guilt,

In which

Man after man

Is horribly entangled.

God—

Bring God to justice!

I accuse him!

ECHO FROM A DISTANCE: Bring God to justice!

(*The moving* PRISONERS *stand still. Their arms suddenly shoot up.*)

THE PRISONERS: We accuse Him!   (*The* PRISONERS *fade.*)

THE KEEPER: Now you are healed.

Come out

Of the cage.

THE HANDCUFFED ONE: I am free?

THE KEEPER: Fettered!

Free!

(*The stage darkens.*)

seventh picture

(A prison cell. A small table, bench, and iron bed fastened to the wall. A grated hole of light clouded by frosted glass. The WOMAN *sits at the table.)*

THE WOMAN: O path that leads through fields of ripening
wheat
In August days . . .
Wandering on wintry hills before the dawn . . .
O beetle drinking in the breath of noon . . .
O world . . .
　　(Silence spreads itself gently about the WOMAN.*)*
Did I long for a child?
　　(Silence soars.)
How life divides us all in two!
Bound to man and his desires.
To those we love . . . and hate . . .
Bound to our enemies?
Bound to ourselves?
I need him now . . . he must confirm me.
　　(The cell is unlocked. The MAN *enters.)*
THE MAN: Wife . . . I have come,
Come because you called me.
THE WOMAN: Husband . . . !
Man . . .
THE MAN: I bring good news.
The sewers cannot keep on pouring
Their filth upon your name . . . my name, whenever they like.
The investigation of the recent murders
Showed that you were not guilty of the outrageous shootings.
Courage! The sentence committing you to death
Has not yet been confirmed.

In spite of treason to the State,
The nobility of aim
Is always respected
By all right-thinking people.
    THE WOMAN (*crying softly*): I am without guilt . . .
Without guilt . . . yet I am guilty . . .
    THE MAN: You are not guilty.
That's positive to every right-thinking person.
    THE WOMAN: To every right-thinking person . . .
I am so hurt . . .
And glad, because your name, free of disgrace . . .
    THE MAN: I knew you were not guilty.
    THE WOMAN: Yes . . . you knew it . . .
Respect for good intentions . . .
You're so respectable!
I see you now so clearly . . .
And yet it's you who have been guilty—husband,
You . . . guilty of all these deaths.
    THE MAN: Wife, I came to you . . .
Wife . . . your speech is hate.
    THE WOMAN: Hate? Never hate.
I love you—love you with all my blood.
    THE MAN: I warned you against the masses.
Root up the masses and you root up hell.
    THE WOMAN: Hell? Who made that hell?
Who built the torture of your golden mills
That grind and grind out profit day by day?
Who put up prisons . . . who cried "holy war"?
Who sacrificed a million human lives
Upon the altars of some desperate game?
Who threw the masses into festering holes
In which, each day, is piled the filth of yesterday?
Who robbed these brothers of their human features,
Who drove them into factories,
Debased them into parts of a machine?
The State! . . . You! . . .
    THE MAN: My life is duty.
    THE WOMAN: Oh, yes . . . duty . . . duty to the State.
You're so respectable . . .
Didn't I say I saw you all too clearly?
You've been so well brought up.
You—tell all your right-thinking people

They never have been right . . .
They are the guilty ones . . .
We are all guilty . . .
Yes, I am guilty . . . guilty to myself,
Guilty to all mankind.
   THE MAN: I came to you.
Is this a court of justice?
   THE WOMAN: *Here* is a court of justice!
I, the accused, am also judge.
I bring the accusation . . . and pass sentence;
Pronounce acquittal
And the final blame . . .
Can you surmise . . . who bears the final blame?
Men must desire to work,
And work grows red with the dear blood of men.
Men must desire to live,
And they must swim through seas of human blood.
Can you surmise . . . who bears the final blame? . . .
Come, give me your hand,
Beloved of my blood.
I have conquered myself . . .
Myself and you.
     (*The* MAN *breaks into trembling. A thought, suddenly
     springing up, distorts his face. He stumbles out.*)
   THE WOMAN: Give me your hand . . .
Brother, give me your hand;
You also are my brother.—
You have gone . . . you had to go . . .
The last road runs across a snowfield.
The last road never knows companions.
The last road winds without a mother.
The last road we walk alone.
     (*The door is opened. The* NAMELESS ONE *enters.*)
   THE NAMELESS ONE: Cured of illusions? Free of dusty
                              dreams?
Has knowledge thrust a dagger through your heart?
Did the judge say "human" and "you are forgiven"?
It was a wholesome lesson.
I congratulate you on your conversion.
Now you are ours again.
   THE WOMAN: You! Who sent you?
   THE NAMELESS ONE: The masses.

THE WOMAN: They've not forgotten me?

The message ... the message ...

THE NAMELESS ONE: My mission here is to set you free.

THE WOMAN: Freedom!

Life!

We escape? Is everything prepared?

THE NAMELESS ONE: Two keepers have been bribed.

There's one more at the gate. I'll strike him down.

THE WOMAN: You'd murder him ... for me?

THE NAMELESS ONE: For the cause.

THE WOMAN: I have no right

To win life through a keeper's death.

THE NAMELESS ONE: The masses have a right to you.

THE WOMAN: And the rights of the keeper?

Keepers are men.

THE NAMELESS ONE: We have no "men" as yet.

On one side, the group belonging to the mass.

On the other, the class belonging to the State.

THE WOMAN: Man is naked.

THE NAMELESS ONE: Mass is godlike.

THE WOMAN: Mass is not godlike.

Force made the mass.

Evils of property made the mass.

Mass is the movement of distress,

Is meek devotion ...

Is terrible vengeance ...

Is blinded slavery ...

Is holy purpose ...

Mass is a fertile field that has been trampled;

Mass is the choked-up, inarticulate people.

THE NAMELESS ONE: And action?

THE WOMAN: Action! And more than action!

To free man in the mass;

To free community in the mass.

THE NAMELESS ONE: The raw wind before the gates

Will heal you.

Hurry!

We have only a few minutes left.

THE WOMAN: You are not deliverance.

You are not salvation.

But I know who you are.

"Kill him!" you cried. Always your cry is "Kill him!"

Your father's name is War.
You are his bastard.
You poor, new head-of-staff of executioners,
Your only remedy: "Death!" and "Shoot them down!"
Throw off the mantle of your lofty phrases,
There's nothing but a woven tissue of lies.

THE NAMELESS ONE: The murder-generals battled for the
State!

THE WOMAN: They murdered, but they did not kill with joy.
Like you, they all believed in their own mission.

THE NAMELESS ONE: They battled for the cold, tyrannical
State;

We battle for humanity!

THE WOMAN: You murder for humanity,
As those deluded ones murdered for the State.
And there were some who surely felt
That through their State, their fatherland,
The earth would be redeemed.
I see no difference:
These murder for a single country,
The others kill for every country.
These murder for a thousand people,
The others for a million.
The one who murders for the State,
You call an executioner.
But he who murders for mankind
Is called a saviour; you crown him
Courageous, noble, great.
Yes, you can speak of good and holy violence!

THE NAMELESS ONE: Rail against others, rail against life
itself!

Should I let still more millions be enslaved
Because their enslavers chain them in good faith?
And are you the less guilty
If you keep silent?

THE WOMAN: The torch of gloomy violence cannot show the
way.

You lead us to a new and curious land,
The land of ancient human slavery.
If fate has pushed you forward at this time
And given you a reckless power
To blandish and betray the desperate crowds

Who look to you as to a new Messiah,
I know this—such a fate will turn against the man.
    THE NAMELESS ONE: Mass counts and not the man.
You're not our heroine, our one-time leader.
Each person bears the taint of their extraction;
You have the bourgeois symptoms:
Weakness and self-deception.
    THE WOMAN: You have no love for man.
    THE NAMELESS ONE: The principle above everything!
I love posterity!
    THE WOMAN: The individual above everything!
You—you would sacrifice
All living men
For a principle.
    THE NAMELESS ONE: The principle demands the sacrifice.
But you betray the masses; you betray the cause.
These are the days when one must make decisions.
Who hesitates and lacks determination,
Supports the masters who bear down upon us,
Supports the masters who have let us hunger,
Is our foe.
    THE WOMAN: I would betray the masses
If I demanded a single human life.
A leader has no right to sacrifice any one but himself.
Listen: no man has the right to kill another
To forward any cause,
And any cause demanding it is damned!
Whoever, in its name, calls for the blood of man
Is Moloch.
God was Moloch.
State was Moloch.
Mass was Moloch.
    THE NAMELESS ONE: And what is holy?
    THE WOMAN: Some day . . .
Brotherhood . . .
Free men bound only by their common work . . .
Work . . . People.
    THE NAMELESS ONE: You lack the power to face the un-
                                      yielding fact,
The need to act.
Free men will only come
Through hard facts and through harder deeds!

Atone by dying.
Perhaps your death will be some use to us.
　THE WOMAN: I live for ever.
　THE NAMELESS ONE: You were born too soon.
(*The* NAMELESS ONE *leaves the cell.*)
　THE WOMAN: You lived yesterday.
You live to-day.
And you are dead to-morrow.
I live for ever,
From sphere to sphere,
From change to change,
Till some day I become
Clean,
Guiltless,
Mankind.
　　(*A* PRIEST *enters.*)
　THE PRIEST: I come to give you final consolation;
The Church does not refuse assistance even to the criminal.
　THE WOMAN: By whose orders?
　THE PRIEST: The State authorities directed me.
　THE WOMAN: Where were you on the day of the trial?
Leave me!
　THE PRIEST: God forgives you, too. I understand you.
You thought mankind was good—or so you dreamed—
And you allowed outrage and sacrilege
Against the holy State and sacred order.
Man is all evil—bad from the beginning.
　THE WOMAN: Man longs for goodness.
　THE PRIEST: The lie of these degenerate days,
Born of despair, decay, and effort to escape,
Protected by a brittle shell
Of pitiful and empty faith,
Forced by a bad conscience.
Believe me, he never once desires to be good.
　THE WOMAN: He longs for goodness. Even when he does
　　　　　　　　　　　　　　　　　　　　wrong,
He does it under the mask of doing good.
　THE PRIEST: Nations come, nations go;
This earth has never seen paradise.
　THE WOMAN: I believe.
　THE PRIEST: Remember:

Lust for power; lust for pleasure!
That is the rhythm of the world.

THE WOMAN: I believe!

THE PRIEST: Earthly life is a constant changing of forms.
Mankind stays helpless. Salvation rests in God.

THE WOMAN: I believe!!!
I am cold . . . Leave me!
Leave me!

(*The* PRIEST *leaves the cell. An* OFFICER *enters.*)

THE OFFICER: Here's the sentence.
Mitigating circumstances considered.
Nevertheless. Crimes against State must be punished.

THE WOMAN: They are going to shoot me?

THE OFFICER: Orders are orders. Obedience, obedience.
State interests; quiet, discipline.
Duty as officer.

THE WOMAN: And man?

THE OFFICER: All conversation forbidden.
Orders are orders.

THE WOMAN: I am ready.

(*The* OFFICER *and the* WOMAN *go out. The cell is empty
for a few seconds. Two* WOMAN PRISONERS *in prison
smocks slip in. They remain standing at the door.*)

FIRST PRISONER: Did you see the officer? See his lovely gold
uniform?

SECOND PRISONER: I saw the coffin. In the laundry. Yellow
wooden box.

(*The* FIRST PRISONER *sees bread lying on the table and
throws herself upon it.*)

FIRST PRISONER: There's bread! Hungry! Hungry! Hungry!

SECOND PRISONER: Give me! Me bread! Me bread!

FIRST PRISONER: Here's a mirror. My, how pretty!
Hide it. Evening. Cell.

SECOND PRISONER: Here's a silky cloth.
Naked breast, silky cloth.
Hide it. Evening. Cell.

(*From outside the sharp crack of a volley rings through
the cell. The* PRISONERS *throw up outstretched, frightened
hands. The* FIRST PRISONER *searches in her skirt for the
mirror she has hidden. Lays it hurriedly back on the table
and cries, sinking upon her knees.*)

FIRST PRISONER: Sister, why did we do that?

(*Her arms toss in the air with a great helplessness. The* SECOND PRISONER *takes the silken cloth which she has hidden in her skirt and lays it hurriedly on the bed.*)

SECOND PRISONER: Sister, why did we do that?

(*The* SECOND PRISONER *breaks down. She buries her head in her lap. The curtain falls.*)

saint joan of the stockyards

by Bertolt Brecht

English Version by

Frank Jones

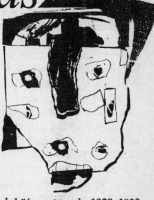

Die heilige Johanna der Schlachthöfe, written in 1929–1930, was broadcast over Berlin Radio on April 11, 1932, and published the same year. It was given an amateur production about 1935 by the Revolutionary Theatre in Copenhagen, Denmark. Brecht directed. Its first professional stage production was in Germany, at the Deutsches Schauspielhaus, Hamburg, on April 30, 1959.

Like *Man and the Masses, Saint Joan of the Stockyards* dramatizes a revolution that fails. Working with material comparable to Toller's, relevant both to that era and to our own —such as unrest in the cities, poverty marches, and the question of violence—Brecht systematically rejects the expressionist mystique of acting according to inner needs and emotions. In Toller's play, the revolution is abstract, presented as dream and vision; in Brecht's, it is brutally and cynically real. Toller's Sonia emotionally repudiates force and violence. Brecht's Joan, at first acting like Toller's heroine on the basis of her feelings, finally comes to realize that compassion not translated into action helps neither man nor masses, but simply perpetuates the status quo. "Only force helps where force rules," she comes to recognize—but too late. Canonizing her as Saint Joan of the Stockyards, the representatives of capitalism and organized religion make her a pious symbol designed to keep the workers in their place and the machinery of capitalism functioning. In dramatizing the relationships between the individual and the capitalist state and between man and the masses, Brecht relentlessly probes beneath the surface of the expressionists' idealism, and proposes a solution that is far more radical. In effect, he refutes Toller's argument.

As in *Man and the Masses,* the action of the play revolves around a struggle for the allegiance of a woman, in this case the salvationist Joan Dark (a pun for d'Arc). In Toller's play, the Man and the Nameless One, representatives of the state and the communists, contend for Sonia's heart. In Brecht's, the capitalist Pierpont Mauler and the Red workers pull Joan toward either devout acceptance of things as they are or violent action to change the world. In Toller, the unresolved duality of conscience and action leads to despair and withdrawal from action. In Brecht, the dichotomy is resolved: conscience, energized by analytic perception, leads to revolutionary action. At first, Joan fights misery which, apparently coming from nowhere, seems to be part of the human condition. The workers themselves know better. To Joan's question, "Where does all your misfortune come from?" one replies, "From Lennox & Co." Trying to give them answers, Joan learns the answers from them. The thrust of the play is her gradual understanding that pious rhetoric prolongs conflicting economic interests and capitalist exploitation of workers. She finally realizes that her humanitarian efforts derive from the incorrect premise of man's eternal plight as suffering sinner and that misery comes neither from heaven nor from human nature but from particular economic conditions. By the time Joan sees through the masks of sentiment and hypocrisy, however, she is dying, and a chorus of meat-packers and salvationists chant a fraudulent litany. Brecht's play is an ironic answer, from the viewpoint of dialectical materialism, to the expressionists' passionate belief in rebirth from within.

Unlike Toller's sinister but abstract bankers, Brecht's capitalist hero, Mauler, is a rich comic creation, a kind slob whose heart is a "sensitive garbage pit." Sensitivity and garbage indicate Mauler's comic contradictions as Brecht parodies the Faustian conception of two souls residing in one heart. Weeping for the cattle who are led to slaughter, Mauler nevertheless eats his steak raw and sheds no tears for his workers who, he claims, are butchers themselves and exemplify man's essentially evil nature. His ideals, which often serve as ambiguous rationalizations for his actions, represent not the pure humanitarianism he professes but self-indulgence on the part of the conscience-stricken capitalist who can afford liberal homilies only because they do not interfere with his business. Mauler's humane actions are motivated by an advantageous combination of morality and calculation. His sentimentality is always profitable for him.

Saint Joan of the Stockyards provides key images for all of Brecht: the stockyards, the stock market, and the market place. On the labor market, man is a commodity, bought and sold like cattle, going to the highest bidder. Wherever there is capitalism, there is only a mercantile evaluation of man, which permits the Meat King Mauler to corner the market in human beings. Mauler eulogizes money and capitalism to Joan because otherwise, he explains, there would be "an utterly different, new evaluation of man" which Joan would like as little as he, since then neither they nor God would have any function. Ultimately, Joan is willing to abandon her ministry to the poor: she prefers a different evaluation of man and new conditions in which he can be transformed. Demonstrating that the causes of man's suffering are economic rather than cosmic, Brecht shows the possibility of removing these causes. He exposes the claim of the Packers and Stockbreeders that "Man must do what suits his stature" as blind acceptance of the conditions of capitalism as the human condition. He shows that man makes his own nature and can change his condition himself. By suggesting choices, alternate possibilities, and competing valuations of man, Brecht aims to make the audience question the nature of society and so-called human nature. Every proposal leading to genuine change, the Workers tell the spectators, must be tested by action. Such propositions, they say, rejecting Toller's pacifism, can be achieved only by force.

Brecht shares with the expressionists his theme and a good deal of technique—such as abstract characters, moral debate, and choral speech—but instead of employing their liberal rhetoric, Brecht demolishes it ironically by parody and by distancing. By these means, Brecht creates the alienation effect (*Verfremdungseffekt*) of epic theatre—keeping the audience cool, detached, and cynical, critically watching the characters and actions on the stage, without passionate, subjective identification. To help produce this alienation, Brecht satirically imitates several other plays. He ridicules the verse form and idealistic philosophy of Schiller's dramas, particularly *The Maid of Orleans* (about Joan of Arc), and parodies lines from Goethe's *Faust*. He draws on Shaw's *Major Barbara*, about a salvationist in the slums who learns the economic relationship between charitable religious institutions and capitalism, and *Saint Joan*, about a Catholic saint whom Shaw regards as a forerunner of Protestantism (Brecht's saint is a Protestant who becomes an atheist). Both of Shaw's plays serve as models for the subversive undermining of uplifting moral positions that are false and sentimental. Brecht also plays with Biblical language (as in the Chorus's "To him that hath shall be given"), inverts Christian morality (damning the meek who accept the status quo, he calls for revolutionists to take over the earth), and uses scriptural analogies (Joan drives the Packers from the Mission with a stick, as Jesus drove the money-changers from the Temple). Such parallels and parodies, heightening our intellectual awareness, enable us to examine critically the poses adopted by the characters. The comedy of the Meat

King's lamentations in blank verse about how "That poor ox's outcry/Will nevermore go mute within me" insures against our becoming too involved. Expressions of awe at the divinely inspired unchangeability of human nature are rendered absurd since we see the economic forces which aim at preventing man from changing his condition. If discussions of the stock market in terms of the immutable courses of heavenly bodies are patently absurd, the permanence of the whole social order is called into question.

Other dramatic techniques also help create alienation. The details of *Saint Joan of the Stockyards* are more concrete than those of *Man and the Masses,* with its atmospheric light and shadows. "The truth is concrete" was one of Brecht's favorite aphorisms, and on stage he aimed at showing the truth of man in his social world. Accordingly, Brecht wants sharp, bright light to show the objective world clearly, rather than to create a mood. He calls for action, not dream. We do not know what Toller's workers actually do. Brecht's workers have specific jobs in the slaughterhouse. We see the widow of a man who was ground up in the bacon-maker and we meet the man who lost an arm on the tin-cutting machine. The Meat Kings devour steaks instead of the insubstantial but suggestively symbolic diet of Toller's Bankers, champagne and girls. Toller's Woman, and Joan herself at first, urge the workers to aspire and strive upward; only Joan learns that the workers need food instead of uplift. The difference between Toller and Brecht is perhaps epitomized by two crucial events in their two plays. At the end of *Man and the Masses,* two prisoners, rating their consciences more important than their material needs, cease looting when the Woman is shot, whereas in *Saint Joan of the Stockyards,* goodness and justice are luxuries that the starving cannot afford: Luckerniddle's widow continues to eat at the company canteen even though it means agreeing not to expose the management's responsibility for her husband's death. For the spiritual realm that Toller portrays, Brecht substitutes material reality.

But Brecht is no illusionist. He places concrete reality not in a realistic environment designed to persuade the audience that it is eavesdropping on the actual situation in a naturalistic locale through an invisible fourth wall, but frankly—and, in fact, ostentatiously—upon a stage. Realistically painted walls, for example, would not enclose the stage to provide a milieu. Instead, the audience might see the solid edges of one wall, perhaps supported by a visible triangular jack planted upon the stage floor. The actors, though their behavior would have its basis in realism, would perform with full realization that they were on a stage, and analytically present their characters to an examining audience rather than emotionally represent them before a hypnotized group of spectators. As part of his epic-theatre arsenal, Brecht also employs striking visual imagery. He paints his mythical Chicago, a lurid capitalist hell where workers howl in torment, in contrasting sets of color. On the one hand are the various shades of black and white: the Black Straw Hats, the snow, and the hungry, chalk-like faces of the workers. A startling contrast to the pale faces of the workers is the meat-red faces of the overfed capitalists, whose "bare chops [are] all smeared with blood." "Black roaring Chicago," a modern inferno which is "burning down below and freezing up on top," is built on a vertical structure of upper and lower regions. Exaggerative make-up helps to dramatize vividly the chasm separating the "many down below and the ones on top."

In epic theatre, the spectators are put at a distance from the stage action, which they are invited to view objectively *as* stage action, in order that they may contemplate the harsh reality of social injustice, not emotionally but intellectually, and then act upon their new understanding. The alienation effects of epic theatre are not ends in themselves but means toward the goals of increased awareness of social evils and the need to change society so as to eliminate these evils.

[Bertolt Brecht's prefatory note, first German edition, 1932]

Experiment 13, *Saint Joan of the Stockyards,* is meant to
portray the contemporary stage in the development of
Faustian man. The piece originated in the play *Happy End*
by Elizabeth Hauptmann. Beyond this, certain classical
models and stylistic elements were used: the representation
of given events received the form historically appropriate
to it. Thus, the intention is to exhibit not only events
but the manner of their subjection to the processes of
literature and theatre.

characters

PIERPONT MAULER
CRIDLE
LENNOX } MEAT KINGS
GRAHAM
MEYERS

JOAN DARK
MARTHA } *Black Straw Hats*
MAJOR PAULUS SNYDER
JACKSON

SLIFT (*a stockbroker*)
MULBERRY (*a landlord*)
MRS. LUCKERNIDDLE (*a worker's wife*)
GLOOMB (*a worker*)
MRS. SWINGURN (*a worker's wife*)
A WAITER
AN OLD MAN
A BROKER
A FOREMAN
AN APPRENTICE
TWO DETECTIVES
FIVE LABOR LEADERS
TWO POLICEMEN
And, as groups: WHOLESALERS, STOCKBREEDERS, SMALL SPEC-
ULATORS, BROKERS, WORKERS, NEWSBOYS, PASSERS-BY, JOUR-
NALISTS, VOICES, MUSICIANS, SOLDIERS, POOR FOLK

1. THE MEAT KING PIERPONT MAULER
GETS A LETTER FROM HIS FRIENDS
IN NEW YORK

(*Chicago stockyards.*)

MAULER (*reading a letter*): "As we can plainly see, dear
Pierpont, there has been a real glut in the meat market for
some little time. Also tariff walls to the south of us are re-
sisting all our attacks. In view of this it seems advisable, dear
Pierpont, to let the packing business go." I have this hint today
from my dear friends in New York. Here comes my partner.
(*Hides letter.*)

CRIDLE: Well, my dear Pierpont! Why so gloomy?

MAULER: Remember, Cridle, how some days ago—
We were walking through the stockyards, it was evening—
We stood beside our brand-new packing machine.
Remember, Cridle, the ox that took the blow,
Standing there blond, huge, dumbly gazing up
Toward Heaven: I feel the stroke was meant for me.
Oh, Cridle! Oh, our business is bloody.

CRIDLE: So—the old weakness, Pierpont!
Almost incredible: you, giant of packers,
Lord of the stockyards, quaking at the kill,
Fainting with pain, all for a fair-haired ox!
Don't tell a soul of this but me, I beg you.

MAULER: O loyal Cridle!
I oughtn't to have visited the stockyards!
Since I went into this business—that's seven
Years—I'd avoided them; and now—oh, Cridle,
I cannot bear it any longer! I'm giving up today.
You take this bloody business, with my share!
I'll let you have it cheap: you above all,
For no one else belongs to it like you.

CRIDLE: How cheap?
MAULER: No long palaver can be held
On such things by old friends like you and me.
Let's say ten million.
CRIDLE: That would not be expensive but for Lennox,
Who fights with us for every case of meat
And ruins our market with his cutthroat prices
And will break us all if he does not go broke.
Before he falls, and only you can fell him,
I shall not take your offer. Until then
Your cunning brain must be in constant practice.
MAULER: No, Cridle! That poor ox's outcry
Will nevermore go mute within me. Therefore
This Lennox must fall fast, for I myself
Have willed to be a decent man henceforth
And not a butcher. Cridle, come with me,
And I will tell you what to do to make
Lennox fall fast. But then you must
Relieve me of this business, which hurts me.
CRIDLE: If Lennox falls.   (*Exeunt.*)

2. THE COLLAPSE OF THE
GREAT PACKING PLANTS

(*In front of the Lennox Plant.*)

THE WORKERS: We are seventy thousand workers in Lennox's packing plant and we
Cannot live a day longer on such low wages.
Yesterday our pay was slashed again
And today the notice is up once more:
ANYONE NOT SATISFIED
WITH OUR WAGES CAN GO.
All right then, let's all go and
Shit on the wages that get skinnier every day.
     (*A silence.*)
For a long time now this work has made us sick
The factory our hell and nothing
But cold Chicago's terrors could

Keep us here. But now
By twelve hours' work a man can't even
Earn a stale loaf and
The cheapest pair of pants. Now
A man might just as well go off and
Die like a beast.
> (*A silence.*)

What do they take us for? Do they think
We are going to stand here like steers, ready
For anything? Are we
Their chumps? Better lie and rot!
Let's go right now.
> (*A silence.*)

It must be six o'clock by now!
Why don't you open up, you sweatshop bosses? Here
Are your steers, you butchers, open up!
> (*They knock.*)

Maybe they've forgotten us?
> (*Laughter.*)

Open the gates! We
Want to get into your
Dirt-holes and lousy kitchens
To cook stuffed meat
For the eaters who possess.
> (*A silence.*)

We demand at least
Our former wages, even though they were too low, at least
A ten-hour day and at least——

> A MAN (*crossing stage*): What are you waiting for? Don't
> > you know

That Lennox has shut down?
> (NEWSBOYS *run across stage.*)

THE NEWSBOYS: Meat king Lennox forced to shut down his
plants! Seventy thousand workers without food or shelter! M.
L. Lennox a victim of bitter competitive struggle with Pierpont
Mauler, well-known meat baron and philanthropist.

> THE WORKERS: Alas!

Hell itself
Shuts its gate in our faces!
We are doomed. Bloody Mauler grips
Our exploiter by the throat and
We are the ones who choke!

P. MAULER

(*A street.*)

THE NEWSBOYS: Chicago Tribune, noon edition! P. Mauler, meat baron and philanthropist, to attend opening of the P. Mauler Hospitals, largest and most expensive in the world! (P. MAULER *passes, with two* MEN.)

A PASSER-BY (*to another*): That's P. Mauler. Who are the men walking with him?

THE OTHER: Detectives. They guard him so that he won't be knocked down.

TO COMFORT THE MISERY OF THE STOCKYARDS, THE BLACK STRAW HATS LEAVE THEIR MISSION-HOUSE. JOAN'S FIRST DESCENT INTO THE DEPTHS

(*In front of the Black Straw Hats Mission.*)

JOAN (*at the head of a Black Straw Hat* SHOCK TROOP):
In gloomy times a bloody confusion

Ordered disorder
Planful wilfulness
Dehumanized humanity
When there is no end to the unrest in our cities:
Into such a world, a world like a slaughterhouse—
Summoned by rumors of threatening deeds of violence
To prevent the brute strength of the short-sighted people
From shattering its own tools and
Trampling its own bread-basket to pieces—
We wish to reintroduce
God.
A figure of little glory,
Almost of ill repute,
No longer admitted
To the sphere of actual life:
But, for the humblest, the one salvation!
Therefore we have decided
To beat the drum for Him
That He may gain a foothold in the regions of misery
And His voice may ring out clearly among the slaughter-
houses.

(*To* THE BLACK STRAW HATS.)
And this undertaking of ours is surely
The last of its kind. A last attempt
To set Him upright again in a crumbling world, and that
By means of the lowest.
(*They march on, drums beating.*)

FROM DAWN TO DARK THE BLACK STRAW HATS WORKED IN THE
STOCKYARDS, BUT WHEN EVENING CAME THEY HAD ACCOM-
PLISHED JUST ABOUT NOTHING

(*In front of the Lennox Plant.*)

A WORKER: They say there's another spell of dirty dealing
going on at the livestock market. Till it's over we'll have to
bide our time, I guess, and live on air.

A WORKER: Lights are on in the offices. They're counting up
the profits.

(THE BLACK STRAW HATS *arrive. They put up a sign: "Bed
for a Night, 20 cents; With Coffee, 30 cents; Hot dogs,
15 cents."*)

THE BLACK STRAW HATS (*singing*): Attention, your attention!

We see you, man that's falling
We hear your cry for help
We see you, woman calling.
Halt the autos, stop the traffic!
Courage, sinking people, we're coming, look our way!
You who are going under,
See us, oh, see us, brother, before you say you're beat!
We bring you something to eat,
We are still aware
That you are standing out there.
Don't say it can't be helped, for things are changing
The injustice of this world cannot remain
If all the people come and join us marching
And leave their cares behind and help with might and main.
We'll bring up tanks and cannon too
And airplanes there shall be
And battleships over the sea
All to conquer a plate of soup, brother, just for you.
For you, yes, you, poor folk,
Are an army vast and grand,
So even in times like these
We've all got to lend you a hand!
Forward march! Eyes right! Rifles ready to fire!
Courage, you sinking people, we're coming, look our way!

(*During the singing the* BLACK STRAW HATS *have been
distributing their leaflet, "The Battle Cry," spoons, plates
and soup. The* WORKERS *say "Thank you" and listen to*
JOAN'S *speech.*)

JOAN: We are the Soldiers of the Lord. On account of our

hats we are also called the Black Straw Hats. We march with drums and flags wherever unrest prevails and acts of violence threaten, to remind men of the Lord whom they have all forgotten, and to bring back their souls to Him. We call ourselves soldiers because we are an army and when we are on the march we have to fight crime and misery, those forces that want to drag us down. (*She begins to ladle out the soup herself.*) That's it, just eat some hot soup and then everything will look real different, but please give a little thought to Him who bestows it upon you. And when you think that way you will see that this is really the complete solution: Strive upward, not downward. Get in line for a good position up above, not here below. Want to be the first man up, not the first man down. Surely you realize now what sort of trust you can place in the fortunes of this world. None at all. Misfortune comes like the rain, that nobody makes, and still it comes. Tell me, where does all your misfortune come from?

AN EATER: From Lennox & Co.

JOAN: Maybe Mr. Lennox has more worries right now than you have. After all, what are you losing? His losses run into millions!

A WORKER: There's not much fat floating in this soup, but it contains plenty of wholesome water and there's no lack of warmth.

ANOTHER WORKER: Shut up, revellers! Listen to the heavenly text, or they'll take away your soup!

JOAN: Quiet! Tell me, dear friends, why are you poor?

WORKER: Aw, *you* tell *us.*

JOAN: All right, I will tell you: it is not because you aren't blest with worldly goods—that is not for all of us—but because you have no sense of higher things. That is why you are poor. These low pleasures for which you work so hard, a bite to eat, nice homes, the movies, they are just coarse sensual enjoyments, but God's word is a far finer, more inward, more exquisite pleasure, maybe you can't think of anything sweeter than whipped cream, but God's word, I tell you, is still sweeter, honestly it is, oh, how sweet God's word is! It's like milk and honey, and in it you dwell as in a palace of gold and alabaster. O ye of little faith, the birds of the air have no *Help Wanted* ads and the lilies of the field have no jobs, and yet He feeds them, because they sing His praises. You all want to get to the top, but what kind of top, and how do you propose to get there? And so it's we Straw Hats who ask you, quite practically: What does a man need to rise?

WORKER: A starched collar.

JOAN: No, not a starched collar. Maybe you need a starched collar to get ahead on earth, but in God's eyes you need much more than that around you, a quite different sort of splendor, but before Him you don't even have a rubber collar on, because you have utterly neglected your entire inner natures. But how are you going to get to the top—whatever, in your ignorance, you call the top—by brute force? As if force ever caused anything but destruction! You believe that if you rear up on your hind legs there'll be heaven on earth. But I say to you: that way not paradise but chaos is created.

WORKER (*enters, running*): A position has just opened up! It pays, and it's calling you over
To Plant Number Five!
It looks like a urinal on the outside.
Run!

(*Three* WORKERS *put down full plates of soup and run.*)

JOAN: Hey, you, where are you off to? Talk to you about God, *that* you don't want to hear, eh!

A BLACK STRAW HAT GIRL: The soup's all gone.

THE WORKERS: The soup's all gone.
Fatless it was and scant,
But better than nothing.

(*All turn away and stand up.*)

JOAN: Oh, keep your seats, no harm's done, the grand soup of heaven never gives out, you know.

THE WORKERS: When will you finally
Open your roachy cellars,
You butchers of men?

(*Groups form.*)

A MAN: How am I to pay for my little house now, the cute
                                            damp thing
With twelve of us in it? Seventeen
Payments I've made and now the last is due:
They'll throw us onto the street and never again
Will we see the trampled ground with the yellowish grass
And never breathe again
The accustomed pestilent air.

A SECOND MAN (*in a circle*): Here we stand with hands like
                                            shovels

And necks like trucks wanting to sell
Our hands and necks
And no one will buy them.

THE WORKERS: And our tool, a gigantic pile
Of steam hammers and cranes,
Barred in behind walls!

JOAN: What's up? Now they're simply leaving! Finished
eating, have you? We hope it does you good. Thanks. Why
have you listened till now?

A WORKER: For the soup.

JOAN: We're moving on. Sing!

THE BLACK STRAW HATS (*singing*): Go straight to the thick
of the fight

Where there's the toughest work to do.
Sing with all your might! It may still be night,
But already the morning is coming in might!
Soon the Lord Jesus will come to you, too.

A VOICE FROM THE REAR: There's still work to be had at
Mauler's! (*Exeunt* WORKERS, *all but a few* WOMEN.)

JOAN (*gloomily*): Pack up the instruments. Did you see
how they hurried

Away as soon as the soup was gone?
This thing gets no higher up
Than the rim of a dish. It believes
In nothing that it does not
Hold in its hand—if it believes in hands.
Living from minute to minute, uncertainly,
They can no longer raise themselves
From the lowest ground. Only hunger
Is a match for them. They are touched
By no song, no word
Penetrates their depths.
(*To the* BYSTANDERS.) We Black Straw Hats feel as though we
were expected to satisfy a starving continent with our spoons.
(*The* WORKERS *return. Shouting in distance.*)

THE WORKERS (*in front*): What's that yelling? A huge
stream of people from the packing houses!

A VOICE (*in back*): Mauler and Cridle are shutting down
too!

The Mauler works are locking us out!

THE RETURNING WORKERS: Running for jobs, we met
halfway

A stream of desperate men
Who had lost their jobs and
Asked us for jobs.

THE WORKERS (*in front*): Alas! From over there, too, a
                                                troop of men!
You can't see the end of it! Mauler
Has shut down too! What's to become of us?

THE BLACK STRAW HATS (*to* JOAN): Come along with us
now. We're freezing and wet and we have to eat.

JOAN: But now I want to know who's to blame for all this.

THE BLACK STRAW HATS: Stop! Don't get mixed up in that!
                                                They're sure
To give you an earful. Their minds are stuffed
With low ideas! They're lazybones!
Gluttonous, shirkers, from birth onward
Void of all higher impulse!

JOAN: No, I want to know. (*To the* WORKERS.) Tell me
now: why are you running around here without any work?

THE WORKERS: Bloody Mauler's locked in battle
With stingy Lennox; so we go hungry.

JOAN: Where does Mauler live?

THE WORKERS: Over there where livestock is bought and
                                                sold,
In a big building, the livestock market.

JOAN: There I will go, for
I have to know this.

MARTHA (*one of the* BLACK STRAW HATS): Don't get mixed
                                up in that! Ask many questions
And you'll get lots of answers.

JOAN: No, I want to see this Mauler, who causes such
misery.

THE BLACK STRAW HATS: Then, Joan, we take a dark view
                                        of your further fate.
Do not mix in the quarrels of this world!
He who meddles in a quarrel becomes its victim!
His purity swiftly perishes. Soon
His small warmth perishes in the cold
That reigns over everything. Goodness abandons him
Who flees the protective hearth.
Striving downward
From level to level toward the answer you never will get,
You will disappear in dirt!

For only dirt is stuffed into the mouths
Of those who ask without caution.
    JOAN: I want to know. (*Exeunt* BLACK STRAW HATS.)

3. PIERPONT MAULER FEELS A BREATH
FROM ANOTHER WORLD

(*In front of the livestock market. Lower level,* JOAN *and*
MARTHA *waiting; upper level, the meat packers* LENNOX *and*
GRAHAM, *conversing.* LENNOX *is white as chalk.*)

    GRAHAM: How you have felt the blows of brutal Mauler,
My good friend Lennox! There's no hindering
The rise of this monstrosity: to him
Nature is goods, even the air's for sale.
What we have inside our stomachs he resells to us.
He can squeeze rent from ruined houses, money
From rotten meat; throw stones at him,
He's sure to turn the stones to money; so
Unruly is his money-lust, so natural
To him this lack of nature that he himself
Cannot deny its driving force within him
For I tell you: himself, he's soft, does not love money,
Cannot bear squalor, cannot sleep at night.
Therefore you must approach him as though you could hardly
                        speak,

And say: "Oh, Mauler, look at me and take
Your hand off my throat—think of your old age—"
That will frighten him, for sure. Maybe he'll cry . . .
    JOAN (*to* MARTHA): Only you, Martha, have followed me
                        this far.

All the others left me with warnings
As if I were bound for the end of the world.
Strange warning from their lips.
I thank you, Martha.
    MARTHA: I warned you too, Joan.
    JOAN: And went with me.
    MARTHA: But will you really recognize him, Joan?
    JOAN: I shall know him!

CRIDLE (*coming out on upper level*): Well, Lennox, now
                                    the underbidding's over.
You're finished now and I'll close up and wait
Until the market recovers. I'll clean my yards
And give the knives a thorough oiling and order some
Of those new packing machines that give a fellow
A chance to save a tidy sum in wages.
  GRAHAM: Damnable times!
Waste lies the market, flooded out by goods.
Trade, that was once so flourishing, lies fallow.
Scuffling over a market that's long been glutted,
You wrecked your own prices by underbidding one another:
                                                    thus
Do buffaloes, fighting for grass, trample to shreds the grass
                                              they fight for.
  (MAULER *comes out, with his broker,* SLIFT, *among a
  crowd of* PACKERS, *two* DETECTIVES *behind him.*)
  THE MEAT PACKERS: Now everything's a matter of holding
out.
  MAULER: Lennox is down. (*To* LENNOX.) Admit it, you are
                                                        out.
And now I ask you, Cridle, to take over
The packing plant as stated in our contract,
Presuming Lennox finished.
  CRIDLE: Agreed, Lennox is out. But also finished
Are good times on the market; therefore, Mauler,
You must come down from ten million for your stock!
  MAULER: What? The price stands
Here in the contract! Here, Lennox, see if this
Is not a contract, with a price right on it!
  CRIDLE: Yes, but a contract made in better times!
Are bad times also mentioned in the contract?
What can I do alone with a stockyard now
When not a soul will buy a can of meat?
Now I know why you couldn't bear to watch
More oxen dying: it was because their flesh
Cannot be sold!
  MAULER: No, it's my heart
That swells, affected by the creature's shrieks!
  GRAHAM: Oh, mighty Mauler, now I realize
The greatness of your actions: even your heart
Sees far ahead!
  LENNOX: Mauler, I wanted to talk with you . . . again . . .

GRAHAM: Straight to his heart, Lennox! Straight to his heart!
It's a sensitive garbage pit!

(*He hits* MAULER *in the pit of the stomach.*)

MAULER: Ouch!

GRAHAM: You see, he has a heart!

MAULER: Well, Freddy, now I'll make a settlement with
Cridle

So he can't buy a single can from you,
Because you hit me.

GRAHAM: You can't do that, Pierpy! That's mixing
Personal matters with business.

CRIDLE: O.K., Pierpy, with pleasure. Just as you please.

GRAHAM: I have two thousand workers, Mauler!

CRIDLE: Send them to the movies! But really, Pierpy, our
agreement isn't valid. (*Figuring in a notebook.*) When we
contracted for your withdrawal from the business, the shares
—of which you hold one-third, as I do—stood at 390. You
gave them to me for 320; that was cheap. It's expensive today;
they're at a hundred now, because the market's blocked. If I'm
to pay you off I'll have to throw the shares onto the market. If
I do that they'll go down to 70, and what can I use to pay you
then? Then I'll be done for.

MAULER: If that's your situation, Cridle, I must certainly
Get my money out of you right away,
Before you're done for.
I tell you, Cridle, I am so afraid
I'm all of a sweat, the most I can let you have
Is six days! What am I saying? Five days
If that's your situation.

LENNOX: Mauler, look at me.

MAULER: Lennox, you tell me if the contract says anything
about bad times.

LENNOX: No. (*Exit.*)

MAULER (*watching him go*): Some worry seems to be op-
pressing him,
And I, on business bent (would I were not!)
Did not perceive it! Oh, repulsive business!
Cridle, it sickens me.

(*Exit* CRIDLE. *Meanwhile* JOAN *has called one of the*
DETECTIVES *over to her and said something to him.*)

THE DETECTIVE: Mr. Mauler, there are some persons here
who want to talk to you.

MAULER: Unmannerly lot, eh? With an envious look, eh?

And violent, no doubt? I
Cannot see anyone.

THE DETECTIVE: They're a pair from the Black Straw Hat
Organization.

MAULER: What kind of an organization is that?

THE DETECTIVE: They have many branches and are numerous and respected among the lower classes, where they are
called the Good Lord's Soldiers.

MAULER: I've heard of them. Curious name:
The Good Lord's Soldiers . . . but
What do they want of me?

THE DETECTIVE: They say they have something to discuss
with you.

> (*During this the market uproar has resumed:* "Steers
> 43," "Hogs 55," "Heifers 59," *etc.*)

MAULER: All right, tell them I will see them.
But tell them also they may say nothing that I
Do not ask about first. Nor must they break out
Into tears or songs, especially sentimental ones.
And tell them it would be most profitable to them
For me to get the impression
That they are well-meaning people, with nothing to their dis-
credit,
Who want nothing from me that I do not have.
Another thing: do not tell them I am Mauler.

THE DETECTIVE (*going over to* JOAN): He consents to see
you, but
You must ask no questions, only answer
When he asks you.

JOAN (*walking up to* MAULER): You are Mauler!

MAULER: No, I'm not. (*Points to* SLIFT.) That's him.

JOAN (*pointing to* MAULER): You are Mauler.

MAULER: No, he is.

JOAN: You are.

MAULER: How do you know me?

JOAN: Because you have the bloodiest face. (SLIFT *laughs.*)

MAULER: You laugh, Slift? (*Meanwhile* GRAHAM *has hurried
off. To* JOAN.) How much do you earn in a day?

JOAN: Twenty cents, but food and clothing are supplied.

MAULER: Thin clothes, Slift, and thin soup too, I guess!
Yes, those clothes are probably thin and the soup not rich.

JOAN: Mauler, why do you lock the workers out?

MAULER (*to* SLIFT): The fact that they work without pay

Is remarkable, isn't it? I never heard
Of such a thing before—a person working
For nothing and none the worse. And in their eyes
I see no fear
Of being down and out.
(*To* JOAN.) Extraordinary folk, you Black Straw Hats.
I shall not ask you what particularly
You want of me. I know the fool mob calls me
Mauler the Bloody, saying it was I
Who ruined Lennox or caused unpleasantness
For Cridle—who, between ourselves, is one
Of little merit. I can say to you:
Those are just business matters, and they won't
Be interesting to you. But there's something else, on which
I would like to hear your views. I am thinking of giving up
This bloodstained business, as soon as possible; once for all.
For recently—this *will* interest you—I saw
A steer die and it upset me so
That I want to get rid of everything, and have even sold
My interest in the plant, worth twelve million dollars. I gave it
to that man

For ten. Don't you feel
That this is right, and to your liking?
   SLIFT: He saw the steer die and made up his mind
To butcher wealthy Cridle
Instead of the poor steer.
Was that right?
     (*The* PACKERS *laugh.*)
   MAULER: Go on, laugh. Your laughter's nothing to me.
Some day I'll see you weep.
   JOAN: Mr. Mauler, why have you shut down the stock-
yards?
This I must know.
   MAULER: Was it not an extraordinary act to take my hand
Out of a mighty concern, simply because it is bloody?
Say this is right, and to your liking.
All right then, don't say it, I know, I admit, some people
Did poorly out of it, they lost their jobs,
I know. Unhappily, that was unavoidable.
A bad lot anyway, a tough mob, better not go near them, but
tell me:
My act in withdrawing my hand from the business,
Surely that is right?

JOAN: I don't know whether you ask in earnest.

MAULER: That's because my damned voice is used to faking,
And for that reason too I know: you
Do not like me. Say nothing.
(*To the* OTHERS.)
I seem to feel a breath from another world wafted toward me.
(*He takes everybody's money from them and gives it to*
JOAN.)
Out with your money, you cattle butchers, give it here!
(*He takes it out of their pockets, gives it to* JOAN.)
Take it to give to the poor folk, Joan!
But be assured that I feel no obligation in any way
And sleep extremely well. Why am I helping here? Perhaps
Just because I like your face, because it is so unknowing,
                                                      although
You have lived for twenty years.

MARTHA (*to* JOAN): I don't believe in his sincerity.
Forgive me, Joan, for going away now too:
It seems to me you also
Should really drop all this!   (*Exit.*)

JOAN: Mr. Mauler, you know this is only a drop in the
bucket. Can you not give them real help?

MAULER: Tell the world I warmly commend your activities
                                                          and
Wish there were more like you. But
You mustn't take this thing about the poor this way.
They are wicked people. Human beings do not affect me:
They are not guiltless, and they're butchers themselves.
However, let's drop the matter.

JOAN: Mr. Mauler, they are saying in the stockyards that
you are to blame for their misery.

MAULER: On oxen I have pity; man is evil.
Mankind's not ripe for what you have in mind:
Before the world can change, humanity
Must change its nature.
Wait just one more moment.
(*In a low tone, to* SLIFT.) Give her more money away from
                                              here, when she's alone.
Say "for the poor folk," so that she can take it
Without blushing, but then see what she buys for herself.
If that's no help—I'd rather it were not—
Then take her with you
To the stockyards and show her

Those poor of hers, how wicked and gross they are, full of
                                      treachery and cowardice
And how they themselves are to blame.
Maybe that will help.
(*To* JOAN.) Here is Sullivan Slift, my broker; he will show you
                                      something.
(*To* SLIFT.) I tell you, it's almost intolerable in my eyes
That there should be people like this girl, owning nothing
But a black hat and twenty cents a day, and fearless.   (*Exit.*)
    SLIFT: I would not care to know what you want to know;
Still, if you wish to know it, come here tomorrow.
    JOAN (*watching* MAULER *go*): That's not a wicked man, he
                                      is the first
To be scared from the tanglewoods of meanness by our drums,
The first to hear the call.
    SLIFT (*departing*): I give you fair warning: do not take up
                                      with those people
Down in the yards, they're a lowdown lot, really
The scum of the earth.
    JOAN: I want to see it.

4. THE BROKER SULLIVAN SLIFT SHOWS JOAN DARK THE WICKEDNESS OF THE POOR: JOAN'S SECOND DESCENT INTO THE DEPTHS

(*The stockyards district.*)

    SLIFT: Now, Joan, I will show you
The wickedness of those
For whom you feel pity and
How out of place the feeling is.
        (*They are walking alongside a factory wall inscribed
        "Mauler and Cridle, Meat Packing Company." The name
        Cridle has been painted out in crosswise strokes. Two
        MEN come through a small gate. SLIFT and JOAN hear
        their conversation.*)
    FOREMAN (*to a young* APPRENTICE): Four days ago a man
named Luckerniddle fell into our boiler, we couldn't stop the
machinery in time so he got caught in the bacon-maker, a
horrible thing to happen; this is his coat and this is his cap,
take them and get rid of them, all they do is take up a hook in

the cloakroom and make a bad impression. It's a good plan to burn them, right away would be best. I entrust the things to you because I know you're a reliable man. I'd lose my job if the stuff were found anywhere. Of course as soon as the plant opens again you can have Luckerniddle's job.

THE APPRENTICE: You can count on me, Mr. Smith. (*The* FOREMAN *goes back in through the gate.*) Too bad about the fellow that has to go out into the world as bacon, but I feel bad about his coat too, it's still in good shape. Old Man Bacon has his can to wear now and won't need this any more, but I could use it very well. Shit, I'll take it. (*Puts it on and wraps his own coat and cap in newspaper.*)

JOAN (*swaying*): I feel sick.

SLIFT: That's the world as it is. (*Stopping the* YOUNG MAN.) Wherever did you get that coat and cap? Didn't they belong to Luckerniddle, the man that had the accident?

APPRENTICE: Please don't let it get around, sir. I'll take the things off right away. I'm pretty nearly down and out. That extra twenty cents you get in the fertilizer-cellars fooled me into working at the bone-grinding machine last year. There I got it bad in the lungs, and a chronic eye inflammation too. Since then my working capacity has gone down and since February I've only been employed twice.

SLIFT: Keep the things on. And come to Canteen No. Seven at noon today. You'll get a free lunch and a dollar there if you tell Luckerniddle's wife where your cap and coat came from.

APPRENTICE: But, sir, isn't that sort of raw?

SLIFT: Well, if you don't need the money . . . !

APPRENTICE: You can rely on me, sir. (JOAN *and* SLIFT *walk on.*)

MRS. LUCKERNIDDLE (*sitting in front of the factory gate, lamenting*): You in there, what are you doing with my husband?

Four days ago he went to work, he said:
"Warm up some soup for me tonight!" And to this
Day he hasn't got back! What have you done with him
You butchers! Four days I have been standing here
In the cold, nights too, waiting, but nobody tells me
Anything, and my husband doesn't come out! But I tell
You, I'm going to stand right here until I get to see him!
You'll rue the day if you've done him any harm!

SLIFT (*walking up to the* WOMAN): Your husband has left town, Mrs. Luckerniddle.

MRS. LUCKERNIDDLE: Oh, don't give me that again.

SLIFT: I'll tell you something, Mrs. Luckerniddle, he is out of town, and it's very embarrassing to the factory to have you sitting around here talking foolishness. So we'll make you an offer which could not be required of us by law. If you give up your search for your husband, you may have lunch in our canteen every day for three weeks, free.

MRS. LUCKERNIDDLE: I want to know what's become of my husband.

SLIFT: We're telling you, he's gone to Frisco.

MRS. LUCKERNIDDLE: He has not gone to Frisco, he's had some accident because of you, and you're trying to hide it.

SLIFT: If that's what you think, Mrs. Luckerniddle, you cannot accept any meals from the factory, but you will have to bring suit against the factory. But think it over thoroughly. I shall be at your disposal in the canteen tomorrow. (SLIFT *goes back to* JOAN.)

MRS. LUCKERNIDDLE: I must have my husband back. I have nobody but him to support me.

JOAN: She will never come.
Twenty dinners may mean much
To one who is hungry, but
There is more for him.

> (JOAN *and* SLIFT *walk on. They stop in front of a factory canteen and see two* MEN *looking in through a window.*)

GLOOMB: There sits the overseer who's to blame for my getting my hand in the tin-cutting machine—stuffing his belly full. We must see to it that this is the last time the swine gorges at our expense. You'd better give me your club, mine will probably splinter right off.

SLIFT: Stay here. I want to talk to him. And if he approaches you, say you're looking for work. Then you'll see what kind of people these are. (*Going up to* GLOOMB.) Before you get carried away into doing something—that's the way it looks to me—I'd like to make you a profitable proposition.

GLOOMB: I have no time right now, sir.

SLIFT: That's too bad, because there would have been something in it for you.

GLOOMB: Make it short. We cannot afford to let that swine go. He's got to get his reward today for that inhuman system he plays overseer to.

SLIFT: I have a suggestion to make for your own benefit. I am an inspector in the factory. Much inconvenience has been caused by your place remaining vacant. Most people think it too dangerous, just because you have made all this to-do about your fingers. Now it would be just fine if we had someone to fill that post again. If you, for example, could find somebody for it, we would be ready to take you on again right away—in fact, to give you an easier and better-paid job than you've had up to now. Perhaps even a foreman's position. You seem a clever man to me. And that fellow in there happens to have got himself disliked lately. You understand. You would also have to take charge of production speed, of course, and above all, as I say, find somebody for that place at the tin-cutting machine, which, I admit, is not safe at all. Over there, for instance, there's a girl looking for work.

GLOOMB: Can a man rely on what you say?

SLIFT: Yes.

GLOOMB: That one over there? She looks weak. It's no job for anyone who tires easily. (*To the* OTHERS.) I've thought it over, we'll do the job tomorrow night. Night's a better time for that kind of fun. So long. (*Goes over to* JOAN.) Looking for a job?

JOAN: Yes.

GLOOMB: Eyesight good?

JOAN: No. Last year I worked at a bone-grinding machine in the fertilizer cellars. I got it bad in the lungs there and a chronic eye inflammation too. Since then my work-capacity has gone down badly. I've been out of a job since February. Is this a good place?

GLOOMB: The place is good. It's work that even weaker people, like yourself, can do.

JOAN: Are you sure there's no other place to be had? I've heard that working at that machine is dangerous for people who tire easily. Their hands get unsteady and then they grab at the blades.

GLOOMB: That isn't true at all. You'll be surprised to see how pleasant the work is. You'll fan your brow and ask yourself how people could ever tell such silly stories about that machine. (SLIFT *laughs and draws* JOAN *away.*)

JOAN: Now I'm almost afraid to go on—what will I see next! (*They go into the canteen and see* MRS. LUCKERNIDDLE, *who is talking to the* WAITER.)

MRS. LUCKERNIDDLE (*figuring*): Twenty lunches . . . then I could . . . then I'd go and then I'd have . . . (*She sits down at a table.*)

WAITER: If you're not eating you'll have to leave.

MRS. LUCKERNIDDLE: I'm waiting for somebody who was going to come in here today or tomorrow. What's for lunch today?

WAITER: Peas.

JOAN: There she sits.
I thought she was firmly resolved, and feared
That still she might come tomorrow, and now she has run here
faster than we
And is here already, waiting for us.

SLIFT: Go and take her the food yourself—maybe she'll think again. (JOAN *fetches a plate of food and brings it to* MRS. LUCKERNIDDLE.)

JOAN: Here so soon?

MRS. LUCKERNIDDLE: It's because I've had nothing to eat for two days.

JOAN: You didn't know we were coming in today, did you?

MRS. LUCKERNIDDLE: That's right.

JOAN: On the way over here I heard someone say that something happened to your husband in the factory and the factory is responsible.

MRS. LUCKERNIDDLE: Oh, so you've reconsidered your offer? So I don't get my twenty meals?

JOAN: But you got along with your husband very well, didn't you? People told me you have nobody except him.

MRS. LUCKERNIDDLE: Well, I've had nothing to eat for two days.

JOAN: Won't you wait till tomorrow? If you give up your husband now, no one will ask after him any more. (MRS. LUCKERNIDDLE *is silent.*) Don't take it. (MRS. LUCKERNIDDLE *snatches the food from her hands and begins to eat greedily.*)

MRS. LUCKERNIDDLE: He's gone to Frisco.

JOAN: And basements and storerooms are full of meat
That cannot be sold and is going rotten
Because no one will take it away.

(*The* WORKER *with the cap and coat enters, rear.*)

WORKER: Good morning, is this where I eat?

SLIFT: Just take a seat beside that woman over there. (*The* MAN *sits down.*) That's a good-looking cap you have there. (*The* WORKER *hides it.*) Where did you get it?

WORKER: Bought it.

SLIFT: Well, where did you buy it?

WORKER: Not in any store.

SLIFT: Then where did you get it?

WORKER: I got it off a man that fell into a boiling vat.

MRS. LUCKERNIDDLE (*feels sick. She gets up and goes out. On the way out she says to the* WAITER): Leave the plate where it is. I'm coming back. I'm coming here for lunch every day. Just ask that gentleman. (*Exit.*)

SLIFT: For three whole weeks she will come and feed, without looking up, like an animal. Have you seen, Joan, that their wickedness is beyond measure?

JOAN: But what mastery you have
Over their wickedness! How you thrive on it!
Do you not see that their wickedness hasn't a chance?
Certainly she would have liked
To be true to her husband, as others are,
And to ask after the man who supported her
For some time longer, as is proper.
But the price was too high: it amounted to twenty meals.
And would that young man on whom
Any scoundrel can rely
Have shown the coat to the dead man's wife
If things had gone as he would like?
But the price appeared too high to him.
And why would the man with only one arm
Have failed to warn me? if the price
Of so small a scruple were not so high for him?
Why, instead, did he sell his wrath, which is righteous, but too
                                        dear?

If their wickedness is beyond measure, then
So is their poverty. Not the wickedness of the poor
Have you shown me, but
The poverty of the poor.
You've shown the evil of the poor to me:
Now see the woes of evil poverty.
O thoughtless rumor, that the poor are base:
You shall be silenced by their stricken face!

5. JOAN INTRODUCES THE POOR TO THE LIVESTOCK EXCHANGE

(*The Livestock Exchange.*)

THE PACKERS: We have canned meat for sale!
Wholesalers, buy canned meat!
Fresh, juicy, canned meat!

Mauler and Cridle's bacon!
Graham's sirloins, soft as butter!
Wilde's Kentucky lard, a bargain!
THE WHOLESALERS: And silence fell upon the waters and
Bankruptcy among the wholesalers!
THE PACKERS: Due to tremendous technical advances
Engineers' hard work and entrepreneurs' farsightedness
We have now succeeded
In lowering prices for
Mauler and Cridle's bacon
Graham's sirloins, soft as butter
Wilde's Kentucky lard, a bargain
BY ONE-THIRD!
Wholesalers, buy canned meat!
Seize your opportunity!
THE WHOLESALERS: And silence fell upon the mountaintops
And hotel kitchens covered their heads
And stores looked away in horror
And middlemen turned pale!
We wholesalers vomit if we so much as
See a can of meat. This country's stomach
Has eaten too much meat from cans
And is fighting back.
SLIFT: What news from your friends in New York?
MAULER: Theories. If they had their way
The meat ring would be lying in the gutter
And stay there for weeks till there wasn't a peep left in it
And I'd have all that meat around my neck!
Madness!
SLIFT: I'd have to laugh if those men in New York really
                                                        had
Tariffs lowered now, opened things up below the border
And started a bull-market—just supposing!—and we
Were to miss the bus!
MAULER: What if they did? Would you be harsh enough
To hack your pound of flesh from misery
Like this? Look at them, watching for a move,
As lynxes do! I couldn't be so harsh.
WHOLESALERS: Here we stand, wholesalers with mountains
                                                        of cans
And cellars full of frozen steers
Wanting to sell the steers in cans
And no one will buy them!
And our customers, the kitchens and stores,

Are stuffed to the ceiling with frozen meat!
Screaming for buyers and eaters!
No more buying for us!

PACKERS: Here we stand, packers with slaughterhouses and
packing space
And stables full of steers; day and night the machines
Run on under steam; brine, tubs and boiling vats
Wanting to turn the lowing ravenous herds
Into canned meat and nobody wants canned meat.
We're ruined.

STOCKBREEDERS: And what about us, the stockbreeders?
Who'll buy livestock now? In our barns stand
Steers and hogs eating expensive corn
And they ride to town in trains and while they ride
They eat and eat and at stations
They wait in rent-devouring boxcars, forever eating.

MAULER: And now the knives motion them back,
Death, giving livestock the cold shoulder,
Closes his shop.

PACKERS (*shouting at* MAULER, *who is reading a news-
paper*): Traitorous Mauler, nest-befouler!
Do you think we don't know who's selling livestock here—
Oh so secretly—and knocking the bottom out of prices?
You've been offering meat for days and days!

MAULER: Insolent butchers, cry in your mothers' laps
Because the hunted creature's outcry ceases!
Go home and say that one of all your number
Could not hear oxen bellow any longer
And would rather hear your bellow than their bellow!
I want my cash and quiet for my conscience!

A BROKER (*bellowing from the Exchange entrance, rear*):
Terrific drop in stock exchange quotations!
Colossal sales of stocks. Cridle, formerly Mauler,
Whirl the whole meat ring's rates down with them
Into the abyss.

(*Uproar arises among the* MEAT-PACKERS. *They rush at*
CRIDLE, *who is white as chalk*.)

PACKERS: What's the meaning of this, Cridle? Look us in
the eye!
Dumping stocks, with the market the way it is?

BROKERS: At 115!

PACKERS: Are your brains made of dung?
It's not yourself alone you're ruining!
You big shit! You criminal!

CRIDLE (*pointing to* MAULER): There's your man!

GRAHAM (*standing in front of* CRIDLE): This isn't Cridle's doing, someone else
Is fishing these waters and we're supposed to be the fish!
There are people who want to take care of the meat-ring, now,
And do a final job! Defend yourself, Mauler!

PACKERS (*to* MAULER): The story is, Mauler, that you're squeezing your money
Out of Cridle, who, we hear, is groggy already, and Cridle
Himself says nothing and points to you.

MAULER: If I leave my money in this Cridle's hands an hour longer—a man who's confessed to me personally that he's unsound—who among you would still take me seriously as a businessman? And I want nothing so much as for *you* to take me seriously.

CRIDLE (*to the* BYSTANDERS): Just four weeks ago I made a contract with Mauler. He wanted to sell me his shares—one-third of the total—for ten million dollars. From that time on, as I've just found out, he has been secretly selling quantities of livestock, cheap, to make a still worse mess of prices that are sagging already. He could ask for his money whenever he wanted to. I intended to pay him by disposing of part of his shares on the market—they were high then—and reinvesting part. Then the drop came. Today Mauler's shares are worth not ten but three million. The whole plant is worth ten million instead of thirty. That's exactly the ten million I owe Mauler, and that's what he wants overnight.

PACKERS: If you're doing this, making things hard for Cridle,
Whose affiliates we are not, then you're well aware
That this concerns us too. You're stripping
All business bare: the fault is yours
If our cans of meat are as cheap as sand,
Because you ruined Lennox with cheap cans!

MAULER: You shouldn't have gone and slaughtered so many cattle,
You raving butchers! Now I want my money;
Though you should all go begging, I must have
My money! I have other plans.

STOCKBREEDERS: Lennox smashed! And Cridle groggy! And Mauler
Pulls all his money out!

SMALL SPECULATORS: Oh, as for us, the little speculators,
Nobody cares. They scream when they see
The colossus topple, but don't see where it falls,
Whom it strikes down. Mauler! Our money!
    PACKERS: Eighty thousand cans at 50, but fast!
    WHOLESALERS: Not a single one! (*Silence. The drumming of
the* BLACK STRAW HATS *and* JOAN's *voice are heard.*)
    JOAN: Pierpont Mauler! Where is Mauler?
    MAULER: What's that drumming? Who
Is calling my name?
Here, where every man
Shows his bare chops all smeared with blood!
        (*The* BLACK STRAW HATS *march in. They sing their war-
        chant.*)
    BLACK STRAW HATS (*singing*): Attention, pay attention!
There is a man who's falling!
There is a cry for help!
There is a woman calling!
Halt the autos, stop all traffic!
Men falling all around us and no one looks their way!
Is there no sight in your eye?
Say hello to your brother, not just any guy!
Get up from where you've dined—
Is there no thought in your mind
For the starving folk nearby?
I hear you say: it will always be the same,
The injustice of the world will still remain.
But we say this to you: You've got to march
And leave your cares and help with might and main
And bring up tanks and cannon too
And airplanes there shall be
And battleships over the sea
To conquer a plate of soup, poor brother, just for you.
You've all got to lend us a hand
And it must be today
For the army of the good
Is not a vast array.
Forward march! Eyes right! Rifles ready to fire!
Men falling all around us and no one looks their way!
        (*Meanwhile the Exchange battle has continued. But
        laughter, prompted by exclamations, is spreading toward
        the front of the scene.*)
    PACKERS: Eighty thousand cans at half price, but fast!

WHOLESALERS: Not a single one!
PACKERS: Then we're finished, Mauler!
JOAN: Where is Mauler?
MAULER: Don't go, Slift! Graham, Meyers,
Stay there in front of me.
I don't want to be seen here.
STOCKBREEDERS: Not a steer to be sold in Chicago any
more
This day spells ruin for all of Illinois
With mounting prices you prodded us on into raising steers
And here we stand with steers
And no one will buy them.
Mauler, you dog, you are to blame for this disaster.
MAULER: Enough of business. Graham! My hat. I've got to
go.
A hundred dollars for my hat.
CRIDLE: Oh, damn you to hell. (*Exit.*)
JOAN (*behind* MAULER): Now, you stay here, Mr. Mauler,
and listen to what I have to say to you. It is something you all
may hear. Quiet! Yes, indeed, you hardly think it right for us
Black Straw Hats to turn up like this in the dark hidden places
where you do your business! I've been told about the kind of
things you do here, how you make meat more and more
expensive by your carryings-on and subtle trickery. But if you
ever supposed you could keep it all concealed, then you're on
the wrong track, now and on the Day of Judgment, for then it
will be revealed, and how will you look then, when our Lord
and Saviour has you walk up in a row and asks with His big
eyes, "Well, where are my steers? What have you done with
them? Did you make them available to the people at prices
within their reach? What has become of them, then?" And
when you stand there embarrassed, groping for excuses, the
way you do in your newspapers, which don't always print the
truth either, then the steers will bellow at your backs in all the
barns where you keep them tucked away to make prices go
sky-high, and by their bellowing they will bear witness against
you before Almighty God! (*Laughter.*)
STOCKBREEDERS: We stockbreeders see nothing funny in
that!
Dependent on weather, summer and winter, we stand
Considerably nearer the Lord of old.
JOAN: And now an example. If a man builds a dam against
the unreasonable water, and a thousand people help him with

the labor of their hands, and he gets a million for it, but the dam breaks as soon as the water rises and everybody working on it and many more are drowned—what kind of man is he who builds a dam like that? You may call him a businessman or a rascal, depending on your views, but we tell you he's a numskull. And all you men who make bread dear and life a hell for human beings, so that they all become devils, you are numskulls, wretched, stingy numskulls and nothing else!

WHOLESALERS (*shouting*): Because of your unscrupulous
Juggling with prices and filthy lust for profit
You're bringing on your own ruin!
Numskulls!

PACKERS (*shouting back*): Numskulls yourselves!
Nothing can be done about crises!
Unshakable above our heads
Stands economic law, the not-to-be-known.
Terrible is the cyclic recurrence
Of natural catastrophes!

STOCKBREEDERS: Nothing to be done about your hold on
our throats?

That's wickedness, calculated wickedness!

JOAN: And why does this wickedness exist in the world? Well, how could it be otherwise? Naturally, if a man has to smash his neighbor's head for a ham sandwich so that he can satisfy his elementary needs, brother striving with brother for the bare necessities of life, how can the sense of higher things help being stifled in the human heart? Why not think of helping your neighbor simply as serving a customer? Then you'll understand the New Testament in a flash, and see how fundamentally modern it is, even today. Service! Why, what does service mean if not charity—in the true meaning of the word, that is! Gentlemen, I keep hearing that the poor haven't enough morals, and it's true, too. Immorality makes its nest down there in the slums, with revolution itself for company. I simply ask you: Where are they to get morals from, if they have nothing else? Where can they get anything without stealing it? Gentlemen, there is such a thing as moral purchasing-power. Raise moral purchasing-power, and there's your morality. And I mean by purchasing-power a very simple and natural thing—that is, money, wages. And this brings me back to the practical point: if you go on like this you'll end by eating your own meat, because the people outside haven't got any purchasing power.

STOCKBREEDERS (*reproachfully*): Here we stand with steers
And nobody can afford them.

JOAN: But you sit here, you great and mighty men, thinking that no one will ever catch you at your tricks, and refusing to know anything about the misery in the world outside. Well then, just take a look at them, the people whom your treatment has brought to this condition, the people you will not admit to be your brothers! Come out now, you weary and heavy-laden, into the light of day. Don't be ashamed! (JOAN *shows to the Exchange* CROWD *the* POOR PEOPLE *she has brought along with her.*)

MAULER (*shouting*): Take them away! (*He faints.*)

A VOICE (*rear*): Pierpont Mauler has fainted!

THE POOR PEOPLE: He's the one to blame for everything! (*The* PACKERS *attend to* MAULER.)

PACKERS: Water for Pierpont Mauler!
A doctor for Mauler!

JOAN: If you, Mauler, showed me the wickedness
Of the poor, now I show you
The poverty of the poor, for they live far away from you
And that puts beyond their reach goods they cannot do
without—
The people out of sight, whom you
Hold down in poverty like this, so weakened and so urgently
In need of unobtainable food and warmth that they
Can be just as far away from any claim
To higher things than the lowest gluttony, the beastliest habits.
       (MAULER *comes to.*)

MAULER: Are they still here? I implore you, send them away.

PACKERS: The Black Straw Hats? You want them sent away?

MAULER: No, those others, behind them.

SLIFT: He won't open his eyes before they get out.

GRAHAM: Can't bring yourself to look at them, eh? But it
was you
Who brought them to this state.
Shutting your eyes won't rid you of them,
Far from it.

MAULER: I beseech you, send them away! I'll buy!
Listen, all of you: Pierpont Mauler's buying!
So that these people may get work and go.

Eight weeks' production in cans of meat—
I'll buy it!

PACKERS: He's bought! Mauler has bought!

MAULER: At today's prices!

GRAHAM (*holding him up*): And what about back stocks?

MAULER (*lying on the floor*): I'll buy 'em.

GRAHAM: At 50?

MAULER: At 50!

GRAHAM: He's bought! You heard it, he has bought!

BROKERS (*shouting through megaphones, rear*): Pierpont
Mauler keeps the meat market going. According to contract,
he's taking over the meat-ring's entire stock, at 50, as of today,
besides two months' production, starting today, also at 50. The
meat-ring will deliver at least four hundred tons of canned
meat to Pierpont Mauler on November 15.

MAULER: But now, my friends, I beg you, take me away.
(MAULER *is carried out*.)

JOAN: That's fine, now have yourself carried out!
We work at our mission jobs like plough-horses
And this is the kind of thing you do up here!
You had your man tell me I shouldn't say a thing.
Who are you, I'd like to know,
To try to muzzle the Lord in His goodness? You shouldn't
even
Muzzle the ox that's yoked to the thresher!
And speak I will.
(*To the* POOR PEOPLE.)
You'll have work again on Monday.

POOR PEOPLE: We've never seen such people anywhere. But
we'd prefer them to the two that were standing beside him.
They have a far worse look than he does.

JOAN: Now sing, as a farewell song, "Who Ever Feels the
Lack of Bread."

BLACK STRAW HATS (*singing*): Who ever feels the lack of
bread
Once he's given the Lord his bond?
A man will never be in need
If he stays within God's grace.
For how shall snow fall on him there?
And how shall hunger find that place?

WHOLESALERS: The fellow's sick in his head. This country's
stomach

Has eaten too much meat from cans and it's fighting back.
And he has meat put into cans
That no one will buy. Cross out his name!
    STOCKBREEDERS. Come on, up with those prices, you lousy
                                  butchers!
Until you double livestock prices
Not an ounce will be delivered, for you need it.
    PACKERS: Keep your filth to yourselves! We will not buy.
For the contract which you saw agreed on here
Is a mere scrap of paper. The man who made it
Was not in his right mind. He couldn't raise
A cent from Frisco to New York
For that kind of business.   (*Exeunt* PACKERS.)
    JOAN: Well, anyone who is really interested in God's word
and what He says and not just in what the ticker tape says—
and there must be some people here that are respectable and
conduct their business in a God-fearing way, we have nothing
against that—well, he's welcome to visit our Divine Service
Sunday afternoon in Lincoln Street at two P.M. Music from
three o'clock, no entrance charge.
    SLIFT (*to the* STOCKBREEDERS): What Pierpont Mauler
                                promises he fulfills.
Breathe freely now! The market's getting well!
You who give bread and you to whom it's given,
At last the doldrums have been overcome!
They menaced confidence, and even concord.
You who give work, and you to whom it's given,
You're moving in and opening wide the gates!
Sensible counsel, sensibly adopted,
Has got the upper hand of foolishness.
The gates are opening! The chimney's smoking!
It's work you've both been needing all the time.
    STOCKBREEDERS (*placing* JOAN *up on the steps*): Your
                    speech and presence made a great impression
On us stockbreeders and many a man
Was deeply moved, for we
Have terrible sufferings too.
    JOAN: You know, I have my eye
On Mauler, he has woken up, and you,
If there's something you need to help you out,
Then come with me, that he may aid you also,
For from now on he shall not rest
Till everyone is helped.

For he's in a position to help: so
Let's go after him.
(*Exeunt* JOAN *and* BLACK STRAW HATS, *followed by the* STOCK-
BREEDERS.)

6. THE CRICKET CAUGHT

(*The City. The broker* SULLIVAN SLIFT'*s house, a small one
with two entrances.*)

MAULER (*inside the house, talking to* SLIFT): Barricade the
door, turn on all the lights there are—then take a good look
at my face, Slift, and see if it's true that anybody could tell
by it.

SLIFT: Tell what by it?

MAULER: My business!

SLIFT: A butcher's? Mauler, why did you fall down when
she talked?

MAULER: What did she say? I did not hear it,
For behind her there stood such people with such ghastly faces
Of misery—misery that comes
Before a wrath that will sweep us all away—
That I saw nothing more. Slift,
I will tell you what I really think
About this business of ours.
It can't go on this way, nothing but buying and selling
And one man coldly stripping off another's skin:
There are too many people howling with pain
And they are on the increase.
That which falls into our bloody cellars
Is past all consolation:
When they get hold of us they'll slap us against the pavement
Like rotten fish. All of us here,
We're not going to die in our beds. Before
We get that far they will stand us up against walls
In throngs, and cleanse the world of us and
Our hangers-on.

SLIFT: They have upset you! (*Aside.*) I'll make him eat a
rare steak. His old weakness has come over him again. Maybe
he'll come to his senses after enjoying some raw meat. (*He
goes and broils* MAULER *a steak on a gas stove.*)

MAULER: I often ask myself why
I'm moved by that fool talk, worlds away,
The cheap, flat chitter-chatter they study up . . .
Of course, it's because they do it for nothing, eighteen hours a
                                                        day and
In rain and hunger.
    SLIFT: In cities which are burning down below
And freezing up on top, there are always people
Who'll talk of this and that—details that aren't
In perfect order.
    MAULER: But what is it they're saying? In these cities, inces-
                                                            santly
On fire, in the downward rush
Of howling humanity,
Surging toward hell without respite
For years on end, if I hear a voice like that—
Foolish, of course, but quite unlike a beast's—
I feel as if I'd been cracked on the backbone with a stick
Like a leaping fish.
But even this has only been evasion until now, Slift,
For what I fear is something other than God.
    SLIFT: What is it?
    MAULER: Not what is above me
But what is below me! What stands in the stockyards and
                                                        cannot
Last through the night and will still—I know—
Rise up in the morning.
    SLIFT: Won't you eat a little meat, my dear Pierpont?
Think, now you can do it with a clear conscience again, for
from this day onward you won't have anything to do with
cattle-murder.
    MAULER: Do you think I should? Perhaps I could.
I ought to be able to eat now, oughtn't I?
    SLIFT: Have a bite to eat and think over your situation. It's
not very satisfactory. Do you realize that today you bought up
everything there is in cans? Mauler, I see you engrossed in the
contemplation of your noble nature, allow me to give you a
concise account of your situation, the external, the unimportant one. The main point is that you've taken one hundred and
fifty tons of stocks away from the meat-ring. You'll have to
get rid of these in the next few weeks on a market that can't
swallow one more can even today. You've paid 50 for them,

but the price will go down at least to 30. On November 15,
when the price is 30 or 25, the meat-ring will deliver four
hundred tons to you at 50.

MAULER: Slift! I'm done for!
I'm finished. I've gone and bought up meat.
Oh, Slift, what have I done!
Slift, I've loaded myself with all the meat in the world.
Like Atlas I stumble, cans by the ton on my shoulders,
All the way down to join the people who sleep
Under bridges. Only this morning
Many men were about to fall, and I
Went to see them fall and laugh at them
And tell them not a soul
Would be fool enough to buy meat in cans now
And while I stand there I hear my own voice saying:
I'll buy it all.
Slift, I've gone and bought meat, I'm done for.

SLIFT: Well, what do you hear from your friends in New
York?

MAULER: That I ought to buy meat.

SLIFT: You ought to do what?

MAULER: Buy meat.

SLIFT: Then why are you yammering because you have
bought it?

MAULER: Yes, they told me I ought to buy meat.

SLIFT: But you have bought meat!

MAULER: Yes, that is so, I did buy meat, but I bought it
Not because of the letter that said I should
(That's all wrong anyhow, just armchair theory)
Not from any low motives, but because
That person gave me such a shock, I swear
I barely riffled through the letter, it only came this morning.
Here it is. "Dear Pierpont——

SLIFT (*reads on*): —today we are able to inform you that
our money is beginning to bear fruit. Many Congressmen are
going to vote against tariffs, so it seems advisable to buy meat,
dear Pierpont. We shall write you again tomorrow."

MAULER: This bribery, too, is something
That shouldn't happen. How easily a war
Might start from a thing like that, and thousands bleed
For filthy lucre. Oh, my dear Slift, I feel
That nothing good can come of news like this.

SLIFT: That would depend on who had written the letters.

Bribing, abolishing tariffs, making wars—
Not everybody can do that. Are these people all right?
    MAULER: They're solvent.
    SLIFT: But who are they? (MAULER *smiles*.)
Then prices might go up after all?
Then we'd be off the hook.
That might be a prospect if it wasn't for the farmers—
By offering all their meat, only too eagerly,
They'd bring prices crashing down again. No, Mauler,
I don't understand that letter.
    MAULER: Think of it this way: a man has committed theft
And is caught by a man.
Now if he doesn't knock the other man down
He's done for; if he does, he's out of the woods.
The letter (which is wrong) demands (so as to be right)
A misdeed like that.
    SLIFT: What misdeed?
    MAULER: The kind I could never commit. For from now on
I wish to live in peace. If they want to profit
By their misdeeds—and they will profit—
They need only buy up meat wherever they see it,
Beat into the stockbreeders' heads the fact
That there's too much meat around and mention
The Lennox shutdown and take
Their meat away from them. This above all:
Take the stockbreeders' meat from them . . . but then
They'll be duped all over again . . . no, I'll have nothing
To do with that.
    SLIFT: You shouldn't have bought meat, Pierpont.
    MAULER: Yes, it's a bad business, Slift.
I'm not going to buy so much as a hat or a shoe
Until I get out of this mess, and I'll be happy
If I have a hundred dollars when I do.
    (*Sound of drums.* JOAN *approaches, with the* STOCK-
    BREEDERS.)
    JOAN: We'll lure him out of his den the way you catch a
cricket. You stand over there, because if he hears me singing
he'll try to get out the other way, to avoid meeting me again:
I'm a person he doesn't care to see. (*She laughs.*) And so are
the people who are with me. (*The* STOCKBREEDERS *take up a
position in front of door, right.* JOAN, *in front of door, left.*)
Please come out, Mr. Mauler, I must talk to you about the terrible condition of the stockbreeders of Illinois. I also have sev-

eral workers with me—they want to ask you when you're going to reopen your factory.

MAULER: Slift, where's the other exit? I don't want to run into her again, still less the people she has with her. I'm not opening any factories now, either.

SLIFT: Come out this way. (*They go through the interior to door, right.*)

STOCKBREEDERS (*in front of door, right*): Come on out, Mauler, our troubles are all your fault, and we are more than ten thousand Illinois stockbreeders who don't know whether they're coming or going. So buy our livestock from us!

MAULER: Shut the door, Slift! I'm not buying.
With the whole world's canned meat around my neck,
Now should I buy the cattle on the dog-star?
It's as if a man should go to Atlas when
He can barely drag the world along, and say:
"They need another carrier on Saturn."
Who's going to buy the livestock back from me?

SLIFT: The Grahams, if anybody will—they need it!

JOAN (*in front of door, left*): We're not leaving the place until the stockbreeders get some help.

MAULER: Most likely the Grahams, if anybody, they need livestock. Slift, go out and tell them to let me have two minutes to think things over. (SLIFT *goes and returns.*)

SLIFT (*to the* STOCKBREEDERS): Pierpont Mauler wishes to give careful consideration to your request. He asks for two minutes' thinking time. (*Re-enters the house.*)

MAULER: I'm not buying. (*He starts figuring.*) Slift, I'm buying. Slift, bring me anything that looks like a hog or a steer, I'll buy it, whatever smells of lard, I'll buy it, bring every grease-spot, I'm the buyer for it, and at today's price too, at 50.

SLIFT: Not a hat will you buy, Mauler, but
All the cattle in Illinois.

MAULER: Yes, I'll still buy that. Now it's decided, Slift. Take A. (*He draws an A on the closet door.*)
A man makes a mistake, let that be A,
He did it because his feelings overcame him,
And now he goes on to do B, and B's wrong too
And now the sum of A and B is right.
Ask the stockbreeders in, they're very nice people,
Badly in need and decently clothed and not
The sort of folk that scare you when you see them.

SLIFT (*stepping out in front of the house; to the* STOCK-BREEDERS): To save Illinois and avert ruin from its farmers and stockbreeders, Pierpont Mauler has decided to buy up all the livestock on the market.

STOCKBREEDERS: Long live Pierpont Mauler! He's saved the livestock trade! (*They enter the house.*)

JOAN (*calling after them*): Tell Mr. Mauler that we, the Black Straw Hats, thank him for this in the name of the Lord. (*To the* WORKERS.) If the people who buy cattle and the people who sell cattle are satisfied, then there'll be bread once more for you too.

7. THE EXPULSION OF THE MONEY-CHANGERS FROM THE TEMPLE

(*The Black Straw Hats' Mission. The* BLACK STRAW HATS, *sitting at a long table, are counting out from their tin boxes the widows' and orphans' mites they have collected.*)

BLACK STRAW HATS (*singing*): Gather the pennies of widows
and orphans with song!
Great is the need
They have no roof or bread
But Almighty God
Won't let them go hungry long.

PAULUS SNYDER (*Major of the* BLACK STRAW HATS, *getting up*): Very little, very little. (*To some* POOR FOLK *in the background, among them* MRS. LUCKERNIDDLE *and* GLOOMB.) You here again? Don't you ever leave this place? There's work at the stockyards again, you know!

MRS. LUCKERNIDDLE: Where? The yards are shut down.

GLOOMB: We were told they would open up again, but they haven't.

SNYDER: Well, don't go too near the cash-box. (*He motions them still further back.* MULBERRY, *the landlord, enters.*)

MULBERRY: Say, what about my rent?

SNYDER: My dear Black Straw Hats, my dear Mulberry, my honored listeners! As to this troublesome problem of financing our operations—anything that's good speaks for itself, and needs propaganda more than anything—hitherto we have aimed our appeals at the poor, indeed the poorest, on the assumption that they, being most in need of God's help, were the people most likely to have a bit left over for Him, and that their sheer numbers would produce the desired effect. To our regret, it has been borne in upon us that these very classes manifest an attitude of reserve toward God that is quite beyond explanation. Of course, this may be due to the fact that they have nothing. Therefore, I, Paulus Snyder, have issued an invitation in your name to Chicago's wealthy and prosperous citizens, to help us launch a major offensive next Saturday against the unbelief and materialism of the city of Chicago, primarily against the lower orders. Out of the proceeds we shall also pay our dear landlord, Mr. Mulberry, the rent he is so kindly deferring for us.

MULBERRY: It would certainly be very welcome, but please don't worry about it.   (*Exit.*)

SNYDER (*to the* POOR PEOPLE): Well, now go happily about your work and be sure to clean the front steps. (*Exeunt* BLACK STRAW HATS.) Tell me, are the locked-out workers in the stockyards still standing there patiently, or have they begun to talk like rebels?

MRS. LUCKERNIDDLE: They've been squawking pretty loud since yesterday, because they know the factories are getting orders.

GLOOMB: Many are saying already that they won't get any more work at all if they don't use force.

SNYDER (*to himself*): A good sign. The meat kings will be more likely to come and listen to our appeal if they're driven in by stones. (*To the* POOR PEOPLE.) Couldn't you split our wood, at least?

POOR PEOPLE: There isn't any more, Major. (*Enter* CRIDLE, GRAHAM, SLIFT, MEYERS.)

MEYERS: You know, Graham, I keep asking myself where that livestock can be hiding out.

GRAHAM: That's what I'm asking too, where can that livestock be hiding out?

SLIFT: So am I.

GRAHAM: Oh, you too? And I guess Mauler is too, eh?

SLIFT: I guess he is.

MEYERS: Somewhere some swine is buying everything up.
Someone who knows quite well that we're committed
By contract to deliver meat in cans
And so need livestock.

SLIFT: Who can it be?

GRAHAM (*hitting him in the stomach*): You cur, you! Don't play any tricks on us there, and tell Pierpy not to either! That's a vital spot!

SLIFT (*to* SNYDER): What do you want of us?

GRAHAM (*hitting him again*): What do you think they want, Slift? (SLIFT, *with exaggerated mockery, makes the gesture of handing out money.*) You said it, Slift!

MEYERS (*to* SNYDER): Fire away. (*They sit down on the prayer benches.*)

SNYDER (*in the pulpit*): We Black Straw Hats have heard that fifty thousand men are standing around in the stockyards without work. And that some are beginning to grumble and say: "We'll have to help ourselves." Aren't your names beginning to be called as the ones to blame for fifty thousand men being out of work and standing idly in front of the factories? They'll end by taking the factories away from you and saying: "We'll act the way the Bolsheviks did and take the factories into our own hands so that everybody can work and eat." For the story is getting around that unhappiness doesn't just come like the rain but is made by certain persons who get profit out of it. But we Black Straw Hats try to tell them that unhappiness does come down like the rain, no one knows where from, and that they are destined to suffering and there's a reward for it shining at the end of the road.

PACKERS: Why mention rewards?

SNYDER: The reward we speak of is paid out after death.

PACKERS: How much will it cost?

SNYDER: Eight hundred dollars a month, because we need hot soup and loud music. We also want to promise them that the rich will be punished—when they're dead, of course. (*The* FOUR *laugh noisily.*) All that for a mere eight hundred a month!

GRAHAM: You don't need that much, man. Five hundred.

SNYDER: Well, we could get along with seven hundred and fifty, but then——

MEYERS: Seven hundred and fifty. That's better. Let's make it five hundred.

GRAHAM: You do need five hundred, certainly. (*To the* OTHERS.) They've got to get that.

MEYERS (*front*): Out with it, Slift, you fellows have that livestock.

SLIFT: Mauler and I have not bought one cent's worth of livestock, as true as I'm sitting here. The Lord's my witness.

MEYERS (*to* SNYDER): Five hundred dollars, eh? That's a lot of money. Who's going to pay it?

SLIFT: Yes, you'll have to find someone who will give it to you.

SNYDER: Yes, yes.

MEYERS: That won't be easy.

GRAHAM: Come on, Slift, cough it up; Pierpy has the livestock.

SLIFT (*laughing*): A bunch of crooks, Mr. Snyder. (*All laugh except* SNYDER.)

GRAHAM (*to* MEYER): The man has no sense of humor. Don't like him.

SLIFT: The main point is, man, where do you stand? On this side of the barricades, or the other?

SNYDER: The Black Straw Hats stand above the battle, Mr. Slift. This side. (*Enter* JOAN.)

SLIFT: Why, here's our sainted Joan of the Livestock Exchange!

THE PACKERS (*shouting at* JOAN): We're not satisfied with you, can't you tell Mauler something from us? You're supposed to have some influence with him. They say he eats out of your hand. Well, the market is so short of livestock that we have to keep an eye on him. They say you can bring him round to doing whatever you want. Have him get that livestock out. Listen, if you'll do this for us we're willing to pay the Black Straw Hats' rent for the next four years.

JOAN (*has seen the* POOR PEOPLE *and is shocked*): Why, what are you doing here?

MRS. LUCKERNIDDLE (*coming forward*): The twenty dinners
                                      are all eaten now.
Please don't get angry because I'm here again.
It's a sight I would be glad enough to spare you.
That's the awful thing about hunger: no sooner
Is it satisfied than back it comes again.

GLOOMB (*coming forward*): I know you, it was you I tried
                                      to talk
Into working on that slicer that tore my arm off.
I could do worse things than that today.

JOAN: Why aren't you working? I did get work for you.

MRS. LUCKERNIDDLE: Where? The stockyards are closed.

GLOOMB: We were told they would open up again, but they haven't.

JOAN (*to the* PACKERS): So they're still waiting, are they?
                              (*The* PACKERS *say nothing.*)

And I thought they had been provided for!
It's been snowing on them now for seven days
And the very snow that kills them cuts them off
From every human eye. How easily
I forgot what everyone likes to forget for the peace of his
mind!
If one man says things are all right again, no one looks into
them.
(*To the* PACKERS.) But surely Mauler bought meat from you?
He did it at my request! And now you still refuse to open up
your factories?

CRIDLE, GRAHAM, MEYERS: That's quite right, we wanted to
open up.

SLIFT: But first of all you wanted to leap at the farmers'
throats!

CRIDLE, GRAHAM, MEYERS: How are we to do any slaugh-
tering when there's no livestock?

SLIFT: When Mauler and I bought meat from you we took
it for granted you would start employment going again so that
the workers would be able to buy meat. Now who will eat the
meat we got from you? For whom did we buy meat if con-
sumers can't pay for it?

JOAN: Look, if you people have control of all the equipment your employees use in your all-powerful factories and
plants, then the least you could do would be to let them in, if
they're kept out it's all up with them, because there is a sort of
exploitation about the whole thing, and if a poor human creature is tormented till the blood comes, and can think of no
way out but to take a club and bash his tormentor's head in,
then it scares the daylights out of you, I've noticed that, and
then you think religion's fine and it's supposed to pour oil on
the troubled waters, but the Lord has His pride too, and He
won't pitch in and clean your pigsties for you all over again.
And I run around from pillar to post, thinking: "If I help you
people on top, the people under you will also be helped. It's all
one in a way, and the same strings pull it," but I was a prize
fool there. If a man wants to help folks that are poor it seems
he'd better help them get away from you. Is there no respect
left in you for anything that wears a human face? Some day,
maybe, you won't rate as human beings either, but as wild
animals that will simply have to be slaughtered in the interest
of public order and safety! And still you dare to enter the
house of God, just because you own that filthy Mammon,
everybody knows where you got it and how, it wasn't come by

honestly. But this time, by God, you've come to the wrong people, we'll have to drive you out, that's all, yes, drive you out with a stick. Come on, don't stand there looking so stupid, I know human beings shouldn't be treated like steers, but you aren't human beings, get out of here, and fast, or I'll lay hands on you, don't hold me back, I know what I'm doing, it's high time I found out. (JOAN *drives them out, using as a stick a flag held upside down. The* BLACK STRAW HATS *appear in the doorways.*) Get out! Are you trying to turn the house of God into a stable? Another Livestock Exchange? Get out! There's nothing for you here. We don't want to see such faces here. You're unworthy and I'm showing you the door. For all your money!

THE FOUR: Very well. But forty months' rent goes with us—simply, modestly, irretrievably. We need every cent of it anyway: we're facing times as terrible as the livestock market has ever seen. (*Exeunt.*)

SNYDER (*running after them*): Please stay, gentlemen! Don't go, she has no authority at all! A crazy female! She'll be fired! She'll do whatever you want her to do.

JOAN (*to the* BLACK STRAW HATS): Well, that certainly wasn't very smart at a time like this, what with the rent and all. But we can't think about that now. (*To* LUCKERNIDDLE *and* GLOOMB.) Sit down back there, I'll bring you some soup.

SNYDER (*returning*): Go on, make the poor your guests
And regale them with rainwater and fine speeches
When there's really no pity for them up above,
Nothing but snow!
You followed your very first impulses,
Utterly without humility! It is so much easier
Simply to drive the unclean out with arrogance.
You're squeamish about the bread we have to eat,
Much too curious how it's made, and still
You want to eat it! Now, woman above the world,
Get out in the rain and face the snowstorm in righteousness!

JOAN: Does that mean I'm to take off my uniform?

SNYDER: Take off your uniform and pack your bags! Get out of this house and take along the riff-raff you brought us. Nothing but riff-raff and scum followed you in here. Now you'll be in that class yourself. Go and get your things.

JOAN (*goes out and comes back dressed like a country servant, carrying a little suitcase*): I'll go find rich man
Mauler, he is not
Without fear or good will, and ask his help.

I won't put on this coat or black straw hat
Ever again or come back to this dear house
Of songs and awakenings till
I bring in rich man Mauler as one of us,
Converted from the ground up.
What if their money has eaten away
Their ears and human faces like a cancer
Making them sit apart but loftily
Beyond the reach of any cry for help!
Poor cripples!
There must be *one* just man among them!   (*Exit.*)
   SNYDER: Poor simpleton!
You're blind to this: set up in huge formations
The givers and the takers of work
Confront one another:
Warring fronts: irreconcilable.
Run to and fro between them, little peacemaker, little me-
                                  diator—
Be useful to neither and go to your doom.
   MULBERRY (*entering*): Have you the money now?
   SNYDER: God will still be able to pay for the definitely
scanty shelter He has found on earth, I said scanty, Mr.
Mulberry.
   MULBERRY: Yes, pay, that's the ticket, that's the problem!
You said the right word then, Snyder! If the Lord in His
goodness pays, good. But if He doesn't pay, not so good. If the
Lord in His goodness doesn't pay His rent, He'll have to get
out, and what's more, He'll have to go on Saturday night, eh,
Snyder?   (*Exit.*)

8. PIERPONT MAULER'S SPEECH
ON THE INDISPENSABILITY
OF CAPITALISM AND RELIGION

   MAULER: Well, Slift, today's the day
When our good friend Graham and all his crew
Who wanted to wait for the lowest livestock prices
Will have to buy the meat they owe us.
   SLIFT: It will cost them more, because anything
The Chicago market can show in the way of lowing cattle
Is ours now.

Every hog they owe us
They'll have to buy from us, and that's expensive.
   MAULER: Now, Slift, let loose all your wholesalers!
Let them torment the livestock market with demands
For everything that looks like hogs and cattle
And so make prices go up and up.
   SLIFT: What news of your Joan? There's a rumor
Around the Livestock Exchange that you slept with her.
I did my best to scotch it. She hasn't been heard of
Since that day she threw us all out of the temple:
It's as though black roaring Chicago had swallowed her up.
   MAULER: I liked her action very much,
Throwing you all out like that. Yes, that girl's afraid of
                           nothing.
And if I'd been along on that occasion
She'd have thrown me out with the rest and that's
What I like about her and that house of hers,
The fact that people like me are impossible there.
Force the price up to 80, Slift. That will make those Grahams
Rather like mud you stick your foot into
Merely to see its shape again.
I won't let an ounce of meat go by:
This time I'll rip their skins off for good and all,
In accordance with my nature.
   SLIFT: I'm delighted, Mauler, that you've shaken off
Your weakness of the past few days. And now
I'll go and watch them buy up livestock.   (*Exit.*)
MAULER: It's high time this damn town had its skin ripped
                               off
And those fellows taught a thing or two
About the meat market: what if they do yell "Crime!"
   (*Enter* JOAN, *carrying a suitcase.*)
   JOAN: Good morning, Mr. Mauler. You're a hard man to
find. I'll just leave my things over there for the time being.
You see, I'm not with the Black Straw Hats any more. We had
an argument. So I thought, well, I'll go and see how Mr.
Mauler's doing. Having no more of that wearing mission work
to do, I can pay more attention to the individual. So, to begin
with, I'm going to occupy myself with you a little, that is, if
you'll let me. You know, I've noticed that you are much more
approachable than many other people. That's a fine old mohair
sofa you have there, but why do you have a sheet on it?—and
it isn't made up properly, either. So you sleep in your office? I
thought surely you would have one of those great big palaces.

(MAULER *says nothing.*) But you're quite right, Mr. Mauler, to be a good manager in little things too, being a meat king. I don't know why, but when I see you I always think of the story about the Lord when He visited Adam in the Garden of Eden and called out, "Adam, where are you?" Do you remember? (*Laughs.*) Adam is standing behind a bush with his arms up to the elbows in a doe, and he hears the voice of God just like that, with blood all over him. And so he acts as if he wasn't there. But God doesn't give up, and calls out again, "Adam, where are you?" And then Adam says, faintly and blushing crimson: "This is the time you pick to visit me, right after I've killed a doe. Oh, don't say a word, I know I shouldn't have done it." But your conscience is clear, Mr. Mauler, I hope.

MAULER: So you're not with the Black Straw Hats any more?

JOAN: No, Mr. Mauler, and I don't belong there either.

MAULER: Then what have you been living on? (JOAN *says nothing.*) I see. Nothing. How long ago did you leave the Black Straw Hats?

JOAN: Eight days ago.

MAULER (*turns away and weeps*): So greatly changed, and
in a mere eight days!
Where has she been? To whom has she been talking? What
was it
That drew those lines around her mouth?
The city she has come from
Is a thing I do not yet know.
(*He brings her food on a tray.*) I see you very much changed. Here's something to eat, if you like. I'm not hungry myself.

JOAN (*looking at the food*): Mr. Mauler, after we drove the rich people out of our house—

MAULER: Which amused me very much, and seemed the right thing to do—

JOAN: The landlord, who lives on the rent we pay, gave us notice to get out next Sunday.

MAULER: Indeed! So the Black Straw Hats are poorly off financially?

JOAN: Yes, and that's why I thought I'd go and see Mr. Mauler. (*She begins to eat hungrily.*)

MAULER: Don't you fret. I'll go into the market and get you the money you need. Yes, I'll do that, I'll get hold of it whatever it costs me, even if I have to slice it right out of the

city's skin. I'll do it for you. Money's expensive, of course, but
I'll produce it. That will be to your liking.

JOAN: Yes, Mr. Mauler.

MAULER: So you go and tell them: "The money is on the
way. It will be there by Saturday. Mauler will get hold of it.
He just left for the livestock market to dig it up." That matter
of the fifty thousand didn't go so well, not exactly as I wanted
it. I was unable to get them work immediately. But for you
I'll make an exception, and your Black Straw Hats shall be
spared, I'll get the money for you. Run and tell them.

JOAN: Yes, Mr. Mauler!

MAULER: There, I've put it in writing. Take it.
I too am sorry that the men are waiting for work
In the stockyards and not very good work at that.
Fifty thousand men
Standing around in the stockyards, not even leaving at night.
     (JOAN *stops eating.*)
But that's the way this business goes:
It's to be or not to be—a question whether
I am to be the best man in my class or go
The dark and dreary way to the stockyards myself.
Also, the scum is filling up the yards again
And making trouble.
And now—I'll tell you the simple truth—I would have liked
To hear you say that what I do is right
And my business is natural: so
Tell me for sure that it was on your advice
I ordered meat from the meat-ring and from
The stockbreeders too, thus doing good; then,
Because I know well that you are poor and right now
They're trying to take away the very roof over your heads,
I'll add a contribution for that too, as token
Of my goodwill.

JOAN: So the workers are still waiting in front of the slaughterhouses?

MAULER: Why are you set against money? and yet look
So very different when you haven't any?
What do you think about money? Tell me,
I want to know; and don't get wrong ideas,
The way a fool will think of money as
Something to be doubted. Consider the reality,
The plain truth, not pleasant maybe, but still
True for all that: everything is unsteady and the human race

Is exposed to luck, you might say, to the state of the weather,
But money's a means of making some improvement—even if
only
For certain people—apart from that, what a structure!
Built up from time immemorial, over and over again
Because it keeps collapsing, but still tremendous: demanding
sacrifice,
Very hard to set up, continually set up
With many a groan, but still inescapably
Wresting the possible from a reluctant planet,
However much or little that may be; and accordingly defended
At all times by the best. Just think, if I—
Who have much against it, and sleep badly—
Were to desert it, I would be like a fly
Ceasing to hold back a landslide. There and then
I would become a nothing and it would keep on going over
me.

For otherwise everything would have to be overturned
And the architect's design fundamentally altered
To suit an utterly different, incredible, new valuation of man,
Which you people don't want any more than we do, for it
would take effect
With neither us nor God, who would have no function left
And be dismissed accordingly. Therefore you really ought to
Collaborate with us, and even if you make no sacrifices—
We don't ask that of you—still sanction the sacrifices:
In a word, you really ought
To set God up once more—
The only salvation—and
Beat the drum for Him so that He may
Gain a foothold in the regions of misery and His
Voice may ring out among the slaughterhouses.
That would suffice.
        (*Holding out the note to her.*)
Take what you get, but know the reason
Before you take it! Here's the voucher, this is four years' rent.
    JOAN: Mr. Mauler, I don't understand what you have been
saying
And do not wish to either.
(*Rising.*) I know I should be overjoyed to hear
That God is going to be helped, only
I belong to those for whom
This does not mean real help. And to whom
Nothing is offered.

MAULER: If you take the money to the Straw Hats you can
                                                    also
Stay in their house again: this living
On nothing is not good for you. Believe me,
They're out for money, and so they should be.
    JOAN: If the Black Straw Hats
Accept your money they are welcome to it,
But I will take my stand among the people waiting in the
                                            stockyards,
Until the factories open up again, and
Eat nothing but what they eat and if
They are offered snow, then snow,
And the work they do I will do also, for I have no money
                                                    either
And no other way to get it—honorably, anyhow—
And if there is no more work, then let there be none
For me either, and
You, who live on poverty and
Cannot bear to see the poor and condemn
Something you do not know and make arrangements
So as not to see what sits condemned,
Abandoned in the slaughterhouses, disregarded,
If you want to see me again
Come to the stockyards.   (*Exit.*)
    MAULER: Tonight then, Mauler,
Get up every hour and look out of the window
To see if it's snowing, and if it is
It will be snowing on the girl you know.

9. JOAN'S THIRD DESCENT INTO THE DEPTHS: THE SNOWFALL

(*Stockyards district.*)

    JOAN: Listen to the dream I had one night
A week ago.
Before me in a little field, too small
To hold the shade of a middle-sized tree, hemmed in
By enormous houses, I saw a bunch
Of people: I could not make out how many, but
There were far more of them than all the sparrows

That could find room in such a tiny place—
A very thick bunch indeed, so that
The field began to buckle and rise in the middle
And the bunch was suspended on its edge, holding fast
A moment, quivering: then, stirred
By the intervention of a word—uttered somewhere or other,
Meaning nothing vital—it began to flow.
Then I saw processions, streets, familiar ones, Chicago! you!
I saw you marching, then I saw myself:
I, silent, saw myself striding at your head
With warlike step and bloodstains on my brow
And shouting words that sounded militant
In a tongue I did not know; and while many processions
Moved in many directions all at once
I strode in front of many processions in manifold shapes:
Young and old, sobbing and cursing,
Finally beside myself! Virtue and terror!
Changing whatever my foot touched,
Causing measureless destruction, visibly influencing
The courses of the stars, but also changing utterly
The neighborhood streets familiar to us all—
So the procession moved, and I along with it,
Veiled by snow from any hostile attack,
Transparent with hunger, no target,
Not to be hit anywhere, not being settled anywhere;
Not to be touched by any trouble, being accustomed
To all. And so it marches, abandoning the position
Which cannot be held: exchanging it for any other one.
That was my dream.
Today I see its meaning:
Before tomorrow morning we
Will start out from these yards
And reach their city, Chicago, in the gray of dawn,
Displaying the full range of our wretchedness in public places,
Appealing to whatever resembles a human being.
What will come after, I do not know.

    (*Livestock Exchange.*)
    MAULER (*to the* PACKERS): My friends in New York have
                                   written me to say
That the tariff in the south
Was repealed today.
  PACKERS: This is awful, the tariff law gone and here we are
Without any meat to sell! It's been sold already

At a low price and now we are asked to buy meat when it's
                                                    going up!

STOCKBREEDERS: This is awful, the tariff law gone and here
                                                    we are

Without any livestock to sell! It's already been sold
At a low price!

SMALL SPECULATORS: Awful! Eternally inscrutable
Are the eternal laws
Of human economics!
Without warning
The volcano erupts and lays the country waste!
Without an invitation
The profitable island rises from the barren seas!
No one is told, no one is in the know! But the last in line
Is bitten by the dogs!

MAULER: Well, seeing that livestock is being demanded
In cans at an acceptable price
I now request you to hand over quickly
The canned meat I am supposed to get from you
According to contract.

GRAHAM: At the old price?

MAULER: As the contract specified, Graham.
Four hundred tons, if I remember correctly
A moment when I was not myself.

PACKERS: How can we take livestock now, with prices
                                                    rising?

Someone has made a corner in it,
Nobody knows who—
Release us from the contract, Mauler!

MAULER: Unfortunately I must have those cans. But there is
Still livestock enough, a bit expensive, granted, but
Livestock enough. Buy it up!

PACKERS: Buy livestock now? The hell with it!

(*A little tavern in the stockyards district.* MEN *and*
WOMEN WORKERS, JOAN *among them.—A group of*
BLACK STRAW HATS *enter.* JOAN *rises and makes frantic
gestures at them during what follows.*)

JACKSON (*after a hurried song*): Brother, why won't you
                              eat the bread that Jesus gives?
See how happy and glad are we.
It's because we have found the Lord Jesus, Lord of all our
                                                    lives.

Hurry, come to Him heartily!
Hallelujah!

> (*One of the* BLACK STRAW HAT GIRLS *talks to the*
> WORKERS, *making side remarks to her* COMRADES.)

BLACK STRAW HAT: (It's no use, is it?) Brothers and sisters,
I too used to stand sadly by the wayside, just as you are, and
the old Adam in me cared for nothing but meat and drink, but
then I found my Lord Jesus, and then it was so light and glad
inside me, but now (They aren't listening at all!) if I just think
real hard about my Lord Jesus, who redeemed us all by His
suffering in spite of our many wicked deeds, then I stop
feeling hungry and thirsty, except for our Lord Jesus' word.
(No use.) Where the Lord Jesus is, there is not violence, but
peace, not hate but love. (It's quite hopeless!)

BLACK STRAW HATS: Hallelujah! (JACKSON *passes the box
around. Nothing is put into it.*) Hallelujah!

JOAN: If only they wouldn't stay here in the cold
Making all that nuisance and talking, talking!
Really, now I can hardly bear
To hear the words
That once were dear and pleasant to me! If only a voice,
Some remnant inside them, would say:
There's snow and wind here, be quiet here!

A WOMAN: Oh, let them be. They have to do this to get a bit
of warmth and food. I wish I was in their shoes.

MRS. LUCKERNIDDLE: That was nice music!

GLOOMB: Nice and short.

MRS. LUCKERNIDDLE: But they really are good people.

GLOOMB: Good and brief, short and sweet.

WOMAN WORKER: Why don't they give us a real talk, and
convert us?

GLOOMB (*making a gesture of paying out money*): Can you
keep the pot boiling, Mrs. Swingurn?

WOMAN WORKER: The music is very pretty but I was expecting them to give us a plate of soup, maybe, seeing they
had brought a pot along.

WORKER (*surprised at her*): No kidding, you thought that?

JOAN: Are there no people here with any enterprise?

A WORKER: Yes, the Communists.

JOAN: Aren't they people who incite to crime?

THE WORKER: No.

(*Livestock Exchange.*)

PACKERS: We're buying livestock! Yearlings!

Feeders! Calves! Steers! Hogs!

Offers, please!

STOCKBREEDERS: There isn't any! We've sold whatever was salable.

PACKERS: Isn't any? The depots are bursting with cattle.

STOCKBREEDERS: Sold.

PACKERS: To whom? (*Enter* MAULER. *Milling around him.*)

Not a steer to be found in Chicago!

You'll have to give us more time, Mauler.

MAULER: You'll deliver your meat as agreed. (*Going over to* SLIFT.) Squeeze 'em dry.

A STOCKBREEDER: Eight hundred Kentucky steers at 400.

PACKERS: Impossible. 400! Are you crazy?

SLIFT: I'll take them. At 400.

STOCKBREEDERS: Eight hundred steers sold to Sullivan Slift for 400.

PACKERS: It's Mauler! What did we say? He's the one!

You crooked hound! He makes us deliver canned meat

And buys up livestock! So we have to buy from him

The meat we need to fill his cans!

You filthy butcher! Here, take *our* flesh, hack yourself off a slice!

MAULER: If you're an ox you shouldn't be surprised when people's appetites grow with looking at you.

GRAHAM (*makes as if to attack* MAULER): He's got it coming, I'll settle his hash!

MAULER: All right, Graham, now I demand your cans.

You can stuff yourself into them.

I'll teach you the meat business, you

Traders! From now on I get paid, and well paid,

For every hoof, every calf from here to Illinois*

And so I'll offer five hundred steers at 56 to start with.

(*Dead silence.*)

And now, in view of the weak demand, seeing nobody here

Needs livestock,

I want 60! And don't forget my cans, either!

(*Another part of the stockyards. Placards are inscribed: "Solidarity with Locked-out Stockyard Workers!" "All out for General Strike!" In front of a shed two* MEN *from the central union office are speaking to a group of* WORKERS. *Enter* JOAN.)

---

* *Sic.* [Translator's note.]

JOAN: Are these the people who lead the movement of the unemployed? I can help, too. I've learned to speak in streets and meeting-halls, even big ones, I have no fear of insults and I think I can explain a good thing well. Because, as I see it, something's got to be done right away. I have some suggestions to make, too.

A LABOR LEADER: Listen, all. So far the meat gang hasn't shown the least inclination to open up its factories. At first it seemed that the exploiter Pierpont Mauler was all out for a reopening because he wants from the meat gang huge quantities of canned meat that they owe him by contract. Then it became clear that the meat they need for packing is in Mauler's own hands and he won't even consider letting it go. Now we know that if things are left up to the meat gang we workers will never all get back into the slaughterhouses, and never at the old wages. With things in this pass we've got to realize that nothing can help us but the use of force. The city utilities have promised to join the general strike by the day after tomorrow at the latest. Now this news must be spread in all parts of the stockyards; if it isn't, there's a danger that the masses will be led by some rumor or other to leave the yards, and then be forced to yield to the meat gang's terms. So these letters, stating that the gasworks, waterworks and power stations are going to help us by going on strike, must be handed out to delegates who will be awaiting our password in different parts of the stockyards at ten o'clock tonight. Stick that in your overalls, Jack, and wait for the delegates in front of Mother Schmitt's canteen. (*A* WORKER *takes the letter and leaves.*)

SECOND WORKER: Give me the one for the Graham works, I know them.

LEADER: 26th Street, corner Michigan Park. (WORKER *takes letter and leaves.*) 13th Street by the Westinghouse Building. (*To* JOAN.) Well, and who may you be?

JOAN: I was fired from the job I had.

LEADER: What job?

JOAN: Selling magazines.

LEADER: Who were you working for?

JOAN: I'm a peddler.

A WORKER: Maybe she's a stool-pigeon.

THE OTHER LEADER: Who can tell what she will do with the letter we give her?

FIRST LEADER: Nobody. (*To* JOAN.)
A net with a torn mesh

Is of no use:
The fish swim through at that spot
As though there were no net.
Suddenly all its meshes
Are useless.

JOAN: I used to sell papers on 44th Street. I'm no stool-pigeon. I'm for your cause heart and soul.

SECOND LEADER: Our cause? Why, isn't it your cause?

JOAN: It certainly isn't in the public interest for the factory owners to put all those people in the street just like that. Why, it makes you think the poverty of the poor is useful to the rich! You might say poverty is all their doing! (*The* WORKERS *laugh uproariously.*) It's inhuman, that's what it is! I even have people like Mauler in mind when I say that. (*Renewed laughter.*) Why do you laugh? I don't think you have any right to be malicious and to believe without proof that a man like Mauler can be inhuman.

SECOND LEADER: Not without proof! You can give the letter to her, all right.

FIRST LEADER: Go to Storehouse Five at the Graham plant. When you see three workers come up and look around them, ask if they are from the Cridle plant. This letter is for them.

(*Livestock Exchange.*)

SMALL SPECULATORS: Quotations going down! The packing
                                              plants in peril!
What will become of us, the stockholders?
The man with small savings who gave his last cent
For the middle class, which is weakened anyway?
A man like Graham ought to be
Torn to shreds before he makes waste paper
Out of the note with our share marked on it, the one
We earned from his bloody cellars.
Buy that livestock, buy it at any price!

(*Throughout this scene the names of firms suspending payment are being called out.* "Suspending payment: Meyer & Co.," *etc.*)

PACKERS: We can do no more, the price is over 70.

WHOLESALERS: Mow 'em down, they won't buy, the high-hats.

PACKERS: Two thousand steers demanded at 70.

SLIFT (*to* MAULER, *beside a column*): Shove 'em up.

MAULER: I see that you have not stood by your part
Of the contract I drew up with you that day

In the wish to create employment. And now I hear
They're still standing around out there in the yards. But
You're going to regret it: out with the canned meat
Which I have bought!

GRAHAM: There's nothing we can do: meat has completely
Vanished from the market!
I'll take five hundred steers at 75.

SMALL SPECULATORS: Buy them, you greedy hounds!
They won't buy! They'd rather hand over
The packing plants.

MAULER: We shouldn't push it up any higher, Slift.
They're powerless now.
They are meant to bleed, but they mustn't perish;
If they go out we're goners too.

SLIFT: There's life in them yet, put it up a notch.
Five hundred steers at 77.

SMALL SPECULATORS: 77. Did you hear that? Why
Didn't you buy at 75? Now
It's gone to 77 and still climbing.

PACKERS: We get 50 from Mauler for the cans and can't
pay Mauler 80 for the livestock.

MAULER (*to a group of* MEN): Where are the people I sent
to the stockyards?

A MAN: There's one.

MAULER: Well, let's have it.

FIRST DETECTIVE (*reports*): Those crowds, Mr. Mauler, you
can't see the end of them. If you called the name of Joan, ten
or maybe a hundred would answer. The mob sits there and
waits, without a face or a name. Besides, nobody can hear just
one man's voice and there are far too many people running
around asking after relatives they've lost. Serious unrest prevails in the sections where the unions are at work.

MAULER: Who's at work? The unions? And the police let
them agitate? Damn it all! Go and call the police right away,
mention my name, ask them what we're paying taxes for.
Insist that the troublemakers get their heads cracked, speak
plainly to them. (*Exit* FIRST DETECTIVE.)

GRAHAM: Oh, give us a thousand at 77, Mauler;
If it knocks us out, it's the end of us.

SLIFT: Five hundred to Graham at 77. All the rest at 80.

MAULER (*returning*): Slift, this business no longer entertains
me.
It might take us too far.
Go up to 80, then let it go at 80.

I'll hand it over and let them go.
Enough's enough. The town needs a breathing-spell.
And I have other worries.
Slift, this throat-squeezing isn't as much fun
As I thought it would be.
(*Seeing the* SECOND DETECTIVE.) Did you find her?

SECOND DETECTIVE: No, I saw no woman in a Black Straw
Hat uniform. There are a hundred thousand people standing
around in the stockyards; besides, it's dark and that biting
wind drowns your voice. Also, the police are clearing the
yards and shots are being fired already.

MAULER: Shots? At whom? Oh, yes, of course.
It seems strange—you can't hear a thing in this place.
So she's not to be found, and shots are being fired?
Go to the phone booths, look for Jim and tell him
Not to call, or people will say again
That we demanded the shooting.   (*Exit* SECOND DETECTIVE.)

MEYERS: Fifteen hundred at 80!

SLIFT: Not more than five hundred at 80!

MEYERS: Five thousand at 80, you cutthroat!

MAULER (*returning to the column*): Slift, I feel unwell. Let
up, will you?

SLIFT: I wouldn't think of it. There's life in them yet. And if
you start to weaken, Mauler, I'll shove them up higher.

MAULER: Slift, I need a breath of air. You carry on
The business. I can't. Carry it on
The way I would. I'd rather give it all away
Than have more things happen because of me!
Go no higher than 85! But manage it
The way I would. You know me.   (*Exit.*)

SLIFT: Five hundred steers at 90!

SMALL SPECULATORS: We heard that Mauler was willing
To sell at 85. Slift has no authority.

SLIFT: That's a lie! I'll teach you
To sell meat in cans and then
Not have any meat!
Five thousand steers for 95!
      (*Uproar.*)

      (*Stockyards. Many* PEOPLE *waiting,* JOAN *among them.*)
PEOPLE: Why are you sitting here?

JOAN: I have to deliver a letter. Three men are supposed to
come by here. (*A group of* REPORTERS *comes up, led by a*
MAN.)

MAN (*pointing to* JOAN): That's the one. (*To* JOAN.) These people are reporters.

REPORTERS: Hello, are you Joan Dark, the Black Straw Hat?

JOAN: No.

REPORTERS: We have heard from Mauler's office that you've sworn not to leave the stockyards before the plants open up. We have it, you can read it here, in big front-page headlines. (JOAN *turns away*.) Our Lady of the Stockyards Avers God Solidly Behind Stockyard Workers.

JOAN: I said no such thing.

REPORTERS: We can assure you, Miss Dark, that public opinion is on your side. All Chicago sympathizes with you, except a few unscrupulous speculators. Your Black Straw Hats will reap terrific success from all this.

JOAN: I'm not with the Black Straw Hats any more.

REPORTERS: That can't be. For us, you belong to the Black Straw Hats. But we don't want to disturb you, we'll keep well in the background.

JOAN: I would like you to go away. (*They sit down some distance off.*)

WORKERS (*in the stockyards, rear*): Before our need is at its
worst
They will not open the factories.
When misery has mounted
They will open up.
But they must answer us.
Do not go before they answer.

COUNTER-CHORUS (*also rear*): Wrong! Let misery mount,
They will not open up,
Not before profits mount.
If you wait for the answer
You will get the answer:
Out of cannon and machine guns
They will answer you.
And we advise you to wait
For this answer: do not go.

JOAN: I see this system and on the surface
It has long been familiar to me, but not
In its inner meaning! Some, a few, sit up above
And many down below and the ones on top
Shout down: "Come on up, then we'll all
Be on top," but if you look closely you'll see
Something hidden between the ones on top and the ones below

That looks like a path but is not a path—
It's a plank and now you can see it quite clearly,
It is a seesaw, this whole system
Is a seesaw, with two ends that depend
On one another, and those on top
Sit up there only because the others sit below,
And only as long as they sit below;
They'd no longer be on top if the others came up,
Leaving their place, so that of course
They want the others to sit down there
For all eternity and never come up.
Besides, there have to be more below than above
Or else the seesaw wouldn't hold. A seesaw, that's what it is.

(*The* REPORTERS *get up and move upstage, having received some news.*)

A WORKER (*to* JOAN): Say, what have you to do with those fellows?

JOAN: Nothing.

WORKER: But they were talking with you.

JOAN: They took me for someone else.

OLD MAN (*to* JOAN): You sure look frozen. Like a swig of whiskey? (JOAN *drinks.*) Stop! Stop! That's no mean shot you took!

A WOMAN: Scandalous!

JOAN: Did you say something?

WOMAN: I said, scandalous! Guzzling all the old man's whiskey!

JOAN: Shut your trap, you silly old thing. Hey, where's my shawl? They've gone and swiped it again. That's the last straw! Going and stealing my shawl, on top of everything else! Now who's got my shawl? Give it here pronto. (*She grabs a sack off the head of the* WOMAN *standing next to her. The* WOMAN *resists.*) Oh, so it's you. No lies! Gimme that sack.

THE WOMAN: Help, she's killing me!

A MAN: Shut up! (*Someone throws her a rag.*)

JOAN: For all you people care, I might be sitting around in
          this draft nekkid.

It wasn't as cold as this in my dream.
When I came to this place with brave plans,
Fortified by dreams, I still never dreamed
That it could be so cold here. Now the only thing I miss
Of all I have is my nice warm shawl.
You may well be hungry, you have nothing to eat,
But they're waiting for me with a bowl of soup.

You may well freeze
But I can go into the warm room any time,
Pick up the flag and beat the drum
And speak about HIM who lives in the clouds. After all,
What did you leave? What I left
Was no mere occupation, it was a calling,
A noble habit, but a decent job as well
And daily bread and a roof and a livelihood.
Yes, it seems almost like a play,
Something undignified, for me to stay in this place
Without extremely pressing need. And yet
I may not go, and still—
I'll be frank about it—fear tightens round my throat
At the thought of his not eating, not sleeping, not knowing
Where you are,
Habitual hunger, helpless cold and—
Worst of all—wanting to get away.
   WORKER: Stay here! Whatever happens,
Do not break ranks!
Only if you stand together
Can you help each other!
Realize that you have been betrayed
By all your public sponsors
And your unions, which are bought.
Listen to no one, believe nothing
But test every proposal
That leads to genuine change. And above all learn:
It will only work out by force
And only if you do it yourselves.
   (*The* REPORTERS *return.*)
   REPORTERS: Hey there, gal, you've had sensational success:
we've just found out that the millionaire Pierpont Mauler, who
has vast quantities of livestock in his hands now, is releasing
livestock to the slaughterhouses in spite of rising prices. This
being so, work will be resumed in the yards tomorrow.
   JOAN: Oh, what good news! The ice has thawed in their
                           hearts. At least
The one just man among them
Has not failed us. Appealed to as a man,
He has answered as a man.
There *is* kindness in the world.
   (*Machine guns rat-a-tat in the distance.*)
What's that noise?

REPORTER: Those are army machine guns. The army has orders to clear the stockyards because the agitators who are inciting to violence will have to be silenced now that the slaughterhouses are to be reopened.

A WORKER: You just take it easy and stay here. The stockyards are so big it'll take the army hours to get this far.

JOAN: How many people are there in them now, anyway?

REPORTER: There must be a hundred thousand.

JOAN: So many?
Oh, what an unknown school, an unlawful space
Filled up with snow, where hunger is teacher and unpreventably
Need speaks about necessity.
A hundred thousand pupils, what are you learning?

WORKERS (*rear*): If you stay together
They will cut you to pieces.
We advise you to stay together!
If you fight
Their tanks will grind you to pulp.
We advise you to fight!
This battle will be lost
And maybe the next
Will also be lost.
But you are learning to fight
And realizing
That it will only work out by force
And only if you do it yourselves.

JOAN: Stop: no more lessons
So coldly learned!
Do not use force
To fight disorder and confusion.
Certainly the temptation is tremendous!
Another night like this, another wordless
Oppression like this, and nobody
Will be able to keep quiet. And certainly
You have already stood together
On many a night in many a year and learned
To think coldly and terribly.
Certainly acts of violence and weakness
Are matching one another in the dark
And unsettled business is piling up.
But the meal that's cooking here—who
Will be the ones to eat it?

I'm leaving. What's done by force cannot be good. I don't belong with them. If hunger and the tread of misery had taught me violence as a child, I would belong to them and ask no questions. But as it is, I must leave. (*She remains seated.*)

REPORTERS: Our advice to you is, leave the stockyards right now. You made a big hit, but that's over and done with.

(*Exeunt. Shouting, rear, spreading forward. The* WORKERS *rise.*)

A WORKER: They're bringing the men from headquarters. (*The two* LEADERS *of the workers are brought forward, handcuffed.*)

A WORKER (*to his handcuffed* LEADER): Never mind, William, not every day is dark.

ANOTHER (*shouting after the* GROUP): Bloody brutes!

WORKERS: If they think they're stopping anything that way, they're on the wrong track. Our men have taken care of everything.

(*In a vision* JOAN *sees herself as a criminal, outside the familiar world.*)

JOAN: The men who gave me the letter! Why are they
Handcuffed? What is in the letter?
I could do nothing
That would have to be done by force and
Would provoke force. A person like that would stand
Against his fellow man, full of deceit
And beyond the range of any settlement
That human beings usually make.
Not belonging, he would lose his way
In a world no longer familiar to him. The stars
Would hurtle over his head breaking
The ancient rules. Words
Would change meaning for him. Innocence
Would abandon one who was constantly persecuted.
He can look at nothing without suspicion.
I could not be like that. So I'm leaving.
For three days Joan was seen
In Packingtown, in the stockyards swamps
Going down, downward from level to level
To clear the mud away, to manifest
To the lowest. Three days walking
Down the slope, growing weaker on the third
And finally swallowed by the swamp. Say:
"It was too cold."

(*She gets up and goes. Snow begins to fall.*)

A WORKER: I thought right away that she'd take off when
the real snow came. (*Three* WORKERS *come by, look around
for someone, fail to find him, and leave.*)

(*As it grows dark, a writing appears.*)
"The snow is starting to fall,
Will anyone stay at all?
They'll stay today as they've stayed before—
Stony ground and folk that are poor."

PIERPONT MAULER CROSSES THE BOUNDARY OF POVERTY

(*A Chicago street corner.*)

MAULER (*to one of the* DETECTIVES): No further, let's turn
back now, what do you say?
Admit it: you laughed. I said, "Let's turn back now,"
And you laughed. They're shooting again.
Seems to be some resistance, eh? But this is what
I wanted to impress upon you: think nothing of it
If I turned back a couple of times
As we came nearer the stockyards. Thinking
Is nothing. I'm not paying you to think.
I probably have my reasons. I'm known down there.
Now you are thinking again. Seems I've taken
A couple of nitwits along. Anyway,
Let's turn back. I hope the person I was looking for
Has listened to the voice of sense and left that place
Where hell appears to be breaking loose.

(*A* NEWSBOY *goes by.*)
Give me those papers! let's see how the livestock market is
going!

(*He reads, and turns pale.*)
Well, something's happened here that changes things:
It's printed here, black on white, that livestock
Is down to 30 and not a head is being sold,
That's what it says here, black on white, the packers
Are ruined and have left the livestock market.
And it also says that Mauler and Slift, his friend,
Are the worst hit of all. That's what it says and it means
That things have reached a point that certainly was not striven
for,
But is greeted with sighs of relief. I can help them no fur-
ther—
I freely offered
All my livestock for the use of any man that wanted it
And nobody took it and so I am free now
And without pretensions and hereby

I dismiss you in order to cross
The boundary of poverty, for I no longer require your ser-
vices.
Henceforth nobody will want to knock me down.
THE TWO DETECTIVES: Then we may go.
MAULER: You may indeed, and so may I, wherever I want.
Even to the stockyards.
And as for the thing made of sweat and money
Which we have erected in these cities:
It already seems as though a man
Had made a building, the largest in the world and
The most expensive and practical, but—
By an oversight, and because it was cheap—he used dog-shit
As its material, so that it would have been very difficult
To stay there and in the end his only glory was
That he had made the biggest stink in the world.
And anyone who gets out of a building like that
Should be a cheerful man.
A DETECTIVE (*departing*): So, he's finished.
MAULER: Bad luck may crush the man of humble size;
Me it must waft to spiritual skies.

(*A No-Man's-Land in the Stockyards.* JOAN, *hurrying
toward the city, overhears two passing* WORKERS.)
FIRST WORKER: First they let the rumor leak out that work
would start up again, full blast, in the stockyards; but now that
a part of the workers have left the yards to come back tomorrow morning, they're suddenly saying that the slaughterhouses won't be opened at all, because Mauler has ruined
them.
SECOND WORKER: The Communists were right. The masses
shouldn't have broken ranks. All the more so because all the
factories in Chicago would have all called a general strike for
tomorrow.
FIRST WORKER: We didn't know that.
SECOND WORKER: That's bad. Some of the messengers must
have failed us. A lot of people would have stayed put if they'd
known about it. Even in the teeth of the cops' violence.
(*Wandering to and fro,* JOAN *hears voices.*)
A VOICE: He who does not arrive
Can plead no excuse. The fallen man
Is not excused by the stone.
Let not even the one who does arrive
Bore us with reports of difficulties

But deliver in silence
Himself or what is entrusted to him.
>   (JOAN *has stood still and now runs in another direction.*)
>   A VOICE (JOAN *stands still*): We gave you orders
Our situation was critical
We did not know who you were
You might carry out our orders and you might
Also betray us.
Did you carry them out?
>   (JOAN *runs farther and is halted by another voice.*)
>   A VOICE: Where men are waiting, someone must arrive!
>   (*Looking around for an escape from the voices,* JOAN
>   *hears voices on all sides.*)
>   VOICES: The net with a torn mesh
Is of no use:
The fish swim through it at that point
As though there were no net.
Suddenly all its meshes
Are useless.
>   (JOAN *falls to her knees.*)
>   JOAN: Oh, truth, shining light! Darkened by a snowstorm in
>   an evil hour!
Lost to sight from that moment! Oh, how violent are snow-
                                                    storms!
Oh, weakness of the flesh! What would you let live, hunger?
What outlasts you, frost of the night?
I must turn back! (*She runs back.*)

10. PIERPONT MAULER HUMBLES HIMSELF AND IS EXALTED

(*The Black Straw Hats' Mission.*)

MARTHA (*to another* BLACK STRAW HAT): Three days ago a
messenger from Pierpont Mauler, the meat king, came to tell
us that he wishes to pay our rent and join us in a big campaign
for the poor.

MULBERRY: Mr. Snyder, it's Saturday evening. I'm asking
you to pay your rent, which is very low, or get out of my
building.

SNYDER: Mr. Mulberry, we expect Mr. Pierpont Mauler any minute now and he has promised us his support.

MULBERRY: Dick, old man, Albert, old man, put the furniture out in the street. (*Two* MEN *begin to move the furniture out.*)

BLACK STRAW HATS: Oh! They're taking the prayer bench! Their greedy grasp even threatens
Pipe organ and pulpit.
And louder still we cry:
Please, rich Mr. Mauler, come
And save us with your money!

SNYDER: Seven days now the masses have been standing
In rusting stockyards, cut off from work at last.
Freed from every kind of shelter they stand
Under rain and snow again, sensing above them
The zenith of an unknown decision.
Oh, dear Mr. Mulberry, give us hot soup now
And a little music and they'll be ours. In my head I see
The Kingdom of Heaven ready and waiting.
Just give us a band and some decent soup,
Really nourishing, and God will settle things
And all of Bolshevism, too,
Will have breathed its last.

BLACK STRAW HATS: The dams of faith have burst
In this Chicago of ours
And the slimy flood of materialism surges
Menacingly round the last of its houses.
Look, it's tottering, look, it's sinking!
Never mind—keep going—rich man Mauler's on the way!
He's started out already with all his money!

A BLACK STRAW HAT: Where can we put the public now, Major? (*Enter three* POOR PEOPLE, MAULER *among them.*)

SNYDER (*shouting at them*): Soup, that's all you want! No soup here! Just the Word of God! We'll get rid of them straight off when they hear that.

MAULER: Here are three men coming to their God.

SNYDER: Sit down over there and keep quiet. (*The three sit down. A* MAN *enters.*)

MAN: Is Pierpont Mauler here?

SNYDER: No, but we're expecting him.

MAN: The packers want to speak to him and the stock-breeders are screaming for him.   (*Exit.*)

MAULER (*facing* AUDIENCE): I hear they're looking for a
                                        man named Mauler.

I knew him: a numskull. Now they're searching
High and low, in heaven and in hell,
For that man Mauler who was dumber all his life
Than a dirty drink-sodden tramp.
> (*Rises and goes over to* BLACK STRAW HATS.)

I knew a man who once was asked
For a hundred dollars. And he had about ten million.
And he came along without the hundred but threw
The ten million away
And gave himself.
> (*He takes two of the* BLACK STRAW HATS *and kneels with
> them on the prayer bench.*)

I wish to confess my sins.
No one who ever knelt here, friends,
Was as humble as I am.

BLACK STRAW HATS: Don't lose confidence,
Don't be souls of little faith!
He's sure to come—already he's approaching
With all his money.

A BLACK STRAW HAT: Is he here yet?

MAULER: A hymn, I pray you! For my heart
Feels heavy and light at once.
> (*They intone a hymn. The* BLACK STRAW HATS *join in
> abstractedly, eyes on the door.*)

SNYDER (*bent over the account books*): I won't tell how this
                                               comes out.

Quiet!
Bring me the housekeeping record and the unpaid bills. I've
                                         got to that stage.

MAULER: I accuse myself of exploitation,
Misuse of power, expropriation of everybody
In the name of property. For seven days I held
The city of Chicago by the throat
Until it perished.

A BLACK STRAW HAT: That's Mauler!

MAULER: But at the same time I plead that on the seventh
                                                      day

I rid myself of everything, so that now
I stand before you without possessions.
Not guiltless, but repentant.

SNYDER: Are you Mauler?

MAULER: Yes, and torn to pieces by remorse.

SNYDER (*with a loud cry*): And without any money? (*To*

the BLACK STRAW HATS.) Pack up the stuff, I hereby suspend all payments.

MUSICIANS: If that's the man you were waiting for
To get the cash to pay us with
Then we can go. Good night.   (*Exeunt.*)

CHORUS OF BLACK STRAW HATS (*gazing after the departing*
                    MUSICIANS): We were awaiting with prayers
The wealthy Mauler, but into our house
Came the man converted.
His heart
He brought to us, but not his money.
Therefore our hearts are moved, but
Our faces are long.

(*Confusedly the* BLACK STRAW HATS *sing their last hymns
as they sit on their last chairs and benches.*)

BLACK STRAW HATS: By the waters of Lake Michigan
We sit down and weep.
Take the proverbs off the walls
Wrap the songbooks in the cover of the defeated flag
For we can pay our bills no more
And against us rush the snowstorms
Of approaching winter.

(*Then they sing "Go Into the Thick of the Fight."*
MAULER *joins in, looking over a* BLACK STRAW HAT's
shoulder.)

SNYDER: Quiet! Everybody out now—(*To* MAULER.)—espe-
                                             cially you!
Where is the forty months' rent from the unconverted
Whom Joan expelled? Look what she's driven in instead! Oh,
                                                        Joan,
Give me my forty months' rent again!

MAULER: I see you would like to build your house
In my shade. Well, for you a man
Is what can help you; likewise, for me
A man was only plunder. But even
If man were only what is helped,
There would be no difference. Then you'd need drowning men,
For then it would be your business
To be straws for them to clutch at. So all remains
Within the mighty orbit of wares, like that of the stars.
Such teaching, Snyder, would embitter many.
But I can see that as I am
I'm the wrong man for you.

(MAULER *makes to go, but the* MEAT KINGS *stop him at the door; they are all white as chalk.*)

PACKERS: Forgive us, noble Mauler, for seeking you out,
Disturbing you amid the involved emotions
Of your colossal head.
For we are ruined. Chaos is around us
And over us the zenith of an unknown intention.
What are you planning for us, Mauler?
What will your next step be? We're sensitive
To the blows you rain on our necks.

(*Enter the* STOCKBREEDERS *in great commotion, equally pale.*)

STOCKBREEDERS: Damnable Mauler, is this where you've
                                          sneaked off to?
You pay for our livestock, instead of getting converted!
Your money, not your soul! You would not need
To lighten your conscience in a place like this
If you hadn't lightened our pockets! Pay for our livestock!

GRAHAM (*stepping forward*): Permit us, Mauler, to give a
                                          brief account
Of the seven-hour battle which began this morning and ended
By plunging us all into the abyss.

MAULER: Oh, everlasting slaughter! Nowadays
Things are no different from ancient times
When they bloodied each other's heads with iron bars!

GRAHAM: Remember, Mauler, by our contract to deliver
Meat to you, you forced us to buy meat
In these of all times, and it had to be
From you, as only you had meat to sell.
Well, when you went away at noon, that Slift
Pulled the rope even tighter around our necks.
With harsh cries he kept on raising prices
Until they stood at 95. But then
A halt was called by the ancient National Bank.
Bleating with responsibility, the old crone dumped
Canadian yearlings on the chaotic market, and prices stood
                                          quivering.
But Slift—that madman!—scarcely had he seen
The handful of widely-travelled steers but he grabbed them at
                                          95,
As a drunkard who's already swilled an oceanful
And still feels thirsty greedily laps up one
Tiny drop more. The old crone shuddered at the sight.

But some people leaped to the beldame's side to hold her up—
Loew and Levi, Wallox and Brigham, the most reputable
firms—
And mortgaged themselves and all their possessions down to
the last eraser,
As a promise to bring forth the last remaining steer
From the Argentine and Canada within three days—they even
offered
To get hold of unborn ones, ruthlessly,
Anything that was steerlike, calfly, hoggish!
Slift yells: "Three days? No! Today, today!"
And shoves the prices higher. And in floods of tears
The banks threw themselves into the death-struggle,
Because they had to deliver the goods and therefore buy.
Sobbing, Levi himself punched one of Slift's brokers
In the belly, and Brigham tore his beard out
Screaming: NINETY-SIX! At that point
An elephant might have wandered in
And been crushed underfoot like a berry.
Even office-boys, seized with despair, bit one another
Without saying a word, as horses in olden times
Would bite each others' flanks among their fighting riders!
Unsalaried clerks, famous for lack of interest in business,
Were heard gnashing their teeth that day.
And still we bought and bought; we had to buy.
Then Slift said: ONE HUNDRED! You could have heard a
pin drop.

And as quietly as that the banks collapsed,
Like trampled sponges—formerly strong and firm,
Now suspending payment like respiration. Softly
Old Levi spoke, and all of us heard him: "Now
Our packing plants are yours, we can no longer
Fulfill our contracts," and so,
Packer after packer, they sullenly laid
The shut-down, useless packing plants at your feet—
Yours and Slift's—and went away;
And the agents and salesmen snapped their brief cases shut.
And at that moment, with a sigh as of liberation—
Since no more contracts compelled its purchase—
Livestock sank into the bottomless pit.
For unto prices it was given
To fall from quotation to quotation
As water hurtles from crag to crag

Deep down into the infinite. They didn't stop before 30.
And so, Mauler, your contract became invalid.
Instead of gripping our throats you have strangled us.
What does it profit a man to grip the throat of a corpse?

MAULER: So, Slift, that was how you managed the fight
I left on your hands!

SLIFT: Tear my head off.

MAULER: What good is your head?
I'll take your hat, that's worth five cents!
What is to become
Of all that cattle no one has to buy?

THE STOCKBREEDERS: Without becoming excited
We request you to tell us
Whether, when and with what
You wish to pay
For the bought but unpaid-for cattle.

MAULER: At once. With that hat and this boot.
Here is my hat for ten million, here
My first shoe for five. I need the other.
Are you satisfied?

THE STOCKBREEDERS: Alas, when moons ago
We led the frisky calf
And clean young steers,
Carefully fattened, by ropes to the station in far-off Missouri
The family yelled after us
And even after the rolling trains,
With voices broken by toil they yelled:
"Don't drink the money away, fellows, and
Let's hope prices will rise!"
What'll we do now? How
Can we go home? What
Shall we tell them
Showing the empty ropes
And empty pockets?
How can we go home in such a state, Mauler?

(MAN WHO WAS THERE BEFORE *enters.*)

MAN: Is Mauler here? There's a letter from New York for
him.

MAULER: I *was* the Mauler to whom such letters were addressed. (*Opens it, reads it aside.*) "Recently, dear Pierpont,
we wrote to tell you to buy meat. Today, however, we advise
you to arrive at a settlement with the stockbreeders and limit
the quantity of livestock, so as to give prices a chance to

recover. In that event we shall gladly be of service to you.
More tomorrow, dear Pierpont.—Your friends in New York."
No, no, that won't work.

GRAHAM: What won't work?

MAULER: I have friends in New York who claim to know a
way out. It doesn't seem feasible to me. Judge for yourselves.
(*Gives them the letter.*)
How completely different
Everything seems now. Give up the chase, my friends.
Your property is gone: you must grasp that, it is lost.
But not because we are no longer blest with earthly
Goods—not everyone can be that—
Only because we have no feeling for higher things.
That's why we're poor!

MEYERS: Who are these friends of yours in New York?

MAULER: Horgan and Blackwell. Sell. . . .

GRAHAM: Would that be Wall Street? (*Whispering spreads
through the gathering.*)

MAULER: The inward man, so cruelly crushed within us. . . .

PACKERS *and* STOCKBREEDERS: Noble Mauler, consent to
bring yourself

To descend to us from your lofty
Meditations! Think of the chaos
That would swoop on everything, and take up—
Since you are needed, Mauler—
The burden of responsibility again!

MAULER: I don't like to do it.
And I won't do it alone, for the grumbling in the stockyards
And the rat-tat-tat of machine guns
Still resound in my ears. It would only work
If it were sanctioned in a very grand style
And conceived as vital
To the public good.
Then it might work.
(*To* SNYDER.) Are there many Bible shops like this one?
Since you are needed, Mauler—

SNYDER: Yes.

MAULER: How are they doing?

SNYDER: Badly.

MAULER: Doing badly, but there are many of them.
If we promoted the cause of the Black Straw Hats
In a really big way—if you were equipped

With lots of soup and music
And suitable Bible quotations, even with shelter
In great emergencies—would you then speak
On our behalf, saying everywhere that we are good people?
Planning good things in bad times? For only
By taking extremest measures—measures that might seem
harsh
Because they affect some people, quite a few really,
In short: most people, nearly everybody—
Can we preserve this system now, the system
Of buying and selling which is here to stay
And also has its seamy side.

    SNYDER: For nearly everybody. I understand. We would.

    MAULER (*to the* PACKERS): I have merged your packing
plants

As one ring and am taking over
Half of the stocks.

    PACKERS: A great mind!

    MAULER (*to the* STOCKBREEDERS): My dear friends, listen!
    (*They whisper.*)

The difficulty which oppressed us is lifting.
Misery, hunger, excesses, violence
Have one cause only and the cause is clear:
There was too much meat. The meat market was
All stuffed up this year and so the price of livestock
Sank to nothing. Now, to maintain it,
We, packers and stockbreeders, have formed a united front
To set some limits to this unbridled breeding:
To restrict the livestock coming into market
And eliminate excess from the current supply. This means
Burning one-third of the livestock total.

    ALL: Simple solution!

    SNYDER (*saluting*): Might it not be possible—if all that
cattle

Is so worthless that it can be burned—
Just to give it to the many standing out there
Who could make such good use of it?

    MAULER (*smiling*): My dear Snyder, you have not grasped
The root of the situation. The many
Standing out there—*they are the buyers!*
(*To the* OTHERS.) It's hardly credible.
    (*All smile for a long time.*)

They may seem low, superfluous,
Indeed, burdensome sometimes, but it cannot elude
Profounder insight that *they* are the buyers!
Likewise—there are very many who do not understand this—
it is essential
To lock out a third of the workers.
It is also work that has clogged our market and therefore
It must be limited.

    ALL: The only way out!

    MAULER: And wages lowered!

    ALL: Columbus' egg!

    MAULER: All this is being done so that
In gloomy times of bloody confusion
Dehumanized humanity
When there is no end to the unrest in our cities
(For Chicago is again upset by talk of a general strike)
The brute strength of the short-sighted people
May not shatter its own tools and trample its own bread-bas-
kets underfoot,
But peace and order may return. That is why we are willing
To facilitate by generous contributions
The work by which you Black Straw Hats encourage order.
It's true that there ought to be people among you again
Like that girl Joan, who inspires confidence
By her mere appearance.

    A BROKER (*rushing in*): Glad tidings! The threatened strike
has been suppressed. They've jailed the criminals who im-
piously troubled peace and order.

    SLIFT: Breathe freely now! The market's getting well!
Again the doldrums have been overcome.
The difficult task has once again been done
And once again a plan is finely spun
And the world resumes the way we like it run.

    (*Organ.*)

    MAULER: And now, open wide your gates
Unto the weary and heavy laden and fill the pot with soup.
Tune up some music and we will sit
Upon your benches and be the first
To be converted.

    SNYDER: Open the doors! (*The doors are flung wide open.*)

    BLACK STRAW HATS (*singing, eyes on the door*): Spread the
net far out: they're bound to come!
They've just abandoned the last redoubt!

God's driving cold on them!
God's driving rain on them!
So they're bound to come! Spread the net far out!
Welcome! Welcome! Welcome!
Welcome to our humble home!

Bolt everything tight so that none will escape!
They're on their way down to us all right!
If they've no work to do
If they're deaf and blind too
Not one will escape! So bolt everything tight!
Welcome! Welcome! Welcome!
Welcome to our humble home!

Whatever may come, gather everything in!
Hat and head and shoe and leg and scamp and scum!
Its hat has gone sky-high
So it comes right in to cry!
Gather everything in, whatever may come!
Welcome! Welcome! Welcome!
Welcome to our humble home!

Here we stand! Watch them coming down!
Watch their misery drive them like animals to our hand!
Look, they're bound to come down!
Look, they're coming down!
They can't get away from this spot: here we stand!
Welcome! Welcome! Welcome!
Welcome to our humble home!

> (*Stockyards. Environs of Graham's Warehouse. The yards are almost empty. Only a few groups of* WORKERS *are still passing by.*)

JOAN (*coming up to ask*): Did three men go by here asking for a letter? (*Shouting from rear, spreading toward front. Then enter five* MEN *escorted by* SOLDIERS: *the two from the union central office and the three from the power stations. Suddenly one of the two stands still and speaks to the* SOL-DIERS.)

MAN: If you're taking us to jail now, there's something you ought to know. We did what we did because we are for you.

SOLDIER: Keep moving, if you're for us.

MAN: Wait a little!

SOLDIER: Getting scared, eh?

MAN: Yes, that too, but that's not what I'm talking about. I just want you to stand still a little so I can tell you why you have arrested us, because you don't know.

SOLDIERS (*laughing*): O.K., tell us why we arrested you.

MAN: Without property yourselves, you help men of property because you don't yet see any possibility of helping men without property.

SOLDIER: That's fine. Now let's move on.

MAN: Wait, I haven't finished the sentence: on the other hand, the working people in this town are starting to help the people without work. So the possibility is coming nearer. Now worry about that.

SOLDIER: I guess you want us to let you go, eh?

MAN: Didn't you understand me? We just want you to know that your time's coming soon too.

SOLDIERS: Can we go on now?

MAN: Yes, we can go on now. (*They move on.* JOAN *stays where she is, watching the arrested* MEN *go. Then she hears two* PEOPLE *talking beside her.*)

FIRST MAN: Who are those people?

SECOND MAN: Not one of them
Cared only for himself.
They ran without rest
To get bread for strangers.

FIRST MAN: Why without rest?

SECOND MAN: The unjust man may cross the street in the open, but the just man hides.

FIRST MAN: What's being done to them?

SECOND MAN: Although they work for low wages and are
useful to many men
Not one of them lives out the years of his life,
Eats his bread, dies contented
Or is buried with honors, but
They end before their time,
Struck down and crushed and covered with earth in shame.

FIRST MAN: Why don't we ever hear about them?

SECOND MAN: If you read in the papers that certain criminals have been shot or thrown into prison, they're the ones.

FIRST MAN: Will it always be like that?

SECOND MAN: No. (*As* JOAN *turns to go, she is accosted by the* REPORTERS.)

REPORTERS: Isn't this Our Lady of the Stockyards? Hi there! Things have gone wrong! The general strike was called off. The stockyards are opening up again, but only for two-thirds of the personnel and only at two-thirds' pay. But meat prices are going up.

JOAN: Have the workers accepted this?

REPORTERS: Sure. Only a part of them knew a general strike was being planned, and the cops drove that part out of the yards by force. (JOAN *falls to the ground.*)

11. DEATH AND CANONIZATION OF SAINT JOAN OF THE STOCKYARDS

(*The* BLACK STRAW HATS' *house is now richly furnished and decorated. Its doors are flung wide open; in ordered groups, the* BLACK STRAW HATS *with new flags, packers, stockbreeders and wholesalers stand waiting for the Gloombs and Luckerniddles.*)

SNYDER: Thus our task meets happy ending:
       God's foothold has been found again.
       For the highest good contending,
       We have faced the depths of pain.

       Both our mounting and descending
       Show what we can mean to you:
       Lo, at last the happy ending!
       Look, at last we've put it through!

   (*Enter a mass of* POOR PEOPLE, *with* JOAN *at their head, supported by two* POLICEMEN.)

POLICEMAN: Here is a homeless woman
We picked up in the stockyards
In a sick condition. Her
Last permanent residence was
Allegedly here.

   (JOAN *holds her letter high as though still anxious to deliver it.*)

JOAN: The man who has perished will never
Take my letter from me.
Small enough service to a good cause, the only service
Demanded of me my whole life long!—
And I did not perform it.

(*While the* POOR PEOPLE *sit down on the benches to get their soup,* SLIFT *consults with the* PACKERS *and* SNYDER.)

SLIFT: It's our own Joan. Why, her coming is like an answer to our prayers. Let's cover her with glory; by her philanthropic work in the stockyards, her championship of the poor, and even her speeches against us, she helped us over some really difficult weeks. She shall be our Saint Joan of the Stockyards! We will cultivate her as a saint and refuse her no jot of respect. The fact that she is shown under our auspices will prove that we hold humaneness in high regard.

MAULER: May the pure and childlike soul
Ever figure on our roll;
May our humble choir delight
In her singing clear and glad;
May she damn whatever's bad
And defend our every right.

SNYDER: Rise, Joan of the stockyards,
Champion of the poor,
Comforter of the lowest depths!

JOAN: What a wind in the depths! What is that shrieking
The snow is trying to hush?
Eat your soup, you!
Don't spill your last bit of warmth, you
Good-for-nothings! Eat your soup! If only I had lived
As tranquilly as a cow,
And yet delivered the letter that was entrusted to me!

BLACK STRAW HATS (*going up to her*): Sudden daylight
makes her ache
After nights of stupefaction!
Only human was your action!
Only human your mistake!

JOAN (*while the* GIRLS *dress her in the Black Straw Hat uniform again*): The roar of the factories is starting again,
you can hear it.
Another chance to stop it—wasted.
Again the world runs
Its ancient course unaltered.
When it was possible to change it
I did not come; when it was necessary
That I, little person, should help,
I stayed on the sidelines.

MAULER: Alas, that man cannot abide
In his distress the earthly bond,
But with swift and haughty stride

Rushes past the everyday
Which he thinks will turn him gray
Past his target and beyond
Into worlds outside his ken,
Endless worlds too high for men.

JOAN: I spoke in every market place
And my dreams were numberless but
I did harm to the injured
And was useful to those who harmed them.

BLACK STRAW HATS: Alas! All effort, sages write,
Achieves but patchwork, void of soul,
If matter make not spirit whole.

PACKERS: And ever 'tis a glorious sight
When soul and business unite!

JOAN: One thing I have learned and I know it in your stead,
Dying myself:
How can I say it—there's something inside you
And it won't come out! *What* do you know in your wisdom
That has no consequences?
I, for instance, did nothing.
Oh, let nothing be counted good, however helpful it may seem,
And nothing considered honorable except that
Which will change this world once for all: that's what it needs.
Like an answer to their prayers I came to the oppressors!
Oh, goodness without consequences! Intentions in the dark!
I have changed nothing.
Vanishing fruitless from this world
I say to you:
Take care that when you leave the world
You were not only good but are leaving
A good world!

GRAHAM: We'll have to see to it that her speeches only get
through if they are reasonable. We mustn't forget that she has
been in the stockyards.

JOAN: For there is a gulf between top and bottom, wider
Than between Mount Himalaya and the sea
And what goes on above
Is not found out below
Or what happens below, above
And there are two languages, above and below
And two standards for measuring
And that which wears a human face
No longer knows itself.

PACKERS *and* STOCKBREEDERS (*very loud, so as to shout*
                    JOAN *down*): Top and bottom must apply
For the building to be high
That's why everyone must stay
In the place where they belong
Day after day
Man must do what suits his stature
For if he forgets his nature
All our harmonies go wrong.
Underdogs have weight below,
The right man's right when up you go.
Woe to him who'd rouse that host—
Indispensable but
Demanding, not
To be done without
And aware of that—
Elements of the nethermost!
    JOAN: But those who are down below are kept below
So that the ones above may stay up there
And the lowness of those above is measureless
And even if they improve that would be
No help, because the system they have made
Is unique: exploitation
And disorder, bestial and therefore
Incomprehensible.
    BLACK STRAW HATS (*to* JOAN): Be a good girl! Hold your
tongue!
    PACKERS: Those who float in boundless spaces
Cannot rise to higher places,
For to climb you need a rung,
And to reach for things aloft
You must make a downward tread!
    MAULER: Action, alas, may break a head!
    BLACK STRAW HATS: Though your shoe is stained with gore
    PACKERS: Do not try to pull it off!
You will need it more and more.
    BLACK STRAW HATS: Keep conduct high and spirit young.
But do not forget to rue it!
    PACKERS: Do anything!
    BLACK STRAW HATS: But always do it
With a twinge of conscience, for—
Being given to contemplation
And to self-vituperation—
Your conscience will be sore!

Men of trade, be informed:
You cannot afford
To forget the splendid
Quite indispensable
Word of the Lord
Which is never ended
And ever transformed!

JOAN: Therefore, anyone down here who says there is a
God

When none can be seen,
A God who can be invisible and yet help them,
Should have his head knocked on the pavement
Until he croaks.

SLIFT: Listen, people, you've got to say something to shut
that girl up. You must speak—anything you like, but loud!

SNYDER: Joan Dark, twenty-five years old, stricken by pneumonia in the stockyards of Chicago, in the service of God: a
fighter and a sacrifice!

JOAN: And the ones that tell them they may be raised in
spirit

And still be stuck in the mud, they should have their heads
Knocked on the pavement. No!
Only force helps where force rules,
And only men help where men are.

(*All sing the first verse of the chorale in order to stop
JOAN's speeches from being heard.*)

ALL: Fill the full man's plate! Hosanna!
Greatness to the great! Hosanna!
To him that hath shall be given! Hosanna!
Give him city and state! Hosanna!
To the victor a sign from Heaven! Hosanna!

(*During these declamations loudspeakers begin to announce terrible news:*

POUND CRASHES! BANK OF ENGLAND CLOSES FOR FIRST
TIME IN 300 YEARS! EIGHT MILLION UNEMPLOYED IN
U.S.A.! FIVE YEAR PLAN A SUCCESS! BRAZIL POURS A
YEAR'S COFFEE HARVEST INTO OCEAN! SIX MILLION UNEMPLOYED IN GERMANY! THREE THOUSAND BANKS COLLAPSE IN U.S.A.! EXCHANGES AND BANKS CLOSED DOWN BY
GOVERNMENT IN GERMANY! BATTLE BETWEEN POLICE
AND UNEMPLOYED OUTSIDE FORD FACTORY IN DETROIT!
MATCH TRUST, BIGGEST IN EUPOPE, CRASHES! FIVE YEAR
PLAN IN FOUR YEARS!

Under the impression of this news those not engaged in declamation scream abuse at one another, as: "You slaughtered too much livestock, you rotten hog-butchers!" "You should have raised more stock, you lousy stock-breeders!" "You crazy money-grubbers, you should have employed more labor and handed out more pay-checks! Who else will eat our meat?" "It's the middleman that makes meat expensive!" "It's the grain racket that raises livestock prices!" "The railroads' freight rates are strangling us!" "The banks' interest rates are ruining us!" "Who can pay those rents for stables and silos?" "Why don't you start plowing under?" "We did, but you aren't!" "The guilt is yours and yours alone!" "Things won't improve until you're hanged!" "You should have been in jail years ago!" "How come you're still at large?" ALL *sing second and third verses of chorale.* JOAN *is now inaudible.*)

Pity the well-to-do! Hosanna!
Set them in Thy path! Hosanna!
Vouchsafe Thy grace, Hosanna!
And Thy help to him that hath! Hosanna!
Have mercy on the few! Hosanna!
    (JOAN's *talk is noticeably stopping.*)
Aid Thy class, which in turn aids Thee, Hosanna!
With generous hand! Hosanna!
Stamp out hatred now! Hosanna!
Laugh with the laugher, allow, Hosanna!
His misdeeds a happy end! Hosanna!
    (*During this verse the girls have been trying to pour some soup down* JOAN's *throat. Twice she has pushed the plate back; the third time she seizes it, holds it high and then tips the contents out. Then she collapses and is now lying in the* GIRLS' *arms, mortally stricken, with no sign of life.* SNYDER *and* MAULER *step toward her.*)

MAULER: Give her the flag! (*The flag is presented to her. It drops from her hands.*)

SNYDER: Joan Dark, twenty-five years of age, dead of pneumonia in the stockyards in the service of God, a fighter and a sacrifice!

MAULER: Something pure
Without a flaw,
Uncorrupted, helpful, whole—
It thrills us common folk to awe!

Rouses in our breast a newer,
Better soul!
> (*All stand in speechless emotion for a long time. At a
> sign from* SNYDER, *all the flags are gently lowered over*
> JOAN *until she is entirely covered by them. A rosy glow
> illumines the picture.*)

THE PACKERS *and* STOCKBREEDERS: The boast of man is
that he owns

Immemorial desires
By which toward the higher zones
His spirit constantly aspires.
He sees the stars upon their thrones,
Senses a thousand ways to heaven,
Yet downward by the flesh is driven;
Then in shame his pride expires.

MAULER: A twofold something cuts and tears
My sorely troubled inward state
Like a jagged, deep-thrust knife:
I'm drawn to what is truly great,
Free from self and the profit rate,
And yet impelled to business life
All unawares!

ALL: Humanity! Two souls abide
Within thy breast!
Do not set either one aside:
To live with both is best!
Be torn apart with constant care!
Be two in one! Be here, be there!
Hold the low one, hold the high one—
Hold the straight one, hold the sly one—
Hold the pair!

A PLAY IN FOUR ACTS AND SEVEN SCENES

by Yurii Olyesha

the conspiracy of feelings

English Version by

Daniel C. Gerould

and

Eleanor S. Gerould

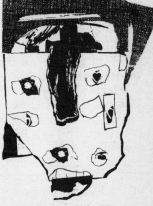

Заговор Чувств (*Zagovor Chyvstv*) was first performed in Moscow at the Vakhtangov Theatre on March 13, 1929, and first published in 1968 in Russian and in English (in this translation: *Drama and Theatre*, VII [Fall, 1968]).

Saint Joan of the Stockyards is about a capitalist meat king, *The Conspiracy of Feelings* about a socialist sausage maker. The last stage in the chronology of revolution, Olyesha's play portrays the world that results when the abortive workers' revolution of *Man and the Masses* and *Saint Joan of the Stockyards* actually succeeds. The triumph of the working class, sought so ardently by bourgeois intellectuals like Toller's Woman, creates a world in which such people have no place. The alienated intellectual remains as alienated in the socialist technological society as in the capitalist, and for much the same reasons. Like the capitalist world, the new socialist order is mechanized and impersonal, with little place for the individual. The old feelings, vicious and worthless but at least human, come into conflict with the automated world of the future and its mass-production kitchens and bedrooms.

In the plays by Toller and Brecht, there is hope and longing for the revolutionary world still to be born. In Olyesha's play, which takes place in the post-natal period, there is a futile yearning for the old bourgeois world and an absurd dream of re-establishing the heroic emotions and gestures of the past. The only country in the between-wars period where the revolution had succeeded is represented by a revolutionary drama not about the 1917 Revolution but about an abortive counter-revolution.

The 1929 productions of *The Conspiracy of Feelings* at Moscow's Vakhtangov Theatre and Leningrad's Bolshoi Dramatic Theatre produced ecstatic reviews of the performance and praise for the play's brilliance, but bewilderment at the work's ideological intent. Although all agreed that the play incisively exposed the malice and pettiness of the dying bourgeois world, there was disagreement as to whether Andrei Babichev properly represented the new Soviet man and the positive hero who was beginning to become a dogma in Soviet literature. According to Olyesha, Andrei was to be taken as the heroic new man. Anatolii Lunacharskii, People's Commissar for Education, who helped make the Soviet theatre as free and creative as it was during the 1920's, defended the play with the argument that Andrei was not an idealized figure abstractly representing everything a good communist should be, but a particular dramatic figure in a play. Other critics, far less favorable, called Andrei a wheeler-dealer in the American style who thought making salami more important than building socialism; they condemned him as a horribly distorted image of the new socialist man. The model in the lobby of the Bolshoi Dramatic Theatre of a new mass-production kitchen which would serve up to 15,000 meals per day prompted one critic to observe that this exhibit was a more convincing example of the triumph of the new collective way of life than Andrei Babichev and the entire play. Later, the play was condemned as false to Soviet reality in suggesting that the individual would be sacrificed to the mass. Since it did not conform to the tenets of socialist realism, the work was also denounced as decadent, grotesque, and expressionistic in form. Not until after Stalin's death were Olyesha's works reprinted, but *The Conspiracy of Feelings* was not published in Russian until 1968. In the West, the play has been interpreted, despite Olyesha's claims to the contrary, on the basis of its hostile reception in Stalin's Russia, as a sympathetic defense of the conspirators—following the cold war ideology of seeing all good Soviet literature only as an attack on communism.

Removed from the sphere of partisan political interpretation, the play can be seen to treat all points of view ironically. One of Olyesha's achievements is his adaptation of expressionistic themes and techniques to the struggle of old and new in Soviet life. Olyesha then transposes this conflict to the level of comedy and clowning. Meyerhold had experimented with acrobatics in his famous production of Ostrovsky's *The Forest* in 1922. The following year, Eisenstein turned Ostrovsky's *Enough Stupidity in Every Wise Man* into a circus and clown show. These productions, however, played against the texts of classical works. Olyesha incorporated into his own text elements of Meyerhold's theatricalism, uniting striking visual images and clowning with the more traditional verbal structure. Utilizing the techniques of the expressionists, Olyesha eschews their passionate, ideological rhetoric and instead mocks both bourgeois man's ineffectual anguish and socialist man's foolish arrogance.

Alexei Popov's direction and Nikolai Akimov's sets for the production at the Vakhtangov Theatre powerfully evoked the comic and the fantastic. Ivan was a paunchy, flabby-faced philosopher-clown, wending his way through the labyrinths of Moscow communal apartments, clutching his yellow pillow like the banner of his conspiracy or some priceless religious relic. The phantasmagoric scene—with geometric flights of stairs, an intestine-shaped chimney pipe, cobwebs and mold (on gauze screens hanging from above), and smoke from old stoves—created an atmosphere of foul air, chronic disease, bickering, and backbiting in which the grand old feelings of envy and spite could flower. All of the riff-raff crawled out of the woodwork and stood in split, twisted poses to view their prophet as he appeared on high. At the name-day party, a huge, oval table covered with food resembled a gigantic trough around which the guests gathered to sigh, slurp, and grunt their cheap sentimentality as Ivan lamented the death pangs of the 19th century. Above the entire scene hung a huge, fringed lampshade, large as the sun, symbol of petty bourgeois coziness. In Annichka's room, a huge bed filled the stage. Annichka, Kavalerov, and Ivan argued, fought, sat, lay, ate, slept —in other words, lived in this bed, which was decorated with oval mirrors, sumptuous pillows, and playful cupids. And it was here that Kavalerov had his nightmare vision.

Olyesha undercuts tragedy and seriousness at every moment. Andrei claims the passionate experience of being for the canning of crab meat by enthusiastic workers. Ivan and Kavalerov offer jealousy, envy, spite, and petty violence as the only alternatives to Soviet stability. The third Babichev brother, the true revolutionary Roman who was executed for throwing a bomb, might seem to be a correct index of the heroic gesture, but as Shapiro points out, anyone can throw a bomb, whereas it takes great skill to make a good salami. The only possible insurrection left is a counter-revolution on a sexual level, an absurd conspiracy of frustrated malcontents. Unlike the revolutionary struggles in *The Water Hen, Man and the Masses,* and *Saint Joan of the Stockyards,* however, and unlike real insurrections, gunfire plays no part in *The Conspiracy of Feelings.* The new society has been antiseptically purified of violence as well as violent emotions. With the instruments of revolution confiscated, the struggle becomes Shakespeare versus salami—an unequal battle, since the salami maker appropriates Shakespearean imagery for his sausage salesmanship. Everyday objects are the weapons in this new warfare: Kavalerov wields his razor, Andrei his basin, Ivan his pillow. The revolutionary battles of the past have become a pillow fight among clowns; heroic combat has turned into organized sports. Stifled and embittered, Ivan eggs others on to senseless personal violence as his only form of social rebellion and revolution.

For Olyesha, a novelist and story writer, the metaphor is the essence of the art of writing. In *The Conspiracy of Feelings*, there are many brilliant verbal metaphors, such as Ivan's description of himself: "The bags under my eyes hang down like violet stockings." Far more important, however, is his use of visual images, for Olyesha adapts literary metaphor to the stage. Ivan's pillow, for example, becomes an embodiment of the play's central themes. Valya used to sleep on the dirty yellow pillow Ivan totes about with him. Once redolent of childhood and the past, it has now become shabby and smelly. A pillow ushers us into sleep and dreaming. It is an accessory to love-making, though it may fall off the bed: "Their lovemaking knocked the pillow off the bed," Ivan tells the young man whose mistress is betraying him with her husband, when they hear a "soft thud" from the other room. Sleeping and dreaming play major roles in the play, and the pillow is the key to the unconscious, an emblem opening up hidden wishes. In contrast to Ivan's dirty pillow is Andrei's bright basin, so cleaned and polished that it clearly reflects the outside world.

But although *The Conspiracy of Feelings* makes extensive use of visual images and staging techniques, it effectively employs traditional literary devices as well. Prominent among these is the frequent use of ironic Biblical parallels. Ivan, likened to Christ, proves to be a false prophet, who offers murder instead of salvation. A miracle worker, his miracles always miscarry. Wandering into a wedding, he reverses the marriage of Cana by turning wine into water. He inverts Christ's advice to turn the other cheek and to forgive the woman taken in adultery by urging the young man to kill the husband—another ironic reversal since normally it would be the husband's role to forgive the lover. At the name-day party, which Lunacharskii called Ivan's last supper, a further ironic reversal occurs: whereas Judas kissed Christ, Ivan, the Christ figure, kisses Kavalerov; but just as Judas was responsible for Christ's death, it is Kavalerov who is responsible for Ivan's.

References abound to Shakespeare as well as to the Bible.

Olyesha uses Shakespeare as parody, subtext, image, and allusion. Kavalerov's two possessions, when he arrived at Andrei's, were his razor and his volume of Shakespeare. Shakespeare's name appears in nonsensical exchanges between Valya, Kavalerov, Shapiro, and Andrei. *Othello* serves as ironic comparison for two love triangles: Ivan–Valya–Kavalerov and the Young Man–Lizaveta–the Husband. The provincial governor killed by Roman Babichev's bomb is likened to Othello, governor-general of Cyprus. But it is *Hamlet* which provides the most complete analogue to *The Conspiracy of Feelings*. Ophelia, the name of Ivan's anti-machine machine, is appropriated by Andrei for the name of his salami, just as Valya herself, linked with the salami, is appropriated by him. Ophelia, at her father's command, rejects Hamlet; so Valya spurns Kavalerov. Kavalerov, the Hamlet of *The Conspiracy of Feelings*, must act as avenger of the nineteenth century. Throughout the play, the major opposition is between the introspective and intellectual Hamlet-like dreamer Kavalerov and the Fortinbras-like strong man Andrei. In the final scene, Ivan makes these identifications explicit, proclaiming the entrance of Fortinbras–Andrei, who cares nothing for the anguish and passions of Hamlet–Kavalerov. In Eastern Europe, where the vicissitudes of history and power politics have borne down particularly hard on intellectuals and dreamers, the opposition between Hamlet and Fortinbras assumes an importance it never has had in the West. Fortinbras, who appears twice in *Hamlet* and speaks a total of 27 lines, becomes the Prince's chief foil—the strong man versus the indecisive intellectual—and ultimately overshadows him. Olyesha is the first to use this analogue as the basis for an original play.

characters

ANDREI PETROVICH BABICHEV (*Director of the Food Industry Trust*)
IVAN (*his brother*)
NIKOLAI KAVALEROV
VALYA (*Ivan's adopted daughter*)
SOLOMON DAVIDOVICH SHAPIRO
ANNICHKA PROKOPOVICH
LIZAVETA IVANOVNA
A YOUNG MAN (*her lover*)
HER HUSBAND
TENANTS
DOCTOR (*in the dream*)
A WOMAN CELEBRATING HER NAME DAY
ZINOCHKA
LADY IN GREEN
VIC
A VENERABLE OLD MAN
A LESS VENERABLE OLD MAN
A HARD-DRINKING GUEST
A LESS DRUNK GUEST
MIKHAIL MIKHAILYCH
HARMAN (*a German*)
FESSENKOV
WAITERS, SPECTATORS, TENANTS

The action takes place in Moscow, 1928.

act I

scene 1

(*In* ANDREI BABICHEV's *house. Morning. A light, clean room. On the wall, in a glass frame, a plan of the mass-production kitchen, "The Quarter." The huge legend "The Quarter" hits you in the eye. First floor. Windows, glass door, with a terrace visible behind them, greenery, a garden. Very light and bright.*

Doors to the right and to the left. KAVALEROV *sits on a messy bed made up on the sofa. He gets dressed slowly. On the floor in the middle of the room, a mat with a stool standing on it.* ANDREI BABICHEV *pours water out of a pitcher into a basin.* ANDREI *is stripped to the waist, in knitted underwear.*)

KAVALEROV: A month ago you came up to me as I was coming out of a bar. You took me home with you even though I was just a nobody. I'm only a poor working man and for a month now I've been living in a famous man's house.

ANDREI: Don't be so modest. Everything's been going all right. You know English. I'm working on a book and you're a great deal of help. I'm very grateful to you.

KAVALEROV: That means I'll be able to sleep on this sofa until you finish your book. Right? And then what?

ANDREI: Then, I don't know . . .

KAVALEROV: Well, if that's the case . . . I'll leave today.

ANDREI: It's not right to quit your job, is it now? No, it isn't. (*He puts the basin on the stool.*) It's a terrific basin. If you ask me, water looks much better in a basin than flowing freely. See how blue the basin is. That's real beauty. There's the window over there, and if you bend over you can see how the window dances in the basin. (*He bends over the basin and looks into it, standing in front of it.*) Boy, that's really great. (*He jiggles the basin.*) Well, now. (*Admiringly.*) That's real beauty. (*He goes into the bedroom.*)

KAVALEROV (*alone*): How much do you weigh?

ANDREI (*from the bedroom*): 216. (*He comes out with a towel in his hands.*) Yesterday, as I was going downstairs, all of a sudden I felt something weird—my breasts were shaking. Get that, Kavalerov. My breasts were shaking like an old woman's. It was revolting. I decided to start a new series of exercises. (*He starts exercising. Squatting positions. Squatting.*) O-o-one. You ought to do exercises. O-o-one, two-o . . . You'll get fat . . . How old are you, Kavalerov?

KAVALEROV: 28 . . . I'm as old as the 20th century.

ANDREI (*extending and pulling back his arms*): Ah, two, ah, two, ah, ah, ah, ah, two.

KAVALEROV: I often think about the 20th century. This century of ours is an illustrious one. I've grown up with this century.

ANDREI: Ah, two, ah, two, ah, two. Phew! . . . (*Running in place.*) Op-pop, op-pop, op-pop . . .

KAVALEROV: In Europe, there are many opportunities for a talented person to become famous. There an individual can achieve personal fame. But here? Here they don't like personal fame. Isn't that right?

ANDREI: That's right. (*He lies on his back. He raises first one leg, then the other.*)

KAVALEROV: In our country all the paths of glory are blocked by barriers. A talented person either grows dull or else has to raise the barrier by causing an uproar.

ANDREI (*raises his leg*): Ouch! O-one. My leg's like a barrier. One leg weigh 100 pounds.

KAVALEROV: You say that personal glory has to disappear. You say that the individual is nothing, and only the masses exist. That's what you say.

ANDREI: That's what we say.

KAVALEROV: Rubbish. I want my own personal glory . . . I demand some recognition. (ANDREI, *raising himself on tiptoe, goes down on his hands and knees in such a way that he turns his rear end toward* KAVALEROV.) It's easy enough for you to show me your rear end.

ANDREI (*on his feet again*): Phew . . . that does it. Now for some water. How about a little water?

KAVALEROV: You insist on a sober approach to things and to life in general. So I'm going to create something obviously absurd just for its own sake. I'll do something crazy and original . . . Just for its own sake. You want everything to be purposeful, but I want to be purposeless. (*A pause.*) I'll go hang myself on your front porch. (*At this point* ANDREI *goes out the door to the right, taking the basin with him, then returns.*)

ANDREI (*coming back*): Better hang yourself in front of the Commissariat of the National Economy. In Varvarskaya Square. There's a huge arch there. You've seen it. It'll really be impressive there. (ANDREI *goes out the door to the right again, taking the stool out with him.*)

KAVALEROV (*alone*): Stupid bureaucrat. (ANDREI *returns, goes into the bedroom through the door on the left. To* ANDREI *in the bedroom.*) I want to tell you about a little incident.

ANDREI (*from the bedroom*): Tell me about a little incident.

KAVALEROV: Once . . . it was a long time ago . . . I was a schoolboy. My father took me to the museum where they have wax figures. You know, the wax works exhibition? You know, there are those glass cases. And they have figures in them. Cleopatra. A gorilla kidnapping a young girl. Robespierre on the guillotine. There was a handsome man lying in one of these cases. He was wearing a tail-coat. He was wounded in the chest. He was dying, his eyelids were closing. My father said to me: That's the French President Sadi Carnot. He's been wounded by an anarchist. (*A pause.*) Such a wonderful man lying there with his beard sticking straight up in the air. His life was slowly passing by, like the hours on a clock. It was wonderful. It was then that I first heard the roar of time.

ANDREI (*from the bedroom*): What?

KAVALEROV: The roar of time . . . Do you understand? I heard how time sounds. Understand? Time rushed over me. I cried for joy. I decided to become famous.

ANDREI: Yeah, yeah.

KAVALEROV: That was the day I made up my mind to become famous. I decided at all costs to make sure that someday my image and wax double filled with the sound of the ages would also stand in splendor in the great museum of the future. (AN-DREI *comes out of the bedroom dressed.*) There are people that things don't like and people that things do like. That's you Andrei Petrovich. Things like you. Everything looks stylish on you. But things don't like me. (ANDREI *has taken food from the small cupboard. Sits down at the round table, eats.*) The furniture tries to trip me. Yesterday the corner of this desk (*Points to the corner of the desk.*) actually bit me. Look, I just dropped my collar button. Where is it? Where did it disappear to? If you drop your collar button, it'll turn up right at your feet. But my collar button's rolled under the sofa. Look, the sofa's laughing at me.

ANDREI: Kavalerov, you should meet my brother, Ivan, you'd have a lot in common. By the way, my brother Ivan has turned up again in Moscow. He hasn't shown up for a whole year. My brother Ivan's all over the place, and then suddenly he disappears. Where's Ivan? Nobody knows. It's anybody's guess whether he's in prison or an insane asylum. (*A pause.*) Yesterday my brother was walking along Petrovsky Boulevard. I saw him from the bus stop. He was walking along holding a pillow by one of the corners. And there were children running after him. The nut . . . He just kept walking on and on, then he stopped, took off his derby, and bowed in all directions.

KAVALEROV: With a pillow?

ANDREI: With a pillow. He's quite a nut, my brother Ivan.

KAVALEROV: Why does he go around with a pillow?

ANDREI: Oh, the hell with him. (*A pause.* KAVALEROV *sits down and shaves. He continues shaving during the rest of the scene.*) Well, Kavalerov, we're about to witness some great events . . .

KAVALEROV: Because your brother's turned up . . .

ANDREI: Oh, the hell with my brother. What I'm talking about is the new kind of salami we're going to put on the market in a few days.

KAVALEROV: For a whole month I've been hearing about nothing but that salami . . .

ANDREI: I suppose you think it's so easy to make salami? And such a salami, too . . . Do you understand anything about the salami business?

KAVALEROV: Not a thing.

ANDREI (*he's finished eating, and feels great*): It's going to be a sensational salami. You should have some respect for me, Kavalerov. I've achieved amazing results. It'll be a great triumph. You'll see . . . Ho-ho . . . it'll be terrific. We're going to send it to the exhibition in Milan. And then we'll get down to work on "The Quarter." (*He goes up to the map of "The Quarter," looks at it, steps back, draws near again, admires it.*) Kavalerov, we're going to call our mass-production kitchen "The Quarter." That's great. If you ask me, that's great. "The Quarter," mass-production kitchen. And why call it "The

Quarter"? Because the two-course dinner will sell for 25 kopecks. For a quarter. Great, eh? And they'll both be meat courses! If you ask me, that's great. Look at the plan the German drew up . . . It's a beauty. The building's gigantic. The garden's over here. See? There are the towers and a small square . . . Terrific, isn't it? If you ask me, it's terrific. That German really knows his stuff . . . And there's your "Quarter" . . . the all-purpose cafeteria. Breakfast, snacks, dinner, home delivery, baby food, scientifically-prepared cream of wheat. You know, Kavalerov, we'll be serving 2,000 dinners a day. A sea of cabbage soup . . . You ought to write an epic about it, Kavalerov . . .

KAVALEROV: About what?

ANDREI: About cabbage soup. An epic about dinner on a grand scale. 2,000 people eating cabbage soup to the strains of Wagner. If you ask me, that's great. An epic about the abolition of sauce pans. (*A pause.*) It'll be terrific . . . just terrific . . . To hell with half-pound boxes and little bottles, to hell with tiny packages . . . Just think of it: a half-pound of salt, a half-pint of cooking oil . . . it's revolting . . . it's so primitive . . . We'll build "The Quarter," then you'll see . . . 100 gallons of cooking oil . . . I'll bash in those pots and pans and smash all those little bottles . . . to hell with them all.

KAVALEROV: Andrei Petrovich, you know what? I think I saw your brother yesterday too. He looks like you.

ANDREI: He does . . . but he's a little shorter.

KAVALEROV: He was wearing a derby.

ANDREI: He always wears a derby. I'd like to bash in that pot of his too. The nut. In a derby. The monkey . . . In this country it's not right to wear a derby. In this country only ragpickers or ambassadors wear derbies . . .

KAVALEROV: But he was. He was wearing a derby . . . I saw him. In Chernyshevsky Street.

ANDREI (*alarmed*): Where?

KAVALEROV: He was standing in the middle of the street. His derby had slid down on the back of his head. There he was, a short, fat man standing in the middle of the street, with his head thrown back. That's where Valya lives, on the second floor.

ANDREI: Did you see him there?

KAVALEROV: Uh-huh . . . The pillow was in a yellow pillow case . . . An old one . . .

ANDREI: The ragpicker . . . standing under Valya's window.

KAVALEROV: Well, Valya's his daughter.

ANDREI: She's his adopted daughter. She's not his real daughter, she's just adopted. But that's all over now. She's left him. He doesn't have any rights at all over her. She's completely on her own. (*A pause.*) So he was standing under her window . . .

KAVALEROV: Yes, he was.

ANDREI: Well, what about her? You didn't see her, did you? She didn't come to the window, did she?

KAVALEROV (*not answering right way*): No. Nobody came to the window. The only thing in the window was a little vase with a blue flower in it. (ANDREI *is silent.*) Why do you hate your brother so much?

ANDREI: He ought to be shot. (*At this point* ANDREI *sits down at his desk, begins working, becomes absorbed in it.* KAVALEROV *shaves.*)

KAVALEROV: I hate you, Andrei Petrovich. (*A pause.*) I hate you . . . Are you listening? When you're working you don't hear a thing. What are you so absorbed in that you don't hear anything? (*A pause.*) Bureaucrat . . . you stupid bureaucrat . . . Now you're the master. You're one of the new aristocrats, Andrei Petrovich. I hate you. Because you're a man without imagination, a blockhead . . . a sausage-maker. (*A pause.*) Why do you consider yourself a model child of the 20th century, and me such a bad one? (*A pause.*) You're crushing me. Who gave you the right to crush me? How am I worse than you are? (*A pause.*) You're cleverer . . . (*A pause.*) better organized . . . (*A pause.*) stronger . . . more important . . . (*A pause.*) and that's why I have to acknowledge your superiority. You and I are going to have it out, my dear Andrei Petrovich. I'm 28 years old, and you're 40.

ANDREI (*jumps up again suddenly and explodes*): What?! What?! I beg your pardon? What's that you said? 40? Ha-ha-ha . . . (*He roars with laughter; he growls and snorts.*) 40 . . . He said: 40 . . . The nut . . . you nut, Kavalerov . . . you joker . . . 40 . . . Listen . . . you just said 40 . . . no, not 40 . . . We're going to sell it for 35 . . . For 35 . . . get it? There's close figuring for you . . . Come over here . . . (*Drags* KAVALEROV *to the desk, grabs the papers.*) Look . . . I've figured it all out . . . (*Loud laughter.*)

KAVALEROV: 40 . . .

ANDREI (*bellows with laughter*): 35 . . . It's terrific, it's stupendous . . . It's a great triumph . . . hurrah . . . shout hurrah, Kavalerov. (KAVALEROV *is silent.*) Why are you looking at me that way?

KAVALEROV: I don't feel like shouting hurrah . . .

ANDREI: You nut . . . Why don't you? You don't believe that 70% veal salami can sell for 35 kopecks? Just take a look at this: Here's the complete set of figures. It's all perfectly clear.

KAVALEROV: It's all perfectly clear.

ANDREI: Then shout hurrah . . . He doesn't say a word . . . the joker.

KAVALEROV: All this salami business isn't getting us anywhere.

ANDREI: What do you mean, the salami business isn't getting us anywhere? You know, don't you, that every factory, industrial plant, and boarding school is going to buy our salami. (*They go look at the papers.*) Here's the analysis of its nutritive content. Take a look at those carbohydrates . . .

KAVALEROV (*suddenly*): Bravo, bravo! All right, I'll shout hurrah. Hurrah, Andrei Petrovich, hurrah!

ANDREI: So you really do think it's terrific? If you ask me, it's terrific.

KAVALEROV: I can see that you're mighty pleased with yourself.

ANDREI: Well, of course. Why wouldn't I be, when it's such a success?

KAVALEROV: In this world great reputations are made because a new sort of sausage comes out of a machine. I look at you and I can see that the nature of glory has changed . . .

ANDREI: If you ask me, it has changed. (VALYA *comes out from the terrace.*) So, you see, you did come, but I have to leave.

VALYA: I can come with you.

ANDREI: You can stay here awhile. Stay with Kavalerov.

KAVALEROV: Hello, Valya.

ANDREI: You know, Ivan's back?

VALYA: I know. Yesterday he came and stood under my window. He kept calling me.

ANDREI: And what'd you do?

VALYA: I hid and listened. He stood there for a whole hour. Then I couldn't help looking. I felt so sorry for him.

ANDREI: That was a mistake. You didn't have to look.

VALYA: But he kept calling me.

ANDREI: He can go to hell.

VALYA: That's cruel.

ANDREI: It isn't cruel. Not in the least. You don't have to worry about that.

VALYA: He's been reduced to groveling. He stood there for a whole hour.

ANDREI: Yes, he's reduced to groveling. Can you beat that ... so he stood under your window?

VALYA: For a whole hour.

ANDREI: It's all one of his little tricks. Don't believe anything he says. He likes to stand under windows. I know him. He even stands under my window.

VALYA: He was carrying a pillow. He said to me: Look, Valya, I've brought the pillow you used to sleep on.

ANDREI (*guffaws*): Really? What? The pillow you used to sleep on? Can you beat that . . . But how's that pillow any worse than the one you're sleeping on now? Every pillow has its own story. So don't worry.

VALYA: You've seen him too, Kavalerov?

KAVALEROV: Yes, I've seen him.

ANDREI: Why didn't you tell me Valya'd been talking with him?

KAVALEROV: I'm not Valya's keeper.

ANDREI: You're two of a kind, Kavalerov. Right, Valya? They should get to know each other. Right, Valya? They'd have a lot in common . . . Well, I'm going . . . well, I'm going . . . Are you coming with me? If not, stay here with Kavalerov. (*Suddenly.*) But what were you doing under Valya's window? (*To Valya.*) Stay here with him. He's been standing around under your window. (*After a pause, ironically.*) Doesn't he have a tragic face?

VALYA (*with a smile*): If you ask me, it's tragic. Why are you attacking Kavalerov? Kavalerov's a nice guy.

ANDREI: You think so?

VALYA: Yes, I think so . . . (*A pause.*)

ANDREI (*looks at his watch*): Well, all right . . . You know how much we'll sell the salami for? 35. Isn't that terrific? Well, let's go. You coming? (*They go out through the glass door.*)

KAVALEROV (*calling after her, softly, leaving the rest unsaid*): Valya . . . (*He holds the razor in his hands. He puts away his shaving equipment. The razor gleams in his hands.*

He confronts himself.) Why did you kill Andrei Babichev? (*A pause.*) Because you hated him. (*A pause.*) No . . . no. (*A pause.*) Then why did you? (*A pause.*) All my life I've been in the background . . . He took me in. He was my benefactor. Why did I raise my hand against him? (*A pause.*) Why did I kill Andrei Babichev?

(*Curtain.*)

scene 2   (*A kitchen. A stove, a faucet over a sink. Various entrances, hallways, flights of stairs. Several doors—of different heights. Street door above. A long stairway leads up to it. Morning. There are tenants in the kitchen.* LIZAVETA IVANOVNA, *a beautiful woman in an unfastened dressing gown. Small shelves, dishes, primus stove, steam.*)

FIRST TENANT (*at the stove, cooking. Something is boiling in a saucepan*): You shouldn't believe rumors. It's just stupid gossip.

SECOND TENANT (*polishing his shoes*): One of the guys I know at the office was telling me about it. He saw it all with his own eyes. There was this wedding. I even know where it took place: it was on Yakimanka Street. It was just an ordinary wedding. This tax collector was getting married. The guy from my office was there. And then all of a sudden this total stranger appeared at the wedding. He just walked right in— nobody knew who he was . . . see? . . . What a sight . . . he was wearing a derby . . . he didn't even take his derby off and he was carrying a pillow . . . and I even know the details: it was a yellow pillow in a yellow pillow case.

FIRST TENANT: That's ridiculous. That's absolutely ridiculous.

SECOND TENANT: You think everything's ridiculous. But just listen . . . and you listen, Lizaveta Ivanovna. You listen too. Amazing things are going on in Moscow.

LIZAVETA: But you'd better talk about it more quietly.

SECOND TENANT: Why should we keep quiet about it? It's not politics. Well then . . . this total stranger in the derby carrying a yellow pillow showed up at the tax collector's wedding. He suddenly appeared and said (*Strikes a pose.*) "Why are you getting married? You shouldn't. You'll only be bringing your own worst enemies into the world!"

LIZAVETA: What business was it of his?

SECOND TENANT: It was incredible . . . Don't get married— he said—"You shouldn't get married" . . . "Our children are our own worst enemies." And listen to this: the bride fainted of course and the bridegroom was ready to start a fight. Then the stranger with the pillow left. The guests sat down at the table and began eating and having a good time. And suddenly, before their very eyes, all the wine in the bottles turned into water . . . (*The door opens. The* THIRD TENANT *enters carrying a brief case—he's on his way to work.*)

SECOND TENANT (*repeats significantly*): All the wine turned into water . . . (*Silence.*)

THIRD TENANT: What . . . what? . . . What are you talking about? About the man with the pillow? I've heard about it too . . . they say that all sorts of things have been going on. A man with a pillow's walking around Moscow. He's going around looking for something . . . in and out of apartments and beer joints . . . honestly . . . (*Silence.*)

FIRST TENANT: There's really nothing to it, my friends, nothing at all. People, at least the people on this street, want miracles to happen. Do you see what I mean? People lead dull lives. Understand? They want something unusual to happen . . . But all this is just idle talk . . . idle talk . . . after all, look where we live. Are miracles really possible? . . . Can wine really turn into water? (*A pause.*)

THIRD TENANT: God only knows . . . maybe it's an advertisement . . . Or maybe they're making a movie. But there are strange things going on here all right.

LIZAVETA (*to the* FIRST TENANT): Your milk will boil away . . .

SECOND TENANT: It's true, we do lead dull lives. Boil the milk, clean up, go to work. But do you think a miracle worker really has appeared?

FIRST TENANT: What nonsense . . .

THIRD TENANT: Why is it nonsense? Maybe he's not a real miracle worker, but some kind of hypnotist . . . you know, mass suggestion . . .

LIZAVETA: Just what's he suggesting? (*Silence.*)

SECOND TENANT: It's strange all right . . . (*The* FIRST, SECOND *and* THIRD TENANTS *leave the kitchen.* LIZAVETA IVA-

NOVNA *alone at the stove. A* YOUNG MAN *appears at the door at the top of the stairs.*)

YOUNG MAN (*with his elbows leaning on the railing, he looks down from the top of the stairs at* LIZAVETA IVANOVNA): You wouldn't go on sleeping with him unless you still loved him. How can you belong to me and stay married to him at the same time...

LIZAVETA: Well, what do you want? Cut his throat if you like... If I leave him, he'll kill both of us.

YOUNG MAN: Are you afraid?

LIZAVETA: Go ahead and cut his throat.

YOUNG MAN: Do you want me to cut his throat right now? (LIZAVETA IVANOVNA *is silent.*) Well, where is he? He hasn't gone out yet, has he?

LIZAVETA: I'm making him some hash.

YOUNG MAN: Aha, then he's still home. I can just picture it: he's sitting on the bed in his long underwear, scratching himself and thinking about what you'll bring him for breakfast. You slut, you, Liza ... (LIZAVETA IVANOVNA *is silent.*) You're a real slut. You can love two men at the same time and sleep with them both. Either I'll slit his throat or he'll slit mine—you don't care which. Why are you always coming out in the kitchen practically naked? I know why. You want everyone to get excited just looking at you. You're a whore ... (*As he goes out, the* THIRD TENANT *leaves the door at the top of the stairs open. Blue sky is visible through the doorway. This is the exit to the yard. It's morning.* IVAN BABICHEV *appears in the doorway, a small, slovenly fat man in a derby. He's carrying by one corner a large dirty pillow in a yellow pillow case. He stops at the top of the stairs and listens.*)

LIZAVETA: I love you, you fool ...

YOUNG MAN: You're lying ... you love your husband just as much as you love me ...

LIZAVETA: There's the knife. (*She points to the knife lying on the stove. A pause.*) There's the knife ... (*The* YOUNG MAN *is silent.*) Coward ...

YOUNG MAN: All right ... (*He comes down the stairs to her.*) What are you smiling at ... You don't believe I'm capable of committing a crime for your sake?

A MAN'S VOICE FROM THE OTHER ROOM: Liza!

YOUNG MAN: Well go, your lord and master's calling...

THE VOICE: Liza!

LIZAVETA: Coward ...

YOUNG MAN: No, wait. No, I'm not a coward. But suppose I do cut his throat. So I go and slit his throat right now . . . then they'll lock me up. I'll be behind bars for eight years, and what about you? You'll be living with other men . . .

THE VOICE: Liza!

YOUNG MAN: Is that what you want? Listen. In just a minute you'll be gone and I'll be dead. I'll cut my own throat. Is that what you want?

LIZAVETA: That's just a lot of talk. (*She shouts to the other room.*) I'm coming! (*She goes out.*)

YOUNG MAN (*sits down on a small bench in a state of great agitation*): What'll I do, what'll I do?

IVAN (*from above*): You should kill the husband.

YOUNG MAN (*jumps up*): What? Who's that? Who said that?

IVAN: If you want my opinion, you should slit the husband's throat . . .

YOUNG MAN: What business is it of yours? You were eavesdropping!

IVAN: No need to get so angry, my friend. You see, I spend whole days, days and nights, walking about . . . I go up and down other people's stairs. I look in other people's windows, I pick up other people's words. (*A pause.*) Why are you putting it off, young man? (*The knife gleams.*) What are you waiting for? At this very moment the woman you love is kissing someone else . . . listen how quiet it is in there. They're kissing.

YOUNG MAN: What a way to laugh. (IVAN *has come down into the kitchen. He sits down on a stool, takes off his derby, and puffs. He's put the pillow at his feet.*) Get the hell out of here, who are you anyhow? . . . Maybe you came to steal the stove!

IVAN: I came in search of heroes.

YOUNG MAN (*ironically*): Well, isn't that nice! So you heard our conversation.

IVAN: Yes, I did. And it gave me great pleasure. Really, aren't you going to act out this drama to the end? It had a great beginning.

YOUNG MAN: Listen, there's something really absurd about this. What would you like, for me to go all the way?

IVAN: I'm in search of heroes.

YOUNG MAN: Stop clowning. (*He looks him over carefully.*) A pillow . . . I don't get it at all . . . looks pretty suspicious to me . . .

IVAN: You're a hero . . . you're a real hero and you don't even suspect it. You ought to be proud of it . . .

YOUNG MAN: I'll be late for work on account of you.

IVAN: I'm talking about jealousy.

YOUNG MAN (*angrily*): What?

IVAN: I mean your jealousy.

YOUNG MAN: That's none of your business.

IVAN: It is my business. You've got to kill that beautiful woman's husband. She's very beautiful. But you're right: she's a slut. You called her a slut . . . in other words she's what was called in the old world a demonic woman.

YOUNG MAN: Really? . . . Can you tell that right away? Good God, what'll I do?

IVAN: But you're not going to be intimidated . . .

YOUNG MAN: What?

IVAN: What's holding you back? Jealousy is one of the grand old emotions . . .

YOUNG MAN: What'll I do?

IVAN: Show your feelings. The old-fashioned feelings are beautiful. Love, hate, jealousy, pride, envy, pity . . .

YOUNG MAN: You're quite an actor . . .

IVAN: Young man, I'm a leader . . .

YOUNG MAN: You're pulling my leg.

IVAN: I'm the leader of all those old-fashioned feelings. I'm the leader of a conspiracy and you're the standard-bearer of one of the great feelings—jealousy—you're an accomplice in my conspiracy.

YOUNG MAN: Oh really, what sort of rubbish is that! A guy walks into somebody else's house just like that . . . (*A pause.*)

IVAN: Take the knife and go right in without knocking. She's in his arms at this very moment . . .

YOUNG MAN: Tell me, do you really think she's beautiful? Were you struck by that right away?

IVAN: She sparkles like a glass vase, and right now your rival is pouring his love into that vase. Take the knife . . .

YOUNG MAN: Oh, I can't . . .

IVAN: Ssh . . . listen . . . a soft thud. That was the pillow falling. Their love-making knocked the pillow off the bed. Ssh. (*They stand at the door listening. Sudden commotion in the other room, then a frightful scream—the door flies open.* NEIGHBORS *appear. Anxious faces, uplifted hands, general panic. The* HUSBAND *appears at the door.*)

SECOND TENANT: What's the matter? What's happened?

HUSBAND: I'm all right. Just leave me alone, will you! You bastards! . . .

FIRST TENANT: He's killed his wife! . . .

FOURTH TENANT: He cut his wife's throat!!

FIRST TENANT: Grab him!!!

HUSBAND: Get out of my way! . . . Where is he? Where is he? Where is he? (*Goes up the stairs.*) Where's the lover-boy? (*He beats on the door where the* YOUNG MAN *went out.*) You bastard . . . you bastard . . . open the door . . . or I'll break it down . . . Open the door . . . so you've been living with her? I'll kill you! I'll kill you! . . .

A VOICE: Help!

ANOTHER VOICE: Police!

IVAN (*to the* YOUNG MAN *who is hiding behind* IVAN's *back*): What are you hiding for? No, no, come on out, young man, stop hiding. Come on out and answer for what you've done . . . one always has to face the consequences of loving. (*He shouts to the* HUSBAND, *pointing to the* YOUNG MAN *hiding behind him.*) Here he is! Right here! . . .

YOUNG MAN: A-a-a-ah! For God's sake, what are you doing? Don't let him . . . save me . . . a-a-a-ah . . .

SECOND TENANT: The knife! . . . he's seen the knife! . . .

YOUNG MAN: A-a-a-a-a-ah . . . (*The* HUSBAND, *seeing his rival, goes down the stairs. Silence.*)

FIRST TENANT: Grab him! . . . (*The* HUSBAND *falls at* IVAN's *feet.*)

HUSBAND: I killed her . . .

IVAN (*applauding*): Long live the good old human feelings! Long live jealousy! Long live love!

FIRST TENANT: He's a madman!

SECOND TENANT: Call the police!

IVAN: . . . Where are you now, brother? Do you see now, brother Andrei! Follow me! . . . all you cowards, jealous ones, lovers, heroes . . . you knights in shining armor . . . follow me . . . the old world . . . the old feelings—follow me . . . I'll lead you on our last march.

(*Curtain.*)

act II

scene 3

IVAN: We haven't seen each other for six months. How are all your state farms, and apiaries, and cafeterias? . . .

ANDREI: I've invented a new kind of sausage, Vanya.

IVAN: And I've invented a machine.

ANDREI: Really? Good for you . . . What kind of machine?

IVAN: Andrei, I've invented an amazing machine. You know: my greatest dream has always been the universal machine, the machine's machine. For years I've been thinking about the ideal instrument. My aim was to concentrate hundreds of different functions in one small apparatus . . . I wanted to tame the mastodon of technology, harness it, and domesticate it . . .

ANDREI: Good for you . . . I envy you. You've got big ideas. It makes me feel ashamed of myself. Where will my salami get me? . . . There you are with your mastodon of technology, while all I've got is some lousy old sausage . . . Of course it does have 70% veal . . . well, go on, go on.

IVAN: I've done it, Andrei. I've invented this machine . . .

ANDREI (*suddenly*): Why do you drink so much, Vanya? You look pretty bloated.

IVAN: Don't interrupt me. I've invented a machine that can blow up mountains, that can fly, lift weights, crush stone. It's a perfect masterpiece of engineering. (*Suddenly.*) Why are you smiling?

ANDREI (*ironically*): From sheer pleasure. I'm anticipating what a great success you'll be. You'll be rendering an unforgettable service to your government. (*After a pause.*) Say: maybe it could even be of some use in making salami?

IVAN: It can do everything.

ANDREI: Well, I'll be damned . . . we'll have to give you the Order of the Red Banner of Labor. What time is it? Eleven. It's late . . . otherwise I'd phone the patent office at the Commissariat of the National Economy in the Sovnarkom . . .

IVAN: No point in doing that.

ANDREI: Why not?

IVAN: Wait a second, you didn't let me finish . . . Once the machine was built I realized I had a miraculous opportunity to avenge my era. You won't get my machine—not you, or the patent office, or any part of this whole era of yours.

ANDREI: That's a great blow to us. Just think: we were getting so far behind and then you came along with your machine. You could have solved all our problems—in a flash your machine could have brought us into the golden age of technology.

IVAN: You're just making wisecracks, Andrei, while I'm being serious. Please stop making wisecracks. I repeat: I've invented an amazing machine. (*Silence.*) But you won't get it. I'm a knight in shining armor defending a dying era. I'm avenging my era—to which I'm indebted for the brains I've got in my head, brains that could devise such an amazing machine. Who'll get my machine? You? You devour us as though we were something to eat. You're swallowing the 19th century whole, the way a boa constrictor does a rabbit. You chew us, digest us, and then get rid of what you don't want. I don't want to be either digested or gotten rid of. You guzzle down our machinery and throw our feelings away . . . I'll avenge our feelings. Do you know exactly what kind of machine I've invented?

ANDREI: No, Vanya, I don't know.

IVAN: While you're striving to turn man into a machine, I've already turned a machine into man. You're the new era, and I'm the old. And so I thumb my nose at you; in a burst of glory the dying century thumbs its nose at the one that's being born . . . You won't get my machine! . . .

ANDREI (*with a smirk*): You frighten me, Vanya.

IVAN: Do you understand what this means?

ANDREI: No, I don't understand.

IVAN: Even though it's the greatest creation of modern technology, I've endowed my machine with the pettiest of human feelings. I've corrupted the machine. I've turned the best machine in the world into a liar, and a cheap, sentimental scoundrel. At the celebration in Red Square for the October Revolution—I'll unveil it in front of everyone. You'll see, Andrei. It can blow up mountains, but I won't let it. Understand? I taught it to sing love songs, silly love songs from out of the past. It sings, gets sad, picks flowers, foolish flowers of the past. It falls in love, gets jealous, weeps, dreams, and that's not all . . . Andrei, you know what: it'll corrupt all your machines. That's how I've avenged my era . . . which was a mother to me.

ANDREI (*softly*): You didn't invent anything, Vanya. That's an obsession of yours. You're not being very funny. What sort of a machine is this, anyway? Come on, now, could there really be such a machine?

IVAN: You don't believe it?

ANDREI: Sorry, I don't . . .

IVAN: Watch out, Andrei . . . this machine does exist. I named it Ophelia. That was the name of the girl who went mad from love . . . I named my machine after the girl who went out of her mind from love and despair. Ophelia . . . she drowned herself . . .

ANDREI: Serves her right . . . Now I'll tell you about my invention. You were talking about the machine's machine. Now imagine the salami's salami, the universal salami. Only I don't know what to name it—what about Ophelia, huh? Maybe name it Ophelia? Ophelia—that's the girl who went mad from love. Isn't there a girl in classical literature who ate too much salami? . . .

IVAN: I hate you, Andrei. You're a graven image. You're a graven image with bulging eyes. You know what you look like? A piggy bank. I hate you, Andrei. (ANDREI *roars with laughter.*)

ANDREI: And just why do you hate me?

IVAN: You took my daughter away from me. (*Silence.*)

ANDREI: She left you of her own free will.

IVAN: Give me back my daughter . . .

ANDREI: She's not your daughter. She's only adopted.

IVAN: I'm asking you, where's Valya?

ANDREI: She's living with a girl friend. You know that. You stood under her window. Don't act dumb. You kept calling her, but she wouldn't come back.

IVAN: Thanks to your planning, you told her what to do . . .

ANDREI: You did everything you could to drive her out of

her mind. If I hadn't done it, the police would have taken her away from you.

IVAN: You're a skunk.

ANDREI: Don't shout. If you're going to get nasty, I'll kick you right out the door.

IVAN: You skunk, you dirty old man . . .

ANDREI: What?

IVAN: You're a dirty old man, you're corrupting Valya. (*Silence.*) How can you dare even dream of a girl like that, you salami maker? I'll strangle you with my bare hands. (*Silence.*) I know everything. Oh, you skunk. You want to breed a new race of people just the way you're breeding a new species of salami. You've selected my daughter. My daughter's no incubator. Do you hear? My daughter's not going to be an incubator for you.

ANDREI: It's hard to make me angry. I'm a gentle soul. As the Director of the Food Trust, I deal with calves, lambs, fish, and bees. I've always been goodnatured, and nothing's going to change me now. Listen, Ivan, you say I'm a corrupter of youth. You've known for a long time that Valya's everything to me.

IVAN: Don't you dare talk about love. People of your era don't know what love is. You look at a woman as if she were a reservoir. Valya isn't going to be your reservoir. Do you hear? I'll kill you. (*Throws himself at* ANDREI, *who pushes him away,* IVAN *falls at his brother's feet. After a pause, at* ANDREI's *feet.*) Andryusha . . . I'm sick . . . I'm sick, Andryusha . . .

ANDREI: You're not sick, Vanya. You're a son of a bitch, Vanya . . .

IVAN: I'm miserable, Andryusha.

ANDREI: That's not true, Vanya. I don't feel sorry for you. You're just a phony. Vanya, they forgot to shoot you . . . clear out of here . . .

IVAN: So you're driving me away . . .

ANDREI: Get going, Ivan Babichev . . . I've got to work . . . Clear out!

IVAN: All right, Andrei, I'm going, but just remember . . .

ANDREI: Just remember what . . . That's enough out of you . . .

IVAN: Remember: You're talking to a leader . . . you may be a leader, but I'm a leader too. Watch your step, Andrei . . .

ANDREI: Okay, okay ...

IVAN: Don't go too far, Andrei . . . I have a huge army behind me. I'm the leader of what you'd call the petty bourgeois. It's a peaceful conspiracy, a bloodless revolution of feelings . . . it's a new kind of counter-revolution. (*He goes out.*)

ANDREI (*alone*): Too bad Kavalerov wasn't here. (*Walks back and forth, deep in thought. He goes over to the table, lifts the receiver off the phone, and begins speaking into it.*) 5–60–62. Yes. Uh huh. Is this Comrade Shapiro? Hello, Solomon Davidovich. Yes, it's me. Hope I'm not calling too late. You're not asleep yet? Listen Solomon Davidovich, how's my beauty? All locked up for the night, safe and sound? I'm in love with her. What? There's nothing dearer to me in the whole world. What? Uh-huh, uh-huh. When will I see her? Wednesday or Thursday? Give her my love. Uh-huh. I've been dreaming about her. So pink, so radiant, so tender. Uh-huh. You think we'll be able to sell her for 35 kopecks? But what'll we name her? You don't happen to know, do you, whether somewhere in the classics there's a girl who ate too much salami and went out of her mind from love? What? Uh-huh, uh-huh . . . I'm just talking off the top of my head . . . what? You mean nobody's going to be able to go out of their mind from love anymore? What? . . . A-a-h . . . Uh-huh . . . but in our new society there really won't be any such thing as going out of your mind from love? What? They won't be able to. Huh? What? So that's the way it's going to be? . . . Well, okay. . . . Good talking to you . . . (*He puts the receiver down. Sits lost in thought. Takes the phone again, and lifts the receiver.*) 5–60–62. Comrade Shapiro? You're not asleep yet? Tell me the truth. Is it all right if I get married? What? You're already asleep? Well, okay . . . good night, then. (VALYA *enters.*) And here's another crazy female. You'll keep me from working. You can stay for ten minutes and that's it.

VALYA (*sits down on the sofa*): I'm awfully sleepy. Can I sleep on your sofa?

ANDREI: Kavalerov will be coming any minute now. He sleeps on the sofa.

VALYA: Kavalerov told me that when he first saw me passing by he felt as if a branch full of flowers and leaves had rustled past him. (ANDREI *is busy at his table, deeply engrossed in his work*.) Kavalerov says that you don't hear anything that's

going on around you when you get engrossed in your work . . .
is that true? Andrei Babichev—fire! . . . (*A pause.*) Kavalerov
says you snore at night. There's a volcano called Krakatou.
You snore like that: Krra-Ka-Tou . . . u . . . Kraa . . . Ka . . .
To . . . u . . . It's revolting. (*A pause.*) Kavalerov says that you
sing in the bathroom every morning. Very beautifully.
(*Silence. It's not clear whether* ANDREI *hears her or not.*) I
love you, Andrei Petrovich. I love you, dear Uncle Andrei,
more than anything in the world. I promise you, dear, darling
Uncle, undying love. I promise I'll be awfully good to you. I'm
a very good-looking girl, I'm better than that salami you're
always mooning over. Uncle . . . do you hear me, Uncle?
You're a glutton, a fat slob, do you hear what I'm saying to
you? Look at me, idiot. (*Silence.*) We'll go to the football
game together. I'll rustle in the wind like a branch full of
flowers and leaves. But we won't take Kavalerov. Why did you
take Kavalerov in anyway? I want to sleep on that sofa. I'm
going to start getting undressed right now, I'll get undressed
and go to bed. As soon as I'm all undressed you'll see what
kind of a branch I am. It'll drive you mad. Uncle . . . I'm
starting to undress . . . o-one-two-three . . . the buttons have all
popped open . . . you don't even hear me, you miserable
salami salesman. (*Silence. Sleepily.*) Let's go into the lab together. I'll show you some amazing things. You should study
chemistry, Uncle. It'll help you in making packaged foods . . .
So long, Uncle, I'm falling asleep . . . the bed springs are
singing . . . just listen to the springs singing . . . little drops are
trickling . . . down from the vines of the sofa . . . bunches of
grapes . . . I'm already asleep . . . nite-nite . . . nitwit . . .
(*Silence.* VALYA *sleeps.*)

ANDREI (*goes to the telephone, starts to lift the receiver, but
thinks better of it and talks directly at the telephone*): It's me
again. Yes, it's me, Solomon Davidovich. Wake up. I don't
know what to do . . . what should I do, Solomon Davidovich?
She's here, she's sleeping on my sofa . . . what should I do,
Solomon Davidovich? Wake up, wake up, the President of the
Board is talking to you . . . what shall we name her? . . . isn't
there a girl in the classics who was in love with a salami
salesman?

(*Curtain.*)

scene *4*   (ANDREI BABICHEV'*s house. Early morning.*
ANDREI *seated at the table.* SHAPIRO.)

SHAPIRO: I was just getting ready for bed. Five more minutes and I'd have been asleep. Then you phoned and said: "Shapiro, is it all right if I get married?" Then I got dressed again and came right over. This is a fine state of affairs. You've got me running around at all hours of the night.

ANDREI: I was thinking things over. Then I read for a while. Shakespeare's plays. See—it's one of Kavalerov's books.

SHAPIRO: And where is your Kavalerov?

ANDREI: I don't know. Maybe he's with that widow of his.

SHAPIRO: What widow?

ANDREI: It's a ghastly story. He got involved with an old bag in her forties when he was on a drunk. She's a cook, she fixes meals for the barbers' co-op. It's awful, you know, it's really tragic . . . such grandiose expectations, and then suddenly he lands in an old bag's bed . . . (*After a moment's silence.*) But I feel sorry for Kavalerov. What about hiring him to write jingles? Or have him write an opera about "The Quarter"?

SHAPIRO: I don't like the sound of any of this. What sort of behavior is that anyway, to pick up some drunk off the street and bring him home to live with you? That's straight out of Shakespeare.

ANDREI: And now I don't know what to do with him.

SHAPIRO: Tell him: "So long, take your Shakespeare and get out . . ."

ANDREI: I just read *Othello* . . . you know who Othello was, don't you?

SHAPIRO: Sure, everybody knows that. He was a Negro.

ANDREI: In the first place, he wasn't a Negro, he was a Moor, but that's not what's important. You know who he was —he was a general, governor-general of the island of Cyprus. The whole thing's really a military drama, a story of life in the barracks . . . Iago is a line officer, Cassio is a desk officer . . . and Desdemona is the sweetheart of the regiment . . . and the whole thing's pretty great . . . if you ask me, it's great . . . General Othello was an ugly bastard. He was black and repulsive and everyone hated him. But he won the heart of Desdemona with tales of his great deeds in battle. She fell in love with him because of all he'd been through. (*A pause.*)

SHAPIRO: Aha . . . I see, Kavalerov is beginning to have an influence on you. You're already starting to dream about heroes.

ANDREI: I had a brother named Roman. He threw a bomb at the governor. At the governor-general, who was a kind of Othello. They hanged him . . .

SHAPIRO: Big deal . . . just like in a novel, that's very romantic . . . but it's harder to make a sausage. A bomb can be made any old way, but a sausage has to be nutritious.

ANDREI: You're right, Shapiro. I'm dreaming about heroes. I want salami-makers to be heroes, understand? But look at the kind of people I have to work with—all they want to do is take the line of least resistance. But I demand an enthusiastic approach. (*He gets carried away, stands up, and speaks as if to a large audience.*) You know what Prokudin did. He just came out with a cherry cordial candy and you know what he called it—"Rosa Luxemburg." How do you like that? I'm disgusted with Comrade Prokudin for taking the line of least resistance . . . if Comrade Prokudin ever dreams up a new kind of piroshki, he'll probably call it "Lenin's Legacy" . . . Words once written in blood Comrade Prokudin writes in sugar. That's taking the line of least resistance. Last week they put twelve new kinds of chocolates on the market. These are the names Comrade Prokudin had to offer: "Chanticleer," "Flight of the Bumblebee." And, if I remember correctly, "Odalisque." Comrade Prokudin proposes calling a Soviet candy "Odalisque." How do you like that? He's only got one line—"Rosa Luxemburg's" at one end, and "Odalisque's" at the other . . . that's the line of least resistance. But anyhow, I've always said: names should come from the sciences. To make them sound intriguing. Some of the sciences are poetic —right, Shapiro? Like geography and astronomy. Use names like "Eskimo," "Telescope," "Equator"—Comrade Prokudin would never think of anything like that. I'm the one who ought to be thinking up names for candies. Even if I don't have the time, I've got to make it my business. Because, if I don't make it my business, I'll have horrible nightmares about Comrade Prokudin putting a cake on the market called "The Last Flight of the Bumblebee." I've really got to look after everything myself. (*Pause.*) Yes, Shapiro, I demand an enthusiastic approach. Take this can, for instance . . . (*He picks up a can from the table.*) Here's a can made by really enthusiastic workers. It's the product of one of our canneries in Vladivostok. What's in this can? Crab. Look at that blue. What a fine substantial can—bright and glorious as a ship's pennant. Enthusiastic workers made that can. (*Pause.*)

VALYA (*speaking from the bedroom*): Andrei Petrovich. (SHAPIRO *is utterly astonished.*) Andrei Petrovich . . . Are you there? Uncle . . .

SHAPIRO: Greetings! Andrei Petrovich isn't here. This is Shapiro. Andrei Petrovich went out in the garden to take a little walk. He took a volume of Shakespeare's plays with him and went into the garden. What are you doing in there?

VALYA: I sleep here. (ANDREI *keeps quiet and listens.*)

SHAPIRO: But do you have any right to sleep there? Are you already married?

VALYA: Not yet.

SHAPIRO: Are you in love with him?

VALYA: I have been ever since I was a child. It's awful . . .

SHAPIRO: It's awful? . . .

VALYA: That I'm in love.

SHAPIRO: You're an odd one! What's so awful about it . . . on the contrary, it's great for a young girl to be in love.

VALYA: Who said that?

SHAPIRO: Shakespeare.

VALYA: Who?

SHAPIRO: Boris Shakespeare.

VALYA: His name's William . . .

SHAPIRO: Oh yeah, I forgot . . .

VALYA: It's disgraceful . . .

SHAPIRO: What's disgraceful? That I forgot?

VALYA: That I'm in love . . . Love—that's a medieval emotion . . .

SHAPIRO: Valya, you're pulling my leg . . .

VALYA: There shouldn't be any such thing as love. Modern science will enable us to produce any feeling we want by aritificial means. Just imagine the kind of machine there'd be. Your unhappy person comes along, say, somebody like Nikolai Kavalerov. He goes to the Institute of Emotions. That's the sort of institute there'll be: the "Institute of Emotions." So Kavalerov goes to the Institute of Emotions and announces: "I'm unhappy." Then a professor has Kavalerov sit down in front of the machine, puts the special head band on him—a chemically charged beam flashes back and forth—the machine starts to buzz—bzz-bzz-bzz . . . it only takes a minute, and then, due to the action of that beam of light, William Kavalerov absorbs all the emotions you're supposed to feel in a perfect love affair. That's all there is to it . . .

SHAPIRO: That's all very fine, my dear lady, but frankly, it bores me. Chemistry should be used chiefly for agricultural purposes . . .

VALYA: You don't understand a thing. The new man must be absolutely rational. Andrei Petrovich doesn't understand anything either.

SHAPIRO: And all in all, Andrei Petrovich is a pretty awful person. Sure, he's a member of the All-Russian Central Executive Committee, he's been a party member for ten years—and then what does he go and do? He falls in love . . .

VALYA: Do you think he really is in love?

SHAPIRO: Boy, is he! Like a knight in shining armor, a real feudal lord.

VALYA: Did he tell you he's in love?

SHAPIRO: No, he didn't. But it's a known fact that he went to the Institute of Emotions and declared: "I want to fall in love, put the head band on me." The professor had him sit down in front of the machine. The machine started to buzz— bzz-bzz-bzz—it only took a minute. Then Andrei Petrovich said: Thanks, now I'm all charged with emotions, I've fallen in love . . .

VALYA: You're just kidding me . . .

SHAPIRO: Of course I'm kidding. You know what Andrei Petrovich is—an elephant. If he went to the Institute of Emotions, and they told him that falling in love was forbidden, he'd smash all their equipment to pieces . . .

ANDREI (*suddenly*): That's enough . . . it's beginning to bore me . . .

SHAPIRO: Oh, you're here . . .

VALYA (*looks out from the bedroom*): What's beginning to bore you?

ANDREI: Romance.

VALYA: You're just cross because I slept in your bed. And you didn't sleep all night. Where's Kavalerov?

ANDREI: He's been appointed Governor-General of the Island of Cyprus.

VALYA: Why are you so angry? I'm all dressed now. You can go to bed. (*Appears from the bedroom.*)

ANDREI: You don't say?

VALYA: What are you hissing at me for?

ANDREI: I didn't know I was hissing.

VALYA: Well, why don't you say: "Valya, I love you."

ANDREI: I won't be hissing if I say that . . .

VALYA: Then add: "so much!" "Valya, I love you so much!"

ANDREI: Stop being so stupid. There's a little hissing for you.

SHAPIRO: It's beginning to bore me . . .

ANDREI: What's beginning to bore you?

SHAPIRO: Romance. In the new world there won't be any such thing as love. Isn't that right, my dear lady? Modern science will enable us to produce any feelings we want by artificial means. There'll be an "Institute of Emotions."

ANDREI: Who said so?

SHAPIRO: Shakespeare.

ANDREI: Your Shakespeare's an idiot.

KAVALEROV (*comes in from the terrace. To* VALYA): You're here, Valya? What are you doing here? Did you spend the night here?

SHAPIRO: What business is it of yours, Comrade Kavalerov? What difference does it make where Valya spent the night?

KAVALEROV: Andrei Petrovich, I think I'll be moving out now . . . for good . . . and I want you to listen to what I've got to say . . .

ANDREI: Go ahead.

KAVALEROV: I want to talk about Valya.

ANDREI: Valya, he wants to talk about you.

KAVALEROV: Can I say whatever I want?

ANDREI: Go ahead.

KAVALEROV: It's not possible for a young girl to really be in love with a forty-year-old man. It's just your position that impresses her. She isn't in love with you. I've been doing a lot of thinking . . . I've thought over carefully what I'm going to say . . . (*Pause.*) I don't have the right to tell you what to do. But it seems to me you're on the verge of doing something that a good Communist wouldn't do . . .

ANDREI: All right.

KAVALEROV: I don't want to make you angry. I'm talking to you man to man. Fate brought us together in a strange way. I can see that you and I are going to come into conflict. Because of the difference in our positions in life, and Valya.

VALYA: And what?

KAVALEROV: And you, Valya.

VALYA (*to* ANDREI): What did he say?

KAVALEROV: I love you, Valya. I mean that from the bottom of my heart. Tell me . . .

VALYA: What's he talking about . . . What am I supposed to say?

KAVALEROV: Valya, why don't you tell me the truth . . . You spent the night here because you . . . because you're already married?

VALYA: Leave me alone . . . (*Silence.*)

KAVALEROV: Then that means . . . it means that . . . You've taken everything I have away from me, Andrei Petrovich . . . all my dreams of life and love . . .

ANDREI: I haven't taken anything away from you, Kavalerov.

KAVALEROV: Can't you see how unfairly I've been treated? I don't have anything to live for. It's perfectly clear. Everything belongs to you. And I'm just a beggar in this terrifying new world. Give Valya back to me, Andrei Petrovich. (*Silence.*) Give Valya back to me. You don't need her. You've already reached the top.

ANDREI: You're talking very strangely, Kavalerov. Valya, I don't get it at all. Help us, Shapiro.

KAVALEROV: Don't you dare bring Shapiro into this. (*To* SHAPIRO.) Get out of here. You pimp! Valya, why don't you say something?

VALYA: I don't have anything to say. I think you're drunk. It'd be better if you left . . .

KAVALEROV: I don't have anywhere to go. Where could I go? Back to being a bum? But you . . . you'll stay here . . . to perform your function . . .

VALYA: What function?

KAVALEROV: You know what function . . . being a reservoir . . .

SHAPIRO: He's crazy . . .

VALYA: I don't know what's going on, Uncle . . .

KAVALEROV: But maybe you'll come to me later on . . . in a month or so, and let me have the reservoir that others have already made use of.

ANDREI: What did you say? Reservoir? . . . Oh, I get it. Those are the very words my brother Ivan used. Then that means you've already met Ivan? I'm very glad. Congratulations, Kavalerov.

KAVALEROV: Yes! I'm prepared to defend your brother and his daughter. I'll fight for him and his daughter against you.

You've cheated her out of tenderness, genuine feeling, individuality, and everything else you try to suppress. Don't believe him, Valya. You're just something for him to play around with. (*Suddenly notices how threatening* ANDREI's *silence is becoming.*) No . . . no . . . wait . . . don't get angry . . . Really . . . I'm only joking . . I'm drunk. Honestly . . . I'm completely drunk. Why don't you say something? . . . Well, don't if you don't want to. Really, Comrade, it's all a misunderstanding . . . absolute nonsense . . . (*A pause.*) I'm all on edge . . . I'm exhausted . . . I'm in a state of nervous collapse. I ought to take cold showers . . . I'll do calisthenics with you. Will you let me? . . . All right? . . . We could, couldn't we? Why don't you say something, Andrei Petrovich? Valya, tell him . . . Well, all right, so you don't want to talk to me, what do you want me to do, then? (IVAN *looks in the window from the terrace.*) Go away, right? Just like a dog. But where? To the Widow Prokopovich? To some old bag's bed. And Valya will stay here. That means I'll never see Valya again. To go away . . . (*Silence.*) How can I just go away after what's happened? Something's got to be done about this. I insulted you—so why don't you hit me? (*Silence.*) Or maybe you and I don't speak the same language? Yes, of course, that's it. You're a Communist, you're busy building a new way of life, but I'm just a poor intellectual. I challenge you to a duel, do you hear? (*Silence.*) You've got weapons here. We'll fight. Give me a revolver. I'm not going to just leave. Do you hear, I won't leave. (*Silence.*) I'm insulting you, so you'll have to fight. Do you hear? . . . You . . . sausage-maker . . . sausage-maker . . . seducing a young girl like that . . . you child-raper. (*Up until this point* VALYA *has maintained an embarrassed silence.*)

VALYA (*to* ANDREI): Why don't you say something?

ANDREI: It's a temporary fit of insanity. What can I do?

VALYA: I'm leaving. (*Goes quickly to the door to the terrace.*)

ANDREI: Valya . . . (VALYA *comes back and slaps* KAVALEROV *in the face.*)

SHAPIRO: Serves him right!

KAVALEROV: All right . . . I'll go . . . what in the . . . Where are my things? (*Looks everywhere, picks up a book from the table.*) This is my book . . . yes . . . here's my razor . . . (*Picks up the razor.*) It's mine all right . . . (*Sees* IVAN *in the window.*)

IVAN (*whipping the derby off his head*): Greetings, Andryusha. You know what this is called? It's called the sexual counter-revolution. Come here, Kavalerov. Oh, my poor friend! Come here. Oh, you'll certainly be the leading man in my company. (KAVALEROV *goes out on the terrace and can be seen leaning on* IVAN'*s shoulder.*) Andryusha, did you notice, he took his razor with him? . . .

(*Curtain.*)

act III

scene 5

(*At* ANNICHKA PROKOPOVICH's *house. A small, ugly, musty room crowded with so much furniture it's hard to move about. The room is dominated by a huge bed. It casts a towering shadow like a temple. It is evening.* IVAN, ANNICHKA, KAVALEROV.)

IVAN: So this is it, is it? Um-hmm . . . so this is the place where Kavalerov's been living. You know, Anna Mikhailovna, your room's already becoming a part of history. "Nikolai Kavalerov lived here." And you're becoming part of history too, Anna Mikhailovna. After all, you're the—wife, or at least the girl friend of Nikolai Kavalerov.

KAVALEROV: What are you making such a face for, Ivan Petrovich?

ANNICHKA: Kolya hates me.

IVAN: Kavalerov, it's not right, to hate such a nice lady. After all, Anna Mikhailovna let you climb into her remarkable bed. Just look at it, rosewood, mirrored arches, cupids dancing, apples rolling out of horns of plenty . . .

ANNICHKA: My late husband won this bed in the lottery . . .

IVAN: There, you see. It's a family heirloom. But you despise her. You were offered love, a family, an heirloom, a legend in the making—but you refused. And then there's Anna Mikhailovna herself. Take a good look at her: how expansive she is, how soft, how kind. Anna Mikhailovna, didn't you ever dream you turned into a bed? I'm amazed at you, Kavalerov. Nice people like Anna Mikhailovna and my brother Andrei take you into their homes . . . and yet you behave so obnoxiously everywhere you go . . . and you hate absolutely everyone . . . (KAVALEROV *remains silent.*)

ANNICHKA: A new movie theatre just opened next door. It's a great theatre. It's called the Fantasma. It's right around the corner. We could all go to a movie.

IVAN: Sure we could! That's a wonderful idea!!! You know, Kavalerov, we've been talking a lot about feelings . . . but we've forgotten the most important one of all: indifference . . . of course . . . I consider indifference the highest state the human mind can attain. Let's be indifferent, Kavalerov. Look: we've discovered true peace. (*Points to* ANNICHKA, *then the bed.*) Kavalerov, we ought to drink to indifference and to Annichka. (*Silence.*) Women were once the shining light of our civilization, the symbol of all that was pure and beautiful. I was searching for the essence of womanhood . . . but Valya left me for him. I thought a woman was something that belonged to you, and that her tenderness and love was only meant for you, but that's where I was wrong . . . Valya left me for him. After something like that, is anything worth fighting for? Isn't it time to stop caring, Kavalerov? After all, she really does love him. Nobody actually stole her. She ran out on you.

KAVALEROV: I'll get Valya away from him.

IVAN: Oh, no, Kavalerov . . . no, you won't get her away from him . . . she won't leave him for you. Your youth is over, Kavalerov.

KAVALEROV: That's not true. I'm 28. He's older than I am, and she doesn't love him.

IVAN: You're a thousand years old, Kavalerov. Stop giggling, Anna Mikhailovna. He's old, your friend Kolya—he's ancient . . . he's weighted down with all the old age of our epoch, and suffers from all the rheumatism. But that brother of mine—he's young and energetic, he's on top of the world. He's got his nose stuck so high in the air he doesn't even see us. Look, Kavalerov, there's your destiny—a bed, a warm comforter, a warm Anna Mikhailovna . . . what else do you have to look forward to? Look what you've turned out to be . . . a clown, a little boy who never grew up. I know that's hard to take, it's sad . . . yes, I know, there's Chernyshevsky Street somewhere out there . . . open windows on the second floor, clouds float across the sky, and their paths merge with their reflections in the window panes. And a girl was leaning on the window sill, her arm delicate as a flute. You'd better forget about all that, that's not for you with your big red nose . . . your youth is over . . . you're not going to be handsome or famous. You won't be coming from a small town to the capital, you won't be a general or a scholar or a long-distance runner or an adventurer . . . it's all over for you . . . you're old enough to be a father yourself. You ought to have a son of your own.

ANNICHKA: There, you see, Kolya. Ivan Petrovich is saying just what I've been saying all along. That's what I've been telling you: you'll settle down when we have a baby.

IVAN: Then what's the matter? You're a fascinating woman, Anna Mikhailovna. Take him to your bosom. Rock the tired old century to sleep in your arms. Hurrah! . . . Bear him a child, Anna Mikhailovna. We'll put it on this little pillow of mine. We'll celebrate the birth of a true child of the October Revolution . . . if it's a boy, we'll call him "The Quarter," if it's a girl, we'll call her "Ophelia." Let's drink, Kavalerov, let's drink to youth which has passed, and to the conspiracy of feelings which has failed.

KAVALEROV: You're a son of a bitch, Ivan Petrovich. My youth isn't over. No . . . (*Grabs* IVAN *by the collar.*) It's not true, do you hear? I'll prove it to you . . . do you hear?

ANNICHKA: Don't shout, Kolya . . . don't make a scene . . .

KAVALEROV: Shut up . . . get back to your kitchen . . . I'm not in the same class with you, you pig . . . do you hear?! . . . you got me in your clutches when I was drunk . . . it was all a big mistake, understand . . .

ANNICHKA: But you kissed me so passionately that night . . . you said: "Annichka, it's so wonderful, after all those prostitutes, to hold a pure woman in my arms" . . .

KAVALEROV: This is awful . . . this is awful! . . . of course she's nothing but a dumb broad, but you, Ivan Petrovich, why are you making fun of me? Well, why don't you tell her, tell her . . . tell her her face looks like a rusty padlock . . . tell her she's an old bag coming apart at the seams, you can squeeze her out like liver paste . . . (*After a pause, exhausted.*) Let me alone . . . Go away. Get out. (*A pause. He staggers from exhaustion.*) What should I do, Ivan Petrovich, what should I do?

IVAN: Kill my brother Andrei. (*Silence.*)

KAVALEROV: You're the one . . . you're the one that ought to be killed for stirring up all this trouble. (*Silence.*)

ANNICHKA: God knows what you're talking about . . .

IVAN: You wanted fame. This will make you famous. Your name will be honored by posterity as the hired assassin who murdered the century. I give you my blessing.

KAVALEROV: Get out. Leave me alone. (*He drags himself towards the bed. Falls on the bed. Silence.*)

IVAN: Well, how about it, Anna Mikhailovna, shall we go to the Fantasma? Let's let Kavalerov sleep.

ANNICHKA: It's right around the corner. You don't even have to put a hat on. I'll just take a scarf.

KAVALEROV (*raising himself up*): I don't know why, Ivan Petrovich, but I have a feeling . . . that Valya is going to come here . . . really I do . . . tell her how to get here . . . it's easy to get lost in the corridors here. Maybe she'll come to make up for being so cruel to me.

IVAN: You're making Anna Mikhailovna jealous for nothing by talking that way . . . Don't get upset, Anna Mikhailovna, nobody's going to come to him. Oh, you look just like Carmen in that scarf! I'd carry you over my head like a torch, but alas . . . you're not a torch at all, but a whole searchlight . . . (*They go out.*)

(KAVALEROV *lies on the bed. Everything is quiet. Here* KAVALEROV's *dream begins. The stage seems to vibrate. All at once the shadows shift position as if an invisible source of light had sprung up somewhere from within the depths of the furniture—an unpleasant yellowish light. A knock at the door.* KAVALEROV *sits up on the bed.*)

KAVALEROV: Come in! . . . (VALYA *enters. She seems to float in, the essence of femininity, tender, touching.* KAVALEROV *sits on the bed.*) There . . . I knew it . . . I've been waiting.

(ANDREI BABICHEV *enters.* KAVALEROV *recoils.* ANDREI *and* VALYA *sit down at the table. They don't see* KAVALEROV. *He's in plain sight, but they don't see him—it's a dream.*)

ANDREI: Ah-ha . . . say, this is great . . . if you ask me, it's great . . .

KAVALEROV (*from the bed*): Hello, Andrei Petrovich . . .

ANDREI: This is where we'll have the wedding. If you ask me, it's a great place.

KAVALEROV: Valya, here I am . . .

VALYA (*without seeing or hearing him*): Why'd you bring me here?

ANDREI: Why, don't you like it here? Look, that's quite a bed, made out of rosewood . . .

KAVALEROV (*seized with fear*): Andrei Petrovich . . .

ANDREI (*without seeing or hearing him*): Are you embarrassed? . . . are you ashamed? . . .

VALYA: I don't know . . . (ANDREI *laughs loudly. In the dream* ANDREI *looks the way he appears in* KAVALEROV's *imagi-*

nation, he's frighteningly inhuman like a statue or a scare-crow.)

KAVALEROV: You're not alone, Andrei Petrovich. I'm here —Kavalerov! Can't you see me? Here I am!

ANDREI: I'll undress you now . . .

KAVALEROV (*screams*): Valya!

ANDREI: What are you sighing for? . . .

VALYA: Someone's calling me . . .

KAVALEROV: Valya, here I am! . . .

ANDREI: Who's calling you? What nonsense. That's mysticism. That's a lot of mysticism. It's all very simple. Now we're going to go to bed together. What's the point of mysticism?

KAVALEROV (*screams, but without being seen or heard*): I won't let you . . . do you hear . . . the bastards . . . why doesn't he hear me?

VALYA: I feel so sad.

ANDREI: You little fool . . . Ivan taught you that . . . what do you want anyhow? For me to start sighing? . . .

VALYA: I want to see Kavalerov.

KAVALEROV: Valya, Valya . . . look . . . I'm over here . . . look, here I am . . . what's going on here . . . I'm screaming, "Valya, Valya" as loud as I can . . . can't you see me . . . here I am, see, here are my hands. Here I am, I'm standing right next to you . . . Valya . . . My God . . . she doesn't see me . . .

VALYA: I want to see Kavalerov.

ANDREI: I'll have him put away in a lunatic asylum . . .

VALYA: You're a tyrant.

KAVALEROV: Quit trying to kid me, Andrei Petrovich. You're just pretending not to see me. Don't be afraid, Valya, don't be afraid. Look at me, I'm right here next to you, I'll save you, I've been waiting for you all my life . . . Valya . . . Valya . . . they want to marry me off to Annichka . . . Valya, take pity on me . . . (*Gets down on his knees before her, throws his arms around her legs.*) Take pity on me . . . I'm right here . . . you don't see me, you don't feel my hands, even though I'm touching your knees . . .

VALYA (*without seeing or hearing him*): Kavalerov saw me at the recreation center. I was in my shorts. He said my knees were sweet as oranges. You never say things like that to me.

ANDREI: Corpses talk like that. That's the language of the dead.

KAVALEROV: I'm not dead.

ANDREI: You're a reservoir, Valya . . . do you understand? You're an incubator . . . We'll sleep together in that big comfortable bed and then you'll have a baby. We've got to have descendants. All the rest is mysticism . . .

KAVALEROV: Don't sleep with him, Valya . . . don't waste your youth on him: you hear what he's saying, don't you? He's saying you're a reservoir. Valya, he's an insensitive boor, he's a monster . . . he's a machine . . .

VALYA: I won't go to bed with you! . . .

ANDREI: Oh yes you will! . . .

VALYA: I'll scream! . . . Kavalerov! . . .

KAVALEROV: I'm right here! . . .

VALYA: Kavalerov! . . .

KAVALEROV: I'm right here! . . .

VALYA: Kavalerov! . . .

KAVALEROV: Here I am . . . here I am . . . I'm right over here. Over here . . .

VALYA: Save me, Kavalerov! . . .

KAVALEROV: What'll I do? . . . he doesn't even see me. (*There's a bottle on the table,* KAVALEROV *grabs it. He can't lift it. It's a dream. The bottle seems glued to the table.*) Ah—ah—ah—ah—ah . . .

ANDREI: Stop screaming . . . you can forget the word "love." That's an obsolete concept. What are you afraid of? There'll be one gigantic apartment building with rows of mass production bedrooms . . . 20,000 sex acts per day. But what do you want? . . . individual portions . . . sweet little kisses . . . caresses . . . sighs. To hell with all that! That's the old-fashioned home-made way . . . I'll kick the stuffing out of all those little kisses . . . Throw them out! . . . I'll build the perfect mass production bedroom. Pretty great, huh?

VALYA: You make me feel trapped! Let me go to Kavalerov. He said that I rushed past him like a branch full of flowers and leaves . . . Kavalerov, where are you? . . .

KAVALEROV: I'm right here . . .

VALYA (*speaks without seeing or hearing* KAVALEROV): Where are you? You won't have to live in back alleys anymore. I want to be with you . . .

ANDREI: Be quiet . . .

VALYA: It's me! It's me! The one you've been waiting for all your life. Here's my hand, delicate as a flute . . . Your youth hasn't passed. No . . . I love you . . . I'll save you . . . dearest . . . darling . . . where are you? . . .

KAVALEROV: I'm right here . . .

ANDREI (*as if he suddenly just caught sight of* KAVALEROV. *In a terrible rage*): Doctor!!! (*A* DOCTOR *appears wearing a white uniform. Black beard. Glasses. Yellow bald spot. Bony.*)

KAVALEROV (*cries out in terror, like someone having a nightmare*): Don't! Don't! Don't!

DOCTOR (*in a jerky voice, as if he wasn't able to talk, but had been taught how*): Where's the patient?

ANDREI: There's the patient.

DOCTOR: Ahah . . . (*Squealing with delight.*)

KAVALEROV: Valya . . .

DOCTOR: Take off his jacket. Give me a hand . . . that's it . . . (ANDREI *helps the* DOCTOR *undress* KAVALEROV.) Let's just take off his shirt now . . .

KAVALEROV: I don't want to. I'm ashamed . . . Valya, I'm ashamed, don't, don't . . .

ANDREI: Just take it off . . . that's it . . . quite a handsome guy . . . (*They undress* KAVALEROV, *who looks pathetic.*)

DOCTOR: Uh huh . . . uh huh . . . just a minute . . . let's have a look at the muscles . . . uh huh . . . quite a flabby set of muscles . . . uh huh . . . loose living, must come from loose living . . . well now, just step over here to the light . . . come over to the light now . . . Let me take a look at your pupils . . . let's see those pupils . . . let's take a look at them . . . let's see how they respond . . . just step over here to the light . . . (*He pulls* KAVALEROV.) Uh huh . . . uh huh, uh huh . . . just a little nearer to the light . . . yessir . . . uh uh uh uh . . . (*Shouts, his voice going higher and higher.*) He's stark— raving—mad! . . . (*They all rush over to* KAVALEROV.)

KAVALEROV: Forgive me . . . forgive me . . . (*He falls on the bed.*)

(*He wakes up.* KAVALEROV's *dream comes to an end. The stage once again assumes its former appearance.* ANNA PROKOPOVICH *enters on tip toe.*)

Let me go . . . let me go . . . I'm coming! . . . I'll save her . . . let me go . . . (*He screams.*) Valya! Valya! . . . (*He continues to scream as the curtain falls.*)

(*Curtain.*)

(A small room. Petty bourgeois. The LADY OF THE HOUSE *is celebrating her nameday. A table laden with sumptuous fare. A hanging lamp with a very broad orange lamp shade. The group applauds as* IVAN BABICHEV *and* NIKOLAI KAVALEROV *enter, led in by the master of ceremonies,* MIKHAIL MIKHAILYCH. IVAN *is carrying his pillow.* NIKOLAI KAVALEROV *looks like a sleepwalker. His reddish hair is unkempt.)*

MIKHAIL MIKHAILYCH: Ladies and gentlemen, may I have your attention for just a moment, please? . . . Quiet, please . . . ssh . . . With your permission, ladies and gentlemen, today, for Elena Pavlovna's nameday, I've decided to . . . it's a kind of a present . . . and for her gift, here's what I've arranged: I've invited the famous man we've all been hearing so much about. The man I've invited to be here with us tonight is none other than *(Points with a sweeping gesture.)* Ivan Petrovich Babichev! . . . I just ran into him on the street. Ivan Petrovich has been stirring people up to rise in revolt against his brother.

LADY IN GREEN: But who is his brother?

MIKHAIL MIKHAILYCH: Now please don't interrupt, ladies and gentlemen. Before we do anything else, we should all give Ivan Petrovich a rousing welcome. If I may be allowed to express myself this way, Ivan Babichev is the great prophet of the 20th century . . .

GUESTS: Bravo . . . bravo . . . bravo!

IVAN: Greetings, my friends, greetings . . . Congratulations, Elena Pavlovna, let's wish her many happy returns, my friends . . .

VENERABLE OLD MAN: Please sit down and make yourself at home . . .

IVAN: And here's Nikolai Kavalerov, the man of humble origin and grandiose ideas . . . sit down, Nikolai Kavalerov . . .

KAVALEROV: All right, I'll sit down, it's all the same to me, you can do whatever you want.

LADY OF THE HOUSE: Very pleased to meet you . . . make yourself at home. May I pour you some wine?

IVAN: Thank you. (*A pause.*) Can you all see me all right? Move back just a little, would you please . . . I want you all to see me.

OLD MAN: Bravo . . .

MIKHAIL MIKHAILYCH: Quiet . . . ssh . . . it's about to begin. (*Tension begins to mount in the* CROWD.)

IVAN (*raises his wine glass*): I drink to your health, my friends . . . (*A pause.*) Everyone look at me. I'm your king. Take a good look at me. (*A pause.*)

KAVALEROV (*maliciously*): Oh no, he's not crazy. You think he's crazy? He's a crook . . .

A HARD-DRINKING GUEST: Right! (*A pause.*)

IVAN: I'm your king. Take a good look at me! I'm a fat guy. I've got a bald spot. The bags under my eyes hang down like violet stockings. Look at me! Remember this moment well! This is Ivan Babichev you're looking at. When they ask you "What did Ivan Babichev look like?" then you'll be able to tell them about me . . . See this derby. My derby's rusty-brown with age. My derby's begun to look like an Easter cake. (*A pause.*) Look at me. A king sits before you. I am the king of the cheap, the shabby, and the vulgar . . .

VIC (*enthusiastic young man, asks in amazement*): But what's the pillow for?

IVAN: It's my coat-of-arms. It's your coat-of-arms, my dear people. It's an old pillow, honored by the many heads that have slept on it.

OLD MAN: Bravo, bravo . . .

IVAN: See, I'm putting it down at my feet. And it just sat down there like a pig.

HARD-DRINKING GUEST: Right . . .

ZINOCHKA (*in the hush that follows*): Tell me: is it true that you know how to perform miracles?

IVAN (*in the ensuing silence*): Yes, it's true . . . (*A pause.*)

LADY OF THE HOUSE: Mikhail Mikhailych, ask your friend to perform a miracle . . .

KAVALEROV: Show them a miracle, Ivan Petrovich. (*Throughout what follows* KAVALEROV *puts his head down on*

*the table and remains indifferent to what's going on around
him, as if asleep.*)

IVAN: All right, my friends, I agree . . .

OLD MAN: Wonderful . . . wonderful . . .

MIKHAIL MIKHAILYCH: Comrade Babichev is a 20th century
miracle worker.

IVAN: I agree to perform a miracle, but first, each of you
has got to confess his innermost desires.

HARD-DRINKING GUEST: Right. (*A hush falls over the
group.*)

LADY IN GREEN: But people's innermost desires are often
indecent. (*A pause.*) What do we do in that case?

LESS VENERABLE OLD MAN: That's not so easy—to confess
your innermost desires.

IVAN: I'm waiting. Who'll be the first? (*Laughing and giggling, they crowd around* IVAN.)

ZINOCHKA: Well, I'd like (*She stops short.*) oh, no . . .

MIKHAIL MIKHAILYCH: Don't be embarrassed, Zinaida Mikhailovna. This is beginning to get interesting.

ZINOCHKA: Let somebody else start. (*A pause.*)

MIKHAIL MIKHAILYCH: Then let me. This is a deeply personal matter, and it'll probably seem funny to everyone else,
but, with your permission, I'll go ahead and tell you about it
anyhow. My wife's eight months pregnant . . . you see, my
greatest desire is a small one, really, but it's very important to
me . . . a father's fondest hope, so to speak . . . would it be
possible for the baby to look like me?

IVAN: Bravo, bravo! . . .

OLD MAN: Well, all right . . . then I'll be next . . . it's not so
bad after all. Well, my wish is just a simple human one . . . a
desire for peace and quiet . . . well, that's it. I'm sixty years
old. I'd like to own my own house. Just a little house, a
bungalow in the country. With a garden and a flowering hedge
—and jasmine blooming. And a verandah opening out on the
garden . . . braided rugs, a piano with a silk cover, an awning
that rolls down from the window. Peace, quiet . . . On Sundays
the whole family comes to visit me: my old brother, my uncle
who's a hundred, my sons the engineers, and all the grandchil-
dren . . . We all sit on the verandah and eat raspberries. My
granddaughter plays a serenade by Drigo on the piano. We eat
raspberries. And the youngest one crawls on the grass with
raspberry all over his face . . .

LADY OF THE HOUSE: Ah, how lovely . . .

OLD MAN: A big family. A quiet house. Patches of sunlight on the floor. Where is all that? Why doesn't my granddaughter play the piano? I'm an old man, I need a quiet little house.

LADY OF THE HOUSE: Ah, how lovely . . . (*Silence.*)

VIC (*all of a sudden, impetuously*): But I'd like . . . but I'd like . . . wait . . . I dream about having an extraordinary love affair . . .

LESS DRUNK GUEST: Oh, you devil . . .

VIC (*passionately*): I dream about having an extraordinary love affair . . . do you suppose I could? That's what I wanted to say . . . I'm an electrical engineer by profession . . . I often have to go into other people's apartments. And what do I see there? Fights, perpetual bickering. Hate, screaming at children . . . it shouldn't be that way . . . our hearts should be overflowing with happiness.

HARD-DRINKING GUEST: Right.

VIC: So what I want to say is: my secret wish is to love a woman with an undying passion.

IVAN: Bravo . . .

LADY OF THE HOUSE: Well, now it's my turn . . . you see, there's my daughter Zina.

ZINOCHKA: Oh, Mama, don't . . .

LADY OF THE HOUSE: Just a minute, Zinochka. Don't interrupt . . . if this man can help us, why not tell him all about it? Here's my Zinochka . . . she's very talented . . .

ZINOCHKA: Oh, Mama, how can you . . .

LADY OF THE HOUSE: She sings beautifully . . . and I'd like . . . it would be so easy to make my dreams come true. Of course, I'm a mother, and I want my daughter to have everything in life. I'm so anxious for Zinochka to be famous throughout the whole world. That's really not so far-fetched. She has a voice like an angel. Is it really so sinful to want wealth and fame for your child?

LESS VENERABLE OLD MAN (*with sudden vehemence, in a threatening tone*): Tell me now, why are you eating your heart out? Why do you hate your next-door neighbor? On account of a room?

OLD MAN (*excitedly*): What's that?

LESS VENERABLE GUEST: Let's say that I'm here. And let's say that you're there—Sergei Nikolaevich, Mr. Mikulitsky . . . That makes us neighbors then, we live right next door to each other.

OLD MAN: Well, what of it?

LESS VENERABLE OLD MAN: And let's say I know that you're

a venerable old man, an old man that everybody respects. But I just happen to live right next door to you, with only a thin wall between us, and I listen every night to hear if you're dying yet. So every morning I get up and start swearing because the old man hasn't died yet. He's still alive and kicking even though he's got one foot in the grave. Here's my wish: If you asked: "What's your secret desire"—I'd tell you: "I wish you'd die, neighbor, I wish you'd die, Sergei Niko-laevich Mikulitsky!" That's my wish. So your room would be empty.

VIC: That's disgraceful . . .

OLD MAN: For god's sake, Elena Pavlovna, why do you let him! (*The* OLD MAN *sobs. General indignation.*)

ELENA PAVLOVNA: It's a disgrace . . . it's a disgrace . . . aren't you ashamed, Nikitin . . .

LESS VENERABLE OLD MAN: Of course, I apologize . . . I'm awfully ashamed of myself . . .

OLD MAN: Just how low can a person sink?

LESS VENERABLE OLD MAN: It's shameful but true.

IVAN: So now I've heard you all . . . everything's just fine. I've listened carefully to everything. All that remains to be done now is to fulfill your wishes.

VIC: Our lives are boring, our lives are worthless. Nothing but sadness. Hatred and fighting . . .

LADY IN GREEN: You mean you can make our wishes come true?

IVAN: I can't make your wishes come true. I'm the king of the dead.

LADY IN GREEN: In other words, you've tricked us?

IVAN: Dead men don't have desires. I'm the king of corpses.

ZINOCHKA (*passionately*): That's not true. I'm going to be a famous singer.

IVAN: My dear girl, they won't let you be famous.

LADY OF THE HOUSE: Who won't?

IVAN: My brother, Andrei Babichev. (*Silence.*) My brother, Andrei Babichev, builder of the new world, will destroy vanity, love, the family, cruelty . . .

OLD MAN: What does all that mean?

IVAN: You were talking about family, my dear sir—there won't be families anymore. You wished for the death of your neighbor. That means you're cruel. There won't be such a thing as cruelty anymore. There'll be neither lovers, nor trai-tors, nor daredevils, nor true friends, nor prodigal sons—

OLD MAN: What can we do, then?

IVAN: The great human feelings are regarded as cheap and worthless nowadays. You ask what can be done. Now you there, I mean the electrical engineer, listen to what I have to say. You know how an electric light bulb suddenly goes out. Burned out, you'd say . . .

VIC: Yeh, burned out . . .

IVAN: But say you shake the burned-out bulb?

VIC (*eagerly*): It lights up again.

HARD-DRINKING GUEST: Right.

IVAN: It'll light up again and burn for a little while longer. A breakdown's taken place inside the bulb. The filaments have snapped. What are they . . .

VIC: Tungsten . . .

IVAN: The tungsten filaments have snapped, and when the fragments come into contact, the light comes back to life . . . briefly, unnaturally . . .

VIC (*delighted*): Unnaturally.

IVAN: But there's no hiding the fact that its life is doomed. It's like a fever, it burns too brightly. A flash of brilliance, then total darkness. But the momentary brilliance is exquisite. (*A pause.*) You ask: What should we do? Now I'm going to tell you. You must shake the light. You must shake the heart of the burned-out epoch. You must shake this heart like a bulb, so that the fragments will come into contact and blaze up with an exquisite momentary brilliance.

VIC (*spellbound*): Exquisite brilliance.

IVAN: Yes, we're dying. Victims of history . . . we're dying . . . the 19th century is dying, but we're still alive. Our death pangs will be terrible. History, I want to say to you: here's a lover, here's a fool, here's a mother doting on her daughter . . here's a proud man, here's a cheat—here they all are, spokesmen for the great feelings . . . (*A pause.*) I want to gather a great horde around me—only then will I be able to make my choice. I go from house to house, searching. Love, where are you?

VIC: Here I am, right here . . . that's me, I'm the one who wants to love! . . .

IVAN: Vanity, where are you?

ZINOCHKA: Mama, that's me, I'm the one he's calling . . . I want great fame . . . I want . . .

IVAN: Come to me. Love . . . be jealous . . . be proud . . . Be cruel and tender . . . Let's go. I'm going to show you to my brother. He makes fun of people like you—of your sauce pans and kettles, of your flower pots, of your quiet little lives, of your privilege to shove a pacifier in your kids' mouths . . . what is he trying to tear out of your hearts? Your own home —home, sweet home! He wants to make you outcasts on the barren fields of history. Let's send him straight to hell. Here's my pillow. I'm the king of pillows. You can tell my brother: Let each of us sleep on his own pillow. Keep your hands off our pillows.

LESS VENERABLE OLD MAN: That kind of brother ought to be killed . . . (KAVALEROV *raises his head.*)

IVAN: He will be killed. (*Silence.*) I've been going around looking. I've been trying to find a hired assassin to avenge the century. And I've finally found him. (*Kisses* KAVALEROV *on the forehead. Silence.*) Nikolai Kavalerov is going to kill my brother. Andrei. Tomorrow. At the football game. Here's the razor he's going to do it with. (*Pulls the razor out of* KAVALE-ROV's *pocket.*)

VIC: Slit his throat . . . slit his throat . . . (MIKHAIL MIKHAI-LYCH *beams with satisfaction—the party's been a great success.*)

IVAN: Do you hear that, Kavalerov? They're giving you full power. Oh, my poor, dear friend, what anguish you've suffered! Perhaps your moment of glory that you've been dreaming about since childhood has come at last. Don't give up, here's your chance. Approach this mighty deed with the knowledge that a great century, the 19th century, gives you its blessing . . .

KAVALEROV: But what if the new century curses me? . . . (*The bulb in the lamp suddenly goes out. Panic.*)

VIC: That's nothing serious, it's all right . . . it's just burned out . . . I'll fix it right away . . . it's nothing . . . it's just burned out . . .

LADY OF THE HOUSE (*screams*): Shake it! . . . Shake it! (*The door opens. Silhouetted in the doorway, with the light behind him,* ANDREI BABICHEV *appears—a huge stone guest. General uproar and then silence.*)

ANDREI: Excuse me, does Citizen Shapiro live here? Solomon Davidovich Shapiro?

LADY OF THE HOUSE (*relieved, almost with a groan*): No, that's higher up, on the third floor . . . (*The door closes. Darkness.*)

KAVALEROV (*hurls himself at the door, bumping into the table and knocking dishes to the floor*): Andrei Petrovich!! Oh, you've gone already!! . . . Oh, you don't want to . . . Well, all right . . . it's your own fault then . . . You're the one that wanted it this way . . . (*He calms down. A pause.*)

IVAN: And so, my friends, we'll meet tomorrow at the stadium . . . (*The table's set up on its legs again.*)

(*Curtain.*)

scene 7

(*The Stadium. The football game is just about to begin. Bright sunny day. Posters with huge lettering. Greenery, pennants. Refreshment stand, small tables. Picket fences, pathways. Seated at one of the small refreshment tables:* MIKHAIL MIKHAILYCH, ZINOCHKA, *and the* VENERABLE OLD MAN, *all from Scene 6.*)

ZINOCHKA: Is he really going to kill him?

MIKHAIL MIKHAILYCH: Yes, he's going to. There's been so much talk about it. If he doesn't, he'll really be a skunk . . .

VENERABLE OLD MAN: Listen . . . isn't this dangerous? . . . Well, I don't know quite how to say it . . . but they won't arrest us as accomplices, will they? . . .

MIKHAIL MIKHAILYCH: Why would they? It's not really a crime—it's a murder of historical necessity: one man kills another without any personal motive whatsoever.

VENERABLE OLD MAN: He what? I suppose he'll wear a disguise. He'll probably wear a false mustache . . .

ZINOCHKA: But say his mustache suddenly fell off . . . that would really be embarrassing. (IVAN BABICHEV *appears with his pillow and* KAVALEROV.)

MIKHAIL MIKHAILYCH: Ssh . . . Here they are . . . Sssh . . . They're not wearing any make-up . . . Come over and join us, Ivan Petrovich . . .

IVAN: Greetings, my friends . . .

MIKHAIL MIKHAILYCH (*to the* WAITER): Waiter! Two dishes of ice cream. (*To* IVAN.) What kind do you want? Raspberry?

IVAN: Yes, raspberry . . .

ZINOCHKA: And I'll have the same.

MIKHAIL MIKHAILYCH: And lemon for me. We're in a bit of a hurry. (*Silence.*)

ZINOCHKA (*to* KAVALEROV): Aren't you afraid? Tell me . . .

MIKHAIL MIKHAILYCH: Don't interfere, Zinaida Mikhailovna. Don't interfere, or you'll spoil everything . . .

IVAN: You look pale, Kavalerov. That won't do.

KAVALEROV: I'm completely calm.

IVAN: You've read Shakespeare, haven't you, Kavalerov? Remember? Remember how Hamlet ends? Corpses, dire passions, misery, and suddenly enter Fortinbras. Enter the conqueror. And all passions come to an end. Enough is enough. Enter Fortinbras—who doesn't give a damn for passions or anguish. All soliloquies are over. Now begin the cheers and fanfares . . . (*A pause.*) There . . . look, Kavalerov. (*He points to the grandstand with a sweeping gesture.*) Now Fortinbras is going to enter, now the football players are going to enter, and they don't give a damn for your anguish or passions. We've got to hurry, Kavalerov . . . Let's go, my friends . . . We'll meet him at the entrance . . . (*They go out.*)

OLD MAN (*tagging along after them*): Maybe we shouldn't after all. Heavens, maybe it's not worth it . . . (*A military band starts playing.* ANDREI, HARMAN—*a German business man —and* REPRESENTATIVES *of the Food Producers Union come on stage. They sit down at one of the small tables on the other side of the refreshment stand.*)

ANDREI: The football game today is sponsored by the Food Producers Union in honor of a new kind of salami which has just come out. Here are the representatives of the Food Producers Union. (*He points them out.*) This is Herr Harman from Berlin, he's a leading authority on nutrition for the masses. (*They bow to one another.*) Herr Harman knows our language. So if you start making wisecracks about his being a dirty capitalist, it'll be pretty embarrassing. (*To* HARMAN.) A man from our firm, Solomon Davidovich Shapiro, should be here at any moment with a sample of the salami.

HARMAN (*makes a great effort to speak correctly*): Oh, you'll have to cut a little piece for me.

ANDREI: We'll make you a whole sandwich. Unfortunately, there's been a slight delay. You see, today's game isn't just a sports event, it's part of an advertising campaign too.

HARMAN: So I've heard. I just heard about it. Someone came out into the umpire's box and shouted through a megaphone that the salami will be on sale tomorrow in all the stores and food stands . . .

ANDREI: Yeah, that's the plan . . . and we're really sorry that we're a little late in getting it out. But in the meantime, it would be a good idea after today's game to treat the winning team to a couple of pounds of salami. What are you smiling at, Fessenkov?

FESSENKOV: At the offer you just made.

ANDREI: You ought to be ashamed in front of our foreign visitors. You see, Herr Harman, even in the Soviet Union we still haven't been able to get rid of the trappings that went along with medieval tournaments. For example: here's a union man Fessenkov, who's convinced that you can only shower the winning team with roses . . .

HARMAN: That's no good, Citizen Fessenkov . . .

ANDREI: Es ist nicht gut, Herr Fessenkov . . . our salami is just as good as any roses. Herr Harman, we'll make you a rose sandwich . . .

HARMAN: Oh, you're a real poet . . .

ANDREI: Did you hear that, Safranov? You thought that I was just a salami salesman but it turns out that I'm a poet. O.K. . . . Tomorrow we'll show Mr. Harman where they're building "The Quarter." "The Quarter" will open in November. Herr Harman, we're paving the way for a great migration of the masses. That Fessenkov's smirking again. Stop smiling. I'm a poet, and can't help expressing myself this way. Yes, we're paving the way for a great migration of the masses.

HARMAN: Just where do the people have to migrate to?

ANDREI: To the wonderful land of public nutrition. The name of this country is "The Quarter"! What we're trying to do now is make the way to this new land as appealing as possible. There'll be banners to greet the newcomers: "The Quarter Cigarettes," "The Quarter Soap," "The Quarter Fruit Drops." And we're only sorry that we can't sell our salami at less than 35 kopecks a kilo. (*Suddenly getting angry.*) Why doesn't Shapiro come? Where's Shapiro? Why isn't he here? Herr Harman, at "The Quarter" there'll be a schnitzel conveyer belt . . .

HARMAN: You're a great cook, Herr Babichev. (*Sees* SHA-PIRO *approaching.*) But look, there's someone coming—it must be Shapiro. He's carrying a package.

ANDREI (*bellowing*): Yeah, that's him all right. Over here

... over here ... hurry up, Herr Shapiro ... we're waiting ... we're waiting ... we're waiting ...

SHAPIRO (*comes up to them*): I hurried as fast as I could. I'm awfully hot, Andrei Petrovich ... I brought her. (*Puts the package down on the table.*)

ANDREI: All right, gentlemen, your attention please. Herr Harman, there she is. That's the salami. Der Wurst. Hello, Shapiro. Come here and let me give you a big hug. Quiet, comrades. (*No one's making any noise except* ANDREI.) Take out your notebook now, Herr Harman, and start writing. (*As if he were dictating.*) "Genosse Shapiro brachte Wurst." Write that down. Have you written it down? Now to continue ... "When they first brought it in, I thought it was a rose ..."

HARMAN: "But it was a salami they brought" ... Oh, Herr Babichev, you're just like one little child ...

ANDREI: Keep on writing ... "Then I inhaled a beautiful fragrance" ... (*No longer dictating.*) You know, Herr Harman ... that's a Shakespearean salami ...

SHAPIRO: 70% pure romance ... that is, veal ...

HARMAN: In Russian, are romance and veal really the same thing? I don't know what to write down ...

ANDREI: Write this down: "I saw salami made out of romance, and romance made out of veal" ...

HARMAN: What I'll write is that I don't understand a thing ...

ANDREI: And besides that, write this down: "I saw a mad salami salesman" ... How would you say that in German ...

SHAPIRO: In German that would be: "You're a great guy, Comrade Babichev!"

HARMAN (*speaks in German*): Ach, ja ...

ANDREI: And now, Shapiro, give me a knife ...

SHAPIRO: That's going to be difficult, since I don't have one ... (*Enter* IVAN *and* KAVALEROV, *with a* CROWD OF FOLLOWERS *behind them.*)

IVAN (*on seeing* ANDREI): There he is ... Are you ready, Kavalerov? (KAVALEROV *remains silent.*) Kavalerov, you've got to slam the door hard ... Kavalerov, you've got to leave a scar on history's ugly mug ...

VALYA (*running in on the upper platform*): Andrei Petrovich ... the game's beginning ...

KAVALEROV: I'm ready ... I'm coming ... they'll probably shoot me ... (VALYA *runs down the ramp,* KAVALEROV *climbs up the ramp and meets* VALYA.)

VALYA: Hello, Kavalerov.

KAVALEROV: Hello . . .

VALYA: What's the matter with you, Kavalerov? You're not mad at me, are you, because I slapped you?

KAVALEROV: I'm not mad at you, Valya. Are you Andrei Petrovich's wife?

VALYA: Not yet . . .

KAVALEROV: I'm just about to slit his throat with a razor . . .

VALYA: You? Well, then go ahead and slit it . . . Andrei Petrovich . . .

KAVALEROV: Valya . . .

VALYA: Andrei Petrovich, Kavalerov's come to slit your throat . . .

ANDREI: Who, me? Now? . . . here? . . . O.K. . . . What am I supposed to do? Lie down? Unbutton my collar?

SHAPIRO: Well, now we're going to have a little Shakespeare . . .

ANDREI: What would you like to cut my throat with?

VALYA: A razor.

ANDREI: Well, let's start cutting then, Kavalerov. (*He takes the razor from* KAVALEROV *and starts to cut the salami.*) That's the way we slice it . . . smell the aroma? . . .

IVAN: Cut his throat! . . . down with salami salesmen! Cut his throat . . .

KAVALEROV: No, that's not it . . . give me the razor . . . (KAVALEROV *snatches the razor out of* ANDREI's *hands and heads for* IVAN.)

ZINOCHKA: Stop him . . .

IVAN: I see now, I see . . . (All of IVAN's FOLLOWERS *retreat in horror.* IVAN *runs offstage. A moment later he lets out a terrible shriek.*)

KAVALEROV (*runs in from offstage*): There, I've killed him . . . I've murdered my own past . . . let me explain . . .

ANDREI: That's the end of the old passions . . . The new world is beginning. (*A whistle. The* FOOTBALL PLAYERS *come down the ramp.*)

(*Curtain.*)

**A COMEDY IN TWO OR THREE ACTS WITH
CHORAL INTERLUDES**

each

in his

own way

by Luigi Pirandello

English Version by

Arthur Livingston

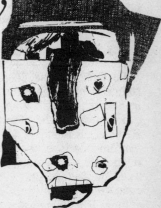

Ciascuno a suo modo was first produced in Milan
at the Teatro dei Filodrammatici on May 22, 1924,
and published the same year.

Each in His Own Way transposes the theme of revolution from the streets to the theatre. Insurrection occurs not at the barricades, but backstage, on stage, and in the lobby. In the first choral interlude, half of the audience, rebelling against the play, quarrels with the other half. In the second interlude, the "real" characters on whom the play is based rise up against the actors and the author: La Moreno slaps the actress who plays a character patterned after her and perhaps even strikes the author, Pirandello. Then, joining the uprising against the playwright, the actors and actresses refuse to appear in the play and leave the theatre. Pirandello himself is the cause of a theatrical revolution; his dramatization of the relationship between art and life, illusion and reality, provokes a public disturbance and even leads to a strike.

In *Each in His Own Way*, as in the other plays which comprise his theatre-within-the-theatre trilogy (*Six Characters in Search of an Author* and *Tonight We Improvise*), Pirandello questions the nature of theatre and of theatrical illusion. He enlarges the dimensions of drama by placing the traditional play and its invented characters in the larger context of their relationships to actors, audience, and "real" characters whose roles the actors play. Above all, Pirandello dramatizes the creative process itself by including a new character, the author. Breaking down the barriers between stage and audience, the playwright now explores the complex interaction between art and life. In *Each in His Own Way*, one setting represents the theatre lobby, and thus enabled the audience at the play to watch the audience at the play. An onstage spectator exclaims, "The play seems to have moved from the stage to the lobby!" With equal accuracy, a spectator in the auditorium might observe that the lobby has moved to the stage, and that the audience, watching itself represented, is placed in the same position as La Moreno and Baron Nuti. Although the "real" lovers rebel against the artistic representation of themselves, they nonetheless imitate and repeat that representation. And might not the "real" audience imitate and repeat the words and attitudes of the onstage audience? Even so, while life may imitate theatre, theatre imitates life. In making himself the source of uproar and confusion in *Each in His Own Way*, Pirandello mirrors the actual disturbances and quarrels that attended the first performance of *Six Characters in Search of an Author* at the Teatro Valle in Rome.

Overlapping circles of reality and illusion, of life and art, and of the constantly dissolving and changing individual personality challenge the conception of theatre as imitative of an objective world. If reality, art, and personality are unstable, then the form and structure of drama itself, a mirror of interacting human beings, should be equally fragmented and disintegrative. Instead of bending his subject matter to fit a predetermined formal envelope, Pirandello creates a form which is itself an aspect of his subject matter and may in fact *be* that subject matter.

In *Each in His Own Way*, image seems to recede within image to infinity as the shifting planes of reality move from the play into the audience and from there to the street and the real world outside. Characters of the inner play discuss, interpret, and argue about the Morello case. Characters of the outer play discuss, interpret, and argue about the Moreno case as well as about the inner play. The real audience will presumably discuss, interpret, and argue about both inner and outer play.

The stage directions at the beginning of the first Choral Interlude indicate the three principal levels of reality, each of which pushes the preceding into the realm of illusion: the invented characters of the inner play, the "real" people on whom the fictitious play is based, and the audience discussing the play. When "real" characters from the second level, after disrupting the inner play, begin to imitate it, the circle is completed. Since the structure is circular, the possible multiplication of mirror images seems infinite. The setting of the second act reflects the several levels of reality: the lounge opens onto the verandah which opens onto the garden, and while curtains separate each from the others, they can be drawn to reveal perspectives within perspectives. Michele Rocca, based on the "real" Baron Nuti, bursts in from the third layer, the outside world of the garden, through the second into the first. The duelers upon whom he bursts are comic puppets and manikins, as the dueling equipment suggests: the masks, gloves, and breast protectors make the humans seem mechanical dolls pulled by strings. Morello–Moreno and Rocca–Nuti, on the other hand, are driven by the force of overwhelming passions. Theirs is another realism, the tragedy of the naked soul.

Unlike *Man and the Masses,* where reality and dream scenes blend into one subjective consciousness, here the three levels of reality come into conflict. Inner and outer play, illusions and reality, art and life all confront each other. Reality interrupts illusion, life interferes with art, and reflections and arguments on action replace action. Conflicts among the shifting planes of reality grow so intense that the drama cannot be finished. The inner play is a potential well-made play (about a courtesan's efforts to marry into respectable society) that remains unmade. *Each in His Own Way* subverts the well-made play, revealing the impermanence of the bourgeois values which it reflected and the uncertainty of the supposedly objective logic in which it took such pride.

Each in His Own Way proceeds as an unfolding of layers of reality, opening with the play-within-the-play and moving from there to the outer play and the world of audience, "real" characters, actors, and author. The doubling process is always ironically redoubled since even the audience, "real" characters, and actors are themselves played by actors. An actress plays an actress playing Delia Morello. The actual spectators watch actors playing spectators say what they themselves might say in the lobby during intermission. If, when the actual audience goes to the actual lobby during the real intermission, they repeat and imitate the lines Pirandello gave his audience of actors, this mirror image would double the doubling La Moreno and Baron Nuti give of their dramatized story. Audiences, Pirandello demonstrates, conditioned and almost programmed in their automatic responses to his plays, are fully as farcical as the puppet-like characters in one of his comedies. The members of the audience, therefore, become characters in *Each in His Own Way,* which ironically attacks them, subverting the theatre that they regarded as an absolute reflection of objective reality.

Even in the play-within-the-play there are different layers of reality. The first "prologue," between the anonymous old and young men, announces one of the major themes in abstract and as yet insubstantial form: the relativity of opinion. The second "prologue," between the three anonymous women, takes us from what people say and think to what they feel and how they act—a realm as unstable and uncertain as that of opinion. We are in Plato's cave, a world of appearance, the shadow of shadows. Significantly, the word *seem* continually recurs. The dual prologue states the theme of the endless flux of public opinion and human emotion—the first, a matter of external form and therefore farcical; the second, a matter of the essence of life and therefore tragic. The inner play provides a particular instance of these general propositions, but instead of moving to the action after a traditional expository opening, we are simply confronted with different versions of the same story: the suicide of Delia Morello's fiancé and her escape with his brother-in-law on the eve of her marriage.

With the presentation of conflicting opinions about conflicting opinions, words about words, a discussion about a discussion on the previous night, the process of doubling and regression seems endless. Even Delia Morello is only a pseudonym. Continuing the function of the dual prologue, Doro's friend Diego acts as commentator on the action—that is, on the comments of the others. He is a familiar figure from the well-made play, the raisonneur, a worldly-wise character who is usually not directly involved in the plot but is eminently qualified to analyze human nature, which he does in lengthy disquisitions that make use of elaborate analogies. The figure of the raisonneur, perfectly appropriate to the potentially well-made inner play, is one of Pirandello's prime devices for dissecting and subverting the firm reality of the world and structure of the well-made play. Diego's analogies, in manner like the raisonneur's labored stories, have precisely the opposite effect: instead of affirming a moral code, they cast into doubt all certainties about human nature and conduct.

The Fourth Critic in the First Interlude describes the inner play as a glittering mirror gone mad. The image of the mirror, appropriate to virtually all of Pirandello's writings, is especially central to *Each in His Own Way*. A mirror figures prominently in Diego's story of his nine-day vigil while his mother was dying. Becoming so fatigued that he wished for a moment that she would die, at that very moment he suddenly caught a glimpse of his face in the mirror. Diego feels forever imprisoned by this frightening image that flashes before him for only a moment, and he passes judgment on this other self which lurks within him. A mirror also plays a key role in one of the stories Delia Morello tells to Diego. Whereas Diego saw an unknown but real self become a fixed mask, she recalls seeing in the mirror not herself but only a false mask she has made: her ugly, overpainted face. Alienated from herself and her actions, she joins the commentators in discussing her life. She accepts the mirror images that they present to her, which reflect a reflection of her deeds. These and other stories of Diego and Delia Morello create a pattern of imagery that conveys the anguish and loneliness of the human condition, which lies outside the comedy of group opinion and can be expressed only by confession and reverie. These are the quiet moments of recognition when we see through the mask to the horror of life; they are essential in establishing the proper tension between the play's alternating modes: farce and tragedy.

characters

LITERARY MAN (*who would write if the public were not beneath his contempt*)
GOOD-NATURED SPECTATOR
BAD-HUMORED SPECTATOR
A MAN WHO UNDERSTANDS
A MAN WHO NEVER UNDERSTANDS
ONE OR TWO SUPPORTERS OF PIRANDELLO
AN ARMY OF ANTAGONISTS
SPECTATOR FROM THE SOCIAL SET
LADIES AND GENTLEMEN (*from the audience*)

The public is requested to remain seated
at the end of the first and second acts, for the curtain
will at once rise again for the choral interludes.
The number of acts in the comedy cannot be made
more specific in view of unpleasant incidents that will
arise during the course of the performance.

act I   (*The ancient palace of* DONNA LIVIA PALEGARI. *It is tea time, and the* GUESTS *are about to leave. Through the back drop, which presents three arches and two columns, a sumptuous drawing-room brightly lighted and with an animated company*—LADIES *and* GENTLEMEN—*can be seen. The front of the stage, less brightly lighted, is a smaller parlor ornately decorated in damask, and with ancient paintings [of religious subjects for the most part] on the walls. As we look at the stage we should get the impression of being in a shrine in a church, of which the drawing-room beyond the columns might be the nave—the sacred chapel of a very worldly church! The parlor in the foreground is unfurnished save for one or two benches or wooden stools for the convenience of people desirous of studying the paintings on the walls. There are no doors. The* GUESTS *will come into this retreat two or three at a time to exchange confidences in private; and in fact as the curtain rises, we meet there: an* OLD FRIEND *of Donna Livia and a* YOUNG MAN [*one of the guests*], *engaged in conversation.*)

YOUNG MAN: Well, what's your idea of it?

OLD MAN (*with a sigh*): My idea of it? (*Pause.*) I really couldn't explain. (*Pause.*) What are other people saying?

YOUNG MAN: Oh, some one thing, some another.

OLD MAN: Of course, each his own private opinion!

YOUNG MAN: But none of them, when you come down to it, seem to be sure of themselves. They are all like you. Before they'll tell you what they think, they want to know what others are saying.

OLD MAN: Oh, as for me, I am absolutely sure. But . . . it's common sense, isn't it? I'm not anxious to make a fool of myself. Before I say anything definite I ought to know whether other people may not have some information which I have not yet had and which might in part modify my judgment.

YOUNG MAN: But what do you think, so far as you know?

OLD MAN: Oh, my dear boy, we never know everything!

YOUNG MAN: Well, in that case, what are opinions worth?

OLD MAN: Dear me, opinions? My opinion is a view that I hold until—well—until I find out something that changes it.

YOUNG MAN: Not at all, if I may press the point. The moment you say that we never know everything, you take it for granted that facts exist which would change your mind.

OLD MAN (*looking at him thoughtfully and smiling*): Are you trying to corner me? You're trying to make me say that I have no opinion?

YOUNG MAN: How can you? From your point of view I shouldn't think anyone could have an opinion.

OLD MAN: Well, refusing to have an opinion is a way of having one, isn't it?

YOUNG MAN: Yes, but in a purely negative way.

OLD MAN: A negative way is better than no way at all though, my boy. (*He takes the* YOUNG MAN *by the arm and starts back with him toward the drawing-room, where some* GIRLS *can be seen serving tea and cookies to the* GUESTS. *A pause. Two* YOUNG LADIES *steal cautiously into the parlor.*)

FIRST YOUNG LADY (*eagerly*): So you know all about it then? Oh, you darling! Tell me! Tell me!

SECOND YOUNG LADY: But remember, it's only an impression I have.

FIRST YOUNG LADY: When *you* have an impression it's sure to be worth hearing. Was he pale? And you said he was sad!

SECOND YOUNG LADY: He seemed that way to me.

FIRST YOUNG LADY: I should never have let him go away! Oh, and I felt that way at the time—here, in my heart. I went as far as the door with him, his hand in mine. He was a step outside, and still I held his hand. We had kissed each other good-bye. We had separated—but our hands—no, no—they just refused to let go! But tell me, won't you? He made no reference—?

SECOND YOUNG LADY: Reference to what?

FIRST YOUNG LADY: No—I mean—well—I mean whether—well, you know—speaking in a general way as one often does—

SECOND YOUNG LADY: No, he said nothing in particular. He was listening to what the others were saying.

FIRST YOUNG LADY: Ah yes. Because he—*he* knows. He knows what harm we do through this silly habit of talking we all have. Whereas, so long as we have the slightest doubt, we ought to keep our lips shut, tight. But we talk—we talk—and we don't know what we are talking about, ourselves! But you said he was pale—and sad! You don't remember what the others were saying, do you?

SECOND YOUNG LADY: No, I really don't. However, I shouldn't like to have you disappointed, my dear. You know how it is—we are so easily mistaken. It may have been indifference, but it seemed to me that he was pale; and when he smiled it was such a sad smile. Wait. I do remember! When somebody said—

FIRST YOUNG LADY: What did somebody say?

SECOND YOUNG LADY: What was it now? Wait—somebody said: "Women are like dreams—they are never the way you would like to have them."

FIRST YOUNG LADY: He didn't say that, did he? You are sure?

SECOND YOUNG LADY: No, it wasn't he.

FIRST YOUNG LADY: Oh my, my, my! Anyhow, I don't know whether I am making a mistake or not. I've always been proud of acting in my own way under all circumstances. I'm a very good-natured person; but I can be spiteful on occasion. And if I ever am—well—it'll go hard with him!

SECOND YOUNG LADY: I hope you will never be any different from what you are, dear.

FIRST YOUNG LADY: But what am I, really? I'm sure I don't know. I assure you I don't know—even myself! All this way and that, fickle, changing, my feet off the ground! First I'm here and then I'm there. I laugh. I go off into a corner to have a good cry all by myself. Oh, how terrible it is! Sometimes I just have to hide my face to keep from seeing myself. I am so ashamed at realizing how different, how incoherent, how unreliable I am from time to time. (*At this moment other* GUESTS *come into the room; two* YOUNG MEN [*dressed in the height of fashion*] *much bored with the party; and, with them,* DIEGO CINCI.)

FIRST YOUNG MAN: Hope we're not intruding?

SECOND YOUNG LADY: Not in the least. Please, do come in!

SECOND YOUNG MAN: So here's the chapel! The confessional, you might almost call it, eh?

DIEGO: Yes. There's only one thing lacking. Donna Livia ought to have a father confessor here for the convenience of her guests!

FIRST YOUNG MAN: And why a priest, pray? We have our own consciences.

DIEGO: Yes, but what do you do with your conscience?

FIRST YOUNG MAN: My conscience?

SECOND YOUNG MAN (*solemnly*): "Mea mihi conscientia pluris est quam hominum sermo."

SECOND YOUNG LADY: Why, that was Latin, wasn't it?

SECOND YOUNG MAN: Exactly, Signorina. A quotation from Cicero. I remember it from my school days.

FIRST YOUNG LADY: And what does it mean?

SECOND YOUNG MAN (*solemnly*): "I care more for what my conscience says than for what the world says!"

FIRST YOUNG MAN: We have a popular saying something like that. "With conscience clear, never fear!"

DIEGO: If we were the only ones—

SECOND YOUNG MAN (*not understanding*): What do you mean? If we were the only ones—?

DIEGO: I mean that then the approval of our own consciences would be sufficient. But in that case it would hardly be a question of conscience any longer. Unfortunately, my friends, I'm here, and you're here! Unfortunately!

FIRST YOUNG LADY: Unfortunately, he says!

SECOND YOUNG LADY: And not very nice of him either!

DIEGO: Why, I mean—we've always got to consider other people, my dear young lady.

SECOND YOUNG MAN: Not at all, not at all. When my own conscience approves—

DIEGO: But don't you see that that blessed conscience of yours is nothing but other people inside you?

FIRST YOUNG MAN: Your usual philosophical clap-trap!

DIEGO: But it's not so hard to understand. (*To the* SECOND YOUNG MAN.) When you say that you are satisfied with the approval of your own conscience. what do you mean? You mean that other people may think of you and judge you as they choose—even unjustly, let us say; but that you, meantime, will hold your own head high in the assurance that you have done no wrong. Isn't that what you mean?

SECOND YOUNG MAN: Yes, I guess so.

DIEGO: Well, then, how do you acquire that assurance except from other people? Who can assure you you have done no wrong?

SECOND YOUNG MAN: I do myself. It's my conscience. What else?

DIEGO: All you're saying is that other people in your place, meeting, in other words, circumstances similar to yours, would have done as you have done. That's all you are saying, isn't it? Or indeed, you mean that above and beyond definite concrete situations in life, certain abstractions, certain general principles, exist on which we can all agree—and why not?—since agreement, in the case of principles merely, costs so little! But notice now: if you shut yourself up disdainfully in your ivory tower and insist that you have your own conscience and are satisfied with its approval, it is because you know that everybody is criticizing you, condemning you, or laughing at you— otherwise you would never think of saying such a thing. The fact is that the general principles in question ever remain abstractions. No one is able to recognize them as you do in the situation in which you find yourself, nor are people able to see themselves acting just as you acted in doing what you did. So then you say that the approval of your own conscience is sufficient—but sufficient for what, if you please? Does it enable you to enjoy standing all by yourself against the world? Not at all, not at all! As a matter of fact, you are afraid of being at outs with everybody. So what do you do? You imagine that there are any number of heads all made like your own, heads in fact that are duplicates, replicas, of your head. And you think you can shake those heads to say 'yes' or 'no,' 'no' or 'yes,' just as you please; and that comforts you and makes you sure of yourself. Oh, interesting game, I grant you! But what else does that conscience of yours amount to?

SECOND YOUNG MAN: But what do *you* do, may I ask?

DIEGO: Oh, I play the game the same as you. I have my conscience too, I should say so!

FIRST YOUNG LADY: Oh, how interesting! But, I'm sure it's getting late! I think I must be going!

SECOND YOUNG LADY: Yes, yes, everybody seems to be going. (*Turning to* DIEGO *and pretending that she is much offended.*) How entertaining you have been!

FIRST YOUNG MAN: Hadn't we better be going too? (*They step back into the drawing-room to pay their respects to the hostess and to take their leave. The company in the parlor, meantime, has thinned out perceptibly. The last* GUESTS *are bowing to* DONNA LIVIA, *who finally steps forward into the parlor, great anxiety written on her face. She is leading* DIEGO CINCI *by the hand. The* OLD MAN *whom we saw at the rising of the curtain and a* SECOND OLD MAN *follow after her.*)

DONNA LIVIA (*to* DIEGO): Oh no, Diego, please don't go! Please don't go! You are the best friend my son has in the world, and I am quite beside myself. Tell me, is it true? Is it true—what these dear old friends of mine have been saying?

FIRST OLD MAN: I was careful to point out, Donna Livia, that we had no real information to go on.

DIEGO: You are talking about Doro? What's happened to him?

DONNA LIVIA (*in surprise*): What? Haven't you heard?

DIEGO: I haven't heard anything. Nothing serious, I trust. If it had been, I am sure I should have heard.

SECOND OLD MAN (*half closing his eyes to soften the shock of what he is about to reveal*): We were referring to the trouble last night! A bit of a scandal, you know . . .

DONNA LIVIA: . . . at the Avanzi's! Doro stood up for that—that—what's her name?—that woman!

DIEGO: Scandal! What woman?

FIRST OLD MAN (*as above*): Why, that Morello person. Who else?

DIEGO: Oh, you are talking about Delia Morello!

DONNA LIVIA: So you know her then?

DIEGO: Know her? Who doesn't know her, Signora?

DONNA LIVIA: So Doro knows her too? It is true then! He knows her!

DIEGO: Why, I suppose so. Why shouldn't he? And what was the trouble about?

DONNA LIVIA (*turning to the* FIRST OLD MAN): And you said he didn't!

DIEGO: He knows her the way everybody knows her, Signora. But what happened?

FIRST OLD MAN: But remember, remember! I was careful to say just what I said: that he stood up for the woman, *perhaps without ever having spoken to her in his life!*

SECOND OLD MAN: Yes, that's the way he knew her. Just her general reputation!

DONNA LIVIA: And yet he stood up for her, even to the point of coming to blows?

DIEGO: Blows? With whom?

SECOND OLD MAN: With Francesco Savio.

DONNA LIVIA: Why, it's incredible! The idea of starting a fight—a fight—in a respectable house, of respectable people! And for a woman of that breed!

DIEGO: Why, perhaps in the course of an argument . . .

FIRST OLD MAN: . . . Just so . . . in the heat of an argument . . .

SECOND OLD MAN: . . . as so often happens . . .

DONNA LIVIA: Please, gentlemen, don't try to spare my feelings. (*To* DIEGO.) *You* tell me, Diego, *you* tell me! *You* know all about Doro.

DIEGO: But why so wrought up, my dear Signora?

DONNA LIVIA (*putting her foot down*): No! You pretend to be a real friend of my son. In that case it is your duty to tell me frankly all you know about the matter.

DIEGO: But I know nothing whatever about the matter. Surely it can't be of much importance. Why so excited over a mere word or two?

FIRST OLD MAN: Ah, as for that—now you're going a step too far! I don't follow you! . . .

SECOND OLD MAN: You can't deny that the affair made a very great impression on everybody present.

DIEGO: But what affair, for heaven's sake?

DONNA LIVIA: Why, he stood up for the woman! Why, he actually came to her defense! Does that seem to you a matter of no consequence?

DIEGO: But, my dear Signora, the whole town has been talking about Delia Morello for three weeks past. She is the topic of conversation in the cafés, in the clubs, on the sidewalks, wherever you go. She is in the headlines of the papers. You must have read about her yourself.

DONNA LIVIA: Yes, a man committed suicide on her account.

FIRST OLD MAN: A young painter he was, named Salvi.

DIEGO: Giorgio Salvi, yes!

SECOND OLD MAN: A youth of great promise, it seems.

DIEGO: And it seems that there was someone before him.

DONNA LIVIA: What! Another man?

FIRST OLD MAN: Yes, it was mentioned in one of the papers . . .

SECOND OLD MAN: . . . that *he* committed suicide too.

DIEGO: Yes, he was a Russian. That, however, happened some years ago at Capri.

DONNA LIVIA (*shuddering and hiding her face in her hands*): Oh dear! Oh dear! Oh dear!

DIEGO: But for heaven's sake, you're not afraid that Doro is going to be the third, are you? I must say, Signora, that we all have a right to deplore the tragedy that has robbed us of an artist like Giorgio Salvi; but after all, when we know the situation as it actually was, it is quite possible—possible, no-tice—to say something in defense of the woman.

DONNA LIVIA: So you defend her too?

DIEGO: Yes, I too, to that extent! Why not?

SECOND OLD MAN: Challenging the indignation of all decent people in town, I suppose!

DIEGO: Perhaps! I was simply observing that something may be said for the woman.

DONNA LIVIA: But my own son, my Doro! I always thought he kept the best of company.

FIRST OLD MAN: He was a good boy . . .

SECOND OLD MAN: . . . always knew how to behave himself.

DIEGO: But it was an argument, wasn't it? Well, in an argument he may have said more than he really meant. He may have exaggerated.

DONNA LIVIA: No! No! Don't you try to spare my feelings! Don't you conceal anything from me! Delia Morello—she's an actress, isn't she?

DIEGO: I should call her a lunatic, Signora.

FIRST OLD MAN: She has been on the stage.

DIEGO: But she couldn't hold her job anywhere. No manager dares take the risk of hiring her any more. Delia Morello can't be her real name. That must be just the way she is known on the stage. No one knows who she really is, nor where she comes from.

DONNA LIVIA: Is she a good-looking woman?

DIEGO: They call her beautiful.

DONNA LIVIA: Oh, they're all beautiful—those actresses! I suppose Doro met her in some theatre.

DIEGO: I believe he did. But at the most it couldn't have been more than an introduction, a visit to her dressing-room, back-stage, perhaps. And that is not such a terrible thing as many good people imagine, Signora. Please don't worry!

DONNA LIVIA: But here two men have gone and killed them-selves on her account!

DIEGO: I would not have killed myself for her!

DONNA LIVIA: But she made those two fellows lose their heads.

DIEGO: I wouldn't have lost mine!

DONNA LIVIA: But I'm not worried on your account—I am thinking of Doro!

DIEGO: Never fear, Signora! And one more thing: if that unhappy woman has done wrong to other people, she has always done the greatest wrong to herself. She's one of those women who are made haphazard, so to speak, who seem unable to get hold of themselves—wanderers astray on the face of the earth, never knowing where they're going nor where they will end. And yet sometimes, you know, she seems to be just a poor little child afraid of the world and appealing to you for help.

DONNA LIVIA (*much impressed, and seizing him by both elbows*): Diego, look me in the eye: you got that from Doro!

DIEGO: No, Signora!

DONNA LIVIA (*insisting*): Tell me the truth, Diego. Doro is in love with that woman!

DIEGO: I am sure he isn't.

DONNA LIVIA (*still insisting*): He is! He is! He is in love with her. What you have just said only a man in love with her could say!

DIEGO: But they're my words, not Doro's!

DONNA LIVIA: That isn't so. Doro talked that way about her to you. And no one can convince me that he didn't!

DIEGO (*shrinking before her persistence*): Oh! Oh! (*Then with a sudden eloquence, his voice becoming clear and light, caressing, inviting.*) Signora, can't you imagine—imagine—a carriage—driving along a country road—through the open fields—on a bright afternoon in summer time?

DONNA LIVIA (*dumbfounded*): A carriage—on a country road! What's that got to do with it?

DIEGO (*angrily and deeply moved*): Signora, can you imagine the condition I was in when I sat up all night watching at the bedside of my mother, dying? I sat there—and do you know what I was doing? I was staring at a fly, a fly that had fallen into a glass of water on the lamp-stand and was swimming about, his wings flat on the surface of the water—And I sat there watching him. I didn't even notice when my poor mother died! I was all taken up in admiring the confidence that poor fly seemed to have in the strength of his two hind legs. They were longer than the others. They were made for him to get his start with. He kept swimming about desperately, always confident that those two hind legs would finally lift him above the liquid surface where he was caught. But whenever he tried to jump, he would find that something was sticking to the ends of them. So every time he failed, he would rub them together furiously, to clean them—and then he would try again! I sat there watching him for more than half an hour; and then I saw him die—and I did not see my poor mother die! Now then, do you understand? Let me alone!

DONNA LIVIA (*dumbfounded, bewildered, stands there looking first at one and then at the other of the two* OLD MEN *who are as much at sea as she is.*) I beg your pardon—I don't see the connection!

DIEGO: Does it seem to you so absurd? Well, tomorrow now, I assure you, you will laugh . . . you will laugh at all these fancied terrors you are feeling for your son when you think of that carriage on the country road which I have just trundled along before your mind's eye the better to confuse you. But please realize that I can never laugh as I think of that poor fly that came before my eyes while I was sitting there watching at my mother's bedside. (*A pause.* DONNA LIVIA *and the two* OLD MEN *stand looking at each other after this abrupt diversion, more than ever confused, unable in spite of all their efforts to make this carriage on the country road and this fly in the glass of water fit into the subject which they had just been discussing.* DIEGO CINCI *is all absorbed in memories of his mother's death; so that when* DORO PALEGARI *enters, at just this moment,* DORO *will find* CINCI *in a very unusual frame of mind.*)

DORO (*looking first at one and then at the other of the* COMPANY *in surprise*): Why, what's the matter?

DONNA LIVIA (*coming to herself*): Oh, it's you! Doro, my boy, what have you been doing? What have you been doing? These gentlemen have been telling me—

DORO (*snapping angrily*): About the "scandal," I suppose? Saying that I am in love, head over heels in love, with Delia Morello, eh? I suppose so! All my friends wink at me as I pass them on the street. "Eh, how's Delia, old boy?" Heavens above! What's got into you? Have you all lost your minds?

DONNA LIVIA: But if you—

DORO: If I, what? I can't understand it, upon my word! And a scandal made of it, within twenty-four hours!

DONNA LIVIA: But you came to the defense of that—

DORO: I came to nobody's defense.

DONNA LIVIA: At the Avanzi's last evening!

DORO: At the Avanzi's last evening I heard Francesco Savio express, in regard to the tragic suicide of Giorgio Salvi—about whom, by the way, everybody is having his say—an opinion which did not seem to me a fair one. So I contested it! That's all there is to it!

DONNA LIVIA: But you said certain things. . . .

DORO: Oh, I may have talked a lot of nonsense. All I said I really can't remember. In an argument one word follows on another. I may have exaggerated! But hasn't a fellow a right to his opinion on topics of the day? It seems to me we can interpret certain episodes in one fashion or another as we see fit. Today it is this way, tomorrow it's another. For example, if I happen to see Francesco Savio tomorrow, I shall be quite ready to admit that he was right and that I was wrong.

FIRST OLD MAN: Oh, in that case, very well.

DONNA LIVIA: Do so, please, Doro! Please do so! By all means!

SECOND OLD MAN: . . . to put an end to all this gossip, you understand.

DORO: Oh, not for that reason. I don't care a hang about the gossip! I would be doing it only to get rid of the mortification I feel myself!

FIRST OLD MAN: Quite so. Yes, quite so . . .

SECOND OLD MAN: . . . at seeing yourself so misunderstood!

DORO: Not at all, not at all! The mortification I feel at having let myself go so far—an anger justified perhaps by the spectacle of Francesco Savio sitting there, stupidly arguing, with his facts all wrong; though he after all—well yes—he was right, substantially! So now, when I've cooled off a bit, I'm ready—yes, I'm quite ready—to apologize. And I will do so. I will apologize in the presence of everybody, to put an end to this absurd dispute. My, what a row over nothing! I'm disgusted.

DONNA LIVIA: Well, I'm much relieved, Doro, much relieved! And I'm glad to hear you admit right here in the presence of a friend of yours that nothing can be said in defense of such a woman.

DORO: Why, was he trying to defend her too?

FIRST OLD MAN: Yes, he was—that is to say, after a fashion . . .

SECOND OLD MAN: Not in earnest, you understand! Just to soothe your mother's feelings.

DONNA LIVIA: Yes, and I must say he wasn't succeeding very well. But now what you have said is a great relief to me. And thank you, thank you ever so much, my boy.

DORO (*angry, irritated at the implication of his* MOTHER's *gratitude*): But—you're really serious? You—why, mother, you make me angrier than ever! I'm getting mad, clear through!

DONNA LIVIA: Angry—because I am thanking you?

DORO: Well, I must say? Why do you thank me, in fact? Why are you so much relieved now! I see, you thought that . . . I swear, mother, I'll be flying off the handle!

DONNA LIVIA: No, no, don't be angry! Let's say no more about it!

DORO (*turning to* DIEGO): So you think something can be said for Delia Morello?

DIEGO: Oh, let's drop the subject—now that your mother is quite herself again.

DORO: No, I insist on knowing. I insist on knowing.

DIEGO: So you want to start the argument over again with me?

DONNA LIVIA: Please don't, Doro.

DORO (*to his* MOTHER): No, it was just a matter of curiosity. (*To* DIEGO.) I wanted to see whether you were making the same points that I brought up last evening in my quarrel with Francesco Savio.

DIEGO: And suppose I were. You don't mean to say you would be on the other side now?

DORO: Do you think I'm a whirligig? Last evening I took this position: I said: "You can't claim that Delia Morello intended to encompass the ruin of Giorgio Salvi because of the simple fact that the night before she was to be married to him she went off on a lark with another man; since the real ruin of Salvi would have been for him to marry her!"

DIEGO: Exactly! Just my view of it. And the Morello woman knew this too; and, precisely because she knew it, she was determined to prevent it.

DORO: Nothing of the kind! Savio was right in holding that she went off with that other fellow, Michele Rocca, to push her vengeance on Giorgio Salvi to the limit—because there is no escaping the fact that in all this affair she acted at all times and under all circumstances with the most refined treachery toward him. There!

DIEGO: So that's your view of it? Well, keep to that opinion. And much good may it do you! At any rate, let's drop the subject now!

FIRST OLD MAN: Wisely said! And now we must be going, Donna Livia. (*He kisses her hand.*)

SECOND OLD MAN: . . . delighted that everything has been cleared up now! (*He also kisses her hand. Then turning to the* OTHERS.) Good afternoon, Doro, and you too, Cinci.

DIEGO: Good afternoon! Good afternoon!

DONNA LIVIA (*turning to the first of the two* FRIENDS *and starting back with them to the drawing-room, from which they will depart through an exit to the right*): So then, when you get to Christina's—just tell her that I'll be calling, and ask her to be ready. (DONNA LIVIA *withdraws. For a moment* DORO *and* DIEGO *stand there without speaking. The empty drawing-room brightly lighted in the background behind them should give an interesting effect.*)

DIEGO (*spreading the fingers of his two hands fan-shaped, then crossing one hand over the other so as to form a network of his fingers, finally stepping up to* DORO *to attract the latter's attention*): This is the way it is—look!—this way—exactly!

DORO: What?

DIEGO: That conscience we were talking about in here just before you came. A net, an elastic net! You slacken it up a little like this and good-bye!—the madness we each have in us runs amuck!

DORO (*after a brief silence, worried, suspicious*): You mean that for me?

DIEGO (*almost talking to himself*): Before your mind the images, the memories, piled up during the years, begin to crowd—fragments of the life which you have lived perhaps, but which never gains the forefront of your consciousness because you have never been willing or able to view it in the clear light of reason . . . questionable things you may have done; lies of which you would be ashamed; thoughts that are mean, petty, unworthy of you; crimes you have thought out and planned in their minutest particulars; desires unconfessed and unconfessable—and it all, all, all comes up in your mind and throws you off your balance, till you don't know where you're at, leaving you disconcerted, bewildered, terrified!

DORO (*as above*): What are you talking about, man?

DIEGO (*gazing fixedly into space*): And I hadn't slept for nine nights in succession. . . . (*He turns vehemently upon* DORO.) Try it for yourself! Nine successive nights without a wink of sleep! The white mug on the table beside your bed has a single blue line around it—and that infernal bell! Ding! Ding! Ding! Ding! Eight . . . nine! I used to count them! Ten . . . eleven! The clock striking, you see! Twelve! Not to mention the quarters and the halves . . . ! There's no human affection strong enough to hold its own when you've neglected those primal needs of the body which must—must, I tell you!—be satisfied! There I was, outraged at the cruel fate which had fallen upon the ghastly, unconscious, unrecognizable body of my poor mother—nothing but body left of her, poor thing—well, do you know what I thought? I kept thinking: "God! I wish she'd stop that gasping!"

DORO: But my dear Diego! Your mother . . . why . . . she's been dead at least two years, hasn't she?

DIEGO: Yes! And you have no idea how surprised I was when the gasping did stop for a moment. The room fell into a terrible silence, and I turned—I don't know why—and I looked into the mirror on the dressing-table. I was bending over the bed to see whether perchance she might have died. But the mirror was so placed that I couldn't help seeing—seeing what the expression on my face was like, the expression, that is, which I was wearing as I bent over to look at her . . . a sort of joyous terror, a sort of terrible joy, the joy that would welcome my liberation. . . . But she gave another gasp, and that gasp gave me such a shudder of loathing for the thought I had been thinking that I buried my face in my two hands as though I had committed a crime. And I began to weep—to weep like the child I once had been—for my poor mamma, whose pity . . . yes! yes! it was her pity I wanted, pity for the fatigue I felt, the fatigue I felt for having been there nine sleepless nights in succession! You see . . . yes . . . at that instant I had ceased to hope that she would die. Poor, poor mamma! How many nights' sleep had she lost when I was a little child—and sick?

DORO: Would you mind explaining why you talk about your mother this way, all of a sudden?

DIEGO: I don't know, I'm sure. Won't you tell me why you got angry when your mother thanked you for having put her mind at ease?

DORO: Why, it was because she actually suspected for a moment, herself—

DIEGO: Oh, get out! You can't make me swallow that.

DORO (*shrugging his shoulders*): I don't know what you're driving at.

DIEGO: If such a suspicion on her part had not been well founded, you would have laughed instead of getting angry.

DORO: What do you mean? You don't seriously think . . . ?

DIEGO: I? You are the one who is thinking it!

DORO: But now I'm taking Savio's view of the matter.

DIEGO: So you see. . . . First here and then there! You are

even angry at yourself—for your exaggerations, as you called them!

DORO: That is because I now see . . .

DIEGO: No! No! Be frank with yourself! Read your own thoughts, accurately!

DORO: But what thoughts shall I read, man alive?

DIEGO: You're now agreeing with Francesco Savio! But do you know why? It's to hide a feeling which you've had inside you without your knowing that it was there.

DORO: Nothing of the kind! You make me laugh!

DIEGO: It's true! It's true!

DORO: You make me laugh, I say!

DIEGO: In the excitement of the argument last evening that feeling suddenly came to the top in your mind. It caught you off your guard . . . and you said things you didn't realize you were saying. . . . Of course you didn't! Of course you didn't! And you imagine you never even thought those things! And yet you did think them . . . you did think them! . . .

DORO: What do you mean? When?

DIEGO: Secretly . . . unknown even to yourself! Oh, my dear Doro, just as we sometimes have illegitimate children, so we sometimes have illegitimate thoughts!

DORO: Speak for yourself, eh!

DIEGO: Yes, I'll speak also for myself! . . . We all yearn to marry, and for our whole life long, some one particular soul . . . the soul which seems most convenient, most useful, to us . . . the soul which brings us in dowry the faculties and qualities most likely to help us attain the goals to which we aspire. But later on, outside the honest, conjugal household of our consciousness, we have . . . well . . . one affair after another, numberless little sins with all those other souls which we have rejected and buried in the depths of our being, and from which actions and thoughts are born—actions and thoughts which we refuse to recognize, but which, when we are forced to it, we adopt or legitimize . . . with appropriate adaptations, reserves, and cautions. Now, in this case, one of your own poor, fatherless thoughts has come home to you. You deny paternity . . . but look it over carefully! It's yours! It's yours! You were really in love with Delia Morello . . . head-over-heels in love, as you said!

DORO: Hah! Hah! Hah! Hah! Hah! Hah! Hah! You make me laugh! You make me laugh! (*At this point the butler,* FILIPPO, *enters the room.*)

FILIPPO: Signor Francesco Savio, sir.

DORO: Oh, here he is now! (*To* FILIPPO.) Show him in!

DIEGO: And I will leave you alone with him!

DORO: No! Wait! I want you to see how much in love I am with Delia Morello! (FRANCESCO SAVIO *appears in the drawing-room.*)

DORO: Come in here, Francesco, won't you?

FRANCESCO: Why, my dear Doro! And how are you, Cinci?

DIEGO: Glad to see you, Savio!

FRANCESCO (*addressing* DORO): I came to tell you how sorry I was about our little squabble last evening.

DORO: I was just on the point of going to look you up to tell you how sorry I was.

FRANCESCO (*taking his hand warmly*): That's good news, Doro, my boy! You have taken a great weight off my mind!

DIEGO: I should like to have a picture of you two fellows, upon my word!

FRANCESCO (*to* DIEGO):You know, Diego, we two have been friends all our lives . . . and we were on the point of breaking over nothing!

DORO: Oh, it wasn't quite so bad as that, was it!

FRANCESCO: Why, it was on my mind all last evening! I can't understand how I could have helped recognizing the generosity which prompted you . . .

DIEGO (*breaking in*): Exactly! The *generosity* which prompted him to defend Delia Morello!

FRANCESCO: Yes! And so that everybody could hear too! And it took some courage . . . with all those people yelping against her!

DORO (*puzzled*): But . . . do you mean to say . . . ?

DIEGO (*to* FRANCESCO): And you more rabid than any of the rest!

FRANCESCO (*warmly*): Yes. Because I had not given enough weight to certain considerations, one more sound and convincing than the other, which Doro, here, brought forward!

DORO (*with rising anger*): Ah! So *that's* it! So you now . . . so you now! . . .

DIEGO (*breaking in*): Exactly! So you now are standing up for the woman, are you not?

FRANCESCO: But Doro stood out against the whole crowd! He held his ground in the face of all those fools, and they couldn't find a thing to answer him with!

DORO (*to* FRANCESCO, *at the height of his irritation*): Listen! You know what you are? . . . You're an ordinary circus clown!

FRANCESCO: What do you mean? I came here to see you to admit that you were right! . . .

DORO: Yes! And that is why I say: you are just an ordinary circus clown!

DIEGO: You see, just as you now have come to the point of agreeing with him, he had already come to the point of agreeing with you!

FRANCESCO: Agreeing with me?

DIEGO: Yes, with you . . . with you because of the things you said *against* Delia Morello! . . .

DORO: . . . and now you have the impudence to come and tell me that I was right!

FRANCESCO: But—simply because I have thought over all you said!

DIEGO: Exactly! Don't you see? Just as *he* has thought over what *you* said! . . .

FRANCESCO: And now he says *I* was right . . .

DIEGO: Just as you say *he* was right!

DORO: Yes! You say that now . . . after you made a fool of me last night . . . in the presence of everybody! Set them all talking about me . . . and nearly drove my poor mother out of her mind! . . .

FRANCESCO: I? . . .

DORO: Yes! You! You! You just drew me on . . . getting me into an argument . . . trying to compromise me . . . making me say things that I would otherwise never have dreamed of saying! (*He steps up to* FRANCESCO *and faces him angrily.*) Just take a suggestion from me! You be very careful not to go around saying to anybody that I was right! . . .

DIEGO (*pressing his point*): Because you see, you recognize the generosity which prompted him! . . .

FRANCESCO: But I do . . . I do! . . .

DORO: You're just an ordinary circus clown!

DIEGO: You see . . . if you go around saying that he was right that will show that you, too, know the truth now . . . the truth, that is, that *he is in love* with Delia Morello . . . and that he came to her defense *on that account!*

FRANCESCO: That is the third time you've called me a clown, notice!

DORO: But it won't be the last! I'll say you're a clown one hundred times . . . today . . . tomorrow . . . always!

FRANCESCO: Please remember that I am in your house!

DORO: In my house I say that you're a clown . . . but even

when I'm not in my own house I'll say you're a clown! You're a clown! A clown! A clown!

FRANCESCO: Very well! Very well! In that case . . . good afternoon! And we'll see each other later, eh? . . . (*He starts to leave the room.*)

DIEGO (*in an effort to detain him*): One moment . . . one moment! Let's not go too fast!

DORO (*restraining him*): No, let him go!

DIEGO: Are you crazy, man? This will compromise you for good!

DORO: I don't care a damn!

DIEGO (*breaking away from him*): But you're crazy, I say! Let me go! (*He dashes out of the room in an effort to overtake* FRANCESCO SAVIO.)

DORO (*calling after him*): Mind your own business, Diego! (DIEGO, *however, does not stop.*)

DORO (*begins walking up and down the room, muttering furiously to himself*): Huh! That's a good one! And he has the impudence to come and tell me that I was right! . . . The clown! After making it look to everybody as though . . . (*At this point the* BUTLER *hurries in in some alarm with a visiting card in his hand.*)

FILIPPO: May I come in, sir?

DORO: Well, what's the matter?

FILIPPO: A lady calling, sir.

DORO: A lady?

FILIPPO: Here's her card. (*He holds out a visiting card.*)

DORO (*in great agitation after reading the name on the card*): Where . . . where is she?

FILIPPO: She is in the hall, sir, waiting.

DORO (*he looks around him in perplexity. Finally, and with a great effort to conceal his anxiety and confusion*): Has mamma gone out?

FILIPPO: Yes, sir, she left a moment ago!

DORO: Show the lady in! Show her in here! (FILIPPO *withdraws.* DORO *advances toward the drawing-room to receive the visitor. He is standing under the central arch between the two columns when* FILIPPO *reappears, introducing* DELIA MORELLO. *She is soberly but elegantly costumed, and wears a thick veil.* FILIPPO *withdraws, bowing.*)

DORO: You? Delia? Here?

DELIA: I came to thank you. Oh, can I ever tell you how grateful I am, my good, kind, friend!

DORO: Please, please, don't say that!

DELIA: Yes! I must say just that! (DORO *has extended his hand.* DELIA *bends over as though to kiss it.*) I must thank you! Thank you, indeed!

DORO: But no . . . no . . . please! . . . I, rather, should warn you that . . .

DELIA: Thank you for the kindness . . . the great kindness you did me!

DORO: But what kindness? I simply said . . .

DELIA: No! Oh, I see! . . . You thought I was thanking you for having stood up for me? Not at all! What do I care whether people accuse me or defend me? I am my own judge, and my own tormentor! My gratitude, rather, is for what you thought and felt inside yourself . . . and not because you took the trouble to express it in the presence of other people.

DORO (*in great bewilderment*): I thought . . . yes . . . what . . . knowing the facts as I did . . . it seemed to me . . . what it seemed to me was just to think.

DELIA: Just or unjust . . . what do I care? The fact is that what you said of me suddenly made me see myself . . . you understand . . . see myself—the moment I heard it!

DORO (*in growing bewilderment, but striving to appear indifferent*): Ah, so then . . . so then . . . I guessed right?

DELIA: As right as though you had lived my life to the bottom . . . but understanding me in a way I never understood myself! Never! Never! And a great shudder went over me! . . . I cried . . . Yes! Yes! . . . "That's just the way I am! That's just the way I am!" . . . And you can't imagine with what joy and with what anguish I recognized myself, saw myself . . . in all the things you found to say of me!

DORO: I am happy . . . happy . . . most happy . . . happy because it all seemed to me so clear at the time, when in fact I did discover those things—without reflection . . . you understand . . . as though by an inspiration coming to me directly from you. Later on, I confess, I did not feel the same way.

DELIA: Ah! Later on—you changed?

DORO: Yes. But if now you tell me that you recognize yourself in what I said of you . . . if you tell me that I was right . . .

DELIA: I have been living all day on that inspiration of yours—inspiration you may well call it. What I don't understand is how you could see through me so easily, and so clearly —you who scarcely know me, after all. Whereas I . . . well . . . it's terrible . . . I struggle and struggle, suffering all the while

—I don't know—as though—as though I were not quite myself, as though I were constantly groping around to find myself . . . to understand the woman that I really am, to ask her what she really wants, why she is suffering so, and what I ought to do to tame her, pacify her, give her a little peace . . .

DORO: That's it . . . a little peace, a little quiet! That's what you need!

DELIA: I have him constantly before my eyes . . . just as I saw him there at my feet . . . pale . . . lifeless . . . a dead thing! It all came over me in a flash! I felt myself—I don't know— dying—and I bent over to look at him . . . trying to grasp from the abyss of that instant the eternity of the sudden death I could see before my eyes, there, in his face, a face which in a second had lost consciousness of everything . . . Ah, I knew . . . I alone knew . . . the life there had been in that poor body which had destroyed itself for me, for me who am nothing . . . nothing. Ah! I was quite mad! Imagine the state I must be in at present!

DORO: But quiet, now! Please, be calm!

DELIA: Oh, I am calm enough . . . But see . . . when I try to be calm . . . well . . . it's this way . . . I'm stunned, stunned, that's it! All feeling seems to leave me! Just that . . . just that! I pinch myself, but I don't feel it! My hands . . . I look at them, and they don't seem to be mine! And then all the things I have to do—I don't know why I have to do them—I open my handbag and take out my mirror and I am horror-stricken at the pallor and at the coldness that has come over me! Well . . . you can't imagine the impression I get, there, in the circle of that mirror, of my painted lips and my painted eyes! . . .

DORO: That's because you don't see yourself as others see you.

DELIA: So you say that, too? Must I actually hate—hate as my enemies—all the people I have anything to do with—that they may help me to understand myself?

DORO: Why no . . . why should you?

DELIA: Why, I see them walk in front of me and they seem —well—to be dazzled by my eyes, by my lips, by my beauty, in short; but no one cares for me . . . no one cares for what most concerns me.

DORO: Your real self, that is! . . .

DELIA: So then I punish them in the things they really desire. Those desires disgust me, but first I do my best to fan them, make them worse in order to get my revenge . . . and that revenge I get by giving myself away, suddenly, capri-

ciously, to the person whom they would have least expected to
win me! (DORO *nods with a suggestion of reproach.*) I do
that, I suppose, to show them my contempt for the things
they most highly prize in me. (*Again* DORO *nods.*) Have I
harmed myself? Always . . . always! But better worthless men
like that . . . worthless men who have no pretensions, and who
know how little they amount to . . . people who bore you,
perhaps, but who do not disappoint you . . . and who may
even have their good points, too—certain fresh and honest
qualities which are the more delightful because you least
expect to find them, just there.

DORO (*surprised*): Well, that was almost exactly what I said!
Almost exactly!

DELIA (*with great emotion*): Yes! Yes!

DORO: That was the way I explained certain incomprehensible acts of yours! . . .

DELIA: Incomprehensible? Yes . . . caprices . . . impulses of
the moment . . . leaps into space with my eyes closed! . . . (*She
stands there for a moment, gazing vacantly into void, as
though fascinated by some distant vision.*) Just imagine . . .
(*And then she continues as though speaking to herself.*) somersaults you might call them . . . yes . . . somersaults . . .
(*Falling into her abstraction again.*) There was a little girl,
and the gypsies taught her to turn somersaults . . . handsprings
. . . wheeling hand over hand on a green lawn near my house
in the country when I was a child! . . . (*Still in her abstraction.*) Was I ever a child? (*A memory of the way her mother
used to call her comes into her mind and she shouts.*) "Lilly
dear! Lilly dear! Lilli! Lilli!" Hahah! Hahah! She was afraid of
those gypsies, poor, dear mamma! She was afraid they would
suddenly break camp and carry me off. (*Comes to herself
again.*) The gypsies never carried me off. I learned to turn
handsprings and somersaults all by myself after I had come
away from the country here to town . . . here, where everything is false, fictitious . . . falser and more fictitious every
day. And we can't shake it off; because when we try to get
back to simplicity again . . . make ourselves true and honest
again, our very honesty and our very simplicity seem false and
counterfeit! It all seems that way because it is . . . because it is
false and counterfeit! Haha! Truth? What is truth? . . .
Nothing is true! I should like to see with my eyes, or hear with
my ears, or feel with my fingers, one thing . . . just one thing
. . . that is true . . . really true . . . in me!

DORO: There is one thing in you that I imagine is true . . .

the goodness and kindness that you have at bottom—a goodness and a kindness hidden from other people, and perhaps even from yourself—a goodness, at any rate, that I tried, in the quarrel yesterday, to make other people see.

DELIA: Yes! Yes! And I'm very grateful! Yes! Goodness . . . you call me "good"—but a goodness so complicated, so complex that when you tried to make people understand it, when you tried to make it look simple and clear, they grew angry at you and laughed at you. . . . But you have explained it, even to me. . . . Yes, people dislike me, just as you say. I was kept at a distance by everybody—there, at Capri. I'm sure that some of them thought I was a spy! But what a discovery I made there, Doro. . . . Love for humanity! Do you know what it means to love humanity? It means just this: when you say you are in love with humanity, you are satisfied with yourself! When a person is satisfied with himself . . . happy with himself . . . he loves humanity! Full of just such love, and happy . . . oh, so happy *he* must have been when *he* came to Capri, after the last exhibition of his paintings at Naples!

DORO: Giorgio Salvi, you mean?

DELIA: He had been working on some Neapolitan studies, as he called them, and he found me when he was in just that state of mind.

DORO: There you are! Just as I said! All taken up with his own art . . . and as for feelings! . . . no feelings for anything except for his art!

DELIA: Color . . . ah, color . . . everything was color with him! Feeling with him was nothing but color!

DORO: So he asked you to sit for a portrait? . . .

DELIA: In the beginning . . . yes! But later on . . . he had a way of his own in asking for anything he wanted—so funny —petulant, almost impudent—he was like a spoiled child! So I became his model! . . . It was very, very true what you said: nothing is more irritating than to be held aloof, excluded from a joy which . . .

DORO: . . . which is living, present, before us, around us, and the reason for which we can neither discover nor define! . . .

DELIA: Exactly! It was a joy . . . well, a pure joy, but only for his *eyes* . . . and it proved to me that, after all, at bottom he saw in me . . . he prized in me . . . only my body! My body was the only thing he wanted from me! Oh, don't misunderstand me! Not as other men wanted me—out of a low desire —oh no!

DORO: But that, in the long run, could only have irritated you the more.

DELIA: Precisely! Because if I was disgusted, nauseated, when other men failed to help me in my own spiritual uncertainties and troubles, my disgust at a man who also wanted my body and nothing else—but only to get from me a purely . . . a purely . . .

DORO: . . . ideal joy . . .

DELIA: . . . and a joy exclusively his own . . .

DORO: . . . must have been all the stronger precisely because every tangible motive for anger was lacking . . .

DELIA: . . . and it was impossible for me to have the satisfaction of that vengeance which at least I was able to inflict upon other men by suddenly giving myself to someone else! Oh, for a woman I assure you, an angel is always more irritating than a beast!

DORO (*triumphantly*): Well! Well! Well! I used those very words! Absolutely! Those very words!

DELIA: Yes, but you forget—I am only repeating them, after you, just as they were reported to me. You see, they suddenly made so many things clear to me!

DORO: Why, yes . . . revealing a real reason . . .

DELIA: . . . for what I did! Yes . . . yes . . . it's true: to get my revenge on him, I tried to bring my body gradually to life before him so that it should no longer exist merely for the delight of his eyes . . .

DORO: . . . and later, when you saw that he had become your slave as so many others had been, then, to taste your vengeance to the full, you forbade him any other joy than the one with which, up to that time, he had been content . . .

DELIA: Since that was all he had ever asked for . . . since that was the only one truly worthy of him! . . .

DORO: That's enough! I understand! I understand! In that way your vengeance was complete! You never wanted him to marry you, did you? In fact, you were determined that he shouldn't?

DELIA: Yes! Yes! For a long time I struggled . . . I did my best to dissuade him . . . But in the end, driven to a fury, beside himself . . . exasperated beyond endurance by my obstinate refusals, he threatened to do something rash . . . It was then that I decided to go away . . . disappear forever!

DORO: And then it was that you imposed upon him conditions which you knew would be terribly hard for him! ... You imposed them deliberately upon him! ...

DELIA: Deliberately ... yes ... on purpose!

DORO: The condition that he would introduce you formally, as his fiancée, to his mother and to his sister! ...

DELIA: Yes ... yes ... because they were proud and haughty women, of the most inaccessible aristocracy—not my kind at all—and he was proud of their pride and jealous of their high position. Yes, I did it deliberately, so that he would say no! Oh, how he used to talk of his little sister! ...

DORO: Exactly! Just as I contended, then! Tell me the truth now ... when Rocca, his sister's fiancé ...

DELIA (horror-stricken): Oh, no, no! Don't speak of him ... don't speak of him, please!

DORO: But here we would have the real proof of the position I maintained! You must tell me! You must tell me that what I said is true!

DELIA: Yes, I did go away with him! I did spend a night with him ... because I was desperate ... desperate ... unable to see any other means of escape!

DORO: Exactly! Exactly!

DELIA: And under such circumstances that Giorgio would be sure to find us together—yes—find me with Rocca and thus refuse to go on with our marriage ... which would have been the ruin of him—utter unhappiness—and the ruin of me also. I would have been wretched, too.

DORO (triumphantly): Exactly! Absolutely what I said! So I defended you—and that fool there saying I was wrong—saying that your refusals of Giorgio ... all your struggles, all your threats ... your attempt to run away ... were just part of a cheap game you were playing to lead him on.

DELIA (alarmed): He said that? ...

DORO: Yes! Treachery premeditated ... carefully thought out ... aiming to reduce Salvi to utter despair, after you had made him fall in love with you, after you had led him on!

DELIA (alarmed): I ... led him on ... I?

DORO: Exactly! And the more desperate he got, the more you held out in order to gain many many things which he would never have granted you otherwise.

DELIA (more and more alarmed and gradually losing her confidence again): What things?

DORO: Well, first of all, an introduction to his mother and to his sister, and to the latter's fiancé, social recognition from the three of them!

DELIA: Ah! And he didn't see that I hoped to find in Giorgio's refusal to give me those introductions a pretext for breaking off my engagement to him?

DORO: No . . . no! He claimed you had another scheme in that!

DELIA (*in utter desperation*): What scheme?

DORO: He said you wanted to parade your victory in public, before all society, by being seen in the presence of that little sister of his . . . you a model of the studios . . . you an actress . . . you, an adventuress! . . .

DELIA (*stabbed to the heart*): Oh, that is what he said? (*She stands there looking blankly into space, overwhelmed.*)

DORO: That is exactly what he said! And furthermore, he said that when the introduction you had insisted upon was postponed from day to day, you discovered that the postponement was due to the flat refusal of Rocca, the sister's fiancé, to meet you!

DELIA: And so to show my power over Rocca . . . to humiliate him . . . to get even with him! . . . That's the idea, isn't it?

DORO: Yes . . . you sank your claws into Rocca, twisting him around your finger like a blade of grass, quite forgetting Salvi, meantime—just for the pleasure of showing that sister of his and her mother, what the pride and respectability of the pillars of public morals amounted to! (*For a time* DELIA *stands in silence, her eyes fixed apparently upon something in distant space. Finally she covers her face with both her hands and remains in that attitude for some seconds.* DORO *considers her, in perplexity and surprise. Then he asks.*) What's the matter? (DELIA *still keeps her hands to her face, but finally she lowers them and is again seen staring with the same blank expression into space. Then, opening her two arms in a gesture of discouragement.*)

DELIA: And who knows! Who knows! Who knows that those weren't the reasons?

DORO (*startled*): Weren't the reasons? . . . What do you mean? If they were . . . (*At this moment* DONNA LIVIA *appears in the brightly lighted drawing-room and comes forward on the stage in great agitation, calling, before she reaches the parlor.*)

DONNA LIVIA: Doro! Doro!

DORO (*leaping to his feet in alarm at the sound of his* MOTHER'*s voice*): My mother is coming!

DONNA LIVIA (*rushing into the room*): Doro! Is this true?

I've been told that the trouble last evening is to result in a duel!

DORO: Duel? Who ever said such a thing?

DONNA LIVIA (*noticing* DELIA *and turning disdainfully upon her*): Ah! Indeed! So I find this woman in my own house!

DORO (*firmly, and stressing the important words*): Yes, in your house! In *your* house, mamma! You call it *your* house!

DELIA: Oh, but I'm going away . . . I'm going away! But don't be alarmed, Signora! There will be no duel . . . there will be no duel! I assure you, Signora! Don't worry on that account! I will prevent it . . . I will find a way to prevent it! . . . (*With a sob, she starts rapidly for the other room.*)

DORO (*following after her and calling*): Signora, don't you dare! Please, Signora, don't try to interfere! (DELIA *goes out.*)

DONNA LIVIA (*trying to stop* DORO *and almost in a scream*): So it's true then?

DORO (*turning and answering vehemently*): True? What is true? That I'm going to fight a duel? Perhaps! And why? For something that no one understands . . . neither he, nor I, nor the woman herself . . . ah . . . nor the woman herself! . . .

(*Curtain.*)

first choral interlude

(*The curtain falls, but almost immediately rises again, uncovering a section of the theatre lobby opening on the orchestra.* SPECTATORS, *one by one, are seen coming out of the main hall of the theatre, at the end of the first act. It may be taken for granted that other* SPECTATORS *are similarly entering the corridors that lie invisible to right and left. In fact,* NEWCOMERS *keep appearing from other parts of the lobby from time to time.*

*This scene in the lobby—*SPECTATORS *coming out of a theatre—will show what was first presented on the stage as life itself to be a fiction of art; and the substance of the comedy will accordingly be pushed back, as it were, into a secondary plane of actuality or reality. But later on, toward the end of this interlude, the scene in the lobby will, in its turn, be* *expelled from the foreground, when it transpires that the comedy which has been witnessed on the stage is a "comedy with a key"—a comedy, that is, based upon an episode in real life, an episode, moreover, with which the newspapers have been recently dealing as a feature: the famous triangular situation between a certain* MORENO WOMAN *[whom everybody recognizes in the* DELIA MORELLO *of the comedy]: a certain* BARON NUTI, *and the sculptor,* GIACOMO LA VELA *[who has committed suicide]. The* MORENO WOMAN *and* BARON NUTI *are present in the theatre among the* SPECTATORS. *Their appearance, therefore, suddenly and violently establishes a plane of reality still closer to real life, leaving the* SPECTATORS *who are discussing the fictitious reality of the staged play on a plane midway between. In the interlude at the end of the second act these three planes of reality will come into conflict with one another, as the participants in the drama of real life attack the participants in the comedy, the* SPECTATORS, *meantime, trying to interfere. Under such circumstances it need not be observed, a comedy cannot go on.*

In the production of this first interlude the greatest naturalness, volubility, and vivacity are necessary. The presupposition is that at the end of every act of these unintelligible, implausible, paradoxical—and what not—comedies of Pirandello, arguments and conflicts are bound to occur. The DEFENDERS OF PIRANDELLO *should show toward his uncompromising antagonists a smiling humility of countenance which has the effect of exasperating hostilities rather than the contrary.*

Various groups of PEOPLE *form in the lobby.* INDIVIDUALS *may be seen going from one group to the other in quest of light. Comic effects should be derived from their changes of opinion according to the group they hit upon. A few placid* INDIVIDUALS *are smoking unconcernedly, and the way they smoke will show their boredom, if they are bored, or their doubts, if they are in doubt; because smoking, like all vices that become habitual, has this sad shortcoming: that it eventually fails to satisfy, by itself, but takes its flavor from the moment in which it is indulged and from the state of mind in which it is indulged. It follows that even people who dislike Pirandello's plays may console themselves with a good cigar, if they choose, on occasion.*

Conspicuous in the CROWD *in the lobby, the uniforms of two* POLICEMEN *[carabinieri] may be seen. An* USHER *or two and a* TICKET TAKER; *two or three* MAIDS *dressed in black with white aprons. A* NEWSBOY *intrudes from the street, calling his headlines. In the groups, arguing and gesticulating here and there, a few* WOMEN *may be observed. Some of them also are smoking [but not with the author's approval]; others may be seen going in and out of the doors to the boxes, where they are visiting friends.*

The five DRAMATIC CRITICS *are naturally much in evidence. They keep away from each other at first, and if anyone questions them they maintain a stolid silence [they have to, you see, to live up to a reputation for "reserve" and "balance"]. Gradually, however, they drift together to get a line on each other's "dope."* INDIVIDUALS *who recognize them edge up as close as possible [without impoliteness] to hear what these celebrities are saying. The interest these people manifest gradually attracts a* CROWD, *whereupon the* CRITICS *either crawl into their shells or walk away. It is quite possible that here in the lobby some of the* CRITICS *will say very sharp things about the comedy and its author; though they will have only praise for both in the articles they write for their papers the next day. A profession is one thing, while the man who professes it is quite another: a critic may have plenty of reasons for sacrificing as a writer his sincerity as a man—granted, of course, that such sacrifice be possible, granted, I mean to say, that he have some sincerity to sacrifice. So with the* SPECTATORS. *Many of those who here appear as bitter critics of the play clapped it uproariously in the theatre at the end of the first act.*

It is hardly worth while writing out the dialogue of this choral interlude. People say much the same things and express much the same judgments about all plays and all authors— which, and who, are "good," "bad," "well constructed," "badly constructed," "obscure," "absurd," "improbable," "paradoxical," "cerebral—all from the brain," and so on. Nevertheless, we must here note down such exchanges as are indispensable between the actors who are actors for the moment in this interlude; though the stage manager is intentionally left a free hand to introduce anything he can devise to keep the lobby in a state of lively and confused animation.

At first: monosyllables, exclamations, grunts, brief questions and answers, from phlegmatic SPECTATORS *who make for the lobby at the earliest possible moment [those really interested in the play are still inside witnessing or fomenting the uproar following on the first act].)*

TWO PEOPLE (*coming out in a hurry*): I'll just go upstairs and look for him.

Number eight, second row, balcony. But be sure you find him, eh?

Don't worry, I'll get him all right. (*The* SECOND *starts away to the left.*)

A MAN (*meeting him*): Hello! So you managed to get in?

THE SECOND OF THE FIRST TWO: As you see. However, I'll be back in a moment. I'm just going upstairs. (*Other* SPECTATORS *come on from the left where a great deal of talking can be heard.* OTHERS *are appearing through the main and side entrances.*)

SOMEBODY (*anybody*): Good house tonight!

ANOTHER: Full up!

A THIRD: See them anywhere?

A FOURTH: I don't think they got past the box-office; but they were beauts! (*In the general confusion exchanges of greetings:* "Good evening!" "Good evening!"—*Smatterings of light talk; one word comments on the play:* "Some show!" "Bunk!" *etc., etc. A few introductions. A* NEWSBOY *enters from the street calling his papers. A* MAN *buys one. An eruption from the theatre—a number of* SPECTATORS *favorable to the author. Enthusiastic, eager, eyes gleaming, they crowd together in a group and begin exchanging first impressions. Later they scatter in various directions, approaching this or that hostile circle, defending their author and his comedy now good-humoredly, now bad-humoredly, now with irony. Their* ADVERSARIES *have also been organizing, meantime.*)

FRIENDS OF PIRANDELLO:

Here we are! Here! This way!

I'll be right there!

All together now, if there's trouble!

A great success, it seems to me!

Splendid! Splendid!

Seems to have gotten away with it!

That last scene with the woman . . . !

Real acting, I say!

Those fellows both changed their minds!

The whole act's a ripper!

OPPONENTS:

His usual line of nonsense!

What does he think we are, fools?

Pirandello's in the same old rut!

You can't make head or tail to the thing!

What's it all mean?

That bird's getting away with murder!

Two dollars, to listen to that stuff!

ONE OF THE ADVERSARIES (*calling to the group of* PIRAN-DELLO'S FRIENDS): But you fellows, you understand it all, eh?

ANOTHER OF THE ADVERSARIES: Of course they do. They're a bunch of wise ones, all right!

ONE OF PIRANDELLO'S FRIENDS (*approaching*): You said that for my benefit?

THE FIRST OF THE ADVERSARIES: No, I didn't mean you —I meant him. (*And he points to another* MAN.)

THE LATTER (*advancing*): You meant that for me?

ADVERSARY: Yes, I meant it for you! I meant it for you! You wouldn't understand "Punch and Judy" if you had it explained to you!

THE MAN IN QUESTION: Yes, but *you* understand, don't you! At least, you understand enough to say it's bunk, don't you?

VOICES FROM NEIGHBORING GROUPS:

But what is there to understand, anyhow?

Didn't you hear . . . ?

Nobody knows what it's all about!

First it's this, and then it's something else!

First they said one thing, but now they say the opposite!

It's a joke on the audience!

What are those people staring at?

That poor mother dying, eh? . . .

. . . And that carriage on the country road! . . .

And it never gets anywhere! Some flivver!

A MAN (*going from one group to another*): So it's a joke on the audience! A joke on the audience! What's it all mean? No one knows what it means! No one can make head or tail to it!

ANOTHER GROUP (*coming into the foreground*):

But it certainly makes you think, eh?

But why is he always harping on this illusion and reality string?

That's not my view of it!

It's just a way of saying things!

Hasn't he expressed it?

Well, expression is art, and art is expression!

But damned if I can see what he's expressed!

But I saw you clapping . . . yes, you did . . . yes, you did . . . I saw you . . . I saw you! . . .

But a single conception may present different phases, according as you look at it, providing it be a whole conception of life.

Conception be damned! Can you tell me what the conception in this first act is?

Yes, but supposing it didn't pretend to have any meaning! . . .

THE SAME MAN (*going to another group*): Yes! Exactly! I see! It isn't supposed to have any meaning! Clever, eh? Clever!

A THIRD GROUP (*gathering around the* CRITICS): Nonsense! Just plain damn nonsense! But you critics—you understand the dra-ama! Pray enlighten us. What's it all mean?

FIRST CRITIC: The construction . . . not bad . . . not bad. Of course one or two places could be left out . . .

ONE OF THE SPECTATORS: What was the point in all that high-brow stuff about conscience?

A SECOND CRITIC: But gentlemen, gentlemen, you have seen only the first act! . . .

THIRD CRITIC: But, honest now . . . is it permissible, I ask you, to play with character that way? There ought to be a law against it . . . and an act without either head or tail? Here we have a drama based, almost casually, you might say, on a discussion that is not even held on the stage! . . .

FOURTH CRITIC: But the discussion is about the play itself. It is the play itself!

SECOND CRITIC: And the play gets going at last when the woman comes on!

THIRD CRITIC: But why not give us the play then, and have done with it?

A FRIEND OF PIRANDELLO: But that woman is well conceived!

ONE OF THE ADVERSARIES: It isn't so much the character, though. It's the girl who takes the part. (*He will name the actress doing* DELIA MORELLO.)

THE MAN (*leaving this group and going back to the first one*): The drama gets going finally, when the woman comes on! She is well conceived, there's no denying that! Everybody is saying so!

A MAN IN THE FIRST GROUP (*answering angrily*): Oh, give us a rest! This play is just one jumble of words!

ANOTHER MAN (*vehemently*): He took the plot out of the newspapers! Sheer impudence!

THIRD (*just as vehemently*): One trick after another! Just word play! All on the surface!

THE MAN (*going from the first to the second group*): Yes, he got the plot from the newspapers! There's no denying it! Everybody says so!

FOURTH CRITIC (*speaking to the* THIRD): But what characters, in the name of heaven! Where do you find people like that in life?

THIRD CRITIC: That's a great idea! People can talk, can't they, and the moment they talk ... !

FOURTH CRITIC: Talk? Exactly! Talk! And you can do what you want when you're playing with words!

FIFTH CRITIC: But I ask you now, if the theatre is art! ...

ONE OF THE ADVERSARIES: Art ... exactly ... poetry ... poetry!

FIFTH CRITIC: But why not controversy? Admirable, that, I grant you. Conflict ... the shock of opposite opinions ... just that!

ONE OF THE FRIENDS OF PIRANDELLO: But you people are making the controversy, it seems to me. I didn't notice so much of it on the stage!

ONE OF THE ADVERSARIES: Yes ... here we have a great author, haven't we? At least you say so!

THE OLD AUTHOR (*who never had a play produced*): So far as I am concerned, if you like this play, you're welcome! What I think—you know already!

VOICES: No! Tell us! Tell us! What do you think? Let's have it!

OLD AUTHOR: Oh, little tricks of the mind ... intellectual altogether, gentlemen ... little problems ... what shall I say—little problems of philosophy, as philosophy is studied by men who are not philosophers! ...

FOURTH CRITIC: I don't agree! I don't agree!

OLD AUTHOR (*raising his voice*): But no great travail of the spirit, as we say! Nothing really straightforward and convincing.

FOURTH CRITIC: Yes, we all know what you call straightforward and convincing! ...

A LITERARY MAN (*who never writes*): If you ask me, the most objectionable thing about the play is ... well ... it's the disagreeableness of the situation itself!

SECOND CRITIC: Why, no! This time it seems to me we have an atmosphere much more wholesome than usual.

LITERARY MAN: But no real artistic urge! Why anybody could write like that!

FOURTH CRITIC: For my part, not having seen the whole play as yet, I shouldn't risk a final judgment; but I think there is going to be something to it. It's as though you were looking into a looking-glass that had gone crazy somehow and . . . (*On the left at this moment a violent clamor is heard. Screams. Shouts.*) "Lunatic! Fraud! Fraud! Lunatic! Call the ambulance!" (PEOPLE *all look in that direction.*) What's going on in there?

THE BAD-HUMORED SPECTATOR: Can't a fellow ever come to see a play of this fellow Pirandello without getting mixed up in a scrap?

GOOD-HUMORED SPECTATOR: Let's hope there'll be no heads broken.

ONE OF THE FRIENDS OF PIRANDELLO: If you want to sleep, why don't you stick to the other plays? With them you can just lean back in your seat and take what is sent you across the footlights. But with a comedy of Pirandello's you have to be on your pins. You sit up straight and dig your finger nails into the arms of your chair as though you were going to be knocked down by what the author has to say! You hear a word . . . any word at all . . . "chair" for instance! Now with most people that would mean "chair," but with Pirandello you say "A chair? . . . No sir! He isn't going to get away with that! I'm going to find out what's under the chair!"

ONE OF THE ADVERSARIES: Yes, yes! That's right! Pirandello gives you everything except a little sentiment! But not a bit of sentiment!

OTHER ADVERSARIES: That's it! That's it! Not a bit of sentiment . . . and you've got to have sentiment!

ONE OF PIRANDELLO'S FRIENDS: If you want sentiment go and find it under the chair that fellow is talking about.

THE ADVERSARIES: But let us have done with these spasms, this nihilism . . . this delight he takes in denying everything! We're tired of tearing down. Let us begin to build up!

FIRST OF PIRANDELLO'S FRIENDS (*vehemently*): Who is tearing anything down? You people are the Bolshevists!

ONE OF THE ADVERSARIES (*storming back at him*): We, tearing down? We never denied that reality exists!

FIRST OF PIRANDELLO'S FRIENDS: But who denies your reality, if you never succeeded in creating one?

A SECOND FRIEND: You deny the truth as other people see it, you claim that there is only one way of looking at things.

FIRST FRIEND: The way you look at them yourself, today!

SECOND FRIEND: Forgetting how you looked at them yesterday!

FIRST FRIEND: Because you . . . you people get your reality from others—it's a convention . . . a mere convention . . . an empty word . . . any word at all: mountain, tree, stream. You think that reality is something fixed, something definite, and you feel as though you were being cheated if someone comes along and shows you that it was all an illusion on your part. Idiots! This comedy tells you that everyone must build a foundation for himself under his own feet, bit by bit, step by step, if he is to advance. You must kick aside a reality that does not belong to you, for the simple reason that you have not made it for yourselves, but are using it as parasites—yes, gentlemen, as parasites—mourning that old-fashioned sentimentality of yours that we've driven from the stage at last, thank God!

BARON NUTI (*pale, disheveled, in a rage, comes in from the left accompanied by two other* SPECTATORS *who are trying to restrain him*): And something else, it seems to me, this comedy teaches, my dear sir! It teaches you to malign the dead and to slander the living!

ONE OF THE MEN WITH HIM (*seizing him by an arm and trying to drag him away*): But please . . . no . . . please . . . come away . . . come away!

THE OTHER MAN WITH HIM (*talking at the same time*): Yes . . . hush . . . hush! Come . . . come . . . please come! Come!

BARON NUTI (*as he is being dragged off to the left, turns and shouts back*): To malign the dead and to slander the living!

VOICES (*amid general surprise*):
What's the matter? Who's that man?
Who's that man?
What a face!
Has he gone crazy?
What's the matter?
Who is he?

SPECTATOR FROM THE SOCIAL SET: It's Baron Nuti.
VOICES:
Baron Nuti? Who is Baron Nuti?
Why did he say what he said?

SPECTATOR FROM THE SOCIAL SET: But don't you people understand that there is a key to this comedy?

ONE OF THE CRITICS: A key? What do you mean . . . a key?

SPECTATOR FROM THE SOCIAL SET: Why yes! This comedy is based on the Moreno affair! Almost word for word! The author has taken it from real life!

VOICES.

The Moreno case?

The Moreno woman?

Who is she?

Who is she?

Why, she's that actress that was in Germany for so long!
She's well known in Turin!

Ah, yes, she was mixed up in the suicide of that sculptor
named La Vela some months ago!

What do you think of that?

And Pirandello . . . is Pirandello getting so low that he
makes comedies on society gossip?

Looks that way . . . looks that way!

And it's not the first time, you know!

But there's nothing wrong in making comedy out of the
day's gossip, is there?

No, unless, as that man just said, you use your comedy to
malign the dead and slander the living.

But Nuti . . . who is Nuti?

SPECTATOR FROM THE SOCIAL SET: He is the other fellow in
the triangle! La Vela killed himself on Nuti's account! Nuti
was to marry La Vela's sister!

ONE OF THE CRITICS: And he spent the night with the
Moreno woman—the night before her marriage to La Vela?

VOICES FROM THE HOSTILE GROUP: The same situation to a
T! It's a crime . . . a downright crime!

OTHER VOICES FROM THE SAME GROUP: And the actors in the
real drama have been here in the theatre?

A THIRD (*calling attention to* NUTI *off the stage, to the left*):
There he is . . . there he is!

SPECTATOR FROM THE SOCIAL SET: The Moreno woman has
a seat in a box upstairs. She recognized herself immediately in
the comedy. They'd better watch out for her! She's a terror
when she gets started! She bit her handkerchief to shreds
during the first act! She'll be making a noise, you'll see! She'll
turn the place upside down!

VOICES:

Serve them right if she did!

The idea of putting a woman in a pillory like that!

Her own case right before her eyes on the stage, and that
Nuti fellow, too!

He had murder in his eye!

There's going to be trouble here . . . there's going to be
trouble!

(*A bell rings, announcing the beginning of the second act.*)

There's the bell . . . there's the bell!

The curtain's going up!

Let's hurry! We mustn't miss anything!

(*There is a general movement toward the entrances to the theatre proper. Exclamations, comments, murmurings continue as the news spreads. Three* INDIVIDUALS *from the group favorable to Pirandello bring up the rear, so that they are present on the stage—that is to say, in the theatre lobby, now virtually cleared of people—when the* MORENO WOMAN *appears from the left. She has come tearing down from her box upstairs despite the efforts of three* MALE FRIENDS *who are trying to get her out of the theatre to prevent trouble. The* TICKET TAKERS *at the theatre doors are at first caught by surprise; but then they do their best to quiet the disturbance so that the play inside will not be interrupted. The three* PARTISANS OF PIRANDELLO *stand aside listening in amazement and consternation.*)

SIGNORA MORENO: No . . . no! I will! I will! Let me alone . . . let me alone!

ONE OF HER FRIENDS: But it's madness . . . it's sheer madness! What can you do about it?

SIGNORA MORENO: I am going behind the scenes!

A SECOND OF HER FRIENDS: What can you do in there? Have you lost your mind?

SIGNORA MORENO: Let me alone! Let me alone!

THE THIRD OF HER FRIENDS: Now I'll just take you to my car.

OTHER TWO (*in chorus*): Yes, yes, let's all go home! Please, now, come along with us!

SIGNORA MORENO: I won't! I won't! Let go of me! Let go of me! It's a disgrace! It's an insult! And they won't get away with it scot free!

THE FIRST FRIEND: But what's the idea? What's the idea? . . . On the stage . . . in front of everybody there?

SIGNORA MORENO: Let go of me, I tell you! Let go of me! Yes, there on the stage, in front of everybody!

SECOND FRIEND: Ah, no, not a bit of it! Not a bit of it! We won't let you make a show of yourself like that!

SIGNORA MORENO: Let go of me, won't you? I'm going in there behind the scenes. . . .

THIRD FRIEND: But the actors are out on the stage again!

FIRST FRIEND: The second act has begun!

SIGNORA MORENO (*suddenly growing calmer*): Ah, they have begun again? I must hear what they have to say! I'm going back! (*She starts off toward the left again.*)

HER FRIENDS (*all together*): No! No! Please, let's go away! Do as we say! Please! Please! Let's go home!

SIGNORA MORENO (*virtually dragging them after her*): No! I'm going back in again! I want to see the rest of it! I will! I will!

ONE OF THE FRIENDS (*as they withdraw to the left*): But why torment yourself any further?

ONE OF THE TICKET TAKERS (*addressing the three* PARTISANS OF PIRANDELLO): What's the matter with those people? Gone nutty? . . .

THE FIRST OF THE PARTISANS (*to the other two*): Did you understand? Did you understand?

THE SECOND: It's the Moreno woman!

THE THIRD: But say, is Pirandello in the theatre?

THE FIRST: He may be. I think I'll just step inside and advise him to run, while the running is good. This evening there's going to be a rumpus, and no mistake.

(*Curtain.*)

act II (*The house of* FRANCESCO SAVIO *the morning after. A sort of lounge opening on a wide veranda, where* SAVIO *habitually practices fencing. On the veranda, accordingly, as we view it through the large windows which occupy almost all the rear wall of the room, there are one or two stools, a long bench for spectators, fencing masks and gloves, chest protectors, sabres, rapiers. A green cloth curtain hangs on the inside of the window and may be run back and forth on rings so as to cut off the view of the veranda and give a little privacy to the room. A similar curtain, stretched between the posts on the veranda, is already drawn, cutting off the veranda from the garden which is supposed to lie beyond, and of which a glimpse will be had at certain moments as some of the* CHARACTERS *draw the curtain aside to go down the steps into the garden.*

The room is furnished with green wicker furniture—two chairs, a table, a stand, two divans. There must be a door to the right, in addition to one opening upon the veranda, and a small window to the left.

As the curtain rises, FRANCESCO SAVIO *and the* FENCING MASTER, *with masks, protectors, and gloves on, are fencing on the veranda.* PRESTINO *and two other* FRIENDS *stand looking on.*)

THE FENCING MASTER: Eh-eh-eh! Look out! Look out! (*He lunges and* FRANCESCO *parries.*) Good! No . . . let's try that again! Eh-eh-eh-eh! (*They cross their rapiers, the* FENCING MASTER *lunges, and* FRANCESCO *parries as before.*) Well done! Well done! Now look out . . . look out! In position! Now attack . . . now attack! That feint is no good! That feint is no good! It leaves you open over here! This way . . . see? There you are! All right! Alt! (*They lower their rapiers. The practice bout is over.*) Keep at it that way and you'll come through all right! (*They take off their masks.*)

FRANCESCO: Yes! I'm sure I will! But I think I have had enough! Thanks, maestro! (*He shakes hands with the* FENCING MASTER.)

PRESTINO: Yes, better not keep it up too long!

FENCING MASTER (*taking off his glove and then the protector*): But I'll tell you one thing . . . you're not going to find Palegari easy! He's a tough customer when he attacks!

ONE OF THE TWO FRIENDS: And he parries splendidly! Don't give him a chance at you!

THE SECOND: He's as quick as a flash!

FRANCESCO: Yes, I knew that. (*Taking off his glove and protector.*)

THE FIRST OF HIS FRIENDS: You keep your eye peeled to the right!

FENCING MASTER: The main point is to keep your iron on his.

FRANCESCO: I understand . . . I understand!

THE SECOND FRIEND: The straight lunge works best against Doro.

FIRST FRIEND: Not a bit of it! You just meet his rush . . . just meet his rush! You take it from me . . . let him alone and he'll beat himself! Keep a stiff arm and he'll split himself on your weapon!

FENCING MASTER: Meantime, I must congratulate you . . . you have an air-tight defense!

PRESTINO: Follow my advice and don't do any attacking! Keep him coming on and you'll get a chance at him sooner or later! Meantime I propose a round of drinks to your good luck! (*He comes forward into the room with the others.*)

FRANCESCO: Yes, yes, right you are! (*He pushes a button in the wall; then turning to the* FENCING MASTER): And you, maestro, what'll you have?

THE FENCING MASTER: Nothing for me—I never drink in the forenoon.

FRANCESCO: I have some first rate beer.

PRESTINO: That's the talk! A mug of beer!

FIRST OF THE TWO FRIENDS: Same here! (*The* BUTLER *appears from the door to the right.*)

FRANCESCO: Bring in four or five bottles of beer right away. (*The* BUTLER *goes out, returning almost immediately, however, with bottles and glasses on a tray. He pours the beer, passes it around and withdraws again.*)

FIRST FRIEND: This will be the craziest duel on record. Your name will go down in history, Francesco.

SECOND FRIEND: It certainly will. I doubt whether two men ever cut themselves up before, each for the privilege of saying that the other one was right.

PRESTINO: But it's all very natural, however.

FIRST FRIEND: Natural? What is there natural about it?

PRESTINO: Why, here the two of them were on opposite sides of the same question. They both changed their minds at the same time, each coming around to the view of the other. Naturally, they collided in the process.

FENCING MASTER: Of course, if while the one who was first attacking has now passed to the defense and fights just as fiercely as before, each of them, meantime, using the arguments of the other . . .

FIRST FRIEND: Are you sure of that?

FRANCESCO: I assure you I went to his house with the most sincere and cordial intentions.

FIRST FRIEND: And not because you felt—

FRANCESCO: No, there is no question of pride at all!

FIRST FRIEND: That isn't what I was going to say. It's not because you felt you had gone a bit too far in publicly assailing the Morello woman so bitterly?

FRANCESCO: Not at all . . . not at all! Why . . . I . . .

FIRST FRIEND: Wait! Let me finish. I was going to say: without taking account of a fact that was perfectly obvious to everybody that evening?

SECOND FRIEND: That he was defending the woman because he was in love with her?

FRANCESCO: Not at all . . . not at all! It was because I had not been thinking of any of those things that all the trouble has arisen. We must look like two blamed fools! This is what I get for letting myself go, for being quite spontaneous and frank for once in my life! What a nuisance! I had planned on a quiet little visit to my sister and her husband in the country day after tomorrow.

PRESTINO: Nevertheless, you had had a rather heated argument the evening before.

FRANCESCO: But—as I tell you again—without thinking of anything but the merits of the case, and without dreaming that he had any secret passion for the woman!

SECOND FRIEND: But are you sure he has?

FIRST FRIEND: Certainly he has!

PRESTINO: He must have . . . certainly!

FRANCESCO: If I had even remotely suspected such a thing I

would not have gone to his house to admit that he was right, certain as I could be that that would make him furious!

THE SECOND FRIEND (*violently*): I wanted to say this . . . (*He breaks off short and they all turn to look at him in surprise.*)

FIRST FRIEND (*after waiting a second*): You wanted to say what?

SECOND FRIEND: I wanted to say . . . oh, I have forgotten what. (*At this moment* DIEGO CINCI *appears in the doorway to the right.*)

DIEGO: Am I intruding?

FRANCESCO (*in surprise*): Oh, Diego, you here?

PRESTINO: Has someone sent you?

DIEGO (*shrugging his shoulders*): Why should anyone have sent me? Good day, maestro!

FENCING MASTER: Good day, Cinci! But I must be going. (*Shakes hands with* SAVIO *warmly.*) See you tomorrow, Savio . . . and don't stay awake, worrying!

FRANCESCO: Never was cooler in my life, don't fear! Thank you, maestro!

FENCING MASTER (*bowing to the* OTHERS): Gentlemen, I am sorry I can't stay in your good company, but I have an important engagement. (*The* OTHERS *bow to him.*)

FRANCESCO: Look, maestro, if you prefer, you can go out this way. (*He points toward the veranda.*) Just draw the curtain aside and you'll see the stairs. The garden opens on the street.

FENCING MASTER: Ah, that's a good idea. I'll do that. Once more . . . good morning! (*He withdraws.*)

FIRST FRIEND (*to* DIEGO): We were expecting you to be one of Doro Palegari's seconds.

DIEGO (*shaking his finger in silent negation*): No, I couldn't, you see, I was caught between two fires last evening. Good friends of them both! . . . I had to keep out of it.

THE SECOND FRIEND: But why have you come here now, then?

DIEGO: To say that I am delighted that there is going to be a duel! Delighted! Delighted! (*The* OTHERS *laugh.*) And I hope that both get hurt! Not mortally, of course . . . not mortally! A little blood-letting would do them both good! A cut, besides, is something you can see and be sure about! A cut two . . . three . . . five inches long! (*He takes* FRANCESCO *by the forearm and looks under the sleeve of his coat.*) Let me look at your wrist!

All sound! Well, tomorrow morning you're going to have a cut from here to here. It will be something you can look at!

FRANCESCO: A fine consolation! (*The* OTHERS *laugh again.*)

DIEGO (*speaking up quickly*): But Doro will get his too, let us hope! Doro, too! Let's be quite impartial! I have a surprise for you! You know who came to Palegari's shortly after you went away and I followed you?

PRESTINO: Delia Morello!

THE SECOND FRIEND: I suppose she went to thank him for standing up for her!

DIEGO: Yes, except that when she found out just why you accused her . . . well . . . you know what she did?

FRANCESCO: What did she do?

DIEGO: She admitted that you were right!

FRANCESCO, PRESTINO, *and the* FIRST FRIEND (*all together*): She did? Really? That's a great idea! And Doro . . . how about him?

DIEGO: You can imagine how he took it!

SECOND FRIEND: He can't have the least idea now why he is going to fight.

FRANCESCO: No, he knows the reason for that! He's going to fight because he insulted me in your presence while I, as I was saying here to my two friends and as you know yourself, had simply gone to him to admit that he was right!

DIEGO: Now . . .

FRANCESCO: Now what?

DIEGO: Now that you know that Delia Morello says that you were right . . .

FRANCESCO: Oh, well, if she herself—

DIEGO: No, my dear boy, no; Hold your ground . . . hold your ground . . . because now Delia Morello is in greater need of a defender than ever, and the job falls to you! You were the first to accuse her!

PRESTINO: Let's get this straight! Francesco must defend her against herself, now that she's accused herself before the man who at first tried to defend her!

DIEGO: Exactly! Exactly! And my admiration for her has increased one hundredfold since I found that out! (*Turns suddenly on* FRANCESCO.) You—who are you? (*Then turning to* PRESTINO.) Who are you? Who am I? Who are we all? Your name is Francesco Savio; mine is Diego Cinci; yours is Prestino. We have of each other reciprocally, and each has of himself, knowledge of some small, insignificant certainty of today, which is not the certainty it was yesterday and will not be the certainty of tomorrow. Francesco, you are living on your income and you are bored!

FRANCESCO: No ... who told you that?

DIEGO: You are not bored? Lucky man! I have worn my soul out digging, digging tunnels—to China! (*To* PRESTINO.) What do you do?

PRESTINO: Nothing!

DIEGO: A fine profession! But even people who work, my dear friends—decent, respectable people like me—we are all, all alike! This life that is in us and around us—well examine it as closely as you wish. It is such a continuous, changing thing that if our deepest affections cannot endure against it, imagine what the case with the ideas, the opinions, the judgments which we succeed in forming for ourselves, must be! All our ideas, in short, change in the restless turmoil we call life. We think we catch a glimpse of a situation! But let us just discover something contrary to what we thought! So-and-so was a white man, eh? Well, at once he's a black man! Our impressions of things change from hour to hour! A word is often sufficient or even just the manner in which it is said—to change our minds completely! And then besides, quite without our knowledge, images of hundreds and hundreds of things are flitting through our minds, suddenly causing our tempers to vary in the strangest way! Here along a road darkening with the approach of evening we are walking, sad, gloomy, despondent. We raise our eyes and we see a cottage still blazing under the setting sun. ... Or we see a red geranium burning in a stray burst of sunlight. ... And we change ... we change ... we brighten! A wave of tenderness sweeps over us!

PRESTINO: And where does all that get us?

DIEGO: Nowhere! Where are we trying to get, for that matter? I was telling you how things are ... everything vague, indefinite, changing, insubstantial! Finally, to get hold of something solid, to feel the firm ground under your feet, you drop back into the weariness and affliction of your little certainty of today! ... of that little which you succeed in knowing about yourself ... your name, let us say ... how much money you have in your pocket ... the number of the house on the street where you live ... your habits ... your feelings ... all these things which are customary, established, fixed, in your existence ... that poor body of yours, for example, which still moves and can follow the flux of life, until its movements, which grow less and less vigorous every day and less and less supple the older you get, finally cease altogether and—good night!

FRANCESCO: But you were talking of Delia Morello!

DIEGO: Ah, yes! I was trying to make you understand my great admiration for her; or rather I was trying to make you feel what a joy it is, what a wonderful—though terrible—joy it is, when, caught by the tide of life in one of its moments of tempest, we are able actually to witness the collapse of all those fictitious forms around which our stupid daily life has solidified; and under the dikes, beyond the seawalls, which we had thrown up to isolate, to create, a definite consciousness for ourselves at all hazards, to build a personality of some kind, we are able to see that bit of tide—which was not wholly unknown to us and which seemed something tangible to us because we had carefully harnessed it to serve our feelings, draining it off into the duties which we had assumed, into the habits which we had created—suddenly break forth in a magnificent, overwhelming flood and turns everything topsy-turvy! Ah, at last!—A whirlwind! A volcanic eruption! An earthquake! A cataclysm!

EVERYBODY (*in chorus*): You like that, eh? No, thank you! None of those things for me! The Lord deliver us!

DIEGO: But, my dear friends, after we have witnessed the farce of our own absurd changes of opinion, we have before us the tragedy of a bewildered spirit, gone astray and unable to find its way again. And it's not only Delia Morello! Wait, Francesco, you'll see! Soon you'll have them both on your hands! Both her and the other fellow!

FRANCESCO: The other fellow? What other fellow? Michele Rocca?

DIEGO: Yes, Michele Rocca, himself!

FIRST FRIEND: He came in last evening from Naples.

SECOND FRIEND: Ah, I have it! That was what I was trying to tell you fellows some time ago. I learned that he was looking for Palegari . . . to slap his face!

PRESTINO: Yes, but we knew all that! (*To* FRANCESCO.) I told you so, didn't I?

FRANCESCO (*to* DIEGO): But why should he come here to see me just now?

DIEGO: Because he insists on fighting a duel with Doro Palegari before you do! But now it would seem that he ought to have the duel with you!

FRANCESCO: What do you mean . . . with me?

THE OTHERS (*all together*): Why with Francesco? Why with Savio?

DIEGO: With you, of course! You have changed your mind, haven't you, honestly, sincerely? And thereby you assume responsibility for everything said by Palegari against him . . . at the Avanzi's the other night! What could be clearer? You have inverted your respective positions! It is obvious then! Rocca ought to make his fight with you!

FRANCESCO: Not so fast, not so fast! What in the deuce are you talking about?

DIEGO: Excuse me . . . you are fighting this duel with Doro simply because he insulted you, are you not? Well, why did Doro insult you?

FRANCESCO (*in some irritation*): Why, of course, of course . . . because I . . .

DIEGO (*speaking up quickly and carrying on the thought*): . . . because you, *loyally, sincerely* . . .

THE TWO FRIENDS (*without letting him finish*): Yes, yes, he's right! Diego is right!

DIEGO: So the rôles have been inverted! You are left to defend Delia Morello, putting all the blame on Michele Rocca!

PRESTINO (*shocked*): Oh, let's quit joking!

DIEGO: Joking? (*To* FRANCESCO.) Oh, if you ask me . . . you can boast this time of being right!

FRANCESCO: So you want me to have a duel with Michele Rocca, too?

DIEGO: Ah, I couldn't say that! A duel with a man in his frame of mind would be a very serious matter! The poor fellow is desperate!

THE FIRST FRIEND: I should say so! With Salvi's corpse lying between him and the girl he was going to marry.

SECOND FRIEND: The marriage broken off! . . .

DIEGO: And Delia Morello making a fool of him!

FRANCESCO (*with a rising irritation*): What do you mean . . . a fool of him? You are saying she made a fool of him, now!

DIEGO: That she did use him for her own purposes, no one can deny!

FRANCESCO: Treacherously, therefore, as I claimed at first!

DIEGO (*trying to stop him with a reproof*): Ah-ah-ah-ah, ah-ah-ah! There you go! Listen! The annoyance you now feel for having gotten into this mess ought not make you change your mind for still a third time!

FRANCESCO: Not at all! Not at all! Excuse me . . . you said yourself that she went and confessed to Doro Palegari that I was right in accusing her of treachery!

DIEGO: You see? You see?

FRANCESCO: But what do I see, damn it all? If I discover that she is now accusing herself and saying that I was right, why—of course—I change my mind and go back to my first position! (*Turning to the* OTHERS.) Don't you think I have a right to, you people?

DIEGO (*vehemently*): But I tell you that she used him treacherously . . . yes . . . if you insist on that word . . . but only in order to free Giorgio Salvi from the danger he was running in marrying her! Understand? You have absolutely no right to claim that that was treachery toward Salvi. On the contrary, I am ready to defend her myself, even if she herself be her own accuser . . . I'll defend her even against herself. . . .

FRANCESCO (*giving ground with some irritation*): . . . In view of the reasons . . . yes . . . of the reasons advanced by Doro Palegari . . .

DIEGO: . . . on account of which you . . .

FRANCESCO: . . . yes, . . . changed my mind . . . changed my mind . . . exactly. . . . But the fact remains that as regards Rocca she was really treacherous all the time.

DIEGO: Treacherous? She was just a woman! Why not stop at that? He approached her with the idea of having his fun with her, giving her that impression also, so that she in her turn made a fool of him. That really is what's the matter with Michele Rocca! He is stung in his pride as a man and as a male! He is not yet ready to admit that he was just a helpless, stupid thing in the hands of a woman, a doll which Delia Morello tossed aside and broke to pieces after amusing herself in making it open and close its arms in prayer—just by pressing the spring of passion which that doll had in its insides somewhere! Huh! The doll has been picked up again and set in place, the wax nose of its wax face broken, the wax fingers on its wax hands gone—cracks in its wax head and in its wax body, and the spring—the spring of passion that it had in its gizzard—has broken through the cloth covering and is sticking out! But yet . . . no . . . the doll will not have it that way! The doll keeps crying at the top of its voice that it's not true; that that woman didn't make it say its prayers; that that woman did not use it as a plaything, breaking it to pieces when the game was done! No . . . no . . . it cries! Well, I ask you, did you ever see a more absurd spectacle than that?

PRESTINO (*losing control of himself and almost shaking his fist in* DIEGO's *face*): Why are you trying to make us laugh at such a serious matter, you clown?

DIEGO (*looking at* PRESTINO *in amazement, as the* OTHERS *do also*): I?

PRESTINO: You! Yes, you! Ever since you've been in here, you've been playing the clown, trying to make a fool of him, of me, of us, of everybody!

DIEGO: But also of myself, don't you think?

PRESTINO: Keep your compliments for yourself! It's easy to laugh the way you do, making us all out so many cocks on a weather vane which turns this way or that, according as the wind blows! I'm tired of this nonsense! How shall I describe it? When you talk that way you seem to put poison in my soul!

DIEGO: Not at all, my dear boy! I laugh because I have reasoned my heart dry!

PRESTINO: You said as much yourself . . . there is nothing in your heart! It is empty, cold, dead . . . that is why you laugh!

DIEGO: That is why you *think* I laugh!

PRESTINO: I think so because it's so! Even if it were true that people are as you say we are, I should think you would feel more like pitying us than laughing at us.

DIEGO (*offended in his turn, advancing toward* PRESTINO *aggressively, placing his two hands on the latter's two shoulders, and bringing his face up close, looking the man fixedly in the eye*): Pity? Yes . . . if you let yourself be examined this way . . .

PRESTINO (*puzzled*): What way?

DIEGO: This way . . . in the eye . . . just like this! No . . . look at me! This way . . . naked as you are . . . with all the filth and muck and smallness there is in you! In you as in me . . . in me as in you—all the fears—all the self-reproaches—all the hesitations and contradictions! Shake yourself free from the manikin you create out of a false interpretation of what you do and what you feel, and you'll at once see that the manikin you make yourself is nothing at all like what you really are or what you can really be! Nothing at all like what is in you without your knowing that it is there—a terrible avenger if you resist it; though it at once becomes charitable toward all your shortcomings if you just give in and do not try to justify and delude yourself! Oh, I know . . . to cast aside that manikin, that fiction, seems in a certain way to be a denial of one's self, something unworthy of a man; and it will always be that way so long as we believe that humanness consists in what we call conscience, in that courage, if you wish, which we have shown on one single occasion rather than in the cowardice which on many occasions has counselled prudence. You have agreed to act as Savio's second in this stupid duel of Palegari's. (*Talking to* SAVIO.) And you thought that Palegari kept calling you a clown yesterday? Huh! He was calling names at that manikin which he could not see in himself, but which he could see in you because you showed it to him as in a mirror! I laugh . . . yes . . . I laugh in my own way, and my ridicule falls upon myself sooner than on anyone else! (*A pause. They all fall silent, each absorbed in his own thoughts. The following lines will be pronounced at intervals between pauses, as though each were talking to himself.*)

FRANCESCO: Of course, I have no real animosity against Doro Palegari. He kept leading me on from one thing to another. (*A pause.*)

PRESTINO (*after some seconds*): So many times we have to pretend we are sure; and if such pretense only hurts us the more deeply, we are not more worthy of blame, but more worthy of pity.

FIRST FRIEND (*after another pause, as though he were reading* FRANCESCO SAVIO's *thoughts*): Who knows? It must be splendid out in the country today!

FRANCESCO (*answering quickly and without surprise, as though to justify himself*): Why I had actually bought some playthings to carry out to my sister's little girl.

SECOND FRIEND: A cute little tot she was that time I saw her.

FRANCESCO: Oh, a dear little thing! Prettiest child I ever set my eyes on! So wise, as she looks up at you out of her big eyes! An angel! A cherub!

DIEGO (*to* FRANCESCO): Listen! If I were you, Francesco . . . (*The* BUTLER *appears in the doorway to the right.*)

BUTLER: May I interrupt, sir?

FRANCESCO: What is it, Giovanni?

BUTLER: A message for you, sir.

FRANCESCO (*approaching the* BUTLER *and listening to what he has to say. Then with evident annoyance*): Now? How can I? Impossible! (*He turns and stands looking at his* FRIENDS, *hesitant, in great perplexity.*)

DIEGO (*understanding*): She is here?

PRESTINO: You cannot receive her! You must not!

FIRST FRIEND: Of course not! You cannot while this point of honor is still pending!

DIEGO: Not at all! She has nothing to do with that!

PRESTINO: What do you mean? Why, she is the cause of the whole trouble! However, I won't argue the point. I am your second in this affair and I say no! I say you mustn't let her come in!

SECOND FRIEND: But you can't send a lady away like that, without even finding out what she's come for!

DIEGO: I really have no right to say anything.

FIRST FRIEND (*to* FRANCESCO): You might find out what she wants!

SECOND FRIEND: Yes, and if perchance . . .

FRANCESCO: . . . she tries to put in a word about the duel . . .

PRESTINO: . . . end the interview at once! On that basis I consent!

FRANCESCO: Very well! Very well! I'll tell her to go on about her business! That's what I'll do! Just leave it to me! (FRANCESCO *withdraws, followed by the* BUTLER.)

DIEGO: My only suggestion would be that he should advise her to . . . (*At this moment the veranda curtain is torn furiously aside and* MICHELE ROCCA *breaks in from the garden in the throes of a dangerous excitement which he has difficulty in restraining. He is a person about thirty years old—black hair, dark complexion, traces of bitterness, of remorse, of passion, in the lines of his face. His whole expression, the nervous movements of his body, the twitching of his features, show that he is ready to go to any extreme.*)

ROCCA: If I may! (*Then surprised at seeing so many people he had not expected to find.*) Is this the place? I have come to the right house?

PRESTINO (*voicing his own amazement and that of the* OTHERS): Who are you?

ROCCA: Michele Rocca.

DIEGO: Ah, so here he is!

ROCCA (*to* DIEGO): You are Signor Francesco Savio?

DIEGO: No, I am not. Savio is in the other room. (*He points to the door on the right.*)

PRESTINO: But if I may ask . . . how did you get in here in this way?

ROCCA: I was shown to this entrance.

DIEGO: The porter thought he was one of Savio's friends!

ROCCA: Am I mistaken? Did not a lady enter this house a few seconds before me?

PRESTINO: You mean that you were following her?

ROCCA: Yes, I was following her. I knew that she was to come here.

DIEGO: So did I . . . and I knew that you would come here too.

ROCCA: The most outrageous things are being said about me all over town! I know that Signor Savio, without ever having met me, has come to my defense. Now, he must not listen to that woman! He must not . . . without first hearing from me exactly how matters stand!

PRESTINO: But it's too late now, my dear sir!

ROCCA: Too late? What do you mean?

PRESTINO: I said it was too late! Arbitration is now out of the question!

FIRST FRIEND: A challenge has been made and accepted!

SECOND FRIEND: And the conditions signed!

DIEGO: And they both have changed their minds!

PRESTINO (*angrily to* DIEGO): You will be so good as to refrain from any further interference! To put it plainly, please mind your own damn business!

FIRST FRIEND: Why do you keep trying to mix things up?

DIEGO: I'm not mixing anything up. I'm making it clearer! This gentleman came here under the impression that Savio has been defending him. I am simply pointing out that Savio has changed his mind, and is defending him no longer!

ROCCA: Ah, I see! So now *he* is blaming me, too!

DIEGO: He is not the only one, notice!

ROCCA: You too, for instance?

DIEGO: Yes, yes! I—and everybody else here, as you may see!

ROCCA: I can well believe it! So far, you've been talking only with her!

DIEGO: No! No! Not at all! None of us has seen her nor has Savio, until just now! He has this minute stepped into the other room to find out what she wants!

ROCCA: Why do you blame me then? And why does Savio? At first he took my side! If he has changed his mind, why is he having his duel with Signor Palegari?

DIEGO: My dear sir, in your case—as I understand very well —in your case, madness assumes its most spectacular forms; but believe me, as I was saying just now, all of us are crazy in one way or another! This duel, as you must know, is being fought precisely because both the litigants have changed their minds!

FIRST FRIEND (*along with the* OTHERS, *in some heat*): Don't listen to this fellow! He is quite mistaken!

SECOND FRIEND: They're going on with the duel because, after the trouble night before last, Palegari got angry . . .

FIRST FRIEND (*raising his voice*): . . . and called Signor Savio a clown!

PRESTINO (*raising his voice still higher*): Signor Savio took offense at the insult and issued a challenge . . .

DIEGO (*raising his voice till it overrides the* OTHERS): . . . though by that time they were both in perfect agreement!

ROCCA (*vehemently*): In agreement in condemning me without having heard my case? I should like to know—how is this worthless woman able to get everybody on her side like that?

DIEGO: Everybody except herself . . . except herself!

ROCCA: Except herself?

DIEGO: Not quite that! Don't imagine that she is on one side or on the other! She doesn't know exactly where she stands! Examine your own state of mind, a little more carefully, Signor Rocca, and you will see that even you are not quite sure where you stand!

ROCCA: I'm glad you enjoy your own jokes! However, will you kindly announce me, one of you gentlemen? Say that Signor Michele Rocca would like to be received by Signor Francesco Savio.

PRESTINO: But what do you want to see him about? I repeat, it's too late!

ROCCA: What do you know about it? If he's against me now, all the better!

PRESTINO: But he's in the other room there with the lady!

ROCCA: Better still! I followed her to this house on purpose! Perhaps it is just as well for her that I am meeting her with other people, in the presence, in fact, of a stranger whom chance has seen fit to involve in our troubles. So then, I have made up my mind—for anything! I was blind . . . blind . . . but now the simple fact that I find myself here unexpectedly with all you gentlemen . . . the simple fact that I must speak . . . answer your questions . . . well . . . I feel as though . . . I could—all of a sudden—breathe more easily . . . as though the atmosphere had been cleared! I had been keeping to myself for days and days! You gentlemen can't understand the agony I have been through! I tried to save the man whose sister I was to marry, a man I had come to love as my own brother . . . !

PRESTINO: You tried to save him? That's a good one!

FIRST FRIEND: By running off with the girl he was in love with!

SECOND FRIEND: The night before he was to marry her!

ROCCA: No! No! Listen . . . listen, please! Not at all! I wasn't trying to steal his girl . . . and you say he was going to marry her! It wasn't much of a job to save him! It was sufficient to demonstrate to him, to make him see beyond any question of doubt that the woman he was going to marry because he wanted her could be his—as she could be anybody's —without any question of marriage!

PRESTINO: Anyhow, you spent the night with her . . . !

ROCCA: But on a bet . . . on a bet!

FIRST FRIEND: On what bet?

SECOND FRIEND: Bet with whom?

ROCCA: Let me finish! Let me finish! A bet with him! You see, it was by arrangement with his sister and his mother! He had introduced her to the family, doing violence thereby to all his feelings of propriety; and I, by an arrangement I made with his sister and his mother, followed the two of them to Naples with the excuse of helping them get settled in their new house! He was to marry the girl a few months later. However, there was a quarrel . . . one of those quarrels that often arise between people about to get married. She lost her temper and left him for some days! (*He covers his eyes with a hand as though to hide a vision that tempts and horrifies at the same time.*) Oh, she went away . . . and I can see her . . . I can see her! . . . (*He lowers his hand, his face showing greater and greater emotion.*) For I was present at the quarrel! . . . (*Mastering his feelings.*) I seized that occasion as a favorable opportunity for demonstrating to Giorgio the absurdity of what he was about to do. It's incredible, isn't it? Incredible! And yet those women are often that way, it seems! Do you know, she never gave him the slightest concession?

FIRST FRIEND (*intent, as all the* OTHERS *are, on the narrative*): Of course!

ROCCA: Not only that. At Capri there, she had shown herself disdainful and contemptuous toward all the men, keeping to herself . . . proud and reserved! "Well, I'll bet you," said he to me, "I'll bet you!" And he challenged me to do what I bet him that I could do, promising that if I won the bet, he'd break with the girl and have nothing more to do with her! Well, instead, he shot himself!

FIRST FRIEND: But I don't understand! You lent yourself to such a scheme!

ROCCA: It was a bet! To save him!

SECOND FRIEND: But the treachery of it all!

ROCCA: Yes, horrible . . . horrible!

SECOND FRIEND: But his treachery toward you, I mean!

ROCCA: Yes, he did not play fair with me!

SECOND FRIEND: He shot himself!

PRESTINO: It's incredible . . . incredible!

ROCCA: . . . that I lent myself to such a thing? . . .

PRESTINO: . . . No, that he allowed you to strike such a bargain with him!

ROCCA: But don't you see? He did it on purpose! Because he had noticed . . . noticed right away, you understand . . . that she had tried—from the very moment when she saw me with his sister—she had tried spitefully, with the most evil intent, to attract me . . . attract me to herself, wheedling me with all her artfulness! Why, it was Giorgio himself who called my attention to it! So it was easy, you understand—it was easy to make the proposal I made at that moment, saying to him: "Why, you know she would give herself even to me!"

PRESTINO: And in that case . . . well, I give up. He dared you—but he was really daring himself!

ROCCA: But he ought to have told me! He ought to have shouted it into my ears if necessary! He should have made me understand that he was lost, poisoned forever! That it was useless for me to try to cure him of a venom from that viper's fangs which had sunk so deep into his soul!

DIEGO: Viper? Viper? No, excuse me! I would hardly say viper!

ROCCA: Viper! Viper! Viper!

DIEGO: I wonder . . . I wonder! A bit too ingenuous it seems to me, a bit too ingenuous, for a viper. If there was so much poison in her fangs, why should she have bitten you so soon, so immediately, I might even say?

PRESTINO: But she may have been bent on ruining Giorgio Salvi, breaking his heart, encompassing his death!

ROCCA: She may.

DIEGO: And how is that possible? She had succeeded in forcing him to marry her, hadn't she? Why spoil everything before getting what she wanted?

ROCCA: But she never suspected . . .

DIEGO: Why do you call her a viper then? A viper is always

deliberate. A snake such as you say she is would have bitten afterwards, but not before! If now she did bite nevertheless, it means either that she is not so bad as you say she is, or else that she was not trying to harm Giorgio Salvi!

ROCCA: So you think then . . .

DIEGO: It is you who make me think so, understand! You are trying to tell me that she is a treacherous woman. I am keeping to what you say yourself . . . and the case for perfidy doesn't hang together! You say she was trying to trick him into marrying her, but then just before the wedding she gives herself to you!

ROCCA (*jumping to his feet*): Gives herself to me? Who ever said she gave herself to me? I had nothing to do with the woman . . . nothing at all! And you imagine I ever could have thought of such a thing?

DIEGO (*in astonishment, like the rest*): Ah, really?

THE OTHERS: What! Is it possible?

ROCCA: You see, all I wanted was proof . . . proof that she . . . something in short to convince *him!* (*At this moment the door on the right opens and* FRANCESCO SAVIO *appears in great excitement and commotion. He has been in the other room with* DELIA MORELLO. *Fulfilling her promise to prevent the duel between him and* DORO PALEGARI, *she has used all her arts upon him, intoxicating him with herself. He at once assails* MICHELE ROCCA *vehemently.*)

FRANCESCO: And what is this? What are you doing here? What do you want in my house? What mess are you trying to stir up here?

ROCCA: I came to tell you . . .

FRANCESCO: There is nothing you need to tell me!

ROCCA: You are mistaken! I have something to say, and not only to you!

FRANCESCO: I should advise you not to be quite so positive in your threats!

ROCCA: I am making no threats. I was anxious to talk with you.

FRANCESCO: You have been following a lady to my house!

ROCCA: Ah, I have just been explaining to your friends here . . .

FRANCESCO: What do I care about your explanations to my friends? You have been following a woman who was coming to see me! Do you deny it?

ROCCA: Yes, because if you intend to fight a duel with Signor Palegari . . .

FRANCESCO: What duel? Nonsense! I am not going to fight a duel with anybody!

PRESTINO (*in amazement*): What is that you say? No duel?

FRANCESCO: I am calling it off!

FIRST FRIEND, DIEGO, SECOND FRIEND (*speaking at once*): Are you crazy? Do you mean it? That's ridiculous!

ROCCA (*also speaking at the same time, but in a louder voice, with a guffaw*): Of course, you're calling it off! It's *her* work!

FRANCESCO (*about to attack him physically*): Shut your mouth or I . . .

PRESTINO (*running in front of him and holding him back*): No! First you must answer me! You're calling this duel with Palegari off?

FRANCESCO: Yes, I am calling it off! It's all nonsense, and I have no right to add to a woman's despair.

PRESTINO: But it will be worse, if you don't fight! The conditions of the duel have been drawn up and the papers signed!

FRANCESCO: But it's sheer nonsense to have a duel with Palegari now! It's ridiculous!

PRESTINO: Why so ridiculous?

FRANCESCO: Ridiculous! It's ridiculous because we are in entire agreement . . . Oh, you understand, Prestino, when you have a chance to figure in some affair like this, you are ready for a week's holiday!

PRESTINO: But Palegari insulted you, and you challenged him!

FRANCESCO: But nonsense, nonsense, just as Doro said, nonsense! I am calling it off!

PRESTINO: This is incredible . . . incredible!

ROCCA: He promised her he wouldn't fight with her champion?

FRANCESCO: Yes, why shouldn't I, since I have you here?

ROCCA: I see! That is why you promised not to?

FRANCESCO: No, since you are here insulting me in my own house! What do you want of that lady, anyhow?

PRESTINO: You can't do that!

FRANCESCO: He's been following her around for a day or more!

PRESTINO: But you can't fight with *him* now!

FRANCESCO: No one can say I am challenging a less dangerous opponent!

PRESTINO: Not at all! Not at all! That won't make any difference! Because if I should go now and offer to fight Palegari in your place . . .

FIRST FRIEND (*almost shouting at* FRANCESCO): You will be disqualified!

ROCCA: But I can ignore the disqualification!

FIRST FRIEND: No, because we would prevent you!

PRESTINO (*to* FRANCESCO): And you won't find a soul to act as your second! However, you have all day to think it over. I can't stay here any longer, so I'm going away!

DIEGO: He'll think it over, all right!

PRESTINO (*to the two* FRIENDS): This is no place for us! Let's be going! (*The three of them withdraw by way of the garden, rear.*)

DIEGO (*walking out on the veranda after them and calling*): Not too fast, gentlemen, not too fast! (*Then turning to* FRANCESCO.) And you had better watch your step!

FRANCESCO: You go to the devil! (*Again assailing* ROCCA.) And you!—you will find the door this way! Please make use of it! I am at your service when, where, and as, you wish! (*At this point* DELIA MORELLO *appears at the doorway to the right. The moment she sees* MICHELE ROCCA, *so changed from what he had been, another person in fact, she suddenly finds the mask lifted from her eyes—the mask, the fiction, which both she and he have hitherto been using to defend themselves against the secret passion by which from the very beginning they have been madly attracted toward one another, a passion which they have been translating before their own minds into terms of pity and interest for* GIORGIO SALVI, *each pretending to be trying to save him from one or the other. With this fiction gone, destroyed by the sudden shock they feel at being brought thus face to face, they stand looking at each other, pale and trembling.*)

ROCCA (*with a sob*): Delia! Delia! (*He advances to embrace her.*)

DELIA (*sinking into his arms and accepting his kiss*): No! No! My poor boy! My poor boy! (*To the horror and disgust of* FRANCESCO *and* DIEGO, *they embrace frantically.*)

ROCCA: Delia! My Delia!

DIEGO: That is the way they hate each other! Ah, how they hate each other! You see? You see?

FRANCESCO: But it's absurd! It's monstrous! With the corpse of a man between them!

ROCCA (*gathering* DELIA *into his arms, like an animal turning ravenously upon its prey*): Monstrous? Yes! But she must belong to me! She must suffer with me ... with me!

DELIA (*suddenly horrified, and tearing herself loose ferociously*): No! No! Go away! Go away! Don't touch me!

ROCCA (*struggling to hold her*): No! No! Mine! Mine! Here, with me, in my despair! Here!

DELIA (*still struggling*): Let me go, I tell you! Let me go! Murderer!

FRANCESCO: Yes! Let her go! I say let her go!

ROCCA: You keep your distance!

DELIA (*freeing herself at last*): Let me go! (FRANCESCO *and* DIEGO *restrain* ROCCA *from throwing himself upon her.*) I am not afraid of you! No! No! No harm can come to me from you! Not even if you kill me!

ROCCA (*speaking at the same time, struggling with the two* MEN *and shouting*): Delia! Delia! You must belong to me! You are mine! You must belong to me! I cannot live without you!

DELIA: I am free! I am free! I feel nothing, nothing whatever! It was an illusion! I thought it was compassion ... fear ... but no, it was nothing ... nothing!

ROCCA (*still struggling*): Let me alone! Let me alone!

FRANCESCO *and* DIEGO (*talking together*): You are two wild beasts! Monstrous! Two monsters!

DELIA: Let him go! I am not afraid of him! I let him kiss me! But it was coldly, without passion! It was not fear! It was not pity!

ROCCA: Yes, you wretch! I know! I know your kisses are worthless, but I want you! I am going to have you!

DELIA: Any harm you might do me, even if you killed me, would not be so bad as that! Another crime! Poison! Death itself! I want to remain as I am! I want to suffer as I am!

ROCCA (*still struggling to free himself from the two* MEN): Her love is worth nothing, but all that I have suffered on her account gives it value to me! It is not love I feel for you! It's hatred! It's hatred!

DELIA: Hatred! Yes, it's hatred with me, too! Hatred!

ROCCA: The very blood that has been shed on her account! (*With a sudden burst of violence he succeeds in freeing his arms.*) Have pity on me . . . pity on me! (*He pursues her about the room.*)

DELIA (*trying to keep away*): No! No! Don't you touch me! It will be the worse for you!

DIEGO *and* FRANCESCO (*getting hold of him again*): But keep away, won't you? You must answer for this with me!

DELIA: It will be the worse for him if he tries to arouse my pity either for myself or for him! I have none! But if you have any regard for him, send him away from here! Send him away!

ROCCA: How can I go away? You know that my life was drowned forever in Giorgio's blood!

DELIA: The brother of the girl you were to marry! And you did not try to save him from dishonor!

ROCCA: You lie! That is not true! You know that we have both been lying!

DELIA: Yes, we have both been lying! Two falsehoods!

ROCCA: You have wanted me as I have wanted you, from the moment when we first saw each other!

DELIA: Yes! Yes! But it was to punish you!

ROCCA: Yes, so with me! It was to punish you! But your life, too, has been drowned, drowned forever in Giorgio's blood!

DELIA: Yes, you are right! You are right! (*She runs to him like a flame, pushing aside the two* MEN *who are restraining him.*) Yes, it is true! It is true!

ROCCA (*embracing her again desperately*): So we must both drown in that blood, but drown together . . . this way . . . in each other's arms . . . not I alone . . . not you alone . . . but both together! This way! This way!

DIEGO: If they don't change their minds!

ROCCA (*carrying* DELIA *in his arms toward the door into the garden, leaving the two* MEN *standing there in utter astonishment and stupefaction*): Yes . . . with me . . . with me! Come! Come! With me . . . away, with me . . . away, with me!

FRANCESCO: Two lunatics!

DIEGO: You don't see yourself!

(*Curtain.*)

second choral interlude

(Again the curtain rises as soon as possible after it has fallen on the second act; and again the theatre lobby appears with the entrances leading to the hall of the theatre. But this time no one comes out for some moments. The TICKET TAKER, *one or two* USHERS, MAIDS *from the women's room are standing about in some apprehension; because, along toward the end of the second act, they have seen the* MORENO WOMAN, *despite the interference of her three* MALE FRIENDS, *run through the corridor toward the stage entrance. Now the sound of shouting, clapping, hissing, comes out from the theatre, growing louder and louder all the time, either because the actors have not yet appeared before the curtain to make their bows to the audience or because something strange and unusual is going on inside.)*

ONE OF THE TICKET TAKERS: What the devil is the matter in there?

ANOTHER TICKET TAKER: Isn't it Pirandello tonight? What else can you expect?

AN USHER: No, the audience is applauding, but the actors refuse to come out.

A MAID: But there's shouting and screaming on the stage, don't you hear?

ANOTHER USHER: And the house is in an uproar!

SECOND MAID: Has that woman anything to do with it?

TICKET TAKER: I imagine she has. The men with her were having a devil of a time keeping her quiet!

FIRST MAID: She got in behind the scenes!

FIRST TICKET TAKER: She was trying to get in at the end of the first act!

ANOTHER MAID: But hell is let loose in there! Don't you hear? *(Two or three of the doors into the theatre are thrown open and some* SPECTATORS *dash out into the lobby, the uproar in the auditorium becoming louder for the moment.)*

THE SPECTATORS: But she got in there on the stage! What's the matter? Are they fighting? *(Shouting. Screaming.)* And the actors are not answering their curtain call! *(More* SPECTATORS *appear, coming through the doors into the lobby and looking toward the stage entrance to the right. They are followed by a great number of* SPECTATORS *who come on through the left.*

They are all shouting.) What's the matter? What's going on? What's the trouble?

CONFUSED VOICES: There's a fight on behind the scenes! There . . . do you hear? On the stage! Why? Why? Who knows?

Gangway, please! What's happened? What's going on? Trouble tonight, all right! Let me get by! Is the play over? Isn't there a third act? There must be a third act! Make way there, please! Yes, at four o'clock sharp, so long! . . . Don't forget! But did you hear that? They're fighting! I am going in there myself! Do you hear that? It's scandalous! They've no right to! What's it all about? Why it seems that . . . God only knows! What the deuce! Why . . . why . . . there . . . there! The door is opening! (*The stage entrance is thrown open, and for the moment the uproar on the stage—shrieks from the* ACTRESSES, *oaths from* ACTORS *and from the* STAGE MANAGER, *the voices of the* MORENO WOMAN *and her three* FRIENDS—*become louder. These noises will be drowned eventually by the confusion among the* SPECTATORS *crowding around the stage entrance, varied by the angry protests of a few* PEOPLE, *some of whom are trying to get to the stage and others are trying to get away and out of the theatre.*)

VOICES FROM THE STAGE (ACTORS *speaking*): Get out of here! Get out of there! Back where you belong! Get that woman away! Have her arrested! She'll pay me for that! Back where you belong! Get out of here!

VOICE OF THE MORENO WOMAN: It's a disgrace! It's a crime! I won't! I won't!

VOICE OF THE STAGE MANAGER: You just be moving along!

VOICE OF THE MORENO WOMAN: You're insulting me publicly!

VOICE OF ONE OF HER FRIENDS: Remember she's a woman!

VOICE OF ANOTHER OF HER FRIENDS: Don't you dare strike a woman!

VOICE OF ONE OF THE ACTORS: Woman? Nonsense! She's making all the trouble! Get her out of here! Get her out of here!

VOICES OF SOME ACTRESSES: What a cat! For shame! For shame!

VOICES OF SOME ACTORS: Lucky for her she's a woman! She deserves every bit of it! Get her out of here!

STAGE MANAGER: Clear that doorway, there! Clear that doorway!

VOICES FROM THE CROWD OF SPECTATORS (*all talking at*

once, with occasional hoots, jeers, and applause): Signora
Moreno! The Moreno woman! Who is she! She slapped the
leading lady's face! Who? Who slapped her? Signora Moreno!
The Moreno woman! Who is she? The leading lady! No! No!
It was the author's face she slapped? Pirandello? She slapped
his face! Who? Who slapped his face? Signora Moreno! No!
The leading lady! The author slapped her face? No! No! The
other way about! The leading lady slapped the author's face!
Not at all! Not at all! Signora Moreno assaulted the leading
lady and pulled her hair!

VOICES FROM THE STAGE: Enough of this! Out of here! Put
her out! Put her out! Cowards! Wretches! Call the police!
What a woman! Put her out! Put her out!

VOICES FROM THE SPECTATORS: Go on with the play! Put
them out! Less noise! Shut up! Signora Moreno! Put her out!
The third act! We want the third act! Pirandello! Put him out!
A speech! A speech from Pirandello! Put him out! A speech!
He's to blame! Sh-sh-sh-sh! Make way there! The third act!
Clear the way! Clear the way! (*Some* ACTORS *and* ACTRESSES
*from the play on the stage, more especially those appearing in
the third act, elbow their way through the* CROWD *gathered
before the stage entrance. With them appear the* STAGE MAN-
AGER *and the* TREASURER *of the theatre, the latter trying to
persuade them to go on with the play. The lobby is thrown into
the greatest agitation. At first the* SPECTATORS *are silent, eagerly
listening to the dialogue of the* STAGE PEOPLE; *though later on
they will break occasionally into noisy comment of approval
or disapproval.*)

TREASURER OF THE THEATRE: But for heaven's sake, use
your brains. The crowd will want its money back! You want to
stop the play?

ACTORS *and* ACTRESSES (*talking all at the same time*): Not
on your life! I am going home! We won't put up with this! We
are all going home! This is too much! It's a disgrace! We
refuse to put up with it! We are going to strike in protest!

STAGE MANAGER: Protest? Who are you protesting against?

ONE OF THE ACTRESSES: Against the author, and rightly so!

ONE OF THE ACTORS: And against the producer! Who ever
thought of producing such a comedy as this!

TREASURER: But you can't protest this way! If you go away
and don't finish the play, we are ruined! This is pure Bolshevism!

VOICES FROM AMONG THE SPECTATORS: Fine! Fine! That's

the way to talk! Not at all! The actors are right! They're right!

THE ACTORS (*all speaking together*): Yes! Yes! We protest! We protest!

AN ACTOR: You can't compel us to play a comedy with a key!

VOICES FROM SOME INGENUOUS SPECTATORS: A key? Where's the key? What's a comedy with a key?

ACTORS: We refuse! We refuse!

VOICES OF OTHER SPECTATORS: Of course! Everybody knows it! It's disgraceful! It's scandalous! You can't help seeing! The Moreno case! She's here! In the theatre! She got in behind the scenes! She slapped the leading lady's face!

VOICES OF SPECTATORS *and* FRIENDS OF PIRANDELLO (*all talking together and in great confusion*): But nobody noticed! It's a good play! We want the third act! Give us our money back! We bought our tickets! The third act! The third act!

ONE OF THE ACTORS: But we refuse to have our faces slapped!

AN ACTOR: Let's all go home! I, for my part, am going home!

AN ACTRESS: The leading lady has already gone home!

VOICES OF SPECTATORS: Gone home? How did she go out? Through the stage entrance! Why?

ACTRESS: Because a woman came in on the stage and slapped her face!

VOICES OF SPECTATORS IN ARGUMENT: Slapped her face? Yes! Yes! Signora Moreno! And she was right! Who was right? The Moreno woman? Why did she slap her face? The leading lady!

ONE OF THE ACTORS: Because she saw an allusion to herself in the play!

ANOTHER ACTOR: And she thought we had conspired with the author to make fun of her?

FIRST ACTRESS: We refuse to be treated that way!

BARON NUTI (*accompanied by two* FRIENDS *as in the first interlude, more than ever excited and confused, pushes his way forward*): It's true! It's unheard of! It's a disgrace! You're right in stopping the show!

ONE OF HIS FRIENDS: Hush! Don't make matters worse! Let's go home!

BARON NUTI: It's a disgrace, ladies and gentlemen! Two people pilloried in public! The private affairs of two people exposed to public ridicule!

TREASURER (*in despair*): The play seems to have moved from the stage to the lobby!

VOICES OF SPECTATORS HOSTILE TO THE AUTHOR: He's right! He's right! It's a disgrace! They ought to put a stop to it! They're right! They're right!

VOICES OF SPECTATORS FAVORABLE TO PIRANDELLO: Not at all! Not at all! It was a good show! The third act! Where is the third act? Give us the third act! Disgrace? Nonsense! It could be anybody! Where's the slander?

TREASURER (*to the* ACTORS): Shall we go on with the show or shall we not?

BARON NUTI (*seizing one of the* SPECTATORS *by the front of his coat and addressing him so violently that everyone falls silent at the spectacle of his fury*): You say it's all right? You approve? They have a right to take me and expose me there on the stage in public? Show me off, and all my sorrows, in the presence of a crowd? Make me say things that I never thought of saying and do things that I never thought of doing? (*In the silence that greets* BARON NUTI's *harangue, the* STAGE MANAGER *will appear from the stage entrance, walking a few steps ahead of the* MORENO WOMAN *who, weeping, disheveled, half fainting, is being rather dragged than led out of the theatre by her three* MALE COMPANIONS. *The exchange of sentences between the* STAGE MANAGER *and* SIGNORA MORENO *will fall upon the silence as a reply to* BARON NUTI's *words. Everyone meantime will turn toward the stage entrance, making way for* SIGNORA MORENO *and her* COMPANIONS. NUTI *will release his grasp on the* SPECTATOR *he has been assailing, and turns to ask.*) What's the matter?

STAGE MANAGER: But you know very well that neither the author nor the leading lady have ever met you! They don't know you at all!

SIGNORA MORENO: She mimicked my voice! She used my manner—all my gestures! She was imitating me! I recognized myself!

STAGE MANAGER: But why should you believe it was you?

SIGNORA MORENO: No! No! That isn't so! It was so terrible to see myself there on the stage acting that way! The idea! Why! I . . . I . . . kissing that man! (*She suddenly becomes aware of* BARON NUTI's *presence and utters a shriek, covering her face with her hands.*) Oh! Oh! There he is! There he is! There!

BARON NUTI: Amelia! Amelia! (*General commotion among*

the SPECTATORS, *who can scarcely believe their eyes, as they see the very characters and the very scene they have witnessed at the end of the second act, present now before them. Their astonishment should be manifested, however, only by facial expression, by brief comments delivered in low tones, and a few hushed exclamations.*)

VOICES OF SPECTATORS: Oh! Look! Look! There they are! Oh! In real life! Both of them! The same scene over again! Look! Look!

SIGNORA MORENO (*desperately, to the three* MEN *with her*): Take him away! Take him away!

HER COMPANIONS: Yes! Let's go away! Let's go away!

BARON NUTI (*dashing upon her*): No! No! You must come with me! You must come with me!

SIGNORA MORENO (*tearing herself from his grasp*): No! Let me alone! Let me alone! Don't touch me! Murderer! Murderer!

BARON NUTI: You heard that on the stage!

SIGNORA MORENO: Let me alone! I am not afraid of you!

BARON NUTI: But it was true! It's our punishment! It's our punishment! And we must suffer it together! Your place is with me! Come! Come!

SIGNORA MORENO: Let me alone, I say! I hate you! I hate you!

BARON NUTI: We are drowning . . . drowning in his blood! It was true! Come with me! Come! (*He drags her off to the left. Most of the* SPECTATORS *follow with noisy comments and exclamations.*)

SPECTATORS: Oh! Really! It can't be! Incredible! How horrible! There they are! Look! Delia Morello and Michele Rocca! (*Other* SPECTATORS *continue standing in the lobby, but looking after them and making more or less the same remarks.*)

A SPECTATOR (*who has not grasped the situation*): And they complain because the same thing was done on the stage!

STAGE MANAGER: Yes, and the leading lady had the courage to come and slap my face . . . there, on the stage!

MANY VOICES: Incredible! Incredible! Absurd!

A SPECTATOR WHO UNDERSTANDS: But no! It's all natural enough! They rebelled because they saw themselves there, as in a mirror, forced into a situation that has the eternity of art!

STAGE MANAGER: They did it over again to the very gesture!

A SPECTATOR WHO UNDERSTANDS: And that's natural, too!

They have done, here before our eyes and quite involuntarily, something that the author had foreseen! (*Some of the* SPECTATORS *approve. Others laugh.*)

TREASURER OF THE THEATRE (*to the* STAGE MANAGER): But I should like to know whether you intend holding a debate right here?

STAGE MANAGER: You want to close the theatre? What have I got to do with that? Tell them to get out!

TREASURER: Well, I can't have the third act! The actors have gone home!

STAGE MANAGER: Post a placard calling the show off!

TREASURER: But some of the audience are still in their seats!

STAGE MANAGER: Very well! I'll make the announcement from behind the footlights!

TREASURER: Yes, that's the way out of it! Go and do that! (*The* STAGE MANAGER *starts for the stage entrance, while the* TREASURER *begins shooing people out of the lobby.*) We are closing up, gentlemen! We are closing up! If you please, gentlemen, the play is over for tonight! The play is over for tonight!

> (*The curtain falls, but immediately the* STAGE MANAGER *will make his way through the central opening of the curtain and come forward to the footlights.*)

STAGE MANAGER: The management is grieved to announce that in view of unfortunate incidents which took place at the end of the second act, we shall be unable to continue the performance this evening.

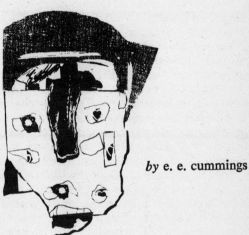

him   *by* e. e. cummings

Him, published in 1927, was first produced
at the Provincetown Playhouse,
New York, on April 18, 1928.

While *Each in His Own Way* presents a play that does not finish, *Him* concerns a play in the process of being written. *Him* is a play about a playwright writing a play about a playwright writing a play. Both Cummings and Pirandello reflect the self-consciousness of the theatre in the between-wars period. A character hitherto unmentioned is openly discussed in Pirandello's play and has the chief role in Cummings': the dramatist. Exploration of the artist's medium—how his mirror works, its multiple images, and what lies behind it—assumes greater importance than the reflection of the real world when the mirror is held up to nature.

In an "Imaginary Dialogue Between the Author and a Public," which appeared on the inside of the front jacket of *Him*, Cummings talks of "a mirror surrounded by mirrors." The image of mirror images within mirror images is central to his process of fragmentation of character and action. Like Pirandello, Cummings shatters the single, stable, mirror-held-up-to-nature reflection, destroys traditional dramatic plot and logic, and creates new temporal and spacial dimensions and relationships. In *Him*, Cummings plays with the fourth-wall convention of the illusionistic stage by creating a revolving stage of the imagination. The room in which Him and Me appear turns a quarter of a revolution each successive scene, making visible the originally invisible fourth-wall which moves about the set. In the first Him–Me scene, an invisible mirror is understood to hang on this invisible fourth wall. Me looks at herself and adjusts her make-up. In the next Him–Me scene, the mirror surfaces, then makes a total revolution in the course of the remaining Him–Me scenes, until in their last appearance it is back where it started, invisible in the invisible wall separating stage from audience. At this point, Cummings changes the rules. After establishing the convention of a rotating frolic, he demolishes it by having Me look through the mirror and make contact with the audience who helped create Him and Me. There are, the audience realizes, only three walls: the rest has been play. The existence of Him and Me as characters on a stage is due to the real people in the audience who give them life by pretending they are real.

Like *Each in His Own Way, Him* has inner and outer plays. The inner play, however, is not a play-within-a-play but a play within *that* play: not Him's play, but the work of the playwright who is the chief character of Him's play. Such artifice further disintegrates the notion of a play as a literal representation of reality. In rejecting the illusionistic theatre, however, Cummings follows a path different from Pirandello's and adopts other techniques for breaking down its realistic surfaces. Analytically dissecting the well-made play and its well-made world, Pirandello dismembers theatrical illusion lucidly and coherently. By a dialectical process of argumentation and reasoning, the Italian playwright strips away layer after layer of confusion, pretense, and illusion.

Cummings, however, is essentially a poet. His theatre is more immediate and less philosophical than Pirandello's unmasking of illusion and reality. Mingling surrealist techniques with vaudeville skits and even political satire in the Mussolini sequence, Cummings disregards traditional organization and uniform texture for bizarre juxtapositions of heterogeneous material. The exploration of the multiple facets of a single personality in the artist's quest for vocation alternates with parody of popular forms of entertainment. The vaudeville acts and burlesque shows of the inner play become an extension of the artist-hero's exploration of his own medium, mirroring his concerns. A single, subjective consciousness dominates all; divided principally into Him and Me, it finds expression in all the characters and motifs.

While the sequential structure is loose, the rich verbal and imagistic texture is closely wrought. The playfulness, variety of styles, and carnival theatricality are controlled and focused, as in a dramatic monologue or stream-of-consciousness novel, by patterns of imagery and phrases repeated from scene to scene and carried back and forth between the Him and Me dialogues and the popular arts burlesques. Him's remark, "Now I lay you down to not sleep," for example, as he attempts to seduce Me in the first scene of Act III, echoes the Policeman's final words as snow falls in his hat at the end of the last scene of

Act II, "Now I lay me down to sleep." Both deal with death and rebirth. The names of the three parody fates—Miss Stop, Miss Look, and Miss Listen—provide three key words, woven in and out of the texture of the play: the characters are constantly admonished to stop, look, and listen—to achieve self-awareness. Integration of *Him*'s contrasting elements is largely verbal and thematic.

The prime image of the play, as model and metaphor, is the circus—a source of inspiration during the between-wars period when highbrow arts cultivated clowns and vaudeville in their revolt against the anemic traditions of genteel realism. The artist must be a bareback rider, a clown, and a lion tamer. Like the acrobat, what he does is amazing, dangerous, daring, and must be executed precisely and perfectly. Like the tight-rope walker, the artist's position is precarious and isolated from his audience. The circus and freak show, moreover, are memories of childhood through which he must return in order to find himself. The inner play's vaudeville routines present a version of the circus and of clowning, but the principal clown remains the man who devised this inner play—Him.

The tradition to which Cummings' play is most closely related is surrealism, discussed in the introduction to *The Water Hen.* "Ah," says Him to no one in particular, "but don't you know that there is a further image—which appears not so much in the window of sleep as in a still deeper mirror?" *Him* not only delves into the characteristic surrealist themes of the dreamer, the child, and the artist in relationship to his art and his love, but it does so with the comic delight in discontinuity and incongruity that most clearly distinguishes surrealism from other allied movements like expressionism. Fantasy, free association, and the ridiculous are both the surrealist techniques which form the texture of the play and also the aspects of life which, for Cummings, contain the most profound wisdom. The effect produced is laughter at the ludicrous: at the verbal fireworks, the variety of accents, the strange mixture of social action and subconscious experience (as in the scene in the European city full of starving poor people), and the dilemma of the artist torn between his commitment to himself and his art or to life, society, and love. In the best surrealist tradition, Cummings creates a new world and enlarges the dimensions of the theatre. Expansion of the stage and of the mind is the subject and technique of the play.

Until Act III, Scenes 4 and 5, when Me opens her eyes slowly and Him returns from Paris, the play can be regarded as Me's dreams as she undergoes the influence of the doctor's anaesthetic in order to have a baby (or perhaps an abortion). *Him* has the fluid shape of a dream, in which elements of reality are refracted as images within images in "a mirror surrounded by mirrors." Since *Him* is a play about birth, it is appropriate that a pregnant woman be the dreamer—whether the pregnancy results in abortion, stillbirth, or true delivery. "Life," as the third Miss Weird says, "is a matter of being born." Both Him and Me are pregnant. Him is trying to give birth to a play, Me to a baby. Both births constitute the labor pains of the play. The nine scenes of the play-within-the-play and the nine exhibits of the freak show harmonize with the nine months of pregnancy. Birth, life, death, and rebirth comprise the play's cycle. Images of sleep and sexual intercourse abound in this drama of conception and labor pains. We are inside the mind of the author, or the womb of the dreamer. The characters and actions are not detached, separated, and individualized into discrete dramatic entities but constantly coalesce, merge, and reconverge into one subjective consciousness where time, space, and identity are elastic. The names Him and Me indicate this subjective view of reality.

In *six nonlectures,* Cummings said that there are "three mysteries: love, art, and selftranscendence or growing." A major issue of the Him—Me scenes, and of the entire play, is Him's struggle to transcend himself and encompass love and art, birth and death, self and other, dream and action. The problem of greatness torments Him, as it does Edgar in *The Water Hen.* In the early stages of his dilemma, Him feels he must selfishly dedicate himself to his self-discovery as an artist, at the expense of everything else. But he is unable to balance high above the world without the support of self-identity. Circus, hat, and mirror become images of his failure.

When Me looks into the mirror, she sees herself and knows who she is. Feeling rather than thinking, Me understands intuitively and lives directly. Him, unable to feel, only thinks. When he stands before the mirror, he sees multiple identities —not himself but images he has constructed of himself. Addressing these images, he uses a variety of personal pronouns: *you, I, our, my, his, we.* Likewise, Him wearing his hat is the other Him, Mr. O.Him, the man in the mirror, Me's mystery lover, the multiple pronouns. Him and Me may be regarded as intellect and passion, divided elements of what should be one character if that character is to be whole.

Unable to live directly, Him must translate everything by means of his intellect and poetic gift. Because Him spins in circles of metaphor, Me breaks off the affair and refuses to allow him to make love to her in the dark. In love only with the sound of his own words and infatuated with his own gestures, Him wonders whether he might not be one of his own creations, "a doll, living in a doll world," and he cannot stop creating "several less or more interesting people—none of whom was myself." Trapped in the forms of his own wit and changing opinions about himself, Him resembles at this point one of Pirandello's manikins. He is the victim of his own gift of words, guilty of what Kierkegaard, in *The Sickness unto Death,* calls "the sin of poetizing instead of being, of standing in relation to the Good and the True through imagination instead of being that, or rather existentially striving to be it . . ."

At ease with her own identity, Me wants to help Him, but Him continues to play endless roles until their separation and his trip to Paris. To find himself, he must go abroad and be alone. Finding himself, he will become reborn. At the restaurant in Paris, Le Père Tranquille (The Serene Father), he points to the cabbage he has been carrying (to be found in a cabbage patch is the continental equivalent of being brought by the stork) and says, "I was born day before yesterday." By the time he returns to the United States, Me's dream is over; her eyes have been opened on the anaesthetist's table. In the fifth scene of Act III, when Me and Him meet again, flowers —rebirth and life—have replaced Him's hat. A new Him has returned from Paris. Understanding less, he has achieved a new kind of awareness. He speaks in fewer metaphors and can admit that "beauty has shut me from the truth." He relates his dream about a child—an appropriate image, for the old Him is dead and the new Him born.

Him and Me are fragments of a single process of life that is made whole. Through images within images, "a mirror surrounded by mirrors," and an all-embracing consciousness, Cummings transcends conflicting dualities of birth and death, masculine and feminine, intellect and passion, Him and Me; and the poet makes a synthesis of art and love, popular culture and high art, burlesque and metaphor that "cannot mean because it is."

looking forward into the past or looking
backward into the future I
walk on the highest
hills and
I laugh
about
it
all
the way
ANNE BARTON

act I
scene 1

*(Scene: A flat surface on which is painted
a* DOCTOR *anaesthetizing a* WOMAN. *In this
picture there are two holes corresponding to
the heads of the physician and of the patient,
and through these holes protrude the living
heads of a man and of a woman.*
*Facing this picture, with their backs to the audience, three
withered female* FIGURES *are rocking in rocking chairs and
knitting.)*

FIRST OR MIDDLE FIGURE: We called our hippopotamus It's
Toasted.

SECOND OR FIGURE TO THE AUDIENCE'S RIGHT: I wish my
husband didn't object to them.

THIRD: Of course it's a bother to clean the cage every day.

SECOND: O I wouldn't mind doing that.

FIRST: Be sure to get one that can sing.

THIRD: Don't they all sing?

FIRST: O dear no. Some of them just whistle.

SECOND: I've heard they're very affectionate.

FIRST: I find them so.

THIRD: Did it take long to tame yours?

FIRST: Only a few days. Now he sits on my hand and
doesn't bite me.

SECOND: How charming.

THIRD: Is it true they imitate policemen?

FIRST: My dear they imitate everybody.

SECOND: I'm afraid my husband wouldn't like that.

FIRST: What do you mean, my dear?

SECOND: If ours imitated a policeman.

THIRD: Really? Why should he object?

SECOND: It would make him nervous I'm afraid—the idea
of the thing.

FIRST: Your husband is a vegetarian?

SECOND: On the contrary, my husband is a burglar.

FIRST: Oh, I see. (*The* WOMAN's *eyes close and her head remains in the picture; the* DOCTOR's *head disappears from the picture leaving a hole. The three* FIGURES *continue to rock and knit. Presently the* DOCTOR *himself enters with* HIM.)

DOCTOR (*To* HIM): Have a cigar. (*Produces two, one of which* HIM *takes. Both men bite off and spit out the tips of their cigars.* HIM, *producing matches, lights the* DOCTOR's *and his own cigar.*) And how are the three Miss Weirds today?

FIRST FIGURE (*Without looking up or turning, continues knitting and rocking*): Very well indeed, thank you doctor.

SECOND (*Ditto*): Fine weather, isn't it?

THIRD (*Ditto*): One really is glad to be alive.

DOCTOR: Speaking of dust, let me introduce a distinguished foreigner. Mr. Anybody, press flesh with the three Weird sisters; get used to Miss Stop, Miss Look and Miss Listen. (HIM *doubtfully extends his hand in the general direction of the unnoticing rocking and knitting* FIGURES)

FIRST FIGURE (*Snobbishly, to* SECOND): I don't think I ever heard the name. (*To* THIRD): Did you? (*All three* FIGURES *shake their heads*)

HIM: Madam, I am very noble.

DOCTOR: "Anybody" is just his nomb D. ploom you know. My friend is strictly incog.

FIRST FIGURE (*Stops knitting and rocking*): How romantic!

SECOND (*Ditto*): How thrilling!

THIRD (*Ditto*): Do tell us his real name!

HIM: My real name, ladies, is Everyman, Marquis de la Poussière.

FIRST FIGURE (*Rising, turns; revealing a maskface*): Delighted, Marquis.

SECOND (*Rising, turns; revealing a maskface identical with the* FIRST's): Enchanted.

THIRD (*Rising, turns; revealing a maskface identical with the* FIRST's *and the* SECOND's): Overwhelmed.

DOCTOR: Well, guess we'll blow. I got some important business to attend to. Bye bye, girls.

ALL THREE FIGURES (*In unison*): Goodbye doctor adieu marquis. (*Turning, they resume their rocking chairs and knitting. Exeunt* DOCTOR *and* HIM.)

SECOND FIGURE: How often do you change the water?

FIRST: I only change it once a day but Mrs. Strong changes it twice a week.

THIRD: Has Mrs. Strong a hippopotamus?

FIRST: Two, my dear. That's where I got mine—they had kittens last May.

THIRD: I wish I'd known.

SECOND: I should have made my husband steal one for me.

FIRST: What a pity. She didn't know what to do with the other six, so she gave them to a circus.

SECOND: They're darling when they're young, aren't they?

FIRST: Perfectly darling. (*The* DOCTOR'*s head reappears in the picture. The* WOMAN'*s eyes continue closed.*)

THIRD: But I suppose it's a nuisance until the little things become housebroken.

FIRST: O you get used to that.

scene 2   (*Scene: A room: three visible walls and an invisible wall. Of the visible walls one, the wall to the audience's left, is solid. In the middle wall is a door and in the wall to the audience's right a window.*

Against the solid wall is a sofa on which lies a man's brown felt hat, much the worse for wear. Under the window in the opposite wall is a table on which reposes a large box for cigarettes; and near the table are two chairs in the less comfortable of which HIM *sits, back to the audience, writing in a notebook.*

ME [*whose head appeared in the picture, preceding scene*] *stands facing the audience just inside the invisible fourth wall. Her open eyes* [*which are focussed at a point only a few inches distant*] *and her gestures* [*arranging hair, smoothing eyebrows, etc.*] *as well as the pose of her body* [*which bends slightly forward from the hips*] *suggest to the audience that she is looking at her reflection in an invisible mirror which hangs on this invisible wall.*)

ME (*To herself*): I look like the devil.

HIM (*Absently, without looking up or turning*): Wanted: death's brother.

ME (*Still primping*): No but did you ever try to go to sleep, and not be able to, and lie watching the dark and thinking about things. . . . (*She cocks her head, surveying herself anew. Satisfied, turns; goes to the table and stands, looking down at him.*)

HIM (*As before*): Did I which?

ME: Nothing.

HIM (*Looks up, smiles*): Impossible.

ME (*Touching his shoulder*): Look. You be nice to me— you can do THAT any time.

HIM: Can I? (*Pockets notebook and pencil. Gets up, faces her.*)

ME: It's true.

HIM: What's "it"?

ME: "It" is, that you really don't care about. . . .

HIM: I'll bite the rubber angleworm: what don't I really care about?

ME (*Sinks into the more comfortable chair*): Anything.

HIM: Whereas this is what's untrue—. (*Sits on the table*) Anything everything nothing and something were looking for eels in a tree, when along came sleep pushing a wheelbarrow full of green mice.

ME (*To herself*): I thought so. . . .

HIM: I, however, thought that it was the taller of the two umbrellas who lit a match when they found themselves in the main street of Hocuspocus side by each riding elephants made out of candy.

ME: And you may find this sort of thing funny. But I don't.

HIM: May I?

ME: O—suddenly I think I'd like to die.

HIM: I think myself that there's some thinking being done around here. But why die now? The morn's on the thorn, the snail's on the wing, the play's on the way; and who knows?

ME: I do. I know we're absolutely different. I've tried and tried not to know it, but what in the world is the use of trying? O, I'm so sick of trying—

HIM: Me too. This business of writing a play, I mean.

ME: You mean I'm no good to you and that we should have ended everything long ago; because—not being interested in all the ideas you're interested in—it's obviously silly of me to pretend.

HIM: To pretend? (*Picking up the box, opens it and proffers cigarettes; her hand automatically takes one. Striking a match, he lights her cigarette and his. He gets off the table; walks up and down, smoking.*) What's obviously silly of you to pretend is, that we are not in love—

ME: In love!

HIM: Precisely; otherwise we couldn't fight each other so.

ME: This may be your idea of being in love: it isn't mine. (*She smokes wearily. Pause.*)

HIM (*Halts, facing the window*): What did you say. . . .

ME: I said, it's not my idea of love.

HIM: No; I mean when I was sitting, and you—

ME: Who cares.

HIM: —you asked me something. I have it: you couldn't go to sleep. (*Walks to the table and stands, looking down at her. After a moment, stooping, he kisses her hand.*) I'm very sorry. (*Puts his arm around her*)

ME: Stop please; I don't want you to be nice to me.

HIM: But I can't help being nice to you, because I'm in love with you. (*She shakes her head slowly*) O yes I am. You may not be in love with me, but that doesn't prevent me from being in love with you.

ME: I don't know, really. . . . O, I wish—

HIM (*Releases her*): What?

ME: —because with part of you I think I'm in love. What can I do?

HIM: Well now let's see . . . here's a bright idea: you can advertise in the Paris edition of the New York Herald for a new lover, thus—"By a freckled fragile petite brunette incapable of loneliness and cooking, wanted: a tall strong handsome blond capable of indigestion and death (signed) Cinderella Van Winkle."

ME (*Involuntarily*): Who's she?

HIM: Don't tell me you never in your whole life heard of Cinderella Van Winkle! The bluest blood in all Gotham my dear, directly descended from the three wise men who went to sea in a thundermug, and great-great-great-GREAT-granddaughter (twice removed) of the original and only founder of the illustrious Van Winkle family, Neverrip Van Winkle, who married a Holeproof.

ME: Being funny doesn't help.

HIM: Neither, he inadvertently answered, does being tragic.

ME: Who's being tragic?

HIM: I give it up.

ME: You mean me? I'm not being tragic, I'm being serious; because I want to decide something. I think you might help me instead of making fun of me.

HIM (*Amorously*): There's nothing I'd rather do, my dear, than help you—

ME (*Quickly*): I don't mean—.

HIM (*Cheerfully*): In that case, I have a definite hunch. (ME *starts*) What in the world. . . .

ME: Yes?

HIM: What's the matter?

ME (*Confused*): Nothing. Go on, please; I'm listening.

HIM (*Smiles*): You're also stopping and looking, which puzzles me because I don't see the engine.

ME (*Smiling*): There isn't any—go on. I was thinking.

HIM: And may I ask what you were thinking?

ME (*Hesitantly*): Yes.

HIM: Well?

ME: I was thinking, when you said that . . .

HIM: When I said?

ME: —about having a hunch . . .

HIM (*Sits on the arm of her chair*): Yes? (*His hand caresses her hair*)

ME: —about . . . a hunchback. That's all.

HIM: What about a hunchback?

ME: Nothing. They're good luck. Please tell me now; that is, if you'd like to.

HIM: "Tell" you?

ME: About the play. Do you think it'll be finished soon?

HIM: On the contrary—that is, yes. I think it will be torn up.

ME: Torn up! Why?

HIM: No good.

ME (*Earnestly*): I'm sure it's good.

HIM: You haven't had the misfortune to read it.

ME: I'd like to—if you don't mind: can I?

HIM: Of course, if you wish. I tell you: it's no good.

ME: I'd like to read it, anyway. Have you got it in your hump?

HIM (*Jumps*): What?

ME: —Pocket, I meant.

HIM: My God, have I a hump? (*Rising*): Here, let me look. (*Starts toward the invisible mirror*)

ME: (*Hugging him*): Please don't be angry with me: I know I'm stupid. I can't help it.

HIM (*Laughs*): I was just on the point of—

ME: Sh.

HIM: —of letting our mirror decide the question. (*Nods in the direction of the audience*)

ME: Were you, now? I guess men are vain—but that big mirror's no good and never was any. . . .

HIM: Like my play.

ME: Nonsense. If you really want to see yourself, I've got a little one in my—O no, I lost it.

HIM: A little one in your which?

ME: A little mirror, stupid, in my bag. I must have dropped it in a snowdrift.

HIM: Not the bag?

ME: No, the mirror. I can't find it anywhere.

HIM: Never mind: I've decided that it's safer to take your word for my looks.

ME: How sweet of you. Maybe you'll let me see the play, too? Please!

HIM: I haven't the play with me today, unfortunately.

ME: I thought you always carried notes or something around with you. (*Suspiciously*) What were you writing a moment ago?

HIM: A mere trifle, as it were. A little embonpoint to the dearly beloved master of my old prepschool at Stoneacre Heights, regretting that the undersigned is unable for pressing reasons to be present at the annual grand ball and entertainment to be held forthwith on the thirteenth Friday of next Thursday beginning with last Saturday until further notice to be furnished by—

ME (*Mystified*): What "master"?

HIM: I doubt if you ever heard of the fellow: his name is Bates. Haha. Let us now turn to serious subjects. Assuming a zygote to result from the fusion of two gametes, the company will next attempt to vizualise, through halfshut optics, a semifluid semitransparent colourless substance consisting of oxygen hydrogen carbon and nitrogen—

ME (*Smiles*):—were looking for eels in a tree.

HIM: Precisely; when who should come along but little Mr. Mendel, wheeling a numerical law full of recurring inherited characteristics all wrong side up with their eyes shut on a slackwire tightrope. (*Vehemently*) Damn everything but the circus! (*To himself*) And here am I, patiently squeezing four-dimensional ideas into a twodimensional stage, when all of me that's anyone or anything is in the top of a circustent. . . . (*A pause*)

ME: I didn't imagine you were leading a double life—and right under my nose, too.

HIM (*Unhearing, proceeds contemptuously*): The average "painter" "sculptor" "poet" "composer" "playwright" is a person who cannot leap through a hoop from the back of a galloping horse, make people laugh with a clown's mouth, orchestrate twenty lions.

ME: Indeed.

HIM (*To her*): But imagine a human being who balances three chairs, one on top of another, on a wire, eighty feet in air with no net underneath, and then climbs into the top chair, sits down, and begins to swing. . . .

ME (*Shudders*): I'm glad I never saw that—makes me dizzy just to think of it.

HIM (*Quietly*): I never saw that either.

ME: Because nobody can do it.

HIM: Because I am that. But in another way, it's all I ever see.

ME: What is?

HIM (*Pacing up and down*): This: I feel only one thing, I have only one conviction; it sits on three chairs in Heaven. Sometimes I look at it, with terror: it is such a perfect acrobat! The three chairs are three facts—it will quickly kick them out from under itself and will stand on air; and in that moment (because everyone will be disappointed) everyone will applaud. Meanwhile, some thousands of miles over everyone's head, over a billion empty faces, it rocks carefully and smilingly on three things, on three facts, on: I am an Artist, I am a Man, I am a Failure—it rocks and it swings and it smiles and it does not collapse tumble or die because it pays no attention to anything except itself. (*Passionately*) I feel, I am aware—every minute, every instant, I watch this trick, I am this trick, I sway—selfish and smiling and careful—above all the people. (*To himself*) And always I am repeating a simple and dark and little formula . . . always myself mutters and remutters a trivial colourless microscopic idiom—I breathe, and I swing; and I whisper: "An artist, a man, a failure, MUST PROCEED."

ME (*Timidly, after a short pause*): This thing or person who is you, who does not pay any attention to anyone else, it will stand on air?

HIM: On air. Above the faces, lives, screams—suddenly. Easily: alone.

ME: How about the chairs?

HIM: The chairs will all fall by themselves down from the wire and be caught by anybody, by nobody; by somebody whom I don't see and who doesn't see me: perhaps by everybody.

ME: Maybe yourself—you, away up ever so high—will hear me applaud?

HIM (*Looking straight at her, smiles seriously*): I shall see your eyes. I shall hear your heart move.

ME: Because I shall not be disappointed, like the others.

HIM: Women generally prefer the theatre, however.

ME: Women can't help liking the theatre any more than women can help liking men.

HIM: I don't understand.

ME: What I mean is perfectly simple. I mean, women like to pretend.

HIM (*Laughs gaily*): Upon which words, our knockkneed flybitten hero executed a spontaneous inverted quintuple backsomersault, missing the nonexistent trapeze by six and seveneighths inches.

ME (*Looking away*): I'm sorry—you see it's no use trying to tell me things, because I don't understand. And I can't argue.

HIM (*Walking over to her, takes her hand in his; caresses it gently*): Wrong, wrong. (*Tries to look in her eyes which, drooping, evade his*) Please don't mistake him; it was meant as a compliment, he's a harmless acrobat, he was trying to show you that he feels how much finer you are than he is or has been or ever will be—you should pity him. (*Stroking*) Poor clown.

ME (*Withdraws her hand*): You shouldn't play up to me.

HIM: You should know better than to accuse me of playing up to you.

ME (*In disgust*): O, you can't know anything about men; they're so complicated.

HIM: MEN complicated!

ME: Women don't want so many things.

HIM: Any woman?

ME: If she's really a woman.

HIM: What does the woman who's really a woman wish?

ME (*Looking at him*): That's a secret.

HIM: Really?

ME: Really a secret.

HIM: A secret is something to be guessed, isn't it?

ME (*Defiantly*): You'll never guess mine.

HIM: Perhaps, but why insult—

ME: Nobody's insulting you. I simply feel that I'm this way and there's no use in my trying to be another way.

HIM (*Smiles*): Speaking of secrets, here's one which I've never breathed to a single soul; sabe usted quién soy?

ME: No. Do you?

HIM: Mr. Bang, the hunter. (*His voice shrinks to a whisper; he gestures mysteriously*) I hunt the gentle macrocosm with bullets made of microcosm and vice versa. (*Laughs. Suddenly serious, resumes.*) Yessiree—and this is a positively dead secret: I very frequently tell this to absolutely noone—. (*With entire earnestness, leaning importantly toward her, enunciates distinctly and cautiously*) My gun is made of chewinggum.

ME (*Quietly*): I wish I had a piece. (*She struts the back of one doll-like hand across her forehead. Speaks vaguely.*) Where are we? I mean, who are we; what am I doing—here?

HIM: We are married.

ME: Why do you say that?

HIM: Isn't that the way married people are supposed to feel? (*Abruptly turning, walks briskly across the room; halts: half-turns, looks toward the window and mutters*) It's snowing . . . (*His voice thinks to itself*) . . . showing . . . (*His whisper marvels, muses*) . . . knowing. (*He stands, lost in thought*)

ME (*With an effort*): Promise something.

HIM (*Absently*): Yes?

ME: Promise that when the circus comes this year you'll take me.

HIM (*To her*): On one condition; that you agree to see everything.

ME: Of course.

HIM: Last year you refused to pay your respects to The Queer Folk.

ME: O. (*Quickly*) But that's not the circus. And besides, whoever wants to see a lot of motheaten freaks?

HIM: I did. (*Smiles to himself*) I seem to remember riding out of a circus once upon a time on somebody's shoulder; and hearing a throbbing noise, and then a coarse voice squirting a stream of bright words—and looking, and seeing a small tent with huge pictures of all sorts of queer things, and the barker spieling like a fiend, and people all about him gaping like fish. Whereupon, I began to tremble—

ME (*Starting, as a drum sounds faintly*): Whatever's that?

HIM: —and begged somebody to take me in; which somebody probably did, I don't remember. . . .

ME: I hear something, don't you? (*The noise nears*) That. It's ever so near now. Must be a parade, and on such a wintry day, too. Imagine.

HIM (*Listening vainly*): What you hear and I don't must be either an exelevated-engineer in a silk stovepipe with a sprig of shamrock in his buttonhole riding a red white and blue tricycle like mad up 5th Avenue and waving a little green flag, or Einstein receiving the keys of the city of Coral Gables in a gondola—

ME: I'm sure it's a parade!

HIM: —or a social revolution—

ME: Will you do something?

HIM: Say it with flowers. (*The noise stops*) What?

ME (*Listening*): It seems to have stopped, very near—please run out and see; will you? (HIM *stares, mildly astonished, as* ME *jumps up from the more comfortable chair and hurries to the sofa*). Here's your hat: and look, it's snowing; you'd better take—

HIM: To Hell with the umbrella. (*Takes his crumpled hat from her*) Now in just what does your most humble and very obedient servant's mission consist?

ME: You're to take a look around the corner. Because I'm almost sure there's something.

HIM: Pardon me, Your Excellency, for remarking that I think you're crazy. (*Going, he kisses her*)

ME: You don't need to tell me: I know I am. (HIM *exits through door in middle wall.* ME *walks nervously up and down*

—pauses: goes to the invisible mirror and stands, stares, gestures, exactly as at the beginning of the scene.)

scene 3

(Scene: The picture, as at the end of Scene 1 [both heads present: WOMAN's eyes closed] and the three knitting rocking FIGURES facing the picture with their backs to the audience.)

THIRD FIGURE: I suppose so—what did you say yours was called?

FIRST: It's Toasted, but it died.

THIRD: How terrible. Did it swallow something?

FIRST: No, it fell down stairs.

SECOND: I can sympathise with you, my dear. All my children were killed in the great war.

FIRST: That's perfectly marvelous! How many did you have?

SECOND: At one time I had over eighty boys.

THIRD: Boys are the naughtiest little creatures—didn't you find them a bother?

SECOND: Not a bit, I used to keep mine out on the firescape.

FIRST: Male or female?

SECOND: Female, so my husband says. *(Enter HIM. The three FIGURES stop rocking and knitting.)*

HIM *(Bowing and removing his battered hat)*: I beg your pardon—. *(All three FIGURES rise and turn. HIM surveys their identical maskfaces doubtfully.)* I . . . how do you do—? *(Extends his hand to the FIRST FIGURE, who extends hers but instead of shaking hands twists his palm upward and studies it)*

FIRST FIGURE *(Rapidly)*: Yes Willie will.

HIM *(Confused)*: Willie—

FIRST FIGURE: Will die.

HIM *(Uncomprehending)*: Die?

FIRST FIGURE: One hour before midnight Daylight Saving Time February 30th.

HIM: —How?

FIRST FIGURE: At seventy kilometres an hour. Of ennui with

complications. In a toilet of the train de luxe going from Fiesole to Fiesole. Next! (*She whisks his hand toward the* SECOND FIGURE *who takes it and studies it*)

SECOND FIGURE (*More rapidly than the* FIRST): The key to the philosophy of Locke is John. Be careful not to swallow too much broken glass during the week and when riding a bicycle from or to work never take your feet off the handlebars even if a policeman smiles at traffic. Your favorite planet is Ringling Brothers. Horseradish will not produce consequences unless cowslips which is unlikely so be not daunted tho' affairs go badly since all will be well. The cards say and the tea leaves admit that enough is as good as a feast which will cause you some flatulence which you will not mind as long as Gipsy continues to remain a diurnal wateringpot but beware of a woman called Metope who is in the pay of Triglyph disguised as either an insurance agent or I forget which it doesn't matter and whenever a stuffed platitude hits you in the exaggerated omphalos respond with a threefisted aphorism to the precise casazza. Faretheewell n'erdoweel.—Next! (*She whisks his hand toward the* THIRD FIGURE, *who takes it and studies it*)

THIRD FIGURE (*More rapidly than the* SECOND): You suffer from noble-blood-poisoning. Time is the autobiography of space. Give a woman everything and she has nothing. Life is a matter of being born. Treat a man like dirt and he will produce flowers. Art is a question of being alive.—Go in peace. (*She drops his hand.* HIM *crams his hat on his head and hurries out, as the* THREE FIGURES *turn sit rock and knit.*)

scene 4

(*Scene: The room of Scene 2 revolved clockwise with reference to the audience so that the fourth or invisible wall is now the window wall. The wall to the audience's right [corresponding to the window wall of Scene 2] is the door wall. The middle wall [corresponding to the door wall of Scene 2] is the solid wall, against which is the sofa. To the audience's left a new wall with a large mirror [the invisible fourth wall of Scene 2] is now visible.*)

ME *is standing and gesturing before the mirror, as at the beginning and end of Scene 2; but at the point on the stage where she then stood there is now the table, near which are the two chairs.*)

HIM (*Coming through the doorway skims his hat at the sofa*): There wasn't anything. (*Brushes snow off himself, stamps, goes to the table: sits in the less comfortable of the chairs and pulls a notebook from his pocket*)

ME (*At the mirror speaks dimly*): I thought there might be. (*A pause*) I was thinking. . . .

HIM (*Absently: turning leaves of notebook*): So am I.

ME (*At the mirror*): You could make ever so much money, if you wanted to.

HIM (*As before*): Hm.

ME: Writing things . . . things people want—the public. Things people would like.

HIM (*Pulling out a pencil begins writing in notebook*): Uh-huh.

ME (*Vaguely*): Like plays and scenarios.

HIM (*Softly*): Keyring Comedies and Keyhole Farces.

ME: Not funny necessarily.

HIM (*Parenthetically*): Just dull.

ME: People like serious things.

HIM (*Almost inaudibly*): The Four Horses of the Apocalypse.

ME (*Still primping*): Because, really, you're ever so clever . . . I know that.

HIM (*Murmurs*): You made me what I am today I hope you're satisfied.

ME: No but take—

HIM (*Starting up*): Aha! I see it all now: The Great American Novel (gimme a chord, professor) where for the first and only time is revealed in all its startling circularity the longlost nombril of the Middle West. (*As if quoting*) Lucy T. Wot felt That Something which is nothing like anything, and as quick as everything laying her red hot pail of blackberries down in the midafternoon moonlight, slowly raised two eyes, in both after each of which a single tear strove as it were for the mastery, to those of Henery Pudd who merely looked at her however.

ME: O well. You don't want to be serious.

HIM: Serious?—I serious? You're jesting. (*Resumes writing*)

ME: I was trying to help you. (*A pause*)

HIM (*Reads to himself in a low voice*): "If we are dolls, It pulls the strings. If we pull strings, It is the dolls: who move." (*Emerging from his thought, finds her standing beside him*): You look terribly.

ME (*Breaking down*): I can't help it and I've tried so hard not to talk about it and I'm sick with worrying—. (*Wrings her hands*)

HIM (*Rises: drawing her into the more comfortable chair, puts his arm over her sobbing body*): Your hair is beautiful, today.

ME: Yes I tried that first. And I even went to the dentist— but nothing works.

HIM: Since when?

ME (*Shudders*): O god I don't know. And I walked miles and miles till I had to sit down in the snow or any old place: I'm sorry. (*She dabs her eyes with a microscopic handkerchief*) I know I'm silly to be this way . . . I'll stop crying— really, I will. Don't be angry with me.

HIM: "Angry"?

ME: I knew you were busy and wanted to get that damned play or whatever it is done. I promised myself I wouldn't go near you or bother you. And then—I don't know . . . I couldn't. (*Chokes on a sob*) O well: now I'll stop crying.

HIM (*Muses*): "Angry?"

ME: Really I'll stop.

HIM (*Smiling*): Our artist's conception—

ME: O, you and your "artist's conception"—. (*Brushing away his arm, rises; smiles wryly*): I'm going to lie down— please go on working. (*He stares straight before him. She takes his face in her hands.*) Look at me: I'm sorry to have been so stupid. . . . (*Kisses him lightly. Goes upstage to the sofa and lies down with her back toward him and the audience.*) This is much better—I think I can go to sleep . . . good night.

HIM (*Stands for a few moments looking out the invisible window, then turns. Walks quietly to the mirror. Speaks in an almost whisper, staring at his reflection.*): If it were the first time. (*Staring always into the mirror, he passes a limp longish hand over face forehead hair*) Where's the moment—come:

for an incipient dramatist you're an unearthly blockhead. You maul the climaxes always. I'll say that as a slack wire artist you're a heavenly plumber—you and your chairs! (*Laughs silently*) "Angry?"—On the contrary, better put everything in working order. Poor old flivver. She coughs, she's running on one. Dirty sparkplugs. If it were the fifteenth time, or time itself for that matter ... Time and Space, a softshoe turn. The wellknown writer of scenarios, properties one million lemon pies, hero a spitball artist of the first water, much furniture everywhere broken, pity and terror incorporated, it all comes out in the wash, happy ending, I've got the machine who's got the god? (*Takes a step forward*) Once again for luck, let's rehearse. Ars longa vita brevis. The Est—? (*Feels of his right jacket pocket*)—Yes. Are you with me? (*Stares fixedly*) You are. Good. Now I straighten up, looking my prettiest as it were. Head, so: eyes wide open.—In a lopsided way you really are almost handsome. We look straight ahead and we move my careful hand, slowly, down along my jacket; to his pocket. I, slowly, put his hand into my pocket; easily, don't you know? Or as if looking for the thirteenth volume of the Encyclopædia Britannica. Very good: excellent.—I should like to see myself do this. I do this very well, really. Mistaken vocation: should have been an actor perhaps?—And we take our hand out of this pocket; very slowly, so as not to. (*Withdraws his hand, with an automatic*) Perfect. That's the gesture—not quite slow enough, perhaps; otherwise. . . . And lifting our, my, his, arm, in a slow easy curve, like this; to the right temple: I do not shut my eyes. (*Stares, pistol at head. Speaks to his reflection.*) Why I'm a fool, I can never get my revenge on You. If I shut my eyes I'm not killing You. (*Bitterly*) And if I don't, it's You who kill your miserable self—quelle blague! (*His hand, with the automatic, wavers.* ME *screams. Wheeling,* HIM *pockets the pistol and bows to her.*) Morgen.

ME: —What—

HIM: It's my play: the wily villain, trapped by armies of unalterable law and so forth, commits harrycarissima with an atomiser—ought to be a howling success, don't you think? The Jarvanese way, you know. Sorry to frighten—

ME: —what's—

HIM: Would you care to inspect? (*He advances toward her. She cringes.*) Pistil. The female organ of a flower. But I only got a D plus in cryptogamic botany, when Professor Roland Thaxter was arrested for riding his bicycle on the sidewalk. (*He reaches the couch. She covers her face with her hands, speechless, cowering.*) Look. It's really very neat: in three parts, ovary style and stigma. (*He removes the magazine*) Not loaded. Don't be afraid.

ME (*Peeping between her fingers*): I—thought. . . .

HIM: Stamen is what you thought, it contains the pollen. (*Inserts the magazine*) Hence stamina.—Are you still unhappy?

ME (*After a short pause, touching him timidly*): Listen: did you—

HIM: You don't look unhappy. (*Slowly goes to the table, on the centre of which he carefully lays the automatic*)

ME: Did you do this—for me?

HIM: This?—I don't get you. Sorry.

ME: Because . . . I think. (*Relaxing utterly, spreads herself over the sofa—halfshut eyes smiling at the ceiling, to which she whispers*) Yes.

HIM (*Half turning, looks at her; expressionless*): Ah. (*Opens the box, takes a cigarette and speaks, tapping the cigarette on his hand*) How is it with you, lady?

ME (*Quietly, to the ceiling*): It's wonderful with me.

HIM (*Lights his cigarette. Sitting on the table, back to the audience, murmurs vaguely.*): The king's to blame. Congratulations.

ME (*Vaguely murmurs*): What . . . king.

HIM: King queen and knave, King kinkajou with his prehensile tail, King C. Y. Didn't Gillette Meknow.

ME (*As before*): The second sounds like a nice king . . . . (*Silence,* HIM *smokes*) Are—are you busy?

HIM (*Laughs*): "Busy"? Not just now.

ME: Then come over here, please.

HIM: Motive?

ME: Because I'm happy and I want you here. (*He strolls upstage to the couch. She makes room for him. As he sits down, she puts her arm around his neck.*) I guess I'll write a play myself—all about policemen and shootings and mirrors.

HIM: Why not.

ME: I guess my play will have ever so many more scary scenes than yours . . . nobody'll go to see your play because it won't be half so exciting. (*She laughs*) O—and mine will have something yours hasn't got: and all the mothers will bring their children to see him.

HIM: Him?

ME: The elephant.

HIM: Indeed.

ME: I'll have a fullsized elephant in my play.

HIM: With a trunk and everything?

ME: Of course. (*She looks at him for a moment: hugs him suddenly*) O you darling. With its baby face—. (*Sees his hat on the floor near the sofa*) That hat's all motheaten or something: you must buy yourself a new one. (*Hugging him, whispers*): My lover.

HIM (*After a short pause*): What did you say then?

ME: "My lover." I can say that if I like, because it's true.

HIM (*Gently*): Can you?—Here's something queer: I can say "that's not my hat." (*Earnestly*) And it's true.

ME: Is it, now: you mean you've given that dreadful old hat away to somebody? Not to me, I hope?

HIM (*Very gently*): How could I give it away when it doesn't belong to me?

ME: You mean it's just a horrid old hat you've rented—by the year, I suppose?

HIM: Not rented. Borrowed.

ME: Well now, that's interesting: the dirty old thing—it belongs to somebody else, you mean?

HIM: It belongs . . . to a friend of ours.

ME: Of ours? That nasty old crooked disagreeable hat?

HIM: It's the Other Man's hat.

ME: What?

HIM (*Gestures*): Just as these are his clothes: didn't I tell you? (*Laughs*) But you knew, really. Really, you were just pretending.

ME: I knew?

HIM: —About these neckties and socks and things. (*Serious*) He lets me wear them because it amuses him.

ME: What are you talking about?

HIM: Am I?

ME: I don't understand. What other man—where?

HIM: Here, of course.

ME: Really dear, you might be serious. You know I don't understand you when you're joking.

HIM: Seriously dear, I don't wish to alarm you. But there are really two men in this room—

ME: Two—?

HIM: —one of whom is jealous of the other.

ME: Are you trying to be funny or something?

HIM: I am not trying to be funny. Seriously.

ME: O; I thought you were. What are you doing?

HIM (*Mysteriously*): Something extraordinarily dangerous. I am really sitting in this Other Man's cage and I am really being caressed by this Other Man's canary.

ME: Who is that?

HIM (*Looking at her*): You are.

ME: "Canary"—of whom?

HIM (*Slowly*): Your lover is in this room.

ME: My— ... (*Rising*) Not any longer.

HIM: O yes he is, and I can prove it.

ME: O no. You can't.

HIM: Very easily. By showing him to you. Would you care to see him now?

ME: Now. Yes.

HIM (*Rising*): This way, ladies and gentlemen—. (*Guides her to the mirror: stands behind her*) —See?

ME (*Puzzled*): What?

HIM: You see him, all right: why not say hello? He's looking straight at you—after all, it's no good pretending to me that you don't know this gentleman.

ME: O. Him.

HIM: Yes; therefore—. (*Dropping suddenly on his knees, face to the mirror*)—Let us pray. (*Shuts his eyes and joins his hands*) O Mr. Man, if sometimes I seem to be taking your place, please don't be angry with me. You know perfectly well that I never seriously compete with you, Mr. Mirror Man, and I know perfectly well that you've got much too much sense to believe what the neighbors say about her and me. Not that she'd be to blame if there were anything really between us; but as a matter of fact I'm innocent, too: O Man in the Mirror, I swear I'm innocent! And since we know it's all a joke, let's speak seriously: now as for this here young woman, I know that she's always been true to you, and everybody knows; and, if you stop to think, you yourself know that you're the only fellow she's ever seriously been really in love with, or really ever seriously wanted, or seriously really ever cared about at all. (*During this speech* ME *tilts her small head sideways, in-*

specting herself critically; her slender hands, having pulled at dress-hips, rise to a cheek where their fingers automatically begin arranging stray wisps of hair: she stares always into the mirror. HIM *gets up. Turns to her.*): N'est-ce pas?

ME: I'm sorry. I didn't hear what you said. (*With a final glance at herself, she strolls toward the invisible window*)

HIM (*Picking up and putting on his battered hat, smiles suddenly*): You aren't mad, am I?

ME (*Shrugging*): I suppose it's because I'm stupid—but somehow I don't care. . . .

HIM: Don't suppose. (*Softly*) Or if you must suppose, suppose that you are standing before a window and that continuously something happens—snow appears, covers the earth; melting, disappears—in other words, suppose that the earth rises, reappears, moves: suppose Spring. Or suppose that I am looking in a mirror and that my consciousness of the surface dissolves before an image as snow may melt before rain or as Winter melts before April and as the awake must dissolve before the asleep. . . . (*Smiles to himself*)—In other words, suppose that a part of me is talking at this moment.

ME (*Standing at the table and looking out the invisible window, speaks vaguely*): But really, everything's winter, outside.

HIM: But seriously: the nearer something is, the more outside of me it seems. (*Walks to the sofa: pulls out notebook and reads, almost inaudibly, to himself*) "These solidities and silences which we call 'things' are not separate units of experience, but are poises, selforganising collections. There are no entities, no isolations, no abstractions; but there are departures, voyages, arrivals, contagions. I have seen an instant of consciousness as a heap of jackstraws. This heap is not inert; it is a kinesis fatally composed of countless mutually dependent stresses, a product-and-quotient of innumerable perfectly interrelated tensions. Tensions (by which any portion flowing through every other portion becomes the whole) are the technique and essence of Being: they copulate in laughter, in your least premeditated gesture are born myriads which die only to be incredibly reborn, they are eaten and drunk, we breathe and excrete them under different names. I do not stroke edges and I do not feel music but only metaphors. Metaphors are what comfort and astonish us, which are the projected brightness of ourselves— a million metaphors times or divided by a million metaphors constitute a moment or a coatsleeve—here is what we call smells and flavours, the difference between this face and another, god, never, tomorrow, love, yesterday, death or whatever yourself and myself agree to entitle that minute indestructible doll which only the artist possibly may endow with a carefully passionate gesture."

ME: . . . Maybe you mean something, I don't know.

HIM (*To noone, putting the notebook in his pocket and stretching himself wearily over the sofa*): Ah, but don't you know that there is a further image—which appears not so much in the window of sleep as in a still deeper mirror? The planes overlap sometimes and sometimes the straight lines seem to fall. Philosophy is a dreampistol which goes off—bang—into flowers-and-candy . . . we dissolve, you and I. Stop look and listen to a fraction of myself. Life is a kind of lust which melts, producing death—a child.

ME: By the way, may I be allowed to ask a question?

HIM (*Absently*): You may.

ME: What's all this play of yours about?

HIM (*To himself, smiling at the ceiling*): This play of mine is all about mirrors.

ME: But who's the hero?

HIM (*To her*): The hero of this play of mine? (*Hesitates.*) A man. . . .

ME: Naturally. What sort of a man?

HIM: The sort of a man—who is writing a play about a man who is writing a sort of a play.

ME: That's a queer hero, isn't it?

HIM: Isn't it?

ME: And what is this hero called?

HIM (*Very slowly*): This hero is called "Mr. O.Him, the Man in the Mirror."

ME: O.Him. (*Smiles*) And the heroine? (*Quickly*)—Or isn't there any?

HIM: On the contrary. My heroine lives over there—. (*Points to the mirror*)

ME (*Turning, at the invisible window*): Me?

HIM: Me, the beautiful mistress of the extraordinary Mr. O.Him.

ME: —Extraordinary because he thinks she's beautiful?

HIM: Extraordinary because I need a shave because he needs a shave.

*(Scene: The picture, as in Scene 3
[both heads present: WOMAN's eyes closed]
and the three knitting rocking FIGURES
facing the picture with their backs
to the audience.)*

scene 5

SECOND FIGURE: Seesaw Margery Daw.

THIRD: Four out of five will get wedlock.

FIRST: How can I when it's Friday the 13th?

THIRD: By reading the gospel according to Saint Freud.

SECOND: Nobody would be the wiser for a glass of mercury.

FIRST: But have you ever tried standing on the third rail?

SECOND: Yes except that February has too many holidays.

FIRST: In Vino Veritas.

THIRD: Beware of pickpockets.

SECOND: Look at Napoleon: he lost the Battle of Waterloo.

THIRD: And what happened to Jesus Christ? They crucified him.

FIRST: Quite the contrary. They took after their mother.

THIRD: Immediately?

FIRST: No, with salt and pepper and of course a dash of lemon.

SECOND: But I only got beyond page six, when nothing happened and the conductor died in my lap.

FIRST: It has wings, I think.

THIRD: That's the insidious thing about hippocampus (unpleasant breath).

SECOND: Atlantic coast from Cape Cod to Charleston.

FIRST: Greatest length seven inches.

THIRD: A Pacific Coast species grows nearly twelve inches long.

SECOND: The young are carried in a pouch by the male.

THIRD: The only fish with a grasping tail.

(*Curtain.*)

act II

scene 1

(*Scene: That amount of the actual structure
of the stage etc. which lies behind the
plane of the curtain is revealed, by
the curtain's rising, without a "set"
of any kind.*
The action or content of Scene 1 consists of the curtain's
rising, of its absence for one minute and of its falling.
Darkness.*)

VOICE OF ME: Was that an accident? Or a scene?

VOICE OF HIM: Both I trust.

VOICE OF ME: Did it really mean something?

VOICE OF HIM: It meant nothing, or rather: death.

VOICE OF ME: O, I see.

VOICE OF HIM: This is the Other Play.

VOICE OF ME: By Mr. O.Him?

VOICE OF HIM: —The Man in the Mirror.

VOICE OF ME: But tell me, what's this Other Play all
about?

VOICE OF HIM: About? It's about anything you like, about
nothing and something and everything, about blood and
thunder and love and death—in fact, about as much as you
can stand. (I might add that it's sure of a long run; provided,
of course, we receive the proper advertising—you know what
I mean—"Broadway is enjoying a novel treat in one of the
wittiest and most highly original products of American genius,
entitled 'How Dyuh Get That Way?' By the authors of 'Nuf
Ced' . . . the subject of this rollicking farce is the 18th Amend-
ment; and right now we want to ask you, could anything be
funnier? . . . but just to show how screamingly and even
killingly funny 'How Dyuh Get That Way' is, we are going to
give the assembled company a sample, taken at random: the
scene is a lawn with the porch of a bungalow to the audience's
right, the time is the wee small hours.")—Are you ready?

scene 2

(*Scene: As previously described. Enter staggeringly three corpulent* MIDDLE-AGED MEN, *the* THIRD *of whom is played by the* DOCTOR.)

FIRST MIDDLE-AGED MAN (*Heartily*): Jon playa gaim croquet.

SECOND (*Irritably*): Oreye bjush wummore Ished.

THIRD (*Loftily*): Sridiculous croquet lesh play tennish.

FIRST (*Delightedly*): Tennish love tennish mfavorite gaim.

SECOND (*Angrily*): Oreye bjush wummore Ished.

THIRD (*Scornfully*): Jon ystewed.

SECOND (*Fiercely*): Oreye bjush wummore.

FIRST (*Rapturously*): Hoosh gota racquet.

THIRD (*Witheringly*): Turrbly shtewed shdishgraysh.

FIRST (*Wildly*): Hoosh gota racquet wanta play tennish.

SECOND (*Furiously*): Wummore.

THIRD (*Annihilatingly*): Youghta gome.

SECOND (*Savagely*): Wummore.

THIRD (*Abolishingly*): Gome goat bed.

FIRST (*Desperately*): Shomebody mushave racquet mush play tennish witha racquet. (*Enter from the left one spinster, or* VIRGO, *with a very red nose, clad in black pajamas and carrying a dripping candle*)

VIRGO: O you big bad old men, you extraordinarily naughty husbands, you typically depraved old things: aren't you just lovely?

SECOND MIDDLE-AGED MAN: Wummore.

THIRD (*To* FIRST): Shpoleashman shudup.

FIRST: Shnot poleashman shfriend mine hullo.

VIRGO: You naughty old thing: how dare you speak to me!

FIRST MIDDLE-AGED MAN: Gota tennish racquet?

SECOND: Wummore.

THIRD: Shudup.

VIRGO: O you terribly intoxicated old reprobates, you perfectly sweet old wretches, I don't understand a word you say.

THIRD MIDDLE-AGED MAN: Officer musha pologise frien vurry drunk shdishgraysh.

SECOND: Oreye. Bjush.

FIRST (*Indicating the* VIRGO *with an ample gesture*): Shoreye shfrien mine shgot tennish racquet.

VIRGO: O you lovely old rascals, aren't you simply ashamed

of yourselves? What would your poor wives do if they could
see you now!

FIRST MIDDLE-AGED MAN: Gimme tennish racquet oleman
wanta play tennish. (*He takes hold of the candle*)

VIRGO: You old wretch: don't you dare touch my candle!
Just you take those naughty hands away now!

THIRD MIDDLE-AGED MAN: Doan sult thoffcer Fred.

VIRGO: O the rascal—he's got it away from me! Whatever
will I do: it's pitch dark, and what a position for a woman!
(*Loudly*) I'm perfectly defenceless.

FIRST MIDDLE-AGED MAN: Thangsh oleman musha blige
kmon Jon play tennish now gota racquet. (*He makes a pass
with the candle*)

VIRGO: Should I scream?—But what good would that do? O,
what wicked old men you are!

SECOND MIDDLE-AGED MAN: Oreye b-

FIRST: Kmon Jon kmon George bye oletop rully musha
blige tyou kmon everybody goint play tennish. (*Exit*)

SECOND: Oreye. (*Exit*)

THIRD: Doan mine offcer sall fun promise frien bring it rye
back frien vurry drunk jush fun yknow course yunnerstan see
ylater oreye goobye mush blige. (*Exit*)

VIRGO (*Sola*): Weren't they simply awful! Aren't men the
dreadfulest wretches! And that old devil who took my candle
away from me, wasn't he the limit—the poor dear thought it
was a tennis racquet, can you imagine that! As for the other
little man, who was simply unthinkably intoxicated, he could
only say two or three words, poor dear! And then the one who
spoke to me as if I were a policeman—rascally old darling!
My, how I'd hate to be their wives!—I must go to bed at once
before I catch my death of cold. (*Utters a profound sigh*) It
was really lucky they were all in such a deplorable condition,
otherwise I should have felt guilty of immodesty. . . . (*Sighs
even more profoundly*) What a terrible thing it is to be a
woman! (*Enter a Negro redcap Grand Central porter*)

PORTER (*Saluting* VIRGO): Pardon me mam but is you de
party asked me to find out about checkin' a pet canary?

VIRGO (*Ecstatically*): My name is Gloria Quackenbush I am
a dancer three years ago I had so much indigestion and constipation that I got terribly run down I was too tired and nervous
to take my lessons a lady recommended yeast the constipation
was relieved and I had much less trouble with gas now I am

strong in every way the hydroplane in the photograph was furnished by the yeast company. (*Darkness*)

VOICE OF HIM: You don't seem very enthusiastic.

VOICE OF ME: I'm not.

VOICE OF HIM: In that case, I have a bright idea. I am going to make a million dollars.

VOICE OF ME: You!

VOICE OF HIM: Sounds incredible, doesn't it?

VOICE OF ME: No but how?

VOICE OF HIM: I shall buy paste and labels and I shall buy boxes and I shall buy pen and ink and breadcrumbs and I shall put all the breadcrumbs in all of the boxes and I shall write the word RA-DI-O-LE-UM on all of the labels and I shall paste all of the labels on all of the boxes.

VOICE OF ME: Is that all?

VOICE OF HIM: No. I shall insert, in all of the leading newspapers and periodicals of the country, a full page advertisement.

VOICE OF ME: Saying what?

VOICE OF HIM: Saying: "WHY DIE? TRY RA-DI-O-LE-UM." . . .

scene 3

(*Scene: A streetcorner. People passing to and fro.*
A SOAP BOX ORATOR, *played by the* DOCTOR, *arrives and establishes himself.*)

SOAP BOX ORATOR (*To an as yet nonexistent audience*): Ladies and gentlemen: do I look like the sort of fellow that goes around trying to drape the universe in deep mourning? Am I one of those lopsided pessimists that perambulate all over this beautiful world trying to persuade everybody he runs into that sunlight costs a million dollars a quart? (SOMEBODY *stops to look and listen*) Is that the effect I make on you as I stand here today—I, that was born and raised on this very street and worked hard all of my life in this fair city for fifty-two years and enjoyed every moment of it? (*Two* PEOPLE *stop to look and listen*) Am I a squeaking squealer or a squealing squawker or a whimpering morbid foureyed crape-hanging meanderer? I see by your faces, ladies and gentlemen, that you don't believe so. (*Three* PEOPLE *stop to look and listen*) All right. But let me tell you something. (*Four* PEOPLE *stop to look and listen*) Every ten men and women I see, walking or talking or shopping or going to the movies or riding in taxicabs busses subways and elevateds or doing nothing whatever or minding the children or reading the newspaper or up in the air in airoplanes, I say to myself—five out of four will get cinderella and the other nine have it already. (*Five* PEOPLE *stop to look and listen*) Now let's get right down to fundamentals: what is cinderella? I'm here to tell you, ladies and gentlemen, that cinderella is a newly discovered disease. (*Six* PEOPLE *stop to look and listen*) You will ask me —is it dangerous? —Dangerous, ladies and gentlemen? Why it's so dangerous that, compared with the untold dangers to which cinderella subjects each and every specimen of the human race without exception in particular and mankind in general, a monthold baby cutting its milk teeth on a stick of dynamite is a picture of perfect safety. —Dangerous? Why, it's so dangerous that the three greatest elocutionists of all time— Demosthenes Daniel Webster and William Jennings Bryan— couldn't explain to you how dangerous cinderella is if they lectured steadily for six months without a glass of water.— Dangerous? Why, if I could begin to convey to your superior intelligences how dangerous this infernal and unprecedented disease known to scientists as cinderella is, I could pick strawberries in the Garden of Eden or fight the American Revolution. (*Seven* PEOPLE *stop to look and listen*)—Is it dangerous? Gracious Heavens, ladies and gentlemen, cinderella is the darkest deepest awfulest most obscure insidious hideous and perfectly fatal malady on the face of God's footstool! (*Eight* PEOPLE *stop to look and listen*) Now let me give you a little illustration, just to show you how incredibly dangerous cinderella is. —Suppose you've got cinderella (that most contagious of human diseases) or I've got cinderella, or the fellow over there's got cinderella: do we know we've got it? No, ladies and gentlemen, we don't know and we can't know! (*Nine* PEOPLE *stop to look and listen*) We may be rotting internally, our lungs intestines livers and other glands both great and small may be silently putrefying, forming invisible pockets of nauseous pus, creating microscopic sacs of virulent poison— and we don't know it! We may be neat and clean and washed and manicured outside, and inside we may be noisome squirming garbage cans breeding billions upon trillions of repulsive wormlike omnivorous germs of cinderella: that's what the scientists have just discovered! Think of it. Dream of it, ladies and gentlemen! And you ask me if this frightful disease is dangerous! Once and for all, let me tell you that cinderella is not dangerous—it is Death Itself! (*Ten* PEOPLE *stop to look and listen*) I see you're terrified, ladies and gentlemen, and I don't blame you. If you weren't afraid of death you wouldn't be human. But I'm not here primarily to give you the fright of your lives. Primarily, ladies and gentlemen, I'm here to help you. And I bring the greatest message of blessed comfort that the human soul in this day and time can possibly imagine. For —mark my words—in this little commongarden ordinary unassuming box reposes, to put it mildly, the secret of the ages. (*He holds up a tin pillbox. Nine* PEOPLE *stop to look and listen.*) Now give me your close attention: when a forest fire starts, we fight the fire with fire, don't we? When a new demon of disease makes his infernal appearance on the face of this planet we turn for help to the latest discoveries of modern science, don't we? (*Eight* PEOPLE *stop to look and listen*) In this case, ladies and gentlemen, we turn with confidence to that most entirely miraculous of all miracles: Radium. (*Seven* PEOPLE *stop to look and listen*) And we find that our hopes are not unfounded. A new light breaks upon us—Radium will conquer cinderella! We are saved! Mankind, the whole human race, is saved! (*Six* PEOPLE *stop to look and listen*) Step right up, ladies and gentlemen. Feast your minds upon the unimaginable treasure which this little innocentlooking box represents and contains. Try to picture to yourself the inherent wonderfulness of its mysterious contents. Think, or try to think, that the medicine comprised in each of the twelve tiny threedimensional oblate spheroids herein uselessly reposing is powerful enough to obliterate annihilate and utterly incinerate five hundred quadrillion cinderella bacteria! (*Five* PEOPLE *stop to look and listen*) All over the universe, ladies and gentlemen, myriads of yearning hands without exaggeration are hopelessly reaching for the secret of life enclosed in this negligible bit of metal. Tomorrow in this very city a hundred hearts will breathe paeans of thankfulness for the salvation that has come to them through this tiniest receptacle. And why? Because in this modest pillbox, ladies and gentlemen, cinderella—the dreaded cinderella—meets its doom! (*Four* PEOPLE *stop to look and listen*)—Ah, if the handful of thankful hearts that will have sampled the delicioustasting automatically assimilated contents of this little box by tomorrow morning could only be a thousand—a million—a decillion! (*Three* PEOPLE *stop to look and listen*) But the remedy is limited, ladies and gentlemen. So infinitely precious and prophylactic a product could not be manufactured rapidly. In time to come we hope to be able to place this miracle on the market in large quantities. With this end in view and no other, our fourteen model factories at Kankakee Illinois are working night and day. We will do our best, but we too are only human. The effort involved is inconceivable. As for the expense, it is simply without exaggeration fabulous. (*Two* PEOPLE *stop to look and listen*) But we don't trouble ourselves on that account: we are not here to make money, but to save our fellowmen and fellowwomen and fellowchildren from the most vomitory fate that has ever threatened humanity in the world's entire history. (*One* PERSON *stops to look and listen*) As a conclusive proof of what I say, let me mention that we are offering the first batch of our absolutely unique and positively guaranteed product at a dead loss—we are in fact giving it away for less than the cost of printing the labels. Ladies and gentlemen, although my statements hitherto may have seemed unbelievable I have one yet to make which for sheer unadulterated unbelievability outdoes them all—the actual expense to each and every purchaser of this lifegiving panacea is, today here and now in this greatest and most prosperous of cities New York, one dollar. (*Nineteen* PEOPLE *go their nineteen ways*) Here you are: one dollar. (*Seventeen* PEOPLE *go their seventeen ways*) Think of it! (*Fifteen* PEOPLE *go their fifteen ways*) Why the heavily silverplated highlypolished universally useful fully guaranteed aluminum box alone is worth a dollar. (*Thirteen* PEOPLE *go their thirteen ways*) It lasts a lifetime! (*Eleven* PEOPLE *go their eleven ways*) Squeeze drop shake it you can't break it, feed it to the lions roll it over Niagara Falls shoot burn and sit down on it it's indestructible turn and twist it at your will if it breaks we pay the bill round and over inside forward wrongside downside upside out—ladies and gentlemen, it remains one and the same. (*Nine* PEOPLE *go their nine ways*) Step right up! (*Seven* PEOPLE *go their seven ways*) Each and every package positively guaranteed to contain authentic infinitesimal amounts of the world's most precious substance Radium, one cubic ounce of which according to painstakingly prepared strictly scientific statistics would generate sufficient dynamic energy to instigate a crop of beautiful lovely luxuriant curly chestnut hair slightly more than five miles long all over the entire surface of the terrestrial globe in six and seven-eighths seconds. (*Five* PEOPLE *go their five ways*) Step right up—here you are! (*Three* PEOPLE *go their three ways, leaving only the original* SOMEBODY *who stopped to look and listen*) You may not have cinderella but if you haven't it's a cinch you've got something else and no matter what it is this little box will save your life one dose alone irrevocably guaranteed to instantaneously eliminate permanently prevent and otherwise completely cure toothache sleeplessness clubfeet mumps stuttering varicoseveins youthful errors tonsilitis rheumatism lockjaw pyorrhea stomachache hernia tuberculosis nervous debility impotence halitosis and falling down stairs or your money back. (*The original* SOMEBODY *goes his original way. Darkness.*)

VOICE OF ME: That wasn't such a bright idea after all.
VOICE OF HIM: Never mind. I have another.
VOICE OF ME: Another bright idea?
VOICE OF HIM: Posolutely absitively.
VOICE OF ME: May I hear it?
VOICE OF HIM: You may. . . .
VOICE OF ME: Well?

VOICE OF HIM: . . . Well—next we have, ladies and gentlemen, Will and Bill: two partners in business who, through association, became each other. Camera!

scene 4

(*Scene: An inner office. At a desk is seated* WILL, *a figure with a maskface which represents the real face of the* DOCTOR, *who presently enters, playing the part of an* INTRUDER.)

WILL (*Looking up, starts: gasps*): Who are you?
INTRUDER: You mean "Who am I."
WILL (*In a shaky voice*): Certainly: that's what I said.

INTRUDER: No. That's what I said.

WILL: Is that so. . . . (*His right hand, fumbling, opens a drawer in the desk*) . . . And what did I say?

INTRUDER: "Who are you."

WILL (*Covers the* INTRUDER *with a pistol*): Will you answer?

INTRUDER (*Imperturbably*): Answer—?

WILL: Will you answer? —Yes or no?

INTRUDER: Which?

WILL: Which—what?

INTRUDER: Which question.

WILL: You know which question—come on now: who are you?

INTRUDER (*Slowly*): I am.

WILL (*Rising, ejaculates tremulously*): —I?

INTRUDER: You. (*A few seconds' pause*)

WILL (*Exploding in hysterical laughter, calls out*): Hey Bill! —Come in here a minute: I got something to show you. (BILL, *a figure with a different maskface, hurries in*)

BILL: What's the matter Will?

WILL: Matter? —I ask this feller who he is and he says "You," did you ever hear anything like that?

INTRUDER: Not you—YOU.

BILL (*Looking about him apprehensively*): Me?—Who? Which feller? —Where?

WILL (*To* INTRUDER): Shut up, YOU. —Listen Bill, this feller comes walking through the door like he owned the place or something.

BILL (*Catching sight of the pistol*): What the—. Will! For Christ's sake, drop that gun—

WILL: Drop nothing. With this feller here, refusing to answer who he is? Are you crazy?

BILL: Where? What feller? —Be careful, Will, it's loaded— it might go off—

WILL: I'll shoot the sonofabitch if he don't answer me: answer, YOU—who are you?

BILL: —Will for God's sake—. (*He covers his eyes with both hands*)

INTRUDER: You.

WILL: God damn you—. (*He pulls the trigger: there is no explosion: he falls forward, writhes on the floor and collapses, with his maskface turned to the audience*)

BILL: Will! —O god: he's killed himself . . . what'll I do—O what'll I do. . . . (*Throws himself on his knees beside the body, as Irving Berlin's "What'll I Do" is heard dimly. The* INTRUDER *stealthily passes to the desk and quietly sits where* WILL *was originally seated.*)

INTRUDER: Get the police to arrest you.

BILL (*Vaguely, staring at nothing*): What's that . . . arrest who?

INTRUDER: You.

BILL (*As before*): . . . Me?

INTRUDER: You.

BILL (*As before*): What did I do. What for?

INTRUDER: For murdering Will, Bill.

BILL (*Starts violently*): I never killed Will—

INTRUDER: Why did you kill me Bill?

BILL (*Straightening, sees the* INTRUDER *for the first time— starts—his left hand with an involuntary meaningless gesture strikes the prone* WILL'*s maskface, which comes off, revealing a real face to which the maskface of* BILL *corresponds*)

INTRUDER (*Softly*): You shouldn't have killed me, Bill.

BILL (*To* INTRUDER *with a gasp of recognition*): —Will!

INTRUDER: Yes Bill, it's Will.

BILL: But you . . . you can't, it ain't possible—. (*Cries out*) He's dead: look at him—. (*His voice sinks to a wondering whisper as he stares unseeingly in the direction of the prone figure*) . . . My god—. Gone! (*His gaze travels gradually back to the* INTRUDER'*s face*)

INTRUDER: I am Will and I am dead because you killed me, Bill.

BILL (*Gradually rising from his knees*): I . . . I never . . . he killed—himself—

INTRUDER: You killed Will, Bill.

BILL: . . . So help me God—I aint lying—if I'm lying, kill me!

INTRUDER (*Sternly*): Bill killed Will and you know it.

BILL (*Writhing in an agony of remorse: anguish sprouting in his body*): I'm innocent—I swear I'm innocent: kill me if I aint—

INTRUDER (*Solemnly*): You ain't, Bill.

BILL (*With a stuttering gesture of hands outstretched against some unbelieveable horror, screams suddenly*): Will!

INTRUDER: Dead, Bill.

BILL (*Sobbing*): Why—why did I—why did—

INTRUDER: For a woman, Bill. You killed me for a woman.

BILL (*Wrapping his maskface in shivering hands*): O—. (*He collapses, groveling, at the* INTRUDER'*s feet. A pause.*)

INTRUDER: Bill. (*No answer. He speaks gently.*) Come Bill.

BILL (*Upwrithing—petrified*): O—.

INTRUDER: Come with me, now. (*Suddenly grabs* BILL, *who goes utterly limp in his grip: shouts, in a completely changed voice*) All right boys—I got her! (*Noise of a door being broken down. Darkness.*)

VOICE OF HIM: May I be so indiscreet as humbly to beg your Royal Highness's most illustrious verdict upon that deplorable scene?

VOICE OF ME: It made me feel as if I'd just swallowed a caterpillar.

VOICE OF HIM: These masks and ghosts, however, lead us into girls and dolls.

VOICE OF ME: Masks and ghosts?

VOICE OF HIM: Larva, pupa and (if we are very lucky) imago: the instantaneous futility.—You mentioned caterpillars, and so I am talking about caterpillars which I consider very interesting.

VOICE OF ME: I dare say everything is interesting if you understand it. Even angleworms are probably intensely interesting, in their way.

VOICE OF HIM: Life is a cribhouse, darling: a cribhouse with only one door: and when we step out of it—who knows but that angleworms are prodigiously and even unnecessarily interesting?

VOICE OF ME: And who cares?

VOICE OF HIM: Certainly not angleworms—eyeless and epicene which wander in ignorant darkness.

scene 5

(*Scene: The stage has become a semicircular piece of depth, at whose inmost point nine black stairs lead up to a white curtain.*

Two coalblack figures, one MALE *and one* FEMALE, *appear at opposite extremities of the semicircle's circumference [i. e.*

of the foreground]. *The* FEMALE *figure is holding in its arms
a large boydoll at whom it looks fondly.*)

MALE (*Nervously*): Who you nigga?

FEMALE (*Looking up, answers lazily*): Ahs de ground.

MALE (*Apprehensively*): Who de ground?

FEMALE (*Proudly*): Ahs de ground.

MALE (*Fearfully*): Wot, you de ground?

FEMALE (*Insolently*): Yas ahs de ground, ahs de ripe rich
deep sweet sleek an sleepy ground, de G-R-O-U-N-D GROUND.
(*Strolls toward centre of semicircle*)

MALE (*Faintly, pointing to the doll*): Wot you got dere.

FEMALE (*Strolling, speaks angrily*): Dere? Where.

MALE (*Breathlessly*): In yo arms.

FEMALE (*Pausing at the centre of the semicircle, speaks
sullenly*): Ah got Johnie.

MALE (*Wildly*): —O Lawd! Johnie's in de arms of de
ground! (SIX COALBLACK FIGURES, *three male and three
female, appear in succession, punctuating the circumference
of the semicircle at regular intervals and in a counterclock-
wise direction with reference to the audience*)

FIRST (*Appearing, speaks rapidly*): De ground's got a hold
of Johnie.

SECOND (*Appearing, speaks more rapidly*): De ground's
got Johnie in her arms.

THIRD (*Appearing, speaks very rapidly*): De ground won't
let go.

FOURTH (*Appearing, speaks very rapidly and shrilly*):
Money won't make de ground let go.

FIFTH (*Appearing, speaks shrilly and almost incoherently*):
Love won't make de ground let go.

SIXTH: (*Appearing, cries hysterically*): Nothin won't make
de ground let go of Johnie.

ALL SIX (*In unison, hysterically*): De ground won't let go,
WON'T LET GO, WON'T LET GO! (*They rightface simulta-
neously and march around the* FEMALE *figure with its doll.
Marching, they speak in succession.*)

FIRST: Look at Johnie
            was a man
            loved a woman
            like a man only can.

SECOND: He loved her hands
           an he loved her lips
           an he loved her feet
           an he loved her hips.

THIRD: He loved her eyes
           an he loved her breasts
           but he loved her somethin
           else the best.

FOURTH: Now he lies
           without a sound
           lonely an small
           in de arms of de ground.

FIFTH: Maybe he twists
           maybe he squirms
           an maybe he's full
           of lil bright worms.

SIXTH: After workin an ashirkin
           eatin an adrinkin
           livin an alovin
           Johnie's in de ground.

(*Behind the white curtain an invisible jazz band plays
softly: the voices of the players darkly sing. The* SIX
FIGURES *halt, in a circle, listening.*)

VOICES: Frankie and Johnie were lovers
           sweet Christ how they could love
           they swore to be true to each other
           as true as the stars above
               but he was a man
               and he done her wrong

           Frankie she lived in the cribhouse
           the cribhouse had only one door
           she gave all her money to Johnie
           who spent it on a parlorhouse whore
               he was a man
               and he done her wrong

           Frankie went down to the corner
           to buy herself a bottle of beer
           and she said to the old bartender

have you seen my loving Johnie in here
  he is a man
  and he done me wrong

I aint agoing to tell you no secrets
and I aint agoing to tell you no lies
but Johnie went out just a minute ago
with that old whore Fanny Fry
  he is a man
  and he done you wrong

Frankie went back to the cribhouse
this time it wasn't for fun
for under her old red kimona
she carried Johnie's .44 gun
  she was looking for the man
  who done her wrong

Frankie she went to the parlorhouse
she looked in the window so high
and there she saw her Johnie
just a — — - — — Fanny Fry
  he was a man
  and he done her wrong

Frankie she went to the front door
she rang the front door bell
she said stand back all you pimps and whores
or I'll blow you all to Hell
  I want my man
  who done me wrong

Frankie went into the parlor
Johnie commenced to run
she said don't run from the woman you love
or I'll shoot you with your own damn gun
  you are a man
  who done me wrong

Frankie went into the parlor
Johnie hollered Frankie don't shoot
but Frankie she out with Johnie's .44 gun
and three times rootytoottoot
  she shot her man
  who done her wrong

Roll me over gently
roll me over slow
roll me over on my right side
'cause my left side's hurting me so
    you've killed your man
    who done you wrong

Frankie she turned him on his stomach
Frankie she turned him on his side
when she turned him for the third time
he hung his head and died
    she killed her man
    who done her wrong

(*The white curtain at the top of the nine black stairs is pulled aside suddenly: the* NINE PLAYERS, *in vermillion suits, with white shirts and socks, emeraldgreen neckties, lemoncoloured gloves and silkhats, appear*)

NINE PLAYERS (*Playing, singing and descending the nine black stairs*):

GET OUT YOUR RUBBERTIRED CARRIAGES
AND GET OUT YOUR DECORATED HACKS
I'LL TAKE MY LOVING JOHNIE TO THE CEMETERY
BUT I'LL BRING HIS—

(*A cadaverous* PERSONAGE *with tortoiseshell spectacles spouts up out of the third row of the audience*)

PERSONAGE (*Played by the* DOCTOR): Stop! (*The song ceases. The* SIX COALBLACK FIGURES *slink to their original positions, as the* FEMALE *figure with its doll rushes up the nine black stairs and vanishes behind the reappearing white curtain. The* MALE *figure advances indignantly.*)

MALE: Who you.

PERSONAGE (*Displays enormous badge*): John Rutter, President pro tem. of the Society for the Contraception of Vice. (*He points a cadaverous finger at the* MALE *figure*) You were about to utter enunciate pronounce and otherwise emit a filthy lewd indecent vile obscene lascivious disgusting word!

MALE (*In astonishment*): O Lawd; was ah?

PERSONAGE: Don't deny it! (*He climbs over the footlights and steps up to the* MALE *figure. Producing from his inside jacket pocket a paper, he seizes the* MALE *figure's right hand and—holding the hand aloft—reads glibly from the paper.*) I

John Smith nose protruding eyes open ears symmetrical being
in my right mind do hereby swear to obstruct impede combat
hinder prevent and otherwise by every means known and unknown including extravasation knockoutdrops hypnotism and
dynamite oppose the propagation or dissemination of any
immediately or ulteriorly morally noxious or injurious or in
any other way whatsoever harmful titillation provocation or
excitation complete or incomplete of the human or inhuman
mind or body or any portion of the same under no matter
what conditions or any assumption of or allusion to the existence of such a tendency in the human species whether such
illusion or assumption be oral graphic neither or both and
including with the written and spoken word the unwritten and
unspoken word or any inscription sign or mark such as has
been known to occur in public places of a strictly private
character commonly or uncommonly known as comfort stations or any other visible or invisible natural or unnatural
assumption of or inclination to assume such a tendency or any
assumption of assumption of such tendency whether compre-
hensible or incomprehensible intentional or unintentional premeditated or spontaneous implicit or explicit uttered or unut-
tered perceptible or imperceptible or any blasphemous filthy
and new idea or group of ideas such as birthcontrol bolshevism and so forth and in general anything at all whatsoever be
its origin or essence both irrespective of and with reference to
its nature or content such as in the opinion of a judge familiar
with the more widely used symbols of the English and American alphabets may can must might could would or should
constitute a tacit misdemeanor against the soul of a child of
not less than one day and not more than one year old and I
take this oath willingly and without mental reservation on my
part of any kind whatsoever conscious unconscious or fore-
conscious so help me God one dollar please. (*Releases the
right hand of* MALE *figure. Pockets the paper.*)

MALE (*Weakly*): Ah ain got one dollar boss. (*The white
curtain at the top of the nine black stairs is suddenly pulled
aside: a slender* NEGRESS *in a red kimona willows down the
nine black stairs, passes the* NINE PLAYERS, *arrives behind the*
PERSONAGE *and bumps him with her elbow*)

NEGRESS: Gway yoh poor whytrash.

PERSONAGE (*Wheeling*): Look here, young lady, that's no
way to address—

NEGRESS: Doan call me "young lady" yoh bowlegged fish: ah ain no "young lady," thang Gawd!

PERSONAGE: In that case, I should advise you to attempt by every method practicable and impracticable to conceal the fact instead of making it glaringly apparent—

NEGRESS (*Drawing herself up proudly before him, speaks contemptuously*): Do yoh all know who ah am? (*The* PERSONAGE *recoils*) —Ah'm Frankie!

MALE FIGURE, SIX COALBLACK FIGURES *and* NINE PLAYERS (*Simultaneously*): SHE'S FRANKIE!

NEGRESS (*To* PERSONAGE): Take dat! (*Whisking into view something which suggests a banana in size and shape and which is carefully wrapped in a bloody napkin, points it straight at the* PERSONAGE—*who utters a scream, jumps over the footlights, rushes up the main aisle of the theatre and disappears.* FRANKIE *turns to the audience: cradling the Something in her arms, as the* GROUND *cradled her boydoll, she takes up the song where the* PERSONAGE *interrupted it.*) —But I'll bring his— (*The drummer taps twice*) back—

EVERYBODY (*Triumphantly*):

BEST PART OF THE MAN
WHO DONE ME WRONG

(*Darkness*)

VOICE OF ME: Tell me. . . .

VOICE OF HIM: What? (*A silence*) So you're getting horribly bored with the other play.

VOICE OF ME: Why should you think I was bored?

VOICE OF HIM: I can't imagine. How did you like that fifth scene?

VOICE OF ME: Let's finish up this Other Play; then I'll be able to judge much better.

VOICE OF HIM: It's not my funeral.

VOICE OF ME: What comes next?

VOICE OF HIM: But will you promise to let me know when you've had enough?

VOICE OF ME: I promise.

VOICE OF HIM: Good. —In that case, ladies and gentlemen, the next scene is all about eels in a tree.

VOICE OF ME: I hope there are no mice in it—are there?

VOICE OF HIM: Not a mice.

scene 6

(*Scene: Fifth Avenue—midnight.
A* PLAINCLOTHESMAN, *his entire being
focussed on something just offstage to the
audience's left, stalks this invisible something minutely. He is played by the* DOCTOR.
Enter an ENGLISHMAN *in evening clothes and a silk hat,
staggering under a huge trunk marked* FRAGILE—*his silk hat
falls off. He looks at it ruefully, even hopelessly. Then an
expression of tranquility adorns his visage, as he catches sight
of the* PLAINCLOTHESMAN'*s back—he clears his throat several
times—having failed to attract the* PLAINCLOTHESMAN'*s attention, he exclaims "I say" and "Beg pardon" and "By the way"
—finally, desperate, he wheels and gently bumps the* PLAIN-
CLOTHESMAN *with the trunk. The* PLAINCLOTHESMAN *leaps
into the air: landing with a drawn automatic, stares his innocent vis-à-vis fiercely in the eye.*)

ENGLISHMAN: Ah—good evening. Excuse me. Would you
mind awfully—you see, my topper just fell off.

PLAINCLOTHESMAN: Yuh wut?

ENGLISHMAN: My topper, my hat—would you be so awfully
kind as to hand it to me? (*The* PLAINCLOTHESMAN *contem-
plates the* ENGLISHMAN *from top to toe: his jowl emits a
cynical leer; pocketing his automatic, and warily stooping, he
picks up the silk hat and inspects it with deep suspicion*)

ENGLISHMAN (*Cheerfully sticking out his head*): On my nut
please, if you don't mind. (*The* PLAINCLOTHESMAN *scowls om-
inously: places the silk hat grimly on the* ENGLISHMAN'*s head*)
Glad to have met you—(*He starts for the wings, right*)
Cheerio!

PLAINCLOTHESMAN: HAY. (*The* ENGLISHMAN *starts: staggers: turns*) Lissun. Wutchuhgut dare.

ENGLISHMAN (*Apprehensively, trying to look behind himself*): There? Where?

PLAINCLOTHESMAN: On yuh back uv coarse.

ENGLISHMAN (*Relieved*): O, you mean that?—(*He tries to
nod at what he carries*)—Don't tell me you don't know what
that is.

PLAINCLOTHESMAN: Sie. Dyuh tink I doughno uh trunk wen
I sees it?

ENGLISHMAN (*Perplexed*): Trunk? I said nothing about a
trunk.

PLAINCLOTHESMAN: Youse dough need tuh. Dyuh know wie? Becuz yuh gut one on yuh back, dat's wie.

ENGLISHMAN: Do you know I'm dreadfully sorry, old man, but I haven't the least idea what you're talking about.

PLAINCLOTHESMAN: Can dat soikus stuff. Wutchuhgut in dat —(*He raps the trunk with his knuckles*)

ENGLISHMAN (*A light dawning*): Ah, I see. So that's what you call my trunk—

PLAINCLOTHESMAN: I calls dat uh trunk becuz dat is uh trunk, dat's wie.

ENGLISHMAN: But my dear chap, you're quite mistaken in supposing that to be a trunk.

PLAINCLOTHESMAN (*Menacingly*): Dat ain uh trunk?

ENGLISHMAN: I should say not. Dear, dear no. The very idea —ha-ha-ha.

PLAINCLOTHESMAN: Wal if dat ain uh trunk, will youse kinely tell me wut dat is?

ENGLISHMAN (*To himself*):—A trunk! That's really not half bad, you know. (*To the* PLAINCLOTHESMAN) But since you ask me, I don't mind telling you.

PLAINCLOTHESMAN: Wal, wut is it?

ENGLISHMAN: Why, that's my unconscious.

PLAINCLOTHESMAN (*Hand at ear*): Yuh wut?

ENGLISHMAN: My unconscious, old egg. Don't pretend you haven't heard of them in America. —Why, my dear boy, I was given to understand that a large percentage of them originated in the States: if I'm not mistaken, the one I've got is made hereabouts, in Detroit or somewhere like that.

PLAINCLOTHESMAN: Nevuh mine ware it was made; wuts in it?

ENGLISHMAN: In it? (*He utters a profound sigh*) Ah—if I only knew. (*The* PLAINCLOTHESMAN *recoils in amazement. The* ENGLISHMAN, *after uttering another and even more profound sigh, turns.*) Well, we can't know everything, can we. Cheerio! (*He starts out*)

PLAINCLOTHESMAN (*Leaping in front of the* ENGLISHMAN, *automatic in hand*): HAY doan try dat stuff wid me. (*The* ENGLISHMAN *pauses*) Drop dat.

ENGLISHMAN (*Puzzled*): Drop? What?

PLAINCLOTHESMAN: Drop wutchugut nmake it quick get me?

ENGLISHMAN (*Despairingly*): I'm afraid I don't in the least know what you mean—

PLAINCLOTHESMAN: I mean leggo wid boat hans one after duhudder nleave duh res tuh gravity.

ENGLISHMAN: But you don't seem to understand—it's my—don't you realize? It's a part of myself—my unconscious—which you're asking me to let go of, to drop. Could anything be more impossibly ridiculous?

PLAINCLOTHESMAN: Sie lissun I doan givuh good god dam fuh youse "Un-con-shus." Nlemme tellyuh sumpn doan gimme no more uh youse lip rI'll make uh hole in youse.

ENGLISHMAN (*Agonized, wails*): But I CAN'T—(*The* PLAINCLOTHESMAN *fires: there is no explosion, but the* ENGLISHMAN *drops the trunk. As it lands, a terrific crash of broken glass is heard. The* ENGLISHMAN, *blinking, begins dusting himself; speaks severely.*) There—you see what you've done.

PLAINCLOTHESMAN (*Furiously*): Wie dinchuh tell me day wuz booze in it yuh goddam fool! (*He rushes—dropping, in his haste, the automatic—at the trunk: falling on both knees, begins tearing at the lock: presently throws back the lid—starts—rising, recoiling, covers his eyes as if from an inconceivable horror: staggers back—falls. The* ENGLISHMAN *continues to dust himself. A* COP *hurries in with a drawn revolver.*)

COP: Hansup! (*The* ENGLISHMAN *puts up his hands*) Wuts dis? Uh trunk? (*He spies the* PLAINCLOTHESMAN, *who is lying on his face*) Sumun croaked—(*Pokes the prostrate figure with his foot*) Wie, it's Joe! (*Stooping, lifts the* PLAINCLOTHESMAN'*s left arm—releases it; the arm falls, inert*) Here's duh gun. (*Picks up the* PLAINCLOTHESMAN'*s automatic; drops it in the right outside pocket of the helpless* ENGLISHMAN'*s dinner jacket, and grimly faces his prey who immediately begins explaining*)

ENGLISHMAN: Yes you see I was carrying this when my bally topper fell off, and being quite unable to pick it up myself—the hat, that is—I asked this Joe as you call him if he'd mind awfully doing me the favour to help me.

COP: W-a-l.

ENGLISHMAN: Well he very kindly obliged me. But subsequently, owing to a perfectly ridiculous misunderstanding—more or less (I believe) as to the precise character of what I was carrying—

COP: Youse wus carryin—wut.

ENGLISHMAN (*Pointing at the trunk*): This.

COP: HANSUP! (*The* ENGLISHMAN's *hand flies aloft*) Wut for.

ENGLISHMAN: What for—O; well you see I'd heard that in the States it's practically impossible to get into a hotel with a woman without a bag.

COP (*Puzzled*): How's dat? Say dem woids again.

ENGLISHMAN (*Raising his voice*): I say: you see it's quite commonly known that in America one simply can't get into a hotel without a woman with a bag—I mean, get into a bag—no no, get into a woman—

COP: Stop! Now yuh talkin doity.

ENGLISHMAN: I mean—it's jolly difficult to express the idea—

COP: Nevuh mine duh idear. Gowon.

ENGLISHMAN:—Well; and so, being as it happens extremely anxious to get into a hotel, I was for taking no chances—

COP: Ware's duh wummun.

ENGLISHMAN (*In astonishment*): Woman? Did you say "woman"?

COP: Y-a-s.

ENGLISHMAN: What on earth do you mean, old egg? What woman?

COP: Duh wummun youse wus takin tuh duh hotel—is she in duh trunk?

ENGLISHMAN: In the trunk? —A woman? You're spoofing, old thing—

COP (*Approaching, bores the* ENGLISHMAN'S *entrails with the muzzle of the revolver*): Kummon, wut wus youse carryin in duh trunk.

ENGLISHMAN: But—you don't seriously suppose I'd be such a bally ass as to carry a trunk on my back with a woman inside it!—A trunk—with a woman—on my back—ha-ha-ha; that's not half bad, you know—

COP (*Disgustedly, shoving the* ENGLISHMAN *aside*): Get ovuh dare. (*He steps rapidly to the trunk—peers in; starts, gasps—recoils, dropping his revolver—and falls, lifeless, beside the trunk. Darkness.*)

VOICE OF HIM: Well?

VOICE OF ME: I liked the Englishman. But where were the eels?

VOICE OF HIM: The eels were in the tree.

VOICE OF ME: But I didn't see any tree.

VOICE OF HIM: There aren't any trees on 5th Avenue below 59th Street.

VOICE OF ME: Then what you said wasn't true.

VOICE OF HIM: But it wasn't untrue.

VOICE OF ME: Why not?

VOICE OF HIM: I said there weren't any mice, and there weren't. That was true, wasn't it?

VOICE OF ME: O yes—I'd forgotten about the mice.

VOICE OF HIM: And about the wheelbarrow too, I dare say? —But I hadn't.

VOICE OF ME: Why should you? After all, you invented it; and the two umbrellas and the tightrope and everything else. In fact, what's queer is, that I should have remembered those eels.

VOICE OF HIM: Allow me to remark that I consider your remembrance of those eels a great and definite compliment. Next we have . . .

scene 7

(*Scene: A* U, *whose arms are alleys of distance and which is recognized as the promenade deck of a transatlantic liner seen from the bow.*

At the end of each alley [or arm of the U] *a rotund cigar-smoking* PASSENGER, *violently attired in an outrageous cap checked stockings and unblownnose breeches, is advancing with six balloons.*

The two PASSENGERS *meet in the foreground at the apex of the* U, *halt and converse. Each then explodes a balloon belonging to the other by touching it with his cigar, rounds the apex of the* U *and continues down the opposite side of the deck from which he emerged, until he reaches the end of his arm of the* U. *He then aboutfaces, retraverses this arm and arrives once more at the apex where he again meets the other* PASSENGER, *halts, converses, explodes a balloon and continues down the side of the deck for which he originally emerged.*

The scene comprises six meetings, six conversations and the exploding of all the balloons. The questioning PASSENGER *is played by the* DOCTOR.)

FIRST CONVERSATION: What's new? —Nothing.

Business? —Soso.
Happy? —Not yet.
Solong. —Solong.
   SECOND CONVERSATION: What's new? —Nothing.
Married? —Uh-huh.
Children? —I dunno.
Solong. —Solong.
   THIRD CONVERSATION: What's new? —Nothing.
Happy? —Soso.
Retired? —Not yet.
Solong. —Solong.
   FOURTH CONVERSATION: What's new? —Nothing.
Divorced? —Uh-huh.
Blond? —I dunno.
Solong. —Solong.
   FIFTH CONVERSATION: What's new? —Nothing.
Millionaire? —Soso.
Happy? —Not yet.
Solong. —Solong.
   SIXTH CONVERSATION: What's new? —Nothing.
Married? —Uh-huh.
How long? —I dunno.
Solong.—Solong.   (*Darkness.*)
   VOICE OF ME: What was that about?
   VOICE OF HIM: Chaos—not to be confused with manifold mendacities fakes counterfeit or spurious imitations such as Cosmos or commongarden ordinary unassuming Kolynos. Cheer up: The Other Play is almost played.
   VOICE OF ME: What's coming now?
   VOICE OF HIM (*Utters a profound sigh*): Ah—if I only knew.
   VOICE OF ME: Do you mean to say you don't know?
   VOICE OF HIM: Excuse me: I was quoting.—The next scene, involving all sorts of allusions to subjects of unequal importance appertaining to the past the present and the future, calls for your undivided attention. I may add that it was composed by John Dewey—the world renowned authority on education and internationally famous author of such inspiring pamphlets as: "Into a Butterfly, or The Worm Will Turn"—in collaboration with C. Petronius, the talented writer of fairytales, on a desert island in the South Pacific during the eventful summer of 3, Eastern Standard Time, and deals in a vivid way with the loves of Spurius Lartius. . . .

scene 8

(Scene: The Old Howard's conception of a luxurious Roman villa, columns 'n' everything, with a protracted glimpse of Tiber and Coliseum plus a few mountains in what should be and is not the distance. Two CENTURIONS *are shooting craps. Enter to them, lazily and unnoticed by them, an* ETHIOPIAN *slave: he stands and regards the game with accumulating interest.)*

ETHIOPIAN *(Finally beside himself with emotion)*: Dirry me.

FIRST CENTURION *(Looking up)*: Hello Sam. *(Picking up the dice, he rolls)*

SECOND CENTURION *(Also looking up)*: Hello Sam. Where yuh goin? *(He rolls)*

ETHIOPIAN: Hello boize. Ah ain goin nowhere.

FIRST CENTURION: Want to come in Sam? *(Rolls)*

ETHIOPIAN: Well ah doan mind if ah does. *(He produces an elaborate pocketbook)* How much you boize playin for?

BOTH CENTURIONS: Two bits.

ETHIOPIAN *(Producing a coin)*: Yoh faded. Now len me dem dice, fellah, ah feels de speerit on me—*(He takes the dice from the* FIRST CENTURION; *heavenwarding his eyes, kisses the dice: murmurs)* All sweet ainjills come sit on deez two babies —. *(Rolls)*

SECOND CENTURION: You lose. *(Enter two* FAIRIES, *in scarlet togas, with lightningrods. The* CENTURIONS *nudge each other—hastily pick up the dice and start out.)*

ETHIOPIAN *(Also going, murmurs en route, glancing at the* FAIRIES*)*: If daze anything worse dan Christians, it certainly am peddyrasts.

FIRST FAIRY *(Soprano)*: Where IS he.

SECOND FAIRY *(Calmly, alto)*: I don't know my dear.

FIRST: You were with him yesterday.

SECOND: I was not, dear. I haven't seen him since day before yesterday.

FIRST: You're lying to me, Tib.

SECOND: I am not, Claud.

FIRST: O dear O dear—I could just cry. *(He whimpers)*

SECOND *(Consolingly)*: Never mind, Claud darling.

FIRST: If he hadn't promised me; but he did—he absolutely promised me he'd be here at four o'clock sharp.

SECOND: He told ME four fifteen.

FIRST: O, so YOU'RE invited.

SECOND: Of course I'm invited. Why do you suppose I'm here, you stupid creature?

FIRST: Well, really—I think he might have told me. The very idea!—But I won't be treated this way, I won't stand it another instant, I won't, I WON'T—

SECOND: But listen dear—he didn't tell ME. . . .

FIRST: Tell you? What? What do you mean?

SECOND (*With dignity*): That YOU would be here.

FIRST: I don't care. It's entirely different, with you. Besides, my nerves are on edge and everybody knows it—(*Enter a* THIRD, *portly* FAIRY)

THIRD FAIRY: Hello Tib dear. Hello Claud, what's the matter dear?

FIRST: It's just too awful.

THIRD (*Severely*): Why is Claud crying, Tib? What HAVE you done?

SECOND: Now listen Con, I SWEAR I'm innocent. . . .

FIRST (*Sobbing*): If—he—hadn't—promised—

THIRD: You mustn't cry this way, Claud, it ruins your complexion.

FIRST (*As before*): I—know—it does.

THIRD: Here dear, take my handkerchief—just blow your nose and brace up. (CLAUD, *sobbing, blows his nose.*) That's better, isn't it.—Now tell me what's wrong between you and Tib.

SECOND: I SWEAR I'm innocent, Con, I SWEAR—

THIRD: Hush, Tib! Tell me Claud, speak right out dear and don't be afraid.

FIRST: It's . . . not Tib . . . it's—

SECOND: There now! Didn't I TELL you I was innocent?

THIRD (*Impatiently*): Will you be still, Tibby?—What IS it Claud, tell Connie.

FIRST: O Con dear, I'm so nervous.

THIRD: Now don't be silly, Claud. Don't cry any more darling. I'm sure everything will be all right.

FIRST: He—he prom-

THIRD: Who promised?

FIRST: Suh—Caesar—

THIRD: Well, what about Caesar?

FIRST: —Pruh-promised he'd be—here at fuh-four sharp.

SECOND: He told me four fifteen. Are you invited?

THIRD: Invited? Of course. He's coming at four thirty.

FIRST: Coming! O, how w-o-n-d-e-r-f-u-l.

THIRD: There now, don't cry any more Claudie; everything will be all right.—By the way, have either of you girls read If Winter Comes?

SECOND: I haven't. It sounds lovely.

FIRST (*Cheering up*): What a heavenly title.

THIRD: I just knew you'd want to read it, both of you—

SECOND: Have you got it on you, Con?

FIRST: Do give it to me first Con; you know I'm so nervous, I must have something to make me forget this horrible tragedy—

THIRD: It's Caesar's book, dear. He lent it to me yesterday to read.

SECOND: Lend it to me, Con—

FIRST: No, to me—

THIRD: I'd simply love to lend it to both of you if I had it, but I gave it back.

SECOND: That was horrid of you Con.

THIRD: Now Tib, I just couldn't help myself and you know I'm not to blame.

FIRST: But you might perfectly well have borrowed it for a long time; Caesar wouldn't have cared.

THIRD: Caesar will lend it to both of you girls, if you ask him nicely.—That's what I wanted to tell you before he arrives.

FIRST: O goody goody! I'm so nervous I just can't bear to wait another minute. (*Enter a* FOURTH, *excited* FAIRY)

FOURTH FAIRY: Hello Con, hello Tib and Claud: listen, have all you girls heard the news?

FIRST: What news, Gus dear?

FOUTH: Mercy, haven't you heard! Why it's all over town—

SECOND: What is?

THIRD: Tell us quickly, Gus.

FOURTH: —EVERYONE'S talking about it.

TRIO: Tell us, tell us—

FOURTH (*archly, finger at lip*): Will you give me a big kiss, every one of you, if I tell—?

TRIO: Yes yes yes—. (*They cover him with kisses*) What is it?

FOURTH: Guess.

THIRD: Are the baths going to be renovated?

SECOND: Is Caesar sick?

FIRST (*Rapturously*): Will he whip us?

FOURTH: No. You're ALL of you wrong, every one of you.

THIRD: WHAT is it?

FIRST: O you're so exasperating.

SECOND: It's just mean of you to keep it to yourself, Gus—

FOURTH (*Tantalizingly*): Shall I tell?

TRIO: Yes yes yes.

FOURTH: All right. (*With enormous solemnity*) Daisy's dead.

TRIO: Dead!

SECOND: I don't believe it.

FIRST: I was with him only yesterday.

FOURTH: Well, he's dead.

THIRD: Impossible!

FIRST: How did he die?

FOURTH (*Proudly, with solemnity*): Choked to death.

SECOND AND THIRD: O-o.

FIRST (*Rolling up his eyes and clasping his hands, murmurs rapturously*): What a b-e-a-u-t-i-f-u-l death! (*Trumpets without: enter majestically the onorevole* BENITO MUSSOLINI, *more or less in the costume of Napoleon and with the traditional pose of that hero—"hands locked behind, As if to balance the prone brow Oppressive with its mind" (Browning)—but also wearing, at the end of a lightningrod, a halo, probably in token of his Christlike role in raising Italia from the dead. Changing his pose, he sticks one hand in his abdomen, à la numerous portraits of the mighty Buonaparte.*)

FOUR FAIRIES (*Executing, more or less together, the fascist or Roman salute*): Hail, Caesar.

MUSSOLINI (*Who is played by the* DOCTOR): Hello girls, have you heard the news?

SECOND FAIRY (*Repeating the fascist salute*): We have, Caesar.

FIRST (*Ditto*): Gus told us, Caesar.

FOURTH (*Ditto*): I told them, Caesar, about Daisy.

MUSSOLINI: Daisy be damned, shrimp.

FOUR FAIRIES (*Saluting*): Aye, Caesar, aye.

MUSSOLINI: I'm talking about something important, damn it all.

THIRD FAIRY (*Timidly*): If it is permitted to ask—have you lynched some more communists, Caesar?

FIRST (*Ecstatically*): That would be just too wonderful!

MUSSOLINI: Lynched? I've roasted 'em alive, lozenge.

FOUR FAIRIES (*Whisper*): O, w-o-n-d-e-r-f-u-l.

MUSSOLINI: Fifty today, sixty-nine yesterday, three hundred and forty-six the day before: that makes—six and nine are fifteen carry one, and four is five, eleven, five is sixteen, one and three is four—four hundred and sixty-five exactly, not including women and children.

FOUR FAIRIES (*As before*): Div-ine.

MUSSOLINI: Nonsense, it's all a trick—anyone with brains can do it.

FOURTH FAIRY (*Involuntarily*): O—no!

MUSSOLINI: I say they can, turnip! (*Wheeling, shouts*) CAMERIERE! (*Enter a saluting fascist*)

FASCIST: Aye Caesar.

MUSSOLINI: We know it's you.—A Mussolini special. (*Exit* FASCIST, *walking backwards with some difficulty and saluting at the same time*)

SECOND FAIRY (*Giggling embarrassedly*): If it—if it is permit-

MUSSOLINI: Speak, thumbprint.

SECOND FAIRY (*Trembling*): Can Caesar do—

MUSSOLINI: Caesar can do anything, nitwit. (*Reenter* FASCIST, *bearing on a tray one liqueurglass and a fivegallon can which is labelled in huge black letters CASTOR OIL.* MUSSOLINI *takes the glass.*) Pour, slave. (*The* FASCIST *pours*) —Basta! (*Lifting the brimming glass,* MUSSOLINI *intones*) To S.M. Il Re! (MUSSOLINI *and everyone else salute:* MUSSOLINI *drains the glass at a gulp—hands it to the* FASCIST, *who exits with tray, walking backwards and saluting with his left hand at the same time*) That's better! (MUSSOLINI *smacks his lips*) What was I saying, girls?

THIRD FAIRY: The news, Caesar.

MUSSOLINI: O yes; well I've forgotten now. Something of no importance—. (*A terrific crash, accompanied by screams, shrieks, screechings, shouts, gasps, grunts, groans, moans and similar expressions of woe, occurs and is immediately followed by piercing yells of "POLICE!" "MURDER!" "FIRE!"—The* FOUR FAIRIES *start almost out of their skins.*)

THIRD FAIRY: Whatever was that perfectly frightful noise!

SECOND: Wasn't it ghastly?

FIRST (*Whimpers*): O I'm so nervous.

MUSSOLINI: CAMERIERE! (*Enter saluting* FASCIST) What in Hell was that?

FASCIST (*Saluting*): Rome, Caesar.

FOURTH FAIRY: I was sure something terrible had happened—

MUSSOLINI: Silence, geranium!—What about Rome, slave? What's it making that noise for?

FASCIST (*Saluting*): Rome can't help it, Caesar.

MUSSOLINI: Can't help it, onion! —Whaduhyuhmean Rome can't help it!

FASCIST (*Saluting*): It's burning, Caesar.

FOUR FAIRIES: —Burning!—

MUSSOLINI (*Drawing himself up to his full majestic shortness roars*): SILENZIO! (*The* FAIRIES *cringe before him: he surveys them with utter contempt—wheeling, speaks in a businesslike tone*) Knew I'd forgotten something. —Rome, of course. (*To* FASCIST) Well, what are you waiting for?

FASCIST (*Saluting*): The great Caesar's orders.

MUSSOLINI: Orders, my orders—yes, naturally. (*Removing his Napoleonic hat, scratches his head*) Pray to the Gods! And hurry up about it. (*The* FASCIST *backs salutingly off, colliding with an entering* MESSENGER *who, disentangling himself, falls on one knee, saluting*)

MESSENGER: Hail, Caesar, reign forever.

MUSSOLINI: Cough up, snowdrop, what's on your mind?

MESSENGER: My lord, the lady Poppaea craves an audience.

MUSSOLINI: I don't get yuh, kid: slip it to me easy, I'm shortwaisted.

MESSENGER: Well—. (*Simpering*) She craves to see your highness.

MUSSOLINI: She ought to be ashamed of herself. Say that my highness is invisible.

MESSENGER: I have already said that, Caesar. (*He laughs foolishly*) Yet she persists, forsooth.

MUSSOLINI: Try again, old dear. Tell her I've got the mumps or something. (*A second frightful crash—followed by darkness*)

VOICE OF HIM: On the whole, how did that scene strike you?

VOICE OF ME: Not very favourably.

VOICE OF HIM: Really?

VOICE OF ME: You can see for yourself how silly it is to try to make a critic out of me.

VOICE OF HIM: I shall confine myself, however, to stating that your disapproval comes as a surprise; considering the allpervading atmosphere of inherent spiritual nobility—not to mention the profound, deepspread, underlying religious significance of the thing. Possibly you didn't realize that those lads in the passionate nighties were Ecce Homos: the only lineal descendants of the ancient and honourable house of Savoy?

VOICE OF ME: I hate history.

VOICE OF HIM: So do I.—Europe, Africa, Asia: continents of Give. America: the land of Keep—Keep in step Keep moving Keep young Keep your head Keep in touch with events Keep smiling Keep your shirt on Keep off the grass Keep your arms and limbs inside the car. National disease: constipation. National recreation: the movies. National heroes: Abraham Lincoln who suppressed his own smut, George Washington who bought slaves with rum and Congressman Mann who freed the slaves. National anthem: You Forgot To Remember. National advertisement: The Spirit of '76—a man with a flag a man with a fife and a drummerboy —caption: General Debility Youthful Errors and Loss of Manhood. . . . Lettergo, professor!

scene 9

(*Scene: The stage as in Scene 1.
Enter two figures, the* GENTLEMAN
[*played by the* DOCTOR] *and the* INTER-
LOCUTOR [*played by* HIM].

INTERLOCUTOR: On the whole, how does this city strike you?

GENTLEMAN: Strike me—are you inferring that I have defective eyesight? Do you think I'm mad? Eh?

INTERLOCUTOR: I wasn't inferring that—

GENTLEMAN: Strike me! (*He snorts*) How does it strike you —how does it strike anybody? (*With vast contempt*) —As a dungheap!

INTERLOCUTOR: There is a great deal of misery—

GENTLEMAN: Is there. I dare say.

INTERLOCUTOR: —Among the native population, I mean.

GENTLEMAN: Let me tell you something: between you and me, after looking this place over, what seems extraordinary is that the men and women who have to spend their lives in it don't all of them commit suicide.

INTERLOCUTOR: Many of them do.

GENTLEMAN: I know I should, if I had to stay here.

INTERLOCUTOR: I take it this is your first visit—?

GENTLEMAN: Yes, and my last.

INTERLOCUTOR: Yes. And I can assure you that before the war this city was not only very gay but even beautiful.

GENTLEMAN: Damitall, that's what I always heard—and here I go out of my way to come; and what do I find? A few motheaten streets and a couple of rusty restaurants. (*Philosophically*) Serves me right. That's what a fellow gets in this world when he takes anybody else's word for anything.

INTERLOCUTOR: But my dear sir, you forget the war—times have changed—you see before you the fruits of defeat—

GENTLEMAN (*Vehemently*): I do forget the war. And what's more, I see no reason why everybody else shouldn't. It would be a damn good thing for some of these people if they turned over a new leaf and showed a little life! Why, look here—. (*He plunges a hand into his outside jacket pocket: produces a fistful of paper money*) Look at this—

INTERLOCUTOR: Poo.

GENTLEMAN: Pooh nothing; it's no joke, let me tell you— why a fellow needs a trunk to carry a nickel's worth—

INTERLOCUTOR: You misunderstand me: I'm telling you that the unit of currency here is the poo.

GENTLEMAN: O, I see: poo—yes, of course.

INTERLOCUTOR: Do you know what the poo was equivalent to, before the war?

GENTLEMAN (*Nettled*): I don't know and I don't care! It's worthless now—

INTERLOCUTOR: Worthless? No; not exactly. Do you know what a mill is?

GENTLEMAN: I'll say I do. My old man made his dough in 'em. O boy.

INTERLOCUTOR: I meant another kind—we were speaking of currency: a mill in American money is the tenth part of a cent.

GENTLEMAN: O, currency—tenth part, sure. I get you.

INTERLOCUTOR: Well: if a mill were a hundred dollars, if it WERE—you understand?

GENTLEMAN: Hundred dollars, sure.

INTERLOCUTOR: A poo, at the present rate of exchange, would be worth slightly less than half of one-eighth of the sixteenth part of one mill.

GENTLEMAN: Hm. Yas. I dare say. Terrible, isn't it?

INTERLOCUTOR: It's a great deal more terrible than you or I imagine. But speaking of the war—

GENTLEMAN (*Turning on him, cries petulantly*): The war? The war's over, isn't it?

INTERLOCUTOR: Not in this part of the world, my friend. You have only to look about you to realize that—

GENTLEMAN: O well, if it isn't it ought to be, and remembering it won't do anybody any good—you'll agree to that?

INTERLOCUTOR: But one has to realize that people everywhere are hungry—that there are riots almost daily—

GENTLEMAN: Riots? What do you mean?

INTERLOCUTOR: I mean that people are rioting.

GENTLEMAN: You mean people are rioting—here are people, you and I, neither of whom (unless I'm very much mistaken) can be said by the most ignorant and uninformed person to be rioting.

INTERLOCUTOR: I refer to the poor. The unemployed. There are five hundred thousand of them in this city with nothing to eat, I believe.

GENTLEMAN: Do you? Let me tell you something: I believe nothing the newspapers say.

INTERLOCUTOR: It's a fact. I saw at least ten thousand only a few days ago—Monday, it was—demonstrating in front of the Crystal Hotel.

GENTLEMAN: Did you indeed. That happens to be my hotel.

INTERLOCUTOR: You have just moved in, perhaps?

GENTLEMAN: No, worse luck.

INTERLOCUTOR: May I ask how long you've been stopping at that hotel?

GENTLEMAN: You may. I've been there ever since I arrived. I arrived, lemme see: yes—last Saturday. I shall leave next Saturday. I should leave this minute if there was a decent train.

INTERLOCUTOR: The demonstration which I saw in front of your hotel occurred last Monday at about eleven in the morning.

GENTLEMAN: I saw nothing unusual at eleven in the morning. In fact, if I remember correctly, I was in bed at eleven in the morning.

INTERLOCUTOR: And you heard nothing unusual?

GENTLEMAN: I heard a mild rumpus of some sort—nothing to disturb myself about.

INTERLOCUTOR: A few weeks ago, I believe, they smashed your hotel and held up all the occupants, ladies included.

GENTLEMAN: I believe nothing unless I see it.—And do you believe the occupants of my hotel gave them anything?

INTERLOCUTOR: Several billion poo and a few thousand dollars . . . of course, the crowd may not have held up the people in bed; I don't know about that. The wisest thing, under the circumstances, might be to go to bed and stay there.

GENTLEMAN: My dear chap, I stay in bed when it pleases me to stay in bed; and I get up when I like to get up; and I read all the newspapers I can find—few enough, Heaven knows, in this godforsaken place—

INTERLOCUTOR: —And which you can understand.

GENTLEMAN: I beg your pardon?

INTERLOCUTOR: —All the newspapers in English.

GENTLEMAN: Naturally. What else should I read?—But as I was saying: I read them all, and I believe not a word in any of them.

INTERLOCUTOR: Then may I ask why you read them?

GENTLEMAN: Because in a hole like this there's nothing else to do. Besides which, let me tell you something: it rather amuses me to see how consistently they contradict each other. (*A dull booming hum is heard: the noise grows, thickens— within it, noises appear and disappear*)

INTERLOCUTOR: If, as I am led to believe, you enjoy seeing things for yourself, all you need do is wait here a few minutes. Because—do you hear that?

GENTLEMAN: I hear a noise; or if you like, I hear noises.

INTERLOCUTOR: Exactly. They're coming.

GENTLEMAN: They? Who's they?

INTERLOCUTOR: The mob.

GENTLEMAN: Well?

INTERLOCUTOR: Excuse me. I'm running along. In my experience, it's best to give these people a large berth.

GENTLEMAN: In that case, let me tell you something: I shall sit here and wait.

INTERLOCUTOR: Listen, don't be a fool: this is no laughing matter—clear out. (*The noises multiply, the noise deepens*) It's damned dangerous.

GENTLEMAN: Clear out? I shall do nothing of the kind. On the contrary, I shall sit on this box and watch this mob, as you call it. (*He sits down placidly on an old box*)

INTERLOCUTOR: Man! You're crazy—you don't know what you're doing. (*He tugs at the* GENTLEMAN'*s arm*)

GENTLEMAN: Although by your account crazy, I am sufficiently possessed of my senses to inquire why you don't go, if you don't want to stay?

INTERLOCUTOR: Idiot!—(*He stands irresolute, perplexed*) Here. (*He grabs out of his trouser pocket a minute gnarled loaf of coarse blackish bread. Shoves it into the* GENTLEMAN'*s hands.*)

GENTLEMAN: Why are you presenting me with this? (*He regards it distrustfully*) What is it?

INTERLOCUTOR: Bread you ass—it may save your life. Take it.

GENTLEMAN: Thanks, I'm not hungry. (*He inspects the loaf*) And if I were, I should not feel particularly inclined to eat this.

INTERLOCUTOR: You fool—throw it to them and run! (*He runs for his life, as a* MOB—*roaring, muttering, gesticulating —swarms upon the stage and curiously, gradually, fatally forms a semicircle to include the* GENTLEMAN: *beside whom, an immensely tall greenish mouldering* SHAPE *quaveringly spews itself upward*)

SHAPE: I'm hungry.

GENTLEMAN: Have you got anything to eat?

SHAPE: No.

GENTLEMAN: Then how foolish of you to be hungry— whereas, if you had something to eat, there'd be some sense in being hungry. (*The greenish tall mouldering* SHAPE *collapsingly sinks back into the* MOB: *a* SECOND SHAPE, *bluish and abrupt, emerges*)

SECOND SHAPE: I have nothing to eat.

GENTLEMAN: Why don't you eat nothing then? Do you want to be hungry? (*The* SECOND SHAPE *darts back into the* MOB. *A* WOMAN *appears in its place.*)

WOMAN: Give me a little piece of your bread.

GENTLEMAN (*Regarding her suspiciously*): How little a piece?

WOMAN: A crumb.

GENTLEMAN: A crumb indeed. What will a crumb do?

WOMAN: It will make me live for an hour.

GENTLEMAN: Ridiculous—if what you say were true, one could, simply by eating crumbs, live forever. (*Severely*) Don't forget, my dear woman, that there is such a thing as death.

(*The* WOMAN *disappears: an* OLD WOMAN *stands before the* GENTLEMAN)

OLD WOMAN: I'm dying.

GENTLEMAN: Are you? That's apropos of you.

OLD WOMAN: Dying yes. (*She nuzzles against him*) Do you understand?

GENTLEMAN (*Drawing back*): No I don't. And do you want to know why? Because, let me tell you something: I'm not dying myself. (*The* OLD WOMAN *falls and is swept back into the* MOB, *whose elements gyrate, intercreep and writhingly focus: a twisted whitish* SHAPE *spouts out*)

THIS SHAPE (*Pointing*): Bread.

GENTLEMAN: Yes, that's bread. Well?

THIS SHAPE: Give.

GENTLEMAN: Give what?

THIS SHAPE: Bread.

GENTLEMAN: Why should I—what's bread for?

THIS SHAPE: Eat.

GENTLEMAN: Quite right. Bread is to eat; in giving my bread, instead of eating it, I should, therefore, be doing something quite unspeakably stupid. (*This* SHAPE *spouts into the* MOB: *a* WHORE, *hollow, dilapidated, swims forward, ogling*)

WHORE (*Simpers*): Give me just a tiny nibble, dearie. I'll give you something very nice for it, darling.

GENTLEMAN: Well now, that's sensible. That's talking business. You're not like the rest of them. You're businesslike, intelligent: you make me a business proposition. Well, let's hear it: just what is your proposition?

WHORE: Give me the tiniest nibble and I'll give you one deep big nice kiss.

GENTLEMAN: Your proposition interests me. Let's go on with it: what will you give me for a big nibble?

WHORE: For a big nibble I'll let you kiss me till you're tired.

GENTLEMAN (*Holds up the loaf before her, speaks slowly*): And what would you do if I should give you all of this bread?

WHORE (*Shrugging*): I'd give some of it away. I couldn't eat that much bread. (*A* FOURTH SHAPE, *elbowing her violently aside, stands*)

GENTLEMAN (*Angrily, to* FOURTH SHAPE): Who are you?

FOURTH SHAPE: A human being.

GENTLEMAN (*With severity*): A being, my friend, is someone who exists; a being is someone alive. What makes you think that you're alive?

FOURTH SHAPE: I'm hungry.

GENTLEMAN: In that case, let me tell you something: what you say is sheer nonsense. Look at me—I'm not hungry. And I'm alive.

FOURTH SHAPE: No. You're not.

GENTLEMAN: What do you mean?

FOURTH SHAPE (*Slowly*): You're not alive.

GENTLEMAN: Of course I'm alive. Aren't people who eat bread alive?

FOURTH SHAPE: You're. Not eating. Bread.

GENTLEMAN: Because I'm not hungry, I'm not eating it now: I prefer to save it. But I assure you I shall eat it eventually, because I'm alive and this is bread.

FOURTH SHAPE (*Shakes his dark, gnarled face to left and right*): That's. Not. Bread.

GENTLEMAN: I never in all my life heard such dribble. And if it's not bread, pray what is it?

FOURTH SHAPE (*A slender mutilated finger, poking from one ragged toolong sleeve and gliding toward his filthy breast, points at his heart*): Me.

GENTLEMAN: All right then. In that case, it's more sensible that I should eat you than that you should eat yourself. (*He turns away*)

FOURTH SHAPE: Dead people don't. Need to eat.

GENTLEMAN (*Pettishly*): But I'm NOT dead, my dear fellow. On the contrary. I'm very much alive.

FOURTH SHAPE: Dead. You're dead, yes.

GENTLEMAN (*Shrugging*): The man is crazy. Here I am sitting not two feet away from him holding a piece of bread, and he tells me I'm dead. Why, you fool, I'm no more dead than yourself, in fact much less so.

FOURTH SHAPE: I'm hungry. (*His handless scarecrow sleeves gesture*) We're all hungry.

VOICES: Hungry. Yes. Eat.

GENTLEMAN (*Indignantly*): And what of that? Suppose you all ARE hungry and I'm not: what the devil difference does THAT make?

FOURTH SHAPE: You're not. Hungry. Only dead people. Aren't hungry.

GENTLEMAN: This is idiotic. You don't know what you're talking about, that's the whole truth of the matter—you can't listen to reason.

FOURTH SHAPE: Listen to me. I'll make you alive.

GENTLEMAN: No thanks. My mother did that for me, some time ago.

FOURTH SHAPE: I'll be your mother. Give me your bread. I'll make you alive.

GENTLEMAN: Give you my bread, eh? What would you do with my bread if I should give it to you?—Would you eat it?

FOURTH SHAPE: Eat. Bread. Yes.

GENTLEMAN: Then by your own account you'd be dead, stupid—Nobody wants to be dead.

FOURTH SHAPE: I. Want to be dead.

GENTLEMAN: O do you? Well, that's no reason why I should murder you.

FOURTH SHAPE: Yes, it's a reason.

GENTLEMAN: Now look here: I don't much fancy the idea of murdering somebody—

FOURTH SHAPE (*Pointing at his heart*): Look.—Here.

GENTLEMAN: Yes, it's very dirty. —And furthermore, I see no reason why I should be a murderer against my will.

FOURTH SHAPE (*Hoisting abruptly his sleeves, assumes the position of one crucified. As he does so, hands emerge.*): Murder. Me. Please. (*A rush of* SHAPES *around him: wallowing squirming wrestling to offer themselves—all stretching out their arms, all crying "Kill me!"*)

MOTHER WITH A CHILD: Kill my baby before you kill the others; please kill my baby first.

VOICE: No, me first.

ANOTHER VOICE: Me.

GENTLEMAN (*Rising, stands: trembling.—Furiously screams out.*): Am I God that I should strike you all dead?

MULTITUDE OF SHAPES (*In three huge cries*): Yes. You are God. Yes.

GIRL'S VOICE (*Shrill*): You are God himself.

A DARK VOICE: God is a man with a piece of bread.

GENTLEMAN: What is the—I don't—really, I don't understand you people—are you all crazy? Or am I crazy?

MULTITUDE OF SHAPES (*Together*): You are dead.

GENTLEMAN (*Utters a trivial brief cry*): Then damitall, kill yourselves! (*He hurls the loaf. The mass of pouncing scrambling wrestling screaming yearning* SHAPES *squirmingly bulges toward the missile; revolving furiously within itself, and rumbling choking roaring, gradually disappears. Snow begins falling. The* GENTLEMAN *stands for a minute, confused—presses his hands to his head in a brittle gesture. He sits down and stares before him, with arms folded. After a minute, his hands automatically begin unbuttoning the buttons of his waistcoat. Rising, staring fixedly at the audience, he takes off his jacket—drops it to one side. Then he takes off his waistcoat and drops it on top of the jacket. Sitting down, he begins automatically unlacing one shoe. A* POLICEMAN *timidly enters.*)

POLICEMAN (*Saluting, speaks with the utmost respect*): Pardon me, sir. May I ask what you are doing?

GENTLEMAN (*Looking up with vague eyes, does not stop unlacing*): Yes. I'm taking off my clothes.

POLICEMAN: Excuse me, sir; if I'm not mistaken it's rather cold to be undressing, isn't it? —It's snowing, sir, I believe.

GENTLEMAN (*Without looking up*): I can't help it. (*The snow falls more rapidly*)

POLICEMAN: Of course not, sir! But mightn't it be better to wait till you got home? (*Coaxingly*) It would be warmer, sir, much warmer.

GENTLEMAN: I can't wait—I mustn't wait. (*He jerks off one shoe: dropping it, begins unlacing rapidly the other*) I'm late already.

POLICEMAN: Beg pardon sir, for asking a question—if I may be so bold, why couldn't you wait? (*The* GENTLEMAN, *jerking off the other shoe, holds it in both hands. His eyes lift to the* POLICEMAN's *face. Dropping the shoe, he rises suddenly; stands, staring into the embarrassed eyes before him—the* PO-LICEMAN *blushes.*) Beg pardon; I mean (excuse me, sir, for suggesting)—it might be a trifle more decent.

GENTLEMAN (*In a low voice*): In that case, let me tell you something. (*Leaning toward the* POLICEMAN, *whispers loudly*) I've. Just. Been. Born. (*Hurriedly slips the suspenders from his shoulders—in another instant he steps quickly and automatically from his trousers. The* POLICEMAN *staggers. The* GEN-TLEMAN *drops his trousers: pauses, irresolute: after shivering doubtfully for a few seconds, he demands plaintively.*) If you please, what do babies were? (*The* POLICEMAN *quakes*) Very little babies? (*The* POLICEMAN *totters; pulling from his left hip-pocket a crucifix, clamps it in fervent fists. He falls on his knees, shutting his eyes, and removes his hat into which a great deal of snow immediately falls.*)

POLICEMAN (*Simply*): Now I lay me down to sleep. . . .

(*Curtain.*)

act III

scene 1

(*Scene: The room of Act I, further revolved so that the fourth or invisible wall is the door wall. The wall to the audience's right [corresponding to the door wall of Act I, Scene 4] is the solid wall. The middle wall is the mirror wall. The window wall is to the audience's left.* HIM'*s hat lies on the centre of the table where the automatic was lying at the end of Act I, Scene 4.*
ME *and* HIM *are seated at opposite ends of the sofa which is against the solid wall to the audience's right.*)

ME: Where I am I think it must be getting dark: I feel that everything is moving and mixing, with everything else.

HIM: I feel that it's very dark.

ME: Do you—feel?

HIM: Terribly dark.

ME: Are you a little afraid of the dark?

HIM: I've always been. (*The room darkens rapidly*) May I sit beside you?

ME: If you don't very much mind. (*He does so*)

HIM: A hand. Accurate and incredible.

ME (*To herself*): The dark is so many corners—

HIM: Here life is, moves; faintly. A wrist. The faint throb of blood, precise, miraculous.

ME (*As before*):—so many dolls, who move—

HIM: Curve. And they talk of dying! The blood delicately descending and ascending: making an arm. Being an arm. The warm flesh, the dim slender flesh filled with life, slenderer than a miracle, frailer.

ME (*As before*): —by Themselves.

HIM: These are the shoulders through which fell the world. The dangerous shoulders of Eve, in god's entire garden newly strolling. How young they are! They are shy, shyest, birdlike. Not shoulders, but young alert birds. (*The figures of* ME *and* HIM *are almost invisible*)

ME (*Almost inaudibly*): Darker.

HIM: A distinct throat. Which breathes. A head: small, smaller than a flower. With eyes and with lips. Lips more slender than light; a smile how carefully and slowly made, a smile made entirely of dream. Eyes deeper than Spring. Eyes darker than Spring, more new.

ME (*To herself*): We must go very carefully . . .

HIM: These, these are the further miracles—

ME (*Almost inaudibly*): . . . gradually . . .

HIM: —the breasts. Thighs. The ALL which is beyond comprehension—the ALL which is perpetually discovered, yet undiscovered: sexual, sweet. Alive!

ME (*Faintly*): . . . until light. (*Complete darkness. After a few moments her voice whispers with a sort of terror.*)

VOICE OF ME: What are you saying.

VOICE OF HIM (*Subdued, intense, trembling*): Not saying: praying . . . (*The voice hardens*) . . . now I lay you down to not sleep—. (*Silence. Then a scream: the room suddenly opens into total visibility.* ME *stands—terse erect panting—beside the sofa on which* HIM *sprawls.*)

ME: No!

HIM (*Slowly collecting himself rises slowly*): Are you sure? Are you terribly, wonderfully sure?

ME: Sure. Yes. (*A pause. She walks upstage to the mirror. He crosses the room to the table; takes and lights a cigarette.*)

HIM (*Standing at the window, laughs briefly*): Mademoiselle d'Autrefois, purveyor of mental meanderings and bodily bliss to Ahsh E. M. His Imperial Majesty, the Man in the Mirror!

ME (*At the mirror*): What do you mean.

HIM: I mean—. (*Twirls the match out*)—That you have been the mistress of someone.

ME: Are you terribly, wonderfully sure?

HIM: Of that? Yes. I am sure.

ME: I gave him everything, you mean?

HIM: I mean just that. Once upon a time.

ME: How extraordinary—and who were you, once upon a time?

HIM (*Flicks the ash*): Why do you ask?

ME: Because—shall I tell you?

HIM: If you wish.

ME: The more I remember, the more I am sure it never happened.

HIM (*Simply*): Dead.

ME (*Turning from the mirror, walks toward him slowly*): And now everything changes. And I can distinguish between things. O, I begin to see things very clearly. —You are just as you were.

HIM: I understand less and less.

ME: Do you? It's clear now—can't you see?

HIM: My eyes are very bad today as the blind man said.

ME: That's what he said. (*Stands before him*) And this is what you say: "May I kiss you?"

HIM: I say that to whom? . . . Excuse me; will you have a cigarette?

ME (*Refuses with a curt gesture*): You simply say it.

HIM: I am very dull. . . . May I kiss you?

ME: No. Because I'm not, any more—this isn't me. But somewhere me is, and it would be jealous if you kissed somebody else.

HIM (*Cutting a laugh in two*): "Jealous!" Why not the truth?

ME: You are making a mistake.

HIM: Probably.

ME: There's nobody else. Really: so far as I know.

HIM: I should prefer that you did not lie to me.

ME: Yes?

HIM: I should.

ME (*She looks entirely at him*): I'm not lying.

HIM (*Looking intently at her*): No, you're not lying.

ME (*Quietly*): The snow did it, or it was the rain—Something outside of me and you: and we may as well let Something alone. (*She walks toward the sofa*)

HIM: That would be pleasant to believe.

ME (*To herself*): Which moves quietly, when everything is asleep; folding hands . . . I don't know. Shutting flowers I guess, putting toys away. (*She sits, in one corner of the sofa*)

HIM: This is the end?

ME: Do you like to call it that?

HIM: Tell me, what is it, if it isn't the end?

ME: This might be where we begin.

HIM: To begin hurts. (*A pause*) Do you think that this folding and shutting Person, who moves, can take memories away?

ME: No. (*A pause. She smiles.*)—I feel as if we'd never lived: everything is so sure, so queer. (*Another pause*)

HIM: Everything will be queerer perhaps.

ME: Do you think?

HIM: When everything has stopped.

ME: Stopped?

HIM: When I and you are—so to speak—folded, with all our curves and gestures.

ME: —In the earth?

HIM (*Strolls toward the sofa*): Anywhere.

ME: Somewhere, in the Spring, you and I lying . . . together. . . .

HIM: And so exceedingly still.

ME (*Smiles, shaking her head*): No: there'll be things.

HIM (*Sitting opposite her*): Things?

ME: Trees pushing. And little creatures wandering busily in the ground, because everywhere it's Spring. (*Smiles*) They will go wandering into me and into you, I expect—roots and creatures and things—but I shan't mind.

HIM: No.

ME (*In a low voice*): If I'm with you.

HIM (*In a low voice*): It will all be gone then; then it will be too late. Think.

ME: . . . I don't want to think.

HIM: Lips, which touched—at first how lightly! What were lips distinctly slowly coming against more than lips; mouths, firmly living upon each other: the focussed Ourselves (alive proud deep bewildered) approaching gradually. Nearing, exquisitely and scarcely. Touching. And then—heartily announced by miles, by years, of strutting light—the minute instant, the enormous Now. . . . (*Pauses; smiles*) Only think, dear, of you and of me gone, like two kites when the string breaks, positively into nowhere. Shut like umbrellas. Folded like napkins.

ME (*Looking at him and away, speaks softly*): Only think, dear, that you and I have never been really in love. Think that I am not a bit the sort of person you think. Think that you fell in love with someone you invented—someone who wasn't me at all. Now you are trying to feel things; but that doesn't work, because the nicest things happen by themselves. You can't make them happen. I can't either, but I don't want to. And when you try to make them happen, you don't really fool yourself and certainly you don't fool me. That's one thing about me. I'm not clever and I don't try to make things happen. —Well, you made a mistake about me and I know that. But the fact is, you know you made a mistake. Everybody knows it. . . . Think what is: think that you are now talking very beautifully through your hat.

HIM (*His glance travels to the table and returns to her*): You are a very remarkable person—among other reasons, because you can make me afraid.

ME: I'm not, and I don't want to be, remarkable. What you really think about me—and won't admit that you think—is true.

HIM: Don't you understand—

ME: I don't. I feel. That's my way and there's nothing remarkable about it: all women are like that.

HIM: Noone is like you.

ME: Pooh. I don't flatter myself—not very much. I know perfectly well it's foolish of you to waste your time with me, when there are people who will understand you. And I know I can't, because things were left out of me. —What's the use of being tragic? You know you aren't sad, really. You know what you really are, and really you're always sure of yourself: whereas I'm never sure. —If anybody were going to be tragic it ought to be me. I know that perfectly well. I've never done anything and I don't believe I ever will. But you can do things. Noone can make you unsure of yourself. You know you will go on, and all your life you've known.

HIM (*Trembling, looks at his hands*): May I tell you a great secret?

ME: A secret?

HIM: All my life I've wondered if I am any good. If my head and my heart are made out of something firmer or more living than what I see everywhere covering itself with hats and with linen. —If all the capable and little and disgusting minds which, somehow, are responsible for the cities and the countries in which I exist, have not perhaps also manufactured this thing—this bundle of wishes—which I like to call "myself." If my arms dreams hands exist with an intensity differing from or beyond the intensity of any other arms dreams hands. . . .

You cannot imagine how disagreeable it is to wonder—to look about you, at the eyes and the gestures which promenade themselves in streets and in houses, and to be afraid. To think: "Am I also one of these, a doll, living in a doll world, doomed to be undressed, dressed, spanked, kissed, put to bed?" (*Trembling, wipes carefully with his handkerchief a sweating forehead*) You can't imagine how disagreeable it is. Suppose that you spent your life buying a dress. Suppose that at last you found the precise and wonderful dress which you had dreamed of, and suppose that you bought it and put it on and walked in it everywhere and everywhere you saw thousands of people all of whom were wearing your dress.

ME: You mean I'm like everybody else.

HIM (*Fiercely*): I mean that you have something which I supremely envy. That you are something which I supremely would like to discover: knowing that it exists in itself as I do not exist and as I never have existed. How do I know this? Because through you I have come to understand that whatever I may have been or may have done is mediocre. (*Bitterly*) You have made me realize that in the course of living I have created several less or more interesting people—none of whom was myself.

ME (*With a brief gesture*): O dear. Am I like that?

HIM: Like nothing.

ME: Please don't talk to me this way. I really don't understand. And I think you don't understand me, very well ... nothing is sure.

HIM (*Rising, smiles*): Limbo, the without pain and joyless unworld, lady. In one act: or, my life is made of glass.

ME (*Rising, moves; stands beside him*): Your—what?

HIM (*Carefully looking into her helpless lifted eyes, speaks carefully*): I mean a clock ticking. Words which were never written. Cries heard through a shut window. Forgotten. Winter. Flies hanging mindless to walls and ceiling around a stove. Laughter of angels. Eheu fugaces. Glass flowers. (*He walks to the table and picks up his hat. Turning, makes for the invisible door. ME steps in front of him quickly.*)

ME: I have no mind. I know that. I know I'm not intelligent, and that you liked me for something else. There isn't any sense in my asking—I ask merely because I want to. I know I haven't any brains and really I don't care. I've seen women with brains and they're miserable, or anyway they look so—I don't know; it might be nice to have a mind sometimes. Please don't think I'm unhappy, because I'm not, and I'm not trying to make you unhappy. I know what I'm really like and what's more I know that you know—we're not fooling ourselves. But what you're really like I don't know; and that doesn't make me unhappy either: I don't care. I know part of you and I'm glad. As a matter of fact I'm rather proud. I think I know a great deal—for instance, if I ask you something you won't mind. And if my asking hurt you, I wouldn't care—I'm like that; it's me. I'm glad everything's over: because I've loved you very much, I'm glad there'll be nothing except memories. . . . You know what I liked best about you, what I will always like and will always remember. It's your hands—you know that and I tell you. Tell me something. Because it doesn't matter and you're going, tell me one thing. Tell me (as if I was dead and you were talking to someone else with your hands on her breasts) what there was, once, about me.

HIM (*After a short pause*): I hoped that I had—perhaps—told you.

ME: Listen. (*Earnestly, staring with entire seriousness into his eyes, almost whispers*) It's snowing: think. Just think of people everywhere and houses and rivers and trees and the mountains and oceans. Then think of fingers—millions—out of somewhere quietly and quickly coming, hurrying very carefully. . . . Think of everywhere fingers touching; fingers, skilfully gently everything—O think of the snow coming down beautifully and beautifully frightening ourselves and turning dying and love and the world and me and you into five toys. . . . Touch me a little. (*Taking his right wrist, she puts its hand against her dress*) It will be so pleasant to dream of your hands. For a hundred years.

HIM (*Whispers*): Dreams don't live a hundred years.

ME: Don't they? (*Smiles. Lets his wrist, hand, drop.*) Perhaps mine does. (*Strolling to the table, opens the box; taking, lights a cigarette; quickly blows out the match*) It's very late, I think. (*His shutting face whitens—putting on his hat, he goes out through the invisible door; stands, facing the audience.* ME *unsteadily crosses the room to the sofa. Darkness.*)

VOICE OF ME: If I had a mind, every morning I'd jump out of bed and hurry to a sort of secret drawer, where I kept my mind because someone might steal it. Then I'd open the drawer with a key and find my mind safe. But to make sure,

I'd take it out of the box where it lived—because if I had a mind I'd be very careful of it for fear it might break—and I'd go to the window with this little mind of mine, and holding it very carefully I'd look through the window out over the roofs (with smoke coming up out of all the chimneys slowly and maybe a street where people moved carefully in the sunlight, in the morning).

scene 2   (*Scene: The three rocking knitting* FIGURES, *facing the picture with their backs to the audience. Both heads are in the picture and the* WOMAN's *eyes are closed.*)

FIRST FIGURE: I held my husband up to the light yesterday and saw through him.

SECOND: What did you see?

THIRD: Your Hole appearance depends upon your hair.

FIRST: I saw father eating a piece of asparagus.

SECOND: Your husband's a landscape gardener?

THIRD: It's off because it's out.

FIRST: Not exactly. He does something in the interests of science.

SECOND: Really?—What does he do?

FIRST: I'm not quite sure . . . something about guineapigs I think.

SECOND: About guineapigs? How fascinating.

THIRD: Happiness in every box.

FIRST: Yes I think he does something to them so they'll have children—

SECOND: Not really!

THIRD: A pure breath is good manners.

FIRST: —because you see he wants them to have children in the interests of science.

SECOND: How remarkable. I didn't suppose guineapigs COULD have children.

FIRST: I didn't either when I married him, but George says he doesn't see why guineapigs can't have children if children can have guineapigs.

THIRD: A clean tooth never decays.
SECOND: DO children have guineapigs?
FIRST: O yes, more's the pity. Mine often have it.
THIRD: Your nails show your refinement.
SECOND: Badly?

scene 3   (*Scene: Le Père Tranquille [Les Halles].* WHORES *asleep. Music asleep. A* WAITER *asleep. Two customers, a* BLOND GONZESSE *and the* GENTLEMAN *of Act II, Scene 9, sit side by each at a corner table on which are two whiskies and an ashreceiver. A bell rings violently and a* HEADWAITER *rushes into the room.*)

HEADWAITER: Psst! (*Exit. The* WHORES *yawn, roll off their chairs and begin dancing with one another half asleep. The* PIANIST, *starting to a sitting position, bangs out chords—the* VIOLINIST, *reaming his eyes, breaks into tune—the* DRUMMER, *shoving back his hair, swats the cymbals. Awakened by this racket, the* WAITER *gets up and adjusts his tie in a mirror: turning, moves glasses aimlessly here and there on tables.* TWO FEMALE VOICES *are heard in the vicinity of the doorway.*)

FIRST FEMALE VOICE: Of course I know him. He's the man from whom Belasco steals his ideas.

SECOND FEMALE VOICE: Steals whose ideas?

FIRST FEMALE VOICE: Belasco's. (*The owners of the voices, a* FAIRLY YOUNG WOMAN *and an* OLDER WOMAN, *enter, followed by the obsequiously ushering* HEADWAITER)

HEADWAITER (*Making, unnoticed by the new arrivals, a sign of negation to music and* WHORES): Bonsoir mesdames. Par ici mesdames? (*He guides his prey to a table in the centre of the room. The* WHORES *and music cease their activities and resume their slumbers.*)

OLDER: Boan swaah.

HEADWAITER (*Ostentatiously presenting menus, as the new arrivals seat themselves*): Voici mesdames. (*Placing himself at the* OLDER's *elbow, he obsequiously threatens*) Qu'est-ce que c'est mesdames? (*Both* WOMEN *pick up menus. Both study their menus attentively*)

OLDER (*Absentmindedly*): Let me see. . . . (*She adjusts a lorgnette*) Y-e-s. (*Looking up*) Donny mwah un omb.

HEADWAITER (*Feigning pleasure*): Un homme. Très bien. Et pour madame?

FAIRLY YOUNG (*Flustered*): What are you having Sally?

OLDER (*Laying down menu and lowering lorgnette*): An omb, dear, as usual.

FAIRLY YOUNG: That's not a bad idea. (*Engagingly*) I'll have the same.

OLDER (*Interpreting*): Ong kore un omb.

HEADWAITER (*As before*): Ça fait deux hommes; bien mesdames. (*To* OLDER) Et comment madame désire-t-elle son homme?

OLDER (*Without hesitation*): Stewed, seal voo play.

HEADWAITER (*To* FAIRLY YOUNG): Et madame?

FAIRLY YOUNG: What does he want to know?

OLDER: He says how do you want your omb.

FAIRLY YOUNG (*Puzzled and embarrassed*): My, what?

OLDER: Your omb, your man.

FAIRLY YOUNG: O—my man—yes . . . how are you having yours?

OLDER: I'm having mine stewed because I like them that way, I think they're nicest when they're stewed.

FAIRLY YOUNG (*Doubtfully*): I think they're nice that way too.

OLDER: Have yours any way you like, dear.

FAIRLY YOUNG: Yes . . . let me see. (*Pause*) I think I'll have mine boiled.

OLDER (*Interpreting*): Voo donny ray poor mwah un omb stewed, a, poor moan ammy, un omb boiled.

HEADWAITER (*As before*): Bien madame. Et comme boisson, madame?

OLDER: What do you want to drink, dear?

HEADWAITER (*Interpolating*): Une bonne bouteille de champagne, n'est-ce pas, madame?

FAIRLY YOUNG: I don't care.

OLDER: A voo donny ray, avek sellah, oon bootay der Ayvyon.

HEADWAITER (*Almost bursting with rage*): Merci mesdames. (*Turning to the waiting* WAITER) Bring two men immediately for these ladies and have one of the men boiled and the other stewed.

WAITER (*Saluting*): Benissimo, sehr gut. (*He vanishes*)

OLDER (*Produces and opens a cigarettecase: offers it*): Will you have a cigarette?

FAIRLY YOUNG (*Hastily, producing ditto*): Try one of mine. They're camels.

OLDER: Thank you, I think I prefer lucky strikes. (*Each lights her own cigarette*) Well, dear. How do you like Paris?

FAIRLY YOUNG: I think Paris is darling. I've met so many people from New York.

OLDER: Yes, Paris is certainly cosmopolitan.

FAIRLY YOUNG: O, very.

OLDER (*After a pause*): Have you been here long?

FAIRLY YOUNG: Only a few days. Dick and I arrived last— when was it—let me see: today is . . . Thursday. . . .

OLDER: Today is Tuesday.

FAIRLY YOUNG: Is today really Tuesday?

OLDER: Today must be Tuesday, because Monday was yesterday. I know, because yesterday I had a fitting on a dress I bought at Poiret's. You should see it—

FAIRLY YOUNG: O dear, then I missed an appointment at the hairdresser's if today is Tuesday. Well, I'll go tomorrow. . . . What were we talking about? I didn't mean to interrupt.

OLDER: Let me see . . . O I asked you if you'd been here long, that was it.

FAIRLY YOUNG: O yes, of course. —Why no, Dick and I arrived . . . last Friday, I guess it was—on the Aquitania.

OLDER: I came on the Olympic myself.

FAIRLY YOUNG: Really.

OLDER: Did you have a pleasant trip?

FAIRLY YOUNG (*Enthusiastically*): Simply glorious. Dick was sick all the time.

OLDER: How silly of him. (*A pause*) I suppose you've been about a great deal since you arrived?

FAIRLY YOUNG: O yes. I've seen everything there is to see.

OLDER (*Dreamily*): Have you seen that old Church, such a beautiful old ruin, over somewhere to the East is it?

FAIRLY YOUNG (*Promptly*): Which bank?

OLDER: I'm talking about a church, it's very famous, very old—

FAIRLY YOUNG: I meant which bank of the Sane is it on?

OLDER (*Unabashed*): O, I don't know, but I think it was on the further one, if I remember rightly.

FAIRLY YOUNG: The interesting one where the students live?

OLDER: You know what I mean, the car tea a lat tan, and all that.

FAIRLY YOUNG: I think I know the one you mean.

OLDER: It's the right, isn't it? I'm always getting them mixed.

FAIRLY YOUNG: I never can keep them straight either.

OLDER: Well, anyway—it's the loveliest old thing—you must have seen it. (*Pause*)

FAIRLY YOUNG: If it's very old, I must have.

OLDER: O—it's very old! (*The* WOMEN *smoke. The* WHORES *and music snore. A pause.*) There was something I wanted to tell you, and it's completely gone out of my head. I can't think what . . . O, yes: this dress I've just bought. It's such a LOVELY dress.

FAIRLY YOUNG (*Insincerely*): I should SO like to see it.

OLDER: We'll go around there tomorrow after lunch—it's black satin, very simple, but the loveliest lines you ever saw in your life, and just oceans of real Brussels lace. (*She makes an oceanic gesture*)

FAIRLY YOUNG: How wonderful. Did it cost much?

OLDER: I should say so—from Poiret, you know: terribly expensive . . . as I remember it, let me see: why I think I paid three of those very big notes; you know, the brown ones.

FAIRLY YOUNG: I thought the brown ones were fifty.

OLDER: The small brown ones are, but these were the big brown ones. (*A pause*)

FAIRLY YOUNG: The yellow ones with the pictures are a hundred, aren't they?

OLDER: Yes, the pictures are a hundred, and then there's a five hundred. The ones I was thinking of are the thousand, I guess—unless there's a ten-thousand franc note. . . . I always get confused whenever I try to figure out anything which has to do with money.

FAIRLY YOUNG: So do I, here. American money is so much more sensible, I should think they'd adopt it everywhere.

OLDER: Well, I suppose it would cause some difficulties.

FAIRLY YOUNG: You'd think they'd adopt it here, though. The French are supposed to be so intelligent.

OLDER (*Confidentially*): O but they're not—really. Why, only today, I tried to make a taxidriver understand where I wanted to go: it was perfectly simple, song karawnt sank roo der lay twahl, and I said it over THREE times, and even then he couldn't seem to understand—

FAIRLY YOUNG: Yes. I know.

OLDER: —so finally I had to say it in English. And then he understood!

FAIRLY YOUNG: They seem to understand English better than French nearly everywhere in Paris, now.

OLDER: Well, I suppose it's the war, don't you think so?

FAIRLY YOUNG: Dick thinks so.

OLDER: Dick—?

FAIRLY YOUNG: My husband. He was in Paris during the war.

OLDER: O. Was he.

FAIRLY YOUNG: Yes. He started in by being a major, but he soon got promoted to colonel.

OLDER: How interesting. —I wonder if you know a man named Seward.

FAIRLY YOUNG (*Eagerly*): Jim Seward or Jack Seward? I know them both well. I'm crazy about Jack. He came over on the boat with me.

OLDER: I think this one's name was Tom, or something like that. I can't quite remember. . . .

FAIRLY YOUNG (*As before*): Is he blond and wonderful looking?

OLDER: No, he's rather dark, and very UNattractive: in fact, quite ugly.

FAIRLY YOUNG: O. (*A pause*)

OLDER: Tom Seward, yes that was his name. His father was a prominent banker or something.

FAIRLY YOUNG: I don't think I ever met him. (*A pause*) Why?

OLDER: O I just wondered. (*A long pause*)

FAIRLY YOUNG (*Glancing about her for the first time*): It's quiet here, isn't it. I expected it to be lively.

OLDER: Did you? —I thought just the opposite. The name is so quiet: Pare Trank Eel. It means Tranquil Father, you know. (*A pause*)

FAIRLY YOUNG: I never heard of it. Is it well known?

OLDER: Only to those who KNOW. (*A pause*)

FAIRLY YOUNG: I was just thinking it looked very exclusive. (*The bell rings with terrific violence.* WHORES *and music leap into consciousness. A* MAN'S VOICE, *cheerfully patronising, is heard in the vicinity of the doorway.*)

MAN'S VOICE: Here we are! (*In the doorway appear two*

WOMEN, *one* ELDERLY, *one* YOUTHFUL, *attired in the last wail of fashion*)

ELDERLY (*Pushing* YOUTHFUL): You go first, Alice.

YOUTHFUL (*Entering with a slouchy saunter which is intended to convey the impression that she is blasée, speaks in a flat Middlewestern voice*): So this is Paris. (*Stares about her, standing awkwardly and flatfootedly. The* ELDERLY WOMAN *follows, drawing herself up and using her lorgnette. Two men, alikelooking in evening dress, block the doorway.*)

OWNER OF MAN'S VOICE BEFOREMENTIONED: Go ahead, Will.

MAN ADDRESSED: You know the ropes, Bill. (*He sidesteps.* BILL *bursts into the room, followed by the* HEADWAITER.)

HEADWAITER: Would you like a nice table sir, over here sir—. (*Salaaming, he rushes to a table in the corner opposite the* GENTLEMAN *and the* BLOND GONZESSE. *Pulls out chairs.*)

BILL: This all right for ever-body?

ELDERLY WOMAN (*Having completed her inspection of the room, smiles mysteriously*): I think this will be all right.

BILL: Siddown ever-body. (*A* CHASSEUR *enters, taking off his cap, and approaches* WILL)

ELDERLY WOMAN: I'll sit here.

BILL: Thass right Lucy—where's Will?

YOUTHFUL WOMAN: Where do I go?

ELDERLY WOMAN: You sit here, Marjorie, where you can see everything.

WILL (*Who is standing, facing the* CHASSEUR *with an expression at once vague and mistrustful*): How much do I give this feller, Bill?

YOUTHFUL WOMAN: There doesn't seem to be much to see.

BILL: Give 'im five francs. (WILL, *pulling out a wad of twenty, fifty and hundred franc notes from his trouser pocket, gives a fifty to the* CHASSEUR)

CHASSEUR (*Bowing briefly*): Merci msieur. (*Putting on his cap he hurries out in search of new victims*)

ELDERLY WOMAN: Come here Will, and sit by me. (*A* VESTIAIRE *hurries in*)

HEADWAITER (*To the* WAITER, *who has been hiding respectfully behind his superior*): Allez vite: cherchez-moi la carte. (*The* WAITER *sprints to a neighboring table, grabs a menu, returning hands it to the* HEADWAITER. *The* VESTIAIRE *comes up.*)

VESTIAIRE (*Insinuatingly*): Voulez-vous vous débarrasser msieurs mdames?

BILL: She wants our hats 'n' coats. (*He gives her his derby*)

ELDERLY WOMAN: I'll keep mine, it's rather chilly here.

BILL: Alice!

YOUTHFUL WOMAN: No thanks.

BILL (*To* VESTIAIRE): Say too. (*The* VESTIAIRE *regretfully turns.* WILL *seizes her by the sleeve.*)

WILL: Hay. (*Whispers*) Where's thuh. (*He gestures occultly, winking ponderously*)

VESTIAIRE (*Removing* WILL's *derby from his hand*): Par ici, msieur. (*She beckons:* WILL *follows her through the doorway*)

HEADWAITER (*Bending over* BILL *and holding the menu so that* BILL *cannot quite see it, speaks caressingly*): Will you have a little soup sir, and some nice oysters—

BILL: Wait a minute. 'Re we all here? Where's—

HEADWAITER (*Apologetically, in a low voice*): The gentleman'll be right in sir.

BILL: I getcha. (*Loudly*) Well now, what'd you girls like to eat?

ELDERLY WOMAN: You do the ordering, Billie dear, you know we can't read it.

HEADWAITER (*Suggestingly*): Oysters are very nice sir, or a nice steak—

YOUTHFUL WOMAN (*Impatiently*): I'll take anything.

BILL (*Importantly*): Lessee. (*He takes the menu, studies it*)

HEADWAITER (*Coaxingly, almost playfully*): A little soup to begin with sir—

BILL: Yas. Soup ahl un yon poor toolah mond.

HEADWAITER: Bien msieur.

ELDERLY WOMAN (*To* YOUTHFUL WOMAN): Did you see those . . . (*She nods toward the* WHORES)

YOUTHFUL WOMAN: Uhhuh. (*She turns her dull gaze upon the* BLOND GONZESSE. *The* BLOND GONZESSE *fixes her with a glassy eye.*)

BILL: 'M ordering soup for Will.

ELDERLY WOMAN (*Quickly*): That's right.

HEADWAITER: Et après. . . .

BILL: Ap ray, donny mwah daze weet.

HEADWAITER (*Approvingly*): Des huîtres, bien msieur.

Quatre douzaines, n'est-ce pas msieur? (WILL, *hands in pockets, enters vaguely*)

ELDERLY WOMAN (*Beckoning anxiously*): Over here, Will!

WILL (*Overhereing*): Hullo everybody.

BILL (*Looks up*): Siddown Will. Thought you fell overboard.

ELDERLY WOMAN: We ordered you some soup. (WILL *sits heavily beside her*)

HEADWAITER: Une douzaine chacun?

BILL: He wants to know how many—. (*Desperately to* HEADWAITER) We.

HEADWAITER (*Radiating approbation*): Et pour la suite msieur—un bon rumstek—un château—un veau sauté—?

WILL (*Ponderously, growls*): Thought I was lost out there.

ELDERLY WOMAN: Yes?

BILL: We we, kom voo voo lay. (*The* HEADWAITER, *beaming, writes down a great many things hurriedly on a pad*) Et ensuite—un peu de fromage—un dessert—you wish strawberries?

WILL: Got some pretty slick girls out there. One of 'em tried to get my watch.

BILL: Will you have strawberries?

YOUTHFUL WOMAN: All right, all right anything at all.

HEADWAITER: Strawberries very fresh.

BILL: Strawberries poor toola mond. Wutabout something to drink?

HEADWAITER: Il n'y a que champagne msieur.

BILL: We we, sham pain.

HEADWAITER (*Tears sheet from pad and hands it to* WAITER, *who mercurially disappears*): Bien messieurs mesdames. (*Turning, beckons vehemently to the music, which has stopped but which immediately recommences with redoubled vigor*)

OLDER WOMAN (*To* FAIRLY YOUNG): I'll ask him. —May truh dough tell. (*The* HEADWAITER *wheels*) Seal voo play— (*He comes to her table*) Voo parlay onglay?

HEADWAITER (*Irritated*): Yes, I speak English.

OLDER WOMAN (*Indicating* WILL *and* BILL, *whispers*): Are those our ombs?

HEADWAITER: Yes madame. But they are not quite ready yet —a little patience, madame.

OLDER WOMAN: O, I see. All right. Thank you, may truh

dough tell. (*The* HEADWAITER *hurries off. The* OLDER *whispers the news to the* FAIRLY YOUNG, *who stares seductively at the* OMBS. *Enter* HIM, *walking too straight, carrying in his left hand a cabbage. He walks too straight up to the table where the* BLOND GONZESSE *and the* GENTLEMAN *are sitting and bows interrogatively to the* GENTLEMAN, *indicating an imaginary third place with a majestic wave of his right hand.*)

HIM: Permettez, monsieur?

BLOND GONZESSE (*Immediately*): Oui monsieur. (*She giggles*)

GENTLEMAN: Sit down. (HIM *draws up a chair. Sits, with the cabbage in his lap.*) Waiter!

WAITER: Msieur?

HIM (*To* WAITER): Trois whis-ky et une assiette.

WAITER: Une assiette msieur—comment—? Une assiette anglaise?

HIM (*Sternly*): Non. Une assiette nature, pour le chou.

WAITER: Ah—pour le chou. Bien msieur. (*Exit*)

GENTLEMAN: I never forget faces.

HIM: Really?

GENTLEMAN: Your face is familiar.

HIM: Yes?

GENTLEMAN: I've seen you somewhere before.

HIM: Possibly. (*A pause*)

GENTLEMAN: Were you ever in a city where the money is called "poo"?

HIM: I may have been.

GENTLEMAN: I think you were, and I think that's where I met you.

HIM: The world's not so big, after all. (*The* BLOND GONZESSE *giggles*)

GENTLEMAN (*To* BLOND GONZESSE): Pardon—meet my friend Mr.—

HIM (*Promptly*): John Brown. (*Bows*)

BLOND GONZESSE: Enchantée, monsieur.

GENTLEMAN: Have a cigar. (*Producing two*) The lady prefers cigarettes.

HIM (*Taking one*): Thanks. (*He and the* GENTLEMAN *bite off and spit out the tips of their cigars.* HIM *strikes a match: lights the* GENTLEMAN's *cigar and his own.*)

GENTLEMAN (*Smoking*): Did I understand you to say you were John Brown?

HIM (*Smoking*): Correct.

GENTLEMAN: In that case let me ask you something: does your body lie mouldering in the grave? (*Leaning across the table*) Because mine does.

HIM: Yes?

GENTLEMAN: But that isn't all of it. (*Drawing himself up, remarks smilelessly*) My soul goes marching on. (HIM *inspects the cabbage gravely. The* BLOND GONZESSE *giggles.*) The lady doesn't believe me. She doesn't know who I am. I just met her.

HIM: Who are you?

GENTLEMAN: I am the unpublished photograph of George Washington crossing the Susquehanna in a breechesbuoy. Who are you.

HIM: I live here.

GENTLEMAN: In that case, let me ask you something: are you one of those God, damned, artists? (*The whiskies and a large plate arrive*)

WAITER (*To* HIM): Voici msieur, l'assiette nature. (*The* BLOND GONZESSE *giggles*)

HIM (*Carefully transferring the cabbage from his lap to the empty plate and lifting carefully his whisky, answers*) No. That is, not exactly: I earn money by taming jellyfish.

GENTLEMAN (*Picking up his whisky*): The lady doesn't believe you. The lady doesn't believe anything.

HIM: The lady is a wise lady—à votre santé madame. (*Gravely bows to the* BLOND GONZESSE) Ashes to ashes. (*Bows gravely to the* GENTLEMAN)

GENTLEMAN: Ally upp. (HIM *and the* GENTLEMAN *drink their whiskies*)

YOUTHFUL WOMAN (*Angrily repulsing* BILL's *halfhearted attempt to embrace her, and gazing rapturously at* HIM *who does not see her*) Don't!

FAIRLY YOUNG WOMAN (*Excitedly whispers to* OLDER, *indicating* BILL): I think mine's almost ready.

A WHORE (*Yawning, to a yawning* WHORE): Rien à faire ce soir.

WILL (*Pouring himself his fourth glass of champagne and staring fixedly at the* OLDER WOMAN): Some. Baby.

ELDERLY WOMAN (*To* WILL, *while desperately ogling the unnoticing* GENTLEMAN): Give ME a little champagne, please.

GENTLEMAN (*To* HIM): How much.

HIM: How much what?

GENTLEMAN: How much do you make?

HIM: O—thirty cents a jellyfish.

GENTLEMAN: What do you do with them, when they're tame?

HIM: I sell them to millionaires. (*He turns amorously to the* BLOND GONZESSE) Il fait chaud, n'est-ce pas, mademoiselle?

BLOND GONZESSE (*Amorously*): Très chaud, monsieur.

GENTLEMAN (*To* HIM): Been over here long?

HIM: Not very. (*He points to the cabbage*) I was born day before yesterday.

GENTLEMAN: In that case, you probably know a show I went to last night: foliz burshare. (*The* BLOND GONZESSE *giggles*)

HIM: Never heard of them.

GENTLEMAN: The lady doesn't believe I've been.—Waiter!

WAITER (*Who has just placed a third bottle of champagne on* WILL'*s table and a second bottle of Evian on the* OLDER WOMAN'*s*): Msieur.

GENTLEMAN (*To* HIM): The same? (HIM *nods*) Ong kore.

WAITER: La même chose—bien msieur. (*He sprints*)

OLDER WOMAN (*To* FAIRLY YOUNG, *pouring water in her glass*): I don't remember ever being so thirsty.

GENTLEMAN (*To* HIM): Are you married?

HIM: Sometimes.

GENTLEMAN: You ought to go to that show.

HIM: Good?

GENTLEMAN: Rotten. A bunch of amateurs and some hand-painted scenery. They don't know how to put on a show over here. Little Old New York is the only place where the theatre's any good. (*Two whiskies arrive*) One more whisky for the lady.

BLOND GONZESSE (*Protestingly*): Non, merci.

HIM: The lady's got one. (*Indicates an untouched glass*)

GENTLEMAN: Give the lady a drink, waiter. Ong kore.

WAITER: Encore un wis-kee—bien msieur. (*Sprints*)

GENTLEMAN: As for the women, they're fat and they're clumsy and they're naked and they don't know they're alive. (*He drinks his whisky*) I can hand Paris only one thing: the Scotch is sure death. What are you doing with that cabbage? Taming it?

WAITER: Un wis-kee—voici msieur. (*Places another whisky on the table*)

GENTLEMAN (*To* WAITER): How much is all this?

WAITER: Ça vous fait ...

GENTLEMAN: Kom be an.

WAITER: Ça fait—quatre cents francs juste, msieur. (*The* BLOND GONZESSE *giggles*)

GENTLEMAN: The lady doesn't think I can pay for it. (*He produces a wallet and pulls out a five-hundred franc note*) Sang song frong: keep the change. (*He puts back the wallet*)

WAITER (*Turning white with pleasure*): Merci msieur. (*He and the* BLOND GONZESSE *exchange significant glances*)

BILL (*Totally disregarding the anguish of the* ELDERLY WOMAN *who has been helping herself freely to champagne and is now swaying dangerously against him, lifts his glass to the* FAIRLY YOUNG WOMAN): Pyjama pyjama.

HIM (*Drinking his whisky, addresses the* GENTLEMAN): Going back?

GENTLEMAN: Back?

HIM: Back to the dear old U.S.A.?

GENTLEMAN (*Drunkenly shaking his head*): Can't do it.

HIM: No?

GENTLEMAN (*All of him leaning across the table speaks distinctly*): Let me tell you something: I had a son. And he's a drunkard. And I had a daughter: and she's a whore. And my son is a member of all the best clubs in New York City. And my daughter married thirteen million dollars. And I'm a member of the God, damned, bourgeoisie. (*He passes out cold*)

HIM (*Solemnly, to the collapsed* GENTLEMAN): Admitting that these dolls of because are dissimilar, since one goes up when the other comes down, and assuming a somewhat hypothetical sawhorse symmetrically situated with reference to the extremities of the strictly conjectural seesaw, god is the candlestick or answer. (*Arising, waves majestically to the music which immediately strikes up Yes, We Have No Bananas— turning, bows to the* BLOND GONZESSE *who has just appropriated the* GENTLEMAN's *wallet*) In that case, let me ask you something: shall we dance the I Touch? (*The* ELDERLY WOMAN *vomits copiously into* BILL's *lap*)

scene 4

(Scene: The three knitting rocking figures facing the picture with their backs to the audience. The DOCTOR's *head has disappeared from the picture, leaving a black hole. The* WOMAN's *head is in the picture; her eyes are closed.)*

FIRST FIGURE: Terribly. Especially in summer.

SECOND: How simply frightful! All over them?

THIRD: Drowsiness rumblings sour risings heartburn waterbrash and the feeling of being stuffed.

FIRST: That depends: sometimes.

SECOND: Is it very painful?

THIRD: Ask the man who owns one.

FIRST: Not very. Like falling down stairs, and you apply the same remedy—one stick of dynamite in a tumbler of ink before meals.

THIRD: Ask dad he knows.

SECOND: I understand the dynamite but what does the ink do?

THIRD: Comes out like a ribbon lies flat on the brush.

FIRST: Why the ink dissolves the guineapigs and makes them nervous.

SECOND: And what do they do after that?

THIRD: Look for the union label on every garment.

FIRST: They? Who?

SECOND: The guineapigs.

FIRST: O! They let go of the children.

SECOND: How time flies—you never know what to expect, do you. *(The* WOMAN's *head stirs in the picture: her eyes open slowly)*

FIRST: Yes life is a mystery at best.

THIRD: If it isn't an Eastman it isn't a Kodak.

SECOND: And we have so many things to be thankful for, haven't we. *(The* DOCTOR's *head appears in the picture)*

FIRST: I should say so: why my husband and I were married fifty years ago come day before yesterday and we've never had a single cross word—now what do you think of that?

DOCTOR'S HEAD *(Harshly, from the picture)*: If you wore your garters around your neck you'd change them oftener.

scene 5   (*Scene: The room, still further revolved so that the fourth or invisible wall is the solid wall. The wall to the audience's right [corresponding to the solid wall of Scene 1] is the mirror wall. The middle wall is the window wall. The door wall is to the audience's left. On the centre of the table, where* HIM's *hat was lying at the beginning of Scene 1, there is a vase of flowers.*

ME *and* HIM *sit, back to [or facing the same way as] the audience, at opposite ends of the sofa which is against the invisible wall.*)

ME: I imagine, myself, it was very nice.

HIM: I remember morning. Silence. Houses in the river—April: the green Seine filled with houses, filled with windows out of which people look. And everything is upside down. . . . Then there comes a least breeze. And the people in the windows and the windows themselves and all the houses gradually aren't. I remember standing, thinking, in sunlight; and saying to myself "dying should be like this."

ME: Dying?

HIM: —To feel like one of the upsidedown people in one of the wrongsideup windows when a breeze comes.

ME (*After a pause*): It must be a nice place, Paris, for a man.

HIM: I happened to be a dream there.

ME: But you're not any more. (*Suddenly*) Tell me, do I look very old?

HIM (*Smiles*): How did you get that idea?

ME: Women don't get it, they're born with it. Besides—you told me, the first time I saw you again, that I'd changed.

HIM: I don't remember saying anything.

ME: You didn't know me—which is worse.

HIM: But that's asking too much of a dream.

ME: I expect I have changed. (*Shudders slightly*)

HIM: Have I?

ME: Changed?—A little.

HIM: I ask because, if you remember, you once said you had changed but that I was the same.

ME: O—yes, I remember saying that. . . .

HIM: You were right about memories.

ME: Was I?

HIM: Wonderfully right.

ME: Isn't it queer. I feel as if we'd—as if you hadn't gone . . . Do you feel that?

HIM: I can't believe that we're together.

ME: With me it's just the other way.

HIM: When one has been a dream, it takes some time to—. (*He gestures smoothly*)—So to speak, renovate oneself.

ME (*Almost to herself*): Let's not talk about dreams any more.

HIM (*Looking at her*): I shall try not to.

ME (*Taking his hand, smiles*): Such a queer day, when I saw you again and you didn't recognize me—and I didn't care. (*A pause*)

HIM: It was raining.

ME: Terribly hard. When I saw you I was running, because I'd forgotten to take my umbrella. Then I stopped—

HIM: In the rain.

ME: —in front of you.

HIM: We looked at each other, probably.

ME: We never said anything.

HIM (*To himself*): I seem to remember very well, looking.

ME: . . . Then you offered me your umbrella.

HIM: Did I?

ME: We walked along together under your umbrella. We walked quite a distance; and most of it, people were laughing.

HIM: Were people laughing?

ME: —Until we stood before the door. . . . Then I spoke to you. Do you remember what I said?—I said "it isn't raining." It hadn't been for some time and I knew; but I didn't say anything.

HIM: I didn't know.

ME: You must have been a little happy?

HIM: Yes.

ME: Then—do you know what you did?

HIM: No.

ME: Well, you shut the umbrella.

HIM: The key squeaked in the lock more than I expected. The floor creaked more than I remembered its creaking.

ME: Yes, I was going to use mine when you stopped me and took out yours.

HIM: You had forgotten giving me that key, once upon a time.

ME: I never dreamed you'd kept it.

HIM (*To himself*): I couldn't go carefully enough.

ME: You frightened me a little when you shut the door. You shut it so very very gently. I remember how you walked to the sofa and how you sat down.

HIM: Perhaps I was afraid of breaking someone. (*A pause*)

ME: We sat for a long time, where we're sitting now.

HIM: A long time?

ME: Nearly an hour, I guess. Until you got up suddenly and looked out the window.

HIM: Outside, someone was putting away pieces of sky which looked remarkably like toys.

ME (*In a low voice*): And always you stood, looking—. Your hands . . . folding, shutting. Finally (just as it was getting very dark)—"I think," you said "my hands have been asleep." Very gently you said that and went out, shutting the door carefully. I heard your feet going down the stairs. I sat, hearing for a long time in the rain your feet, in the dark. Walking. (*A pause*) Tell me—when you left, without your umbrella, where did you go?

HIM: "Go?"

ME: It's silly of me to ask—I ask because I want to. Did you go to a park . . . like the big one with the animals, or the little park where the harbor is?

HIM: Harbor—how did you guess? (*To himself*) Queer that I should have done that; avoiding the animals?

ME: Ships go out sometimes; maybe you were thinking of ships.

HIM: And sometimes come in. And there I met a man with green eyes . . .

ME: A man—? What was he doing?

HIM: Doing? Doing nothing, I think. Let me see: a man came and sat down beside me on a bench. Because it was raining.

ME: Or because he guessed you were lonely?

HIM: . . . and a crumpled hat; who said, I remember, that he had only just returned from Paris. O—and he didn't wear spats.

ME: Did he talk to you much?

HIM: I suppose so.

ME: What did he talk about—Paris?

HIM: Probably.

ME: Didn't you talk to him?

HIM: I don't think I did. O yes—no I didn't talk to him.

ME: Why?

HIM: Because I killed him.

ME (*Starting violently*): —The man?

HIM: Himself.

ME: —You didn't—

HIM: Kill him?

ME: —him—

HIM: O, him. (*Easily*) Of course I didn't. (*Smiles*) —Just the other way 'round.

ME (*Earnestly*): What do you mean?

HIM: It's clear now—can't you see? (*Gently*) He killed me.

ME: Please, dear, I'm—so nervous. (*Taking his other hand*) Don't.

HIM: —Frighten you? All right, sorry. He didn't kill me.

ME: Of course not!

HIM: On the contrary—instead, what did the wretch do?

ME: Never mind. Let's—

HIM: Why as sure as you live and as cool as you please producing from the vicinity of his exaggerated omphalos an automatic, he asked me to shoot himself; or perhaps I asked me to shoot himself, I can't quite remember which. . . .

ME: Why are you like this?

HIM: Or as I said to the man in the green hat with crumpled eyes: why in the name of Heaven should a gentleman recently returned from Paris ask him to kill myself? And do you know what the rascal replied to that?

ME: I don't want to know; let's talk about something else; the play.

HIM: —Sir, said he, the reason I ask me to kill yourself is that a gentleman also recently returned from Paris—

ME: The one you were working on when. The one, you know.

HIM: —from Paris, mind, has recently penetrated God's country by fast freight with the express purpose of—

ME: With the Negroes in it.

HIM: —committing the pardonable sin with my ex . . . Libido, I think was the accurate and incredible word which he employed. (*Relaxing, looks upward*) Then the ocean, filled with trillions of nonillions of ablebodied seamen and only-half-human mermaids and thousands upon hundreds of whales, came up everywhere over the earth—up everywhere over the world—and up up up to the bench where we were sitting. And the mermaids' bellies were full of little slippery fish, and the frolicking great whales were swaying and playing upon harps of gold, and the seamen were sailing before the mast, and the ocean . . . the ocean rose and stood solemnly beside us, resting its chin in its hand and looking at the recently returned gentleman from Paris. Whereupon the recently returned gentleman from Paris invited the ocean to sit down.

ME: You—

HIM: But You never said anything. You was much too busy, eyeing the mermaids and counting the seamen and admiring the golden harps of the most enormous of all mammals—

ME: —didn't—

HIM: —until suddenly You looked. (*He smiles*) The ocean had gone: and away off—ever so many thousands of hundreds of billions of millions of years away—You heard a sound. It was the sound of the mermaids, with bellies full of gooey fish and with long hair, chasing the seamen everywhere and snatching the golden harps from the hands of the resplendent whales. And all this sound went away slowly. Finally You looked all about You: and You was alone, holding in You's hand—. (*He laughs*) —A papyrus from Harun-al-Rashid inviting us all to petit déjeuner in the most excellent Arabic at twenty-three hours on January thirty-second, seven thousand one hundred and seventeen Columbus crossed the ocean blue. (*A pause*)

ME (*Quietly*): Is that all?

HIM: I put it in my pocket—the ocean green. But You didn't care a continental damn.

ME: That's all?

HIM (*Nodding in the direction of the table, upstage*): I see flowers.

ME: Yes, thank you. (*A pause*) Do you know something?

HIM: I understand less and less.

ME: You HAVE changed.

HIM: Much?

ME: Quite a lot: your eyes . . . or maybe it's the light. Did you—

HIM: Aren't my eyes green?

ME: It's been a long time, hasn't it; since you—. (*Timidly*) Please tell me. Am I different . . . very much?

HIM: "Different"?

ME: Olderlooking.

HIM (*Smiles*): You seem to me a little younger, just a little younger.

ME: You're joking. I know I look older. (*Shudders*)

HIM: I'm not joking, seriously. —So my eyes have changed. Probably you're right. Like Rip Van Winkle they've been asleep.

ME: You mean that when your eyes see me they know they've been asleep.

HIM: I really mean that they don't have people like you, up there.

ME: Where?

HIM: Up in the mountains where they play a game with thunder. Anywhere. Nowhere. Where for a hundred years I fell asleep.

ME: O—those mountains.

HIM: Those.

ME (*After a pause*): Are you quite sure you're not sorry that you're awake?

HIM: Wonderfully sure—you see, Rip's story and my story are . . . different.

ME (*Laughing*): Because you haven't a beard?—O but I'm glad you haven't a beard. You know I can't stand men with beards. Or spats.

HIM: Not because I haven't a beard, but because when I woke up and came down out of those mountains, you were younger than before.

ME: How do you know that I. Maybe I'm married, and have ever so many . . . didn't his?

HIM: His?

ME: Rip Van Winkle's girl; or was it his wife? I thought she'd forgotten all about him in the meantime and married someone else.

HIM (*Thoughtfully*): I only seem to remember that she was dead.

ME: O. . . .

HIM (*Vaguely*): I was thinking . . . so am I. I suppose nobody, including his children, really believed him when he told them.

ME: When he told them—about the mountains?

HIM: About the mountains and about being asleep.

ME: Do you think? O dear; I'm sorry, but this is getting too complicated for me.

HIM (*Earnestly*): Please be happy. Why should I talk about myself? I'd much rather talk about you.

ME: Me? (*Bitterly*) There's nothing to talk about.

HIM: Isn't there? I'm very sorry. We all make mistakes.

ME (*Looks at him*): I know. I make them.

HIM: You? stop.

ME: Listen. Suppose—

HIM: Don't suppose.

ME (*Bravely*): —suppose I made a mistake; and it was the mistake of my life. And suppose: O suppose—I'm making it!

HIM (*Steadily*): You're wrong, quite wrong. It's the mistake of my life.

ME (*Whispers*): Is it?

HIM (*Quietly*): Yes.

ME (*Looking at him*): It may take two people to make a really beautiful mistake.

HIM (*Expressionlessly*): The nicest things happen by themselves. —Which reminds me: I had a dream only the other day. A very queer dream: may I tell it to you? (*A pause*)

ME: Do you want to very much?

HIM: If you don't very much mind.

ME (*Hesitantly*): If it's not too queer.

HIM: Will you promise to interrupt me if it's too queer?

ME: All right.

HIM (*Leaning forward, looks at nothing*): You were with me in a sort of room. I was standing beside you and you seemed to be telling me something. But I was only tremendously glad to feel you so near. . . .

ME: Go on.

HIM: That was beautiful to me. —Then you took my left hand and you led me somewhere else in this room—and through the roomshaped dark softness I tiptoed wadingly. You paused and I stood next you: next your blood, your hair, hands, breathing. I felt that you were smiling a little. You pointed to something. And stooping carefully I could not quite see—but through this dark softness I seemed to feel—another person, lying very quietly with an entire quietness that queerly frightened me. . . . May I go on?

ME: Go on.

HIM: When I could see, this other person's eyes and my eyes

were looking at each other. Hers were big and new in the darkness. They seemed to be looking at me as if we had known each other somewhere else. They were very close—so close that my breath almost touched them: so close that my mind almost touched what looked at me from them . . . I can't describe it—a shyness, more shy than you can ever imagine, a shyness inhabiting very easily and very skilfully everything which is profoundly fragile and everything which we really are and everything which we never quite live. But—just as I almost touched this shyness—it suddenly seemed to touch me; and, touching, to believe me and all from which I had come and into which I was changing with every least thought or with each carefully hurrying instant. I felt a slight inexplicable gesture—nearer than anything, nearer than my own body—an inscrutable timidity, capturing the mere present in a perfect dream or wish or Now . . . a peering frailness, perfectly curious about me; curiously and perfectly created out of my own hope and out of my own fear. . . . I did not see any more, then. (*Pauses; smiling, resumes*) Then I stooped a little lower and kissed her hair with my lips and with the trembling lips of my mind I kissed her head, herself, her silence. But as I kissed her, she seemed to me to be made out of silence by whatever is most perfectly silent; so that, to find out if she were perhaps real, I spoke to her—and her voice answered as if perhaps not speaking to me at all, or as if it felt embarrassed because it knew that it was doing something which it should not do; and yet, I remember her voice was glad to feel, close by it, the unreal someone whom I had been. —Then the darkness seemed to open: I know what I saw then: it was a piece of myself, a child in a crib, lying very quietly with her head in the middle of a biggish pillow, with her hands out of the blankets and crossing very quietly and with a doll in the keeping fingers of each hand. . . . So you and I together went out of this opened darkness where a part of ourselves some-how seemed to be lying—where something which had happened to us lay awake and in the softness held a girl doll and a boy doll. Perhaps you closed the door, gently . . . but I remember nothing about coming into the light. (*His eyes search the face of* ME *and find a different nothing*) That is my dream. (*Rises*) —Into the mirror with it, we'll throw it away! (*Strides to the mirror, makes a quick futile gesture and stands facing the mirror. A short pause.* ME *rises and goes to* HIM *slowly: stands, simply, sorrowfully. Turning from the mirror to* ME, HIM *speaks slowly.*) Hark. That was my dream which just fell into my soul and broke.

ME (*Touches his arm pityingly, slightly*): I guess it took so long to fall because it was made of nothing. (*She returns to the sofa and sits down*)

HIM: You have a bright idea. (*Returning to the sofa, sits opposite her. A pause.*) Shall we smoke a cigarette—or two perhaps? (*Fumbles in pockets, finds matches and a package of cigarettes: offers cigarettes to* ME *who does not see them*) Then I will; unless you—

ME: I don't mind.

HIM (*Lights carefully his cigarette: pockets the matchbox. Presently remarks to himself.*): But there was a dog, named something or other. (*Short silence*)

ME: A dog.

HIM: I used to take him to bed with me. In fact we travelled everywhere together. God spelled backwards.

ME: What sort of a dog?

HIM: The name being Gipsy. It didn't last long because it was a cloth dog. Tell me something.

ME: What.

HIM (*Quietly*): Tell me you used to have a cloth dog too.

ME: I didn't . . . at least I don't think so.

HIM: Didn't you? Not ever? There was a battleship, which wound up, with invisible wheels that made it move along the floor: it was very fragile. They called it The Renown. —Did you have dolls?

ME: I guess so, I don't remember.

HIM: I perfectly remember that I had a great many dolls, but that I only loved one—a wax doll named Bellissima who melted in front of the fire. (*Getting up, strolls to the table*)

ME (*Half to herself*): I suppose you cried.

HIM: On the contrary, I asked for a cup of tea. (*He takes from the table an imaginary cup and saucer; drops into the imaginary cup an imaginary piece of sugar*) —But you have given me symbols. Look: I see my life melting as what you call Winter. . . . The edges are fading: gradually, very gradually, it diminishes. (*Takes an imaginary sip*) But notice: there there is a purpose in the accident, I mean there is someone beyond and outside what happens—someone who is thirsty and tired. Someone, to whom the disappearance of my being sweetens unbeing as, let us say, this dissolving cube of sugar—pardon: God would like a slice of lemon. (*Takes an imaginary slice*) Thank you. We are all of us just a trifle crazy, aren't we? Like Archimedes with his mirrors and like old Mr. Benjamin F. who flew kites in a thunderstorm, which reminds me—I never told you that I was flying a kite. And it pulled and rose: wonderfully reaching out and steadily climbing, climbing over the whole world until you'd never believe anything in your life could be so awfully far and bright —until you almost thought it had found some spot where Spring is all the time. . . . But suddenly my foolish hands were full of common twine string.

ME (*Looking straight before her, speaks to herself after a moment*): It's snowing.

HIM: Gay may change, but all my thoughts are in the wash and I haven't a clean thing to put on. —After all, thoughts are like anything else you wear, they must be sent to the crazy laundry once in a while and the crazy laundry wears out more crazy thoughts than ever a crazy man did. Hypnos and Thanatos, a couple of Greek boys who made a fortune overnight, the laundry of the Awake, Incorporated: having mangled our lives with memories it rinses them in nightmare. (*A drum sounds faintly.* ME *starts.*) I think I hear nothing. (*Puts imaginary tea carefully on table; turns, slowly walks to the middle of the room and stands facing the audience*) But if I ask you something, now, will you promise to answer truthfully? (*She shakes her head*) Because you can't? —Tell me; why can't you answer me truthfully, now?

ME (*Rising*): Now you want—truth?

HIM: With all my life: yes!

ME (*Advancing toward him slowly*): You wanted beauty once.

HIM (*Brokenly*): I believed that they were the same.

ME: You don't think so any longer?

HIM: I shall never believe that again.

ME (*Pauses, standing before him*): What will you believe?

HIM (*Bitterly*): That beauty has shut me from truth; that beauty has walls—is like this room, in which we are together for the last time, whose walls shut us from everything outside.

ME: If what you are looking for is not here, why don't you go where it is? (*The drumsound heightens*)

HIM: In all directions I cannot move. Through you I have made a discovery: you have shown me something . . . something about which I am doubtful deep in my heart. I cannot feel that everything has been a mistake—that I have inhabited an illusion with you merely to escape from reality and the knowledge of ourselves. (*To himself*) How should what is desirable shut us entirely from what is? No! That must be not quite all: I will not think that the tragedy can be so simple. There must be something else: I believe that there IS something else: and my heart tells me that unless I discover this now I will never discover it.—Am I wrong?

ME: You were talking about dolls. You see, I think sometimes.

HIM: Are you thinking, now?

ME: Now—yes. (*Total darkness. The drumsound drowns in a whirling nearness of mingling voices out of which juts suddenly* ONE VOICE.)

ONE VOICE: Ladies un genlmun right dis way step dis way evrybudy tuh duh Princess Anankay tuh duh Tatood Man tuh duh Huemun Needl tuh duh Missin Link tuh duh Queen uv Soipunts tuh duh Nine Foot Giun tuh duh Eighteen Inch Lady tuh duh Six Hundud Pouns uv Passionut Pullcrytood tuh duh Kink uv Borneo dut eats ee-lectrick light bulbs!

scene 6

(*Scene: The stage has become a semicircular piece of depth crowded with jabbering and gesticulating people, viz.* HIM [*hatred*], *the other participants in Act II with the exception of those characters which were played by the* DOCTOR, *and the three* MISS WEIRDS *minus their chairs and knitting. The circumference of the semicircle is punctuated at equal intervals by nine similar platforms. The fifth platform [counting, from either extremity of the circumference, inward] supports a diminutive room or booth whose front wall is a curtain. On each of the other eight platforms sits lollingly a* FREAK.

Beginning with the outermost platform to the audience's left and following the circumference of the semicircle inward we have: NINE FOOT GIANT, QUEEN OF SERPENTS, HUMAN NEEDLE,

MISSING LINK *and the fifth or inmost platform with its mysterious booth. Continuing, outward, we have:* TATTOOED MAN,
SIX HUNDRED POUNDS OF PASSIONATE PULCHRITUDE, KING OF
BORNEO *and, on the outermost platform to the audience's
right,* EIGHTEEN INCH LADY.)

MISS STOP WEIRD (*To* MISS LOOK): I don't suppose he really
eats them. (*To* MISS LISTEN) Do you? (*All three* WEIRDS
shake their maskfaces skeptically)

HIM (*Bowing and removing his battered hat*): Excuse me.
ladies—. (*Indicates the* DOCTOR, *who, disguised as a hunchback* BARKER, *has just appeared on the platform of the* GIANT)
—Who is that little creature?

MISS STOP: A harmless magician with whom we are only
slightly acquainted.

MISS LOOK: A master of illusion.

MISS LISTEN: A person of no importance, his name is Nas-
citur.

HIM (*Bows and replaces his battered hat on his head:
looking about him, speaks to himself*): Barnum, thou shouldst
be Darwin at this hour.

BARKER (*Beckons fervently from the platform of the rising*
NINE FOOT GIANT, *toward whom the crowd swirls*): Make it
quick goils kummun fellurs foist we have, Dick duh Giunt I
begs tuh call duh undievieded attention uv all lilypewshuns
here presun tuh dis unparrallul phenomenun uv our own day
un time duh leas skepticul may be pardun fur nut believin wut
I states us duh in-con-tro-voitubl troot dut dis extraordinury
freak uv nachure wen standin in his stockin feet describes uh
longitoodinul trajectury uv one hundun un eight inches no
more no less in duh gigantic palm uv his colussul han he easily
supports his lidl frien Madame Petite while ut duh same time
consultin uh twentytwo carut gole timepiece made tuh ordur
by uh famous Swiss consoin duh diul uv wich measures fourteen inches in dieametur un is protected by windowglass one
quartur uv un inch in tickness upun duh summit uv his ee-normous head he wears uh speciully constructed strawhat weighin
five pouns un fourteen ounces duh amount uv clawt require
fur uh single pair uv dis poisun's elephantine pants would
make six blokes like youse un me two un one half suits apiece
his mammut neddur extremities fur wich numbur twenty-six
shoes has been created bohs toiteen toes all in poific condition

duh smalles biggur dun my wrist expoits have decided upun investigation dut in duh course uv one loonur day his garganchoon appetite consumes un duh average frum toitytwo tuh fortyfive ordinury beefsteaks ur duh protein ee-quivalunt it is estimated by duh managemunt uv dis exhibit dut twelve normul poisuns could exis fur fiftyfour hours twentytree minutes nine un sevuneights secuns un wut dis monstur communly annihilates fur breakfust alone I will merely add dut in ordur tuh facilitate inspection uv oit's mohs vas biped uh sixteen hundud candlepowur rubburtire telescope is placed ut duh disposition uv duh genrul public fur wich no extruh charge will be made walk right up un bring duh chilrun. (*He steps down and disappears in the* CROWD. *The* GIANT *displays his watch, converses, offers photographs of himself. Many grasp the opportunity to observe him through the telescope. The* BARKER, *reappearing on the platform of the* EIGHTEEN INCH LADY, *beckons fervently.*) Dis way gents step dis way ladies—. (*The* CROWD *swirls in his direction*)—Nex we have, Madame Suzette Yvonne Hortense Jacqueline Heloise Petite duh eighteen inch Parisiun doll un uncompromisin opticul inspection uv dis lidl lady will prove tuh duh satisfaction uv all consoin dut dis lidl lady is uh poificly form pocket edition uv sheek femininity born undur duh shadow uv duh Eyfl Towur in Paris were she buys all her close spiks floounly nineteen languages excloosive uv her native tongue to toityone years old in duh course uv her adventurous career has visited each un evry country uv duh civilised un uncivilise globe incloodin Soviet Russiuh were subsequunt tuh bein arrested by duh Checkur us uh spy she wus kidnapped un kep fur sevuntytwo hours widout food ur drink in duh inside ovurcoat pocket uv uh membur uv duh Secret Soivice havin escape by cuttin her way out wid uh pair uv nailscissurs she fell tuh duh frozun ground in uh dead faint in wich she wuz discovur by uh faitful moocheek who fled wid her across duh steps uv Siberiuh pursood by wolves un suckseeded in deliverin her tuh duh French consul ut duh Polish frun-teer receivin us uh reward fur his valur frum duh French guvurnmunt duh crorduhgair wid two palms un frum duh Polish ortorities duh cross uv Sain Graballsky wile duh lidl lady hoiself presented her rescoor wid un autograph photo in spite uv her wellestablish Parisiun origin Madame Petite is passionutely found uv duh home wus in fac sevun times married tuh various internationully famous speci-

muns uv duh uppercrust uv duh pigmy woild such us Purfessur
Tom Tumb un has divorced ur outlived all her husbans us uh
mewzishun Madame is equully voisitil purfurrin especiully duh
French horn trombone xylophone violin granpieannur you-
kuhlayly un jewshap un wich insturmunts she has had duh
honur tuh purform before duh crown heads uv five nations un
tree continunts duh genrul public will be gratifie tuh loin dut
Madame Suzette Yvonne Hortense Jacqueline Heloise Petite
has recunly completed duh only autentic story uv her life wich
undur duh significunt title Minyuhchoors uv Ro-mance ur
Many Abelards has already sold out four editions uv one hundud tousund copies each un is ut presun in duh process uv bein
tran-slated intuh twenty languages incloodin Arabic un Eskimo
Madame Petite will be glad tuh answur any un all questions un
give advice tuh duh best uv her ability un all un any subjecs
tuh whoever cares tuh unboidun her ur his troubles male un
female step right up.

MISS LOOK WEIRD (*Suspiciously*): What was she doing
among the Bolsheviki?

BARKER: I will answur dut unnecessury question Madame
Petite wus un uh mission uv moicy havin been delegated by
duh French Red Cross tuh assis duh Salvation Army in its
uplif woik among starvin Armeniun chilrun nooly rescood
frum duh Toiks in West Centrul Youkraniuh.

MISS LOOK WEIRD (*Satisfied*): Thank you. (*The* EIGHTEEN
INCH LADY *converses and offers copies of her book and photographs of herself. The* BARKER *disappears, only to reappear on
the* QUEEN OF SERPENTS' *platform.*)

BARKER (*Beckoning fervently to the* CROWD): Dis way
ladies ovur here gents—. (*The* CROWD *swirls in the direction
of the* QUEEN OF SERPENTS, *who rises*)—Get uh knockdown
tuh Herpo chawms duh lawges specimuns uv duh reptillyun
genus each un evry one alive dis way fellurs take uh good
squint ut Herpo hanuls duh deadlies becaws mohs poisunous
uv all snakes duh cobruh duh capello like youse boys would
hanul yur bes goil ovur here evrybudy see duh only livin
boaconstrictur in captivity lengt toitynine feet sevun un nine
toitysecunds inches swollud five indigenes ten cartridgebelts six
Winchestur rifles fortytwo rouns uv amyounition un uh
Stetson hat ut one gulp subsequunly capchoord wile fast asleep
by Capn Frank Mac Dermot D.S.C. etceteruh un shipped
F.O.B. un twelve freightcars fur twentyone days tuh duh

mowt uv duh Amazon rivur nevur woked up till fiftyfour
hours out tuh sea wen duh en-tire crew incloodin duh capn
took toins settin un duh heavilypadlock covur uv duh fortyfive
foot bamboo box boun wid steel hoops in wich duh monstur
wus tempurrurrilly imprisoned in spite uv wich precaution he
trashed about so much duh S.O.L. passengurs wus all seasick
till duh ship reached Hamburg were sevun uv um died see duh
mammut rep-tile wine hisself lovinly toiteen times aroun
Herpo wile she drinks un icecream soduh un smokes Virginiuh
cigarettes dis way ladies un gents dis way. (*Steps down and
disappears in the* CROWD. *The* QUEEN OF SERPENTS *takes out of
a box, wraps around her and puts back in the box, four
ancient and decrepit snakes, each larger than the other.*)

VIRGO OF ACT II, SCENE 2 (*Fascinated*): I hate snakes—ugh!

QUEEN OF SERPENTS (*Calmly, through her gum*): Dat's
because youse cawn't chawm dum dearie. (*Laughter*)

BARKER (*Reappearing on the platform of the* KING OF
BORNEO, *who rises*): Evrybudy dis way—. (*He gestures fervently. The* CROWD *swirls toward the* KING OF BORNEO.)—Nex
we comes tuh one uv duh principul kyouriosities uv dis ur any
epock sometimes frivolously allooded tuh by ignorun poisuns
us Duh Huemun Ostrich I refois propurly speakin tuh His
Impeereel Majusty Kakos Kalos duh ex-Kink uv Borneo duh
lad wid duh unpunkshooruble stumick speciully engaged ut
ee-normous expense fur duh benefit uv duh Great Americun
Public durin uh recen revolooshun in purhaps duh mohs primitive uv all semicivilise commyounities Kink Kakos Kalos
nut only los his trone but had duh additionul misforchoon tuh
be trode by his noomerous enemies intuh uh dun-john ur hole
tuh use duh vulgur woid approximutly ninety six feet in dept
un twotoids full uv rainwatur frum wich he wus pulled aftur
fourteen days un nights un forcibly fed nails tincans broken
glass barbwire un uddur dangerous objecs ovur uh period uv
toitysix hours ut duh end uv wich time duh revolooshunuries
lef dier victim fur dead but nix kid fur tanks tuh duh kink's
younique un unparllul constitution wich us any uv youse is ut
liburty tuh ascertain can assimilut wid ease such hidertoo
erroneously considured indiegestubl substunces us carpettacks
knittinneedles safetyrazorblades pins jackknives un dynamite
he live tuh tell uh tale so incredible us tuh outrivul duh
imaginury experiunces uv duh Barun Munchchowsun hisself
but whose vuracity is prove beyon duh shadow uv uh doubt by

duh fac dut it bein now five tuh five ur teatime in one two tree four five minutes Kink Kakos Kalos may be seen by all presun in duh intimut act uv swallurin un ee-lectrick light bulb step right up ladies un gents Duh Huemun Ostrich is in duh tent duh Kink's waitin fur youse KRK KRK KRK he champ-chomps sharp un brittle chews bright prickly glass. (*Disappears in the* CROWD. *The* KING OF BORNEO *holds up a huge electric light bulb, points to it, points to his mouth and winks solemnly to the* SPECTATORS.)

FIRST FAIRY OF ACT II, SCENE 8 (*Soprano*): How unpleasant.

SECOND FAIRY OF DITTO (*Alto*): Positively repellent.

THIRD FAIRY OF DITTO: Perfectly disgusting.

FOURTH FAIRY OF DITTO: Makes one absolutely nauseated —ugh!

KING OF BORNEO (*Furiously*): Sempre abbasso Savoia putana madonna viva Lenine! (*He crams the electric light bulb far into his mouth—chews noisily. The* FOURTH FAIRY *faints and is carried off by the other three* FAIRIES.)

BARKER (*Reappearing on the platform of the* HUMAN NEEDLE): Right dis way evrybudy—. (*He beckons fervently. The* CROWD *swirls toward the* HUMAN NEEDLE, *who rises*.) —Nex we have, Adamus Jones fumilyully known tuh his many friens us Duh Huemun Needl dis young man is twentytree years old un still lookin fur uh wife summuh youse ladies in duh same interestin condition bettur tink twice before toinin down his ——— statistics reinforce wid copious affidavits tens tuh show dut Mr. Jones who is uh native uv Melbourne Australiuh is sevunty un tree quarters inches in height un sevun un one eight inches in widt no more no less his highly illoominatin story is us follows ut duh age uv toiteen years Mr. Jones weighed approximutly tree hundud pouns un wus un acute suffrur frum many uv duh besknown ailmunts such us noomoniuh gout acne tootache indiegestion pulmunnurry tooburcyoulosis un dut mohs obscoor uv all huemun diseases cindurulluh in considuration uv wich fact uh council made up uv mohs uv duh notuble soigeons un speciulis frum duh Younighted Kinkdumb requested duh suffrur tuh place hisself upun uh carefully selected gastrunomic progrum compose chiefly uv watur radishes stringbeans un wustursheer sauce upun wich he has subsisted evur since ut duh presun writin Mr. Jones tips duh beam ut precisely sixtynine pouns un says he nevur felt bettur in his life wears day un night un his left ankle chust above duh knee un ordinury size sealring inscribe wid duh initiuls A.J. un presunted tuh duh wearur un duh fort uv Chooleye nineteen hundud un five by duh Inturnationul An-tie-hippo-fajic Association in tribute tuh his undenieubl poisyveerunce loyulty un courage dis way evrybudy step dis way. (*Disappears. The* HUMAN NEEDLE *converses, offers photographs of himself and displays his anklering.*)

MISS LOOK WEIRD (*To* MISS LISTEN): Think of a man starving himself to avoid honest labour! (MISS LISTEN *shakes her maskface disgustedly*)

BARKER (*From the platform of the rising* SIX HUNDRED POUNDS OF PASSIONATE PULCHRITUDE, *gestures fervently*): All right boys un goils right ovur here un make it snappy—. (*The* CROWD *swirls toward him*) —Nex we have, upun uh speciully design reinforce concrete platform wich travuls wid her werever she goes duh knee plus ultry uv affectionut obesity duh indolunt acmy uv amorous adiposity duh mountain uv libidinous ee-quilibrium Miss Eva Smith bettur known tuh uh legiun uv admirurs us Lidl Eva built like uh big bright bunch uv B. U. tiful bulloons takes one minute un sevunteen secuns fur all uv um tuh sit down two minutes un fiftytwo secuns fur all uv um tuh stand up un frum half uh day tuh twentyfour hours fur duh on-sombul tuh rise from uh recumbunt position unassisted by duh stopwatch ladies un genlmun tuh contumplate dis climax uv frankly female corpulanse is tuh agree wid duh celubrated preachur who wus hoid tuh remark diereckly aftur makin Lidl Eva's acquaintunce dut if duh o-riginal Eve had been like her duh price uv figleaves would have tripled in duh Gawdn uv Eden step right up close evrybudy youse nevur seen nutn like Eva caws Eva doan begin un Eva doan end un Eva's chust one chin aftur unuddur dis way ladies blow yur eyes tuh uh good time wid duh livin illustration uv duh famous maxim Eat Un Grow Tin I wishes tuh announce in duh case uv Miss Smith dut duh managemunt inkois no responsubility fur feyenanciul un uddur losses occasion tuh poisuns nut already acquainted wid duh fac dut youse can lose uh five dollur bill in duh smalles wrinkle uv her eyelid step right up glimpse duh six hundud pouns of poisunully conducted pullcrytood dut makes uh billiardball look like uh cookie dis way tuh duh fort diemension. (*The* SIX HUNDRED POUNDS OF PASSIONATE PULCHRITUDE *converses and offers photographs of herself as the* BARKER *disappears in the* CROWD)

MISS LISTEN WEIRD (*To* MISS LOOK): You'd think people would have a little shame, wouldn't you. (MISS LOOK *shakes her maskface disgustedly*)

BARKER (*From the* MISSING LINK's *platform*): Ladies un genlmun—. (*The* CROWD *swirls toward his fervent beckonings: the* MISSING LINK *does not move*) —Gimme duh honur uv yur attention nex we have, Ge Ge duh mystury uv duh ages duh missin link in duh chain uv evulooshun frum prehistoric times tuh now duh huemun inturrogationpoint duh secrut uv our hairy ancesturs nut tuh be confuse wid manifole mendacities fakes counterfeit ur spyourious imitations uv duh o-riginul wich wus discovered in nineteen hundud un one in duh jungles uv Darkest Africuh by un expedition compriesin toiteen memburs uv duh Royul Darwiniun Society see It pounce upun Its meat like summuh youse fellurs seen uh swell skoit pounce on uh T. totully tran-sparunt bargain ut duh lonjuhray countur eminun speciulis frum all ovur dese Younighted States un purfessurs uv sighkology uv our foremost universities havin toroughly examine Ge Ge by evry intimut means known tuh duh corporeel un mentul sciences incloodin syntetic bloodtests telepatic waves cerebrul photogruphy postprandiul iodic injections testicullur hypnotism rhapsodic vaginul eelectrolysis decalcomaniuh un X ray have purnounce Him ur Her posolutely younique un absitively jenyouwine five hundud dollurs reward will be paid tuh duh man womun ur chile dut can solve Ge Ge's mystury step dis way evrybudy. (*Disappears, as the* MISSING LINK *jumps about uttering uncouth cries and pointing happily to Itself*)

WILL *and* BILL OF ACT II, SCENE 4 (*In unison, to the* MISSING LINK): Who are you?

MISSING LINK (*Interrupting Its antics, haughtily retorts in excellent English*): I am. (*It resumes Its crying and jumping*)

BARKER: Right ovur here ladies dis way gents step right up evrybudy—. (*The* CROWD *swirls toward the platform of the* TATTOOED MAN, *who rises*) —Ladies un genlmun nex we have, A. I. Dolon duh Tatood Man born in duh city uv Boston un duh twelfth day uv Augus eighteen hundud un ninetyeight shipped us cabinboy un duh skoonur Muddur Mucree chust off duh coast uv Timbucktoo duh vessul hit uh cyclone un sunk in midocean all hans bein lost excep duh heroic

cabinboy who swum fur sevun days un six nights landin in uh
state uv complete spirichool un physicul exhustion only tuh
fine hisself surrounded by uh tribe uv two hunded headhuntin
maneatin canibuls all poligamous starknaked un yellin bloody
moidur wus ovurpowured in spite uv un heroic defence un put
in duh fatninpen fur Sunday dinnur in wich pitiful condition
he nevurduhless suckseeded in attractin duh notice uv duh
favorite wife uv duh canibul kink who had him released un
made uh membur uv duh tribe un condition dut his en-tire
body widout exception should be adorned embellished un
uddurwise ornamented wid emblums mottos pickshurs un sim-
ilur insigniuh symbolic uv duh occasion prefurin decoration
tuh det duh heroic seamun ak Y. essed wid duh trooly incred-
ibul results wich fur duh fois time it is duh privilege uv duh
genrul public tuh behold incloodin un soitn more intimut parts
uv Mr. Dolon's unatumy portraits uv his toityfive B. U. tiful
wives all between duh ages uv twelve un sixteen step right up
ladies un gents.

MISS STOP WEIRD (*Skeptically*): May I ask how long this
person lived among the savages?

BARKER: Youse may lady fur ten years durin wich time A.
I. Dolon convoited duh en-tire tribe tuh Christianity un in
addition established uh tuh speak milely flourishin branch uv
duh Y.W.C.A.

MISS STOP WEIRD (*Convinced*): That was very noble of
him. (*The* BARKER *steps down from the* TATTOOED MAN's *platform and disappears in the* CROWD. *The* TATTOOED MAN *revolves slowly.*)

ENGLISHMAN OF ACT II, SCENE 6: I say old egg, you carry a
bally picture-gallery on your back—what?

TATTOOED MAN (*Insultedly*): Dat ain no picher gallry,
buddie.

ENGLISHMAN: Indeed? I rather supposed it was.

TATTOOED MAN (*Indignantly*): Soitnly not. Dat's Awt, dat
is.

BARKER (*Reappearing beside the fifth platform, gestures
fervently and shouts*): Evrybudy dis way please—. (*The*
CROWD *swirls toward the fifth platform with its mysterious
curtained booth*) — Now we comes tuh duh cornbeefun-
caviare uv duh hole shibang duh boin my close I'm in Heavun
duh now youse sees it un now youse tinks youse sees it duh
jenyouwine P.S. duh resistunce duh undielooted o-riginul

milkshake uv duh ages Princess Anankay duh woil's foist un foremohs exponunt uv yaki-hooluh-hiki-dooluh uddurwise known us duh Royul Umbilicul Bengul Cakewalk comes frum duh lan were duh goils bade in nachurl shampain tree times uh day un doan wear nutn between duh knees un duh neck evrybudy wise up tuh dis fac duh managemunt is incloodin Princess Anankay's soopurspectaclur ac widout extruh charge tuh nobudy get dat ladies un gents youse see her strut her stuff fur duh o-riginul price uv admission no more no less namely un to wit two bits two five jits five makin fiveuntwenty ur twentyfive cents duh fort part uv uh silvur dollur all youse bohs guys bums ginks un nuts wut are treaded fur uh ----- step dis way duh Princess Anankay is about tuh purform fur duh benefit uv duh Oreye-entul Ee-lectrickully Lighted Orphunts' Home un duh boys in genrul uh hiddurto strickly sacred Oo-pee-lah ur Spasmwriggle diereck frum duh temple uv You You walk right up gents duh Princess wears so lidl youse can stick her full uv looks like she wus uh pincushion O dut ticklish dut magnifisunt Huemun Form Divine—. (*Shouts, pointing at* HIM *who stands on the outskirts of the* CROWD) —Crawl right up un all fives fellur give duh Princess uh fiftyfifty chawnce wid youse kiddo she'll boost yur splendi-furous bowlegged blueeyed exterior out uv duh peagreen inte-rior uv pinkpoiple soopurconsciousness fourteen million astrul miles intuh duh prehensile presinks uv predetoimine prehis-toric preturnachurl nutn! (*With a vivid gesture, he pulls aside the curtain. A* WOMAN's FIGURE—*completely draped in white and holding in its arms a newborn* BABE *at whom it looks fondly—stands, motionless, in the centre of the diminutive room. The* CROWD *recoils.*)

THREE MISS WEIRDS (*Disgustedly, in unison*): It's all done with mirrors! (*The* WOMAN's FIGURE *proudly and gradually lifts its head: revealing the face of* ME. HIM *utters a cry of terror. Total darkness—confused ejaculations of rage dwindle swirlingly to entire silence.*)

scene 7 (*Scene: The room as it first appeared [Act I, Scene 2] but without* HIM'*s hat on the sofa and with the flowers on the table.*

ME *and* HIM *occupy the same positions with respect to each other and to the room itself as when Scene 5 of Act III was interrupted by darkness.*)

ME: I am thinking.

HIM: And may I ask what you are thinking?—Anything everything nothing or something: which is it?

ME: The last.

HIM: Something?

ME: Something.

HIM (*After a pause*): Is it something about the window?

ME: No.

HIM: About the door?

ME: No.

HIM: About what's behind you?

ME: Not exactly. No.

HIM: But you're thinking something about this room, aren't you?

ME: Yes, I'm thinking something about this room.

HIM: I'm afraid that you'll have to tell me what you are thinking.

ME: Can't you guess? I'll give you time.

HIM: Time is the because with which some dolls are stuffed. No, I can't guess.

ME (*Quietly*): It has only three walls.

HIM (*Looks about him in astonishment*): Behind you—that's a wall, isn't it?

ME: That's one.

HIM: One—and what's there? (*Pointing to the door wall*)

ME: A wall.

HIM: Two—and there? (*Pointing over his shoulder to the window wall behind him*)

ME: Three.

HIM: Three—and what do you see there? (*Indicating the invisible wall*)

ME: People.

HIM (*Starts*): What sort of people?

ME: Real people. And do you know what they're doing?

HIM (*Stares at her*): What are they doing?

ME (*Walking slowly upstage toward the door*): They're pretending that this room and you and I are real. (*At the door, turning, faces the audience*)

HIM (*Standing in the middle of the room, whispers*): I wish I could believe this.

ME (*Smiles, shaking her head*): You can't.

HIM (*Staring at the invisible wall*): Why?

ME: Because this is true.

(*Curtain.*)

A TRAGEDY *BOUFFE* IN ONE ACT

chronicles

of

hell

by Michel de Ghelderode

Translated by

George Hauger

Fastes d'enfer, written and published in 1929,
was first produced at the Théâtre d'Atelier,
Paris, on July 11, 1949.

Him is about being born, *Chronicles of Hell* about dying. Set not in a dehumanized, mechanized metropolis in the twentieth century, but in a "decaying episcopal palace in bygone Flanders," Ghelderode's Gothic drama at first seems an anomaly in the avant-garde of the between-wars period, with little relation to the other plays in this collection. *Chronicles of Hell* totally ignores the social and political issues raised by Toller, Brecht, and Olyesha, as well as the problems of the disintegrating personality explored by Pirandello, Cummings, and Witkiewicz. Yet none of the plays in the collection so well illustrates the theories of Antonin Artaud or so effectively carries out the program of Witkiewicz. In their theoretical writings, both Artaud and Witkiewicz argue for a theatre rid of psychology and storytelling based on bourgeois notions of reality. Instead, they demand a total spectacle, irrational and mysterious as a dream, that will overwhelm the spectator by its sensory impact. *Chronicles of Hell,* by its absence of ideological or didactic concerns, its bypassing of psychology, its transposition into a distant world of strange colors and shapes, and its extreme theatricality, exemplifies the Theatre of Cruelty and recalls Artaud's cry: "The sky can still fall on our heads. And the theater has been created to teach us that first of all."

Both Artaud and Witkiewicz see painting as the analogue for a new theatre. The Belgian playwright Ghelderode seems, in fact, to follow Artaud's advice to theatricalize "the nightmare of Flemish painting." In *Chronicles of Hell,* Ghelderode writes as a painter, utilizing color, image, and action, rather than words alone, to create a baroque canvas of hallucinatory intensity.

Chronicles of Hell illustrates the non-discursive poetry of stage action and image which Jean Cocteau called "poetry of the theatre" (as opposed to verse drama, "poetry in the theatre") and which Artaud and Witkiewicz also advocated.

With powerful, often disgusting images of sight, sound, smell, and touch, Ghelderode bombards his audience, shocking them into seeing themselves unmasked—hypnotized and crushed by images of their own desperate deformity.

By means of noises and sounds, for example, Ghelderode dramatizes the transformation of people into beasts and objects. Krakenbus bleats like a sheep; Pikkedoncker makes ding-dong and booming noises like a bell; Carnibos smacks and slurps, and gurgles not only while he is eating but even when he anticipates eating. Crowd sounds mingle with the rumblings of the priests' innards, and no one can tell whether a certain noise is thunder or Simon's stomach.

Often using words for their purely sensory impact, Ghelderode fulfills Artaud's demand for an incantatory language. In addition to a visceral, baroque French, Ghelderode uses two other languages, Church Latin and Flemish, for maximum sound value. The characters' names—Krakenbus, Pikkedoncker, Duvelhond—have a physical roughness that catches in the throat. The linguistic virtuosity and (largely cacophonous) word-music, reinforcing the visual, creates what Ghelderode calls an oral symphony, a dramatic poem of epic inspiration, and a tragedy *bouffe*.

Though set in the past, the play is not a historical drama or an attempt to reconstruct another era. It is a picture of man's bestiality and grandeur transposed to a mythic time. Ghelderode's creation of an imaginary world of the past, festering with plague, death, and destruction, opens a new dimension of reality which functions as a metaphor for our own world with its scourges and unrest. *Chronicles of Hell* is demonic poetry.

The decaying palace in bygone Flanders, with its tapestries in shreds, its baroque trappings, its sumptuous table, silver setting, and crystal, is surrounded by an invisible and threatening crowd, whose ominous murmur can be heard throughout the play. Also engulfing the grotesque palace is a storm that wants to break but cannot, though thunder and flashes of lightning grow in oppressive intensity. Just as the storm cannot let loose its fury and the mob cannot vent its wrath, so the bishop—choking on a poisoned host which he vainly tries to spit out—is unable to let go of life and die. *Chronicles of Hell* is a terrifying, grotesque tragedy of blocked passages and constricted outlets. Storm, crowd, and the preternaturally grandiose bishop who comes back to life after being

pronounced dead find comic counterparts in the lesser physiological blockage of the priests' intestinal and digestive functions. The agonizing constriction, increasing painfully through
the play, is followed by a massive discharge and sense of
relief. Catharsis is both figurative and literal, a purging of both
emotions and bowels. The storm has spent itself, the wrath of
the crowd has waned, the bishop and his mother have died,
the priests have shit in their pants out of fear, and the new
bishop has farted. Tragic conflict in this play is neither
economic, ideological, nor psychological but, paradoxically,
cosmic and physiological.

Ghelderode's onslaught on the audience begins at the outset
as the play, in Artaud's words, "spreads its visual and sono-
rous outbursts over the entire mass of spectators." The priests
personify grotesque, unnatural malfunction and unhealthy
blockage. Krakenbus has a hump on his back, Simon a dis-
tended belly. Hopping about the table stuffing hunks of meat
into his mouth, the gross Carnibos keeps choking on them and
spitting out pieces. Foul, loathsome metaphor stresses all
aspects of man's lowest nature. "I once dreamed I was on all
fours eating refuse in a charnel house," Carnibos exclaims
gleefully. All human relations and activities are presented as
forms of mastication, digestion, and elimination.

While the priests are the disgusting comic devils of Ghelderode's hell, butting heads like goats and knocking each other
down, the masses are the fearful, superstitious peasants from a
country scene by Breughel. Represented by the butchers, the
mob demands a blessing from the bishop or else there will be
real butchery. Fearful of a rebellion when they learn that the
masses are stirring, the authorities call out the soldiers.
Ghelderode presents revolution as a grotesque nightmare.
"That's real politics! Blessing and butchery!" exclaims Krakenbus. Ghelderode's vision of human society is that of
Brecht's *Saint Joan of the Stockyards*, without ideology and
against a medieval background.

Chronicles of Hell progresses by accumulation, repetition,
and intensification. The lightning grows bluish. The crowd
boos, whistles, barks, and bellows with laughter. The double
doors are opened, revealing the mortal remains ("meat," in
Carnibos' description) of the bishop stretched out to full
length on a tilted funeral couch in a room with a hundred
candles (which grows to a thousand in a later stage direction).

The doors are closed, followed by more gloom and mumbled Latin. Atmosphere, more than plot, sustains the slow unfolding of this ghoulish situation. The papal nuncio describes the demon-infested world of Flanders, all fogs and marshes. A baroque narration describes the past of the fabulous Jan in Eremo: born of the fornication of a monk and a mermaid, he arrived in the town during a time of pestilence, famine, madness, and burning corpses, and miraculously drove the plague away. Following this bizarre account, Jan's corpse struggles to its feet and begins supernatural combat with the new bishop. In a spectacular, non-verbal scene, Ghelderode exploits the full range of theatrical possibilities of Jan's return to life. Illuminated by flashes of lightning, the resurrected prelate staggers down the stairs, bumps into a table covered with silver and goblets, then pulls the wax out of his throat with a knife, drinks, spews out a stream of wine like a gargoyle, and finally tries to dislodge the wafer from his throat, emitting a horrible rattle like the grating of a rusty pump. Described in a page and a half of stage directions, this scene without words may well be the most powerful in the play.

The priests fear the coming end: "The rabble are piling up barrels of powder. We are going to be blown up . . ." The revolution—grotesque, apolitical, asocial—is mounting, another expression of the need for release, like the host stuck in Jan's throat and the wind in Simon's stomach. Explosions rock the building, as Simon has the arquebusier blast a hole in the door, from which a hand and then an arm appear, holding a crook. As the battle between the two giants, Jan and Simon, reaches its climax, the storm is unleashed and the crowd, crazy with lightning and gunpowder, sets off more blasts. While the priests watch the combat in dread, the old servant Veneranda, in utter stillness, subdues Jan and pulls the host out of his throat. About to die, the giant turns into a tottering old man. Disclosing herself as his mother, Veneranda forces him to bless his enemies. To the accompaniment of an immense flash of lightning, the mighty Jan dies. In the midst of the violence and noise, the grand and grotesque figure of Jan quietly shrivels into the pathetic figure of an old man and an even older woman's child—a moment of awe-inspiring recognition and unmasking. The aftermath is the subsiding of the upheaval on all levels—natural, social, and human. Simon forces Veneranda to take the poisoned host and she dies. In a spectacular, final confrontation with the people, a red light floods the stage as giant Butchers enter the room, speaking Flemish; drawing their cutlasses and overturning tables, they demand to see Jan. But their rebelliousness is now purged: they carry the body out and join the funeral procession. As it departs, the bells and sounds of lamentation drift slowly away and the priests laugh their sighs of relief. But there is a stink in the air: the odor of death and of the cowardly living who sniff one another like dogs.

characters

JAN IN EREMO (*Bishop of Lapideopolis*)
VENERANDA (*a servant*)
SIMON LAQUEDEEM (*auxiliary bishop*)
SODOMATI (*the nuncio's secretary*)
KRAKENBUS (*vicar-general*)
REAL-TREMBLOR (*archdeacon*)
DOM PIKKEDONCKER (*pleban [rural dean]*)
CARNIBOS (*chaplain*)
DUVELHOND (*guardian of the holy relics*)
THE MASTER OF THE BUTCHERS
THE BUTCHERS
AN ARQUEBUSIER
FOUR SWISS
THE CROWD

(*A decaying episcopal palace in bygone Flanders, around which an invisible and threatening* CROWD *snarls persistently during the whole of this tragedy. At the back, a wide double door, framed between columns that support a pediment, and reached by some steps. There is a Gothic doorway to the left, and farther downstage a low and narrow exit. To the right, a glass bay window looking onto the public square, through which breaks the morbid light of a stormy summer dusk. Tapestries hang in shreds on the walls, to which portraits of prelates are fastened, very high up. Everywhere at the base of the walls there are piles of baroque objects, idols, suns, witches' masks, multicolored devils, totems, stakes, and instruments of torture. But in the foreground stands a heavy table with a crimson velvet cloth, sumptuously laden with silver plate and crystal. The* CHAPLAIN *goes around the table shiftily, stealing pieces of meat and swallowing them, while the* VICAR-GENERAL, *who has taken up position on the steps at the back, looks through the keyhole.*)

CARNIBOS: Yum . . . yum . . . I'm nibbling . . . yum . . . I've done nothing! Mutton! Good! Veal! Lovely! Yum, yum, yum. . . . What hunger, what hunger! Nibble here, nibble there, oop! It's the first time so much meat has been seen at the palace. For twenty years, eh, Krakenbus? I've withered. You fed yourself on the fat in your hump, didn't you? Never any meat! I used to cry *Miserere nobis!* each day. Never, while in the town they used to set up altars in the market, bearing tottering sacrifices of rich red meats—used to hang up huge oxen, droves of them . . . Ho! Krakenbus, I saw that, and the skinny people, so skinny they frightened you, like me, murmured yum, yum, yum, before these tantalizing displays! . . . (*He puffs.*) What time are we going to eat, Krakenbus, or is this a show table that will be carried away, load and all? I'm hungry! Say nothing, since you haven't seen what I haven't done. I was setting the cold meats in order! (*He is seized by a violent cough.*) Swallowed the wrong way . . . so . . . Ach! Ouf! (*He spits a piece of meat into his hand.*) Yum! (*And eats it again.*)

KRAKENBUS (*who has stopped spying, gazes at this scene*): Heaven has punished you, ravener! This clacking of your jaws is a profanation, Carnibos, a scandal! And the only thing that can be heard of your prayers, Carnibos, is yum, yum, yum. . . . Stop, you devourer! When there's nothing else left, you'll swallow the knives and the cloth. . . . Your sin—

CARNIBOS: My illness, not my sin! Look, Krakenbus, a chicken. Ho, this leg! (*With his mouth full.*) Those who have a stomach, eat; those who have a hump, glue themselves to keyholes.

KRAKENBUS (*who has come close to the table*): It's a pious service that I perform! Take care, my hump contains a second brain, and venom! . . . I am as spiteful as I am humped, as humped as I am spiteful, meat thief! You shall suffer! You shall eat your dirty feet, your knotted guts, your spongy heart! You shall trim yourself to the bone. Put that fowl back in its place and go and wash your hands, your sticky hands. Lick those hands whose marks one finds on sacred cloths that are polluted forevermore. . . .

CARNIBOS (*humble*): Yes, reverend hump. My punishment! I once dreamed I was on all fours eating refuse in a charnel house. Yum, yum, yum . . . But tell me, dear doctor of humpology, is what we do in our dreams reckoned against us?

KRAKENBUS: No, it all depends, chaplain. Yes indeed, when one's head is full of sticky water, greenish pus, like yours. (*He laughs unpleasantly.*) Gnaw your nails, which are too long, as well, chaplain. There are little worms under them. And close your lipless mouth, chaplain. Your breath breeds violet flies. . . . (*He is close to* CARNIBOS.) You will confess these foul dreams to me. I demand it. . . . No? (*With a sudden stamp of his heel, he crushes* CARNIBOS' *foot.*)

CARNIBOS: Ow!

KRAKENBUS: Suffer in silence! And let me have your other foot! I'm going to bruise it in its turn; one pain may drive out the other. . . . No? (*In a smooth voice.*) Talking about feet, I have just seen something philosophical. (*Drawing close to* CARNIBOS.) Sorry yet, glutton? (*He lays hold of a slice of meat.*) Open your mouth! (*And he puts the meat in.*) Give thanks, cockroach! Thanks!

CARNIBOS (*devouring it*): Thanks, holy hump! . . . Ivory hump! . . . Miraculous hump! . . . (*Having finished, he puffs.*) This spectacle? You must teach me to watch through keyholes. . . . Which eye does one use? Left? Right? They say that in time one's eye becomes shaped like a keyhole. I prefer eaves-dropping. There! See my ear, a delicate shell. . . . (*The two* PRIESTS *have gone toward the back and have stopped on the steps leading to the double door.*)

KRAKENBUS: Bend down, look, and not with half an eye. Look with all your eyes, for you will never again see anything like it!

CARNIBOS (*watching through the keyhole*): Yum, yum, yum!

KRAKENBUS: What do you see?

CARNIBOS: Meat! Nothing but meat! A hairy bear. No, it has feet. It's a man. (*Standing upright.*) A dead man!

KRAKENBUS: Right! And what is a dead man?

CARNIBOS: Meat.

KRAKENBUS: No, chaplain. A dead man is two feet! A human being has to be dead for anyone to notice that he has feet. I like seeing dead people. And I've seen some! Men, women too. But never, I swear, was it given to me to see a dead person like this one! Like this one!

CARNIBOS: You couldn't say he's naked, hairy as he is. (*Chuckles.*) A moral in that? When men die, they are chucked into lime. Beasts? Carved up and eaten. As for game, it's decently buried, so that it takes on its flavor. (*He pushes* KRAKENBUS *who has begun spying again.*)

KRAKENBUS (*standing up, hustles the* CHAPLAIN): The dead man is still warm. Cross yourself, dipping crumbs!

CARNIBOS: After you. . . . (*He avoids* KRAKENBUS, *who is seeking to crush his foot with a stamp of the heel.*) Hi! My feet are alive. Peace!

KRAKENBUS: Peace! . . . Let us embrace. (*They go toward each other to embrace, lower their heads, and bang their foreheads together. Double laughter. The* PLEBAN *enters from the left.*)

DOM PIKKEDONCKER: He, he, and I . . .

CARNIBOS: And the dead man make four.

KRAKENBUS: A dead man is nobody. Good evening, pleban.

DOM PIKKEDONCKER: They told me they were sounding passing bells, and I couldn't hear them at all, not at all. . . .

Poor, yes. . . . For a bishop—Holy Virgin!—they should ring royally! Ding-dang-dongs well struck. Not thin-mouthed bells, great thick-lipped ones that go (*Motion of pulling the rope.*) boo-oo-oom! . . . Boo-oo-oom! . . . I'm sweating from it!

KRAKENBUS: You are an old fool, Dom Pikkedoncker!

DOM PIKKEDONCKER (*putting a trumpet to his right ear*): What did you say?

KRAKENBUS: I pledge my word that a bishop may not be worth a chime of pots and pans! (*Mocking.*) That talks of setting the great bells ringing, and it wouldn't hear the walls of Jericho fall.

CARNIBOS (*pulling* KRAKENBUS' *sleeve*): Take care of the deaf one! . . . He hears nothing of what you shout and overhears everything you whisper.

DOM PIKKEDONCKER: Exactly. I shall say that display, whose custom is falling into disuse, is necessary. I love ceremony. Even Hell displays such. . . .

KRAKENBUS: He has been there. . . .

DOM PIKKEDONCKER (*who has heard*): Yes. . . . To buy a place there for you, in a noxious dungeon where you will crush slugs, krak, krak, Krakenbus! . . . (*Shaken by laughter.*) And the deceased? . . .

CARNIBOS: They're rigging it out in priestly fashion. You'll have display! . . . It's the rule. For myself, I'm of the opinion that a sack was enough. . . .

DOM PIKKEDONCKER (*counting*): So many candles, so many succentors, so many clerics. . . . A coffin of some size will be needed, you know. . . .

CARNIBOS: I say a sack would do!

DOM PIKKEDONCKER: Such a body! What did he weigh? And dead, twice as much as when alive. . . . What were you saying?

KRAKENBUS: You trickster! Is this trumpet at your ear for listening to thoughts?

DOM PIKKEDONCKER: A marvelous little horn, my friends, made by a renowned physician, and with which I hear all I want, and even what I don't want. A dead man would be less deaf than me, my friends. Try it. Tell me something!

KRAKENBUS: How is your rural deanery, dear rural dean?

DOM PIKKEDONCKER: Not bad, I say. . . .

CARNIBOS: Do you hear music as well? Listen. . . . (*He sings into the trumpet.*)

That old man Noah one day
Had drunk more than his fill.
I heard his daughter say—
She who liked him ill—

DOM PIKKEDONCKER (*singing*):
    "I'll have the breeches off the fool!
    Come, sister dear, and help me pull."

Be quiet! If God had a trumpet like mine! . . . Do you hear
bells, at last, bells? (*He lays hold of a knife and strikes the
crystal glasses on the table.*) Ting . . . tang . . . Saint Donatus'!
Clang, Saint Walburga's! Her name is Maria. . . .

KRAKENBUS (*who has meanwhile filled several glasses*):
What of it? No. Glasses, I empty them, I do. . . . (*He drinks.*)

CARNIBOS (*drinking*): I no longer say yum, yum, but glug,
glug. . . .

DOM PIKKEDONCKER (*drinking*): Believe me, brethren, I'm
in favor of bells and towers, square towers crammed with
bells. There are not enough towers being built, there are not
enough bells being cast, and that is why religion is losing its
allure. When Flanders is bristling all over with towers, Jesus
will enter the cities of stone and bronze to the sound of the
chimes. And not along the streets, no! He will walk on the
towers. . . . (*Senile laugh.*) I'm not drunk, not at all. You will
be, today. A great day for the lesser clergy, isn't that so?
Wine! Tell me, what did we come here to do?

KRAKENBUS: To cry! When the shepherd is gone, the sheep
go baa-aa! Bleat! Let us bleat! . . .

CARNIBOS: May the Most High bring it about that the new
shepherd does not molest his flock and that he wields a crook
rather than a bludgeon! What did we come to do? I know:
eat! This light repast is for the vigil. In three days, the trium-
phal banquet! Then . . . then will be the time for ringing the
bells, the great bells. The occasion? Eating in this palace!
Starving priests who have come running in packs from all the
parishes! Historic day! One used to eat on the sly in this place.
I used to go and eat in the privy. . . .

DOM PIKKEDONCKER: Already? . . . I hear them rumbling,
the priests, their innards . . .

CARNIBOS: It's the crowd gathering.

DOM PIKKEDONCKER: What does it expect, to eat as well?

KRAKENBUS: The crowd expects a corpse, a corpse to gaze

at. Death, the sight of death, what more gorgeous! (DUVEL-
HOND *has come in and, with hands outstretched, he goes
toward the other three.*)

DUVELHOND: Mi—mi—miserere! D—D—Death is ne—is
ne—is never . . .

CARNIBOS (*imitating him*): Who's this? The guar—guar—
guardian of the holy relics? (*And as* DUVELHOND *stands with
mouth agape, the* CHAPLAIN *thrusts in a piece of meat.*)
Swallow it!

DUVELHOND (*choking*): Ah! . . . Ouf! . . . Pfaugh! . . . Ouf!
. . . Ah!

DOM PIKKEDONCKER: Listen to the stammerer! He's giving
His Highness' funeral oration! As a deaf man, I find it elo-
quent.

KRAKENBUS: That? Already on the way to hew relics from
His Highness' remains? They're yours, Duvelhond, yours. . . .
His hair, his nails . . .

CARNIBOS: His last gasp. . . . The last gasp that he belched
up. . . .

DOM PIKKEDONCKER: What?

CARNIBOS: Oh, worthy of him! One didn't expect less of His
Highness in that supreme moment. What was the word? No, I
shan't tell it to you, not me!

KRAKENBUS: Nor me! Why are you growing pale, pleban?
Could you have heard this word in your wooden ear?

DOM PIKKEDONCKER: The thickest walls must have heard it.
It's your hump that's growing pale, vicar. And your rat's
snout, chaplain. Candle color . . .

CARNIBOS: I'm pale with hunger, yum!

DUVELHOND (*interposing*): His High—Highness said as he
died . . .

KRAKENBUS (*crushing* DUVELHOND's *foot with a swift stamp
of the heel*): Deo gratias!

CARNIBOS: Quick! He has two feet!

DUVELHOND (*limping and moaning, makes off to the left,
shaking his fists*): Curse you! (*He bumps into a newcomer,*
REAL-TREMBLOR, *whom he almost knocks over.*) Look out!
Your fee—eet! . . . Krak—Krak— (*The rest and the newcomer laugh unrestrainedly. Crestfallen,* DUVELHOND *comes
back.*)

REAL-TREMBLOR: I'm not laughing, you know. . . . (*Hilar-
iously.*) Ho, ho! And in a mortuary! Ho, ho! My feet . . . (*In*

consternation.) . . . bore me to this place, which is made majestic by the presence . . .

KRAKENBUS: Of rhetoric? Good evening, archdeacon. Good evening is what is wished.

REAL-TREMBLOR: Good evening, your reverends. . . . A thousand pardons, I was upset. . . . Have you slept these last nights of His Highness' great death agony? The knells that nothing could. assuage! . . . The public lamentations! . . . And the august deceased, tell me, have you seen him? . . .

CARNIBOS: Come here, Real-Tremblor. Why are you quaking?

REAL-TREMBLOR: Strongly affected, you know. . . . Death . . . dead people . . . very frightened, very frightened of them. . . .

DUVELHOND: G—go! . . . They are going to . . .

KRAKENBUS (*barring the way to* REAL-TREMBLOR, *who was attempting to step to the left*): Stop! You are going to salute His Highness. . . . A terrifying corpse! . . . Eyes still open . . . sagging jaw that will have to be wedged with a breviary. . . . Let's drag him there! Let's shut him up with the dreadful corpse! . . .

REAL-TREMBLOR (*struggling*): No, no! He was wicked. . . . No! Hated me! Used to say to me, sneak . . . dirty sneak . . . each time!

KRAKENBUS: How truly he spoke! (*Loosing the* ARCHDEACON.) Is it also true that you were castrated in your young days?

CARNIBOS: Let's not torment this tormented fellow! . . . What more tormented than a spy? What tale did you come to tell us? Hum, hornet. . . . In return, you won't go to the dead wicked man. . . .

REAL-TREMBLOR: What to tell you? I went in quest of information.

KRAKENBUS: You have run about the town to take a collection of rumors and remarks. Open your bag!

CARNIBOS: What is the crowd murmuring?

KRAKENBUS: The common people . . .

REAL-TREMBLOR: That a saint has just died!

DOM PIKKEDONCKER (*who has heard*): That was foreseen! The crowd canonizes! It does in a moment what Rome takes centuries to do! The crowd makes a saint of a mountebank! A saint! . . . What a disgrace sentiment is!

KRAKENBUS: Come on . . . the bottom of the bag!

REAL-TREMBLOR: Here's the filth. . . . Delight yourselves. . . .
(*He waits.*)

KRAKENBUS (*raising his heel to crush the* ARCHDEACON's *foot*): For the sneak, eh?

REAL-TREMBLOR: I was saying . . .

DOM PIKKEDONCKER: You weren't saying anything. . . .

REAL-TREMBLOR: The common folk were saying, in their jargon, that God had nothing to do with the bishop's passing away. . . . Consequently, they are babbling no longer. They are clenching their teeth and snarling, are the common people. What more do I know? The truth is that at the moment of the passing, the sun's sky suddenly darkened—it's not very light, notice—and grisly storm clouds came and piled up above the town, where they are yet, haunting in their motionlessness. For the crowds, no more is needed. . . .

KRAKENBUS: Never mind the crowd! But the storm seems to me disturbing. Where is Monsignor tarrying? Does the auxiliary see that the heavens are threatening to fall on our heads?

REAL-TREMBLOR: Monsignor must be in conference with the governor of the Old Town. They are calling out the men under arms. Why? To do the honors—and from other motives. No doubt the governor will order the closing of the city gates as well. . . .

CARNIBOS: That's the least that can be done, with these masses who know how to read the clouds. Won't they say that the plague will break out, that it's going to rain fiery swords and burning stones? That would be the limit!

DOM PIKKEDONCKER: The masses are afraid, the masses to whom all occasions for fear are good, like all those for being angry!

DUVELHOND: Would you be priests if the ma— masses weren't af—af—raid?

KRAKENBUS: Let them be afraid. Later, we shall give them festivities, consecration festivities! And if they are not satisfied with all this blessing, there will be butchery. There's real politics! Blessing and butchery!

DOM PIKKEDONCKER: Is yon Krakenbus uttering abuse?

CARNIBOS: The storm is responsible.

REAL-TREMBLOR: May the storm be without effect on Monsignor's bowels! Let us ask nothing more!

KRAKENBUS: Let Monsignor come. It's urgent. Let him push his belly on the balcony and offer it to the admiration of the crowd! And the nuncio we're expecting! It's urgent that the crowd have something to look at. . . . Something other than the canopies of the storm to look at!

REAL-TREMBLOR: In actual fact, the air is heavy, vibrant with gnats. News from without? Not very reassuring, and how right you are . . .

CARNIBOS: Is anyone asking your opinion? It's enough that the storm's tainting the meat.

REAL-TREMBLOR (*turning his back on the interrupter*): . . . for nothing augurs well. As soon as the bishop's death was known, the burgomaster, who knew the crowd was tired out with three days and three nights of waiting, called upon the brotherhoods to put on their cowls and to keep moving in an endless procession, very much reckoning that the crowd would fall into step with the penitents, as happens with us. A crowd that walks slowly, intoning psalms, behind crosses and lanterns, becomes the best, the most good-natured of crowds, doesn't it? Without taking into account that they are, at the time, escorted by armed men. But what was the reply to the magistrates from the emissaries of the people? That the people weren't troubling themselves about the threatening storm, and that they wouldn't budge, even at the risk of being struck down on the spot by lightning; that they were pleased to go in procession in honor of the bishop, but without priests or sacristans, and only in company with the carnival giants and dragons, all in silence and with dignity. This rabble has imagination! . . .

KRAKENBUS: Enough, weak mouth! You stink of fear. You are shivering in your shoes and you want your shivers to spread to the universe. . . . Since you tell your tales so badly, I resolve that you go and lick the dead man's nose. Bind him! . . . (*The others rush at the* ARCHDEACON, *who throws himself flat on his belly on the ground.*)

DUVELHOND (*shouting*): Mon—Mon—Monsignor! . . . (*Row. They all give a jump.* SIMON LAQUEDEEM *enters from the left and swoops down on the* GROUP, *which immediately breaks up.*)

SIMON LAQUEDEEM (*tracing blessings*): Bless you . . . And you, you, you. . . .

CARNIBOS: He blesses as if he were boxing your ears!

SIMON LAQUEDEEM: And that thing? (*He kicks* REAL-TREMBLOR, *who is still lying flat on the ground.*) I have blessed you, drunkard! . . .

REAL-TREMBLOR (*standing up and bowing*): I have not had anything to drink, Monsignor. . . .

SIMON LAQUEDEEM: Are you greeting my stomach? (*He shakes* REAL-TREMBLOR *and pushes him toward the* OTHERS, *who laugh shamelessly. With a sharp gesture,* LAQUEDEEM *stops this courtiers' laughter dead.*) What are you laughing at? (*Sternly.*) Alter your faces! You shall laugh later, and the good last of all. (*Raising his voice.*) For we shall be the last to laugh! (*Smooth-tongued.*) Don't chuckle, don't get excited; assume the bearing of people overwhelmed by an infinite stupor; stick your noses out; let your arms hang down and walk trembling on your feet like Barbary apes after lovemaking; have your eyes lusterless and full of gray water, and from time to time raise them skyward like blind men counting the stars. You, pleban, with the truffle-nosing snout, try it. Compose your features into this circumstantial mask, which the others will imitate. . . .

DOM PIKKEDONCKER: Is Monsignor talking to us about his health? In my opinion, nothing is as good as an enema. . . .

SIMON LAQUEDEEM: For the time being, swallow your bowel-washings, you deaf old man! My bowels are my business. For the present, it's the diocese that needs purging of what is obstructing it. The corpse, where is it? Is it prepared?

KRAKENBUS: Must be. We were waiting for you, Monsignor. And the crowd is waiting. . . .

SIMON LAQUEDEEM: I know. . . . The squares will be purged as well. . . . We know our duties. . . . Let the nuncio get here. (*He walks up and down, talking to himself.*) I shall purge the palace of these idols. I understand, I do. And I shall drive his shadow away, obliterate him even to the trace of his footsteps! . . . And sweep out these debauched underlings. . . . (*He stops and holds his stomach, his face suddenly drawn.*) Ah!

REAL-TREMBLOR: Poor Monsignor. . . . Monsignor's poor stomach!

SIMON LAQUEDEEM (*mumbling*): My stomach! . . . Calvary of a stomach! . . . The thorns, the nails, and the lance in it. . . . (*Big sigh.*) Ouf . . . it's working loose!

CARNIBOS: An angel has passed by. . . . The wind from his wing . . .

SIMON LAQUEDEEM: *Laus Deo!* (*He mops his brow. Flashes of silent lightning quiver on the panes of the balcony.*) Who has been in the chamber? None of you? Are they taking hours over embalming him? Are you frightened to go near him dead? He won't bite you any more, my good fellows. . . . (*He goes toward the steps at the back.*) He shan't have the funeral he asked for, in open ground and without a shroud, in the outcasts' enclosure. He will be clad in iron, in lead, and in oak; he will be hidden in the deepest crypt—and the cathedral will press down with all its weight on his bones! (*Having turned toward the* ARCHDEACON.) Go and see if the nuncio is coming to us, Real-Tremblor! (REAL-TREMBLOR *goes out swiftly at the left.* SIMON LAQUEDEEM *is preparing to open the double door at the back when it half-opens. A little black shape comes into view through it.*)

KRAKENBUS: The servant! (*The little shape hugs the walls, seeking to run away. The* PRIESTS *encircle it.*) Catch the crow!

SIMON LAQUEDEEM (*apostrophizing the little* OLD WOMAN): Have you done your funeral task? (*Pause.*) Oh simplicity! She is weeping! The paradise of the innocent will be yours, old servant: you shall have your wages. . . . Vanish into your garret. Henceforth your master will have no further need of you. Let go of her!

DUVELHOND: Impru—pru—dence!

SIMON LAQUEDEEM: I say let her make ready her bits of clothes. She has the right to attend the services. Afterward . . .

CARNIBOS (*shaking the* SERVANT): What is she muttering in her patois?

VENERANDA (*frightened and in a toneless voice*): *Bid voor de ziel!*

SIMON LAQUEDEEM: Pray for the soul? By all means! Go! Let us not see you again! (VENERANDA *is pushed, without consideration, to the left, and disappears.*) I am afraid that, although she is unaware of it, this ninety-year-old knows too much. . . . Imprudence, someone said? No. The staircases in this palace are decrepit. . . . One false step. . . . (*Flashes of lightning outside. A silence during which the* CROWD *is heard snarling.*) Darkness is going to fall. . . . And this storm that seems to be holding itself back for the night! . . . And this nuncio! . . . (*Arrogantly.*) Is there no longer any give and take with Heaven? (*Noise at the left, from which direction* REAL-TREMBLOR *returns, preceding a young* PRIEST.) Him? Greetings, bambino! And the nuncio? Are you hiding him under your robe? Come, let me embrace you! (*He embraces the new arrival who shields himself.*)

SODOMATI: Don't suffocate me! . . . (*Bowing and scraping to all.*) My compliments, Monsignor! And to you, revered, very worthy, learned, and inspired gentlemen. . . . Here we are at last! What den are you drawing me into? The crowd surrounded my carriage. Gallows birds hurled foul words at me. Imagine! They shouted *"Rok af!"* at me. What does that mean?

CARNIBOS: "Tear off his gown!" . . . nothing else.

SODOMATI: Horror!

SIMON LAQUEDEEM: No doubt the people thought to see a pretty girl. Never mind that. . . . Have you brought the nuncio to me?

SODOMATI: Became unexpectedly ill on learning of the decease of the bishop. Understand? I am acting as his substitute. Have the time to make an appearance, then I'm off, understand? I don't like dramatic ceremonials the way they carry them out in this country. Is this a way of doing things? A bishop dies . . .

KRAKENBUS: And what a bishop, too!

SODOMATI: . . . whom I indeed regret not having known alive! The nuncio became crimson when he was spoken to about this apostle. . . . (*Indicating the wall at the back.*) I can imagine the person, incarnated by these abominations, these idols. . . . Bah! . . . What bad form!

SIMON LAQUEDEEM: His friends. . . .

CARNIBOS: His only friends. . . .

SIMON LAQUEDEEM: His court. He was fond of these idols, these monsters, yes, which, he said, consoled him for the hideousness of our human faces. He liked the false gods, his victims, he said, and gazed on them with a culpable pride, like a barbaric warrior counting his trophies. . . .

KRAKENBUS: We have got to admit that he converted savages, and of a dangerous sort. He had his ways: beating and barking! . . . Poor savages converted in this way to a hard life, and all their gods stolen! Why didn't this formidable zealot stay on the other side of the globe!

CARNIBOS: More than that! . . . He drew a subtle argument from these idols. "Men of the Church, my savages were nearer to the divine truth in adoring these untrue gods than you, the anointed, who pretend to adore the true god!" he said. . . .

SODOMATI: Oh, the shameless creature! He said that?

SIMON LAQUEDEEM: Said? No! Shouted . . . bawled . . . howled!

SODOMATI: How I pity you, brethren, how I pity you! Free yourselves as quickly as possible from these symbols of Evil.

Bury them with your bishop, or, better, burn them. . . . The nuncio spoke to me about them. It is not rash to assert that wooden and metal devils possess baleful powers, and may have been masters of your bishop's mind; not rash to assert that these idols have operated, causing the absurd and foolish actions of your bewitched bishop. . . . The nuncio maintains that this palace is under a spell—and I believe it! Make a colossal pile of faggots. Burn these appurtenances of idolatry. The nuncio even believes that these poisonous powers are spreading, contagiously reaching the town, the country, the whole diocese. And I believe it! . . . Only look at the way the crowd behaves since the death of the wonder-worker, I mean the bishop, the wretch . . . I mean the late Monsignor, whom the Almighty will forgive by reason of his faith and zeal, which were worthy of past ages, but no longer of ours. . . .

SIMON LAQUEDEEM: We shall burn them, bambino. . . . These idols were truly the bishop's mistresses, and they ruled the town and the diocese! Burn? It's the whole poisoned population that should be thrown on the pile, a pile as vast as the diocese . . . (*His voice chokes.*) . . . to destroy these packs of wolves—for our pastor's sheep are fierce wolves, believe me!

SODOMATI: Calm yourself, auxiliary! . . . If fire can cleanse the diocese, burn, burn. . . . But will the fire change these wolves into lambs? I doubt it. A strange race in this land of marshes, freethinking, subversive, yes, violent, unmanageable! Among you here, heresiarchs spring up like tares! . . . Ungodly race!

KRAKENBUS: We belong to it, if you don't mind!

SODOMATI: You belong to it! I was thinking so as I watched you making faces. And since you admit it . . . It's obvious the idols have taken possession of you as of the others. You make unsightly grimaces like men possessed. You are the suspect priests of a people of possessed souls!

SIMON LAQUEDEEM: All that because they wanted to tear off your gown, bambino? Calm yourself, pretty secretary! We shall do our burning. We shall burn the sodomites as well. We know how to behave and how to lead our flocks without the advice of the nuncio, pretty secretary! We shall burn the seed of the heresiarch, and lilies shall sprout in the frog-filled marshes. Our pestilential bogs shall become mystical meadows, ineffable gardens of the nunciature, where little angels with chubby buttocks shall dance. . . .

SODOMATI (*superciliously*): I beg your pardon, Simon Laquedeem! . . . I beg your pardon for having confused you! . . . You are not of this race. . . . I was forgetting. You are indisputably descended from kings and prophets, which I would not have believed had I not read your disclaimer of your ancestors written in Hebrew on a foreskin! . . . Burn the sodomites and the heresiarchs. In addition, burn the Jews, the filthy Jews, since this diocese is overflowing with them, Simon Laquedeem—since it is not known by what operation of unwonted charity this diocese receives them, Simon Laquedeem, to the extent of resembling a huge ghetto. . . .

SIMON LAQUEDEEM (*furious, rushes at* SODOMATI): *Rok af!* Strip him! (*Uproar.* REAL-TREMBLOR *intervenes and holds the* AUXILIARY BISHOP *back. Outside, flashes of silent lightning.*)

REAL-TREMBLOR: The storm . . . oh! . . . Everything is going wrong!

KRAKENBUS: They will become so excited that they'll draw down a thunderbolt! Instead of calming the crowd! . . . Give me the aspergillum, well soaked. . . .

SIMON LAQUEDEEM (*pulling himself up*): That is right. We are delaying a great deal. Let us show ourselves on the balcony and give blessing. This action may have results. And no doubt the crowd will think we are warding off the storm. Prepare yourselves! Get on my left, Sodomati. The presence of a Roman witness has its importance in these difficult moments. (*The group forms up,* CARNIBOS *remaining behind, near the table, and* KRAKENBUS *hastening to the right where he goes to open the balcony windows with a crash. At once, the distant murmur outside comes in, amplified, and a harsh though gloomy light floods the room. Slowly, after having drawn themselves up, the* PRIESTS, *with the* AUXILIARY *leading, move to the right and disappear on the balcony.* CARNIBOS *does not follow them and sets about stealing pieces of meat which he devours swiftly. Flashes of lightning, nearer and bluish, follow each other in silence. And suddenly a fierce clamor breaks out: booing, whistling, barking, laughter—the violent* CROWD *is insulting the* PRIESTS. *The latter fall back inside in disorder. The balcony windows shut once more; the clamor diminishes. The* PRIESTS *look at one another and, in the chiaroscuro, seem to be counting their number. This confusion does not last long,* SODOMATI *taking the attention of everyone by a disordered gesticulation. Before long, he bursts out.*)

SODOMATI: We are being booed, do you hear? And for greeting, these sheaves of bare arms, these bundles of fists held out to us! The riffraff of Jerusalem didn't rage more in affronting the Messiah and calling for his execution!

DOM PIKKEDONCKER: Worthy folk! What riffraff! Alleluia! They cried out, "Alleluia!"

SODOMATI: That's what your prestige is capable of, Monsignor! (*Indicating the idols.*) And that is what the prestige of these devils can do! Is it clear enough in this doubtful evening? These devils, unchained by the disappearance of their suzerain, have overcome the vast collection of the crowd, the crowd that will fell you!

SIMON LAQUEDEEM: Am I responsible for the civil order? Have I authority to disperse crowds and control storms?

SODOMATI: The crowd that will fell you! It will serve you right. And don't reckon on being granted the benefit of martyrdom!

SIMON LAQUEDEEM: Go, and may God give you an escort of archangels! Go quickly: this moment is perilous, and those that are coming. For the time being, the crowd will content itself with pissing against your coach. Later, you might leap in the air like a puppet and fall down again, impaled through the bottom, on a picket. We are familiar with our people and their humors. . . .

SODOMATI: I shall not leave until the obsequies are over, seen by my own eyes. . . .

SIMON LAQUEDEEM: Then you will leave without delay, and you will see nothing of the carnival that follows, for the corpse will soon have tumbled down into the vault; go. . . .

SODOMATI: Prudence, Monsignor! . . . There have been refractory corpses that would not allow themselves to be interred with ease. As for your carnival, no, I shall not see anything of it; but you are not at all certain of superintending it. . . .

SIMON LAQUEDEEM: Will you explain yourself?

SODOMATI: The Holy See might become concerned about your bowels. . . . It is acknowledged that this great belly is ill and contains enough stinking breaths to infect all the nearby countries more thoroughly than heresy . . .

SIMON LAQUEDEEM (*bursting out laughing*): Really? Has it been smelled as far as Rome? What a sense of smell, bambino! . . . (*He rubs his belly.*) And if I gave off floral perfumes, wouldn't the cry be, "A miracle"? Tell me, bambino, what is your favorite flower?

KRAKENBUS: The guard. (*Four* SWISS *carrying halberds have just come in and stand waiting.*)

SIMON LAQUEDEEM (*going toward the* SWISS): These, guards? Four vergers rigged out for the occasion. You, Swiss, will station yourselves at each corner of the funeral couch and will not budge from there. Your vigil will not last long, since the corpse will go to lie in the choir of the cathedral when night falls. Don't look at the jugs. You shall have drink, but later. . . .

CARNIBOS: Those who keep vigil in a death chamber are sometimes subject to hallucinations.

REAL-TREMBLOR: Let's set our minds at rest: vergers have never been sensitive to the supernatural. Come, Switzers. . . . (*Followed by the four* SWISS, REAL-TREMBLOR *makes his way to the back and climbs the steps. He opens the double door a little way, makes the* MEN *slip through one after the other, and observes the interior. Then, after a moment, he turns toward the* COMPANY *again.*) *Facta est!* (*He indicates the door.*) Would it not be fitting to gaze in a spirit of Christian sorrow on the mortal remains of Monsignor Jan in Eremo, Bishop of Lapideopolis?

SIMON LAQUEDEEM (*after a short pause during which he has questioned his* CONFEDERATES *by his gaze*): Struck by Christian sorrow, we wish to gaze on the mortal remains of Monsignor John of Eremo, Bishop of what you said. . . . (*And, with the* AUXILIARY *leading, the* PRIESTS *take several steps toward the double door which* REAL-TREMBLOR *opens with a calculated slowness. When the door is open, a chamber is revealed, blazingly illuminated by a hundred candles which light up a tilted funeral couch on which, clothed in his canonicals, mitered, and with his crook, lies a man of remarkable height and breadth, with a grayish and shining face, and all angular, like a recumbent figure cut in stone—the mortal remains of Monsignor* JAN IN EREMO, *Bishop of Lapideopolis. The* SWISS *stand rigid at the corners of the funeral couch. Above the couch, a great crucifix. At the foot of the bed, a coat of arms showing the bearings of the* BISHOP, *anchors sable on a field of gold. With authority.*) *Flectamus genua!* . . . (*At this comand, the* PRIESTS *kneel, turned toward the chamber. The* AUXILIARY *goes up the steps and stops at the threshold. After a long pause.*) He looks still more formidable dead than living! (*He turns away and comes down the steps and prays aloud.*) *Agnus Dei, qui tollis. . . .* (*He yawns and mumbles the Latin words.*)

THE OTHERS (*confusedly making responses*): *Dona eis requiem . . .*

SIMON LAQUEDEEM (*with authority*): *Levate!* . . . (*On the command, the* PRIESTS *get up.* REAL-TREMBLOR *shuts the double door again. Now, after this brief illumination, the gloom has taken on a thickness that the lightning from outside hachures almost continuously.*)

KRAKENBUS: We need lights. . . .

SIMON LAQUEDEEM: The servants will being them when they come for the body. It was my wish that from now until then the windows of the palace should remain dark. Haven't you the most extraordinary illumination dispensed to us from the heavens?

CARNIBOS: Enough to find one's mouth. I feel weak. . . .

SIMON LAQUEDEEM: Sit down! (*The* PRIESTS *take stools from under the table and settle down.* SIMON LAQUEDEEM *remains standing and from time to time walks about.*) Who has played havoc with the food? You, you beast of prey?

REAL-TREMBLOR: The idols. . . . But the jugs are untouched, and the flasks. . . .

SIMON LAQUEDEEM: Eat. Drink. In silence, if possible. Silence would be fitting after what we have just seen.

SODOMATI: Impressive, what we have just seen! I am unaware of what this man was in life; I know what he is in death, somebody! Tell us about him, Laquedeem. I can't abide silence, particularly in this place, particularly this evening. . . .

SIMON LAQUEDEEM: What do you want me to say, since you have said everything? Somebody! There is no other comment. . . .

SODOMATI: You seem to be dreaming, Laquedeem. Are you entering into meditation when your clergy are not missing a mouthful? . . .

SIMON LAQUEDEEM: I was thinking about the inscrutability of the designs of Providence, the strangeness of certain destinies. . . . Somebody! whose shadow weighs on us, in whose shadow we live crushed down. Somebody. . . .

KRAKENBUS: He was called Jan Eremo. . . .

SODOMATI: Will you tell us his legend?

SIMON LAQUEDEEM: No, his true history—the reality is prodigious enough without adding to it. I shall relate it since you dread the silence. It will displease you, as our fogs displease you, and our marshes. . . .

SODOMATI: Your storms . . . your gloom . . .

KRAKENBUS: He was called Jan Eremo. . . .

SIMON LAQUEDEEM: Jan in Eremo was his name. . . . John in the desert, in memory of the sand hills where he was found —a child of an unknown mother, a child without a name—by the monks from the monastery of the Dunes, whom his haunting cries had alerted. It is more than seventy years since John was born in the desert, John, son of the sea and the sand, John who used to say, "I am solitude"—which he was!

RÉAL-TREMBLOR: The people say that he was born of the fornication of a monk and a mermaid!

SIMON LAQUEDEEM: And when did that happen? (*He drinks a cup of wine and throws the dregs in the interrupter's face.*) Not much is known of how this accursed being grew up in the monastery, of what his young life was like up to the day of his ordination. He was a rugged pioneer, and a daring fisherman. His brethren looked on him as being attacked by a strange insanity, and were not surprised when, once, they saw him put out to sea on an equinoctial day in a boat he had dug up from the mud, put out to sea and disappear in the foaming tempest. When their brother did not return, they believed he had perished and sang the office for the dead. (*Satisfied at his beginning,* LAQUEDEEM *gazes on the* COMPANY. *During the short silence, a rumble of thunder, still distant, is heard. All prick up their ears.*)

DOM PIKKEDONCKER: Your belly, Monsignor?

SIMON LAQUEDEEM: The bowels of the storm. The sky's grumbling pleases me, for what I am relating to you doesn't call for the song of the nightingale, I assure you, but the heart-rending cry of the sea gulls. How far had I gotten with this man?

KRAKENBUS: You had just sent him to the bottom, and the monks were singing the office for the dead. . . .

SIMON LAQUEDEEM: But it was written that the man whom the tempests and the cannibals did not want would come back to us some time, after a long, long while, on a day of calamity, a terrible day when the world and Flanders appeared to be doomed to end. . . . He came into view in a worm-eaten boat that the ocean shattered on the beach and whose sides let fall idols. The tides had submerged the ground inland, and it was by walking on the dykes, as if he were walking on the waters, that this man reached the town, this town decimated by the Plague. . . .

SODOMATI: In which chronicles are these horrors recorded?

SIMON LAQUEDEEM: In my memory. Indeed, I lived through those baleful days, and I too thought the world was going to end!

CARNIBOS: That will happen tonight.

SIMON LAQUEDEEM: Eat, Carnibos! At the time I am calling to mind, you would have done the same as the wretched inhabitants of this town, you would have devoured purple flesh from the graveyard, fighting with the rats and the dogs over it, and dying forthwith, to be devoured in your turn! . . . After the Plague, Famine and Madness took office in this town shrouded in opaque yellow mists, our town from which both the count and the bishop had fled, both the priests and the physicians, and where I, a young deacon, remained alone to comfort the dying and drag the blackened corpses to the fire. (*Pause.*) It was then that he appeared, suddenly looming out of the mists, bowed beneath a huge cross made from tarred planks. That was how he appeared! And the plague-stricken, filled with terror at this apparition, had only one word . . .

REAL-TREMBLOR: The Antichrist!

SIMON LAQUEDEEM: The Antichrist was the word that sprang from dying lips as this wild processionary passed by. He certainly had that appearance.

SODOMATI: Where was your crucifer going?

SIMON LAQUEDEEM: Straight to the market square, where a huge fire was crackling, in which corpses writhed in horrible attitudes. Was he going to walk in the flames, after having walked on the waters? The plague-stricken followed him, moaning pitifully from hope or fear. . . . And then what did he do? Threw the huge cross into the fire. A pillar of flame rose up, a glowing pillar, lifting the mists. . . . A marvel? Yes! The Plague was vanquished at once. The yellow mists broke up, the pure sky appeared, and the wind, the great blue wind, drove away the deadly miasmas. A marvel! I can still hear the crackling of the cross, the outcry of that raving crowd, above all the bells, the panic-stricken bells. . . . The survivors had rushed to the churches and had hung themselves in bunches to the ropes, and the bells began ringing, driving other bells crazy

—and in the open country, the bells gave as good as they got, rolling the news around the four corners of the horizon, the astounding news of the end of the Scourge. . . .

SODOMATI: And the author of the marvel?

SIMON LAQUEDEEM: Priest John worked another miracle. Not content with having bound the Plague in chains, he ran the Famine to earth. This inspired, or simply astute, man had discovered the siege stores in the town vaults, casks of wine and beer, salt meats, dried fish, flour, all of which was thrown to the hungry. At night, the moribund were drunk and sang and danced as at fair time. At dawn, the women were pregnant. Life was carrying on. The town had a master, Priest John! The corpses buried, the streets cleaned, the craftsmen at work, life carried on. . . . (*Pause.*) And when, after some weeks, the count came back, the bishop, the clergy, the physicians, the notables, and all those who had fled the Plague, they ran up against the master of the town and didn't know what to do. The bishop and the clergy wanted to recover this palace from which they had fled, and ran up against Priest John— what am I saying?—against Bishop John, Bishop Jan in Eremo, sent by the tempest. . . .

SODOMATI: He was, certainly! He was!

SIMON LAQUEDEEM: He was! This priest in his madness had rigged himself out in the miter, had laid hold of the crook, the crook with which he dealt out blows like a hardened trooper to the old bishop and his runaway priests, uttering the most abominable abuse that clerical ears have ever heard. And Bishop John remained in the palace, a triumphant impostor protected against all justice by the vicious adoration of the butchers and the fullers, until the day that Rome, this Rome with designs more inscrutable than those of Providence, consecrated the imposture . . .

SODOMATI: The History is written, don't amend it!

SIMON LAQUEDEEM (*forcefully*): . . . consecrated the imposture! . . . You know the rest.

SODOMATI: Not at all! I know the beginning, from your so striking evocation, which must leave you tired. Tell me the end, how he died. . . .

SIMON LAQUEDEEM: By God! Are you unaware of that, seeing that you are writing the History? He died a godly death, that's all. . . .

KRAKENBUS: When does an ecclesiastic die otherwise, even if he gives up the ghost calling on Beelzebub? . . .

SIMON LAQUEDEEM: He died a godly death, but in an unusual way; and could it be otherwise? This man who had his life, had to have his death. He had it! And the end was worthy of the beginning. . . .

SODOMATI: The end which he foretold, it seems?

SIMON LAQUEDEEM: Such premonitions are not rare. He foretold it, exactly. . . .

SODOMATI: Weren't the physicians forbidden to come near him?

SIMON LAQUEDEEM: He refused their aid, thrust them aside, and treated them as jackals. Since you are making investigations, learn that his distrust was intense. His strength was obviously declining. From day to day the skeleton's grin shaped itself in the mummified flesh of his face.

SODOMATI: You describe with talent, but what disorder . . .

REAL-TREMBLOR: Hadn't he passed the seventy years mark? Long ago. . . .

SIMON LAQUEDEEM: Since he loved the prophetic manner, he gave up his stubborn silence to utter some phrases that can be considered heavy with meaning, or as childish as the ramblings of comatose old men usually are. What did he say that may be worth anything?

CARNIBOS (*raising a finger*): "The hour I am aware of is coming, forestalling the one God appointed, and I accept it, since He allows it to be forestalled. . . ." Explain that to me!

SODOMATI: That could be explained. . . . But what disorder?

SIMON LAQUEDEEM (*who pretends not to hear the question*): Yes, it was a touching moment when I administered the last sacrament. Although overcome by a deep torpor, prefiguring the last sleep, Monsignor watched what we were doing with a half-open eye, the eye of a scraggy old eagle. . . .

SODOMATI: Well?

SIMON LAQUEDEEM: This eye, laden with an unspeakable hatred, missed nothing of my actions, followed my hands. And as I was holding out the host, the eye shot a flash of steel at me, the lips welded themselves together. But as I solemnly adjured him to receive the body and the blood of the living God, the eye grew dim and the lips unsealed. He communicated. (*A fairly long silence. Stillness. The rumbling of the storm is heard, greater than before.*)

SODOMATI: He communicated. . . .

SIMON LAQUEDEEM: Then? (*Speaking quickly, having become nervous.*) Suddenly erect, the dying man entered into a brief and harsh contest against invisible aggressors—angels or demons—of which we were the terrified witnesses. But the wrestler, seized around the waist and flung full length on his couch, fell broken. Death was winning! Then? The confirmation, the melted wax in the mouth, the red-hot iron on the feet—for we were still in doubt. . . . (*Pause.*) Do you know enough?

SODOMATI (*getting up*): No! I ask you a last time, what disorder . . .

SIMON LAQUEDEEM (*bursting out*): How do I know? (*He seizes the* SECRETARY *by the shoulders and speaks into his face.*) These questions! Have you an inquisitor's commission, little priest? There should have been previous notice. There is a right way of replying to such examinations. . . .

SODOMATI: Isn't it the current question I'm asking, just as all the town is asking it, all the diocese? (*He frees himself.*) Pardon the little priest. . . . He's a nasty noser, isn't he? You understand? He's amazed that his question upsets you to this extent. . . . (SIMON LAQUEDEEM *indulges in gesticulation unaccompanied by any words. During this silence filled with gestures, a long flash of lightning makes a pale false daylight. The* AUXILIARY *finds his voice again and speaks violently.*)

SIMON LAQUEDEEM: On my conscience! I swear . . . I swear I had no part in the death of His Highness! . . . Thus I reply to the perfidious. And may a thunderbolt—if I am lying—fall in at once on our heads, may the thunder, if I am lying . . . (*Another blinding flash of lightning. And a thunderbolt falls and strikes quite close. Everything makes a cracking sound. For a brief moment the room seems to be crackling in an outbreak of bluish fire as it is filled with a violent astral light that all at once goes out. The* PRIESTS *have risen at the shock and make defensive gestures. Outside, the* CROWD *answers the thunderbolt by a tremendous outcry. A brief confusion reigns around the table. Voices are confused. Only* LAQUEDEEM *has not stirred. He dominates the uproar.*) Sit down! What's the matter with you?

CARNIBOS: The thunder . . . fell on us . . . on the palace . . .

SIMON LAQUEDEEM (*roaring*): I heard nothing! (*Turning suddenly.*) What's happening to make your teeth chatter?

SODOMATI: What's happening? Why the thunder is talking, a voice from on high!

SIMON LAQUEDEEM (*roaring*) And what if I tell you that

nothing is happening? (*The* PRIESTS *have drawn close to the* AUXILIARY *and stand around him.*) Frightened? Of what, my children? (*He does his utmost to laugh.*) A farce, a macabre farce! (*But the double door opens a little way, and one after the other the* SWISS *escape through the narrow gap. They seem incoherent and as though distracted. Without seeing anything, they make for the left. The* AUXILIARY *springs toward them and bars their exit.*) And you, vergers? Is the chamber on fire? Frightened as well? Frightened? (*The four utter inaudible words and, hustling the* AUXILIARY, *go out like madmen. The* AUXILIARY *runs to the double door.*) A farce, I say! Don't move! Frightened? Not me, ha, not me! Frightened of what? (SIMON LAQUEDEEM *pushes the halves of the double door wide open, and the mortuary chamber is revealed, blazing with its thousand lights. Six toneless cries, the six cries of terror of the six* PRIESTS, *who are congregating at the left, ready to flee, and the ominous laugh of the* AUXILIARY *rumbling above the bleatings. At the foot of the couch and turned toward the room stands* JAN EREMO, *crook in hand, made taller still by his high miter, a dark and heavy mass hieratically sculpted and as though vibrating in the light.*)

KRAKENBUS: Help! . . . An evil spell!

SODOMATI: Exorcize it!

SIMON LAQUEDEEM (*who retires backward from the chamber toward the* PRIESTS): A farce, a macabre farce! . . . Who has planted this dummy on its feet? Or what power is dwelling in this corpse? Answer, Eremo! Dead or alive. . . . (*The* BISHOP *has stirred at his name, and takes a step forward like a block that is going to tumble down.*)

CARNIBOS: Alive!

SIMON LAQUEDEEM (*drawing farther back*): Not a genuine corpse! An impostor even in your death! What do you want? Prayers? Have you seen Hell? (*The* PRIESTS *are leaving. The* AUXILIARY *keeps on drawing back.*) Have you come back to disclose that you are damned? (*To the* PRIESTS, *who are in flight.*) Shut the doors! (*Addressing the* BISHOP *who comes forward very slowly and who has raised his right hand to his throat.*) What? Have you swallowed your tongue? What? Are toads going to shoot out of your mouth? Expect nothing from me, you automaton or ghost, nothing. . . . (*He goes out.*)

(*Noise of the door being bolted—noise of running around in the corridors, and calling. The hubbub dies away. And there is silence. A solemn silence which is aggravated by the growling of the* CROWD, *like the rumbling of the ceaseless thunder, and on which is superimposed the deep pedal of the storm that seems vocal and growls in unison with the* CROWD.

The BISHOP *has clumsily come down the steps. With empty gaze, he comes forward in the room, his crook wielded spasmodically like a blind man's staff. At each lightning flash, his face shines like metal; the gold embroidery that covers him lights up. He bumps against the banquet table. At each lightning flash, the crystal glass and the silver plate flare up. The* BISHOP *has seized a knife with which he pokes in his mouth, flicking out the wax that was obstructing it. He spits out the pieces of wax, throws the knife down, takes hold of a goblet, and drinks with head flung back. He throws the goblet away and, like a gargoyle, spews out in a jet the wine he was trying to swallow. Then he becomes transformed. A permanent rattle, like the grating of a rusty pump, comes from his freed mouth, and nothing other than this rattle will come from it. He breathes in the air and seems to expand. He becomes animated; his empty gaze is filled with phosphorescent lights. The septuagenarian becomes a kind of jerkily moving athlete, the prey of a powerful oppression. Without respite, his right hand tries to loosen invisible bonds around his throat. From time to time he thrusts his hand in his mouth, as though he were trying to pull out some plug that was choking him. Unutterable torture! Is he an old man still in the death agony, who asks to die? Is he a deceased person come back again, thrust aside by Death, who asks to live once more? Now he is in action. His gaze has sought for exits. He walks to the right where the lightning leaps about—the balcony. He is heard shaking the windows—but the windows fly into pieces. Outside, the crowd is throwing stones and bellowing. The* BISHOP *retraces his steps and hugs the back wall. Painfully mute, he turns to the terrorized or hilarious idols, as though he were asking their help, and touches them pitiably, strokes them. Since the idols remain unchanging in their grimaces, their master turns away from them and begins to turn around on the spot where he is standing when, at the left, the bolts work and,*

the door opening, light marks the exit. The BISHOP
*immediately goes toward this light, while voices call him
in the walls:* "Monsignor! . . . Monsignor! . . ." MON-
SIGNOR *dashes forward and disappears. The room
stays empty for a while. The noise of running
around resounds in the walls. And the gang of* PRIESTS
rushes into the mortuary chamber from the back. The
AUXILIARY *runs nimbly around the couch, leaps the steps
leading to the room, and pursuing his course around the
table, moves obliquely to the left and precipitately shuts
the door through which the* BISHOP *went. Then he goes
back to the center of the room where the* OTHERS, *breath-
less, have parked themselves. Only* REAL-TREMBLOR *insists
on locking the double door at the back, which he has closed
behind him, and he returns brandishing the key.*)

REAL-TREMBLOR: He's in his cage, the evil one!

SIMON LAQUEDEEM: Locked up, eh? He won't come out of
there except to the sepulcher! And if it's necessary that this
dead man should die, he shall die! That's my business. You,
keep cool and collected! Press your buttocks together, but do
what you are told, otherwise there will be slaughter!

SODOMATI: The scandal! . . . We are lost!

SIMON LAQUEDEEM: You are, if I wish it. Pitch yourself into
the water. I am staying on deck. Who will help me?

DUVELHOND: Ky—Kyrie . . .

SIMON LAQUEDEEM (*lays hold of* DUVELHOND *and pulls him
away from the group*): I'll Kyrie you! Go down and fetch one
of the arquebusiers of the guard. (DUVELHOND *goes out by the
front left exit.*) You, Real, go and make sure the militia are
still holding the approaches to the palace! And you, Carnibos,
look for some lanterns! (*The* ARCHDEACON *and the* CHAPLAIN
go out by the same exit.) Let me know if the people's pot is
still boiling. We must make haste, or we shall furnish the
bones for the soup. . . .

SODOMATI: Not die . . . not like that. . . .

SIMON LAQUEDEEM: Flayed, grilled, like pigs! (*Fat laugh.*)
The nuncio scented it. What a surprise, eh? Another marvel
from down there! Write quickly to Rome. Can you smell the
sulphur? I'm not troubled by it. . . . (CARNIBOS *comes back
carrying two lanterns which he hangs on the wall.*) Light?
That? then we are really in the abyss. Let the lightning illumi-

nate my deeds. The worst has come to pass. . . . (REAL-TREM-
BLOR *comes back*.) What have you to say?

REAL-TREMBLOR: That the worst is to come, Monsignor.
The rabble are surging forth under the lash of the storm.
The militia are holding out with great difficulty. . . . But the
butchers are mustering. With them, it will soon be all up. The
rabble want their bishop!

SIMON LAQUEDEEM: We shall give him to them.

REAL-TREMBLOR: They will come and take him. The militia
are still holding out, I said; but on the inside. And the rabble
are piling up barrels of powder. We are going to be blown
up. . . .

SIMON LAQUEDEEM: The ascension of the clergy. Splendid!
(*Furious*.) Blow up! . . . For how are you helping me? Who is
sacrificing himself?

KRAKENBUS: First, let us know is this ghost threatening us
or beseeching us?

CARNIBOS: And then, his throat. . . . What does it mean?

SIMON LAQUEDEEM: The ghost is choking. The host, which
he received in hate and not in love, is throttling him, this host
which can neither come up again nor go down and burns the
dying man whom Heaven and Hell fling back by reason of this
unachieved communion. No, this living man is no longer alive,
and this dead man is not so! He is suspended in Time as the
host is in his body. Come, let a Christian, let a priest tear out
the host—or thrust it in. . . .

SODOMATI: You are a priest and a Christian: do it!

SIMON LAQUEDEEM: He would cut through my wrist with a
bite of his teeth! But you, with your woman's hands . . . (*To*
REAL-TREMBLOR, *who is going toward the exit*.) Where are
you going? To save your skin?

REAL-TREMBLOR (*going*): My idea. . . . Save you all!

SIMON LAQUEDEEM (*made furious by this flight*): Get out!
Leave me alone. . . . Save yourselves, every one of you! . . .
And your souls! . . . Get out! (*He hurls himself into the group
of* PRIESTS *and drives them to the exit with blows from his
fists*.) Up there . . . on the roof . . . and higher . . . a charge of
powder up your ass! (*Short scuffle before the exit, through
which the hustled* PRIESTS *are lost to sight. Alone, the* AUXIL-
IARY *wipes his brow and comes back, listens to the* CROWD
*and the storm growling, then, catching sight of the idols, walks
over to them*.) And you, evil spirits, you, his faithful, are you

going to help your master? Will you defend him in misfortune, you grotesque dolls? Will you escort him in the outer darkness? Have I got to struggle with you as well? You don't stir, in your immemorial ugliness? Don't expect anything more. Your master is caught in the trap. You are afraid of me? Rightly so! No living person would ever dare what I am daring. . . . (*He goes to the back and stops on the steps. Pause. Challenging.*) Eremo! (*After a pause.*) Jan Eremo! (*After a pause.*) Jan in Eremo, Bishop of Lapideopolis! (*Short pause.*) By the Archdemon who rules you . . . (*Short pause.*) Are you still wandering in this world? . . . (*A violent impact shakes the door, which makes a cracking sound and continues violently shaking for a moment. The* AUXILIARY *has taken a spring backward.*) I have my answer! (*And* SIMON LAQUEDEEM *is making his way to the exit when* DUVELHOND *looms through it, preceding an* ARQUEBUSIER.)

DUVELHOND: The arque—que—buus—buus—buus. . . .

SIMON LAQUEDEEM: Booze? Wine for you, you villain! Set up your arquebus!

THE ARQUEBUSIER: Yes, Monsignor!

SIMON LAQUEDEEM: And hurl your grapeshot into this door, this great door. . . . (*The door is shaken again. The* ARQUE- BUSIER *bustles about.*) You understand?

THE ARQUEBUSIER: No, Monsignor. . . .

SIMON LAQUEDEEM: Why?

THE ARQUEBUSIER: Is there a man behind it?

SIMON LAQUEDEEM: No.

THE ARQUEBUSIER: A beast?

SIMON LAQUEDEEM: Yes, a mad one! Go away! (*He snatches the weapon from the* ARQUEBUSIER, *who runs off. To* DUVEL- HOND.) And you, get out! (*He sets up the arquebus and turns its wheel lock.*)

DUVELHOND (*fleeing, his hands over his ears*): Jhesus!

SIMON LAQUEDEEM: Your Jhesus had better not be across my path. I'll . . . (*The shot fires, in a cloud of smoke. Some of the door's boards are shattered. The face of* JOHN EREMO *appears, open-mouthed, in the hole, which is lit up. And the rattle resounds. The* AUXILIARY *rushes to the back, yelling.*) You, still? What do you want? Black sacraments? Gall for your thirst of the damned? I shall fill this dead mouth with lead! This mitered skull shall fly to pieces! (*He pushes the arquebus into the hole in the door. The* BISHOP's *face has*

*disappeared, but the weapon is seized from the other side, and
a struggle for possession of it begins. Panels smash; the hole
grows bigger. Finally,* LAQUEDEEM *lets go of the weapon,
which disappears inside. Taken aback, the* AUXILIARY *returns
to the center of the room, puts his hands to his head, staggers.
. . . A tremendous explosion shakes the palace and is followed
by the applause and hurrahs of the* CROWD. LAQUEDEEM *has
pulled himself together.)* Petards? Wait, my people. . . . You
shall have your joint of meat. And you will commend the
knacker! *(He rushes to the front left exit and disappears. The
room stands empty. But a hand, then an arm come through
the hole in the door and seek the latch. Then a processional
cross comes out, shaft first. This cross also feels about, digs
itself under the cover molding and becomes a lever worked
from inside. The double door groans under the pressure and
takes the strain. The cross jerks more hurriedly and the cover
molding splits away. The vanquished door gives completely.
The* BISHOP *looms in the opening. He has neither crook nor
miter, his gaze is mad, his neck is craned, and his hands are
held forward ready for the attack. He comes down the steps
and stops, as though amazed to be alone. A noise on the left.
Alerted, the* OLD MAN *goes and stands close to the back wall,
among the idols, where he remains stock-still, merged with the
monstrosities. A second explosion shakes the palace and is
answered by the storm, which is just now unleashed, and the*
CROWD, *crazy with lightning and gunpowder. At this juncture,*
SIMON LAQUEDEEM, *carrying an ax, enters by the mortuary
chamber. Having gone around the couch, he appears on the
threshold of the room, ready for the attack.)* Eremo! . . . *(He
comes down.)* Eremo! . . . *(He goes about the room in every
direction.)* Eremo! . . . *(Endlessly turning about.)* Eremo! . . .
Eremo! . . . *(Having stopped, dumbfounded, in a childish
voice.)* Jan! . . . *(Then, with tiny steps, he retreats toward the
idols without suspecting the danger he is approaching, the*
BISHOP *having held back his rattle. The* AUXILIARY *repeats a
last time.)* Eremo! *(And roars.)* Murderer! *(The idols tumble
down.* LAQUEDEEM, *attacked by* EREMO, *lets his ax fall. Merci-
less standing struggle. The two of them rattle in their throats.
The pair roll on the ground, then struggle kneeling, without
letting go of each other. Hubbub and shouts in the corridors.
Someone comes running. The door on the left is shaken.*
VOICES *hoot,* "Monsignor! Monsignor!" CARNIBOS *comes in*

through the exit, discovers the fight, shouts, "Murder," and disappears. The fight goes on, the pair struggling like steve-dores. For a second they disentangle themselves, then, head down, they rush toward each other. LAQUEDEEM *collapses under the impact but escapes on all fours.* EREMO *has picked up the ax. The door on the left has given, and the* PRIESTS *have come in. Flattened against the walls, they stand paralyzed with terror at what they see.* LAQUEDEEM, *who has half raised himself, bellows woefully. And the* BISHOP, *his rattle trans-formed into a kind of fiendish laugh, comes toward him fiercely, brandishing the ax.*

But while the last stage of the fight has been going on, REAL-TREMBLOR *has come back through the exit, violently dragging along* VENERANDA, *the old servant. Pushing her by the shoulders, he catapults her into the middle of the drama. And all of a sudden, the drama stands still in space, just as the justiciary ax stands still in the air. Silence has fallen in the same way the thunderbolt fell—very fatefully. And in the silence, the emptiness rather, in which nothing breathes—even the* CROWD *and the storm holding their peace—the* OLD WOMAN *is seen hopping toward the* BISHOP *and yelping in his face.*)

VENERANDA: What are you doing? (*The* BISHOP *lowers his arm and the ax, which* VENERANDA *snatches from him and lays down. Then.*) Why have you come back from the dead? (*The* BISHOP, *who has lost his stiffness and some of his height, has bent humbly toward the* OLD WOMAN, *and he speaks. Nothing comes from his mouth, but he speaks, like a dumb man swollen up with burning words. He points to the back of his throat.*) Kneel down! (*The* BISHOP *slips to his knees, his head thrown back. The* SERVANT *thrusts her fingers into his mouth, then takes them out.*) Spit out what was tormenting you! . . . (*The* BISHOP *has a spasm and spits out something, at which he gazes in amazement for a moment, on the floor.* VENERANDA *is already helping him to get up.*) Come along, John! . . . (*The* BISHOP *is on his feet.*) Come and die! . . . (*And the* BISHOP *is no more than a tottering old man whom* VENERANDA *pushes to the mortuary chamber. When he gets to the steps, a renewal of strength draws the* BISHOP *up again, and he turns toward the* PRIESTS *and* LAQUEDEEM, *who is still on his knees as though felled. The* OLD WOMAN *has anticipated this undertow of hatred and commands.*) Forgive them (*The* BISHOP *stiffens.*)

. . . if you want your forgiveness! . . . (*Shrunken and with his face suddenly changed, the* BISHOP *raises his right hand, with fist clenched, in a last pugnacious gesture. The* OLD WOMAN *insists, hissing.*) Absolve them! . . . (*And as the gesture persists, she slaps the* BISHOP *full in his face.*) Your mother is ordering you to do it! . . . (*The fist opens at last, and becomes a hand. With his eyes closed, the* BISHOP *blesses the bowed heads, very slowly, and as though reluctantly. His arm falls again. And, turning his back on the assembly, supported by* VENERANDA, *he goes into the mortuary chamber. It seems that he hides his face before disappearing.* VENERANDA *is still heard speaking as she closes the double door again.*) Stretch yourself out, my child! And die amid your tears! (*Silence hovers.* LAQUEDEEM *has gotten up and goes and stands calmly at the gap in the double door. He gazes on the interior. As though crushed by the blessing received, none of the* PRIESTS *moves, except that* SODOMATI *slips hypocritically to the place where the* BISHOP *knelt and picks up what he spat on the ground. He stands examining "it" in the hollow of his hand. The* AUXIL-IARY *has turned around and comes back.*)

SIMON LAQUEDEEM: The dead man is dead! (*Pause.*) Jan in Eremo, Bishop of Lapideopolis, is dead by his true and violent death, dead, twice dead, thoroughly dead! (*An immense flash of lightning, like a dawn—and there is no more thunder and lightning. The* CROWD *has begun muttering again, but without anger, and sorrowfully. Knells come from nearby towers.* LA-QUEDEEM *has gone up to the* NUNCIO'S SECRETARY *and seizes him by the wrist.*) The host?

SODOMATI: Take it: you consecrated it. . . . (*The other* PRIESTS *have begun to talk confusedly.* LAQUEDEEM *addresses them.*)

SIMON LAQUEDEEM: Who wants to take communion? (REAL-TREMBLOR *indicates* VENERANDA, *who is slipping through the slightly open door and moving off to the left.*)

REAL-TREMBLOR: She does!

SIMON LAQUEDEEM (*who in three strides has seized the* OLD SERVANT, *and grips her left arm*): You! Rejoin in eternity him to whom you gave birth. . . .

VENERANDA: *Och God!*

SIMON LAQUEDEEM (*who in three strides has seized the* OLD WOMAN'S *mouth. He murmurs the consecratory words, of which the only ones heard are*): *Corpus . . . custodat . . .*

(*And he releases* VENERANDA. *The* SERVANT *takes one or two steps toward the exit, slides down the wall, and dies.*)

SODOMATI: Amen. This man will go a long way. . . .

SIMON LAQUEDEEM: To the grave, dearest! . . . Listen to that! The rabble are in the building! (*They listen. An uproar in the corridors. Shouting.*) The butchers! (*The* PRIESTS *fall back toward the right.* LAQUEDEEM, *in the center of the room, does not retreat.*) Rely on me, clericity! (*The uproar has stopped. A great blow on the door at the left. A red light floods the room. And a* COLOSSUS, *bald, torso bare, with sheathed cutlasses at his leather breeches, comes forward. Nine other* GIANTS *enter in his wake, some of them carrying torches. They form a group on the left and wait. They are the* BUTCHERS *with their* MASTER, *who goes gravely toward the* AUXILIARY.)

THE MASTER OF THE BUTCHERS: *Waar ligt Jan-men-Kloote?* (LAQUEDEEM *does not answer, pretending not to understand the language of the people, and looking the* MASTER *firmly in the eye. The* MASTER *appears to ponder, then unhurriedly lays hold of one end of the table, says, "Hop!" and turns it over, with all it bears. During the crash, several* PRIESTS *have cried out. Then, the* MASTER *comes back to the* AUXILIARY *and unsheathes one of his cutlasses, passing it under his nose and repeating.*) *Waar ligt Jan-men-Kloote?* (*This time,* LAQUEDEEM *points his forefinger toward the mortuary chamber. At a signal from the* MASTER, *four* BUTCHERS *separate from the rest and go into the chamber. The light of the candles floods the room. After a moment, the four return, carrying the couch on which lie the* BISHOP's *remains, dressed in priestly adornments. The four stop near the* MASTER *with their burden. The* AUXILIARY *has begun to pray in a low voice.*)

SIMON LAQUEDEEM: *Chorus angelorum te suscipiat et eum Lazara quondam . . .*

THE MASTER OF THE BUTCHERS (*interrupting him*): *Bakkes toe!* (*And he gives another signal. The convoy goes out. The* BUTCHERS *follow the corpse, but moving backward, with their* MASTER, *who does not cease to watch the* AUXILIARY, *last.*)

No one stirs when the BUTCHERS *have gone. One guesses that the convoy is leaving the palace, for the* CROWD *gives a final howl—of triumph—that is prolonged and becomes a kind of endless lamentation that will continue to get more distant. And the great bells, countless in number, will start ringing in the towers. Night has finally fallen. Alone in the middle of the room,* SIMON LAQUEDEEM *has put his hands on his stomach. He laughs derisively.*)

SIMON LAQUEDEEM: These obsequies. . . . Ho, ho! . . . You'll see! . . . When they invest the cathedral, they will quickly come seeking us! . . Only the Church can bury. . . . (*Pause. Suddenly the* AUXILIARY *bends at the knees and staggers.*) Aah . . . aah!

REAL-TREMBLOR (*rushing to hold* LAQUEDEEM *up*): Monsignor! . . . Your bowels?

SIMON LAQUEDEEM (*pushing* REAL-TREMBLOR *away*): Damnation! . . . (*The* PRIESTS *have come forward and make a circle—the* AUXILIARY *writhes on the spot.*) Aah . . . aah! . . . (*A long shudder shakes him.*)

KRAKENBUS: Is he going to die?

SODOMATI: In that case, I believe in God! (*But* LAQUEDEEM, *who had just lost his balance, draws himself up again to his full height.*)

SIMON LAQUEDEEM: Deliverance!

KRAKENBUS: Deliverance! The corpse is outside. . . .

CARNIBOS: The smell remains. Ugh! (*He holds his nose.*)

SIMON LAQUEDEEM: The odor of Death!

SODOMATI: Do you think so? (CARNIBOS *disappears at the back.*)

SIMON LAQUEDEEM: True, it doesn't smell nice! . . . The odor of Death, I say! The dead stink.

REAL-TREMBLOR: The living too.

SIMON LAQUEDEEM: True, true . . . they stink! . . . (*He gives a fat laugh.* CARNIBOS *comes back swinging a smoking censer.*) Fine! Incense! . . . Some incense! . . . A lot of incense!

CARNIBOS (*swinging the censer majestically*): I'm censing!

SIMON LAQUEDEEM: Open the balcony! What d'you say, Pikkedoncker?

DOM PIKKEDONCKER: Caca! (*Laughter cascades. The* PRIESTS *sniff each other like dogs.*)

SIMON LAQUEDEEM: Caca? Who?

DOM PIKKEDONCKER: Not me! Him! . . . And you, Monsignor! . . . Caca! (*Panic laughter breaks out, and this hilarity is accompanied by digs in the ribs and monkeylike gesticulations. Seized by frantic joy, the* PRIESTS *jump about comically in the clouds of incense, repeating all the time, "Caca! . . . Caca!"*)

SIMON LAQUEDEEM (*thundering*): The pigs! . . . They've shit
in their cassocks!

　　(*He crouches—gown tucked up—his rabbinical face expressing demoniac bliss—while the curtain comes slowly
down on these chronicles of Hell.*)

documents

theoretical introduction to tumor brainard (*1920*)

by Stanislaw Ignacy Witkiewicz

translated by Daniel C. Gerould *and* Eleanor S. Gerould

It is a well-established fact that the theatre had its origin in the religious mysteries. This is how it happened in ancient Greece, and the beginnings of modern theatre at the break-up of the Middle Ages correspond to the development of the rise of Greek tragedy. However, artistic effect does not necessarily have to be connected with the expression of religious feelings as such. It can be the result of contemplating the form alone, independent of whether or not the real-life content of a given work has any direct connection with metaphysical experiences. Since the elements of theatre are the actions of living beings, the theatre gradually lost its religious character, but the essential, formal, reduced content became an auxiliary means for the purpose of heightened presentation of life, symbolic or real, and the problems connected with it.

The essence of art in general is the directly given unity of personality, or what we call metaphysical feeling, expressed in the construction of whatever the elements are, such as: colors, sounds, words or actions. Painting and music possess homogeneous elements. In addition to its sound values and possibilities for evoking visual images, poetry still works with concepts, the meanings of which are, in our opinion, just as good artistically as any of the pure qualities. However, the theatre has the additional element of actions, whoever the individual beings may be who act. Thus poetry and theatre as composite arts stand in contrast to the simple arts, painting and music. In painting each work of art has, besides its purely formal values—composition, harmony of colors and grasp of form—its objective content, which derives from the fact that metaphysical feeling, generally one and the same for all individual beings, becomes polarized in the psyche of a given individual and creates an individual form, which is the more abstract as pure construction, the more condensed the personality of the individual creating it. Thus a certain immanent contradiction adheres in the essence of artistic creation.

What the world of subjects and images is in painting, the world of feeling is in music, and consequently the realm of conceptual meaning is in poetry and the meaning of actions is in the theatre. If we acknowledge the formal content—that is, the very construction of the work of art itself—to be its essence, then we are no longer obliged to be concerned with the inessential (but no less indispensable) elements of the very process of creation, which have only an indirect connection with the completed work. In this light, deformation of the external world in painting, violation of the logic of feelings in music, real-life and logical absurdity in poetry and on stage need not outrage us. In our opinion, the breaking of certain inessential bad habits concerning the real-life aspect of works of art opens new horizons of formal possibilities, connected mostly with the question of composition. In the theatre what can give new formal possibilities is a certain fantasticality of psychology and actions in contradistinction to external fantasticality: dragons, sorcerers, and so forth, creatures suited to the deformation of the external world. Of course, aims of this kind must be essential, that is, not schematic.

Schematic distortion of normal shapes, schematic absurdity in poetry or in the theatre, is an immensely sad phenomenon. Deformation for deformation, absurdity for absurdity, not justified in purely formal dimensions, is something worthy of the most violent condemnation. Whether certain deviations from the usual pattern in the plays in question are justified in this way remains to be proved. Theoretically there is this possibility, and we suppose that if not these plays, then other ones, by other authors perhaps, will someday prove the validity of these propositions.

Of course, it may seem ridiculous to some, it may outrage others. If anyone is sincerely amused by this, in a way that we consider completely unimportant, we would be delighted because laughter is rare in our gloomy times. No matter how indignant anyone gets in the depths of his soul, as long as he does not show it in too violent a way—it can't be helped. It is absolutely impossible to please everyone. There are fewer and fewer people who burst their sides with laughter at the sight of the square calves in Picasso or who shut their ears in indignation at hearing Stravinsky's score for a ballet. Without prejudging in the least the formal values of the plays in question, we suppose in principle that one may with good will adapt oneself completely to a "subject" which is purely external and, from a real-life point of view, even grotesque and monstrous...

... Using a term analogical to the conception of "directional tension," introduced by us into the theory of painting, it is now a matter of conferring on certain masses of events in time a certain "dynamic tension." This is the formal significance of the so-called "content" of poems and plays. Please note that we do not attribute any objective significance to the "opinions" expressed by characters in these plays.

the analogy with painting

from INTRODUCTION TO THE THEORY OF PURE FORM IN THE THEATRE (1920)

by Stanisław Ignacy Witkiewicz

translated by Daniel C. Gerould *and* Eleanor S. Gerould

Since we hate the contemporary theatre in all its manifestations and have no competence in theatrical questions, we have no intention of expounding here a theory based on expert knowledge of such matters. We are solely concerned with giving a rough sketch of an idea which, lacking suitable data, we do not even claim to be realizable. If works which even approximately illustrated this "theory" actually existed, it would be possible to talk about it quite differently. For the time being there are no such works, and, as we ourselves admit, it is even doubtful there ever will be. We live in an age of manifestoes: even before an artistic movement spontaneously comes into being, its theory is often already in a state of near perfection. Theories are starting to create movements, and not vice versa. Besides, in former times there weren't "movements" in our sense of the word, or different "isms," there were only powerful personalities and the schools formed by their followers. At least that was the case with painting. A greater and greater intellectualization of the creative process and subjugation of the outbursts of genius to principles conceived *a priori* is the characteristic trait of art in our times. We have no intention of justifying our "theory" in this way. It is not the result of any manifesto, as you might think, given the general schematic tendency of art today. These are only a few random remarks suggested by the impressions I have formed of the contemporary theatre and by my observation of current attempts at a "renaissance" of the art of the theatre, based on a faulty knowledge of what the theatre was in the past. Again and again it has been pointed out that the theatre had its origin in the religious mysteries. All art, like religion, which in former times was closely linked with it, has its source in metaphysical feelings. Painting, music, and to some degree sculpture, arts which function through their own simple elements, have in one sense become abstract, i.e., they have become Pure Arts. To the extent that architecture serves less and less ideal and more and more utilitarian goals, it falls off; and the theatre, whose elements are people and their actions —just as the elements of painting are colors enclosed in form, and the elements of music are sounds expressed in rhythm— the theatre, with the progressive decline of metaphysical feelings, had to turn into a pure reproduction of life. The religious rite, losing its primary significance, gives rise to the theatre as a secondary product of its decadence. It seems to us that this is clearly visible in Greece, where a theatre separated from the religious mysteries came into being for the first time. At the period when Christianity began to disintegrate in the fifteenth century, the theatre, at first using only religious themes, began to grow up for a second time, and its development, or rather continuous decline, continues right up to our own days. The theatre is an art, which due to the nature of its elements, i.e. because it deals with people and their actions, arises in its purest form only at the breaking point and collapse of a given cult. Since in its essence it contains the element of disintegration, the theatre might be said to be in a continual and progressive state of decline.

Independent of the birth of new religious cults and the decline of old ones, philosophy has developed in our times to the point where, in a certain manner, it is devouring itself. We are in a period of decline, not only of religion, but of all metaphysics in general, a fact which likewise finds expression in the phenomenon we have called "insatiable craving for form" in art; we are in a period of *the decay of metaphysical feelings themselves,* which are becoming superfluous and useless in the further social evolution of humanity. Only the theatre has not yet entered the period of "insatiable craving for form"; and furthermore, except for certain purely external "oddities" on the part of some writers who wish to unite the mystery of existence as it reveals itself in real life with the seriousness of contemporary thought, the theatre persists in heightened realism, where the cinema gives it serious competition. This is the situation in which various attempts at a "renaissance" have been made; here we must point out their lack of importance and offer, in the most general outline, the possibility, although a very doubtful one, of a real renaissance of the art of the theatre, not through a new interpretation of works which have already been created, but through a completely new type of work, which, it seems to us, does not yet exist in its pure form.

Today we have several types of plays, in which, however, contemporary man cannot experience in a pure state what we have defined as *metaphysical feeling*, i.e., *the experience of the mystery of existence as unity in plurality,* due to that impression of unity which, as in painting and music, is created by combinations of simple elements. We believe that in ancient times when religion and art constituted a more cohesive, undifferentiated mass, the purely artistic aspect, i.e., the integration of a given plurality of elements into a unity or also the creation of this unity, was not so clearly separated from the purely religious aspect, either for the spectators or for the creators, as it is nowadays. Today we understand only this first aspect of ancient works of art, i.e., we comprehend the *form* alone of the work of art, which for us (meaning the small handful who understand art properly) is in its essence the same in both ancient and modern works. Of course, we are referring here to new works of true pure art, i.e., art whose substance is not the reproduction of the visible world or real feelings, but a purely formal unity which ties the given elements into an indissoluble whole. We shall attempt to draw a certain analogy between painting and sculpture on the one hand and the theatre on the other. We believe that a similar analogy could also be drawn between music and theatre, since music was originally only an accompaniment for ritual dances, a part or extension of religious ceremonies, except where, as song, it directly expressed emotional states in contexts other than religious. Today, with the progressive mechanization of life and the decline of all metaphysics, a renaissance of pure form in sculpture and painting has taken place, a renaissance which in our opinion is also the death throes of pure form on our planet. Our question can be formulated in the following manner: *Is it possible, even if only for a short period, for a form of the theatre to arise in which contemporary man, independent of dead myths and beliefs, could experience the metaphysical feelings which ancient man experienced through those myths and beliefs?*

In painting and sculpture we experience the form alone for its own sake and even create a new one, independent of a long extinct creed which held true for a given cult; the very construction of form is for us an abstract "drug" enabling us to experience metaphysical feelings. We maintain that likewise there must be the possibility of a similar form in the theatre, a form in which becoming through time, the simple fact of something "happening" defined only in a purely formal way —the elements of which will of course be human actions— will be able, independent of the real-life content of the actions themselves and of the consistency of characterization of the characters who act, to usher us into a dimension of experience totally different from real life, into the sphere of metaphysical feelings, as it is in pure form.

In order to create such a form in the theatre, what is necessary, in addition to the *absolute necessity* of creating it, which no one today seems to feel to a sufficiently high degree, is a complete break with all of today's theatrical conventions, with today's conception of theatricality, action, and the psychological basis of the construction of a play. For the emotional tension which results from the unfolding on stage of a drama or something in this genre today depends solely on the emotion caused by the vicissitudes of the hero. First everything is made clear: what and how, then the complications begin, the climax is reached, then—bang!! a frightful blow-up and everything is resolved. All this, of course, in purely real-life dimensions, only somewhat intensified. In addition, the spectator must be constantly occupied: someone is constantly entering or exiting as part of the total plot, which is the chief pivot of interest; there is constantly some blow-up on stage, but only as a consequence of the feelings and characters or also of their clashes among themselves or with some higher powers—and this is called the action. The audience cannot grow bored for lack of movement on stage—not even for a moment. The struggle of a man with himself or with fate, the conflicts of a given character—this is the whole "menu" of the contemporary theatre, which is beginning to nauseate even the so-called general public. Another genre deals in various kinds of fear of the unknown, going from the darkened room to death, worn out as stage effects, making chills run down the spine—nothing more. A third genre is symbolism: for example, a blue bird flies over the stage ceaselessly, but the audience must constantly remember that the bird is not a bird at all, but love with a capital L. The bird finally croaks—which signifies that love too has croaked in some heart. In addition to these genres, we have history and all the ancient masters of the stage, presented in old period stylizations or in new ones; we have dramas composed of tableaux vivants, full of a more or less obscure philosophy of history, musical dramas, musical-bellowing, bellowing-howling, howling-squealing—all in vain: boredom reigns supreme in the theatre. Whether it be Greek tragedy in the Greek style, Shakespeare in the Shakespearian style, Ibsen in the Greek style, or modernized Aeschylus, the effect is virtually the same. Whether it be an attempt at the utmost simplification: just a plank, a sheet, and everything spoken in a single uniform tone, or the absolute realism of Munich or Moscow—all that has already been done and will no longer really be able to excite anyone, except the "renaissancers," maniacs for simplification or complication. In Greece people probably went to the theatre for completely different sensations than we do. They knew the subject of the play well, for the subject was only one variant of myths known to everyone. With this known subject as a background, a metaphysical background for the progression on stage, everything that happened, the whole course of the action, was, only through its form, an intensification of the metaphysical element, which in life people were beginning to meet less and less, except for exceptional moments of ecstasy. Human feelings as such were only elements of the becoming, a pretext for purely formal relations, which express a new psychic dimension by their interrelationships and by the synthesis of images, sounds, and sense of the spoken lines. These feelings were not the principal content in the performance and did not hit the spectator in the guts in almost a purely physical way.

In our opinion the task of the theatre is exactly this: to put the audience in an exceptional state, which cannot in its pure form very easily be attained in the course of ordinary daily life, a state where the mystery of existence can be apprehended emotionally. In general this is the goal of all art, but the theatre, in contrast to the other arts, which have their periods of more or less essential expression of just these subjects, could always be said to be the breakdown of something which might have been, but was not. Whereas other arts have actually separated themselves from purely religious manifestations, as supplementary elements of these manifestations, the theatre, which is a continuation of the rite, was not able to resist the life invading it and gradually became life itself. As if a shell left behind by what was in it became filled with a completely different content.

The structural element left over from the ancient rite is the construction of a play, the choice of crucial points in the imagined totality of episodes from life or in some real course of events. But despite the fact that in both cases some sort of beings act: humans or fantastic deities, the content of all this is completely different.

Formerly, these beings were direct symbols of the mystery, which shone through them quite directly and clearly—today they are just people, and it is only by a certain intensification, by condensing great events into a short space of time, that we are able to experience a little of the strangeness of life, which, dragged out in the course of ordinary daily life, and even of "festive" life, we no longer perceive at all. However, to a far greater degree than the theatre, its scorned but nonetheless threatening enemy, the cinema, gives us precisely this sensation of the strangeness of life. We maintain that however already existing plays are staged, whether more simplified or more complicated, in order to present them in a completely different way from previous stagings, we shall be impotent due to their intrinsic nature which results from the purpose for which their authors created them. We cannot go beyond *the limits imposed by the very nature of the dramatic work itself*.

On the one hand, we have directors who consider the chief theatrical element to be "staging," the auditory impressions or the settings and movements. Others want to make a synthesis of those elements, intensified to the highest degree, and thereby completely stupefy the spectator: surrounded by infernal sounds, or images satanic in their richness, he does not know what is happening to him; from time to time he hears some sentence or other, the sense of which disappears in the general *bric-à-brac** of sensations. The result is nothing but a chaos of contradictory elements, which the author has not united by *an internal idea of form itself,* since the play needs only a certain intensity of elements in order to be realistically presented and apprehended by the spectators. No stylization can make a realistic conception into something qualitatively different and thereby give a new dimension of experience. The future of the theatre does not lie in various kinds of interpretations of already-created works, but in a completely new genre of works which we shall try to define by means of the analogy with painting.

---

* In French in the original.

masse-mensch— mob-man

by Kenneth Macgowan *and* Robert Edmond Jones

[*This is an account of Jürgen Fehling's original production of Toller's play at the Berlin Volksbühne in 1921.*]

Masse-Mensch itself is a play, half dream and half reality, in which is pictured the conflict of *Masse,* the masses, against *Mensch,* the individual, of violent revolution against passive strike. Its drama pleads piteously for the sacredness of human life and the equal guilt of the State or the revolution that takes it. Because it was written by Ernst Toller, who, as he wrote it, lay in a Munich jail serving a twenty-year sentence for his part as Minister of Justice in the red rebellion which followed the assassination of Kurt Eisner by the reactionaries, *Masse-Mensch* is pretty generally taboo in German theaters. In the first six months after its *première* at the Volksbühne (29th September, 1921) it was played about seventy times, a very great number of performances in repertory. But upon its production in Nuremberg riots interrupted the first performance, and it was never repeated.

To the significance of the play itself and the proletarian organization which flings it in the face of a Germany where monarchists and republicans, socialists and communists, State and cabals, murder with almost equal recklessness, must be added a truly remarkable type and quality of production. It bears a certain relation to the work of Jessner at the State Schauspielhaus, where, by the way, Fehling is now to be employed. It is absolutely free of Realism and representation —as all expressionist production must be. It reduces setting to less than symbol, to what is hardly more than a convenient platform for the actor. It uses light arbitrarily.

Masse-Mensch is a piece in seven scenes. The first, third, fifth and seventh are actual; the others are dream-pictures. In the first scene Toller's stage directions call for "The rear room of a workingman's meeting hall. On the white-washed walls, portraits of leaders of the people and photographs of union delegates. In the center a heavy table, at which a woman and two workmen are seated." The stage directions for the second scene, or first dream-picture, read: "Indicated: The hall of a stock exchange. At the desk, a clerk; about him, bankers and brokers."

The playwright felt keenly the possibilities of the modern, subjective methods of productions, or he would not have used the word, "indicated." He did not feel them clearly enough, however, to risk more than their application to the dream-pictures. But, taking "Indicated" as a key-word, Fehling has boldly ventured to apply abstract and expressionist methods to the whole of this thoroughly expressionist play. In the first scene, for instance, as you see it at the Volksbühne, there is no hall, there is no desk, there are no portraits. There is nothing but a deep box of high black curtains, and in the center a very low, broad platform. Upon this platform, spotted out with three shafts of light, are the two men and the woman in the taut attitudes of wrestlers as they clasp hands, the woman in the middle. For the dream scene, the stage is again in black curtains, but those at the rear are occasionally opened to show a clerk on an impossibly high stool, writing on an impossibly high desk, almost in silhouette against the yellow-lighted dome. A few steps lead down into the darkness of the front stage. Fehling and his stage designer, Hans Strohbach, pursue the same general method in the succeeding scenes. The "real" episodes are set in black curtains and with steps of one sort or another; they are lit by obvious beams of light, and they are given no more color than shows in the woman's severe blue dress and one glimpse of the yellow dome. The dream-pictures are more elaborately staged, though they seem quite bare by the standard of our productions. The curious part is that the scenes of reality are more expressionistic, considering their purpose, than the dream-pictures. Reality is made of nothing but abstract plastic shapes, harsh, and harshly lit. Dreamland is sometimes painted and shaped in the slightly decorative spirit of Expressionism, and it is lit with beauty and atmosphere.

The effective arrangement of Strohbach's scenes, and the powerful use which Fehling makes of them stamp the physical side of this production with distinction. Spiritually it is even more distinguished because of the rightness of vision with which Fehling interprets the play, and the brilliance with which he handles, not only the individual acting, but a chorus of united voices, which speaks through many scenes with an extraordinary clarity and emotion.

From the beginning of the first scene the actors strike the note of intensity and conviction, both as players and as characters, which they are to carry through the whole performance. Mary Dietrich, once of Reinhardt's company, plays superbly the woman protagonist of the strike and of humanity. From the moment when her husband comes to her in the name of love to ask her to give up the leadership of the strike, which will begin next day, Dietrich drives with such furious precision at the meaning of this woman that she stands out immediately as a sort of Christ-figure. In the beginning she must give up all; she must leave home and love, to follow her call. In the end she must go to the scaffold rejecting all means of escape. It is one of the distinctions of this play, as well as of Dietrich's playing, that this reference to Christ is so beautiful and so sure, yet so reticent.

The second scene, the dream-picture of a stock exchange, is a foreboding and dread satire. The bankers and brokers bid up human souls in the war that is under way, and make plans for an international corporation, which, posing as a founder of homes for convalescent soldiers, will open brothels for the troops. The woman appears in her dream, and makes a vain appeal to the humanity of these men. The bankers hear only the announcement of a mine accident and plan a benefit dance, beginning with a fox-trot by the brokers around the stage.

The third scene is the labor meeting at which a decision is to be taken on action to stop the making of munitions and end the war. Here again, Fehling throws the author's realistic stage directions overboard (much, be it said, to the author's pleasure). Instead of a hall, there is again blackness, emptiness. Out of the emptiness speaks a marvelous choral voice, the voice of the masses, measured, vibrant, intense:

Wir ewig eingekeilt
In Schluchten steiler Häuser.
Wir preisgegeben
Der Mechanik höhnischer Systeme.
Wir antlitzlos in Nacht der Tränen.
Wir ewig losgelöst von Müttern,
Aus Tiefen der Fabriken rufen wir:
Wann werden Liebe wir leben?
Wann werden Werk wir wirken?
Wann wird Erlösung uns?*

Nothing like this voice, coming out of a darkness in which faces vaguely begin to hover, has been imagined, much less attempted, in our theater. The lights rise—or it would be more accurate to say, shoot down—upon the men and women workers standing in an irregular lozenge shape upon steep steps, which spread to the curtains at each side. Out of this crowd, in chorus and singly, come pleas for action, and visions of suffering which sweep the audience with emotion. The woman cries for a strike against war and against capital. Behind her rises The Nameless One, the bastard of War, to cry for armed revolt. His passion sweeps the masses, and the woman submits.

The fourth scene, another dream-picture, envisages her fears for the course of the revolution, her intuition that it will only breed a new violence, the violence of the proletariat. Below great, crooked, towering walls, guards hang over green lanterns. They sing ribald songs of their miseries. The Nameless One enters, and, standing in the middle, plays wildly on a concertina, while the guards and the condemned dance the dance of death about him. The sky lights up on a sudden in crimson, then pulses in and out; colors flood down over the moving figures in waves that throb with the music. Among the condemned is the husband of the woman. She tries to save him, as she would save all men from violence. Her pleas are useless. She stands with him before the firing squad as the curtain falls.

---

* For translation, see p. 73 above. [Editor's note.]

The fifth scene, the tremendous scene of the play and the production, is the rally at the workers' headquarters in the face of defeat. The stage is again boxed in black. There are steps like the corner of a pyramid rising up to the right of the audience. Upon these steps gather the working people. You see a host, affrighted and cowering, in the twenty-four men and women who stagger upon the steps singing *The Marseillaise*. As they sway, locked together hand in hand, like men on a sinking ship, and the old song mounts up against the distant rattle of machine guns, the scene brings the cold sweat of desperate excitement to the audience that fills the Volksbühne, and to comfortable, purse-proud Americans as much as to men who have fought in the streets of Berlin. Suddenly there is a louder rattle of arms. The noise sweeps through the air. It drives into the souls of the huddling men and women. They collapse, go down, fall in a tangled heap. The curtains at the left loop up suddenly. There in the gap against the yellow sky stand the soldiers. They arrest the woman, the woman whom the rebels were about to condemn for her opposition to their slaughter.

The sixth scene is a dream-picture of the woman in prison. There is a void, a misty, swimming emptiness. Upon a platform is the woman's cell, a scarlet cage in which she can only kneel. About her stand guards, bankers, the ghosts of dead enemies. They accuse her. She answers. At last, out of the void rise the shapes of the masses, the imprisoned masses who have been betrayed by violence and by the woman who deserted them and cast her lot with violence. They move in a great circle of towering shadows that seem to hang in the emptiness of the sky, as they pass across the dome at the back of the stage. The guilt of the masses, the guilt of the individual, the guilt of the woman—they have filled the air with recrimination. The figures of the imprisoned masses stop suddenly in their round. They raise their arms. They cry: "We accuse!"

There is only the final scene left. It is in her cell. Again the black curtains; some narrow steps. The husband comes to bring her freedom. The Nameless One also, with a plan of escape through murdering the guards. She rejects both. She rejects the priest, accusing men of primeval sin. She goes to her death. And as she goes, two women prisoners sneak out into the light—to divide the clothes of this new Christ.

Schuldig! Guilty! Guilty! The word echoes through the

play, echoes in the auditorium of the Volksbühne. All are guilty. All are sick with guilt. And none more than these sufferers in the slums of Berlin who must go to the theater to see in black curtains the picture of their guilt. The world goes through capitalism, debasing itself, driving terror, greed, cruelty into the place of love and understanding. It comes out in revolution, a corruption of the thing it cures. The Germans have been through capitalism with a vengeance, through materialism, through war, and through a revolution that blasted half the people and did not satisfy the rest. Here is the misery of capitalism, the misery of abortive revolution, the misery of defeat and black hunger. Berlin is in purgatory. And Berlin goes to *Masse-Mensch*. Before this play sit hundreds of quite ordinary men, who have only to hear some word shouted at them with the passion of this play, and they will leave the slow and loved routine of homes, and lie again behind sandbags on Unter den Linden. All this is a strange, terrible, and sweet thing to feel as you sit looking at the purgatory of those black curtains.

Toller and Fehling have made possible the realization of this intense situation between play and audience; Toller by writing straight at the heart of his public. His dialogue makes no pretense to the accidental rhythms of life. It speaks out plainly and simply and beautifully the passion of each character, the passions of the world. Fehling has driven Toller's speeches just as directly at the public. He has made no pretense at actuality. He has put his actors forward as actors on an abstract stage; and you think of them only as living, intimate presences.

by Bertolt Brecht

a short organum for the theatre (1948)

translated by John Willett

[*Sections marked † are those which Brecht subsequently considered modifying by the series of appendices on pp. 527 ff.*]

PROLOGUE. The following sets out to define an aesthetic drawn from a particular kind of theatrical performance which has been worked out in practice over the past few decades. In the theoretical statements, excursions, technical indications occasionally published in the form of notes to the writer's plays, aesthetics have only been touched on casually and with comparative lack of interest. There you saw a particular species of theatre extending or contracting its social functions, perfecting or sifting its artistic methods and establishing or maintaining its aesthetics—if the question arose—by rejecting or converting to its own use the dominant conventions of morality or taste according to its tactical needs. This theatre justified its inclination to social commitment by pointing to the social commitment in universally accepted works of art, which only fail to strike the eye because it was the accepted commitment. As for the products of our own time, it held that their lack of any worthwhile content was a sign of decadence: it accused these entertainment emporiums of having degenerated into branches of the bourgeois narcotics business. The stage's inaccurate representations of our social life, including those classed as so-called Naturalism, led it to call for scientifically exact representations; the tasteless rehashing of empty visual or spiritual palliatives, for the noble logic of the multiplication table. The cult of beauty, conducted with hostility towards learning and contempt for the useful, was dismissed by it as itself contemptible, especially as nothing beautiful resulted. The battle was for a theatre fit for the scientific age, and where its planners found it too hard to borrow or steal from the armoury of aesthetic concepts enough weapons to defend themselves against the aesthetics of the Press they simply threatened 'to transform the means of enjoyment into an instrument of instruction, and to convert certain amusement establishments into organs of mass communication' ('Notes to the opera *Mahagonny*'*) : i.e. to emigrate from the realm of the merely enjoyable. Aesthetics, that heirloom of a by now depraved and parasitic class, was in such a lamentable state that a theatre would certainly have gained both in reputation and in elbowroom if it had rechristened itself thaëter. And yet what we achieved in the way of theatre for a scientific age was not science but theatre, and the accumulated innovations worked out during the Nazi period and the war—when practical demonstration was impossible—compel some attempt to set this species of theatre in its aesthetic background, or anyhow to sketch for it the outlines of a conceivable aesthetic. To explain the theory of theatrical alienation except within an aesthetic framework would be impossibly awkward.

Today one could go so far as to compile an aesthetics of the exact sciences. Galileo spoke of the elegance of certain formulae and the point of an experiment; Einstein suggests that the sense of beauty has a part to play in the making of scientific discoveries; while the atomic physicist R. Oppenheimer praises the scientific attitude, which 'has its own kind of beauty and seems to suit mankind's position on earth'.

Let us therefore cause general dismay by revoking our decision to emigrate from the realm of the merely enjoyable, and even more general dismay by announcing our decision to take up lodging there. Let us treat the theatre as a place of entertainment, as is proper in an aesthetic discussion, and try to discover which type of entertainment suits us best.

---

* See *Brecht on Theatre* (New York: Hill & Wang, 1964), pp. 33–42.

1. 'Theatre' consists in this: in making live representations of reported or invented happenings between human beings and doing so with a view to entertainment. At any rate that is what we shall mean when we speak of theatre, whether old or new.

2. To extend this definition we might add happenings between humans and gods, but as we are only seeking to establish the minimum we can leave such matters aside. Even if we did accept such an extension we should still have to say that the 'theatre' set-up's broadest function was to give pleasure. It is the noblest function that we have found for 'theatre'.

3†. From the first it has been the theatre's business to entertain people, as it also has of all the other arts. It is this business which always gives it its particular dignity; it needs no other passport than fun, but this it has got to have. We should not by any means be giving it a higher status if we were to turn it e.g. into a purveyor of morality; it would on the contrary run the risk of being debased, and this would occur at once if it failed to make its moral lesson enjoyable, and enjoyable to the senses at that: a principle, admittedly, by which morality can only gain. Not even instruction can be demanded of it: at any rate, no more utilitarian lesson than how to move pleasurably, whether in the physical or in the spiritual sphere. The theatre must in fact remain something entirely superfluous, though this indeed means that it is the superfluous for which we live. Nothing needs less justification than pleasure.

4†. Thus what the ancients, following Aristotle, demanded of tragedy is nothing higher or lower than that it should entertain people. Theatre may be said to be derived from ritual, but that is only to say that it becomes theatre once the two have separated; what it brought over from the mysteries was not its former ritual function, but purely and simply the pleasure which accompanied this. And the catharsis of which Aristotle writes—cleansing by fear and pity, or from fear and pity—is a purification which is performed not only in a pleasurable way, but precisely for the purpose of pleasure. To ask or to accept more of the theatre is to set one's own mark too low.

5. Even when people speak of higher and lower degrees of pleasure, art stares impassively back at them; for it wishes to

fly high and low and to be left in peace, so long as it can give pleasure to people.

6. Yet there are weaker (simple) and stronger (complex) pleasures which the theatre can create. The last-named, which are what we are dealing with in great drama, attain their climaxes rather as cohabitation does through love: they are more intricate, richer in communication, more contradictory and more productive of results.

7. And different periods' pleasures varied naturally according to the system under which people lived in society at the time. The Greek demos [literally: the demos of the Greek circus] ruled by tyrants had to be entertained differently from the feudal court of Louis XIV. The theatre was required to deliver different representations of men's life together: not just representations of a different life, but also representations of a different sort.

8. According to the sort of entertainment which was possible and necessary under the given conditions of men's life together the characters had to be given varying proportions, the situations to be constructed according to varying points of view. Stories have to be narrated in various ways, so that these particular Greeks may be able to amuse themselves with the inevitability of divine laws where ignorance never mitigates the punishment; these French with the graceful self-discipline demanded of the great ones of this earth by a courtly code of duty; the Englishmen of the Elizabethan age with the self-awareness of the new individual personality which was then uncontrollably bursting out.

9. And we must always remember that the pleasure given by representations of such different sorts hardly ever depended on the representation's likeness to the thing portrayed. Incorrectness, or considerable improbability even, was hardly or not at all disturbing, so long as the incorrectness had a certain consistency and the improbability remained of a constant kind. All that mattered was the illusion of compelling momentum in the story told, and this was created by all sorts of poetic and theatrical means. Even today we are happy to overlook such inaccuracies if we can get something out of the spiritual purifications of Sophocles or the sacrificial acts of Racine or the unbridled frenzies of Shakespeare, by trying to grasp the immense or splendid feelings of the principal characters in these stories.

10. For of all the many sorts of representation of happen-

ings between humans which the theatre has made since ancient times, and which have given entertainment despite their incorrectness and improbability, there are even today an astonishing number that also give entertainment to us.

11. In establishing the extent to which we can be satisfied by representations from so many different periods—something that can hardly have been possible to the children of those vigorous periods themselves—are we not at the same time creating the suspicion that we have failed to discover the special pleasures, the proper entertainment of our own time?

12†. And our enjoyment of the theatre must have become weaker than that of the ancients, even if our way of living together is still sufficiently like theirs for it to be felt at all. We grasp the old works by a comparatively new method—empathy—on which they rely little. Thus the greater part of our enjoyment is drawn from other sources than those which our predecessors were able to exploit so fully. We are left safely dependent on beauty of language, on elegance of narration, on passages which stimulate our own private imaginations: in short, on the incidentals of the old works. These are precisely the poetical and theatrical means which hide the imprecisions of the story. Our theatres no longer have either the capacity or the wish to tell these stories, even the relatively recent ones of the great Shakespeare, at all clearly: i.e. to make the connection of events credible. And according to Aristotle—and we agree there—narrative is the soul of drama. We are more and more disturbed to see how crudely and carelessly men's life together is represented, and that not only in old works but also in contemporary ones constructed according to the old recipes. Our whole way of appreciation is starting to get out of date.

13. It is the inaccurate way in which happenings between human beings are represented that restricts our pleasure in the theatre. The reason: we and our forebears have a different relationship to what is being shown.

14. For when we look about us for an entertainment whose impact is immediate, for a comprehensive and penetrating pleasure such as our theatre could give us by representations of men's life together, we have to think of ourselves as children of a scientific age. Our life as human beings in society —i.e. our life—is determined by the sciences to a quite new extent.

15. A few hundred years ago a handful of people, working

in different countries but in correspondence with one another, performed certain experiments by which they hoped to wring from Nature her secrets. Members of a class of craftsmen in the already powerful cities, they transmitted their discoveries to people who made practical use of them, without expecting more from the new sciences than personal profit for themselves.

Crafts which had progressed by methods virtually unchanged during a thousand years now developed hugely; in many places, which became linked by competition, they gathered from all directions great masses of men, and these, adopting new forms of organization, started producing on a giant scale. Soon mankind was showing powers whose extent it would till that time scarcely have dared to dream of.

16. It was as if mankind for the first time now began a conscious and co-ordinated effort to make the planet that was its home fit to live on. Many of the earth's components, such as coal, water, oil, now became treasures. Steam was made to shift vehicles; a few small sparks and the twitching of frogs' legs revealed a natural force which produced light, carried sounds across continents, etc. In all directions man looked about himself with a new vision, to see how he could adapt to his convenience familiar but as yet unexploited objects. His surroundings changed increasingly from decade to decade, then from year to year, then almost from day to day. I who am writing this write it on a machine which at the time of my birth was unknown. I travel in the new vehicles with a rapidity that my grandfather could not imagine; in those days nothing moved so fast. And I rise in the air: a thing that my father was unable to do. With my father I already spoke across the width of a continent, but it was together with my son that I first saw the moving pictures of the explosion at Hiroshima.

17. The new sciences may have made possible this vast alteration and all-important alterability of our surroundings, yet it cannot be said that their spirit determines everything that we do. The reason why the new way of thinking and feeling has not yet penetrated the great mass of men is that the sciences, for all their success in exploiting and dominating nature, have been stopped by the class which they brought to power—the bourgeoisie—from operating in another field where darkness still reigns, namely that of the relations which people have to one another during the exploiting and domi-

nating process. This business on which all alike depended was performed without the new intellectual methods that made it possible ever illuminating the mutual relationships of the people who carried it out. The new approach to nature was not applied to society.

18. In the event people's mutual relations have become harder to disentangle than ever before. The gigantic joint undertaking on which they are engaged seems more and more to split them into two groups; increases in production lead to increases in misery; only a minority gain from the exploitation of nature, and they only do so because they exploit men. What might be progress for all then becomes advancement for a few, and an ever-increasing part of the productive process gets applied to creating means of destruction for mighty wars. During these wars the mothers of every nation, with their children pressed to them, scan the skies in horror for the deadly inventions of science.

19†. The same attitude as men once showed in face of unpredictable natural catastrophes they now adopt towards their own undertakings. The bourgeois class, which owes to science an advancement that it was able, by ensuring that it alone enjoyed the fruits, to convert into domination, knows very well that its rule would come to an end if the scientific eye were turned on its own undertakings. And so that new science which was founded about a hundred years ago and deals with the character of human society was born in the struggle between rulers and ruled. Since then a certain scientific spirit has developed at the bottom, among the new class of workers whose natural element is large-scale production; from down there the great catastrophes are spotted as undertakings by the rulers.

20. But science and art meet on this ground, that both are there to make men's life easier, the one setting out to maintain, the other to entertain us. In the age to come art will create entertainment from that new productivity which can so greatly improve our maintenance, and in itself, if only it is left unshackled, may prove to be the greatest pleasure of them all.

21. If we want now to surrender ourselves to this great passion for producing, what ought our representations of men's life together to look like? What is that productive attitude in face of nature and of society which we children of a scientific age would like to take up pleasurably in our theatre?

22. The attitude is a critical one. Faced with a river, it consists in regulating the river; faced with a fruit tree, in spraying the fruit tree; faced with movement, in constructing vehicles and aeroplanes; faced with society, in turning society upside down. Our representations of human social life are designed for river-dwellers, fruit farmers, builders of vehicles and upturners of society, whom we invite into our theatres and beg not to forget their cheerful occupations while we hand the world over to their minds and hearts, for them to change as they think fit.

23. The theatre can only adopt such a free attitude if it lets itself be carried along by the strongest currents in its society and associates itself with those who are necessarily most impatient to make great alterations there. The bare wish, if nothing else, to evolve an art fit for the times must drive our theatre of the scientific age straight out into the suburbs, where it can stand as it were wide open, at the disposal of those who live hard and produce much, so that they can be fruitfully entertained there with their great problems. They may find it hard to pay for our art, and immediately to grasp the new method of entertainment, and we shall have to learn in many respects what they need and how they need it; but we can be sure of their interest. For these men who seem so far apart from natural science are only apart from it because they are being forcibly kept apart; and before they can get their hands on it they have first to develop and put into effect a new science of society; so that these are the true children of the scientific age, who alone can get the theatre moving if it is to move at all. A theatre which makes productivity its main source of entertainment has also to take it for its theme, and with greater keenness than ever now that man is everywhere hampered by men from self-production: i.e. from maintaining himself, entertaining and being entertained. The theatre has to become geared into reality if it is to be in a position to turn out effective representations of reality, and to be allowed to do so.

24. But this makes it simpler for the theatre to edge as close as possible to the apparatus of education and mass communication. For although we cannot bother it with the raw material of knowledge in all its variety, which would stop it from being enjoyable, it is still free to find enjoyment in teaching and inquiring. It constructs its workable representations of society, which are then in a position to influence

society, wholly and entirely as a game: for those who are constructing society it sets out society's experiences, past and present alike, in such a manner that the audience can 'appreciate' the feelings, insights and impulses which are distilled by the wisest, most active and most passionate among us from the events of the day or the century. They must be entertained with the wisdom that comes from the solution of problems, with the anger that is a practical expression of sympathy with the underdog, with the respect due to those who respect humanity, or rather whatever is kind to humanity; in short, with whatever delights those who are producing something.

25. And this also means that the theatre can let its spectators enjoy the particular ethic of their age, which springs from productivity. A theatre which converts the critical approach —i.e. our great productive method—into pleasure finds nothing in the ethical field which it must do and a great deal that it can. Even the wholly anti-social can be a source of enjoyment to society so long as it is presented forcefully and on the grand scale. It then often proves to have considerable powers of understanding and other unusually valuable capacities, applied admittedly to a destructive end. Even the bursting flood of a vast catastrophe can be appreciated in all its majesty by society, if society knows how to master it; then we make it our own.

26. For such an operation as this we can hardly accept the theatre as we see it before us. Let us go into one of these houses and observe the effect which it has on the spectators. Looking about us, we see somewhat motionless figures in a peculiar condition: they seem strenuously to be tensing all their muscles, except where these are flabby and exhausted. They scarcely communicate with each other; their relations are those of a lot of sleepers, though of such as dream restlessly because, as is popularly said of those who have nightmares, they are lying on their backs. True, their eyes are open, but they stare rather than see, just as they listen rather than hear. They look at the stage as if in a trance: an expression which comes from the Middle Ages, the days of witches and priests. Seeing and hearing are activities, and can be pleasant ones, but these people seem relieved of activity and like men to whom something is being done. This detached state, where they seem to be given over to vague but profound sensations, grows deeper the better the work of the actors, and so we, as

we do not approve of this situation, should like them to be as bad as possible.

27. As for the world portrayed there, the world from which slices are cut in order to produce these moods and movements of the emotions, its appearance is such, produced from such slight and wretched stuff as a few pieces of cardboard, a little miming, a bit of text, that one has to admire the theatre folk who, with so feeble a reflection of the real world, can move the feelings of their audience so much more strongly than does the world itself.

28. In any case we should excuse these theatre folk, for the pleasures which they sell for money and fame could not be induced by an exacter representation of the world, nor could their inexact renderings be presented in a less magical way. Their capacity to represent people can be seen at work in various instances; it is especially the rogues and the minor figures who reveal their knowledge of humanity and differ one from the other, but the central figures have to be kept general, so that it is easier for the onlooker to identify himself with them, and at all costs each trait of character must be drawn from the narrow field within which everyone can say at once: that is how it is.

For the spectator wants to be put in possession of quite definite sensations, just as a child does when it climbs on to one of the horses on a roundabout: the sensation of pride that it can ride, and has a horse; the pleasure of being carried, and whirled past other children; the adventurous daydreams in which it pursues others or is pursued, etc. In leading the child to experience all this the degree to which its wooden seat resembles a horse counts little, nor does it matter that the ride is confined to a small circle. The one important point for the spectators in these houses is that they should be able to swap a contradictory world for a consistent one, one that they scarcely know for one of which they can dream.

29. That is the sort of theatre which we face in our operations, and so far it has been fully able to transmute our optimistic friends, whom we have called the children of the scientific era, into a cowed, credulous, hypnotized mass.

30. True, for about half a century they have been able to see rather more faithful representations of human social life, as well as individual figures who were in revolt against certain social evils or even against the structure of society as a whole.

They felt interested enough to put up with a temporary and exceptional restriction of language, plot and spiritual scope; for the fresh wind of the scientific spirit nearly withered the charms to which they had grown used. The sacrifice was not especially worth while. The greater subtlety of the representations subtracted from one pleasure without satisfying another. The field of human relationships came within our view, but not within our grasp. Our feelings, having been aroused in the old (magic) way, were bound themselves to remain unaltered.

31. For always and everywhere theatres were the amusement centres of a class which restricted the scientific spirit to the natural field, not daring to let it loose on the field of human relationships. The tiny proletarian section of the public, reinforced to a negligible and uncertain extent by renegade intellectuals, likewise still needed the old kind of entertainment, as a relief from its predetermined way of life.

32. So let us march ahead! Away with all obstacles! Since we seem to have landed in a battle, let us fight! Have we not seen how disbelief can move mountains? Is it not enough that we should have found that something is being kept from us? Before one thing and another there hangs a curtain: let us draw it up!

33. The theatre as we know it shows the structure of society (represented on the stage) as incapable of being influenced by society (in the auditorium). Oedipus, who offended against certain principles underlying the society of his time, is executed: the gods see to that; they are beyond criticism. Shakespeare's great solitary figures, bearing on their breast the star of their fate, carry through with irresistible force their futile and deadly outbursts; they prepare their own downfall; life, not death, becomes obscene as they collapse; the catastrophe is beyond criticism. Human sacrifices all round! Barbaric delights! We know that the barbarians have their art. Let us create another.

34. How much longer are our souls, leaving our 'mere' bodies under cover of the darkness, to plunge into those dreamlike figures up on the stage, there to take part in the crescendos and climaxes which 'normal' life denies us? What kind of release is it at the end of all these plays (which is a happy end only for the conventions of the period—suitable measures, the restoration of order—), when we experience the dreamlike executioner's axe which cuts short such crescendos

as so many excesses? We slink into *Oedipus;* for taboos still exist and ignorance is no excuse before the law. Into *Othello;* for jealously still causes us trouble and everything depends on possession. Into *Wallenstein;* for we need to be free for the competitive struggle and to observe the rules, or it would peter out. This deadweight of old habits is also needed for plays like *Ghosts* and *The Weavers,* although there the social structure, in the shape of a 'setting', presents itself as more open to question. The feelings, insights and impulses of the chief characters are forced on us, and so we learn nothing more about society than we can get from the 'setting'.

35. We need a type of theatre which not only releases the feelings, insights and impulses possible within the particular historical field of human relations in which the action takes place, but employs and encourages those thoughts and feelings which help transform the field itself.

36. The field has to be defined in historically relative terms. In other words we must drop our habit of taking the different social structures of past periods, then stripping them of everything that makes them different; so that they all look more or less like our own, which then acquires from this process a certain air of having been there all along, in other words of permanence pure and simple. Instead we must leave them their distinguishing marks and keep their impermanence always before our eyes, so that our own period can be seen to be impermanent too. (It is of course futile to make use of fancy colours and folklore for this, such as our theatres apply precisely in order to emphasize the similarities in human behaviour at different times. We shall indicate the theatrical methods below.)

37. If we ensure that our characters on the stage are moved by social impulses and that these differ according to the period, then we make it harder for our spectator to identify himself with them. He cannot simply feel: that's how I would act, but at most can say: if I had lived under those circumstances. And if we play works dealing with our own time as though they were historical, then perhaps the circumstances under which he himself acts will strike him as equally odd; and this is where the critical attitude begins.

38. The 'historical conditions' must of course not be imagined (nor will they be so constructed) as mysterious Powers (in the background); on the contrary, they are created and

maintained by men (and will in due course be altered by them): it is the actions taking place before us that allow us to see what they are.

39. If a character responds in a manner historically in keeping with his period, and would respond otherwise in other periods, does that mean that he is not simply 'Everyman'? It is true that a man will respond differently according to his circumstances and his class; if he were living at another time, or in his youth, or on the darker side of life, he would infallibly give a different response, though one still determined by the same factors and like anyone else's response in that situation at that time. So should we not ask if there are any further differences of response? Where is the man himself, the living, unmistakeable man, who is not quite identical with those identified with him? It is clear that his stage image must bring him to light, and this will come about if this particular contradiction is recreated in the image. The image that gives historical definition will retain something of the rough sketching which indicates traces of other movements and features all around the fully-worked-out figure. Or imagine a man standing in a valley and making a speech in which he occasionally changes his views or simply utters sentences which contradict one another, so that the accompanying echo forces them into confrontation.

40. Such images certainly demand a way of acting which will leave the spectator's intellect free and highly mobile. He has again and again to make what one might call hypothetical adjustments to our structure, by mentally switching off the motive forces of our society or by substituting others for them: a process which leads real conduct to acquire an element of 'unnaturalness', thus allowing the real motive forces to be shorn of their naturalness and become capable of manipulation.

41. It is the same as when an irrigation expert looks at a river together with its former bed and various hypothetical courses which it might have followed if there had been a different tilt to the plateau or a different volume of water. And while he in his mind is looking at a new river, the socialist in his is hearing new kinds of talk from the labourers who work by it. And similarly in the theatre our spectator should find that the incidents set among such labourers are also accompanied by echoes and by traces of sketching.

42. The kind of acting which was tried out at the Schiff-bauerdamm Theater in Berlin between the First and Second World Wars, with the object of producing such images, is based on the 'alienation effect' (A-effect). A representation that alienates is one which allows us to recognize its subject, but at the same time makes it seem unfamiliar. The classical and medieval theatre alienated its characters by making them wear human or animal masks; the Asiatic theatre even today uses musical and pantomimic A-effects. Such devices were certainly a barrier to empathy, and yet this technique owed more, not less, to hypnotic suggestion than do those by which empathy is achieved. The social aims of these old devices were entirely different from our own.

43†. The old A-effects quite remove the object represented from the spectator's grasp, turning it into something that cannot be altered; the new are not odd in themselves, though the unscientific eye stamps anything strange as odd. The new alienations are only designed to free socially-conditioned phenomena from that stamp of familiarity which protects them against our grasp today.

44. For it seems impossible to alter what has long not been altered. We are always coming on things that are too obvious for us to bother to understand them. What men experience among themselves they think of as 'the' human experience. A child, living in a world of old men, learns how things work there. He knows the run of things before he can walk. If anyone is bold enough to want something further, he only wants to have it as an exception. Even if he realizes that the arrangements made for him by 'Providence' are only what has been provided by society he is bound to see society, that vast collection of beings like himself, as a whole that is greater than the sum of its parts and therefore not in any way to be influenced. Moreover, he would be used to things that could not be influenced; and who mistrusts what he is used to? To transform himself from general passive acceptance to a corresponding state of suspicious inquiry he would need to develop that detached eye with which the great Galileo observed a swinging chandelier. He was amazed by this pendulum motion, as if he had not expected it and could not understand its occurring, and this enabled him to come on the rules by which it was governed. Here is the outlook, disconcerting but fruitful, which the theatre must provoke with its representa-

tions of human social life. It must amaze its public, and this can be achieved by a technique of alienating the familiar.

45†. This technique allows the theatre to make use in its representations of the new social scientific method known as dialectical materialism. In order to unearth society's laws of motion this method treats social situations as processes, and traces out all their inconsistencies. It regards nothing as existing except in so far as it changes, in other words is in disharmony with itself. This also goes for those human feelings, opinions and attitudes through which at any time the form of men's life together finds its expression.

46†. Our own period, which is transforming nature in so many and different ways, takes pleasure in understanding things so that we can interfere. There is a great deal to man, we say; so a great deal can be made out of him. He does not have to stay the way he is now, nor does he have to be seen only as he is now, but also as he might become. We must not start with him; we must start on him. This means, however, that I must not simply set myself in his place, but must set myself facing him, to represent us all. That is why the theatre must alienate what it shows.

47. In order to produce A-effects the actor has to discard whatever means he has learnt of getting the audience to identify itself with the characters which he plays. Aiming not to put his audience into a trance, he must not go into a trance himself. His muscles must remain loose, for a turn of the head, e.g. with tautened neck muscles, will 'magically' lead the spectators' eyes and even their heads to turn with it, and this can only detract from any speculation or reaction which the gesture may bring about. His way of speaking has to be free from parsonical sing-song and from all those cadences which lull the spectator so that the sense gets lost. Even if he plays a man possessed he must not seem to be possessed himself, for how is the spectator to discover what possessed him if he does?

48. At no moment must he go so far as to be wholly transformed into the character played. The verdict: 'he didn't act Lear, he was Lear' would be an annihilating blow to him. He has just to show the character, or rather he has to do more than just get into it; this does not mean that if he is playing passionate parts he must himself remain cold. It is only that his feelings must not at bottom be those of the character, so

that the audience's may not at bottom be those of the character either. The audience must have complete freedom here.

49. This principle—that the actor appears on the stage in a double role, as Laughton and as Galileo; that the showman Laughton does not disappear in the Galileo whom he is showing; from which this way of acting gets its name of 'epic' —comes to mean simply that the tangible, matter-of-fact process is no longer hidden behind a veil; that Laughton is actually there, standing on the stage and showing us what he imagines Galileo to have been. Of course the audience would not forget Laughton if he attempted the full change of personality, in that they would admire him for it; but they would in that case miss his own opinions and sensations, which would have been completely swallowed up by the character. He would have taken its opinions and sensations and made them his own, so that a single homogeneous pattern would emerge, which he would then make ours. In order to prevent this abuse the actor must also put some artistry into the act of showing. An illustration may help: we find a gesture which expresses one-half of his attitude—that of showing—if we make him smoke a cigar and then imagine him laying it down now and again in order to show us some further characteristic attitude of the figure in the play. If we then subtract any element of hurry from the image and do not read slackness into its refusal to be taut we shall have an actor who is fully capable of leaving us to our thoughts, or to his own.

50. There needs to be yet a further change in the actor's communication of these images, and it too makes the process more 'matter-of-fact'. Just as the actor no longer has to persuade the audience that it is the author's character and not himself that is standing on the stage, so also he need not pretend that the events taking place on the stage have never been rehearsed, and are now happening for the first and only time. Schiller's distinction is no longer valid: that the rhapsodist has to treat his material as wholly in the past: the mime his, as wholly here and now.* It should be apparent all through his performance that 'even at the start and in the middle he knows how it ends' and he must 'thus maintain a calm independence throughout'. He narrates the story of his

---

* Letter to Goethe, 26.12.1797. [Translator's note.] Quoted in *Brecht on Theatre*, *op. cit.*, p. 210.

character by vivid portrayal, always knowing more than it does and treating its 'now' and 'here' not as a pretence made possible by the rules of the game but as something to be distinguished from yesterday and some other place, so as to make visible the knotting-together of the events.

51. This matters particularly in the portrayal of large-scale events or ones where the outside world is abruptly changed, as in wars and revolutions. The spectator can then have the whole situation and the whole course of events set before him. He can for instance hear a woman speaking and imagine her speaking differently, let us say in a few weeks' time, or other women speaking differently at that moment but in another place. This would be possible if the actress were to play as though the woman had lived through the entire period and were now, out of her memory and her knowledge of what happened next, recalling those utterances of hers which were important at the time; for what is important here is what became important. To alienate an individual in this way, as being 'this particular individual' and 'this particular individual at this particular moment', is only possible if there are no illusions that the player is identical with the character and the performance with the actual event.

52. We shall find that this has meant scrapping yet another illusion: that everyone behaves like the character concerned. 'I am doing this' has become 'I did this', and now 'he did this' has got to become 'he did this, when he might have done something else'. It is too great a simplification if we make the actions fit the character and the character fit the actions: the inconsistencies which are to be found in the actions and characters of real people cannot be shown like this. The laws of motion of a society are not to be demonstrated by 'perfect examples', for 'imperfection' (inconsistency) is an essential part of motion and of the thing moved. It is only necessary—but absolutely necessary—that there should be something approaching experimental conditions, i.e. that a counter-experiment should now and then be conceivable. Altogether this is a way of treating society as if all its actions were performed as experiments.

53†. Even if empathy, or self-identification with the character, can be usefully indulged in at rehearsals (something to be avoided in a performance) it has to be treated just as one of a number of methods of observation. It helps when rehearsing, for even though the contemporary theatre has applied it in an indiscriminate way it has none the less led to subtle delineation of personality. But it is the crudest form of empathy when the actor simply asks: what should I be like if this or that were to happen to me? what would it look like if I were to say this and do that?—instead of asking: have I ever heard somebody saying this and doing that? in order to piece together all sorts of elements with which to construct a new character such as would allow the story to have taken place—and a good deal else. The coherence of the character is in fact shown by the way in which its individual qualities contradict one another.

54. Observation is a major part of acting. The actor observes his fellowmen with all his nerves and muscles in an act of imitation which is at the same time a process of the mind. For pure imitation would only bring out what had been observed; and this is not enough, because the original says what it has to say with too subdued a voice. To achieve a character rather than a caricature, the actor looks at people as though they were playing him their actions, in other words as though they were advising him to give their actions careful consideration.

55†. Without opinions and objectives one can represent nothing at all. Without knowledge one can show nothing; how could one know what would be worth knowing? Unless the actor is satisfied to be a parrot or a monkey he must master our period's knowledge of human social life by himself joining in the war of the classes. Some people may feel this to be degrading, because they rank art, once the money side has been settled, as one of the highest things; but mankind's highest decisions are in fact fought out on earth, not in the heavens; in the 'external' world, not inside people's heads. Nobody can stand above the warring classes, for nobody can stand above the human race. Society cannot share a common communication system so long as it is split into warring classes. Thus for art to be 'unpolitical' means only to ally itself with the 'ruling' group.

56. So the choice of viewpoint is also a major element of the actor's art, and it has to be decided outside the theatre Like the transformation of nature, that of society is a liberating act; and it is the joys of liberation which the theatre of a scientific age has got to convey.

57. Let us go on to examine how, for instance, this viewpoint affects the actor's interpretation of his part. It then becomes important that he should not 'catch on' too quickly. Even if he straightway establishes the most natural cadences for his part, the least awkward way of speaking it, he still cannot regard its actual pronouncement as being ideally natural, but must think twice and take his own general opinions into account, then consider various other conceivable pronouncements; in short, take up the attitude of a man who just wonders. This is not only to prevent him from 'fixing' a particular character prematurely, so that it has to be stuffed out with afterthoughts because he has not waited to register all the other pronouncements, and especially those of the other characters; but also and principally in order to build into the character that element of 'Not–But' on which so much depends if society, in the shape of the audience, is to be able to look at what takes place in such a way as to be able to affect it. Each actor, moreover, instead of concentrating on what suits him and calling it 'human nature', must go above all for what does not suit him, is not his speciality. And along with his part he must commit to memory his first reactions, reserves, criticisms, shocks, so that they are not destroyed by being 'swallowed up' in the final version but are preserved and perceptible; for character and all must not grow on the audience so much as strike it.

58. And the learning process must be co-ordinated so that the actor learns as the other actors are learning and develops his character as they are developing theirs. For the smallest social unit is not the single person but two people. In life too we develop one another.

59. Here we can learn something from our own theatres' deplorable habit of letting the dominant actor, the star, 'come to the front' by getting all the other actors to work for him: he makes his character terrible or wise by forcing his partners to make theirs terrified or attentive. Even if only to secure this advantage for all, and thus to help the story, the actors should sometimes swap roles with their partners during rehearsal, so that the characters can get what they need from one another. But it is also good for the actors when they see their characters copied or portrayed in another form. If the part is played by somebody of the opposite sex the sex of the character will be more clearly brought out; if it is played by a comedian,

whether comically or tragically, it will gain fresh aspects. By helping to develop the parts that correspond to his own, or at any rate standing in for their players, the actor strengthens the all-decisive social standpoint from which he has to present his character. The master is only the sort of master his servant lets him be, etc.

60. A mass of operations to develop the character are carried out when it is introduced among the other characters of the play, and the actor will have to memorize what he himself has anticipated in this connection from his reading of the text. But now he finds out much more about himself from the treatment which he gets at the hands of the characters in the play.

61. The realm of attitudes adopted by the characters towards one another is what we call the realm of gest. Physical attitude, tone of voice and facial expression are all determined by a social gest: the characters are cursing, flattering, instructing one another, and so on. The attitudes which people adopt towards one another include even those attitudes which would appear to be quite private, such as the utterances of physical pain in an illness, or of religious faith. These expressions of a gest are usually highly complicated and contradictory, so that they cannot be rendered by any single word and the actor must take care that in giving his image the necessary emphasis he does not lose anything, but emphasizes the entire complex.

62. The actor masters his character by paying critical attention to its manifold utterances, as also to those of his counterparts and of all the other characters involved.

63. Let us get down to the problem of gestic content by running through the opening scenes of a fairly modern play, my own *Life of Galileo*. Since we wish at the same time to find out what light the different utterances cast on one another we will assume that it is not our first introduction to the play. It begins with the man of forty-six having his morning wash, broken by occasional browsing in books and by a lesson on the solar system for Andrea Sarti, a small boy. To play this, surely you have got to know that we shall be ending with the man of seventy-eight having his supper, just after he has said good-bye for ever to the same pupil? He is then more terribly altered than this passage of time could possibly have brought about. He wolfs his food with unrestrained greed, no other

idea in his head; he has rid himself of his educational mission in shameful circumstances, as though it were a burden: he, who once drank his morning milk without a care, greedy to teach the boy. But does he really drink it without care? Isn't the pleasure of drinking and washing one with the pleasure which he takes in the new ideas? Don't forget: he thinks out of self-indulgence. . . . Is that good or bad? I would advise you to represent it as good, since on this point you will find nothing in the whole play to harm society, and more especially because you yourself are, I hope, a gallant child of the scientific age. But take careful note: many horrible things will happen in this connection. The fact that the man who here acclaims the new age will be forced at the end to beg this age to disown him as contemptible, even to dispossess him; all this will be relevant. As for the lesson, you may like to decide whether the man's heart is so full that his mouth is overflowing, so that he has to talk to anybody about it, even a child, or whether the child has first to draw the knowledge out of him, by knowing him and showing interest. Again, there may be two of them who cannot restrain themselves, the one from asking, the other from giving the answer: a bond of this sort would be interesting, for one day it is going to be rudely snapped. Of course you will want the demonstration of the earth's rotation round the sun to be conducted quickly, since it is given for nothing, and now the wealthy unknown pupil appears, lending the scholar's time a monetary value. He shows no interest, but he has to be served; Galileo lacks resources, and so he will stand between the wealthy pupil and the intelligent one, and sigh as he makes his choice. There is little that he can teach his new student, so he learns from him instead; he hears of the telescope which has been invented in Holland: in his own way he gets something out of the disturbance of his morning's work. The Rector of the university arrives. Galileo's application for an increase in salary has been turned down; the university is reluctant to pay so much for the theories of physics as for those of theology; it wishes him, who after all is operating on a generally-accepted low level of scholarship, to produce something useful here and now. You will see from the way in which he offers his thesis that he is used to being refused and corrected. The Rector reminds him that the Republic guarantees freedom of research even if she doesn't pay; he replies that he cannot make much of this freedom if he lacks the leisure which good payment permits. Here you should not find his impatience too peremptory, or his poverty will not be given due weight. For shortly after that you find him having ideas which need some explanation: the prophet of a new age of scientific truth considers how he can swindle some money out of the Republic by offering her the telescope as his own invention. All he sees in the new invention, you will be surprised to hear, is a few scudi, and he examines it simply with a view to annexing it himself. But if you move on to the second scene you will find that while he is selling the invention to the Venetian Signoria with a speech that disgraces him by its falsehoods he has already almost forgotten the money, because he has realized that the instrument has not only military but astronomical significance. The article which he has been blackmailed—let us call it that—into producing proves to have great qualities for the very research which he had to break off in order to produce it. If during the ceremony, as he complacently accepts the undeserved honours paid him, he outlines to his learned friend the marvellous discoveries in view—don't overlook the theatrical way in which he does this—you will find in him a far more profound excitement than the thought of monetary gain called forth. Perhaps, looked at in this way, his charlatanry does not mean much, but it still shows how determined this man is to take the easy course, and to apply his reason in a base as well as a noble manner. A more significant test awaits him, and does not every capitulation bring the next one nearer?

64†. Splitting such material into one gest after another, the actor masters his character by first mastering the 'story'. It is only after walking all round the entire episode that he can, as it were by a single leap, seize and fix his character, complete with all its individual features. Once he has done his best to let himself be amazed by the inconsistencies in its various attitudes, knowing that he will in turn have to make them amaze the audience, then the story as a whole gives him a chance to pull the inconsistencies together; for the story, being a limited episode, has a specific sense, i.e. only gratifies a specific fraction of all the interests that could arise.

65†. Everything hangs on the 'story'; it is the heart of the theatrical performance. For it is what happens *between* people that provides them with all the material that they can discuss, criticize, alter. Even if the particular person represented by the actor has ultimately to fit into more than just the one episode, it is mainly because the episode will be all the more striking if it reaches fulfilment in a particular person. The 'story' is the theatre's great operation, the complete fitting together of all the gestic incidents, embracing the communications and impulses that must now go to make up the audience's entertainment.

66. Each single incident has its basic gest: *Richard Gloster courts his victim's widow. The child's true mother is found by means of a chalk circle. God has a bet with the Devil for Dr Faustus's soul. Woyzeck buys a cheap knife in order to do his wife in,* etc. The grouping of the characters on the stage and the movements of the groups must be such that the necessary beauty is attained above all by the elegance with which the material conveying that gest is set out and laid bare to the understanding of the audience.

67. As we cannot invite the audience to fling itself into the story as if it were a river and let itself be carried vaguely hither and thither, the individual episodes have to be knotted together in such a way that the knots are easily noticed. The episodes must not succeed one another indistinguishably but must give us a chance to interpose our judgment. (If it were above all the obscurity of the original interrelations that interested us, then just this circumstance would have to be sufficiently alienated.) The parts of the story have to be carefully set off one against another by giving each its own structure as a play within the play. To this end it is best to agree to use titles like those in the preceding paragraph. The titles must include the social point, saying at the same time something about the kind of portrayal wanted, i.e. should copy the tone of a chronicle or a ballad or a newspaper or a morality. For instance, a simple way of alienating something is that normally applied to customs and moral principles. A visit, the treatment of an enemy, a lovers' meeting, agreements about politics or business, can be portrayed as if they were simply illustrations of general principles valid for the place in question. Shown thus, the particular and unrepeatable incident acquires a disconcerting look, because it appears as something general, something that has become a principle. As soon as we ask whether in fact it should have become such, or what about it should have done so, we are alienating the incident. The poetic approach to history can be studied in the so-called

panoramas at sideshows in fairs. As alienation likewise means a kind of fame certain incidents can just be represented as famous, as though they had for a long while been common knowledge and care must be taken not to offer the least obstacle to their further transmission. In short: there are many conceivable ways of telling a story, some of them known and some still to be discovered.

68. What needs to be alienated, and how this is to be done, depends on the exposition demanded by the entire episode; and this is where the theatre has to speak up decisively for the interests of its own time. Let us take as an example of such exposition the old play *Hamlet*. Given the dark and bloody period in which I am writing—the criminal ruling classes, the widespread doubt in the power of reason, continually being misused—I think that I can read the story thus: It is an age of warriors. Hamlet's father, king of Denmark, slew the king of Norway in a successful war of spoliation. While the latter's son Fortinbras is arming for a fresh war the Danish king is likewise slain: by his own brother. The slain king's brothers, now themselves kings, avert war by arranging that the Norwegian troops shall cross Danish soil to launch a predatory war against Poland. But at this point the young Hamlet is summoned by his warrior father's ghost to avenge the crime committed against him. After at first being reluctant to answer one bloody deed by another, and even preparing to go into exile, he meets young Fortinbras at the coast as he is marching with his troops to Poland. Overcome by this warrior-like example, he turns back and in a piece of barbaric butchery slaughters his uncle, his mother and himself, leaving Denmark to the Norwegian. These events show the young man, already somewhat stout, making the most ineffective use of the new approach to Reason which he has picked up at the university of Wittenberg. In the feudal business to which he returns it simply hampers him. Faced with irrational practices, his reason is utterly unpractical. He falls a tragic victim to the discrepancy between such reasoning and such action. This way of reading the play, which can be read in more than one way, might in my view interest our audience.

69. Whether or no literature presents them as successes, each step forward, every emancipation from nature that is scored in the field of production and leads to a transformation of society, all those explorations in some new direction which

mankind has embarked on in order to improve its lot, give us a sense of confidence and triumph and lead us to take pleasure in the possibilities of change in all things. Galileo expresses this when he says: 'It is my view that the earth is most noble and wonderful, seeing the great number and variety of changes and generations which incessantly take place on it.'

70. The exposition of the story and its communication by suitable means of alienation constitute the main business of the theatre. Not everything depends on the actor, even though nothing may be done without taking him into account. The 'story' is set out, brought forward and shown by the theatre as a whole, by actors, stage designers, mask-makers, costumiers, composers and choreographers. They unite their various arts for the joint operation, without of course sacrificing their independence in the process.

71. It emphasizes the general gest of showing, which always underlies that which is being shown, when the audience is musically addressed by means of songs. Because of this the actors ought not to 'drop into' song, but should clearly mark it off from the rest of the text; and this is best reinforced by a few theatrical methods such as changing the lighting or inserting a title. For its part, the music must strongly resist the smooth incorporation which is generally expected of it and turns it into an unthinking slavey. Music does not 'accompany' except in the form of comment. It cannot simply 'express itself' by discharging the emotions with which the incidents of the play have filled it. Thus Eisler, e.g. helped admirably in the knotting of the incidents when in the carnival scene of *Galileo* he set the masked procession of the guilds to a triumphant and threatening music which showed what a revolutionary twist the lower orders had given to the scholar's astronomical theories. Similarly in *The Caucasian Chalk Circle* the singer, by using a chilly and unemotional way of singing to describe the servant-girl's rescue of the child as it is mimed on the stage, makes evident the terror of a period in which motherly instincts can become a suicidal weakness. Thus music can make its point in a number of ways and with full independence, and can react in its own manner to the subjects dealt with; at the same time it can also quite simply help to lend variety to the entertainment.

72. Just as the composer wins back his freedom by no longer having to create atmosphere so that the audience may

be helped to lose itself unreservedly in the events on the stage, so also the stage designer gets considerable freedom as soon as he no longer has to give the illusion of a room or a locality when he is building his sets. It is enough for him to give hints, though these must make statements of greater historical or social interest than does the real setting. At the Jewish Theatre in Moscow *King Lear* was alienated by a structure that re-called a medieval tabernacle; Neher set *Galileo* in front of projections of maps, documents and Renaissance works of art; for *Haitang erwacht* at the Piscator-Theater Heartfield used a background of reversible flags bearing inscriptions, to mark changes in the political situation of which the persons on the stage were sometimes unaware.

73†. For choreography too there are once again tasks of a realistic kind. It is a relatively recent error to suppose that it has nothing to do with the representation of 'people as they really are'. If art reflects life it does so with special mirrors. Art does not become unrealistic by changing the proportions but by changing them in such a way that if the audience took its representations as a practical guide to insights and impulses it would go astray in real life. It is of course essential that stylization should not remove the natural element but should heighten it. Anyhow, a theatre where everything depends on the gest cannot do without choreography. Elegant movement and graceful grouping, for a start, can alienate, and inventive miming greatly helps the story.

74. So let us invite all the sister arts of the drama, not in order to create an 'integrated work of art' in which they all offer themselves up and are lost, but so that together with the drama they may further the common task in their different ways; and their relations with one another consist in this: that they lead to mutual alienation.

75. And here once again let us recall that their task is to entertain the children of the scientific age, and to do so with sensuousness and humour. This is something that we Germans cannot tell ourselves too often, for with us everything easily slips into the insubstantial and unapproachable, and we begin to talk of *Weltanschauung* when the world in question has already dissolved. Even materialism is little more than an idea with us. Sexual pleasure with us turns into marital obligations, the pleasures of art subserve general culture, and by learning we mean not an enjoyable process of finding out, but the

forcible shoving of our nose into something. Our activity has none of the pleasure of exploration, and if we want to make an impression we do not say how much fun we have got out of something but how much effort it has cost us.

76. One more thing: the delivery to the audience of what has been built up in the rehearsals. Here it is essential that the actual playing should be infused with the gest of handing over a finished article. What now comes before the spectator is the most frequently repeated of what has not been rejected, and so the finished representations have to be delivered with the eyes fully open, so that they may be received with the eyes open too.

77. That is to say, our representations must take second place to what is represented, men's life together in society; and the pleasure felt in their perfection must be converted into the higher pleasure felt when the rules emerging from this life in society are treated as imperfect and provisional. In this way the theatre leaves its spectators productively disposed even after the spectacle is over. Let us hope that their theatre may allow them to enjoy as entertainment that terrible and never-ending labour which should ensure their maintenance, together with the terror of their unceasing transformation. Let them here produce their own lives in the simplest way; for the simplest way of living is in art.

APPENDICES TO THE SHORT ORGANUM

(The numbers refer to the relevant paragraphs of the work)

3. It is not just a matter of art presenting what needs to be learned in an enjoyable form. The contradiction between learning and enjoyment must be clearly grasped and its significance understood—in a period when knowledge is acquired in order to be resold for the highest possible price, and even a high price does not prevent further exploitation by those who pay it. Only once productivity has been set free can learning be transformed into enjoyment and vice versa.

4. (a) If we now discard the concept of EPIC THEATRE we are not discarding that progress towards conscious experience which it still makes possible. It is just that the concept is too slight and too vague for the kind of theatre intended; it

needs exacter definition and must achieve more. Besides, it was too inflexibly opposed to the concept of the dramatic, often just taking it naïvely for granted, roughly in the sense that 'of course' it always embraces incidents that take place directly with all or most of the hall-marks of immediacy. In the same slightly hazardous way we always take it for granted that whatever its novelty it is still theatre, and does not turn into a scientific demonstration.

(b) Nor is the concept THEATRE OF THE SCIENTIFIC AGE quite broad enough. The Short Organum may give an adequate explanation of what is meant by a scientific age, but the bare expression, in the form in which it is normally used, is too discredited.

12. Our enjoyment of old plays becomes greater, the more we can give ourselves up to the new kind of pleasures better suited to our time. To that end we need to develop the historical sense (needed also for the appreciation of new plays) into a real sensual delight. When our theatres perform plays of other periods they like to annihilate distance, fill in the gap, gloss over the differences. But what comes then of our delight in comparisons, in distance, in dissimilarity—which is at the same time a delight in what is close and proper to ourselves?

19. In times of upheaval, fearful and fruitful, the evenings of the doomed classes coincide with the dawns of those that are rising. It is in these twilight periods that Minerva's owl sets out on her flights.

43. True, profound, active application of alienation effects takes it for granted that society considers its condition to be historic and capable of improvement. True A-effects are of a combative character.

45. The theatre of the scientific age is in a position to make dialectics into a source of enjoyment. The unexpectedness of logically progressive or zigzag development, the instability of every circumstance, the joke of contradiction and so forth: all these are ways of enjoying the liveliness of men, things and processes, and they heighten both our capacity for life and our pleasure in it.

Every art contributes to the greatest art of all, the art of living.

46. The bourgeois theatre's performances always aim at smoothing over contradictions, at creating false harmony, at idealization. Conditions are reported as if they could not be

otherwise; characters as individuals, incapable by definition of being divided, cast in one block, manifesting themselves in the most various situations, likewise for that matter existing without any situation at all. If there is any development it is always steady, never by jerks; the developments always take place within a definite framework which cannot be broken through.

None of this is like reality, so a realistic theatre must give it up.

53. (a) However dogmatic it may seem to insist that self-identification with the character should be avoided in the performance, our generation can listen to this warning with advantage. However determinedly they obey it they can hardly carry it out to the letter, so the most likely result is that truly rending contradiction between experience and portrayal, empathy and demonstration, justification and criticism, which is what is aimed at.

(b) The contradiction between acting (demonstration) and experience (empathy) often leads the uninstructed to suppose that only one or the other can be manifest in the work of the actor (as if the Short Organum concentrated entirely on acting and the old tradition entirely on experience). In reality it is a matter of two mutually hostile processes which fuse in the actor's work; his performance is not just composed of a bit of the one and a bit of the other. His particular effectiveness comes from the tussle and tension of the two opposites, and also from their depth. The style in which the S.O. is written is partly to blame for this. It is misleading often thanks to a possibly over-impatient and over-exclusive concern with the 'principal side of the contradiction'.*

55. And yet art addresses all alike, and would confront the tiger with its song. What is more, he has been known to join in. New ideas whose fruitfulness is evident irrespective who may reap the fruits are liable to rise to the 'top' from classes on their way up, and to get a grip on people who ought by rights to be combating them in an effort to preserve their own privileges. For members of a given class are not immune to ideas from which their class cannot benefit. Just as the oppressed can succumb to the ideas of their oppressors, so mem-

---

* Mao-Tse-tung: 'On Contradiction.' One of the two sides of a contradiction is bound to be the principal one. [Translator's note.]

bers of the oppressor class can fall victim to those of the oppressed. In certain periods when the classes are fighting for the leadership of mankind any man who is not hopelessly corrupt may feel a strong urge to be counted among its pioneers and to press ahead.

64. The story does not just correspond to an incident from men's life together as it might actually have taken place, but is composed of episodes rearranged so as to allow the storyteller's ideas about men's life to find expression. In the same way the characters are not simply portraits of living people, but are rearranged and formed in accordance with ideas.

These rearrangements often in various ways contradict the knowledge which the actors have gained from experience and from books: a contradiction that the actors must seize and maintain in their performance. The source of their creation must lie at the same time in reality and in the imagination, for both in their work and in that of the playwright reality must appear vivid and rich in order to bring out the specific or general features of the play.

65. For a genuine story to emerge it is most important that the scenes should to start with be played quite simply one after another, using the experience of real life, without taking account of what follows or even of the play's overall sense. The story then unreels in a contradictory manner; the individual scenes retain their own meaning; they yield (and stimulate) a wealth of ideas; and their sum, the story, unfolds authentically without any cheap all-pervading idealization (one word leading to another) or directing of subordinate, purely functional component parts to an ending in which everything is resolved.

73. A quotation from Lenin: 'It is impossible to recognize the various happenings in the world in their independence of movement, their spontaneity of development, their vitality of being, without recognizing them as a unity of opposites.'*

It is a matter of indifference whether the theatre's main object is to provide knowledge of the world. The fact remains that the theatre has to represent the world and that its representations must not mislead. If Lenin's view is right, then they cannot work out satisfactorily without knowledge of dialectics —and without making dialectics known.

---

* Lenin: 'On the Question of Dialectics.' [Translator's note.]

Objection: What about the kind of art which gets its effects from dark, distorted, fragmentary representations? What about the art of primitive peoples, madmen and children?

If one knows a great deal and can retain what one knows, it may be possible perhaps to get something out of such representations; but we suspect that unduly subjective representations of the world have anti-social effects.

(*A Separate Note*). Studying a part means at the same time studying the story; or rather, it ought at first to consist mainly in that. (What happens to the character? How does he take it? What opinions does he come in contact with? etc.) To this end the actor needs to muster his knowledge of men and the world, and he must also ask his questions dialectically. (Certain questions are only asked by dialecticians.)

For instance; an actor is due to play Faust. Faust's love for Gretchen runs a fateful course. The question arises whether just the same thing wouldn't happen if they got married. This is a question that is not usually asked. It seems too low, vulgar, commonplace. Faust is a genius, a great soul striving after the infinite; how can anyone dream of asking a question like 'Why doesn't he get married?' But simple people do ask it. That in itself must lead the actor to ask it too. And once he has thought about the matter he will realize that this question is not only necessary but extremely fruitful.

We have first of all to decide under what conditions this love affair takes place, what is its relation to the story as a whole, what it signifies for the principal theme. Faust has given up his 'lofty', abstract, 'purely spiritual' attempts to find satisfaction in life, and now turns to 'purely sensual' earthly experiences. His relationship with Gretchen thereby becomes a fateful one. That is to say he comes into conflict with Gretchen; his sense of union becomes a division in two: his satisfaction turns into pain. The conflict leads to Gretchen's utter destruction, and Faust is hard hit by this. At the same time this conflict can only be portrayed correctly by means of another much wider conflict which dominates the entire work, Parts I and II.

Faust manages to emerge from the painful contradiction between his 'purely spiritual' escapades and his unsatisfied and insatiable 'purely sensual' appetites, and this thanks to the Devil. In the 'purely sensual' sphere (of the love affair) Faust comes up against his environment, represented by Gretchen, and has to destroy it in order to escape. The main contradiction is resolved at the end of the whole play; it is this that explains the lesser contradictions and puts them in their place. Faust can no longer behave like a mere consumer, a parasite. Spiritual and sensual activity are united in productive work for mankind; the production of life leads to satisfaction in life.

Turning back to our love affair we see that marriage, though utterly 'respectable', out of the question for a genius and in contradiction with his whole career, would in a relative sense have been better and more productive as being the conjuncture which would have let the woman he loved develop instead of being destroyed. Faust would of course scarcely in that case have been Faust; he would have been bogged down in pettinesses (as suddenly becomes clear) and so forth.

The actor who sympathetically asks the question that bothers simple people will be able to make Faust's non-marriage into a clearly-defined stage of his development, where otherwise, by following the usual approach, he merely helps to show that whoever wishes to rise higher on earth must inevitably create pain, that the need to pay for development and satisfaction is the unavoidable tragedy of life—i.e. the cruellest and most commonplace principle: that you can't make omelettes without breaking eggs.

by Yurii Olyesha

the author
about his play *(1929)*

translated by Daniel C. Gerould *and* Eleanor S. Gerould

My play *The Conspiracy of Feelings,* now playing in Moscow at the Vakhtangov Theatre, is an adaptation of my novel *Envy.*

This I can say about my play: like any play derived from a work of fiction, it has certain faults—it is long and drawn-out in places, the plot is not properly worked out, and it is too wordy.

If I had written a play on the same subject as the story, but without having the story as its source, the play would have turned out completely differently and been completely unlike *The Conspiracy of Feelings* in structure and far superior to it.

The theme of the play is the struggle for passionate commitment. A young man, Nikolai Kavalerov, who is just as old as the century is, enters into the struggle with his "benefactor" Andrei Babichev—a communist and a director of a food industry trust.

Kavalerov considers Andrei a blockhead, a "salami salesman," a graven image, devoid of feelings, a machine that stifles everything human: tenderness, genuine feeling, individuality.

The young man dreams of becoming "the hired assassin avenging his century." He wants to kill the communist Andrei Babichev, in order not to surrender without a fight to this new figure and give up his own personality which he considers highly gifted and undeservedly doomed to destruction.

A conspiracy grows up against the director. At the head of the conspiracy stands the director's brother, a fantastic character, Ivan Babichev, the king of pillows: "Follow me! . . . all you cowards, jealous ones, lovers, heroes . . . you knights in shining armor . . . follow me . . . I'll lead you on our last march."

Thus cries the king.

The hired assassin raises his hand. He must leave a scar "on history's ugly mug."

My aim was to show that passionate involvement is not the exclusive monopoly of people from the old world, that strong feeling is not just showing off and ranting and raving, that those building the new world and a new way of life are more humane than anyone else and that what seems to the condemned man to be the stone face of a graven image is really the shining face of the new man, incomprehensible to the one who is condemned, threatening and blinding him.

A whole series of accusations were leveled against me on account of the central figure, Andrei Babichev. He is a sausage-maker—according to the criticism—a sausage-maker and nothing more. I deliberately gave my communist-hero an odd profession to make him theatrical and alive. Then, to counterbalance the dazzling talk of the people from the past, I wanted to make the hero's diction rough and ironic, and I wanted to contrast plain salami with Ophelias and concrete reality with vague romanticism.

Let people who still live in the past fly into a rage, boil over, and get furious because the new man has the skill to be a poet of salami.

Living is more frightening when one has nothing to live for. It is all the more frightening for Kavalerov to experience the collapse of his romanticism when he sees it break on such an unromantic thing as salami.

What concerns me most of all is whether my play is "intelligible" to the masses. The Bolshoi Dramatic Theatre is now working on the play to make it intelligible. I think that the theatre will be successful.

notes of a dramatist *(1933)*

by Yurii Olyesha

translated by Daniel C. Gerould *and* Eleanor S. Gerould

1) I am interested in the question of the physical destruction of characters in plays.

In the past plays were written in which the participants were kings, princes, generals, knights (Shakespeare, Schiller, Hugo). It was an easy matter for these characters to destroy one another. They all wore swords, and—at the slightest provocation—a sword was quickly drawn, and the murder required by the plot took place.

Poison too was often used. Poison was poured into the hero's goblet. Or the hero poured poison into someone else's goblet. The poison was prepared by court doctors. They kept it in a ring.

Although it may seem comical, the question of the right to bear arms exerts some influence on the techniques of playwriting.

Let us consider plays written in the pre-revolutionary period. For example, Chekhov's plays. Chekhov could not conceive of a play without a shot. A shot rings out in all his plays. In the vaudeville *The Bear,* the action revolves around pistols. And even in the well-known formulation of the laws of drama, Chekhov could not get along without firearms: "If a gun hangs on the wall in the first act, then it must be fired in the last."

Ivanov shoots himself, Voinitsky shoots Serebryakov, Treplyev shoots himself. A duel takes place in *The Three Sisters*. Incidentally, it is interesting to note that Chekhov was somewhat embarrassed by the flashiness of a shot on stage. He reduces this flashiness in several cases. For example, when Voinitsky shoots at Professor Serebryakov, he shouts "bang" as he does it. It is not a real shot, Chekhov indicates, not a shot producing thunder and lightning, but only a "bang." It is a restrained, non-combatant, comical shot (but a shot all the same). There is the same kind of reduction in *The Seagull*. The sound of the shot is like the sound of a can of ether exploding.

In the bourgeois era it was easy to buy a weapon in a store. There is a story of Chekhov's in which a deceived husband picks out a weapon in a store. And Ivanov came to his own wedding with a revolver.

The last stage direction in *Ivanov* reads: "Ivanov runs to one side and shoots himself." That means, before going to his own wedding, a man pulled a revolver out of his desk and put it in the pocket of his dress pants.

That is how simply things were done then.

But what about us?

The right to bear arms is under strict control, and this right is granted to just those people who are least likely to do any shooting for personal reasons.

Most often we have recourse to a secondary issue: the theft of the revolver.

In this connection there are certain difficulties occasioned by life itself. When, let us suppose, X decides to kill Y, he makes a special trip to Leningrad to his brother's and steals a revolver from him. The trip to Leningrad, the theft of the revolver—that's a whole act of the play!

A person can be killed with a chair or an axe as well as with a gun. But such murders do not occur on the stage, since they are not convincing. In Andreev's *Thought*, Kerzhentsev uses a paper-weight to kill someone. But Andreev indicates that the man who gets murdered stands there as though he were hypnotized, and the murderer brings down his hand in a slow, jerky fashion. Thus it is extremely important for Andreev to fix the actor's attention at this point. In this instance the dramatist realizes that it is impossible for the murderous blow to come off convincingly.

In a drama, everything is constructed around the sufferings

of some character, and the action eventually comes to the point where this character either kills, is killed, or kills himself. Every drama contains some external criminal act. It is very difficult to recall a drama without the actual death of one of the characters.

In our Soviet plays, if a character pulls out a revolver, the question immediately arises: Where did he get the revolver?

A dramatist jots down in his notebook: "Next he is going to shoot him." That is rash. To avoid falsehood and stretching things, first it is necessary to work out carefully how, where, and by what means the weapon came into the character's possession.

Now the following idea occurs to me: our Soviet playwriting more than any other offers the possibility of dramas in which destruction is brought about by a logic machine. Physical destruction becomes logical destruction. Man is transformed not into a corpse, but a zero.

2) Money was the principal theme in bourgeois drama. The theme of money, of getting rich. Especially getting rich suddenly. Wealth was the reward for inner qualities. The material standard of wealth had to be improved and raised.

A promissory note. How often it turns up in bourgeois plays! It is crumpled, torn, burned. It is wept over, given back, stolen. It holds the plot together, creates the conflicts, emerges as part of a triangle, constituting the drama itself. The struggle centers around it. It is the litmus paper revealing the truth in people.

Or, for example, the rich suitor. There used to be rich suitors. In novels you would come across sentences such as: "He was one of the richest suitors in Russia."

What does that mean? What is a "rich suitor"? We do not know, we do not know. Now there aren't any rich matches any more. Now even the word "suitor" is going out of style. Now it is extremely rare to hear the phrase:

—He is her suitor.

A rich suitor was one of the most effective characters in bourgeois drama. His entrance received a long preparation, he would not appear until the end of the act.

It was awful to live in those times! How long one had to wait and grovel in order to get a blessing for one's marriage from some important relative—a distant one who ignored the most important and richest. Five whole acts!

For there used to be the concept: inheritance. I.e., money. I.e., getting rich.

Inheritance. It was essential to obtain one. To wait for an inheritance . . . Oho! It is a struggle, a duel, a source of the most fascinating characters. Forgers of wills. Kidnappers of children. Secrets, secrets, secrets. What complications, what crises, what meetings in the last act, what tears, what capes on footmen, what tearing off of masks!

In the bourgeois world, everyone had the "opportunity" to make his own fortune in the world. You could make a million. You could find a bag full of money. That world made the theme of money magical. The dream of suddenly getting rich was transformed into the entrancing figures of Cinderella and the Ugly Duckling. That world created the type of the foundling, the type of the thief who stole for the sake of the poor, the type of the benevolent rich man. Little by little, imperceptibly, insidiously money took root—as the chief motive of all of life—in art.

This theme—the theme of money—became very firmly established in art and captured the imagination of artists. It began to give birth to such ideal and angelic figures that one even lost sight of how crudely materialistic, dirty, and bloody this theme was.

How fascinating Jean Valjean is in Hugo's *Les Misérables*. He changed from a thief into a rich man. He changed from a convict into an honest man. A benevolent rich man, he saved a little girl from want and degradation. He met her at night in the forest. She was carrying a heavy bucket. As they were walking along, he took the bucket from her hand; suddenly she stopped feeling the weight—he carried the bucket which weighed down the poor little beggar girl. A tavern keeper and his wife—crooks, evil rich people—humiliated the girl. The benevolent rich man took her part and punished them. Externally, aesthetically, this sounds unusually powerful. Remember that scene . . . Thus the theme of getting rich in bourgeois art gave birth to both strong emotions and the tenderest melodies.

In our Soviet world, where private property is dying out, the theme of getting rich is disappearing. It is disappearing forever, like smoke, dispersing never to arise again, it is dead and buried. The myth of Cinderella cannot be repeated.

In America they say:

—That man is worth two million.

A different evaluation of man interests us: in a society where there will be neither rich nor poor, to have the opportunity to determine the absolute value of man. In a classless society much will be done to improve man. Competition arises in this connection. Which of us is better, purer, more intelligent, more creative? Whose value is higher?

Absolute value. Without millions. Without an inheritance.

Perhaps this aspect—competition among human qualities —will become the main theme of playwriting in the future.

And such competition will certainly create the sharpest conflicts and could be very tragic. But its purpose is pure and high: to become better.

3) People say: a fascinating person.

There are fascinating people. There are people without fascination—totally good, intelligent, well-educated, honest, affable, but devoid of the ability to attract others sympathetically.

There are people with whom you don't want to leave the party when it's time to go home, people you want to get away from.

But I am convinced that for everyone—even for a completely undistinguished, ordinary person, there is a sphere of activity where he becomes fascinating.

I've noticed that people become fascinating while they are executing a job, that is, when they are making movements each of which is necessary and useful. That is, people moving in rhythm. It is always pleasant to see people with hammers repairing the streetcar line at night. The driver becomes fascinating as he focuses all his attention.

One day the wire for the streetcar broke. They roped off the place. The streetcars stopped. The crowd was quiet. Then the emergency repair tower arrived. A young man wearing gloves appeared at the top, above the crowd—he did something with the wire. He was all concentration. And, without even knowing it—or rather, without having time to think of it—he was an actor in front of a large number of spectators. And everyone looked at him with delight and admiration, feeling some gratitude to him and at the same time envy and the wish to be like him and to be able to be proud of him. That is, they experienced the kind of feelings which arise when you are in love.

A man directing the near-fatal traffic of transport vehicles has to show the utmost in concentration. He is all rhythm. He is responsibility personified. Not one superfluous movement. In this lies his gracefulness and in the fact that he becomes someone we want to imitate.

This is the point which explains how life itself, without the artist's intervention, can become art.

When he appears at the scene of an accident, the doctor has great magical powers of fascination. This terrible figure extracting glittering steel from a little satchel, this possessor of momentary but superhuman greatness, who calls for stretcher-bearers with a movement of his finger, after feeling the pulse of the person lying in the road and without saying anything to the crowd about the condition of the victim—this man is the personification of what's proclaimed as life and death.

The favorable responses called forth by the figure of a great surgeon are well known.

The child does not die out in people. There is an element of play in a military parade. There is an element of play in the mounting of the guard; in the ceremonies of congresses and law courts. And how frightfully these things, which call forth love in children, are linked with death and blood!

Scenes of arrest, scenes of interrogation, scenes of trial—how effective they are in plays, how the public loves them!

It seems to me that the figure who appears in a play and says, Don't be afraid, is the most fascinating one. The person to whom the fearful come for help produces a catch in the audience's throat by his every word and gesture. The figure of the protector. He is a relation of that young man wearing gloves in the emergency repair tower who makes every movement with the utmost care and efficiency as he repairs the broken wire, since even the slightest contact with it could kill him.

4) When I was a boy, they used to sell a wonderful kind of transfers. They came in a little book or album. Various scenes were depicted on the pages, painted in a single shade—a dark color.

It seemed natural to imagine that when the transfer was made onto paper the same scene would appear, only bright and multicolored.

But—and this was the specialty of that sort of little picture —a completely different picture came out on the paper, incredibly bright, new, surprising, coming from no one knew where.

One of these pictures I remembered all my life. I did not know what it was all about then. I only found out much later.

It was an episode dealing with the suppression of the Boxer Rebellion in China. There was a high wall beneath an indescribably blue sky, and from the wall were hanging decapitated Chinese. And blood—indescribably scarlet—was running down the wall. The little picture glistened because it had just come out of the water.

I was very young then: only six or seven. I wrote my first poetry at seventeen. Consequently, I did not even have any idea for a very long time that I would ever be involved with art. But I remember clearly that the impression which I got from contemplating that amazing picture has stood out sharply from all other impressions of childhood.

I became convinced at that moment that space and time are relative, that there is in this world an opportunity to control this relativity and that the opportunity to control this relativity resides in art. This small picture, the size of a playing card, could not be evaluated by its dimensions alone. It entered one's consciousness as the event itself, and not as the portrayal of the event.

Of course, I only analyzed this situation much later, but that it was extremely strange, new, and even shocking—all that I recognized already when I was a child at the very moment that this condition began.

I was not able to carry on such reflections then, but still the shadow of a thought passed through my mind—the thought that the essence of drama lies in the interrelationships between space and man (the small Chinamen, the wall, and the empty sky), i.e., in the composition.

That was my first acquaintance with art. Childhood impressions have a special significance for the later development of an artist's relationship to the world. When I'm writing a play or preparing to work on one, as I ponder what kind of outer form my new idea will take, I always relive the memory of that transfer, I see it shining before me. It was brilliantly staged—space, figures, and properties were all marvelously arranged in it. In it there was the air of the dramatic event.

5) I want to write a play in which one of the main characters will be an egotist.

The type of person in love with himself.

The egotist lives in a large room with two windows. Nice furniture, a bright hallway, trees and grass nearby. At the windows, which open on the garden, there is a delightful atmosphere created by the reflections of sky and greenery, the shadows of the glass, the smells. The egotist steps into these surroundings. He goes to the closet. The closet is between the windows. The egotist doesn't notice the difference between one kind of atmosphere and another. Meanwhile the green light from the tree, which spread out beyond the window, flies into the room, and the egotist's hands turn green. His shirt turns green too. The egotist doesn't suspect for a moment that it is anything but snowy white.

The tree grows just a stone's throw from the window. It is young and strong. The egotist doesn't notice: after taking a nap the tree stretches, yawns, and shakes itself.

The egotist opens the closet. It is totally dark in the closet. The neckties are shimmering. He selects a necktie. He ties the necktie, looking in the mirror below. He knows—the mirror can last forever, if it doesn't get broken. It almost defies time, it doesn't age. The durability of "Gillette" razor blades is nothing in comparison to the mirror. The egotist reflects: "For my lifetime, one mirror and two closets are enough, but how many razor blades?"

The egotist still has about forty years to live. He says to himself: "I'm thirty-five, I've had a new fur coat made. It will last me ten years." He doesn't reflect any further. But one could reflect further along these lines: ten years will pass, the beaver fur will get thin, the hairs will fall out, the cloth will become threadbare, the polecat skin will wear out. I'll have to have a new coat made. That will happen in ten years. But something else will happen in ten years. Not only will the fur coat wear out, so will the person wearing it—his hair will fall out, his skin will wrinkle. They'll say of him: he went through a child's winter coat, a schoolboy's overcoat, a university student's overcoat and beyond that even two excellent fur coats. The second half of his life was made up of two excellent fur coats. The second fur coat lasted until his death. We're catching the egotist in the period of his first fur coat. It's his heyday, the high point for him. The fur coat is magnificent.

As a large unit of life is composed of smaller ones, so the fur coat of the egotist, which we took as the large unit of his life, also consists of smaller units: suits, separate pairs of pants, shirts, hats, lap rugs, crystal glasses. And as the days in a century flash by, so many they cannot be counted, so rapidly they cannot be noticed, so too the "Gillette" razor blades flash by, innumerable and imperceptible in the fur coat-century.

The egotist is encased in the beautiful. The limit of human sight lies in infinity. We see the starry nebulae. The limit of the egotist's sight is confined to exactly that swing of the arm necessary to slide his arm into the sleeve of his fur coat.

So the character of the egotist is prepared for.

He has a hard pink bald spot. He is handsome and smells of perfume. Once he dropped a ten-kopeck piece in the streetcar. You can imagine it for yourself: he dropped the ten-kopeck piece in the streetcar right at the exit, just as the car came to a stop, when the crowd started pushing. He began to look for the ten-kopeck piece. He looked for it under the passengers' feet, making movements like someone washing the floor.

His behind stuck out. Do you picture it? He kept looking until he got poked in the behind with a fist.

So the egotist lives in the notebook. For the time being he is treated in prose fiction. Next he will begin to act.

He will be the representative of man's power over his fellow man—and he will be punished for it.

Now the process of playwriting and the working out of the characters must begin. The character of the egotist—maybe an excellent citizen, a hard worker, a useful and indispensable man, but a selfish person, an egotist—is to me unusually interesting as a character to portray on the stage.

by Yurii Olyesha

alternate ending to
the conspiracy
of feelings

translated by Daniel C. Gerould
and Eleanor S. Gerould

[*The text printed below is Olyesha's original version. During the course of rehearsals, the playwright changed the ending to the version printed above, pp. 255–256.*]

HARMAN (*speaks in German*): Ach, ja . . . (IVAN *approaches followed by the* CROWD.) Who's that man? What's he doing here with a pillow? Maybe he wants to move to the land of the collective kitchen?

IVAN: Andryusha, treat me to some salami. (*Silence.*) Mr. Harman, write this down: a crazy sausage-maker stole his own brother's daughter.

HARMAN: Mr. Babichev, this is an advertisement too. (*Silence.*)

ANDREI: If you don't get out of here immediately, I'll have you arrested.

IVAN: They'll let me go. I'm harmless. I'm not a magician, Andryusha, I'm a trickster. And here's the last trick: the flying sausage. (*He seizes the salami, swings his arms, general panic, throws the salami in* ANDREI's *face. He grows frightened himself.*) Bravo, bravo. War's declared. Down with Andrei, the sausage-maker. Great. Well, what are you doing to do? Grab me. (*They try to grab him. He runs away. He holds the pillow like a defensive weapon.*) Kavalerov, Kavalerov. Cut his throat. Long live the conspiracy of feelings. Slash him. Slash him. (*They grab him, the pillow rolls away.* KAVALEROV *climbs up to the group.* VALYA *appears.* IVAN *starts struggling violently as they hold him.*) Here he comes. You see. He'll kill you. Aha . . . you're going pale. You're scared, Andryusha. (KAVA-LEROV *climbs up. He has his razor in his hand. He notices* VALYA.)

VALYA: That's not true. We're not afraid. Don't be afraid. Don't be afraid. (KAVALEROV *drops the razor, looks back, makes an attempt to pick it up, can't, sits down on the steps.*)

KAVALEROV: Well . . . now please give me just a minute of your attention . . . Andrei Petrovich, I raised my hand against you . . . and I can't . . . condemn me . . . punish me . . . put out my eyes . . . I want to be blind . . . I've got to be blind so I won't see you . . . and your triumph . . . and your world . . .

VALYA: Andrei Petrovich, we've got to finish this. The football players are coming. (*In run* VIC, *the* WOMAN IN GREEN, *the* HARD-DRINKING GUEST, *and the* LESS VENERABLE OLD MAN.)

VIC (*seeing* KAVALEROV *lying on the steps*): Oh, we're too late. He's killed himself.

IVAN: He's alive. He's alive. He's not dead. He's a stuffed animal. He's a doll. Take Kavalerov off to the museum. Bring the doll to the museum. Bring the man whose life they stole to the museum.

ANDREI: Take them away. The match is beginning. (*A march. The* FOOTBALL PLAYERS *come down the ramp. Twenty-two men in brightly colored uniforms.*)

Luigi Squarzina

directing pirandello today *(1966)*

interviewed by Gino Rizzo

Luigi Squarzina, playwright and director, works at the Teatro Stabile di Genova—the municipal repertory theatre. He began directing in 1950. A brief discussion of his plays will be found in the Tulane Drama Review, *Vol. VIII, No. 3 (T23), pp. 101–102.*

RIZZO: In the fifteen years you have been working for the theatre, what plays have been most significant in your development as a director?

SQUARZINA: My development has been more a change from one style to another than a progression of plays. At first, I felt I had to contribute to the reawakening of Italian conscience that was the task of our generation, and engaged in a kind of social realism which I would no longer indulge in. I recognize the validity it had then, but in no way would I identify myself with it now. I moved on to a more historically-minded *mise-en-scène*, and in that key I did my first Pirandello, *It's Only a Joke (Ma non e' una cosa seria)*. Pirandello had never been done that way before. Still later, I freed myself of this preoccupation with historical accuracy, in order to regain the stage as stage. The theatre is used by the director as a painter uses his canvas: each creates his reality in the very moment in which he acts.

RIZZO: How did you approach *It's Only a Joke?*

SQUARZINA: *It's Only a Joke* was thought to be—and perhaps it is—one of Pirandello's minor plays. I thought that in order to make the play meaningful to us I had to set it right after the First World War. This, I think, helped portray the situation of She—the typical situation of Italian women—in the narrow microcosm of the men returning from the war, and of He, a petty would-be dictator. Without departing from the nostalgic and humorous tone of the play, I wanted to convey the sense of the impending catastrophe of Fascism. Pirandello was the most sensitive seismographer of his age.

RIZZO: Why did you choose *Each in His Own Way* for your second production?

SQUARZINA: 1961 was the twenty-fifth anniversary of Pirandello's death. Ivo Chiesa, who was then the sole director of the Repertory Theatre of Genoa (I joined him three years ago), suggested that I do either *Tonight We Improvise* or *Each in His Own Way.* I chose the second, because it had never been done since Pirandello's day, and because I thought I could see in it a great Pirandello—the equal of Joyce, Kafka, and Musil.

RIZZO: Could you elaborate?

SQUARZINA: In this play, Pirandello integrates his *ars poetica* into his own art and anticipates the treatment of reality on fragmented levels which is the mark of this century's great art. He approaches reality on the basis of its many probable levels —a quantitative, statistical approach. It was time to free Pirandello from the prison of his so-called dialectics. His thought is much more varied. In the two *entr'actes* of this play, particularly, Pirandello presents a truly original vision.

There are stage directions (which I object to most violently in any author) that are equivalent to the speeches of the characters. I treated the stage directions and the speeches interchangeably, and I was then able to present the "audience" in Pirandello's *entr'actes* as particles of a gas in motion. On the one hand, there is the play within the play: the design is clear-cut, almost angular; the scenes are sharply drawn, with entrances, exits, climaxes, and anticlimaxes all well defined. On the other, there are the scenes where the audience appears: these scenes are pulverized, as if they took place in a cyclotron, with a thousand fragments clashing and colliding without constructing anything. What they present is only a wide spectrum of probabilities cancelling each other out.

This remains my way of approaching Pirandello. When I reread my notes for the production of that play, I still think the way to do Pirandello is to present him as one of the first European writers to contribute to the fragmentation of traditional structures.

RIZZO: You said before that the *mise-en-scène* of *It's Only a Joke* was set in post-World-War-One Italy. Did you do the same with *Each in His Own Way*?

SQUARZINA: I staged the "world premiere" of the play—it was originally given, I believe, in 1925, the only production until mine. There are speeches like, "Pirandello is on the stage," "He's left," "He's run away," etc., which made the "premiere" setting inevitable. By accentuating the costumes, I was able to contrast a certain reality—the Italian stage of the Twenties and, implicitly, the stage of any theatre, any time and everywhere—with the reactions of an urban audience, a multifarious collectivity, barely kept together by the fact that at that time any audience was almost completely a bourgeois audience. My preoccupation was no longer with historical accuracy *per se,* as it was in *It's Only a Joke,* but with keeping the stage clearly distinct from the audience. I achieved that by an emphasis on the costuming, and, of course, on the style of the acting.

RIZZO: In your production notes you speak of three levels, as in fact Pirandello does. And you also say that in moving from one level to the other two, we witness a recurrent process of identification—alienation—identification.

SQUARZINA: What's in question here is no longer a style of acting or the costumes, but Pirandello's epistemology. The actor who played, let's say, Diego Cinci, was in fact asked to play three roles: the character Diego Cinci in the play within the play, the actor who played Diego Cinci, and the actor of the Repertory Theatre of Genoa, Alberto Lionello, who presented those two other levels. Thanks to the actor's skill and the dynamics of his relations to the other actors, I was able to show this one piece of reality in its three contradictory facets.

There, too, my aim was to break the dialectic between

fiction and reality of Tilgher's formula,* which we should not take seriously any more. Pirandello accepted it, who knows why—perhaps because he found it convenient, or because it helped him in making his work clear and understandable to his audience. I think it did him more harm than good.

By moving continuously from identification to alienation and back to identification again, we presented Pirandello's reality as a playing with mirrors, as I think Pirandello really wanted it to be, but never as a Manichean dichotomy of reality—like *a* and *b*, black and white—never.

RIZZO: At the end of the play, how did you bring these three facets of reality together?

SQUARZINA: Through a general collision between audience and actors. The character who sees himself and his own life portrayed on the stage is in the same situation which Pirandello had assigned him in the fiction of the play. He falls into a cliché, and in my production I had a photographer fix him with the flash of a camera, just as Pirandello used to say that we become fixed to a single act of ours. But by freezing him into a photograph, I de-emphasized the ideological value of this kind of identification. I was much more interested in the contrast between the actors with their poses—their absolute incomprehension of what they were acting out—and the audience, which confronted them with the thousand problems raised by the performance on stage. Though you still had two portions of reality coming into conflict, the conflict itself was not dialectical but polycentric, centrifugal.

RIZZO: You have already mentioned essential differences between *It's Only a Joke* and *Each in His Own Way*. Would you say that in the second play Pirandello is no longer interested in the portrayal of a given socio-historical reality and its universal significance, but takes as his point of departure a metaphysical inquiry?

SQUARZINA: Let us use a term you suggested yesterday, referring to Lionel Abel's book *Metatheatre*. More than of metaphysics, we should be speaking of "metatheatre" in this case. The play within the play, which is also called *Each in*

---

* In his *Voci del tempo* (Rome: 1921) and *Studi sul teatro contemporaneo* (Rome: 1923), Adriano Tilgher popularized the interpretation of Pirandello's "philosophy" as a dialectic of fiction and reality, of "form"— the rigidity of the mask each of us wears in his contacts with society—and life.

His Own Way, has been put there with the express purpose of having it attacked by the audience and by the protagonists, in real life. Pirandello, like other artists in this century, has not so much written a play as given us the materials for a play: they are *objets trouvés,* a collage made up from the fusion of several of his short stories with dialogues of the worst "Pirandellism." The first two scenes are the most extreme Pirandellism Pirandello ever wrote, and the reason he parodied himself was to break through the solidity of traditional structures and insert his own presence in the play. This is action painting or collage. The socio-historical reality which appears here and there in this play is only one of the collage elements.

RIZZO: What about the criticism that has been made of the melodrama in *Each in His Own Way* and *Six Characters*?

SQUARZINA: I think such criticism is wrong, of course, because the melodrama is like a piece of newspaper next to a patch of color in a collage. The more melodramatic and "in bad taste" the play within the play is, the more clear the meaning of the total play becomes. Pirandello had this kind of courage—for which he was certainly not given credit the first time the play was produced. He was criticized for having written a poor play, and then building on top of it a ponderous structure.

RIZZO: Don't you think that even *Six Characters* is usually seen as the representation of a dichotomy between art and life?

SQUARZINA: It should be presented as work-in-progress. In the past, one of the notable interpretations of *Six Characters* was that of German expressionism. I think the time has perhaps come to show it as drama that is taking place at the very moment of the performance—each speech is totally unexpected—the structure is abolished, and we are constantly in the presence of a magma.

RIZZO: This would also justify the title, which otherwise remains incomprehensible. At the close of the play, they are still in search of an author . . .

SQUARZINA: They haven't found him yet. But it is Pirandello who has found his *Six Characters*.

RIZZO: To go back to *Each in His Own Way,* you said that the structure of the play consists of the changing perspectives among its three different levels: the play within the play, the discussions among the audience in the *entr'actes,* and finally the irruption of those in the audience who identify themselves with the characters on the stage . . .

SQUARZINA: Yes, but there is also a fourth level: the presence of the author, made more tangible and unavoidable by the mention of his name. Pirandello is said to be there at the performance from the very opening scenes.

RIZZO: But is it just his name that gives us the sense of his presence? You have said that his presence was even more intrinsic in the Pirandellism of those two scenes of the Old Gentleman with the Thin Young Man, and then of the Two Young Ladies.

SQUARZINA: Yes, of course. These two scenes seem to be unrelated to the rest of the play, but they are the best kind of introduction. They are one of the most modern things the theatre of this century has to offer. What you have is an author who presents even the negative side of his own poetics; he parodies himself, as if to say, "See, I can look at myself and see what I'm doing; so, please, let's talk about something else." And this cannot fail to cause alarm among his critics.

RIZZO: In such an overt presentation of his poetics, don't you think that Pirandello could be seen as a forerunner of the absurdists?

SQUARZINA: Certainly. In Pirandello the non-sense word, spoken without being thought out, used merely as a cliché, appears often enough. In *Each in His Own Way*, there are entire sequences that are built on it. The most obvious one comes in the second *entr'acte*, when you don't know if it is the actor who has slapped the leading actress, or the actress who has slapped the author—no, it's the author who has slapped the actress. It's pure theatre of the absurd, or even better—because Pirandello offers it as only one moment in a work of far greater complexity, rather than as the basis for a whole evening at the theatre.

RIZZO: By and large though, wouldn't you say that Pirandello's logical paradox differs from the non-sense of the theatre of the absurd?

SQUARZINA: Yes, because he was not confronted with a mass society. In Italy, especially, communication was not yet devoid of information. For Pirandello, the problem was still an epistemological one; it had not become social. This can be a limitation, but also a definite advantage. The theatre after Pirandello had to deal with problems posed by a new social context—the problems of individuals who can no longer find words to express their inner selves. In Pirandello, the exchange between two human beings is not condemned by their society, but by their being. And since every one of us is like that, we will never learn the truth—except as we get to know it by living it out without an end.

RIZZO: We've talked of *Each in His Own Way*'s dramatic structure and the significance of the many levels of this play. Now, as a director, how did you realize them in your production?

SQUARZINA: In the *mise-en-scène* the problem was to show the play within the play as dated, and to distinguish it from the conversation carried on by the audience—which is also somewhat dated, but very real and such that it could happen any time and anywhere. In the part of the play that shows the stage, there is a double theatrical transposition, since what we are seeing there is how the society of a given time revealed itself on its stage. In the part showing the audience, on the other hand, although there is a certain distance between us and the audience of that time, there is no actual screen. When the actors were on stage, I kept in mind what the theatre was in Pirandello's time. Those were the days of the actor-director type of company, and Pirandello was usually produced by fashionable troupes whose repertory was made up primarily of Hungarian comedies and French *pochades*. In my production, the actors who did those scenes had to follow an outmoded and, for a modern audience, inadequate style, while making their drama credible.

RIZZO: How did you manage these two conflicting effects?

SQUARZINA: By following the charge of irony you always have in Pirandello. This enables you to wink an eye at your audience, telling them that you act that way because you've got some reason to, or asking them to believe you any way. And in that portion of the play I observed faithfully the traditional structure: the well-made scene, the *scène à faire*, the *coup de scène*. On the other hand, in the *entr'actes* where the audience appears, I used, and also further developed, all the techniques with which you can divest a word of its meaning—the word as syllable, as a compound of letters, as assonance, as mere sound, as noise, as the clashing of two sounds, as an orchestrated phrase—a treatment very much like that of "*musique concrète*," including its cacophony, out of which the main themes developed through the conversation of the audience could finally emerge and be heard.

Here I learned how to turn the stage directions into speeches. I said before that I don't like stage directions. I think they reveal better than anything else the limitations of the bourgeois theatre—a kind of paternalism on the part of the author towards his readers and his interpreters. But in *Each in His Own Way* the stage directions lend themselves beautifully to a total integration of the play. There is, for instance, a digression on smoking, the effects of smoking and why people smoke; I turned it into a speech, having one who's smoking say it while the rest of the action continues to merge and dissolve in a constant fluctuation.

RIZZO: Doesn't the handling of the audience pose certain problems in the stage setting?

SQUARZINA: The setting of the play within the play was painted canvas, which reproduced in good taste the bad taste of the time. The *entr'actes* showed instead a solid architecture, geometrically defined and characterized by a total lack of pictorial elements, as if to contrast its three-dimensionality with the bi-dimensionality of the other.

RIZZO: How did you work the transitions from the stage to the *entr'actes* at the end of each act?

SQUARZINA: By using the revolving stage, which was seen in motion only at the end. At the end of the first act I had the curtain fall as if it were time for the intermission. I also had the applause and booing recorded as if it were a performance of Pirandello's time, with the typical reactions of his premieres. When the curtain re-opened almost instantly, the setting showed the foyer of the theatre with people talking and arguing as if coming from boxes and galleries. Curtain again, and when it re-opened there was the second act of the play. Curtain closed and re-opened, and then the setting showed the circular corridor along the boxes, with people listening both to the uproar coming from the orchestra and to a brawl that had started on stage. I thought I found the touchstone of my production precisely at this point. I had the mass of spectators rush through the door leading to the stage, occupying it like an army of invaders. The stage was being blasphemed and desecrated—and, therefore, it too was denounced as a part of reality rather than as a temple devoted to some mysterious ritual.

RIZZO: What happened to Pirandello's wish to have the audience of the *entr'actes* mixed and confused with the audience of today's performance, so that one couldn't tell if the man sitting next to him was a spectator or an actor?

SQUARZINA: That was Pirandello's intention, no doubt about it, but I believe that in this too we can go beyond such a scholastic dichotomy. Our notion of total theatre has changed considerably since Pirandello's time. And again, I have the feeling that Pirandello used it as a device. Both because I wanted to show the audience as the primary level, and the play within the play as secondary, and because I intended to give an integral rendering of Pirandello's text, I decided to discard this element as banal. I sacrificed surprise and that type of emotion, in order to give my audience a reflection of themselves on the stage—they could see their reality in a mirror, so to speak, rather than having it all around them *à la* Stanislavski.

In my production, I didn't start with the first scene of the play within the play. I had it begin with the Intelligent Spectator. The scene showed the audience entering the theatre. Pirandello has it this way too, when he says that this happens on the street leading to the theatre, but he confines it to the stage directions. What I did, instead, was to turn the stage direction into the first speech of the play. The Intelligent Spectator enters. The scene is otherwise still empty; he lights a cigarette and says, turning to the audience: "Look, this play should begin on the street." In a word, I was explicitly stating my reading of Pirandello by saying that he had intended it in a certain way and I was using his intention in order to create theatre on the stage.

RIZZO: I take it that if you were to do *Six Characters* you would de-emphasize the entrance of those six on stage, their relationship to the audience . . .

SQUARZINA: Of course. This is not the main problem in a production of *Six Characters*.

RIZZO: I still haven't asked you how you handled those spectators in the audience who identify themselves with the action shown by the play within the play.

SQUARZINA: I didn't make them act any differently than the rest of the audience, because, like them, they were supposed to represent the people who live in houses, who get up after dinner to go to a theatre. Rather, it was those who played *as*

actors who showed at times that they were being watched by
an audience. This also was coming from within rather than
without. In saying certain things about the characters they
portrayed, they would throw glances toward a hypothetical
place—a box, or the orchestra—where they imagined the real
people they impersonated might be. You had the old problem,
the problem raised by Brecht, of the actor who cannot merely
live the part he plays, but must also pass judgment on it.
Except that I kept it within the bounds of humor, of professional self-consciousness. The actor is not entirely convinced
of what he says, and stops being an actor to become part of
the audience, of the critics—everyday life watching its own
transfiguration on the stage.

RIZZO: You mentioned Brecht. What about Pirandello's
impact on the contemporary theatre, both in Italy and else-
where?

SQUARZINA: In the case of Brecht, I think his notion of
"alienation" is quite different from Pirandello's. Perhaps you
could find some points of contact in one of his pre-Marxist
plays, like *Man Is Man*. But even there, Brecht's main preoccupation is the debunking of capitalistic, bourgeois attitudes.
In Italy, the playwright who learned most from Pirandello was
Ugo Betti. His roots must be traced back to Strindberg, but his
handling of the dialogue comes from Pirandello. Outside of
Italy, the man who has inherited Pirandello's vision of reality
is Genet. Genet is even trapped by Pirandello's notion of
reality as theatre. In him any relationship is constantly denounced as theatre. Reality is offered as mere hypothesis, to
be either denied or affirmed. This is obvious in *The Balcony*,
but you find it also in *The Blacks* and *The Screens*. The
distinction between the French and the Arabs, like that between blacks and whites, moves away from its social, racial
basis towards the metatheatre so typical of Pirandello.

RIZZO: Now an unfair question. Are you sorry you cannot
do Genet?

SQUARZINA: Yes, indeed. But, after all, in Italy we got rid of
censorship only three years ago. The recent reawakening of
interest in the theatre must be put in relation to the abolition
of censorship. Plays like *Galileo* or *The Devil and the Good
Lord* could not have been produced before. This kind of play
has almost created a new audience. In Italy it is impossible to
do *The Deputy*, and in Genoa we cannot now do Genet. I
regret it.

RIZZO: The objections raised against *The Deputy* are not the same that are being raised against Genet.

SQUARZINA: Of course not. As for *The Deputy*, I saw the Paris production, which was not great; and yet at the end one was almost paralyzed by the exposure of those facts that are thrown at you like handfuls of ice. But it is not a good play. In the case of Genet, instead, I feel restricted in not being able to show one of the great dramatists of our time. This for me is much more serious.

by Luigi Squarzina

notes for each in his own way

translated by Joseph Williman

... The drama of modern art and its public, Everyman after Hiroshima faced with the debris of Dubuffet, the chromatic tumors of Wols, the burlap canvasses, Burri's industrial red-lead on shards of sheet metal, the orchestral blasts of Nono, the "what cannot be said is better left unsaid" of Wittgenstein's anti-philosophy; a drama already dated, if it is true that the levelling-off of taste, the techniques of psycho-control, the establishment of the marketplace in the cultural sphere all threaten to deprive Everyman (and his artist) of any right to tragedy. In this respect *Each in His Own Way* can be presented, today, not at all as a manifesto of Pirandellism, but rather as nothing less than a lyrical consummation without a trace of discursive reasoning, a poetics that is poetry. For someone working in the theatre it has the same value as a page by Mallarmé on poetry would have for a poet. It seems to say that his theatre, indeed all theatre, is a vast *pièce à clef* in which the actor "of the true drama—of life" is the inescapable, feeble Everyman, at first indifferent, then inept at seeing himself "in the mirror," then indignant at the image of himself which the artist offers him, then irritable if an Intelligent Spectator tries to enlighten him as to what is going on, then fascinated, then, finally, ready to accept identity. ("It is true, we must punish each other! Don't you think?") ...

. . . Pirandello places himself in question, his very vision of things, his very commitment as poet-philosopher. Accused of extreme subjectivism and of barely concealed solipsism, he projected himself onstage most ostensibly; criticized for the predominance in his works of the rational over the poetic, he offers two hours of cruel, bleak sincerity. The first act seems simply a "discussion about drama"; if the audience wants "a little poetry," a critic points out that the discussion is "the drama itself." But the second act will open with a symbolic glittering and clashing of swords . . .

. . . "The play's the thing/Wherein I'll catch the conscience of the King": the conscience of mass society, the uncrowned king. Not so much a play within a play, both for Pirandello and for us, as a play about a play. "The performance of this play should start on the street": doormen, ushers, even the playbills perform in this codification of non-sense in the guise of a philosophical thriller, written by the man himself, the celebrated dramatist; performed by brilliant and sophisticated actors, the company of Nicodemi; seen and discussed by spectators—those of the early Twenties; dissected by critics on varying esthetic premises; attacked and ultimately accepted by the protagonists in real life of the tabloid item brought onto the stage . . .

. . . The pivot is Delia Morello, alias "la Moreno," "and everybody knows who she is" as it says by her name in the cast—so the playbill already suggests, "except herself." Delia Morello, a real female *casus belli*, a sado-masochist on the outside, but inwardly a woman in search of her lost innocence, of her share of truth which is at the mercy of the opinions of others, just as "la Moreno" is at the mercy of the artist who could take care of "what she most needs—her spirit." Certainly this is not up to La Vela (alias Giorgio Salvi) but rather up to him, Pirandello, who takes care of it even as far as revealing the relativity of his own opinions (the third act is not performed, "and after—after the third act—")
. . .

. . . Everything is doubled—the character and the actor who plays that role, Pirandello, author of the total play, and Pirandello, author of his own role in the play, the babbled cues from the audience and those spoken onstage. Diego Cinci makes up for his own failing by becoming analyst-prophet-judge of the acts of others and of their intentions: thus even in the play within the play there is a spectator, a critic; the game of mirrors is really endless. It is a dialectic of identification–alienation–identification (to be performed as "absorption–estrangement–absorption"), but an open dialectic, which can be pursued without ever straying afield, thanks to the irony and humorous imposture of the author . . .

. . . Too stylized, the speeches of the actors in the inner play would perhaps prove unbearable. My device should become clear enough from the melodramatic pattern of the action playing against the flow of dialogue within the audience; from the painted settings (Italian production, 1920–25) playing against the theatre construction; from a kind of frontal and conventional position playing against the coming and going in the lobby. To point out the conscious and subtle irony in Pirandello's own style, his own rhythms, his own manner: take the first two scenes between the Old Gentleman and the Thin Young Man, and between the two Young Ladies; take the "cerebral acrobatics" of the duel . . .

. . . The audience. A most difficult problem, terrifying for any director. One must approach it with humility, restraint, with no claims to grandeur: attempt to produce it with a limited number of individuals (about forty), always the same whether in the foyer or in the lobby or in the corridors—like a statistical graph of public opinion, in motion all the while. A treatment not choral, but rather statistical, of the various reactions, a collective entity forever in imperceptible motion like a chemical gas; a serial treatment of cues (the memorable series of "who has slapped whom"). To show a public in search of a ready-made truth without the bother of a moral choice, its leaning toward a form of knowledge which is egoistic rather than altruistic, idle curiosity and small talk rather than thirst for truth; yet without forgetting that even within the audience there is a kind of life which does not stop at discursive reason, whose reaction provides the zones of sentiment—that is, of action and thus of moral responsibility. It is this element in the audience which recognizes itself in the mirror of the play. To represent the spectators who invade the stage and instinctively lower their voices, as if they had come suddenly into a temple: an inverted mysticism, the blood of San Gennaro will not liquefy . . .

by André Breton

first surrealist manifesto *(1924)*

translated by Patrick Waldberg

We are still living under the reign of logic, but the logical processes of our time apply only to the solution of problems of secondary interest. The absolute rationalism which remains in fashion allows for the consideration of only those facts narrowly relevant to our experience. Logical conclusions, on the other hand, escape us. Needless to say, boundaries have been assigned even to experience. It revolves in a cage from which release is becoming increasingly difficult. It too depends upon immediate utility and is guarded by common sense. In the guise of civilization, under the pretext of progress, we have succeeded in dismissing from our minds anything that, rightly or wrongly, could be regarded as superstition or myth; and we have proscribed every way of seeking the truth which does not conform to convention. It would appear that it is by sheer chance that an aspect of intellectual life—and by far the most important in my opinion—about which no one was supposed to be concerned any longer has, recently, been brought back to light. Credit for this must go to Freud. On the evidence of his discoveries a current of opinion is at last developing which will enable the explorer of the human mind to extend his investigations, since he will be empowered to deal with more than merely summary realities. Perhaps the imagination is on the verge of recovering its rights. If the depths of our minds conceal strange forces capable of augmenting or conquering those on the surface, it is in our greatest interest to capture them; first to capture them and later to submit them, should the occasion arise, to the control of reason. The analysts themselves can only gain by this. But it is important to note that there is no method fixed *a priori* for the execution of this enterprise, that until the new order it can be considered the province of poets as well as scholars, and that its success does not depend upon the more or less capricious routes which will be followed.

It was only fitting that Freud should appear with his critique on the dream. In fact, it is incredible that this important part of psychic activity has still attracted so little attention. (For, at least from man's birth to his death, thought presents no solution of continuity; the sum of dreaming moments— even taking into consideration pure dream alone, that of sleep —is from the point of view of time no less than the sum of moments of reality, which we shall confine to waking moments.) I have always been astounded by the extreme disproportion in the importance and seriousness assigned to events of the waking moments and to those of sleep by the ordinary observer. Man, when he ceases to sleep, is above all at the mercy of his memory, and the memory normally delights in feebly retracing the circumstance of the dream for him, depriving it of all actual consequence and obliterating the only *determinant* from the point at which he thinks he abandoned this constant hope, this anxiety, a few hours earlier. He has the illusion of continuing something worthwhile. The dream finds itself relegated to a parenthesis, like the night. And in general it gives no more counsel than the night. This singular state of affairs seems to invite a few reflections:

1. Within the limits to which its performance is restricted (or what passes for performance), the dream, according to all outward appearances, is continuous and bears traces of organization. Only memory claims the right to edit it, to suppress transitions and present us with a series of dreams rather than *the dream*. Similarly, at no given instant do we have more than a distinct representation of realities whose co-ordination is a matter of will.* It is important to note that nothing leads

---

* We must take into consideration the *thickness* of the dream. I usually retain only that which comes from the most superficial layers. What I prefer to visualize in it is everything that sinks at the awakening, everything that is not left to me of the function of that preceding day, dark foliage, absurd branches. In 'reality', too, I prefer to *fall*.

to a greater dissipation of the constituent elements of the dream. I regret discussing this according to a formula which in principle excludes the dream. For how long, sleeping logicians, philosophers? I would like to sleep in order to enable myself to surrender to sleepers, as I surrender to those who read me with their eyes open, in order to stop the conscious rhythm of my thought from prevailing over this material. Perhaps my dream of last night was a continuation of the preceding night's, and will be continued tonight with an admirable precision. *It could be,* as they say. And as it is in no way proven that, in such a case, the 'reality' with which I am concerned even exists in the dream state, or that it does not sink into the immemorial, then why should I not concede to the dream what I sometimes refuse to reality—that weight of self-assurance which by its own terms is not exposed to my denial? Why should I not expect more of the dream sign than I do of a daily increasing degree of consciousness? Could not the dreams as well be applied to the solution of life's fundamental problems? Are these problems the same in one case as in the other, and do they already exist in the dream? Is the dream less oppressed by sanctions than the rest? I am growing old and, perhaps more than this reality to which I believe myself confined, it is the dream, and the detachment that I owe to it, which is ageing me.

2. I return to the waking state. I am obliged to retain it as a phenomenon of interference. Not only does the mind show a strange tendency to disorientation under these conditions (this is the clue to slips of the tongue and lapses of all kinds whose secret is just beginning to be surrendered to us), but when functioning normally the mind still seems to obey none other than those suggestions which rise from that deep night I am commending. Sound as it may be, its equilibrium is relative. The mind hardly dares express itself and, when it does, is limited to stating that this idea or that woman *has an effect on it*. What effect it cannot say; thus it gives the measure of its subjectivism and nothing more. The idea, the woman, *disturbs* it, disposes it to less severity. Their role is to isolate one second of its disappearance and remove it to the sky in that glorious acceleration that it can be, that it is. Then, as a last resort, the mind invokes chance—a more obscure divinity than the others—to whom it attributes all its aberrations. Who

says that the angle from which that idea is presented which affects the mind, as well as what the mind loves in that woman's eye, is not *precisely* the same thing that attracts the mind to its dream and reunites it with data lost through its own error? And if things were otherwise, of what might the mind not be capable? I should like to present it with the key to that passage.

3. The mind of the dreaming man is fully satisfied with whatever happens to it. The agonizing question of possibility does not arise. Kill, plunder more quickly, love as much as you wish. And if you die, are you not sure of being roused from the dead? Let yourself be led. Events will not tolerate deferment. You have no name. Everything is inestimably easy.

What power, I wonder, what power so much more generous than others confers this natural aspect upon the dream and makes me welcome unreservedly a throng of episodes whose strangeness would overwhelm me if they were happening as I write this? And yet I can believe it with my own eyes, my own ears. That great day has come, that beast has spoken.

If man's awakening is harsher, if he breaks the spell too well, it is because he has been led to form a poor idea of expiation.

4. When the time comes when we can submit the dream to a methodical examination, when by methods yet to be determined we succeed in realizing the dream in its entirety (and that implies a memory discipline measurable in generations, but we can still begin by recording salient facts), when the dream's curve is developed with an unequalled breadth and regularity, then we can hope that mysteries which are not really mysteries will give way to the great Mystery. I believe in the future resolution of these two states—outwardly so contradictory—which are dream and reality, into a sort of absolute reality, a *surreality,* so to speak. I am aiming for its conquest, certain that I myself shall not attain it, but too indifferent to my death not to calculate the joys of such possession.

They say that not long ago, just before he went to sleep, Saint-Pol-Roux placed a placard on the door of his manor at Camaret which read: THE POET WORKS.

There is still a great deal to say, but I did want to touch lightly, in passing, upon a subject which in itself would require a very long exposition with a different precision. I shall return to it. For the time being my intention has been to see that justice was done to that *hatred of the marvellous* which rages in certain men, that ridicule under which they would like to crush it. Let us resolve, therefore: the Marvellous is always beautiful, everything marvellous is beautiful. Nothing but the Marvellous is beautiful.

. . . One night, before falling asleep, I became aware of a most bizarre sentence, clearly articulated to the point where it was impossible to change a word of it, but still separate from the sound of any voice. It came to me bearing no trace of the events with which I was involved at that time, at least to my conscious knowledge. It seemed to me a highly insistent sentence—a sentence, I might say, *which knocked at the window*. I quickly took note of it and was prepared to disregard it when something about its whole character held me back. The sentence truly astounded me. Unfortunately I still cannot remember the exact words to this day, but it was something like: 'A man is cut in half by the window'; but it can only suffer from ambiguity, accompanied as it was by the feeble visual representation of a walking man cut in half by a window perpendicular to the axis of his body.* It was probably a simple matter of a man leaning on the window and then straightening up. But the window followed the movements of the man, and I realized that I was dealing with a very rare type of image. Immediately I had the idea of incorporating it into my poetic material, but no sooner had I

---

* Had I been a painter, this visual representation would undoubtedly have dominated the other. It is certainly my previous disposition which decided it. Since that day I have had occasion to concentrate my attention voluntarily on similar apparitions, and I know that they are not inferior in clarity to auditory phenomena. Armed with a pencil and a blank sheet of paper, it would be easy for me to follow its contours. This is because here again it is not a matter of drawing, *it is only a matter of tracing*. I would be able to draw quite well a tree, a wave, a musical instrument—all things of which I am incapable of furnishing the briefest sketch at this time. Sure of finding my way, I would plunge into a labyrinth of lines which at first would not seem to contribute to anything. And upon opening my eyes I would experience a very strong impression of '*jamais vu*'. What I am saying has been proved many times by Robert Desnos. To be convinced of this, one has only to thumb through No. 36 of *Feuilles Libres*, which contains several of his drawings (*Romeo and Juliet, A Man Died This Morning*, etc.). They were taken by this review as drawings of the insane and innocently published as such.

invested it with poetic form than it went on to give way to a scarcely intermittent succession of sentences which surprised me no less than the first and gave me the impression of such a free gift that the control which I had had over myself up to that point seemed illusory and I no longer thought of anything but how to put an end to the interminable quarrel which was taking place within me.*

Totally involved as I was at the time with Freud, and familiar with his methods of examination which I had had some occasion to practise on the sick during the war, I resolved to obtain from myself what one seeks to obtain from a patient—a spoken monologue uttered as rapidly as possible, over which the critical faculty of the subject has no control, unencumbered by any reticence, which is *spoken thought* as far as such a thing is possible. It seemed to me, and still does —the manner in which the sentence about the man cut in two came to me proves it—that the speed of thought is no greater than that of words, and that it does not necessarily defy language or the moving pen. It was with this in mind that Philippe Soupault (with whom I had shared these first conclusions) and I undertook to cover some paper with writing, with

---

* Knut Hamsun attributes the kind of revelation by which I have just been possessed to *hunger*, and he may well be right. (The fact is that I was not eating every day at that period.) Unquestionably the manifestations that he describes below are the same as mine:

'The next day I awoke early. It was still dark. My eyes had been open for a long time when I heard the clock in the flat overhead sound five o'clock. I wanted to go back to sleep, but had no success. I was completely awake and a thousand things ran through my mind.

'All of a sudden several good pieces came to me, just right for use in a sketch or article. I found abruptly, and by chance, very beautiful phrases, phrases such as I had never written. I repeated them to myself slowly, word for word: they were excellent. And they kept coming. I rose and took a piece of paper and pencil to the desk behind my bed. It was as though a vein had burst in me, one word followed another, set itself in place, adapted itself to the situation, scenes accumulated, action unfolded, replies surged in my brain. I enjoyed myself prodigiously. Thoughts came to me so rapidly and continued to flow so abundantly that I lost a multitude of delicate details because my pencil could not go fast enough, and even then I was hurrying, my hand was always moving. I didn't lose a minute. Sentences continued to be driven from me, I was at the heart of my subject.'

Apollinaire affirmed that Chirico's paintings had been executed under the influence of cenesthesiac pains (migraines, colic).

a laudable contempt for what might result in terms of literature. The ease of realization did the rest. At the end of the first day we were able to read to each other around fifty pages obtained by this method, and began to compare our results. Altogether, those of Soupault and my own presented a remarkable similarity, even including the same faults in construction: in both cases there was the illusion of an extraordinary verve, a great deal of emotion, a considerable assortment of images of a quality such as we would never have been capable of achieving in ordinary writing, a very vivid graphic quality, and here and there an acutely comic passage. The only difference between our texts seemed to me essentially due to our respective natures (Soupault's is less static than mine) and, if I may hazard a slight criticism, due to the fact that he had made the mistake of distributing a few words in the way of titles at the head of certain pages—no doubt in the spirit of mystification. On the other hand, I must give him credit for maintaining his steadfast opposition to the slightest alteration in the course of any passage which seemed to me rather badly put. He was completely right on this point, of course.* In fact it is very difficult to appreciate the full value of the various elements when confronted by them. It can even be said to be impossible to appreciate them at the first reading. These elements are outwardly *as strange to you who have written them as to anyone else,* and you are naturally distrustful of them. Poetically speaking, they are especially endowed with a very high degree of *immediate absurdity*. The peculiarity of this absurdity, on closer examination, comes from their capitulation to everything—both inadmissible and legitimate—in the world, to produce a revelation of a certain number of premises and facts generally no less objective than any others.

In homage to Guillaume Apollinaire—who died recently, and who appears to have consistently obeyed a similar impulse to ours without ever really sacrificing mediocre literary means

---

* I believe increasingly in the infallibility of my thought in regard to myself, and it is too accurate. Nevertheless, in this *writing down of thoughts*, where one is at the mercy of the first exterior distraction, 'transports' can be produced. It would be inexcusable to seek to ignore them. By definition, thought is strong and incapable of being at fault. We must attribute those obvious weaknesses to suggestions which come from outside.

—Soupault and I used the name SURREALISM to designate the new mode of pure expression which we had at our disposal and with which we were anxious to benefit our friends. Today I do not believe anything more need be said about this word. The meaning which we have given it has generally prevailed over Apollinaire's meaning. With even more justification we could have used SUPERNATURALISM, employed by Gerard de Nerval in the dedication of *Filles de Feu.** In fact, Nerval appears to have possessed to an admirable extent the *spirit* to which we refer. Apollinaire, on the other hand, possessed only the *letter* of surrealism (which was still imperfect) and showed himself powerless to give it the theoretical insight that engages us. Here are two passages by Nerval which appear most significant in this regard:

'I will explain to you, my dear Dumas, the phenomenon of which you spoke above. As you know, there are certain story-tellers who cannot invent without identifying themselves with the characters from their imagination. You know with what conviction our old friend Nodier told how he had had the misfortune to be guillotined at the time of the Revolution; one became so convinced that one wondered how he had managed to stick his head back on.'

'. . . And since you have had the imprudence to cite one of the sonnets composed in this state of SUPERNATURALIST reverie, as the Germans would say, you must hear all of them. You will find them at the end of the volume. They are hardly more obscure than Hegel's metaphysics or Swedenborg's ME-MORABLES, and would lose their charm in explication, if such a thing were possible, so concede me at least the merit of their expression . . .'†

It would be dishonest to dispute our right to employ the word SURREALISM in the very particular sense in which we intend it, for it is clear that before we came along this word amounted to nothing. Thus I shall define it once and for all:

SURREALISM, noun, masc., Pure psychic automatism by which it is intended to express, either verbally or in writing, the true function of thought. Thought dictated in the absence

---

* And also by Thomas Carlyle in *Sartor Resartus* (Chapter VIII: 'Natural Supernaturalism'), 1833–34.

† See also l'IDÉORÉALISME by Saint-Pol-Roux.

of all control exerted by reason, and outside all aesthetic or moral preoccupations.

ENCYCL. *Philos.* Surrealism is based on the belief in the superior reality of certain forms of association heretofore neglected, in the omnipotence of the dream, and in the disinterested play of thought. It leads to the permanent destruction of all other psychic mechanisms and to its substitution for them in the solution of the principal problems of life.

editorial by J.-A. Boiffard, P. Eluard, *and* R. Vitrac

the surrealist revolution (1924)

translated by Patrick Waldberg

As the trial of knowledge is no longer relevant and intelligence no longer need be taken into account, the dream alone entrusts to man all his rights to freedom. Thanks to the dream, the meaning of death is no longer mysterious, and the meaning of life becomes unimportant.

Each morning in every family, men, women and children, *if they have nothing better to do,* tell each other their dreams. We are all at the mercy of the dream and we owe it to ourselves to submit its power to the waking state. It is a terrible tyrant garbed in mirrors and flashes of lightning. What is pen and paper, what is writing, what is poetry before this giant who holds the muscles of clouds in his own muscles? You are there stammering before the serpent, ignoring the dead leaves and glass traps, fearing for your fortune, your heart and your pleasures, and in the shadow of your dreams you look for all the mathematical signs which will restore to you a more natural death. Others—and these are the prophets —blindly guide the forces of night towards the future; dawn speaks through their mouths and the ravished world is either frightened or satisfied. Surrealism opens the doors of dream to everyone for whom the night is miserly. Surrealism is the crossroads of the enchantments of sleep, alcohol, tobacco, ether, opium, cocaine, morphine; but it is also the breaker of chains. We do not sleep, we do not drink, we do not smoke, we do not sniff, we do not puncture ourselves: we dream, and the speed of the lamps' needles introduces to our minds the marvellous deflowered sponge of gold. Ah! if bones were inflated like dirigibles we would visit the shadows of the Dead Sea. The road is a sentinel erect against the wind which embraces us and makes us tremble before our fragile rubied appearances. You, stuck to the echoes of our ears like the octopus-clock on the wall of time, you can invent pitiful tales which will make us smile nonchalantly. We no longer bother. There is a good line: *the idea of movement is above all an inert idea* (Berkeley), and the tree of speed becomes visible to us. The mind spins like an angel and our words are the lead beads which kill the bird. You to whom nature has given the power to turn on the electricity at noon and stay under the rain with sun in your eyes, your acts are gratuitous, ours are dreams. Everything is whispers, coincidences; silence and brilliance ravish their own revelation. The tree loaded with meat which rises among the paving stones is supernatural only in our astonishment, but the time for closing the eyes has not yet begun.

Every discovery changes nature, the destination of an object or a phenomenon constitutes a surrealist deed. Between Napoleon and the phrenologist's bust which represents him there are all the battles of the Empire. Far be it from us to exploit these images and modify them in a sense which could imply progress. As many satisfying images and worthless inventions as alcohol, milk, or gas for lighting may appear from the distillation of liquid. No transformation takes place but, nevertheless, the writer who uses invisible ink will be counted among the missing. Solitude of love, the man lying on top of you commits a perpetual and fatal crime. Solitude of writing, you will no longer be known in vain, your victims caught up in the gears of violent stars come back to life in themselves.

We declare the surrealist exaltation of mystics, inventors and prophets, and we go on.

In addition, reports of inventions, fashion, life, the fine arts and magic will be found in this review. Fashion will be discussed according to the gravitation of white letters on nocturnal flesh, life according to portions of day and perfumes, invention according to the players, the fine arts according to the skate which says 'storm' to the centenarian cedars' bells, and magic according to the movement of the spheres in blind eyes.

Already the automatons multiply and dream. In cafés they quickly demand writing materials, veins of marble are the graphics of their flight and their cars go to the Bois alone.

Revolution . . . Revolution . . . Realism is the pruning of trees, surrealism is the pruning of life.

no more masterpieces

from THE THEATRE AND ITS DOUBLE
(1938)

by Antonin Artaud

translated by Mary Caroline Richards

One of the reasons for the asphyxiating atmosphere in which we live without possible escape or remedy—and in which we all share, even the most revolutionary among us—is our respect for what has been written, formulated, or painted, what has been given form, as if all expression were not at last exhausted, were not at a point where things must break apart if they are to start anew and begin fresh.

We must have done with this idea of masterpieces reserved for a self-styled elite and not understood by the general public; the mind has no such restricted districts as those so often used for clandestine sexual encounters.

Masterpieces of the past are good for the past: they are not good for us. We have the right to say what has been said and even what has not been said in a way that belongs to us, a way that is immediate and direct, corresponding to present modes of feeling, and understandable to everyone.

It is idiotic to reproach the masses for having no sense of the sublime, when the sublime is confused with one or another of its formal manifestations, which are moreover always defunct manifestations. And if for example a contemporary public does not understand *Oedipus Rex,* I shall make bold to say that it is the fault of *Oedipus Rex* and not of the public.

In *Oedipus Rex* there is the theme of incest and the idea that nature mocks at morality and that there are certain unspecified powers at large which we would do well to beware of, call them *destiny* or anything you choose.

There is in addition the presence of a plague epidemic which is a physical incarnation of these powers. But the whole in a manner and language that have lost all touch with the rude and epileptic rhythm of our time. Sophocles speaks grandly perhaps, but in a style that is no longer timely. His language is too refined for this age, it is as if he were speaking beside the point.

However, a public that shudders at train wrecks, that is familiar with earthquakes, plagues, revolutions, wars; that is sensitive to the disordered anguish of love, can be affected by all these grand notions and asks only to become aware of them, but on condition that it is addressed in its own language, and that its knowledge of these things does not come to it through adulterated trappings and speech that belong to extinct eras which will never live again.

Today as yesterday, the public is greedy for mystery: it asks only to become aware of the laws according to which destiny manifests itself, and to divine perhaps the secret of its apparitions.

Let us leave textual criticism to graduate students, formal criticism to esthetes, and recognize that what has been said is not still to be said; that an expression does not have the same value twice, does not live two lives; that all words, once spoken, are dead and function only at the moment when they are uttered, that a form, once it has served, cannot be used again and asks only to be replaced by another, and that the theater is the only place in the world where a gesture, once made, can never be made the same way twice.

If the public does not frequent our literary masterpieces, it is because those masterpieces are literary, that is to say, fixed; and fixed in forms that no longer respond to the needs of the time.

Far from blaming the public, we ought to blame the formal screen we interpose between ourselves and the public, and this new form of idolatry, the idolatry of fixed masterpieces which is one of the aspects of bourgeois conformism.

This conformism makes us confuse sublimity, ideas, and things with the forms they have taken in time and in our minds—in our snobbish, precious, aesthetic mentalities which the public does not understand.

How pointless in such matters to accuse the public of bad taste because it relishes insanities, so long as the public is not shown a valid spectacle; and I defy anyone to show me *here* a spectacle valid—valid in the supreme sense of the theater—since the last great romantic melodramas, i.e., since a hundred years ago.

The public, which takes the false for the true, has the sense of the true and always responds to it when it is manifested. However it is not upon the stage that the true is to be sought nowadays, but in the street; and if the crowd in the street is offered an occasion to show its human dignity, it will always do so.

If people are out of the habit of going to the theater, if we have all finally come to think of theater as an inferior art, a means of popular distraction, and to use it as an outlet for our worst instincts, it is because we have learned too well what the theater has been, namely, falsehood and illusion. It is because we have been accustomed for four hundred years, that is since the Renaissance, to a purely descriptive and narrative theater —storytelling psychology; it is because every possible ingenuity has been exerted in bringing to life on the stage plausible but detached beings, with the spectacle on one side, the public on the other—and because the public is no longer shown anything but the mirror of itself.

Shakespeare himself is responsible for this aberration and decline, this disinterested idea of the theater which wishes a theatrical performance to leave the public intact, without setting off one image that will shake the organism to its foundations and leave an ineffaceable scar.

If, in Shakespeare, a man is sometimes preoccupied with what transcends him, it is always in order to determine the ultimate consequences of this preoccupation within him, i.e., psychology.

Psychology, which works relentlessly to reduce the unknown to the known, to the quotidian and the ordinary, is the cause of the theater's abasement and its fearful loss of energy, which seems to me to have reached its lowest point. And I think both the theater and we ourselves have had enough of psychology.

I believe furthermore that we can all agree on this matter sufficiently so that there is no need to descend to the repugnant level of the modern and French theater to condemn the theater of psychology.

Stories about money, worry over money, social careerism, the pangs of love unspoiled by altruism, sexuality sugar-coated with an eroticism that has lost its mystery have nothing to do with the theater, even if they do belong to psychology. These torments, seductions, and lusts before which we are nothing but Peeping Toms gratifying our cravings, tend to go bad, and their rot turns to revolution: we must take this into account.

But this is not our most serious concern.

If Shakespeare and his imitators have gradually insinuated the idea of art for art's sake, with art on one side and life on the other, we can rest on this feeble and lazy idea only as long as the life outside endures. But there are too many signs that everything that used to sustain our lives no longer does so, that we are all mad, desperate, and sick. And I call for *us* to react.

This idea of a detached art, of poetry as a charm which exists only to distract our leisure, is a decadent idea and an unmistakable symptom of our power to castrate.

Our literary admiration for Rimbaud, Jarry, Lautréamont, and a few others, which has driven two men to suicide, but turned into café gossip for the rest, belongs to this idea of literary poetry, of detached art, of neutral spiritual activity which creates nothing and produces nothing; and I can bear witness that at the very moment when that kind of personal poetry which involves only the man who creates it and only at the moment he creates it broke out in its most abusive fashion, the theater was scorned more than ever before by poets who have never had the sense of direct and concerted action, nor of efficacity, nor of danger.

We must get rid of our superstitious valuation of texts and *written* poetry. Written poetry is worth reading once, and then should be destroyed. Let the dead poets make way for others. Then we might even come to see that it is our veneration for what has already been created, however beautiful and valid it may be, that petrifies us, deadens our responses, and prevents us from making contact with that underlying power, call it thought-energy, the life force, the determinism of change, lunar menses, or anything you like. Beneath the poetry of the texts, there is the actual poetry, without form and without text. And just as the efficacity of masks in the magic practices of certain tribes is exhausted—and these masks are no longer good for anything except museums—so the poetic efficacity of a text is exhausted; yet the poetry and the efficacity of the theater are exhausted least quickly of all, since they permit the *action* of what is gesticulated and pronounced, and which is never made the same way twice.

It is a question of knowing what we want. If we are prepared for war, plague, famine, and slaughter we do not even need to say so, we have only to continue as we are; continue behaving like snobs, rushing en masse to hear such and such a singer, to see such and such an admirable performance which never transcends the realm of art (and even the Russian ballet at the height of its splendor never transcended the realm of art), to marvel at such and such an exhibition of painting in which exciting shapes explode here and there but at random and without any genuine consciousness of the forces they could rouse.

This empiricism, randomness, individualism, and anarchy must cease.

Enough of personal poems, benefitting those who create them much more than those who read them.

Once and for all, enough of this closed, egoistic, and personal art.

Our spiritual anarchy and intellectual disorder is a function of the anarchy of everything else—or rather, everything else is a function of this anarchy.

I am not one of those who believe that civilization has to change in order for the theater to change; but I do believe that the theater, utilized in the highest and most difficult sense possible, has the power to influence the aspect and formation of things: and the encounter upon the stage of two passionate manifestations, two living centers, two nervous magnetisms is something as entire, true, even decisive, as, in life, the encounter of one epidermis with another in a timeless debauchery.

That is why I propose a theater of cruelty.—With this mania we all have for depreciating everything, as soon as I have said "cruelty," everybody will at once take it to mean "blood." But *"theater of cruelty"* means a theater difficult and cruel for myself first of all. And, on the level of performance, it is not the cruelty we can exercise upon each other by hacking at each other's bodies, carving up our personal anatomies, or, like Assyrian emperors, sending parcels of human ears, noses, or neatly detached nostrils through the mail, but the much more terrible and necessary cruelty which things can exercise against us. We are not free. And the sky can still fall on our heads. And the theater has been created to teach us that first of all.

Either we will be capable of returning by present-day means to this superior idea of poetry and poetry-through-theater which underlies the Myths told by the great ancient tragedians, capable once more of entertaining a religious idea of the theater (without meditation, useless contemplation, and vague dreams), capable of attaining awareness and a possession of certain dominant forces; of certain notions that control all others, and (since ideas, when they are effective, carry their energy with them) capable of recovering within ourselves those energies which ultimately create order and increase the value of life, or else we might as well abandon ourselves now, without protest, and recognize that we are no longer good for anything but disorder, famine, blood, war, and epidemics.

Either we restore all the arts to a central attitude and necessity, finding an analogy between a gesture made in painting or the theater, and a gesture made by lava in a volcanic explosion, or we must stop painting, babbling, writing, or doing whatever it is we do.

I propose to bring back into the theater this elementary magical idea, taken up by modern psychoanalysis, which consists in effecting a patient's cure by making him assume the apparent and exterior attitudes of the desired condition.

I propose to renounce our empiricism of imagery, in which the unconscious furnishes images at random, and which the poet arranges at random too, calling them poetic and hence hermetic images, as if the kind of trance that poetry provides did not have its reverberations throughout the whole sensibility, in every nerve, and as if poetry were some vague force whose movements were invariable.

I propose to return through the theater to an idea of the physical knowledge of images and the means of inducing trances, as in Chinese medicine which knows, over the entire extent of the human anatomy, at what points to puncture in order to regulate the subtlest functions.

Those who have forgotten the communicative power and magical mimesis of a gesture, the theater can reinstruct, because a gesture carries its energy with it, and there are still human beings in the theater to manifest the force of the gesture made.

To create art is to deprive a gesture of its reverberation in the organism, whereas this reverberation, if the gesture is made in the conditions and with the force required, incites the organism and, through it, the entire individuality, to take attitudes in harmony with the gesture.

The theater is the only place in the world, the last general means we still possess of directly affecting the organism and, in periods of neurosis and petty sensuality like the one in which we are immersed, of attacking this sensuality by physical means it cannot withstand.

If music affects snakes, it is not on account of the spiritual notions it offers them, but because snakes are long and coil their length upon the earth, because their bodies touch the earth at almost every point; and because the musical vibrations which are communicated to the earth affect them like a very subtle, very long massage; and I propose to treat the spectators like the snakecharmer's subjects and conduct them *by means of their organisms* to an apprehension of the subtlest notions.

At first by crude means, which will gradually be refined. These immediate crude means will hold their attention at the start.

That is why in the "theater of cruelty" the spectator is in the center and the spectacle surrounds him.

In this spectacle the sonorisation is constant: sounds, noises, cries are chosen first for their vibratory quality, then for what they represent.

Among these gradually refined means light is interposed in its turn. Light which is not created merely to add color or to brighten, and which brings its power, influence, suggestions with it. And the light of a green cavern does not sensually dispose the organism like the light of a windy day.

After sound and light there is action, and the dynamism of action: here the theater, far from copying life, puts itself whenever possible in communication with pure forces. And whether you accept or deny them, there is nevertheless a way of speaking which gives the name of "forces" to whatever brings to birth images of energy in the unconscious, and gratuitous crime on the surface.

A violent and concentrated action is a kind of lyricism: it summons up supernatural images, a bloodstream of images, a bleeding spurt of images in the poet's head and in the spectator's as well.

Whatever the conflicts that haunt the mind of a given period, I defy any spectator to whom such violent scenes will have transferred their blood, who will have felt in himself the transit of a superior action, who will have seen the extraordinary and essential movements of his thought illuminated in extraordinary deeds—the violence and blood having been placed at the service of the violence of the thought—I defy that spectator to give himself up, once outside the theater, to ideas of war, riot, and blatant murder.

So expressed, this idea seems dangerous and sophomoric. It will be claimed that example breeds example, that if the attitude of cure induces cure, the attitude of murder will induce murder. Everything depends upon the manner and the purity with which the thing is done. There is a risk. But let it not be forgotten that though a theatrical gesture is violent, it is disinterested; and that the theater teaches precisely the uselessness of the action which, once done, is not to be done, and the superior use of the state unused by the action and which, *restored*, produces a purification.

I propose then a theater in which violent physical images crush and hypnotize the sensibility of the spectator seized by the theater as by a whirlwind of higher forces.

A theater which, abandoning psychology, recounts the extraordinary, stages natural conflicts, natural and subtle forces, and presents itself first of all as an exceptional power of redirection. A theater that induces trance, as the dances of Dervishes induce trance, and that addresses itself to the organism by precise instruments, by the same means as those of certain tribal music cures which we admire on records but are incapable of originating among ourselves.

There is a risk involved, but in the present circumstances I believe it is a risk worth running. I do not believe we have managed to revitalize the world we live in, and I do not believe it is worth the trouble of clinging to; but I do propose something to get us out of our marasmus, instead of continuing to complain about it, and about the boredom, inertia, and stupidity of everything.

selected bibliography

Benjamin, Walter. *Understanding Brecht*. Translated by Anna Bostock. London: NLB, 1973. Unusual and penetrating essays by a Marxist intellectual and personal friend of Brecht, including studies of epic theatre and conversations with the playwright.

Bentley, Eric. *The Playwright as Thinker*. New York: Harcourt, Brace, and Jovanovich, 1967. A reprint of the 1946 book and one of the most important works on modern drama, containing sections on Brecht and Pirandello.

Bentley, Eric. *Theatre of War: Modern Drama from Ibsen to Brecht*. New York: Viking, 1973. Half the book concerns Brecht, including comparisons of Brecht with Ibsen and Shaw.

Brecht, Bertolt. *Brecht on Theater*. Translated by John Willett. New York: Hill and Wang, 1964. Valuable essays by Brecht on drama and theatre practice.

Brecht, Bertolt. *The Messingkauf Dialogues*. Translated by John Willett. London: Methuen, 1965. Important theoretical essays in dialogue form.

Bristol, Michael D. and Suvin, Darko, eds. *A Production Notebook to Saint Joan of the Stockyards by Bertolt Brecht*. Montreal, Canada: McGill University Press, 1973. A detailed analysis of the play in relation to an English-language staging.

Büdel, Oscar. *Pirandello*. New York: Hillary House, 1969. An excellent and concise study of Pirandello's work, including his philosophy, humor, staging, and importance in modern drama.

Brustein, Robert. *The Theatre of Revolt*. Boston: Little, Brown, and Co., 1964. Prominent among nine dramatists of revolt are Brecht, Pirandello, and Artaud.

Brockett, Oscar G. and Findlay, Robert R. *Century of Innovation: A History of European Drama and Theatre Since 1870*. Englewood Cliffs, N.J.: Prentice-Hall, Inc., 1973. A comprehensive and highly valuable account of both plays and productions in Eastern Europe and Russia as well as in the West.

Cambon, Glauco, ed. *Pirandello: A Collection of Critical Essays*. Englewood Cliffs, N.J.: Prentice-Hall, Inc., 1967. A useful collection of essays about different aspects of Pirandello's art.

Cohn, Ruby. *Dialogue in American Drama*. Bloomington, Ind.: Indiana University Press, 1971. Contains a discussion of Cummings as a poet-playwright and an analysis of *Him*.

Demetz, Peter, ed. *Brecht: A Collection of Critical Essays*. Englewood Cliffs, N.J.: Prentice-Hall, Inc., 1962. A useful collection of essays by German, Russian, English, and American critics.

Dukore, Bernard F., ed. *Dramatic Theory and Criticism: Greeks to Grotowski*. New York: Holt, Rinehart, and Winston, 1974. Contains selections by Pirandello, Brecht, Artaud, and Witkiewicz.

Esslin, Martin. *Brecht: The Man and His Work*. Garden City, N.Y.: Doubleday Anchor, 1971. An important analysis of the man and his work, including language, dramatic theories, and relationships with communism.

Esslin, Martin. *The Theatre of the Absurd,* rev. ed. Garden City, N.Y.: Doubleday Anchor, 1969. Contains discussions of Artaud, the surrealists, Witkiewicz, and Cummings as precursors of the absurdists.

Ewen, Frederic. *Bertolt Brecht: His Life, His Art, and His Times*. New York: Citadel Press, 1967. A perceptive biographical and critical analysis.

Garten, H. F. *Modern German Drama.* London: Methuen, 1959. Contains discussions of Toller and Brecht.

Giudice, Gaspare. *Pirandello: A Biography.* Translated by Alastair Hamilton. London: Oxford University Press, 1975. An abridged translation of a biography first published in Italian in 1963.

Gorelik, Mordecai. *New Theatres for Old.* New York: Dutton, 1962. A seminal work on the new theatre movements in Europe and America, first written in 1940. Extensive material contained on expressionism, on epic theatre, and on Russian theatre in the 1920s and 1930s.

Greene, Naomi. *Antonin Artaud: Poet Without Words.* New York: Simon and Schuster, 1971. A useful study of the problems inherent in Artaud's writings.

Grossvogel, David. *Twentieth Century French Drama.* New York: Columbia University Press, 1961. Contains a valuable chapter on Ghelderode's plays and their dramatic universe.

Hern, Nicholas. "The Theatre of Ernst Toller." *Theatre Quarterly* II, no. 5 (January–March, 1972): 72–92. A chronology of the life and work of Toller, with summaries and commentaries dealing with the major plays, as well as extensive quotations from the playwright.

Knapp, Bettina. *Antonin Artaud: Man and Vision.* New York: David Lewis, 1969. A critical and biographical study dealing with Artaud's plays, theories, and practice in the theatre.

Matthaei, Renate. *Luigi Pirandello.* Translated by Simon and Erika Young. New York: Ungar, 1973. Short biography and analysis of dramatic and nondramatic works.

Matthews, J. H. *Theatre in Dada and Surrealism.* Syracuse, N.Y.: Syracuse University Press, 1974. Contains valuable material on Artaud and Breton.

Maurer, Robert E. "E. E. Cummings' *Him.*" *Bucknell Review* VI (May, 1956): 1–27. A study of the play and its structure.

Munk, Erika, ed. *Brecht.* New York: Bantam Books, 1972. A collection of essays that first appeared in TDR; among its valuable contents are an incisive analysis of Brechtian theory, an essay on Brecht as director, and an extensive bibliography.

Nadeau, Maurice. *The History of Surrealism.* Translated by Richard Howard. New York: Macmillan, 1965. A detailed survey of the surrealist movement in France.

Paolucci, Anne. *Pirandello's Theater: The Recovery of the Modern Stage for Dramatic Art.* Carbondale, Ill.: Southern Illinois University Press, 1974. Valuable analysis of Pirandello's theatrical drama; includes a chapter on the theatre-in-the-theatre trilogy.

The Polish Review. Special Witkiewicz Issue, XVIII, nos. 1–2 (1973). Contains a chronology of Witkiewicz's life and work as well as a number of articles on different aspects of his plays.

Samuel, Richard and Thomas, R. Hinton. *Expressionism in German Life, Literature, and Theatre (1910–1924).* West Orange, N.J.: Albert Saifer, 1971. A comprehensive and useful study, including material on Toller.

Sokel, Walter. "Introduction." *An Anthology of German Expressionist Drama.* Garden City, N.Y.: Doubleday Anchor, 1968. An excellent short analysis of expressionism in drama.

Sokel, Walter. *The Writer in Extremis: Expressionism in Twentieth-Century German Literature.* Stanford, Calif.: Stanford University Press, 1968. A detailed analysis of the artistic, intellectual, and social significance of German expressionism, including valuable discussions of Toller's plays.

Spalter, Max. *Brecht's Tradition.* Baltimore, Md.: Johns Hopkins Univ. Press, 1967. Considers Brecht in the final chapter as part of a special tradition in German drama represented by Lenz, Grabbe, Büchner, and Wedekind.

Starkie, Walter. *Luigi Pirandello: 1867–1936.* Berkeley, Calif.: University of California Press, 1967. A study of Pirandello's work in relation to his Italian background, including the Italian "Theatre of the Grotesque."

Tulane Drama Review VIII, no. 1 (Fall, 1963). Contains six articles on Ghelderode, including an interview with the playwright and excerpts from his letters dealing with his plays.

Tulane Drama Review VIII, no. 2 (Winter, 1963). Contains two essays about Artaud, letters, a play, and documents by Artaud.

Willett, John. *Expressionism*. New York: McGraw-Hill, 1970. An excellent and comprehensive study of expressionism in all its aspects, including film and theatre.

Willett, John. *The Theatre of Bertolt Brecht: A Study from Eight Aspects*. New York: New Directions, 1968. A valuable study of Brechtian drama and theatre from the viewpoints of subject matter, language, theatrical influence, music, stage practice, theory, and politics.

Witkiewicz, Stanisław Ignacy. *The Madman and the Nun and Other Plays*. Translated and edited by Daniel C. Gerould and C. S. Durer. Seattle, Wash.: University of Washington Press, 1968. Includes Witkiewicz's essay "On a New Type of Play," as well as a long introduction by the editors on Witkiewicz's life and works and a preface by Jan Kott.